THE COMPLETE CHRONICLE

Cliff Richard

THE COMPLETE CHRONICLE

Cliff Richard

FOREWORD BY HANK MARVIN

MIKE READ • NIGEL GOODALL & PETER LEWRY

HAMLYN

Editor: **Mike Evans**
Design: **Margaret Sadler**
Production Controller: **Michelle Thomas**
Picture Research: **Anna Smith**

First published in 1993 by
Hamlyn, an imprint of
Reed Consumer Books Limited,
Michelin House, 81 Fulham Road,
London SW3 6RB
and Auckland, Melbourne, Singapore and Toronto
Revised and reprinted 1995

A Catalogue record for this book is available from the British Library
ISBN 0-600-58858-0

Produced by Mandarin Offset
Printed and bound in China

AUTHORS ACKNOWLEDGEMENTS
For assistance in the research and reporting of Cliff's recording sessions, thanks to Bill Latham, David Bryce, Malcolm Smith, Roger Bruce, Peter Gormley, Gill Snow and all at the Cliff Richard Organisation; Terri Anderson; Ken Townsend, Lou Swoffer, Richard Lee, Peter Vince and Adrian McKinney at EMI Abbey Road Studios; Ruth Edge, Jenny Keen, and Sarah Hobbs at EMI Music Archives; Jill Betts, Amanda Rabbs, Vanessa Burrows, Matt Duffy, and Mike Heatley at EMI Records (UK); Gill Reading at PMI; Bruce Welch, Malcolm Addey, Mike Sammes, Ashley Howe and Tony Clark; Paul Moessl; Gerry Kitchingham, Ben Robbins and Leanne Dearsley at RG Jones Studios; Sarah Foley, Mike Stock, Matt Aitken and Pete Waterman at PWL; John Hudson at Mayfair Studios; Air Studios; Sarm Studios; Mike Gardner at Eden Studios; Gerry Bron at Roundhouse Recording Studios; Tania Howlett and Denise Love at the Hit Factory; Bob Morgan, Keith Bessey and Stuart Colman; See For Miles Records and John Waller at Polydor Records; Clem Cattini; Steve Maycock at Sotheby's; Graham Cousins, Peter Day, Keith Allfrey, Bob Leal, Christine Whitehead, Mogens Troelsen and Harry de Louw.
Special thanks to Susan Willer
And very special thanks to Cliff Richard

'I dedicate this book to my children Adam and Kim.' Nigel

'I dedicate this book to my wife Carole.' Peter

CONTENTS

A Guide to the Session Listings

The following is an explanation of the session listings throughout this chronicle.

SAMPLE ENTRY

12 JULY

ABBEY ROAD
Studio session

A Forever Kind Of Love (11)	*Forever Kind Of Love EP*
Razzle Dazzle (sp)	*Cliff Richard*
Reelin' And Rockin' (3)	*Cliff Richard*

Lead Vocal:	**Cliff Richard**
Guitars:	**Hank Marvin/Bruce Welch**
Bass:	**Brian Locking**
Drums:	**Brian Bennett**
	The Norrie Paramor Orchestra

Producer:	**Norrie Paramor**
Engineer:	**Peter Bown**
Recorded in:	**Studio 2**
Session hours:	**7.00pm-10.45pm**

The first three lines show the date the recording was made, the location of the recording and the type of recording. This is followed by a list of each of the titles recorded at that particular session followed by, in brackets, the take/master number where known and the record on which the track first appeared, or in the case of the track being unreleased the entry will read (Unissued). The last two sections list the musicians and vocalists on the tracks followed by technical details about the session, producers, engineers, studio used and session hours. Footnotes are used where necessary to explain further details relating to the session.

It should be noted that not all the sessions are laid out as above and the following points should be noted:

For example, where an entry reads:

Miss You Nights *See 11 September*

The date refers to the date that Cliff added his vocal to the basic track, and it is on that date you will find the relevant information about the release.

Tracks recorded by the Shadows only, but featured on one of Cliff's albums are listed in the session entries.

Where known details of BBC Radio broadcasts are listed. These were supplied to Radio Stations in the form of a Transcription Disc and were not available to the public.

Unfortunately, the information on the sessions is not always complete, and in these instances a space will be left. We cannot accurately determine whether the unissued tracks listed in this book are complete, incomplete takes or simply unsuitable for commercial release.

With regards to the information on the recording sessions, it should be noted that the information is taken from official sources, but this may sometimes be inaccurate, and unfortunately we cannot determine what is accurate and what is not.

Malcolm Addey Reminisces

It took a while to sink in but after pondering over what to write as my contribution to this book, I realised what a long time ago it all was. Although a lot of things cannot easily be forgotten - that first session and 'Move It' - over the considerable span of thirty five years (!) some of the details can get mislaid. This prompted me to climb to the top shelf of my pokey little closet of an office to pull down that box-file labelled memorabilia. Armed with the yellowing newspaper clippings, photographs and the proofs of the complete recording sessions I was able to jog my memory. They were certainly exciting times in the British recording industry.

It seems to be generally accepted that 'Move It' was somewhat of a landmark historically, being the first truly all-British rock record. It has to be remembered that almost everything at that time was a 'cover' of some already established American hit. Except for 'Schoolboy Crush', which was structured and arranged for professional musicians and singers, this session was in the forefront of songwriting and arranging on the spot, in the studio. I clearly remember Ian Samwell lying on the floor scribbling some adjustments to the lyrics and later 'teaching' Ernie Shear that now familiar guitar introduction. Sammy knew what he wanted to hear but was unable to play the guitar well enough.

The question I get asked the most is how does one get a start as a recording engineer? This is a hard one as nearly all my colleagues seem to have differing backgrounds. Most certainly it helps to have some knowledge of audio electronics and music but the main qualifications are good ears and good luck. My opportunity came strangely enough by way of opera! I had recently been promoted to the well established pop recording team of engineers Peter Bown and Stuart Eltham at EMI's Abbey Road studios. Although I had already been entrusted with some minor sessions but always with Peter or Stuart supervising, this time I was left on my own. My chance had come because Peter Bown was a big opera fan and that night had tickets for a performance he was not going to give up. After a take or two into 'Schoolboy Crush', convinced I could manage on my own, off he rushed to the opera and the rest, as they say, is history!

That first session was recorded only in mono as stereo was still in the experimental stage at that time. Some of the photographs of that period show Cliff singing into two microphones - one was routed to the mono control room - the other to the stereo control room. In fact every microphone on the session was duplicated in this way except for a short time when we occasionally tried doing mono and stereo simultaneously on the same mixing console. This was not a success as we were unable to listen to the two systems at the same time, so one had to suffer. Usually it was the stereo, because few record buyers owned stereo players and for quite a few years stereo releases were rare in the UK for pop material. This, of course, accounts for the fact that some sessions were simply not covered in stereo and therefore not available for re-release compilations in that format today.

The arrival of multiple track recording changed all that, for now we were able to separate individual microphones or sections of the accompaniment to discrete tracks. We used 4 track machines initially, recording on one-inch-wide tape, and this allowed us not only to re-mix the original session at a later date but to overdub a new vocal track or instrument. It is amusing to me that the producers at EMI were very slow at first to be convinced of the usefulness of this technique - but once this flexibility was experienced, they couldn't get enough! Cliff, I remember, did not need to overdub his voice very often (except in the case of foreign language versions) being very much a professional performer.

It's interesting that recently there has been a swing back to direct to stereo recording, triggered largely by the need to boast 'direct to digital'. This is mainly in the kind of music in which I am now involved - jazz and classical. It would be impossible to do rock records that way today as the multiple track machine has become an integral part of the art of rock.

This book is a definitive history of Cliff's career and it's a pity that he is not more widely known in the USA where I have been based for the last 25 years. My colleagues in the recording industry over here are always surprised to learn that there was a valid British rock 'n' roll long before the Liverpool invasion! I am both proud and feel privileged to have been a part of that history.

Malcolm Addey - 1993

Technical Terminology

Acetate
A disc cut for evaluation purposes only, and often taken away by the artist.

Backing tracks
Pre-recorded tape on which an artist will overdub his vocals and/or other instruments.

Cut
The process of making a lacquer from the master tape.

Demo
Disc usually used for artistic evaluation.

Edit Piece
Section of tape spliced in to improve or replace an existing piece.

Fade in
Gradual raising of a signal from infinity to an audible level.

Fade out
Gradual reduction of a signal to infinity, often used at the close of a song.

False start
A very short duration incomplete take lasting usually a few seconds, often caused by the artist or musician singing or playing a wrong note.

Master
The version finally chosen for release.

Mixing
Process whereby the level of individual sections of the recording can be altered.

Mono remix
Remix down from multiple track to a single track.

Out-take
Other versions of a song that were not used as the master.

Overdubs
Process of adding extra vocals/instruments to an already existing track.

Reduction
Mixing together existing tracks and transferring them onto a fewer tracks on another tape, thus vacating recording tracks.

Spiral
A gap inserted between tracks on the finished record, usually a few seconds.

Stereo remix
Remix down from multiple track to a stereo (2-track) master.

Splice
See Edit.

Superimposition
See Overdub.

Tape-to-tape
Transfer from one tape machine to another.

2-track / 4-track / 8-track / 16-track / 32-track
Tape with 2 / 4 / 8 / 16 / 32 tracks respectively for recording.

FOREWORD

When I was asked by the publishers to write the foreword to this new book on Cliff, I felt very privileged and excited, particularly when a fee was mentioned, sadly it hasn't been mentioned again. This oversight though has in no way diminished my enjoyment and appreciation of Mike Read's painstakingly researched diary-style account of Cliff's professional activites.

Back in September 1958 when a seventeen-year-old Cliff and the even younger Drifters (as we were known then) had our first rehearsal in the front room of Cliff's parents' home in Hertfordshire, I felt even then he had a special quality, something different to the rest of us, then suddenly it hit me, he had no pimples. Nevertheless an enduring friendship developed and today as I read through the Chronicle of the early period of his career, a time when he and the Shadows were inseparable, the memories came flooding back. Situations long forgotten and never before published were recalled vividly, such as the time in Germany when after a show, which had ended in a riot complete with police water cannon etc, Cliff and the Shadows took over the best club in town and fell asleep with a cup of cocoa. Exciting times.

The details of recording sessions, films, broadcasts and other information that Mike's collaborators Nigel Goodall and Peter Lewry have obtained are truly amazing – take the recording sessions for example. We are told the dates, the studios used, the titles recorded and whether they turned out to be A-sides, B-sides, foreign releases or were unissued. The names of the musicians, the producer and even the session times, i.e. 7.00pm-10.00pm are given. Do I sound impressed? I am, but despite this evidence of diligent detective work, I was just a little surprised, disappointed even, that more effort was not put into unearthing the really important session details, such as what times were the tea breaks? How long were they? Who took sugar and who didn't?

Seriously though, I congratulate everyone involved in producing this ripping idea of a book, (wish I'd thought of it) that chronicles the career of a great star, and is a must for every one of his admirers. Now about that fee.

Hank Marvin

1940–1959

The Records 1958 – 1959

When Cliff's first single hit the shops, 'Schoolboy Crush' was the intended A-side, but the teenagers' reaction to the B-side resulted in the disc being flipped, sending 'Move It' into the charts to peak at No.2. It is interesting to note that on the 'Move It' test pressing Cliff's surname is spelt "Richards". This mis-spelling has dogged Cliff throughout his career, and even some recent EMI test pressings and acetates bear the name "Cliff Richards". Though the follow-up singles did not equal the success of 'Move It', they all did extremely well. 'High Class Baby', 'Livin' Lovin' Doll' and 'Mean Streak' all managed to sail into the top twenty. The next two singles, however, proved to be very strong indeed with both 'Living Doll' and 'Travellin' Light' reaching the No.1 position. So successful was the latter that even the B-side climbed into the top twenty to reach No.16, while 'Living Doll' became the longest running chart-topper of the year. The B-side of this one featured a rehearsal take of 'Apron Strings' which Columbia had released by mistake. Album sales were impressive as well. The brilliant debut album CLIFF reached the fourth position on the album chart but, surprisingly, the TV soundtrack album OH BOY!, on which Cliff featured on seven tracks, failed to register at all. The picture was definitely better as far as the second album was concerned, with CLIFF SINGS reaching the No.2 slot.

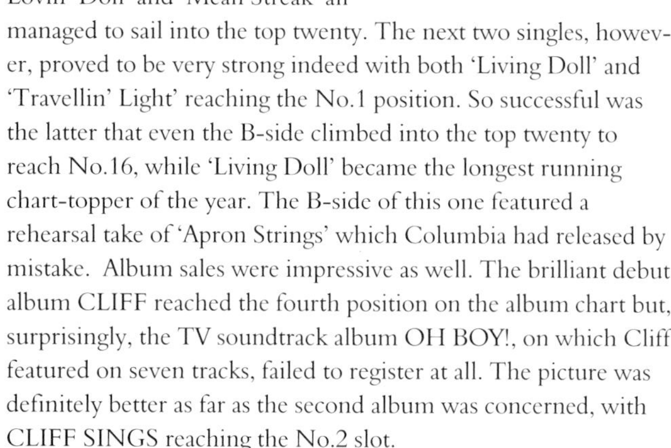

The EPs turned out to be big sellers too, although these were issued before a chart for them had been introduced. SERIOUS CHARGE was hooked up to the release of the film, but in fact was a studio recording. CLIFF No.1 and CLIFF No.2 are the earliest examples of the common practice of issuing an artist's most recent album on a series of EPs several months after its initial release, and these two together comprised two-thirds of the debut CLIFF album.

The Sessions 1958 – 1959

The first known studio recordings can be traced back to mid-1958, when Cliff Richard and The Drifters – with the line-up of Cliff on guitar and vocals, Terry Smart on drums, and Ian Samwell, Norman Mitham and Ken Pavey on guitars – cut their first demo at the recording studio located on the first floor of the HMV record store in London's Oxford Street. It was here that 'Breathless' and 'Lawdy Miss Clawdy' were recorded, providing Columbia producer Norrie Paramor with a demonstration tape that resulted in an audition, and Cliff being signed by EMI to their Columbia label on 9th August 1958. Although rumour suggests that acetates were made at the time of these recordings, John Foster, Cliff's first manager, cannot recall having acetate records. He is certain the original tape was used when approaching Norrie Paramor through agent George Ganjou, and considers it possible the tape was retained by one of them, and either they or someone within the EMI organisation had one or more acetates made, which would explain why there are quite a few around today. The discs would have been 10" acetates playing at 78rpm. There are indications, however, that John had the tape transferred to record for Cliff on 11th September at the same studio where the recordings had been made.

The first Columbia session took place in the EMI studios at Abbey Road on 24 July, strangely enough, 16 days before signing to EMI, although this is regarded as normal procedure as the session was needed to produce both sides that could be released as a single. To minimise any problems of recording with the untried Drifters, session men Ernie Shear on guitar and Frank Clarke on bass were called in to back Cliff, while Terry Smart and Ian Samwell were the only members of the Drifters to work on the session.

The material selected for recording was a cover of a track by American Bobby Helms, 'Schoolboy Crush', as the intended A-side. On the flip was to be a British rock 'n roll original, written by Ian Samwell, but as was noted earlier, the disc was flipped, and 'Move It' became the smash hit.

In October, both sides for the follow-up single – 'High Class Baby' and 'My Feet Hit The Ground' – were taped. A third track 'Don't Bug Me Baby' was also recorded, but has remained unreleased. Unfortunately, we have not been able to track down the names of the musicians on this session, but it seems likely that it was the same line-up as in July. The session on 21st October was for soundtrack recordings for ABC-TV's OH BOY! album, with Cliff recording the vocals after the rhythm track sessions. The seven tracks recorded here all appeared on the album.

The November sessions provided some A-side singles, and was the first time that the Drifters worked with Cliff in the studio, although by now the line-up had changed to Jet Harris on bass, Hank Marvin and Bruce Welch on guitars and Terry Smart on drums. For the next sessions in February 1959, Tony Meehan had replaced Terry Smart, and the Mike Sammes Singers helped out on the back-up vocal work. The sessions on the 9th and 10th

Some impromptu drumming practice before going on stage.

that another seminal English rock'n'roller, Marty Wilde, had a hit with the same song around this time.

At another session only weeks later Cliff taped a version of 'We Had It Made'. An acetate of this song later turned up on both a 7" and 10" Emidisc, although it is unknown whether this is the unreleased version from this session or the version on the ME AND MY SHADOWS album recorded over a year later. It is interesting to note that at this session a further two tracks 'There's A Reason' and 'All That I Need' were originally listed on the Red Form documentation that was originated at EMI Manchester Square and sent to Abbey Road listing the songs due for recording, but both these titles had been scratched out. It is therefore uncertain if these were new titles, or simply early working titles of tracks that would be recorded at a later date.

The September 1959 sessions provided the material for the CLIFF SINGS album, and for the first time two control rooms were utilised, with two groups of engineers, one recording and mixing in mono and one in stereo. Some fine orchestral arrangements of standards in the ballad genre were taped with accompaniment by the Norrie Paramor Strings, which would make up fifty percent of the album content. To be included on the other half of the album were some excellent covers of rock 'n roll material with the backing by the famous Drifters line-up, who by this time had become the Shadows, due to the UK success of an American vocal group also using the Drifters tag. The album showed that Cliff could do other things than just sing rock 'n' roll and for that reason alone fully deserved the praise Cliff received for it in 1959. We must remember it was a time when teěnagers usually preferred to buy singles rather than albums, but with this one, the buying patterns had appeared to change. The album was released in mono, but for certain tracks on the stereo issue Norrie Paramor went back to the original session tapes to choose an alternative version and, in the case of 'I Gotta Know' and 'The Snake And The Bookworm', a further session was held to re-record these two titles for the stereo release which at the time was regarded as of secondary importance to the mono issue.

The sessions running through to December produced soundtrack recordings for Cliff's second feature film *Expresso Bongo* as well as a number of A and B sides. Interesting to note that the version of 'A Voice In The Wilderness' recorded on 8 September is the one featured on the EP and in the film, while the version re-recorded on 20 December was the one on the single. Although we cannot track down the sessions at which two unreleased tracks 'Who's Gonna Take You Home' and 'Let's Stick Together' were recorded, both titles did turn up on a 7" double-sided acetate during this period and were supposedly taped sometime during 1959.

were live recordings taped before a specially invited audience of 200 fans during two nights at Abbey Road's studio 2, and provided the material for the debut album CLIFF. However, it is unclear which tracks were recorded on which evening, and therefore both the sessions have been listed together. It is also unclear whether any test recordings were made of the rehearsal sessions that took place during the afternoon of each day. Of the material, interest was focused on a string of spirited performances of mostly solid rock repertoire, with the Drifters playing solo, and without Cliff, on three of the tracks. Although both 'It's Only Make Believe' and 'Kisses Sweeter Than Wine' were recorded, they were dropped from the final selection on the album. It is uncertain for what reason, but in all probability it was likely to have been for over-running the duration time of the album. There are, of course, other possibilities such as copyright entanglements or artistic valuations.

The next few sessions turned up some items of interest. In April, Cliff cut the soundtrack sides for his first feature film *Serious Charge* but re-recorded a new country version of 'Living Doll' for record release as the version in the film had to bear an authentic rock 'n' roll stamp in keeping with the setting of the movie. From a commercial point of view, the film version was not satisfactory for release as a single or album track. For the next session in May, Cliff put down his vocal for 'A Teenager In Love' during a Drifters remake session of 'Jet Black' and 'Driftin''. This track was never commercially released probably for the reason

OCTOBER 14 1940

Harry Rodger Webb is born in Lucknow, India to Rodger and Dorothy Webb.

1943

Harry's sister Donella is born.

1945

Harry attends his first school which is attached to St Thomas's Church in Lucknow, where he sings in the choir.

1948

Harry's second sister Jacqueline is born.
7-year old Harry and his family undertake the three-week voyage to Tilbury, England, on the SS Ranghi.

SEPTEMBER

With just £5 to their name the Webb family move in to a single room in Carshalton, Surrey.

SEPTEMBER

Harry is enrolled at Stanley Park Road Primary School in Carshalton.

1949

For much of the year Harry's father is unemployed and finds it hard to make ends meet.
Harry's first girlfriend is pony-tailed school friend Elizabeth Sayers.

1950

The Webb family move to Waltham Cross in Hertfordshire where Harry's father starts work for Ferguson's Radio at Enfield and his mother works at a factory in Broxbourne.
Harry enrols at his new school, King's Road Primary in Waltham Cross.
Harry's third sister, Joan, is born.

1952

Harry fails his eleven-plus and goes to Cheshunt Secondary Modern School. The Webb family move into a red-brick three-bedroomed council house in Hargreaves Close, Cheshunt, where Rodger Webb makes furniture for their new home out of packing cases.

1953

Harry plays 'right-back' for the school and Hertfordshire under-14 football teams.

1954/55/56

Harry becomes a leading light in the school dramatic society, taking on the role of Ratty in Toad Of Toad Hall and Bob Cratchit in Dickens' A Christmas Carol. Harry becomes friends with two of the teachers at his school, Mrs Norris and Bill Latham.

1957

Harry is stripped of his prefect's badge for playing truant from school to go to a cinema in Edmonton to watch visiting American Rock 'n' Roll stars Bill Haley and the Comets.
Harry leaves Cheshunt Secondary Modern School with a GCE 'O' level in English.
Harry and some of his school friends, Beryl Molyneux, John Vince, Freda Johnson and Betty Clark perform as The Quintones at the local Holy Trinity Church Youth Club.
Harry works as a credit control clerk at Atlas Lamps Enfield for £4 15s 0d a week.

1958

Drummer Terry Smart co-opts Harry into the local Dick Teague skiffle group as a vocalist and rhythm guitarist.
Terry Smart and Harry break away from the skiffle group to form the Drifters in order to play more rock 'n' roll based music. They enlist an old schoolfriend of Harry's, guitarist Norman Mitham and rehearse at the Webbs' house.
18-year-old teddy boy John Foster, an employee at the local sewage works, is so impressed by Harry after watching him perform at the Five Horseshoes in Hoddesdon that he offers to become his manager. Harry agrees.
A ballroom manager at a hall in Derby where Harry and the boys were appearing said he couldn't bill them as Harry Webb and the Drifters as it wasn't a particularly good name for a rock 'n' roll singer. After initial suggestions of Cliff Russard and Russ Clifford, John Foster suggests Cliff Richard.
Following an appearance by Cliff at the 2i's Club in London's Old Compton Street, guitarist/bass player Ian Samwell joins the group.

EARLY SUMMER

John Foster's parents put up the then-substantial sum of £10 for Cliff to make a demonstration record with cover versions of Lloyd Price's 'Lawdy Miss Clawdy' and Jerry Lee Lewis' 'Breathless' at a recording studio in London's Oxford Street.

MID-1958

HMV Records, Oxford Street, London
Private Recordings

Lawdy Miss Clawdy	*(Unissued)*
Breathless	*(Unissued)*

Lead Vocal:	**Cliff Richard**
Guitar:	**Ian Samwell/Norman Mitham/ Ken Pavey**
Drums:	**Terry Smart**
Engineer:	
Session hours:	

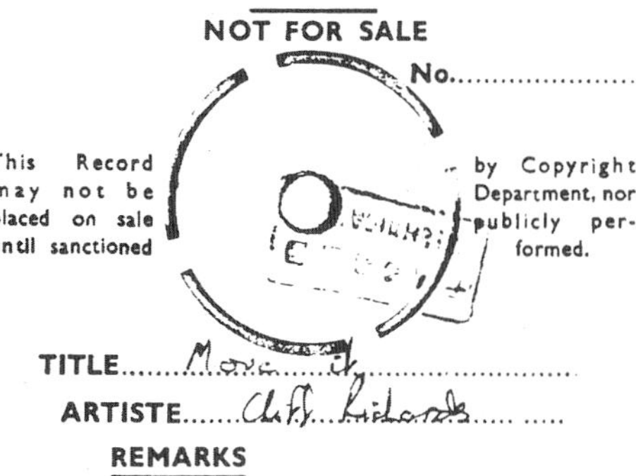

MID-SUMMER

Cliff closes the bill at a Carroll Levis talent contest at the Gaumont Theatre in London's Shepherd's Bush, and a month later, at another appearance there, agent George Ganjou attends and is impressed.

LATE SUMMER

Record producer Norrie Paramor agrees to take Cliff and the Drifters on after hearing their demonstration record.

24 JULY

Abbey Road
Studio session

Schoolboy Crush	*B-side*
Move It	*A-side*

Lead Vocal:	**Cliff Richard**
Guitar:	**Ernie Shear/ Ian Samwell**
Bass:	**Frank Clarke**
Drums:	**Terry Smart**
Vocals:	**Mike Sammes Singers- 7.00pm-9.00 pm only**
Producer:	**Norrie Paramor**
Engineer:	**Malcolm Addey**
Recorded in:	**Studio 2**
Session hours:	**7.00pm-10.30pm**

LATE SUMMER

George Ganjou signs them to his agency.

AUGUST

With Ken Pavey replacing Norman Mitham, Cliff and the Drifters play a 9-week residency at Butlin's holiday camp, Clacton-on-Sea.

AUGUST 9

Cliff signs a long-term contract with Columbia records.

AUGUST

Cliff's first single 'Move It'/'Schoolboy Crush' is released.

SEPTEMBER 12

'Move It' enters the chart.

SEPTEMBER 13

Cliff makes his TV debut on ABC TV's *Oh Boy!* singing 'Move It' and 'Don't Bug Me Baby!'.

SEPTEMBER

Through contacts at the 2i's coffee bar, Cliff recruits two more Drifters, Hank B. Marvin and Bruce Welch. Formerly with the Railroaders skiffle group, and the Chesternuts, they join Terry Smart, Ian Samwell and Cliff to become the new line up of the Drifters. Ken Pavey in no longer a member of the group.

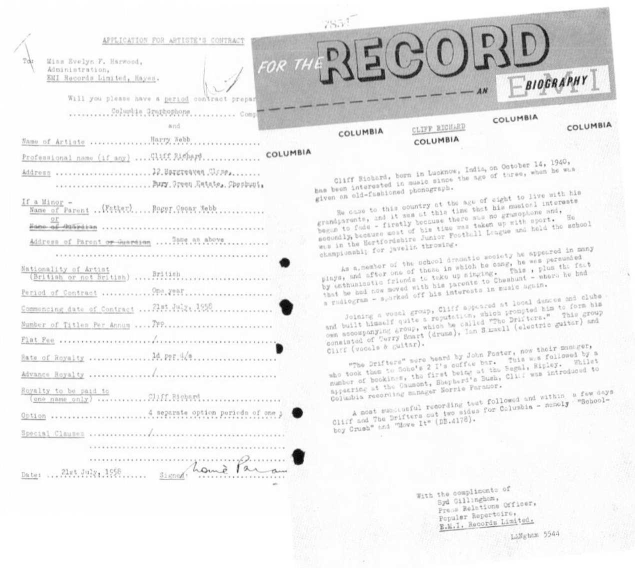

APPLICATION FOR ARTISTE'S CONTRACT

To: Miss Evelyn F. Harwood,
Administration,
EMI Records Limited, Hayes.

Will you please have a period contract prepar[ed] ... Columbia Graphophone ... Comp[any] and

Name of Artiste ... Harry Webb
Professional name (if any) ... Cliff Richard
Address ... 12 Hargreaves Close, Bury Green Estate, Cheshunt.
If a Minor - Name of Parent (Father) ... Roger Oscar Webb
~~Name of Guardian~~
Address of Parent ~~or Guardian~~ ... Same as above
Nationality of Artist (British or not British) ... British
Period of Contract ... One year
Commencing date of Contract ... 21st July, 1958
Number of Titles Per Annum ... Two
Flat Fee ... /
Rate of Royalty ... 1d per d/s
Advance Royalty ... /
Royalty to be paid to (one name only) ... Cliff Richard
Option ... 4 separate option periods of one y[ear]
Special Clauses ... /

Date: 21st July, 1958 Signed: Norrie Param[or]

FOR THE RECORD — AN EMI BIOGRAPHY

COLUMBIA CLIFF RICHARD COLUMBIA

Cliff Richard, born in Lucknow, India, on October 14, 1940, has been interested in music since the age of three, when he was given an old-fashioned phonograph.

He came to this country at the age of eight to live with his grandparents, and it was at this time that his musical interests began to fade - firstly because there was no gramophone and, secondly, because most of his time was taken up with sport. He was in the Hertfordshire Junior Football League and held the school championship for javelin throwing.

As a member of the school dramatic society he appeared in many plays, and after one of these in which he sang, he was persuaded by enthusiastic friends to take up singing. This , plus the fact that he had now moved with his parents to Cheshunt - where he had a radiogram - sparked off his interests in music again.

Joining a vocal group, Cliff appeared at local dances and clubs and built himself quite a reputation, which prompted him to form his own accompanying group, which he called "The Drifters." This group consisted of Terry Smart (drums), Ian Samwell (electric guitar) and Cliff (vocals & guitar).

"The Drifters" were heard by John Foster, now their manager, who took them to Soho's 2 I's coffee bar. This was followed by a number of bookings, the first being at the Regal, Ripley. Whilst appearing at the Gaumont, Shepherd's Bush, Cliff was introduced to Columbia recording manager Norrie Paramor.

A most successful recording test followed and within a few days Cliff and The Drifters cut two sides for Columbia - namely "Schoolboy Crush" and "Move It" (DB.4178).

With the compliments of
Syd Gillingham,
Press Relations Officer,
Popular Repertoire,
E.M.I. Records Limited.

LANgham 5544

3 OCTOBER

ABBEY ROAD
Studio session

High Class Baby	*A-side*
My Feet Hit The Ground	*B-side*
Don't Bug Me Baby	*(Unissued)*

Lead Vocal:	**Cliff Richard**
Guitars:	
Bass:	
Drums:	
Bongos:	

Producer:	**Norrie Paramor**
Engineer:	**Malcolm Addey**
Recorded in:	**Studio 2**
Session hours:	**2.00 pm-7.30pm (Rehearsal 2.00pm-3.00pm)**

OCTOBER 5

Cliff begins a tour with the Kalin Twins. The Most Brothers, who are also on the bill, lend Cliff their bass player Jet Harris for some appearances during the tour.

OCTOBER

Immediately after the tour, Ian Samwell leaves the Drifters to concentrate on songwriting and is replaced by Jet Harris.

OCTOBER

Franklin Boyd becomes Cliff's manager but John Foster still continues to work with Cliff in a similar capacity.

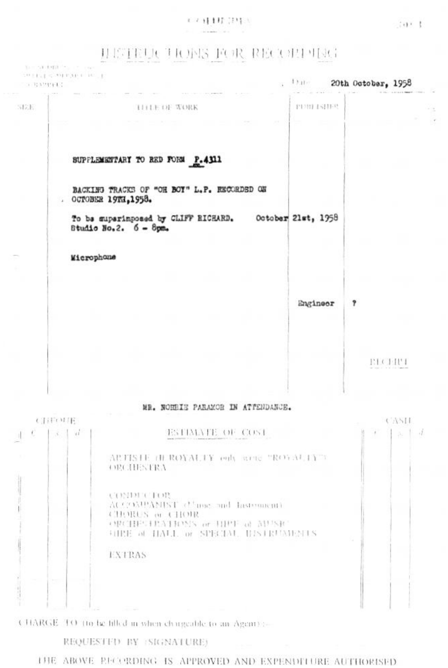
INSTRUCTIONS FOR RECORDING

Date 20th October, 1958

TITLE OF WORK | PUBLISHER

SUPPLEMENTARY TO RED FORM P.4311

BACKING TRACKS OF "OH BOY" L.P. RECORDED ON OCTOBER 19TH,1958.

To be superimposed by CLIFF RICHARD. October 21st, 1958
Studio No.2. 6 – 8pm.

Microphone

Engineer ?

MR. NORRIE PARAMOR IN ATTENDANCE.

ESTIMATE OF COST

ARTISTE (IF ROYALTY only write "ROYALTY")
ORCHESTRA

CONDUCTOR
ACCOMPANIST (Name and Instrument)
CHORUS or CHOIR
ORCHESTRATIONS or HIRE of MUSIC
HIRE of HALL or SPECIAL INSTRUMENTS

EXTRAS

CHARGE TO (to be filled in when chargeable to an Agent):
REQUESTED BY (SIGNATURE)
THE ABOVE RECORDING IS APPROVED AND EXPENDITURE AUTHORISED

21 OCTOBER

ABBEY ROAD
TV soundtrack recordings for ABC TV

TV Hop	*Oh Boy!*
King Creole	*Oh Boy!*
High School Confidential	*Oh Boy!*
Rockin' Robin	*Oh Boy!*
Early In The Morning	*Oh Boy!*
Somebody Touched Me	*Oh Boy!*
I'll Try	*Oh Boy!*

Producer:	**Norrie Paramor**
Engineer:	**Backing tracks – Norman Newell** **Vocal tracks – Malcolm Addey**
Recorded in:	**Studio 2**
Session hours:	**6.00pm-10.00pm**

Backing tracks were recorded on the 19 October.
Musical direction: Harry Robinson/Geoff Love

OCTOBER 25

Cliff makes his radio debut on the BBC Light Programme's *Saturday Club.*

NOVEMBER

Columbia release Cliff's second single 'High Class Baby'/'My Feet Hit The Ground'.

14 NOVEMBER

ABBEY ROAD
Studio session

Livin' Lovin' Doll	*A-side*
Mean Streak	*A-side*

Lead Vocal:	**Cliff Richard**
Guitar:	**Hank Marvin/Bruce Welch**
Bass:	**Jet Harris**
Drums:	**Terry Smart**
Piano:	

Producer:	**Norrie Paramor**
Engineer:	**Malcolm Addey**
Recorded in:	**Studio 2**
Session hours:	**6.00pm-9.20pm**

NOVEMBER 17

Cliff makes his debut on the still-thriving Variety circuit, where rock'n'roll stars were something of a novelty, at the Metropolitan Theatre, Edgware Road in London.

Right from early in his career, Cliff used session musicians as well as The Shadows.

19 NOVEMBER

ABBEY ROAD
Studio session

Never Mind	*(Unissued)*
Steady With You	*B-side*

Lead Vocal:	**Cliff Richard**
Guitar:	**Hank Marvin/Bruce Welch**
Bass:	**Jet Harris**
Drums:	**Terry Smart**
Piano:	
Vocals:	**Mike Sammes Singers**
Producer:	**Norrie Paramor**
Engineer:	**Malcolm Addey**
Recorded in:	**Studio 2**
Session hours:	**2.00pm-5.30pm**

NOVEMBER 21

'High Class Baby' enters the chart, eventually peaking at No. 7.

DECEMBER

Cliff rehearses for the part of Curly Thompson in the forthcoming movie *Serious Charge*.

JANUARY

Cliff makes his first appearance with the new Drifters at Manchester's Free Trade Hall. On the bill with them at the various appearances which follow are the outrageous singer with the flaming orange hair, Wee Willie Harris, Tony Crombie and His Rockets, and 'the sensational new comedian from Liverpool', compere Jimmy Tarbuck.

JANUARY

Franklin Boyd and John Foster receive dismissal letters from Cliff's father.

JANUARY

Cliff's third single 'Living Loving Doll'/'Steady With You' is released. Despite Hank Marvin, Bruce Welch and Jet Harris making their debut on a Cliff single it only reaches No. 20 in the chart.

JANUARY 30

'Living Loving Doll' enters the chart, which is also a historical moment as it's the first time the current group have played on a Cliff Richard single. The Drifters also release their debut single 'Feelin' Fine'/'Don't Be A Fool With Love'.

FEBRUARY

Despite the *NME*'s comments about Cliff's gyrations on ABC TV's *Oh Boy*, he wins the paper's 'Best New Single' award.

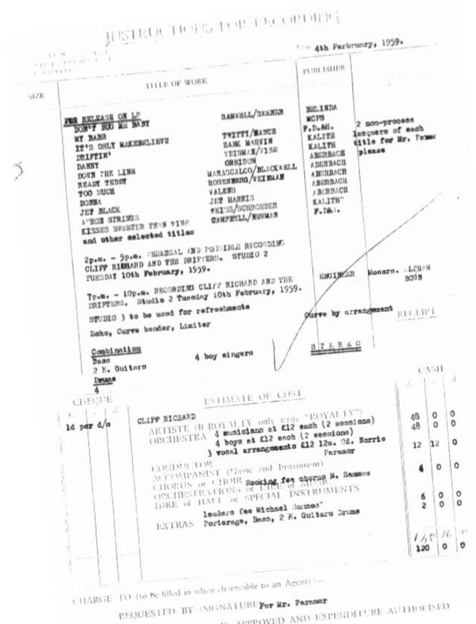

INSTRUCTIONS FOR RECORDING

4th Ferbruary, 1959.

TITLE OF WORK

FOR RELEASE ON LP
DON'T BUG ME BABY
MY BABE — TWITTY/NANCE
IT'S ONLY MAKEBELIEVE
DRIFTIN' — HANK MARVIN
DANNY
DOWN THE LINE — ORBISON
READY TEDDY — MARASCALCO/BLACKWELL
TOO MUCH — ROSENBERG/WEINMAN
DONNA — VALENS
JET BLACK — JET HARRIS
APRON STRINGS — WEISS/SCHROEDER
KISSES SWEETER THAN WINE — CAMPBELL/NEWMAN
and other selected titles

PUBLISHER: BELINDA, MCPS, F.D.&H., KALITH, KALITH, ABERBACH, ABERBACH, ABERBACH, ABERBACH, ABERBACH, KALITH, F.D.&H.

2 non-process lacquers of each title for Mr. Paramor please

2p.m. – 5p.m. REHEARSAL AND POSSIBLE RECORDING CLIFF RICHARD AND THE DRIFTERS. STUDIO 2 TUESDAY 10th February, 1959.

7p.m. – 10p.m. RECORDING CLIFF RICHARD AND THE DRIFTERS. Studio 2 Tuesday 10th February, 1959.

STUDIO 3 to be used for refreshments

Echo, Curve bender, Limiter

Combination
Bass
2 E. Guitars
Drums
4

4 boy singers

ENGINEER

Curve by arrangement

STEREO

ESTIMATE OF COST

CHEQUE		CASH
1d per d/s	CLIFF RICHARD	
	ARTISTE / ORCHESTRA: 4 musicians at £12 each (2 sessions)	48 0 0
	4 boys at £12 each (2 sessions)	48 0 0
	3 vocal arrangements £12 12s. 0d. Norrie Paramor	12 12 0
	CONDUCTOR / ACCOMPANIST	4 0 0
	CHORUS or CHOIR: Booking fee chorus M. Sammes	
	ORCHESTRATIONS or SPECIAL INSTRUMENTS	6 0 0
	HIRE of HALL: leaders fee Michael Sammes	2 0 0
	EXTRAS: Porterage, Bass, 2 E. Guitars Drums	
		120 0 0

CHARGE TO (to be filled in when chargeable to an Agent) :—
REQUESTED BY (SIGNATURE) For Mr. Paramor
THE ABOVE RECORDING IS APPROVED AND EXPENDITURE AUTHORISED

FEBRUARY
Tito Burns is appointed Cliff's manager.

FEBRUARY
Terry Smart leaves the Drifters, eventually joining the Merchant Navy and is replaced by a drummer suggested by Jet Harris – Tony Meehan. Tony had previously played with the Worried Men skiffle group behind Adam Faith, Vince Eager, Vince Taylor and the Vipers.

9/10 FEBRUARY

ABBEY ROAD
Live studio session

It's Only Make Believe	*(Unissued)*
Apron Strings	*Cliff*
My Babe	*Cliff*
Down The Line	*Cliff*
I Got A Feeling	*Cliff*
Jet Black	*Cliff*
Baby I Don't Care	*Cliff*
Donna	*Cliff*
Move It	*Cliff*
Ready Teddy	*Cliff*
Too Much	*Cliff*
Don't Bug Me Baby	*Cliff*
Driftin'	*Cliff*
That'll Be The Day	*Cliff*
Be Bop A Lula	*Cliff*
Danny	*Cliff*
Whole Lotta Shakin' Goin' On	*Cliff*
Kisses Sweeter Than Wine	*(Unissued)*

Lead Vocal: **Cliff Richard**
Guitar: **Hank Marvin/Bruce Welch**
Bass: **Jet Harris**
Drums: **Tony Meehan**
Vocals: **Mike Sammes Singers**

Producer: **Norrie Paramor**
Engineer: **Malcom Addey**
Recorded in: **Studio 2**
Session hours: **7.00pm-10.00pm (Rehearsal 2.00pm-5.00 pm)**

9 MARCH

ABBEY ROAD
Studio session

Never Mind	*B-side*
Choppin' And Changin'	*(Unissued)*
Dynamite (5)	*(Unissued)*

Guitar: **Hank Marvin/Bruce Welch**
Bass: **Jet Harris**
Drums: **Tony Meehan**

Lead Vocal: **Cliff Richard**
Producer: **Norrie Paramor**
Engineer: **Malcom Addey**
Recorded in: **Studio 2**
Session hours: **7.00pm-midnight**

APRIL
The first album is released, simply entitled 'Cliff'.

28 APRIL

ABBEY ROAD
Film soundtrack recordings

Living Doll (4)	*A-side*
No Turning Back (9)	*(Serious Charge) EP*
Mad About You (3)	*(Serious Charge) EP*
Chinchilla (9)	*(Serious Charge) EP*

Lead Vocal:	**Cliff Richard**
Guitar:	**Hank Marvin/Bruce Welch**
Bass:	**Jet Harris**
Drums:	**Tony Meehan**
Producer:	**Norrie Paramor**
Engineer:	**Malcolm Addey**
Recorded in:	**Studio 2**
Session hours:	**2.30pm-5.30pm**

Chinchilla is an instrumental by the Drifters featured in the movie and on the soundtrack EP.

4 MAY

ABBEY ROAD
Studio session

A Teenager In Love	*(Unissued)*

Lead Vocal:	**Cliff Richard**
Guitar:	**Hank Marvin/Bruce Welch**
Bass:	**Jet Harris**
Drums:	**Tony Meehan**
Producer:	**Norrie Paramor**
Engineer:	**Malcolm Addey**
Recorded in:	**Studio 2**
Session hours:	**6.00pm-9.45pm**

Tito Burns, who took over as Cliff's manager in February.

MAY 8

Cliff's fourth single 'Mean Streak' enters the chart, only to be followed into the hit parade the following week by the other side 'Never Mind'.

MAY

Cliff appears in the film *Serious Charge* starring Anthony Quayle, Andrew Ray and Sarah Churchill. Cliff says, 'The people who made the film must have been daft. I was cast as Curly, but instead of simply changing the name of the character, they went through the painful and complicated procedure of curling my hair with hot tongs every morning before the day's shooting.'

SERIOUS CHARGE

Eros Films, 1959. Running time: 99 minutes. Cliff's first feature film.

Synopsis:
Curly Thompson (Cliff) is the brother of the leader of a gang of youngsters who were into speed and lived for the next joy ride

Cast:
Anthony Quayle, Sarah Churchill, Andrew Ray, Irene Brown, Percy Herbert, Cliff Richard.

Credits:
Producer: Michael Delamar. Director: Terence Young. Photography: Georges Perinal. Musical score: Leighton Lucas.

Songs:
'Living Doll', 'No Turning Back', 'Mad About You' performed by Cliff Richard and The Drifters. 'Chinchilla' performed by The Drifters (on soundtrack only)

25 MAY

ABBEY ROAD
Studio session

Apron Strings	*B-side*
We Had It Made	*(Unissued)*

Lead Vocal:	**Cliff Richard**
Guitars:	**Hank Marvin/Bruce Welch**
Bass:	**Jet Harris**
Drums:	**Tony Meehan**
Producer:	**Norrie Paramor**
Engineer:	**Malcolm Addey**
Recorded in:	**Studio 2**
Session hours:	**6.30pm-10.00pm**

JUNE

'Cliff No.1' EP is released.

JULY 10

Cliff's fifth single 'Living Doll', written by Lionel Bart, enters the chart and goes on to win him his first Gold Disc.

JULY

'Cliff No.2' EP is released. Due to confusion with the American Drifters, Cliff's backing group change their name to the Shadows. This is suggested by bass guitarist Jet Harris.

25 JULY

ABBEY ROAD
Studio session

Choppin' And Changin' (34)	*(Unissued)*
Dynamite (51)	*Rock on With Cliff*
Travellin' Light (15)	*A-side*

Lead Vocal:	**Cliff Richard**
Guitars:	**Hank Marvin/Bruce Welch**
Bass:	**Jet Harris**
Drums:	**Tony Meehan**
Producer:	**Norrie Paramor**
Engineer:	**Malcolm Addey**
Recorded in:	**Studio 2**
Session hours:	**6.00pm-10.00pm**

26 JULY

ABBEY ROAD
Studio session

I Gotta Know (13)	*Cliff Sings-Mono version*
The Snake And The Bookworm (11)	*Cliff Sings-Mono version*
I'm Willing To Learn (13)	*Me and My Shadows- Mono version*
We Have It Made (63)	*Me and My Shadows- Mono version*

Lead Vocal:	**Cliff Richard**
Guitars:	**Hank Marvin/Bruce Welch**
Bass:	**Jet Harris**
Drums:	**Tony Meehan**
Producer:	**Norrie Paramor**
Engineers:	**Mono – Malcolm Addey/David Lloyd** **Stereo – Peter Bown / Stuart Eltham**
Recorded in:	**Studio 2**
Session hours:	**6.00pm-10.00pm**

Engineer Malcolm Addey in the control room during the recording of the Cliff Sings album.

AUGUST 21

Cliff appears on the front cover of the *NME* 'as you will see him in the film *Expresso Bongo*'. Classified small ads in the paper offer '12 different pictures of Cliff in action for only 2/9d'.

AUGUST 29

Cliff is best man at the wedding of Shadow Bruce Welch to Anne Findlay at St Stephen's Church, Westminster.

SEPTEMBER 4

Cliff meets Michael Delamar, producer of *Serious Charge*, to discuss his next film.

6 SEPTEMBER

ABBEY ROAD
Studio session

Choppin' And Changin'	*Me and My Shadows- Mono version*
Dynamite	*A-side*
I Gotta Know	*Cliff Sings-Stereo version*
The Snake And The Bookworm	*Cliff Sings-Stereo version*
Here Comes Summer (6)	*Cliff Sings*
Twenty Flight Rock	*Cliff Sings*

Lead Vocal:	**Cliff Richard**
Guitars:	**Hank Marvin/Bruce Welch**
Bass:	**Jet Harris**
Drums:	**Tony Meehan**
Producer:	**Norrie Paramor**
Engineers:	**Mono – Malcolm Addey/Alan Kane**
	Stereo – Peter Bown/Norman Smith
Recorded in:	**Studio 2**
Session hours:	**6.00pm-9.50pm**

7 SEPTEMBER

ABBEY ROAD
Studio session

Blue Suede Shoes (7)	*Cliff Sings*
Mean Woman Blues (3)	*Cliff Sings*
Pointed Toe Shoes (12)	*Cliff Sings*

Lead Vocal:	**Cliff Richard**
Guitars:	**Hank Marvin/Bruce Welch**
Bass:	**Jet Harris**
Drums:	**Tony Meehan**
Producer:	**Norrie Paramor**
Engineers:	**Mono – Malcolm Addey/Alan Kane**
	Stereo – Stuart Eltham/Norman Smith
Recorded in:	**Studio 2**
Session hours:	**7.00pm-10.00pm**

1167

25th May, 1959.

7XCA APRON STRINGS
24877 (remake for single)
7XCA 24878 THERE'S A REASON
7XCA 24879 WE HAD IT MADE
7XCA 24880 ALL THAT I NEED

D.J. lacq's reqd.
D.J. lacq's reqd.
D.J. lacq's reqd.
D.J. lacq's reqd.

To be recorded by Cliff Richard and the Drifters
Monday 25th May, 1959. Studio 2. 6.30p.m. – 9.30

2 non-process lacquers of each title for Mr. Paramor please

Echo
Curve bender
Limiter

Curve by arrangement

Combination
2 guitars
Bass
Drums
4

Engineers:- Bown
Eltham

MR. NORRIE PARAMOR IN ATTENDANCE

14. per a/c CLIFF RICHARD

4 musicians at £6 each — 24 0 0

Porterage. Bass, 1.E.Gtr. Drms. — 1 10 0

25 10 0

FOR NORRIE PARAMOR

8 SEPTEMBER

ABBEY ROAD
Studio session

I'm Walkin' (5)	*Cliff Sings*
A Voice In The Wilderness (25)	*Expresso Bongo EP*
Love (5)	*Expresso Bongo EP*

Lead Vocal:	**Cliff Richard**
Guitars:	**Hank Marvin/Bruce Welch**
Bass:	**Jet Harris**
Drums:	**Tony Meehan**
Producer:	**Norrie Paramor**
Engineers:	**Mono – Malcolm Addey /Alan Kane**
	Stereo – Stuart Eltham/ Norman Smith
Recorded in:	**Studio 2**
Session hours:	**7.00pm-10.00pm**

9 SEPTEMBER

ABBEY ROAD
Studio session

That's My Desire (5)	*Cliff Sings*
Little Things Mean A Lot (6)	*Cliff Sings*
I'll String Along With You (1)	*Cliff Sings*
Somewhere Along The Way (10)	*Cliff Sings*

Lead Vocal:	**Cliff Richard**
	The Norrie Paramor Orchestra
Producer:	**Norrie Paramor**
Engineers:	**Mono – Malcolm Addey /Alan Kane**
	Stereo – Stuart Eltham/ Norman Smith
Recorded in:	**Studio 2**
Session hours:	**7.00pm-10.00pm**

10 SEPTEMBER

ABBEY ROAD
Studio session

Embraceable You (14)	*Cliff Sings*
I Don't Know Why (3)	*Cliff Sings*
As Time Goes By (14)	*Cliff Sings*
The Touch Of Your Lips (4)	*Cliff Sings*

Lead Vocal:	**Cliff Richard**
	The Norrie Paramor Orchestra
Producer:	**Norrie Paramor**
Engineers:	**Mono – Malcolm Addey/ Alan Kane**
	Stereo – Stuart Eltham/ Norman Smith
Recorded in:	**Studio 1**
Session hours:	**7.00pm-10.15pm**

ARTISTE CLIFF RICHARD AND THE SHADOWS
CLASS (TALENT)
LANGUAGE
ACCOMPANIMENT
CONDUCTOR
ARTISTES DEPT. REPRESENTATIVE Mr. NORRIE PARAMOR
RECORDINGS BY MA, FG.
FOR (COY.) Columbia
DATE 19. 10. 59
TIME 02.30 pm
START 02.30 pm.
FINISH 05.30 pm.

"THE SHRINE ON THE SECOND FLOOR"
"FALL IN LOVE WITH YOU"
"BONGO BLUES"

(2 non-process lacquers of each title for Mr Norrie Paramor please.)

SEPTEMBER 18

NME describes Cliff as, 'The most electrifying and dynamic vocal talent to emerge in recent years'.

SEPTEMBER 25

Only a year after his first hit and the article in which they had referred to him as 'a crude exhibitionist', the *NME* include a four-page tribute to Cliff in their September 25 issue. In the supplement Cliff pays tribute to his producer Norrie Paramor, the guy who is by now his manager, Tito Burns, his agent George Ganjou and TV producer Jack Good. Cliff says, 'One short year and yet I seem to have accomplished so much – I've been very lucky. Without the public there would be no Cliff Richard success story – I shall never forget what they've done for me.'

SEPTEMBER 25

Cliff says: 'Marriage is my ultimate aim – but not until I'm 27.' 'In spite of all the insults hurled at today's teenagers, I think they're a great crowd. I should know after all, I'm one of them.'

SEPTEMBER

Cliff gives his own top 10:
Elvis Presley – 'Heartbreak Hotel' 'This was Elvis's first record to break really big.'
Connie Francis – 'Sailor Boy' 'Connie is one of my favourite female artists.'
Frank Sinatra – 'It Happened In Monterey' 'This was the first Sinatra disc that I ever bothered to listen to.'
Ricky Nelson – 'I Believe What You Say' 'Ricky is a big favourite of mine ...this is one of the best beat numbers ever recorded.'
Lena Horne – 'At The Waldorf Astotia'(LP) 'There is really only one thing you can say about her. Perfection.'
Drifters – 'Jet Black' 'Jet Black is one of my favourite instrumentals.'
Carmen Jones (LP) 'I like opera, but I listen to it in a way that's understandable to me.'
Elvis Presley – 'Don't Be Cruel' 'I just like it.'
Ferlin Husky – 'Boulevard Of Broken Dreams' (LP) 'This man is one of the sincerest singers I know.'
Marty Wilde – 'Fire Of Love' 'Marty is a close friend of mine. This is one of his best records.'
Quotes about Cliff:
Marty Wilde 'We aren't rivals.'
'One of the few things we have in common is a liking for Chinese food.'
Craig Douglas 'Cliff is so good-looking, I'd hate to have to follow him on a show.'
Lionel Bart 'I think Cliff & the Shadows' unique rendition of my 'Living Doll' is merely a rung on the ladder towards far bigger things.'
Jack Good 'One of the greatest performers in the country.'
'He always knows the keys in which he sings!'
Jayne Mansfield 'I think Cliff Richard is the "Most".'

Johnny never had it so good – or lost it so fast!
LAURENCE HARVEY
SYLVIA SYMS
YOLANDE DONLAN
EXPRESSO BONGO
CLIFF RICHARD
Written for the screen by WOLF MANKOWITZ
Directed and Produced by VAL GUEST
A VAL GUEST PRODUCTION
PG
Virgin

EXPRESSO BONGO

British Lion Films, 1959. Running time: 111 minutes
Cliff's second feature film.
Synopsis:
Bert Rudge (Cliff), a young beat singer becomes world famous as Bongo Herbert, managed by the rather unscrupulous Johnny Jackson (Laurence Harvey).
Cast:
Laurence Harvey, Sylvia Syms, Yolande Donlan, Cliff Richard.
Credits:
Producer & Director: Val Guest. Story: Wolf Mankowitz.
Photography: John Wilcox.
Songs:
'Love', 'A Voice In The Wilderness', 'The Shrine On The Second Floor' performed by Cliff Richard and The Shadows. 'Bongo Blues' performed by the Shadows.

SEPTEMBER

'My ultimate ambition is to make a Western with Elvis', declares Cliff, adding 'If I had the choice to pick any girl actress to play opposite me in a film, I'd pick Sandra Dee without hesitation. I think she's just fabulous.'

SEPTEMBER/OCTOBER

Cliff films *Expresso Bongo* in which he plays the part of up-and-coming rock 'n' roller 'Bongo Herbert'. Laurence Harvey portrays his manager, who is decidedly more keen on his percentage than his protege's well-being. A more sympathetic ear comes from Harvey's girl-friend in the film, Sylvia Sims. Yolande Donlan is cast as a fading singer who becomes the rising star's would-be seductress. The film, which runs for 1 hour 48 minutes, is produced and directed by Val Guest with screenplay by Wolf Mankowitz.

SEPTEMBER 28

National headlines proclaim: 'Military help Glasgow police control Cliff Richard crowds.'

OCTOBER 2

Keith Fordyce reviews Cliff's new single 'Travellin' Light': 'Cliff Richard's latest is very good, but not tipped for the top spot.' 'Living Doll' enters the US *Billboard* Top 100 at No. 80.

OCTOBER 9

Cliff is voted 'Top British Male Singer' in the *NME* annual poll, while 'Living Doll' is voted 'Disc of the Year'.

OCTOBER 9

Both sides of Cliff's sixth single 'Travellin' Light'/'Dynamite' enter the charts.

OCTOBER 14

Cliff is given a surprise birthday party in Leeds. Among the guests are his parents, manager Tito Burns, impresario Arthur Howes, fan club secretary Jan Vane and the Shadows. Cliff receives over 2,000 cards and presents. 'I can honestly say it is the happiest day of my life.'

19 OCTOBER

ABBEY ROAD

Film soundtrack recordings for Expresso Bongo

The Shrine On The Second Floor (6)	*Expresso Bongo EP*
Fall In Love With You	*(Unissued)*
Bongo Blues (3)	*Expresso Bongo EP*

Lead Vocal:	**Cliff Richard**
Guitars:	**Hank Marvin/Bruce Welch**
Bass:	**Jet Harris**
Drums:	**Tony Meehan**
Producer:	**Norrie Paramor**
Engineers:	**Mono – Malcolm Addey**
	Stereo – Stuart Eltham/Alan Kane
Recorded in:	**Studio 2**
Session hours:	**2.30pm-5.30pm**

Bongo Blues is an instrumental by the Shadows featured in the movie and on the soundtrack EP.

OCTOBER 26

Cliff broadcasts live from Radio Luxembourg, with DJs Barry Alldis, Don Moss and Ted King. The mainland Europe-based commercial station was at the time the premier pop broadcasting outlet, long before the days of pirate radio, independent UK radio or the BBC's 'enlightened' Radio 1 and Radio 2.

OCTOBER 30

Cliff Richard Picture Parade Album is published, containing more than 120 photographs of his friends, car, girl-friends, family and various other candid shots – and all for just 3/6d!

OCTOBER 30

The natural consequences of a flip side getting as high as No. 16 in the charts would be that the sales and Top 30 positions of the top side would be seriously affected. Regardless of such logistics, 'Travellin' Light' zooms to Number One, deposes Bobby Darin's 'Mack The Knife' and stays in the top position for five weeks. For the second time in a row, Cliff knocks Darin off the pole position. 'Travellin' Light' eventually earns Cliff a silver disc.

OCTOBER

Cliff and the Shadows tour Scandinavia. Drummer Tony Meehan is hospitalised with appendicitis and his place is taken by Laurie Joseph.

NOVEMBER 1

Millions of television viewers see compere Bruce Forsyth present Cliff with a Silver Disc for 'Living Doll' during the singer's debut on the peak-viewing *Sunday Night at the London Palladium*. Shadow Tony Meehan is allowed out of hospital for a few hours to appear on the show.

NOVEMBER 6

Following Elvis in the serious merchandising stakes, Cliff Richard necklets and heart lockets become available at the knockdown price of 4/11d.

6 NOVEMBER

ABBEY ROAD

Studio session

Don't Be Mad at Me (12)	*(Unissued)*
Johnny Otis Hand Jive (12)	*(Unissued)*

Lead Vocal:	**Cliff Richard**
Guitars:	**Hank Marvin/Bruce Welch**
Bass:	**Jet Harris**
Drums:	**Tony Meehan**
Producer:	**Norrie Paramor**
Engineers:	**Mono – Malcolm Addey/Alan Kane**
	Stereo – Stuart Eltham/Peter Bown
Recorded in:	**Studio 2**
Session hours:	**2.30pm-5.30pm**

NOVEMBER 13

Cliff writes an article for the world's top film magazine *Photoplay*, in which he insists that he's not another Elvis and gives his reasons.

NOVEMBER

'Cliff Sings' LP is released.

17 NOVEMBER

ABBEY ROAD
Studio session

Fall In Love With You *(Unissued)*
Don't Be Mad At Me *(Unissued)*

Lead Vocal: **Cliff Richard**
Guitars: **Hank Marvin/Bruce Welch**
Bass: **Jet Harris**
Drums: **Tony Meehan**

Producer: **Norrie Paramor**
Engineers: **Mono – Malcolm Addey/Alan Kane**
Stereo – Stuart Eltham/Peter Bown
Recorded in: **Studio 2**
Session hours: **7.00pm-10.00pm**

19 NOVEMBER

ABBEY ROAD
Studio session

Fall In Love With You (35) *A-side*
Don't Be Mad At Me (14) *B-side*
Willie And The Hand Jive (10) *B-side*

Lead Vocal: **Cliff Richard**
Guitars: **Hank Marvin/Bruce Welch**
Bass: **Jet Harris**
Drums: **Tony Meehan**

Producer: **Norrie Paramor**
Engineers: **Mono – Malcolm Addey/Alan Kane**
Stereo – Stuart Eltham/Peter Bown
Recorded in: **Studio 2**
Session hours: **7.00pm-10.00pm**

NOVEMBER 20

The movie *Expresso Bongo,* a satirical look at the music business, is premiered at the Carlton Cinema in London. The critics dubious comments include 'Not enough numbers', 'Not enough professionalism', and 'No colour'.

DECEMBER 6

Cliff voted 'King of Rock 'n' Roll' on Radio Luxembourg's *Swoon Club.*

DECEMBER

Cliff and the Shadows appear in the pantomime *Babes in the Wood* at the Stockton Globe, Cliff playing the part of the Sheriff's troubadour.

Cliff's producer Norrie Paramor with Malcolm Addey at Abbey Road Studios.

DECEMBER

The EP 'Expresso Bongo' is released, three of the tracks have been written by Cliff's producer Norrie Paramor, and by Christmas passes the 30,000 sales mark.

20 DECEMBER

ABBEY ROAD
Studio session

A Voice In The Wilderness *A-side*
Gee But It's Lonesome *(Unissued)*

Lead Vocal: **Cliff Richard**
Guitars: **Hank Marvin/Bruce Welch**
Bass: **Jet Harris**
Drums: **Tony Meehan**

Producer: **Norrie Paramor**
Engineer: **Malcolm Addey**
Recorded in: **Studio 2**
Session hours: **11.15am-1.00pm**

DECEMBER 25

Cliff appears on Hughie Green's AR-TV's Christmas Day Special singing 'Living Doll' to thank the viewers who had voted him the artist they wanted most in the world to appear on the show.

DECEMBER 28

Cliff is voted 'Best British Male Vocalist of the Year' on the TV pop programme *Cool For Cats.* Because of pantomime commitments his mother collects the 'Cat's Whisker' award on his behalf.

1960–1961

The Records 1960 – 1961

Compared with the impact Cliff made on the charts in 1958 and 1959, the following two years proved to be exceptional. Not only did all nine singles hit the top four, but two of them reached the top spot. 'A Voice In The Wilderness' was Cliff's last single to be issued in 78rpm format and reached No.2, and 'Please Don't Tease' became the first ever single to return to No.1 after dropping from the summit. 'Gee Whiz It's You' became the first ever European single to chart in Britain, although the disc was never officially released there. Another single pressed in the United Kingdom for overseas distribution only that found its way briefly into UK record outlets was 'What'd I Say'/'Blue Moon' (Columbia DC 758) which were two tracks taken from the LISTEN TO CLIFF album and EP. Album sales were as exceptional as the singles. Two of the four albums reached No.2, while 21 TODAY and THE YOUNG ONES provided the first two consecutive No.1's on the album chart. ME AND MY SHADOWS set a precedent in British music as most of the material featured on the sixteen-track set had been written by the Shadows.

The EPs all did well too. Ten of the twelve that were released featured previously available material, so the only reason can be the value for money aspect. CLIFF SINGS, ME AND MY SHADOWS, and LISTEN TO CLIFF were all culled from the respective albums, while CLIFF'S SILVER DISCS grouped together four recent singles which boasted four A-sides. From mid-1962 the hits EPs of this nature would give less value for money by grouping together both sides of two recent singles. The most successful EP of this period was the one containing the soundtrack recordings from *Expresso Bongo* which became the first to climb into the singles chart.

The Sessions 1960 – 1961

The March 1960 recording sessions were the first of that year and as usual were held at EMI's Abbey Road studio 2. Work was geared towards producing some hit singles, B-sides and album tracks. 'Nine Times Out Of Ten', 'Please Don't Tease' and 'Gee Whiz It's You' were the gems from these sessions that pioneered the sound Cliff would keep to for the next few years. Usually the sessions started around 7pm and lasted three hours, allowing three or four tracks to be laid down. Throughout the early sixties this became the basic procedure for recording, with Cliff working the same way, simply and fast, usually putting down in one session complete takes that could later be chosen as the released master, and keeping overdubbing to a minimum. In fact, the only additional recording work on these sessions was done on the 17th when Hank Marvin carried out some guitar solo overdubs on 'I Love You So' taking up to an hour of studio time, presumably after the actual session had finished. The sessions that began in late June were recordings made at the London studios of Radio Luxembourg. The resulting tapes were then sent out to their studios in the continental Grand Duchy of Luxembourg for broadcast on a weekly series of shows called "Me And My Shadows". These shows featured material from Cliff's and the Shadows' own catalogues as well as cover versions of the rock 'n' roll standards – most now considered classics – of the time. The material included titles that Cliff never recorded in the studio. 'Dim Dim The Lights', 'Save My Soul', 'Rovin' Gambler' and 'Rock 'n' Roll Machine' were among the many performed on the programmes which opened and closed with a typically fifties arrangement of 'Me And My Shadows'.

The shows were usually sponsored by Ever Ready Batteries and Ilford Film, although it is probable that there were other sponsors over the period of transmission, which survived until April 1963. For the sessions that produced the tracks for the ME AND MY SHADOWS album the same procedure was employed as on CLIFF SINGS by re-recording some titles for the stereo issue. These were done on 24 June when 'I'm Willing To Learn', 'We Have It Made' and 'Choppin' And Changin' ' were taped. The session on 27 September was set originally to record 'A Girl Like You' but, for reasons unknown, was not in fact taped until 28 January 1961 which would seem an unusual length of time between the scheduled date and that of actual recording. Most of the recordings during this period featured the usual Shadows line-up of Hank Marvin, Bruce Welch, Jet Harris and Tony Meehan. On the last two 1961 sessions, however, drummer Brian Bennett was brought in as a replacement for Tony Meehan. Another change in the musician line-up was seen on the sessions that provided the material for the LISTEN TO CLIFF album, when the accompaniments were shared between the Shadows and the Norrie Paramor Orchestra, each representing the rhythm and ballad content of the album respectively, originally to be called STRINGY AND SWINGY.

The first foreign language recordings by Cliff were done towards the end of 1960, when he taped German versions of 'Fall In Love With You' and 'A Voice In The Wilderness' for future release in that country. Similar versions for non-English markets would be made from time to time over the next fifteen years.

Cliff went back into the studios again early in 1961, and the sessions on 4 March can be seen as remake sessions. Cliff re-recorded three songs that had first been attempted the previous October, and were needed to fill out the LISTEN TO CLIFF album.

The first session for *The Young Ones* film soundtrack was set for May, although it is unknown whether the tracks recorded here are the versions featured in the film, as the studio documentation relates to Associated British Pictures at Elstree. What is known, however, is that separate recordings for the albums were usually done some time after the film had been completed. The soundtrack recordings were usually done on the Sound Stage at Elstree, and the album tracks at Abbey Road Studios, which would explain the different versions on some of the songs. One of the reasons for this procedure was to rectify the slight discrepancies of lip movement, and of perspective when sound needed to appear either closer or further away. Also, quite often in a film score the music may not fit into the close of a sequence, but change mood into the next camera shot, and therefore so much of it would have to be re-recorded to make sure it all looked "in synch". The next sessions were designed to try some different material, and provided a number of master takes for the 21 TODAY album. The soundtrack sessions resumed in July and ran through into August. Co-star Grazina Frame recorded her vocal for overdubbing on to Carole Gray's duet with Cliff on 'Nothing Is Impossible' and also put down her solo vocal for 'No One For Me But Nicki'. Both these performances are the ones featured in the movie and on the soundtrack album.

The single version of 'The Young Ones' was also cut at the August sessions, while the strings were added at a session on 5 December. It is interesting to note that an undubbed version of the song was released, but only overseas, and never in the United Kingdom. Almost all of the recording work for the remainder of the year supplied Columbia with some material that would later surface on Cliff's only studio album of 1962.

Cliff and his *Young Ones* co-star Carole Gray.

There were also some unusual spoken items recorded by Cliff during this period which included seasonal Christmas messages for EMI and a specially recorded personal message that was later issued as a souvenir flexi-disc, given away with the *Serenade* teen magazine.

JANUARY 1

Cliff, Lonnie Donegan, Marty Wilde and Russ Conway outstrip all their American counterparts (including Elvis) by taking the top four places in the *NME* end-of-year points table.

JANUARY 15

'A Voice In The Wilderness' is released. Keith Fordyce reviews the record and says,'It's a great pity that an artist of Cliff's calibre should be burdened with a song that many people will find a bit distasteful.'

JANUARY 17

Cliff tops the bill on *Sunday Night at the London Palladium*, which also stars the Platters, and shatters previous viewing records when 19.5 million viewers in 6,853,000 homes become the biggest audience for a light entertainment show in the history of British TV.

JANUARY 18

Despite a car crash on Januray 7, involving two members of the Shadows, Hank Marvin and Jet Harris, Cliff and the group fly to the United States for their first tour of the United States, scheduled to run for 38 days and including shows in Pittsburgh, Milwaukee, Oklahoma City, Kansas City, San Antonio and Houston.

JANUARY

The American tour is advertised as having 'the biggest stars of 1960', and features not only Cliff and the Shadows but top US teen idols Frankie Avalon and Freddie Cannon, plus rhythm and blues top-liners Clyde McPhatterand Sammy Turner, and vocal group the Clovers.

JANUARY 21

Cliff appears on the *Pat Boone Show* on American TV singing 'Forty Days', 'Living Doll', 'Dynamite', 'A Voice In The Wilderness' and 'Whole Lotta Shakin', Pat Boone introduces Cliff as 'Britain's most important singing and record star – a young British lad – terribly young, terribly rich, who tonight makes his television debut. Welcome, Cliff Richard!' Cliff's opening number 'Living Doll' draws comments of 'Wizard', 'Smashing' and 'Top-hole' from Pat Boone. A conversation ensues:

Cliff: 'What? What'd he say?'

Pat: 'I simply said, "Wizard, smashing".'

Cliff: 'Excuse me a moment, please. (consults American-English dictionary). Oh, you mean crazy!'

Pat: 'Well, yes, if you prefer technical terminology. You know, Cliff, I've been reading up on you and I see that you were born in India, but left for England at the age of seven. How come?'

Cliff: 'Frankly, Pat, when you've shot one elephant you've shot them all. Besides, I was getting to be quite a burden on the family. A year old and I hadn't had a single hit record yet!'

Pat: 'That's the most tragic story I've heard since Death of a Salesman. By the way, we're all looking forward to your new picture *Expresso Bongo*.'

Cliff: 'Oh, thank you Pat, it was a fun thing to make.'

Pat: 'Fun thing? Oh dangerous, eh? But what does the title Expresso Bongo mean?'

Cliff: 'Don't know exactly. I believe it has to do with Italian coffee served in a drum.'

Pat: 'Oh, that's a fun joke. I love British humour, it's so quaint.'

Cliff: 'Thank you! You know, one of England's favourite humorists happens to be an American star?'

Pat: 'Oh, really.'

Cliff: 'Oh, indeed! Matter of fact, I'd like to sing a little tribute to him – if you'd care to join me.'

Pat: 'Charmed – what'll it be?'

Cliff: 'It's called 'Pretty Blue Eyes'. I hope you like it, Mr Jack Benny...'

Cliff and Pat then duet on 'Pretty Little Blue Eyes.' After the show Pat Boone says, 'Cliff should have a long and impressive show business career.' One of the production team on the show says, 'I'd call Cliff a younger Pat Boone.'

AMERICAN TOUR 1960

Cliff Richard and the Shadows first American tour was set up to capitalise on the stateside success of Living Doll which had enterd the US *Billboard* Chart at the end of 1959. The tour was advertised as featuring 'The Biggest Stars of 1960', and also on the bill were Frankie Cannon, Clyde McPhatter, Sammy Turner, the Clovers, Bobby Rydell, Johnny and the Hurricanes, The Isley Brothers, Linda Laurie and the Crests. Cliff, backed by the regular Shadows line-up, opened his act with 'Forty Days' followed by 'My Babe'. The other songs featured in his set were 'A Voice In The Wilderness', 'Living Doll' and 'Whole Lotta Shakin Goin On'. When it was discovered, later on, that 'Dynamite' was a favourite with the American fans it was decided to feature this song in place of 'My Babe' which was dropped from his act.

JANUARY 22
The Forum, Montreal

JANUARY 23
Community War Memorial Auditorium, Rochester, New York

JANUARY 24
Armoury, Pennsylvania

JANUARY 25
Maple Leaf Gardens, Toronto

JANUARY 26
Kitchner Memorial Auditorium, Kitchner, Ontario

JANUARY 27
Indiana Theatre, Indianapolis, Indiana

JANUARY 28
Veteran's Memorial Auditorium, Columbus, Ohio

JANUARY 29
Stanbaugh Auditorium, Youngstown, Ohio

JANUARY 30
North Side Gym, Elkhart, Indiana

JANUARY 31
Olympia Stadium, Michigan

FEBRUARY 1
Coliseum, Indiana

FEBRUARY 2
Armory, Kentucky

FEBRUARY 3
Syria Mosque, Pittsburgh, Pennsylvania

FEBRUARY 4
The Mosque, New Jersey

FEBRUARY 5
Sports Arena, Hershey, Pennsylvania

FEBRUARY 6
Municipal Auditorium, Virginia

FEBRUARY 7
The Mosque, Richmond, Virginia

FEBRUARY 8
Memorial Coliseum, Winston-Salem, North Carolina

FEBRUARY 9
Memorial Auditorium, Greenville, North Carolina

FEBRUARY 10
Coliseum, North Carolina

FEBRUARY 11
Memorial Auditorium, North Carolina

FEBRUARY 12
Township Auditorium, South Carolina

FEBRUARY 13
Will Rogers Memorial Auditorium, Fort Worth, Texas

FEBRUARY 14
Sam Houston Coliseum, Houston, Texas

FEBRUARY 15
Municipal Auditorium, San Antonio, Texas

FEBRUARY 16
Memorial Auditorium, Dallas, Texas

FEBRUARY 17
Coliseum, Lubbock, Texas

FEBRUARY 18
Municipal Auditorium, Oklahoma City, Oklahoma

FEBRUARY 19
The Forum, Wichita, Kansas

JANUARY 23

A member of the official Elvis Presley Fan Club of Great Britain meets Elvis in Paris and says of Cliff Richard: 'He's at the top in Britain at present, but no doubt you will put him back in his rightful place when you get back to the civilian life.' Elvis is not pleased with the statement and retorts, 'There is room at the top for everyone.'

FEBRUARY

'Cliff Sings No.1' EP is released.

FEBRUARY 5

Cliff's manager Tito Burns reports to the British press on his return from the American tour: 'The entire company on the bill, which included Frankie Avalon, Freddie Cannon, Johnny and the Hurricanes and Sammy Turner, stood and cheered Cliff at the end of the tour.'

FEBRUARY 12

Pop television producer Jack Good, speaking out in an interview, says, 'I don't think Cliff Richard would have existed at all as a singer without Elvis. He certainly wouldn't be the singer he is today. The initial impetus of Cliff's singing was entirely due to Elvis Presley's influence.'

Cliff forms his own publishing company Eugene Music. His mother and father, Mr and Mrs Rodger Webb, are on the board of directors.

FEBRUARY 19

Marty Wilde supports Jack Good's theory when he comments in an interview: 'Without Elvis Presley the main influence of rock 'n' roll would never have appeared, so neither would Cliff Richard.'

Tito Burns disagrees: 'Tommy rot! I can't believe Jack really meant it in his heart.'

Michael Holliday: 'Cliff undoubtedly had the quality to enable him to develop on his own.'

Norrie Paramor: 'Absolute nonsense! In fact, but for fate decreeing that Elvis should come on the scene first, the Presley-Richard situation could easily have happened in reverse.'

Lionel Bart: 'I must concede that Jack Good is being perfectly reasonable when he states that Cliff was considerably influenced by Elvis.'

FEBRUARY 19

Cliff leaves Wichita, Kansas, by plane.

FEBRUARY 20

At 10pm Cliff arrives at London Airport four hours late after running into bad weather, and goes home to Cheshunt. The Shadows remain in the States, committed to fulfil tour dates.

FEBRUARY 21

Cliff appears at the *NME* Poll Winners' Concert before 10,000 people, with a group called the Parker Royal Four backing him. He shares the Number 1 dressing room with Marty Wilde.

In the evening Cliff appears on *Sunday Night at the London Palladium*, again with the Parker Royal Four, who comprise 20-year-old car mechanic Norman Sheffield on drums, two 18-year-old clerks Norman Tracey and John Rogers on guitar and bass respectively and leader Brian Parker, a 20-year-old accountant who was once a member of the same skiffle group as Cliff. Cliff says, 'They come closer to the Shadows than any other group I've ever heard.' The group is Cliff's choice, as opposed to that of manager Tito Burns who had hoped to arrange an accompaniment which included Cherry Wainer and Don Storer, as well as three guitarists and a percussionist!

Cliff has the last word on the Elvis/Cliff controversy; 'I feel that without Elvis I certainly wouldn't be the singer I am today. I'd like to go on record as saying that in my opinion Elvis Presley is the greatest.'

MARCH

'Cliff Sings No.2' EP is released.

MARCH 4

In an interview in Germany just prior to leaving the army, Elvis singles out Cliff, Marty Wilde and Tommy Steele as three British singers with whom he is specially familiar and whose records he has in his collection.

MARCH 14

Cliff receives the coveted Carl-Allan Award for the artist who made the most popular record during 1959, for his best-selling 'Living Doll'.

MARCH 15

Expresso Bongo opens at the Sutton Theatre, New York.

15 MARCH

ABBEY ROAD

Studio session

Nine Times Out Of Ten (11)	*A-side*
I Don't Know (16)	*Me And My Shadows*
Thinking Of Our Love	*(Unissued)*

Lead Vocal:	**Cliff Richard**
Guitars:	**Hank Marvin/Bruce Welch**
Bass:	**Jet Harris**
Drums:	**Tony Meehan**
Producer:	**Norrie Paramor**
Engineers:	**Mono – Malcolm Addey/Norman Smith**
	Stereo – Peter Bown/Alan Kane
Recorded in:	**Studio 2**
Session hours:	**7.00pm-10.00pm**

16 MARCH

ABBEY ROAD
Studio session

Thinking Of Our Love (5)	*B-side*
Evergreen Tree (5)	*Me And My Shadows*
You're Just The One To Do It (15)	*Me And My Shadows*
Left Out Again (5)	*Me And My Shadows*

Lead Vocal:	**Cliff Richard**
Guitars:	**Hank Marvin/Bruce Welch**
Bass:	**Jet Harris**
Drums:	**Tony Meehan**
Harmonica:	**Jerry Furst**
Producer:	**Norrie Paramor**
Engineers:	**Mono – Malcolm Addey/Norman Smith**
	Stereo – Peter Bown/Alan Kane
Recorded in:	**Studio 2**
Session hours:	**7.00pm-10.00pm**

17 MARCH

ABBEY ROAD
Studio session

Gee Whiz It's You (10)	*A-side*
I Love You So (16)	*Me And My Shadows-Mono version*
She's Gone (7)	*Me And My Shadows*
Speech by Cliff	*(Unissued)*

Lead Vocal:	**Cliff Richard**
Guitars:	**Hank Marvin/Bruce Welch**
Bass:	**Jet Harris**
Drums:	**Tony Meehan**
Producer:	**Norrie Paramor**
Engineers:	**Mono – Malcolm Addey/Norman Smith**
	Stereo – Peter Bown/Alan Kane
Recorded in:	**Studio 2**
Session hours:	**7.00pm-10.00pm**

MARCH 18

Cliff's 8th single 'Fall In Love With You'/'Willie And The Hand Jive' is released, earning a Silver Disc. Reviewer Keith Fordyce says, 'It's a pretty ditty that will appeal to a wide audience.'

MARCH 19

Cliff stars in ATV's *Saturday Spectacular* with Peter Elliott, Janette Scott and Al Saxon as his guests.

MARCH 22

Cliff stars in the BBC's Royal Albert Hall concert with Ted Heath, Edmundo Ross and Chris Barber.

25 MARCH

ABBEY ROAD
Studio session

Please Don't Tease	*A-side*
Tell Me	*Me and My Shadows-Stereo version*
Interview for BBC Birmingham	

Lead Vocal:	**Cliff Richard**
Guitars:	**Hank Marvin/Bruce Welch**
Bass:	**Jet Harris**
Drums:	**Tony Meehan**
Producer:	**Norrie Paramor**
Engineer:	**Malcolm Addey**
Recorded in:	**Studio 2**
Session hours:	**7.00pm-10.00pm**
	(Interview recorded after session 10.15-10.45)

MARCH 28

Cliff is presented to Prince Philip, the Duchess of Kent and Princess Alexandra at the Royal Film Performance at Leicester Square Odeon.

Prince Philip: 'How long have you been back from America and was it hard work?'

Cliff: 'Yes, it has been.'

Prince Philip: 'Yes, I know work doesn't seem to stop.'

Cliff: 'It's a good job it doesn't, sir!'

MARCH 30

Along with sixteen other artists, Cliff helps to raise £3,750 at a Wembley concert in aid of spastics.

30 MARCH

ABBEY ROAD
Studio session

Tell Me (11)	*Me And My Shadows-Mono version*
Where Is My Heart (7)	*B-side*
Lamp Of Love (5)	*Me And My Shadows*
I'm Gonna Get You (10)	*Me And My Shadows*
I Cannot Find A True Love (4)	*Me And My Shadows*

Lead Vocal:	**Cliff Richard**
Guitars:	**Hank Marvin/Bruce Welch**
Bass:	**Jet Harris**
Drums:	**Tony Meehan**
Producer:	**Norrie Paramor**
Engineers:	**Mono – Malcolm Addey/Norman Smith** **Stereo – Peter Bown/Alan Kane**
Recorded in:	**Studio 2**
Session hours:	**7.00pm-10.00pm**

MARCH 31

Cliff is the guest of Eamonn Andrews on BBC TV's *Crackerjack.*

1 APRIL

ABBEY ROAD
Studio session

Working After School (sp)	*Me And My Shadows*
You And I (7)	*Me And My Shadows*
I Live For You (11)	*Listen To Cliff*
What'd I Say (1)	*(Unissued)*

Lead Vocal:	**Cliff Richard**
Guitars:	**Hank Marvin/Bruce Welch**
Bass:	**Jet Harris**
Drums:	**Tony Meehan**
Producer:	**Norrie Paramor/J. Schroeder**
Engineers:	**Mono – Malcolm Addey/Norman Smith** **Stereo – Peter Bown/Alan Kane**
Recorded in:	**Studio 2**
Session hours:	**7.00pm-10.00pm**

APRIL

'Cliff Sings No.3' is released

APRIL

Cliff moves into a semi-detached corner house in Winchmore Hill with his parents and three sisters. The dining-room has a 1960 Design Award mahogany suite with red upholstery. The kitchen floor is covered in grey lino with harlequin colours on the chairs and pink wallpaper. Cliff's bedroom wallpaper is green at one end of the room, with natives and yaks all over it, the other three walls being sunshine yellow. By the side of his bed is a reading lamp presented by the 59 Teenage Club of the Eton Mission in Hackney Wick. Cliff's youngest sisters Jacqueline and Joan share a bedroom, while Donna has her own room with a little balcony. Cliff's grey Sunbeam Alpine sports car is invariably parked outside.

APRIL 4

Cliff starts a week of variety at the Glasgow Empire. The crowds create traffic chaos, and national press coverage follows.

APRIL 11

Week of variety at Coventry Theatre.

APRIL 13

Me & My Shadows ten-minute ATV show.

APRIL 17

Six and a half thousand people pack Blackpool's Opera House to see Cliff and the Shadows. Several hundred fans smashed down a side door in an attempt to get to their idol.

APRIL 18

Week of variety at Sheffield Lyceum.

APRIL 30

The coach driver taking Cliff and the other artists from Norwich to Bradford turns up three hours late, and three thousand fans chant 'We Want Cliff' at Bradford's Gaumont Theatre when the show starts two hours late.

MAY 2

Cliff's Sunbeam Alpine, worth £1,000, disappears in Derby.

MAY 3

The Sunbeam Alpine turns up 300 miles away in Dundee.

MAY 13

On being told that he has again been chosen for the Royal Variety Show, Cliff says, 'When I was chosen for the last Royal Variety in Manchester, I felt that I had then reached a peak, so I'm completely knocked out at being selected again! In fact, everything is going so well at the moment I'm scared to breathe in case something goes wrong. Nervous? Of course I am. My stomach is turning seventy-five cartwheels every minute at the thought of next Monday'.

MAY 14

Cliff's nationwide series of one-night-stands comes to an end at Clacton Essoldo.

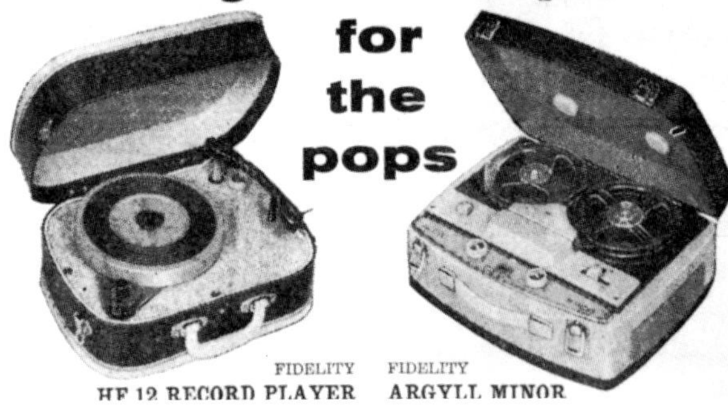

For Cliff Richard–
they're the tops
for
the
pops
FIDELITY
HF 12 RECORD PLAYER
FIDELITY
ARGYLL MINOR

Vol. 3. No. 6. June, 1960

1d

UNDER-21s ARE GIVEN THE VOTE!

A Beat Ballot to decide Cliff Richard's new record

A BIG 'HELLO' from Cliff to all his fans. This is one of many exciting new pictures of the Columbia recording star to be found in this edition of Record Mail.

AT LAST — the under-21s have been given the vote! But this ballot — held recently in the Conference Room of E.M.I Records' new London headquarters in Manchester Square — was a ballot with a difference. Call it, if you like, a Beat Ballot.

The occasion was a unique one in the history of the recording industry — for these under-21s were given the opportunity of helping to decide which should be Cliff Richard's new disc release. And they made their choice from 21 sides he had already recorded.

The Beat Ballot happened this way. Cliff had his songs "in the can" — but neither he nor recording manager Norrie Paramor could make up their minds which sides to issue next. So the teenage voters were called in.

LISTENING SESSION

As Norrie Paramor himself put it: "We thought it was about time that the fans themselves had a say in deciding Cliff's new release and that it would be a good idea to arrange a listening session at which all 21 sides were played."

This, then, was done. From a dozen youth clubs in and around London came 24 boys and girls — one boy and one girl from each of the clubs. Then there were two dozen members of Cliff's own fan club plus several of the younger members of E.M.I Records' own staff.

INTRODUCTIONS

The session began at 6.15 p.m. and, after introductions had been made, each member of the teenage panel was handed a voting slip. The discs were played — it took just one hour and a quarter to play them all — and the votes were cast.

Then the ballot papers were collected and personnel from the statistical department of E.M.I Records began immediately to work out the results. While all this activity was going on a "Coke and Doughnut Bar" was opened — with great success!

BIG SURPRISE

Big surprise of the evening was the arrival of Cliff Richard himself. The teenagers were waiting to hear which sides had been voted into top places — when in walked Cliff to make the announcement.

And the result of the Beat Ballot? A number called "Please don't tease" written by Cliff's rhythm guitarist, Bruce Welch. Runner-up was "Gee wiz its you". Look out for them — they were the teenagers' choice.

EXCLUSIVE! PHOTO-FEATURE SPOTLIGHTS CLIFF ON TOUR page 9

MAY 16

Cliff appears on a Royal Variety Show which includes Russ Conway, Diana Dors, Lonnie Donegan, Liberace, Max Bygraves, Adam Faith, Nat King Cole and Billy Cotton.

MAY 19

Cliff's discovery Dave Simpson enters the chart with a song called 'Sweet Dreams'. He is backed by his group the Hunters – previously the Parker Royal Four who had deputized for the Shadows backing Cliff in February.

MAY 21

Cliff has Bobby Rydell as his guest on ATV's *Saturday Spectacular.*

MAY 23

Columbia throw a party for eighty teenagers to help them decide which of the twenty-four sides recorded by Cliff the previous month will be his new single. The teenagers are drawn from youth organisations, Cliff's Fan Club and EMI staff and after listening to the tracks vote for their favourites.
After allotting their respective marks, the four most popular are evaluated.

1. 'Please Don't Tease'	758
2. 'Gee Whiz It's You'	714
3. 'Nine Times Out Of Ten'	708
4. 'I'm Willing To Learn'	672

JUNE

Cliff and the Shadows – along with Joan Regan, Russ Conway, Edmund Hockridge and Des O'Connor – open in the long-running London Palladium season Stars In Your Eyes. Cliff performs five numbers a night with the Shadows, as well as appearing in a novelty song 'Open Up The Doghouse' with Davis Kossoff.

24 JUNE

ABBEY ROAD
Studio session

I'm Willing To Learn (13)	*Me And My Shadows-Stereo*
We Have It Made (60)	*Me And My Shadows-Stereo*
Choppin' And Changin' (34)	*Me And My Shadows-Stereo*
Interview with Dave Sampson	*(Unissued)*

Lead Vocal:	**Cliff Richard**
Guitars:	**Hank Marvin/Bruce Welch**
Bass:	**Jet Harris**
Drums:	**Tony Meehan**
Producer:	**Norrie Paramor**
Engineers:	**Mono – Malcolm Addey/Norman Smith**
	Stereo – Peter Bown/Alan Kane
Recorded in:	**Studio 2**
Session hours:	**2.30pm-5.15pm**

JUNE 1960-MARCH 1961/NOV-DEC 1961

RADIO LUXEMBOURG STUDIOS, 38 HERTFORD STREET, LONDON

Radio Luxembourg Transcriptions

Willie Did The Cha Cha	*(Unissued)*
Baby I Don't Care	*(Unissued)*
Rock And Roll Shoes	*(Unissued)*
Me And My Shadows	*(Unissued)*
I Gotta Know	*(Unissued)*
9 Times Out Of 10	*(Unissued)*
Me And My Shadows	*(Unissued)*
Gee Whiz It's You	*(Unissued)*
Let The Good Times Roll	*(Unissued)*
Sick And Tired	*(Unissued)*
Where Is My Heart	*(Unissued)*
Baby I Don't Care	*(Unissued)*
Me And My Shadows	*(Unissued)*
I Got A Woman	*(Unissued)*
Save My Soul (River Jordan)	*(Unissued)*
All I Do Is Dream Of You	*(Unissued)*
Dim, Dim The Lights	*(Unissued)*
Me And My Shadows	*(Unissued)*
My Babe	*(Unissued)*
Willie Did The Cha Cha	*(Unissued)*
Rock And Roll Shoes	*(Unissued)*
Me And My Shadows	*(Unissued)*
Reeling And Rocking	*(Unissued)*
It's Me And I'm In Love Again	*(Unissued)*
I Got A Woman	*(Unissued)*
Roving Gambler	*(Unissued)*
Razzle Dazzle	*(Unissued)*
Me And My Shadows	*(Unissued)*
I'll See You In My Dreams	*(Unissued)*
Apron Strings	*(Unissued)*
My Babe	*(Unissued)*
Don't Bug Me Baby	*(Unissued)*
Move It	*(Unissued)*
The Snake And The Bookworm	*(Unissued)*
Travelling Light	*(Unissued)*
My Babe	*(Unissued)*
Blue Suede Shoes	*(Unissued)*
Move It	*(Unissued)*
You Were Meant For Me	*(Unissued)*
Fall In Love With You	*(Unissued)*
Whole Lotta Shakin' Goin On	*(Unissued)*
Me And My Shadows	*(Unissued)*
Hey Everybody	*(Unissued)*
I Got A Woman	*(Unissued)*
Me And My Shadows	*(Unissued)*
Kansas City	*(Unissued)*
Me And My Shadows	*(Unissued)*
I Want You To know	*(Unissued)*
What'd I Say	*(Unissued)*
Let's Have A Party	*(Unissued)*
Me And My Shadows	*(Unissued)*
Me And My Shadows	*(Unissued)*
Lamp Of Love	*(Unissued)*
Teenagers Romance	*(Unissued)*
20 Flight Rock	*(Unissued)*
Me And My Shadows	*(Unissued)*
I Want You To Know	*(Unissued)*
Me And My Shadows	*(Unissued)*
I'm Gonna Get You	*(Unissued)*
I Love You So	*(Unissued)*
Forty Days	*(Unissued)*
Me And My Shadows	*(Unissued)*
I'll See You In My Dreams	*(Unissued)*
Dim, Dim The Lights	*(Unissued)*
Me And My Shadows	*(Unissued)*
The Young Ones	*(Unissued)*
Me And My Shadows	*(Unissued)*
Me And My Shadows	*(Unissued)*
We Say Yeah	*(Unissued)*
Anyone Sweeter Than You	*(Unissued)*
Without You	*(Unissued)*
Willie Did The Cha Cha	*(Unissued)*
Razzle Dazzle	*(Unissued)*
Reeling And Rocking	*(Unissued)*
Rock And Shoes	*(Unissued)*
Dim, Dim The Lights	*(Unissued)*
Young Love	*(Unissued)*
Roseilea Come Back To Me	*(Unissued)*
I'm In Love Again	*(Unissued)*
I Wanna Know	*(Unissued)*

Lead Vocal: **Cliff Richard**
Guitars: **Hank Marvin/Bruce Welch**
Bass: **Jet Harris**
Drums: **Tony Meehan**

JULY 1

NME publish the British chart entry score for January-June 1960 with 30 points for Number 1, 29 for number 2, 28 for number 3, etc, down to 1 point for number 30.

1. Adam Faith	779
2. Cliff Richard	713
3. Anthony Newley	609
4. Johnny Preston	531
5. Emile Ford	471

JULY 7

Me & My Shadows 13-week Sunday night series on Radio Luxembourg commences. Each show runs fifteen minutes.

JULY 11

The *London Evening News* starts a series 'What Are They Really Like – the pop stars adored by millions?', inviting the readers to 'look behind the glossy facade'. They feature the personal story of Cliff.

JULY 15

Columbia A & R manager and Cliff's producer Norrie Paramor says he's confident that the sales of 'Travellin' Light' will pass the million mark within a few weeks, making him only the second British artist to win two Gold Discs. (The other was pianist Winifred Atwell.)

JULY 22

'Please Don't Tease' knocks Jimmy Jones' 'Good Timin'' off the Number One spot.

Fans notice that the Cliff crucifix normally around Cliff's neck has recently been replaced by a St Christopher. Cliff answers: 'The crucifix was given to me when I first began in show business, but when I heard a false rumour that I condemned Protestants and that I was Catholic, I left it off. I'm a Protestant myself, but I have many good friends in other denominations and wouldn't dream of condemning any religious body.'

When asked who he thinks his biggest rivals will be by the summer of 1961, Cliff replies 'Kenny Lynch and Dave Sampson'.

JULY 23

Cliff admits that he would like to have recorded two songs that are current hits – 'Angela Jones' and 'When Johnny Comes Marching Home' – and that if he had to select any personality to entertain him for one evening, it would be Ray Charles.

JULY

The Shadows have the first of many hits which are to span more than two decades.

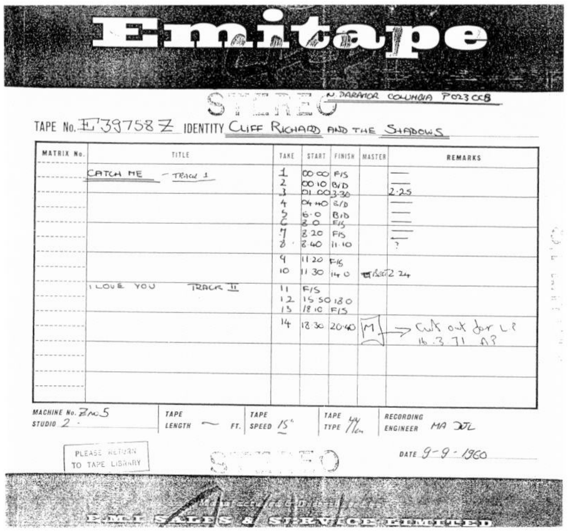

Emitape

STEREO N. PARAMOR COLUMBIA PO23CCB

TAPE No. E 39758 Z IDENTITY CLIFF RICHARD AND THE SHADOWS

MATRIX No.	TITLE	TAKE	START	FINISH	MASTER	REMARKS
	CATCH ME – TRACK 1	1	00.00	F/S		—
		2	00.10	B/D		—
		3	01.00	3.30		2.25
		4	04.40	B/D		—
		5	6.0	B/D		—
		6	8.0	F/S		—
		7	8.20	F/S		—
		8	8.40	11.10		?
		9	11.20	F/S		
		10	11.30	14.0		2.24
	I LOVE YOU TRACK II	11	F/S			
		12	15.50	18.0		
		13	18.10	F/S		
		14	18.30	20.40	M	→ Cut out for LP 16.3.71

MACHINE No. 2 No 5 STUDIO 2 · TAPE LENGTH — FT. · TAPE SPEED 15" · TAPE TYPE · RECORDING ENGINEER MA JL

PLEASE RETURN TO TAPE LIBRARY · STEREO · DATE 9-9-1960

E.M.I. SALES & SERVICE LIMITED

26 JULY

ABBEY ROAD

Studio session

Memories Linger On (10)	*Listen To Cliff*
It's You (5)	*Listen To Cliff*
Now's The Time To Fall In Love (9)	*(Unissued)*

Lead Vocal:	**Cliff Richard**
Guitars:	**Hank Marvin/Bruce Welch**
Bass:	**Jet Harris**
Drums:	**Tony Meehan**
Producer:	**Norrie Paramor**
Engineers:	**Malcolm Addey/Norman Smith**
Recorded in:	**Studio 2**
Session hours:	**2.00pm-5.00pm**

JULY 29

Cliff approves the story for his third film, which it is announced is to be adapted from Margery Allingham's novel *Hide My Eyes.* Negotiations are under way to secure American actress Carol Lynley as co-star. Cliff says, 'I've been an admirer of Carol since I saw her in Blue Jeans. She is my automatic idea of a co-star.'

JULY 31

Cliff Richard stars in *Saturday Spectacular* for ATV, where producer Norrie Paramor presents him with a golden car mascot.

AUGUST 5

'Please Don't Tease' is No.1 for the third week running.

AUGUST 12

Cliff buys a new Ford Thunderbird from Lex Garages in London's Lexington Street.

AUGUST 19

'Please Don't Tease' deposed by the Shadows' 'Apache'.

23 AUGUST

ABBEY ROAD

Studio session

Interview with Cliff Richard

Session hours: **2.00pm-3.00pm**

AUGUST 26

The music press pays tribute to Cliff's second anniversary in show business.

SEPTEMBER 1

Cliff meets American actress Annette Funicello after learning that she couldn't get tickets for his Palladium review Stars In Your Eyes. He invites Annette and her mother to be his guests at the show and takes them out for dinner afterwards. Annette says, 'Cliff is very like Paul Anka, who is a great friend of mine; his manner is almost identical.'

9 SEPTEMBER

ABBEY ROAD
Studio session

I Love You (10)	*(Unissued)*
'D' In Love (3)	*B-side*
Catch Me (10)	*21 Today*
I Love You (14)	*A-side*
Speech for South Africa	

Lead Vocal:	**Cliff Richard**
Guitars:	**Hank Marvin/Bruce Welch**
Bass:	**Jet Harris**
Drums:	**Tony Meehan**
Producer:	**Norrie Paramor**
Engineers:	**Malcolm Addey/David Lloyd**
Recorded in:	**Studio 2**
Session hours:	**2.00pm-5.00pm**

SEPTEMBER 16

Cliff's 10th single 'Nine Times Out Of Ten'/'Thinking Of Our Love' is released and sets up a new record for advance sales for a single in Britain (nearly 180,000).

20 SEPTEMBER

ABBEY ROAD
Studio session

Michelle (3)	*(Unissued)*
Now's The Time To Fall In Love (sp)	*B-side*

Lead Vocal:	**Cliff Richard**
Guitars:	**Hank Marvin/Bruce Welch**
Bass:	**Jet Harris**
Drums:	**Tony Meehan**
Producer:	**Norrie Paramor**
Engineer:	**Malcolm Addey**
Recorded in:	**Studio 2**
Session hours:	**2.00pm-5.00pm**

Now's The Time To Fall In Love is an edit of takes 41 and 42.

SEPTEMBER 22

'Nine Times Out Of Ten' goes straight into the top 10, while 'Please Don't Tease' is still well-placed in the top 20.

27 SEPTEMBER

ABBEY ROAD
Studio session

Until The Right One Comes Along	*(Unissued)*
First Lesson In Love (32)	*(Unissued)*
True Love Will Come To You (6)	*Listen To Cliff-Stereo version*

Lead Vocal:	**Cliff Richard**
Guitars:	**Hank Marvin/Bruce Welch**
Bass:	**Jet Harris**
Drums:	**Tony Meehan**
Producer:	**Norrie Paramor**
Engineer:	**Malcolm Addey**
Recorded in:	**Studio 2**
Session hours:	**2.00pm-5.00pm**

SEPTEMBER

CLIFF SINGS No 4 EP released.

OCTOBER 1

Cliff and the Shadows appear on TV's *Oh Boy* and among other tracks perform 'Evergreen Tree' from their new album.

OCTOBER 3

Cherry Wainer, making her first tracks for EMI, records a song written by Cliff, 'Happy Like A Bell (Ding Dong)'.

OCTOBER 7

The album 'Me And My Shadows' is released, and the music paper headlines boldly proclaim, 'No home should be without this album by Cliff.' The sixteen tracks comprise what is thought by many fans of Cliff and the Shadows to be their greatest LP together.

OCTOBER 9

Cliff receives an early birthday present of a silver St Christopher mascot for his car, from the Mayor of Bexhill-on-Sea .

13 OCTOBER

ABBEY ROAD
Studio session

True Love Will Come To You (6)	*Listen To Cliff-Mono version*
What'd I Say (5)	*(Unissued)*
First Lesson In Love (6)	*Listen To Cliff*
Unchained Melody (1)	*(Unissued)*
I Want You To Know	*Listen To Cliff-Stereo version*

Christmas message for EMI International
Christmas message for EMI South Africa

Lead Vocal:	**Cliff Richard**
Guitars:	**Hank Marvin/Bruce Welch**
Bass:	**Jet Harris**
Drums:	**Tony Meehan**
Producer:	**Norrie Paramor**
Engineer:	**Malcolm Addey**
Recorded in:	**Studio 2**
Session hours:	**2.00pm-5.00pm**

True Love Will Come To You/What'd I Say/First Lesson In Love are listed as remakes on the EMI session sheets.

OCTOBER 14

It is announced that Cliff will star in his own television series on ATV, commencing in the early part of 1961. Six half-hour shows are envisaged, on which he will be supported by the Shadows and the Vernons Girls vocal group, with bandleader/drummer Jack Parnell as musical director.

OCTOBER 16

Cliff co-stars in ATV's Sunday afternoon show *Birthday Honours* with an unknown science student, Fred Chiftenden. Hosted by Godfrey Winn, the programme traces the careers of the two young men, who were both born on the same day, October 14 1940 – Cliff, the £1,000 per week singing star, and Putney-based Fred, a student at the Imperial College of Science living on a modest £6 per week.

OCTOBER

Cliff signs a new contract with his manager Tito Burns

OCTOBER 19

EMI managing director, Len Wood, reveals that in the two years since his career started, Cliff Richard has sold a remarkable 5.5 million single records.

OCTOBER 21

Cliff receives another solid silver St Christopher, this time a key-ring from his South African fan club, and a box of Polynesian cakes from fans in Honolulu.

OCTOBER 28

Cliff's first published composition 'Happy Like A Bell (Ding Dong)' is released on the Columbia label.
Performed by *Oh Boy!* organist Cherry Wainer, it features Shadow Bruce Welch on guitar and Cliff singing the 'ding-dongs'!

OCTOBER 28

NME poll results are published, and Cliff receives the following positions:

World Male Singer – 2nd to Elvis Presley

British Male Singer – 1st

British Vocal Personality – 2nd to Lonnie Donegan

World Musical Personality – 5th behind Duane Eddy, Elvis Presley, Sammy Davis, and Russ Conway

Best British Disc of the Year – 'Please Don't Tease' is 2nd to the Shadows' 'Apache'

His 'runner-up to Elvis' in the World Male Singer section is the highest position ever attained by any British artist in a worldwide category.

OCTOBER 28

Cliff's autobiography entitled *It's Great To Be Young*, is published by Souvenir Press, at 12/6d.

OCTOBER

Secret transatlantic negotiations are apparently under way for Cliff to make a film in Hollywood. Names linked with the venture are Elvis Presley's manager Colonel Tom Parker and Paramount Pictures' Hal Wallis (who has Elvis under an exclusive film contract).

OCTOBER 30

Cliff and the Shadows appear at the annual concert at Cliff's old school in Cheshunt, in aid of the town's youth club building. Also featured are Cliff's cousin Johnny Carson and singer Neil Christian.

NOVEMBER 1

Casting is scheduled to commence for Cliff's third cinema film, based on the novel *Hide My Eyes*, a murder thriller in which he will sing at least three songs.
Production shooting on the movie is due to commence at the end of January, 1961.

17 NOVEMBER

ABBEY ROAD
Studio session

We Kiss In The Shadow (7)	*Listen To Cliff*
Idle Gossip (5)	*Listen To Cliff*
Blue Moon (3)	*Listen To Cliff*
Temptation (2)	*Listen To Cliff*

Lead Vocal:	**Cliff Richard**
	The Norrie Paramor Orchestra
Drums:	**Tony Meehan**
Producer:	**Norrie Paramor**
Engineers:	**Malcolm Addey/Norman Smith**
Recorded in:	**Studio 2**
Session hours:	**1.30pm-5.00pm**

NOVEMBER 20

Cliff is featured in a 40-minute broadcast on the BBC's Home Service, in conversation with Steve Race and poet Royston Ellis. He discusses his career, private life, Elvis, girl-friends and money.

NOVEMBER 25

Cliff's 11th single 'I Love You'/'D In Love' is released. The 'A' side is written by Shadow Bruce Welch.

DECEMBER 1

'I Love You' moves straight into the Top Ten, and goes on to earn a Silver Disc.

DECEMBER 1

'Cliffs Silver Discs' EP released.

DECEMBER 1

Cliff performs in front of the Queen Mother in a Royal version of 'Stars In Your Eyes' with Judy Garland, Bruce Forsyth, the Shadows and the Norrie Paramor Orchestra.

DECEMBER 2

Cliff buys himself out of his film contract with producer Mickey Delemar, allegedly for a sum running well into five figures.

5 DECEMBER

ABBEY ROAD
Studio session

Bin Verliebt (Fall In Love With You)	*German A-side*
Die Stimme Der Liebe (A Voice In The Wilderness)	*German B-side*

Lead Vocal:	**Cliff Richard**
Guitars:	**Hank Marvin/Bruce Welch**
Bass:	**Jet Harris**
Drums:	**Tony Meehan**
Producer:	**Norrie Paramor**
Engineer :	**Malcolm Addey**
Recorded in:	**Studio 2**
Session hours:	**7.00pm-10.00pm**

DECEMBER 9

Cliff vows, 'After being at the London Palladium for six months, I shall never, never stay at the same theatre for more than two weeks in future.'

DECEMBER 12

Cliff takes his first holiday for eighteen months when he flies to Spain with his mother, two of his sisters and road manager Mike Conlin.

DECEMBER 27

Cliff's father Rodger Webb, ill with heart trouble, enters a North London hospital.

DECEMBER 28

EMI Chairman Sir Joseph Lockwood claims that the company had no less than a quarter of the world's total sales during 1960, and Cliff is their best-selling artist, having topped the charts not only in Britain but in overseas territories includingAustralia, Holland, New Zealand, Sweden, Singapore and South Africa.

JANUARY 6

NME's analysis of the best-selling charts for 1960 is published. With 30 points for each week at number 1, down to 1 point for the number 30 position, final placings are:

1	Cliff Richard	1,416
2	Adam Faith	1,386
3	Elvis Presley	1,104
4	Everly Brothers	965
5	Anthony Newley	965
6	Connie Francis	915
7	Jimmy Jones	758
8	Duane Eddy	732
9	Johnny & the Hurricanes	684
10	The Shadows	655

JANUARY 6

Cliff places an ad in the music press:
'My sincere and grateful thanks to all of my friends who sent such wonderful cheery letters and gifts to my father Rodger Webb in hospital. These gestures have been most appreciated, and I am certain will help him on the road to recovery. Once again, my sincere thanks.'

JANUARY 7

ATV announce that Cliff's half-hour series will start on 16 February. Among the guests on the show will be Alma Cogan, Marty Wilde, Cliff's cousin Johnny Carson and Dave Sampson.

11 JANUARY

ABBEY ROAD
Studio session

Almost Like Being In Love (3)	*Listen To Cliff*
Lover (8)	*Listen To Cliff*
Beat Out Dat Rhythm On A Drum	*Listen To Cliff*
Sentimental Journey (6)	*Listen To Cliff*

Lead Vocal:	**Cliff Richard**
	The Bernard Ebbinghouse Orchestra
Producer:	**Norrie Paramor**
Engineer:	**Malcolm Addey/David Lloyd**
Recorded in:	**Studio 2**
Session hours:	**7.00am-10.00pm**

JANUARY 15

Cliff headlines a show at the Royal Albert Hall for the dependants of Jack Conway (recently killed in a car crash), an associate of Cliff's manager Tito Burns.
Cliff opens his act with 'Whole Lotta Shakin' ', followed by 'Willie And The Hand Jive', 'Please Don't Tease', 'I Love You' and finishes with his version of Ray Charles' 'What'd I Say'. Also on the bill are the Shadows, Cliff's protege Dave Sampson, Bert Weedon, the Kaye Sisters, Cherry Wainer, the Vernons Girls, Jackie Rae and Janette Scott, and skifflers Chas McDevitt and Shirley Douglas.

JANUARY 16

Cliff's producer Norrie Paramor goes into the EMI Abbey Road Studios to produce 'Please Don't Treat Me Like A Child', the debut recording by a 14-year-old schoolgirl vocalist from London, Helen Shapiro. She joins the Columbia label and becomes Cliff's stablemate.

JANUARY 18

Cliff records two programmes for the BBC's transcription service, backed by Ted Heath and his Orchestra. Cliff is also featured in sketches with singer Dickie Valentine, who was once a resident vocalist with the Heath band..

JANUARY 19

Cliff appears on the BBC TV children's programme *Crackerjack,* hosted by Eamonn Andrews.

JANUARY 20

Cliff and the Shadows' manager Peter Gormley meet for talks.

JANUARY 23

'Cliff and Elvis choose their favourite love songs for you', reads the newspaper advertisement for the *Mirabelle* girls' magazine. A special song supplement pull-out includes the lyrics of 'Nine Times Out Of Ten' and 'Living Doll'.

JANUARY 28

Cliff's father leaves hospital.

28 JANUARY

ABBEY ROAD
Studio session

Theme For A Dream	*A-side*
Tough Enough (4)	*21 Today*
Poor Boy (8)	*(Unissued)*
Mumblin' Mosie	*B-side*
A Girl Like You	*A-side*

Lead Vocal:	**Cliff Richard**
Guitars:	**Hank Marvin/Bruce Welch**
Bass:	**Jet Harris**
Drums:	**Tony Meehan**
Bongos:	**Jerry Furst**
Vocals:	**Mike Sammes Singers-2pm-4pm only**
Producer:	**Norrie Paramor**
Engineer:	**Malcolm Addey**
Recorded in:	**Studio 2**
Session hours:	**2.00pm-5.00pm/7.00pm-10.00pm**

JANUARY 29

Cliff reveals that he's a great fan of Dakota Staton.

30 JANUARY

ABBEY ROAD

Studio session

How Wonderful To Know (3)	*21 Today*
A Mighty Lonely Man (5)	*21 Today*
To Prove My Love For You (6)	*21 Today*
Outsider (4)	*21 Today*
Fifty Years For Every Kiss (4)	*21 Today*
When The Girl In Your Arms	*A-side*

Lead Vocal:	**Cliff Richard**
	The Norrie Paramor Orchestra
Vocals:	**Mike Sammes Singers**
Producer:	**Norrie Paramor**
Engineer :	**Malcolm Addey**
Recorded in:	**Studio 2**
Session hours:	**3.00pm-5.15pm/7.00pm-9.45pm**

FEBRUARY 5

Cliff begins a tour starting at the Birmingham Hippodrome, headlining a bill that includes Cherry Wainer, Chas McDevitt and Shirley Douglas, Dave Sampson and the Hunters and Norman Vaughan.

FEBRUARY 10

A banner headline in the music press asks, 'Should the Shadows part from Cliff?'

FEBRUARY 16

Cliff begins a TV series which is to include Marty Wilde, the Kaye Sisters and Jill Browne – star of TV's *Emergency Ward 10* in which she plays nurse Carole Young – with whom Cliff sings a duet.

FEBRUARY 17

T. Birckby of Huddersfield sparks off a mini-storm with his letter of the previous week to the music papers which ended '…Cliff Richard, Adam Faith and Fabian are poor singers and the songs they record are trash.' Hundreds of letters pour in to the music press – some agreeing, but most up in arms. Ruth Esau of Virginia Waters in Surrey has the most sensible remark to make, stating in one of the few non-hysterical reactions that 'One man's meat is another man's poison."

FEBRUARY 18

Cliff has five songs in India's Top Ten!

FEBRUARY 18

Impresario Leslie Grade reveals that Cliff could earn around £30,000 from a forthcoming film which is planned, The picture will co-star actor Robert Morley and feature the Shadows, but is as yet unnamed.

SHOULD THE SHADOWS PART FROM CLIFF?

A break in rehearsals, and, while Jet and Hank read a fan letter, Bruce and Tony take it easy.

The instrumentalists give Derek Johnson their answer . . .

THE future career of the Shadows must be a continual source of speculation and controversy among their thousands of supporters, now that they are irrevocably established as Britain's top instrumental group, a position which is overwhelmingly confirmed by the advent of their latest Columbia release, "F.B.I.", in the NME Charts this week.

Has the time not come for this talented group to branch out on their own? That's the question NME readers in their dozens are asking in their letters to us. Surely, they say, Cliff Richard is a powerful enough artist in his own right, and no longer needs to retard the Shadows in the pursuance of their own career?

known as the Shadows' personal manager. And Peter, in his own modest way, prefers to belittle his own achievement, claiming that the bulk of the credit should go to the boys.

"It's true I dreamed up a sort of basic theme," he explained. "But as in the case of any instrumental they select, the Shadows interpreted my original contribution in their own particular way. The theme is always embellished and extended by them in their arrangement—they even put in bits the composer never had anything to do with!"

This is actually Peter's first successful composition, although he has dabbled to some extent in songwriting with Frank Ifield. But what I wanted to know was—how did he come to hit upon the intriguing title of "F.B.I."?

"Well the truth of the matter is—I didn't select the title myself," said Peter. "It was the boys who chose the name. They are all keen filmgoers, and they particularly enjoy detective and gangster pictures—so this title just happened to fall into place."

The Shadows attach the utmost importance to suitable choice of titles for their material. They told me that, when they receive a new song which appeals to them, they frequently look at the title afresh—and occasionally they suggest a new, and more effective one, to the composer.

Composers

As is widely known, the boys themselves have enjoyed a wide measure of success as composers—with Bruce Welch and Hank Marvin the most prolific writers of the quartet. Between them they've been responsible for several Cliff Richard hits (including "Please Don't Tease," "I Love You" and the flip-side of "Nine Times Out Of Ten"), Frank Ifield's latest release "That's The Way It Goes," a new recording by the Bachelors—plus nearly all the material on the "Me and My Shadows" LP, which was written in conjunction with Ian Samwell and Peter Chester.

In view of their recent disc successes, together with the issue of their first EP last month, it occurred to me to wonder whether there was any likelihood of the Shadows cutting an LP on their own in the near future.

"We've thought about this very seriously," they assured me. "And we've come to the decision that we don't want to make an LP just for the sake of making one—you know, three quick sessions, and then it's over and done with. We would much rather take our time in preparing an album—selecting the best possible material, as and when it becomes available.

"And that's exactly what we're doing at the moment. Taking our time over it! And it's a policy with which our recording manager, Norrie Paramor, wholeheartedly agrees."

So the fans will be pleased to know that a Shadows' LP is definitely in the offing—though we may have to wait some little while for it.

One final point—there's a rumour currently circulating to the effect that there was actually an additional guitarist brought into the recording session for "Apache." One of London's top session guitarists helped out on the disc, says this story.

Well, after broaching the subject with the Shadows, I can now once and for all discredit that rumour. Cliff Richard was featured on the session as a bongo player, as has been widely publicised.

But an extra guitarist—no! After all, with this quartet's talent and ability, they don't really need a helping hand, do they?

EPs by ALLEN EVANS

FEBRUARY 19

Cliff dines with American singer Bobby Rydell.

FEBRUARY 23

Cliff duets with Marty Wilde on 'Rubber Ball' on ATV.

FEBRUARY 24

Cliff's 12th single 'Theme For A Dream'/'Mumblin' Mosie' is released. One reviewer calls it, 'A light and pretty number, easy on the ear, with a good tune which will set you humming.

FEBRUARY 24

Cliff appears on a radio documentary *Teen Beat* hosted by Steve Race and subtitled. 'A survey of a teenage idol and his music!'

FEBRUARY 27

EMI reveal that advance orders for 'Theme For A Dream' exceed 200,000.

FEBRUARY

Columbia release 'Me And My Shadows No.1' EP.

MARCH 1

Cliff on BBC TV's *Parade of the Pops.*

MARCH 1

It is announced that Australian Peter Gormley, who came to Britain at the end of 1959 with Frank Ifield, is to be Cliff's new personal manager. Peter has already been looking after the Shadows since July 1960.

4 MARCH

ABBEY ROAD
Studio session

I Want You To Know (38)	*Listen To Cliff-Mono version*
Unchained Melody (31)	*Listen To Cliff*
What'd I Say (33)	*Listen To Cliff*
My Blue Heaven (1)	*(Unissued)*

Lead Vocal:	**Cliff Richard**
Guitars:	**Hank Marvin/Bruce Welch**
Bass:	**Jet Harris**
Drums:	**Tony Meehan**
Producer:	**Norrie Paramor**
Engineers:	**Malcolm Addey/David Lloyd**
Recorded in:	**Studio 2**
Session hours:	**mid-day-3.00pm**

I Want You To Know/Unchained Melody/What'd I Say are all listed as remakes on the EMI session sheets.

MARCH 5

In the afternoon Cliff appears at the *NME* Poll Winers' Concert at Wembley's Empire Pool. In the evening he tele-records a London Palladium Special for the NBC to be networked across the United States. Comedian Charlie Drake and the Tiller Girls dancing troupe are also on the show, which is compered by Laurence Harvey.

MARCH 6

Cliff and the Shadows experience a 4.5 hour delay at London Airport as they attempt to fly to South Africa to start a tour south of the equator, and end up going to see a horror film in Hounslow! They eventually take off six hours late. As well as South Africa, the tour takes in, Australia, New Zealand, Singapore and Malaya.

MARCH 7

Cliff and the Shadows arrive in Salisbury, Rhodesia, to be greeted by a 3,000 strong crowd.

MARCH 10

Cliff reveals that the co-star in his new but as yet unnamed film will be a German girl, Heidi Bruhl. He says, 'She sings extremely well and looks a million dollars. My own thought is that I would like to see young Helen Shapiro in the film. She's only 14 years old, but she has immense potential and could well become one of the biggest names in show business.'

MARCH 13

Cliff is nominated 'Star of Stars' by *Weekend* magazine. As he's in South Africa, his sister Donella collects the award on his behalf at London's Lyceum Ballroom.

MARCH

'Me And My Shadows No.2' EP is released.

MARCH 13/14

Ten thousand teenage fans disrupt traffic in Johannesburg as they surround Cliff's hotel, causing scenes never before witnessed in South Africa. Police, the Flying Squad and the traffic department combine to maintain a constant guard on the Carlton Hotel, to prevent girls getting in. At one stage Cliff addresses the massive crowd from the balcony, but can hardly be heard except for the words '...this is the most fantastic sight I've ever seen.'

MARCH 15

EMI South Africa record Cliff's entire act before a capacity audience at the Johannesburg Colosseum. This is the first time that Cliff and the Shadows have been recorded at a public concert.

MARCH 17

The March issue of *Hit Parade* magazine (2/-) features an article personally written by Cliff.

MARCH

Top South African DJ Bob Holness interviews Cliff for his Durban *Calling to Youth* show, prior to leaving the Union to seek a broadcasting career in Britain.

APRIL 7

On his return from South Africa Cliff talks to journalist Derek Johnson: 'The only minor upset of the tour was the controversy over the colour bar, which prevented some of the non-Europeans from seeing our show. When we were first offered the contract to go to South Africa, we didn't realise there would be those problems, and when they arose we found ourselves in rather an awkward position. We overcame this situation to the best of our ability by offering to do a couple of shows especially for the non-Europeans, with the proceeds going to charity. Those shows took place in Cape Town and Salisbury. Despite this colour bar policy I found that the whites were very tolerant towards the coloureds.'

APRIL 7

'Gee Whiz It's You'/'I Cannot Find A True Love' enters the Top 20. So many copies were unofficially imported into this country that EMI recognise its potential and belatedly release it as Cliff's 13th single.

APRIL

'Me And My Shadows No.3' EP is released.

APRIL

It is announced that Cliff and the Shadows will undertake a summer season at Blackpool Opera House, commencing on Monday 28 August.

APRIL

A mail order firm starts selling the 'Cliff Richard two-way shirt' in black and white for 32/6d.

APRIL 8

Cliff makes his debut on BBC Television's top-rating *Juke Box Jury*, discussing the week's new releases along with actresses Dora Bryan and Janet Munro, and DJ Ray Orchard. There are a couple of hiccups for the normally unruffled chairman David Jacobs, as he wrongly announces that Dave King's 'Young In Love' is a remake of Tab Hunter's 'Young Love', and then accidentaly plays 'Intermezzo', the B-side of Manuel's 'Mountain Carnival'.

APRIL 9

Cliff begins a short series of countrywide one-night stands, topping the bill with the Shadows on a line-up which includes the Brook Brothers, Ricky and Geoff, and Patti Brooks. After the opening show, which is at the Liverpool Empire, all the artists help celebrate Brook Brother Geoff Brook's birthday at a back-stage party.

10 APRIL

ABBEY ROAD
Studio session

Theme For A Dream	*German A-side*
Vreneli	*German B-side*

Lead Vocal:	**Cliff Richard**
Guitars:	**Hank Marvin/Bruce Welch**
Bass:	**Jet Harris**
Drums:	**Tony Meehan**
Producer:	**Norrie Paramor**
Engineer:	**Malcolm Addey**
Recorded in:	**Studio 2**
Session hours:	**7.00pm-9.00pm**

19 APRIL

ABBEY ROAD
Studio session

Poor Boy (12)	*21 Today*
My Blue Heaven (6)	*21 Today*
Got A Funny Feeling (7)	*B-side*

Lead Vocal:	**Cliff Richard**
Guitars:	**Hank Marvin/Bruce Welch**
Bass:	**Jet Harris**
Drums:	**Tony Meehan**
Piano:	**Norrie Paramor**
Producer:	**Norrie Paramor**
Engineers:	**Malcolm Addey/Norman Smith**
Recorded in:	**Studio 1**
Session hours:	**mid-day-3.15pm**

Poor Boy/My Blue Heaven are listed as remakes on the EMI session sheets.

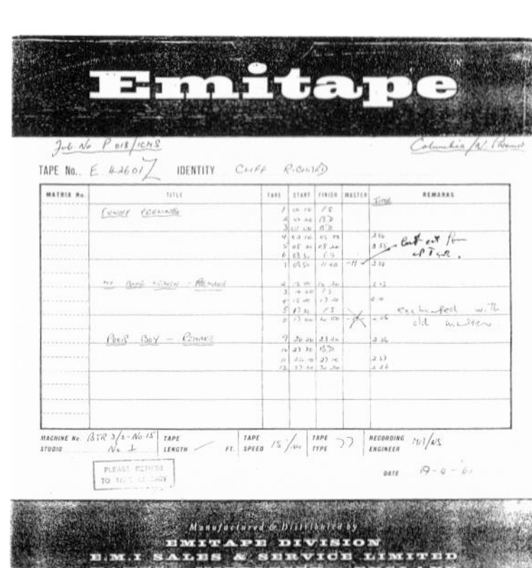

APRIL 21

Cliff has two discs in the Top 10: 'Theme For A Dream' and 'Gee Whiz It's You'.

APRIL 21

'Listen To Cliff' LP is released. Cliff is accompanied by the Shadows on eight of the tracks, by the Norrie Paramor Orchestra on four numbers, and on the remaining four by the Bernard Ebbinghouse Band.

APRIL 22

Cliff appears on BBC Light Programme's *Saturday Club.*

APRIL 26

Cliff is on BBC's *Parade of the Pops.*

APRIL 28

In an interview with journalist Mike Hellicar, Cliff speaks out about the fact that for the first time in his career he has two records in the Top 10: 'I wasn't at all pleased when I found out that 'Gee Whiz It's You' was available as a single in Britain. I thought quite honestly that the decision to release the disc in Britain was a bad one.

APRIL 28

It is announced that the shooting of Cliff's as yet unnamed new film will be delayed until the end of May. Also revealed is that Robert Morley – cast as Cliff's father in the film – probably won't be available and the role may be taken by veteran actor Stanley Holloway of *My Fair Lady* fame.

APRIL 30

Listeners to BBC's Network Three magazine programme *Sound* hear part of an actual Cliff recording session in progress, with the voices of producer Norrie Paramor conducting the orchestra, recording engineer Malcolm Addey and his assistant David Lloyd. The songs being recorded are 'Lover' and 'It's Almost Like Being In Love' for the album 'Listen To Cliff'.

4 MAY

ABBEY ROAD
Studio session

Dream (6)	*Dream EP*
All I Do Is Dream Of You (13)	*Dream EP*
I'll See You In My Dreams (13)	*Dream EP*

Lead Vocal:	**Cliff Richard**
Guitars:	**Hank Marvin/Bruce Welch**
Bass:	**Jet Harris**
Drums:	**Tony Meehan**
Producer:	**Norrie Paramor**
Engineer:	**Malcolm Addey**
Recorded in:	**Studio 2**
Session hours:	**7.00pm-10.00pm**

MAY 8

Network Three programme *Sound* is repeated.

MAY 11

Cliff, along with the Shadows, is featured in a 20-minute cabaret spot at the NSPCC Pied Piper Ball. Cliff's appearance is at the specific request of Princess Margaret who attends with her husband Anthony Armstrong-Jones.

MAY 12

It is revealed that Cliff's new film is to be called *The Young Ones*, and there is likely to be a major role for actress Diana Dors. Robert Morley is to be reinstated in the part of Cliff's father in the film.

RECORD MAIL

A MONTHLY REVIEW AND DETAILS OF THE LATEST "POPULAR" RECORDS ISSUED BY E.M.I. RECORDS LTD. H.M.V., Capitol, Columbia, Parlophone, M-G-M, Mercury, Top Rank.

Vol. 4 No. 5 — May, 1961 — 1d

'GEE WHIZ!' SAYS CLIFF

RECORD MAIL REPORTER

ANOTHER success for Columbia singing star Cliff Richard — but this time it's a success with a difference. It concerns his recording of a song called "Gee whiz it's you" — and it might well be put under the heading of The Mystery of the Unsung Hit. 'Unsung' meaning unheralded, of course.

For — unannounced, unpublicised, unexpectedly (and unheralded) — "Gee whiz it's you" raced into the British Hit Parade. 'Unexpected' because it had never been released officially as a 'single' in this country. Taken from Cliff's "Me And My Shadows" LP, it was, in fact, issued several months ago for the overseas market only.

SPECIAL REQUEST

Said a spokesman of E.M.I Records: "We issued this disc of 'Gee whiz' last December at the special request of our overseas distributors. We couldn't release it on the home market at the same time because we had only just issued his 'I love you' single.

"Then came his 'Theme for a dream' — and, as far as we were concerned, 'Gee whiz' was still only a special overseas issue. But somehow — and we don't know how — word of it got back to his British fans. They then asked their dealers for it and the next thing we knew was that it was in the Hit Parade."

ANOTHER SILVER DISC

News of this latest success comes to Cliff at the same time as the announcement that he has won his eighth Silver Disc (awarded by 'Disc') to mark the quarter-million-plus sales

MAY 12

Christine Porter of Reading and Gloria Vingue of Wembley, both BBC TV employees leaving for jobs in the United States, have a 'last request' granted when they are taken to meet Cliff at BBC's Television Theatre.

12 MAY

ABBEY ROAD
Studio session

When I Grow Too Old Too Dream (8)	*Dream EP*

Lead Vocal:	**Cliff Richard**
Guitars:	**Hank Marvin/Bruce Welch**
Bass:	**Jet Harris**
Drums:	**Tony Meehan**
Producer:	**Norrie Paramor**
Engineer:	**Malcolm Addey**
Recorded in:	**Studio 2**
Session hours:	**7.00pm-10.00pm**

MAY 15

Cliff's father Rodger Webb dies, aged 57.

MAY 19

A virtually unknown actress from London's East End is named as Cliff's co-star in *The Young Ones*. She is 21-year old Annette Robertson, who was in the original production of *Fings Ain't What They Used T' Be*. On the same day Cliff talks about Radio Luxembourg on their 30th anniversary: 'I feel sure that thanks to

Radio Luxembourg, I have made a whole army of newe friends. I have the greatest possible admiration for this organisation, which is an absolute boon to youngsters – and, of course, a blessing to recording artists like me!'

23 MAY

ABBEY ROAD
Film soundtrack recordings for The Young Ones

The Young Ones (36)	*(Unissued)*
When The Girl In Your Arms (7)	*(Unissued)*
Gotta Funny Feeling (7)	*(Unissued)*

Lead Vocal:	**Cliff Richard**
Guitars:	**Hank Marvin/Bruce Welch**
Bass:	**Jet Harris**
Drums:	**Tony Meehan**
Producer:	**Norrie Paramor**
Engineers:	**Malcolm Addey/Norman Smith**
Recorded in:	**Studio 2**
Session hours:	**7.00pm-10.15pm**

In the EMI ledgers these three tracks from the film The Young Ones are marked as remakes and also there is mention of Associated British Picture Corporation. From this we can assume that they are the versions featured in the film.

25 MAY

ABBEY ROAD
Film soundtrack recordings for The Young Ones

Peace Pipe	*The Young Ones*
The Savage	*The Young Ones*

Guitars:	**Hank Marvin/Bruce Welch**
Bass:	**Jet Harris**
Drums:	**Tony Meehan**
Producer:	**Norrie Paramor**
Engineers:	**Malcolm Addey/Norman Smith**
Recorded in:	
Session hours:	

MAY 26

South African Carole Gray, a dancer in the stage musical *West Side Story*, is signed up to play Cliff's girl-friend in *The Young Ones*, while Annette Robertson (originally reported as starring in the role) will now have another part in the film.
On the same day Cliff presents awards at the Methodist Association of Youth Clubs' annual get-together at London's Royal Albert Hall.

JUNE 2

Cliff takes part in a Charity show in aid of the African Bureau at London's Victoria Palace. Also in the show are Georgia Brown, Cleo Laine and the casts of *Fings Ain't What They Used T'Be* and *Beyond The Fringe.*

JUNE

In the June issue of *Hit Parade*, Cliff describes his dream year.

JUNE 9

Cliff talks about *The Young Ones*: 'It's not often that I get nervous, but boy, those butterflies really got at me for the whole of the first day's shooting – and stayed for almost the rest of the week.'

JUNE 12

Cliff buys a powder-blue Hillman Automatic for his mother Dorothy Webb.

JUNE 16

Cliff's 14th single (the 13th being the imported 'Gee Whiz It's You') is released – 'A Girl Like You'/'Now's The Time To Fall In Love'. A favourite song of Cliff's late father, it is described by one reviewer as 'the prettiest song that Cliff has got hold of since 'Living Doll' – it stands every chance of getting to Number One.'

JUNE 17

Cliff sings his new single on BBC's *Saturday Club*. His projected tour of Scandinavia is confirmed for August.

JUNE 25

In top hat and tails, Cliff duets with Russ Conway on BBC TV's *Billy Cotton Band Show.*

JUNE 26

Along with Helen Shapiro, Cliff stars in Radio Luxembourg's hour-long *Monday Spectacular,* hosted by Muriel Young and Shaw Taylor. The show is recorded in front of a hundred eager teenagers.

JUNE 30

'Theme For A Dream' tops the chart in New Zealand.

JULY 3

Cliff's producer Norrie Paramor and his wife Joan celebrate their 18th wedding anniversary.

4 JULY

ABBEY ROAD
Studio session

Tea For Two (8)	*21 Today*
Forty Days (5)	*21 Today*
The Night Is So Lonely (5)	*21 Today*

Lead Vocal:	**Cliff Richard**
Guitars:	**Hank Marvin/Bruce Welch**
Bass:	**Jet Harris**
Drums:	**Tony Meehan**
Producer:	**Norrie Paramor**
Engineer:	**Malcolm Addey**
Recorded in:	**Studio 2**
Session hours:	**7.00pm-10.30pm**

JULY 7

Cliff is booked for the *Jo Stafford Show* being recorded at ATV's Elstree Studios for transmission in the United States.

JULY 7

The *NME*'s chart points table for January-June 1961 is published, with 30 points for each week at number 1, down to 1 point for each week at number 30.

1 Elvis Presley	916
2 Cliff Richard	581
3 The Shadows	519
4 Everly Brothers	488
5 Matt Monro	374
6 Adam Faith	365
7 Bobby Vee	356
8 Temperance Seven	355
9 Duane Eddy	341
10 Allisons	314

11 JULY

ABBEY ROAD
Studio session

Without You (4)	*21 Today*
Y'Arriva (18)	*21 Today*
Shame On You (20)	*21 Today*

Lead Vocal:	**Cliff Richard**
Guitars:	**Hank Marvin/Bruce Welch**
Bass:	**Jet Harris**
Drums:	**Tony Meehan**
Producer:	**Norrie Paramor**
Engineer:	**Malcolm Addey**
Recorded in:	**Studio 2**
Session hours:	**7.00pm-10.15pm**

JULY

Robert Hofschroer and Kevin Sparrow, winners of the National Deaf Children's Society film script competition, win a visit to Elstree to watch *The Young Ones* being shot and to meet Cliff.

28 JULY

ABBEY ROAD
Studio session

Happy Birthday (21)	*21 Today*
We Say Yeah (6)	*The Young Ones*
Lessons In Love (10)	*(Unissued)*

Lead Vocal:	**Cliff Richard**
Guitars:	**Hank Marvin/Bruce Welch**
Bass:	**Jet Harris**
Drums:	**Tony Meehan**
Producer:	**Norrie Paramor**
Engineers:	**Malcolm Addey/Norman Smith**
Recorded in:	**Studio 2**
Session hours:	**7.45pm-10.30pm**

AUGUST 4

As pictures from the set of *The Young Ones* are released, Cliff admits, 'I have benefited enormously as a result of working with such a fine actor as Robert Morley. I've been getting along wonderfully with Carole (Gray) – she's a great girl and everyone likes her. In fact, the other evening she invited the company to a barbecue at her home.'

AUGUST 6

Cliff attends the marriage of his 18-year old sister Donella to Paul

Stevens at Waltham Abbey in Essex. Norrie Paramor and the Shadows are guests at the wedding.

9 AUGUST

ABBEY ROAD

Film soundtrack recordings for The Young Ones

Vaudeville Routine (Part 1) (5)	*The Young Ones*
Vaudeville Routine (Part 2) (8)	*The Young Ones*
Vaudeville Routine (Part 3) (13)	*The Young Ones*
Vaudeville Routine (Part 4) (15)	*The Young Ones*
Vaudeville Routine (Part 5) (22)	*The Young Ones*
No One For Me But Nicki (2)	*The Young Ones*
Nothing Is Impossible (4)	*The Young Ones*
Night (See You At The Dance) (8)	*The Young Ones*
All For One	*The Young Ones*
Mambo	*The Young Ones*

Lead Vocal:	**Cliff Richard**
	The Stanley Black Orchestra
Duet Vocals:	**Grazina Frame (Nothing Is Impossible)**
Vocals:	**Grazina Frame (No One For Me But Nicki)**
Producer:	**Norrie Paramor**
Engineers:	**Malcolm Addey/Alan Kane**
Recorded in:	**Studio 2**
Session hours:	**2.30pm-6.00pm/7.00pm-10.00pm**

Tracks on Vaudeville Routine: What Do You Know We Got A Show/Have A Smile For Everyone You Meet/Tinkle, Tinkle/The Eccentric/Algy The Picadilly Johnny/Captain Ginjah/Joshua/Where Did You Get That Hat/What Do You Know We Got A Show/Living Doll

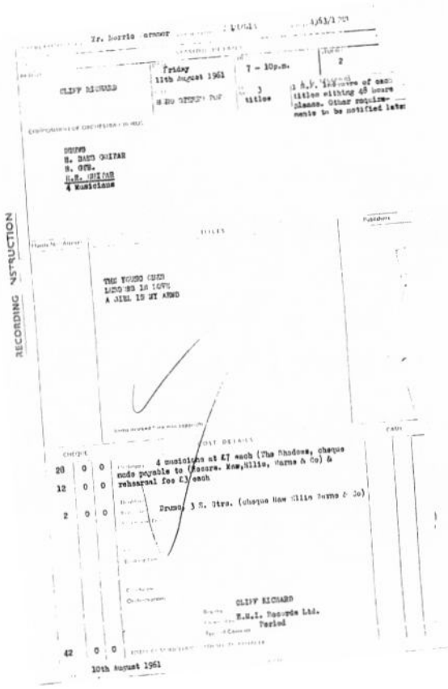

AUGUST 11

Discussing their forthcoming debut LP 'The Shadows',on which Hank Marvin performs a solo vocal 'Baby My Heart', Hank jokes, 'Cliff's scared to death as a result of this unexpected competition.' And on the subject of Bruce Welch's vocal solo, Hank adds, 'Cliff's not so worried about this one!'

11 AUGUST

ABBEY ROAD

Film soundtrack recordings for The Young Ones

The Young Ones (36)	*See 5 December*
Lessons In Love (36)	*The Young Ones*
What Is There To Say (11)	*(Unissued)*

Lead Vocal:	**Cliff Richard**
Guitars:	**Hank Marvin/Bruce Welch**
Bass:	**Jet Harris**
Drums:	**Tony Meehan**
Producer:	**Norrie Paramor**
Engineers:	**Malcolm Addey/David Lloyd**
Recorded in:	**Studio 2**
Session hours:	**7.00pm-10.30pm**

See session dated 5 December for more on The Young Ones

AUGUST 13

Cliff hosts a birthday dinner for his mother Dorothy Webb.

AUGUST 18

The Young Ones producer Kenneth Harper reveals that, 'Interest in the advance prints of the film has been so great that we had no hesitation in beginning an immediate search for a new script for Cliff and the Shadows – we have decided to start production in May or June 1962.'

AUGUST

Cliff buys a record shop for his newly married sister Donella and her husband Paul.

AUGUST

In Norway, Cliff is presented with a Silver Disc for 'Living Doll' at a concert in Oslo. He becomes the first British artist to win the award, which is made by the Norwegian newspaper *Arbeiderbladet* and handed to him by DJ Erik Heyerdahl.

AUGUST 28

Cliff and the Shadows start a six-week season at Blackpool's Opera House.

SEPTEMBER

Cliff's 'A Girl Like You' is at No.7 in the British charts and No.3 in New Zealand. His version of 'Beat Out Dat Rhythm' is at No.5 in Holland, and in South Africa 'Gee Whiz It's You' is also at No.5.

SEPTEMBER 5

Cliff's protege Dave Sampson leaves the Columbia label to join Fontana.

SEPTEMBER 9

An enteritis epidemic – which has been causing havoc among many artists appearing in Blackpool summer shows – lays low Bruce Welch. Lonnie Donegan's lead guitarist Les Bennett joins the Shadows to back Cliff for one night only.

SEPTEMBER 10

Bruce Welch recovers sufficiently to rejoin Cliff and the Shadows when they appear at the *NME*'s all-star concert at Wembley's Empire Pool. A number of girl fans vault the protective rail separating the stage from the auditorium to throw roses at Cliff.

SEPTEMBER

During the Blackpool season, Cliff shares a house with the Shadows a couple of miles down the coast at Lytham St Annes, which had been prepared by his mother during their Scandinavian tour.

SEPTEMBER 14

A fan sends Cliff a 303-page letter!

SEPTEMBER 15

'A Girl Like You' tops the chart in Hong Kong. A newspaper claims that Delia Wicks, who sings in Johnny Leyton's backing group the Angels, is a 'close' friend of Cliff's.

SEPTEMBER 17

Cliff appears at the Royal Albert Hall with the Shadows, Adam Faith, Helen Shapiro and the John Barry Seven at a concert promoted by the *Daily Mirror* for the printers' pension fund.

SEPTEMBER 22

The wives of Shadows Hank Marvin and Bruce Welch arrive in Blackpool. Shadow Jet Harris moves into a bungalow with Cliff.

SEPTEMBER 29

Connie Francis reveals that she would like Cliff or Adam Faith to make a guest appearance in her forthcoming film tentatively titled *Cook's Tour*, which would feature pop talent from Britain and the Continent.

Playing to a slightly reserved audience.

SEPTEMBER 29

Southport fans present Cliff with a ten-week-old Pyrennean Mountain Dog puppy.

SEPTEMBER 30

Cliff watches Preston North End play Leyton Orient at Preston's Deepdale ground as a guest of impresario Leslie Grade.

SEPTEMBER

In a New Zealand disc popularity survey, Connie Francis comes top, followed by Elvis Presley with Cliff third.

OCTOBER

'Listen To Cliff' No1.EP released.

OCTOBER 6

Cliff's 15th single is released: 'When The Girl In Your Arms Is The Girl In Your Heart'/'Got A Funny Feeling'. Both tracks are from the Associated British film *The Young Ones*. On the same day, drummer Tony Meehan leaves the Shadows and is replaced by Krew Kats drummer Brian Bennett.

OCTOBER 7

Cliff appears on *Thank Your Lucky Stars*, his first television programme since *The Billy Cotton Band Show* on 24 June.

Publicity shot from *The Young Ones*.

OCTOBER 13

Cliff and his *Young Ones* co-star Carole Gray appear on the front cover of the *NME*. The paper includes a four-page tribute to Cliff as he comes of age the following day.

Mr Ludovic Stewart, Music Advisor for Cambridgeshire schools says in his annual report: 'Mr Cliff Richard and his associates have done more to continue some children's musical education than the whole world of music teachers and administrators. There is no doubt that some outlay on guitars would benefit an enormous proportion of the secondary school community.'

OCTOBER 14

Many show business personalities pay tribute to Cliff on his 21st Birthday.Cliff's producer Norrie Paramor recalls the early days of his career in 1958:

'He was broke, scared and wondering whether 'Move It' would ever really move! I find Cliff exceptionally easy to get along with and I would give him full marks for his ability to take direction, his genuine humility and his directness of opinion.'

Jet Harris, leader of the Shadows, says, 'Cliff's whole character was summed up for us when our recording of 'Apache' became a hit... Cliff's attitude was one of sheer delight... we were really touched by the real pleasure he derived from our record hit.'

Hank Marvin of the Shadows: 'Cliff has been the perfect ambassador of British show business wherever he has travelled.'

Bruce Welch of the Shadows: 'Despite all the success that has come his way, he hasn't become the slightest bit big-headed.'

Tony Meehan, former Shadows drummer: 'He is undoubtedly one of the finest people character-wise with whom I have ever come into contact. He has great quality and patience, and is a wonderful example to all the young people who admire him.'

Cliff himself looks back over the previous three years: 'It seems incredible that so much has been crammed into such a short spell. If I was asked to nominate the supreme highlight of my career to date, I expect I would settle for the day when I received my Gold Disc for 'Living Doll' at the London Palladium.'

A London palmist and clairvoyant scrutinises a photograph of Cliff's hands without knowing who they belong to. She says: 'I feel the subject is very famous, but although he is a very big personality, he is very humble and never forgets people who have helped him, nor does he consider himself too big to mix with ordinary people. He gets very nervous and tensed-up at times. He is religiously minded, and I forsee that anything he prays for will be answered in time. He will marry at one stage in his career and continue to be successful while he enjoys personal happiness. Although this subject is slightly psychic and would enjoy doing this sort of work, he doesn't know that a protective spirit is watching over him. It tells me he will rise to take on even more power. When he marries he will choose someone of refinement and taste. He will have three big romances and lots of little ones, and on his security finger there is a blonde woman, slim and of medium build. There are lots of "sevens" jumping around him, but I am confused to say why. Some of the sevens are forming into groups of five… the number fourteen keeps recurring. I feel it is very important to him. It is as though he lives two lives, but this could be because he probably has two names. I can see various letters, but I can't identify them as they are such a jumble. I see H-R-Y though!' (Cliff's real name is Harry.)

OCTOBER 14

At Cliff's 21st Birthday Party at EMI's headquarters in London, Sir Joseph Lockwood – the head of EMI – presents him with a Gold Disc for sales of more than 250,000 albums, and a camera.

OCTOBER 14

Jane Maughn of Sanderstead in Surrey presents Cliff with a letter containing no less than 700 sides of writing and 56,000 words on his departure from London Airport.for a tour of Australia and the far east.

OCTOBER 15

Cliff and the Shadows are involved in a drama at Singapore Airport when their airliner makes two unsuccessful attempts to land in heavy mist.

OCTOBER 16/19

In Singapore and Kuala Lumpur.

OCTOBER 19/20/21

Cliff appears at Sydney, Australia in front of 12,000 people each night, before going on to Melbourne, Perth, Adelaide and Brisbane. New Zealand appearances in Auckland, Wellington, Dunedin and Christchurch follow.

OCTOBER 21/22

The Sydney *Daily Mail* says: 'Cliff Richard proved a good entertainer and an engaging personality in his Sydney Stadium show. His voice, too, was pleasing – when you could hear it above the din of screaming, screeching fans.'
Noted violinist Florian Zabach, on the bill with Cliff and the Shadows at Sydney, is booed by the audience while he is playing. Florian says, 'I would have been much happier appearing with the Sydney Symphony.'

OCTOBER

Cliff and touring co-star, the singer Mark Wynter, are guests of honour at a Melbourne Teenage Ball.

NOVEMBER 10

American singing star Connie Francis releases a cover version of 'When The Girl In Your Arms Is The Girl In Your Heart' in the United States, with an appropriate change of gender in the title and lyrics.

NOVEMBER 17

It is anounced that Cliff's next cinema film – another Technicolor musical – concerns a group of youngsters vacationing in a double-decker bus, and will probably be called *Summer Holiday*.

NOVEMBER 20

On their return to Britain from their far east and Australasian tour, Cliff tells the press that during the thirty-five days they were away, he and the Shadows undertook twenty-eight different aircraft flights.

DECEMBER 1

In the annual *NME* poll, Cliff appears in the following categories:
British Male Singer – 1st
World Male Singer – 2nd to Elvis Presley
British Vocal Personality – 2nd to Adam Faith
World Musical Personality – 4th behind Elvis Presley, Duane Eddy and Sammy Davis
Best British disc of the year – 4th with 'When The Girl In Your Arms Is The Girl In Your Heart'
Cliff says, 'I simply can't explain to you how an artist feels when he reads that he has won an honour of this magnitude.'
The same day, producer Norrie Paramor says that he plans five recording sessions for Cliff and the Shadows, to take place before Christmas.

DECEMBER 2

Cliff is impresario Leslie Grade's guest at Leyton Orient v Norwich City football match.

4 DECEMBER

ABBEY ROAD
Studio session

I Wake Up Cryin' (4)	*32 Minutes And 17 Seconds*
Spanish Harlem (5)	*32 Minutes And 17 Seconds*
Let's Make A Memory (8)	*32 Minutes And 17 Seconds*
Do You Remember	*(Unissued)*

Lead Vocal:	**Cliff Richard**
	The Norrie Paramor Orchestra
Vocals:	**The Mike Sammes Singers**
Producer:	**Norrie Paramor**
Engineers:	**Malcolm Addey/Norman Smith**
Recorded in:	**Studio 2**
Session hours:	**2.30pm-5.45pm**

5 DECEMBER

Abbey Road
Studio session

Secret Love	*Love Songs EP*
How Long Is Forever (3)	*32 Minutes And 17 Seconds*
The Young Ones	*A-side*
Falling In Love With Love (6)	*32 Minutes And 17 Seconds*

Lead Vocal:	**Cliff Richard**
	The Norrie Paramor Orchestra
Producer:	**Norrie Paramor**
Engineer:	**Malcolm Addey**
Recorded in:	**Studio 2**
Session hours:	**2.30pm-5.30pm**

The version of The Young Ones shown here is the released version. Strings were overdubbed onto the track at this session.

THE YOUNG ONES

Warner Pathe, 1961. Running time: 108 minutes.
Cliff's third feature film.

Synopsis:
Nicki (Cliff), is the leader of a youth club. Their headquarters is a rundown hut in an equally deteriorating London district. A rich property owner (Robert Morley) wishes to buy the land on which the club stands. A many-variation fight follows between developer and youth group.

Cast:
Cliff Richard, Carole Gray, Robert Morley, Richard O'Sullivan, Melvyn Hayes, The Shadows.

Credits:
Producer: Kenneth Harper. Director: Sidney J Furie. Choreographer: Herbert Ross. Original screenplay and story: Peter Myers and Ronald Cass. Background score, orchestrations and musical direction Stanley Black. Photography: Douglas Slocombe.

Songs:
'Friday Night', 'Mambo: 'Mood Mambo' performed by the ABS Orchestra. 'Got A Funny Feeling', 'Nothing's Impossible', 'The Young Ones', 'All For One', 'Lessons In Love', 'What Do You Know We've Got A Show' Vaudeville routine: 'Have A Smile For Everyone You Meet'/'Tinkle Tinkle Tinkle'/'Algy The Piccadilly Johnny'/'Captain Ginjah'/' Joshua'/'Where Did You Get That Hat?'/'What Do You Know We've Got A Show'/'Living Doll', 'When The Girl In Your Arms Is The Girl In Your Heart' 'Mambo: 'Just Dance', 'We Say Yeah' performed by Cliff Richard and The Shadows. 'The Savage' performed by The Shadows. 'No One For Me But Nicky' performed by Grazina Frame.

DECEMBER 8

The Young Ones is heralded by the critics as 'The best musical Britain has ever made – and the finest teenage screen entertainment produced for a long time – anywhere!' The plot of *The Young Ones* revolves around a youth club which is due to be torn down in a redevelopment scheme by a company owned by Nicky's (Cliff Richard) father Hamilton Black (Robert Morley). Inevitably Nicky is at loggerheads with his father until the wealthy businessman is won over by the enthusiasm of Nicky's crowd at the youth club, who stage a concert to raise £2,000. The cast includes Robert Morley, Carole Young, Richard O' Sullivan, Melvyn Hayes, Teddy Green, Annette Robertson and Sonya Cordeau. *The Young Ones* is directed by Sidney J. Furie and produced by Kenneth Harper, with screenplay by Peter Myers and Ronald Cass.
Meanwhile the press erroneously announce that the 'B' side of the forthcoming 'Young Ones' single will be 'I'll Wake Up Crying'.

DECEMBER 10

Cliff appears on *Sunday Night at the London Palladium*, for the first time since 16 October 1960.

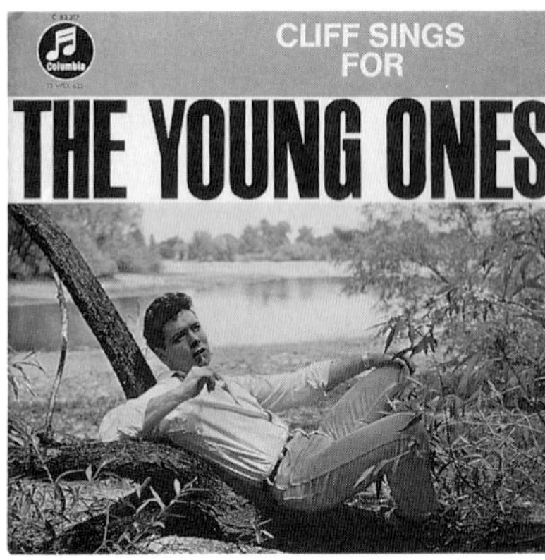

11 DECEMBER

Abbey Road
Studio session

Love Letters (2)	*Love Songs EP*
I'm Looking Out The Window (2)	*A-side*
Fly Me To The Moon (In Other Words) (8)	*Love Is Forever*
Who Are We To Say (6)	*32 Minutes And 17 Seconds*

Lead Vocal:	**Cliff Richard**
	The Norrie Paramor Orchestra
Producer:	**Norrie Paramor**
Engineer:	**Malcolm Addey**
Recorded in:	**Studio 2**
Session hours:	**2.30pm-5.30pm**

DECEMBER 13

The Young Ones is premiered at London's Warner Theatre.

DECEMBER 14

'The Young Ones' LP is released.

18 DECEMBER

ABBEY ROAD
Studio session

You Don't Know (7)	*32 Minutes And 17 Seconds*
Take Special Care	*(Unissued)*
So I've Been Told (10)	*32 Minutes And 17 Seconds*

Lead Vocal:	**Cliff Richard**
Guitars:	**Hank Marvin/Bruce Welch**
Bass:	**Jet Harris**
Drums:	**Tony Meehan**
Producer:	**Norrie Paramor**
Engineer:	**Malcolm Addey**
Recorded in:	**Studio 2**
Session hours:	**2.30pm-5.30pm**

DECEMBER 19

A clip from *The Young Ones* is screened by BBC TV in *Picture Parade.*

19 DECEMBER

ABBEY ROAD
Studio session

Do You Want To Dance (3)	*B-side*
Since I Lost You (12)	*B-side*

Lead Vocal:	**Cliff Richard**
Guitars:	**Hank Marvin/Bruce Welch**
Bass:	**Jet Harris**
Drums:	**Tony Meehan**
Producer:	**Norrie Paramor**
Engineer:	**Malcolm Addey**
Recorded in:	**Studio 2**
Session hours:	**2.30pm-5.30pm**

DECEMBER 20

Cliff appears at the Cheshunt Boys Club charity show at the Edmonton Royal.

DECEMBER 22

Cliff has two records in the South African Top Ten: 'Tea For Two' (No.) and 'A Girl Like You' (No.10). 'When The Girl In Your Arms' is a chart-topper in Norway and 'Now's The Time' is No.4 in India.

DECEMBER 23

Cliff and his mother fly to South Africa to attend *The Young Ones* being premiered at Johannesburg, Cape Town and Durban.

DECEMBER 26

The single of 'The Young Ones' is favourably reviewed in a special Boxing Day edition of *Juke Box Jury*. Hosted by David Jacobs, the panel comprises DJs Peter Murray and Jean Metcalfe, Hayley Mills and Coronation Street star Alan Rothwell.
The same day Cliff tops the bill in ATV's *All Kinds Of Music* which had been tele-recorded the previous Tuesday. The Kaye Sisters appear on the show, but the Shadows are absent due to engagements in Paris.

DECEMBER 31

Along with Lonnie Donegan, Alma Cogan, Jack Parnell, Vera Lynn, Roy Castle and Bert Weedon, Cliff is showcased in a special *Sunday Night at the London Palladium* for ATV.

1962 – 1963

The Records 1962 – 1963

The years 1962 and 1963 were the most successful for Cliff since the late fifties. Of the eight singles released in this period 'The Young Ones' was the first to be released to advance sales of more than one million copies and was to become the biggest seller of all of Cliff's singles so far. It entered the charts straight at No.1 and stayed on the chart for an amazing 21 weeks.

The remaining singles did extremely well, all hitting the top four and two of them reaching the top spot. 'I'm Looking Out The Window'/'Do You Want To Dance' proved to be a very strong release indeed with both sides fighting each other all the way up the charts, thus probably preventing either of them reaching the top spot. Eventually they made it to an impressive 2nd and 10th placing. 'The Next Time'/'Bachelor Boy' did even better with both sides reaching the No.1 spot, and 'Summer Holiday' repeated the success of 'Please Don't Tease' by returning to No.1 after dropping from the summit.

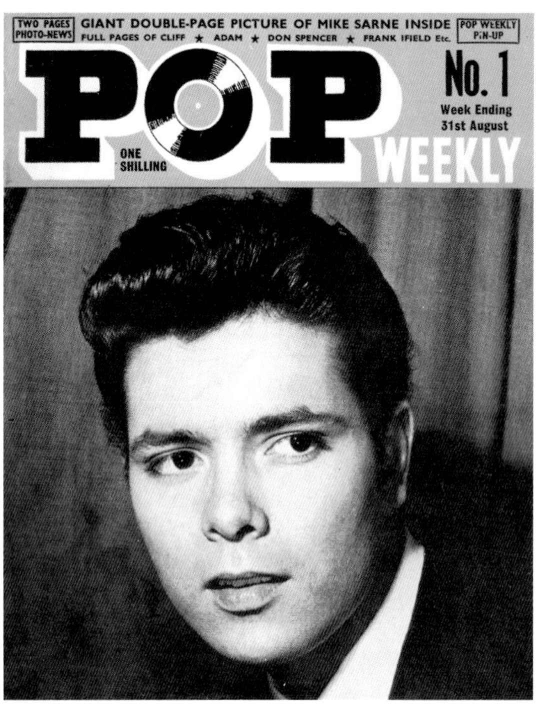

TWO PAGES PHOTO-NEWS
GIANT DOUBLE-PAGE PICTURE OF MIKE SARNE INSIDE
POP WEEKLY PIN-UP
FULL PAGES OF CLIFF ★ ADAM ★ DON SPENCER ★ FRANK IFIELD Etc.
POP
No. 1
Week Ending 31st August
ONE SHILLING
WEEKLY

Cliff's album sales were just as impressive. The film soundtrack album from *Summer Holiday* enjoyed a spell at the pinnacle of the charts, although ironically the only regular album of 1962 – 32 MINUTES AND 17 SECONDS – reached the third position, whereas the compilation CLIFF'S HIT ALBUM reached the No.2 spot, largely as a result of the clever idea of collecting fourteen of Cliff's singles on one album. Another sign of Cliff's broadening popularity was the eighth position reached on the British album chart by the foreign language recording WHEN IN SPAIN, despite the fact that most British fans could not understand any of the lyrics!

Although none of the EPs showed up on the singles bestseller charts during this period, they all proved to be consistent sellers. The only two to feature new material were HOLIDAY CARNIVAL and LOVE SONGS, while the others recycled tracks from recent singles and albums.

The Sessions 1962 – 1963

Cliff visited EMI's Abbey Road Studios to do some regular recording work in January, and laid down two more tracks for 32 MINUTES AND 17 SECONDS, although another session was set for May to complete the album. In the meantime and to collect sufficient material for a live album of Cliff and the Shadows on tour, Columbia taped the first and second houses at the ABC Theatre, Kingston-Upon-Thames on 7 March. However, information on the tape box indicates a number of technical faults, particularly distortion and level changes probably due to the conditions under which it was recorded although these were remedied at a later date when a copy tape was made from the first house versions, as the tapes for the second house have been heavily cut and subsequently edited.

It is known that EMI still possess tapes containing completely finished album sides of the Shadows set on side one, and Cliff's set on side two, showing that Columbia were at the time well advanced with their plans for the CLIFF RICHARD SHOW album. A tantalising piece of information about these recordings is that Cliff performed a number of songs that were never recorded in the studio. These included a great rocker 'Dim Dim The Lights', the country orientated 'Rovin' Gambler', the rousing gospel treatment of 'Save My Soul' and the R & B classic 'I Got A Woman'. When the idea of the album was dropped, attention shifted towards the production of the *Summer Holiday* soundtrack.

Work began in April, and continued at a series of recording dates through the year to November, producing such classics as 'Summer Holiday', 'The Next Time', 'Bachelor Boy' and 'Dancing Shoes'. Some mystery surrounds the song 'Bachelor Boy', however. The version that was originally recorded for the film is slightly different to the version that was eventually released and, according to one tape box, there is also a special version for the USA, which seems likely to be a remix of the record version. Not all the sessions during this period were restricted to soundtrack recordings, and some other material was taped. Of these, the reworking of the Jerry Lee Lewis hit 'It'll Be Me' was the most successful, providing Columbia with an obvious choice for a single release. 'Razzle Dazzle' and 'Save My Soul' had been listed for recording at this session , but for reasons unknown were not, although the former was taped at the next session in July and, while the latter was again listed, it was never recorded. As usual, all the sessions took place in Studio 2 at Abbey Road with the regular Shadows line-up.

There was only one change, from the 5 May recording date, when Jet Harris left, and his place was taken by Brian Locking. We should note here that, before Jet's departure, versions of 'Summer Holiday' and 'Dancing Shoes' had been recorded which remain unheard as the released versions featured new Shadow Brian Locking. For the August and November soundtrack

Publicity photo from *Summer Holiday*.

sessions the Stanley Black Orchestra provided the orchestral arrangements, and the Mike Sammes Singers the vocal backing on the production numbers. April 1963 saw Cliff back in the recording studios again. One session in December provided an English version of 'Perfidia', a song Cliff would later record in Spanish at the WHEN IN SPAIN sessions.

These began towards the end of April 1963. However, the location had changed from Abbey Road to EMI's studio in Barcelona, Spain. During four nights, a total of 12 tracks were laid down that would become the first foreign language album WHEN IN SPAIN. Overdubbing of the Norrie Paramor Strings and backing vocals by Bruce and Cliff were carried out at Abbey Road's Studio Two between 14 and 28 May. In August more foreign language recordings were taped; this time the setting was the Jubilee Hall in Blackpool. The songs Cliff was to record were a collection of popular French hits. 'J'Attendrai' and 'C'est Si Bon' had both enjoyed chart success in France and 'La Mer' and 'Boum' were two of the most famous songs from the pen of the great Charles Trenet. These four tracks found their way onto the WHEN IN FRANCE EP. The next few sessions were aimed at producing new singles and the first batch of material for the WONDERFUL LIFE soundtrack album.

Cliff Richard wins young girls' hearts

CHANTING queues, souvenir touts, and traffic jams greeted the arrival in Kingston on Wednesday evening of Britain's leading pop singer, Cliff Richard, who made two personal appearances in shows at the A.B.C. cinema.

Needless to say, there were no empty seats at either show, though there were a surprisingly large number filled by mums and dads.

Whether they went of their own free will, or merely to ensure that their offspring did not get trampled in the rush, is not certain.

Compere Tony Marsh, obviously an old hand at dealing with predominately teenage audiences, provided an amusing line of smooth patter between the acts.

Sustained, ear-piercing shrieks greeted the appearance of the Shadows, reproduced every time any of the three guitarists lifted their feet, bent their knees or swayed their hips.

Bundle of talent

Their rendering of "F.B.I." nearly brought the house down.

The ovation given to Cliff Richard was, in fact, so tumultuous that it was impossible to hear a single word of his first song.

Undoubtedly this 21 years-old singer has looks, charm, a melodious voice and a bundle of talent. He seems incredibly unassuming, and yet more professional with each public appearance.

It was a pity that his more gentle love songs were ruined by members of the "see-who-can-scream-in-the-quietest-part" clan.

He is bouncing with rhythm every minute he is on stage, a dynamic personality. But oh, those screams!

Cinema staff were on hand to ensure that no one got over-enthusiastic and tried to clamber on to the stage.

Final impressions were of moon-struck girls in the front rows frantically throwing embroidered hearts on to the stage before the curtain came down.

BAPTIST DEACONS' CONFERENCE

Kingston Baptist Church welcomed church officers of the Thames Valley group of Baptist Churches on Thursday last week at a specially convened Deacons' conference.

An address was given by Mr. W. R. Booth, of Ruislip, president of the London Baptist Association. Mr. Booth spoke on Christian Stewardship, and his address was followed by questions and discussion.

Thanks were given to Mr. Booth and to the women members of the church who had organised the catering, by Mr. C. W. Jarrett, secretary of Whitton Baptist Church and vice-president of the Thames Valley group.

The president of the group and Minister of Kingston Baptist Church (the Rev. Herbert E. Ward) presided.

JANUARY

There are several reports in the press that Cliff is to marry 17 year old Valerie Stratford – a claim that Cliff dismisses as 'crazy'.

JANUARY

Cliff's 16th single 'The Young Ones'/'We Say Yeah' is released. Both tracks are from the film *The Young Ones*.

JANUARY 11

'The Young Ones' goes straight into the chart at No.1 becoming only the fourth single to achieve this feat in Britain, the others being Al Martino's 'Here In My Heart' (on the first ever chart) and Elvis Presley's 'Jailhouse Rock' and 'It's Now Or Never'.

JANUARY 11

'The Young Ones' becomes Cliff's 5th chart topping single, knocking Danny William's 'Moon River' off the No.1 spot and staying there for six weeks before being deposed by Elvis Presley's 'Rock A Hula Baby'/'Can't Help Falling In Love'.

18 JANUARY

ABBEY ROAD
Studio session

Turn Around (8)	*32 Minutes And 17 Seconds*
I'm On My Way	*32 Minutes And 17 Seconds*

Lead Vocal:	**Cliff Richard**
	The Norrie Paramor Orchestra
	The Mike Sammes Singers

Producer:	**Norrie Paramor**
Engineer:	**Malcolm Addey**
Recorded in:	**Studio 2**
Session hours:	**7.00pm-10.30pm**

7 MARCH

ABC, KINGSTON, SURREY
Live Recordings

Apache-Shazam	*(Unissued)*
Shadoogie	*(Unissued)*
Wonderful Land	*(Unissued)*
All My Sorrows	*(Unissued)*
Quarter To Three	*(Unissued)*
Nivram	*(Unissued)*
Little B	*(Unissued)*
FBI	*(Unissued)*

Do You Wanna Dance	*(Unissued)*
Dim Dim The Lights	*(Unissued)*
My Blue Heaven	*(Unissued)*
Razzle Dazzle	*(Unissued)*
Roving Gambler	*(Unissued)*
Save My Soul	*(Unissued)*
When The Girl In Your Arms	*(Unissued)*
I Gotta Woman	*(Unissued)*
The Young Ones Medley:	*(Unissued)*
Lessons In Love	
Got A Funny Feeling	
The Young Ones	
We Say Yeah	

Lead Vocal:	**Cliff Richard**
Guitars:	**Hank Marvin/Bruce Welch**
Bass:	**Jet Harris**
Drums:	**Brian Bennett**

Producer:	**Norrie Paramor**
Engineers:	**Malcolm Addey/Ken Townsend**
Session hours:	**1st House**

Birthday kiss

Ann Solkhon, daughter of Mr. John Solkhon, manager of the ABC cinema, Kingston, got a birthday kiss from singing star Cliff Richard on Wednesday. Ann was 15 that day, and in the evening went to her father's cinema to see Cliff's one-night show, which is reviewed on page 18.

7 MARCH

ABC, Kingston, Surrey

Live Recordings

Apache-Shazam	(Unissued)
Shadoogie	(Unissued)
Wonderful Land	(Unissued)
All My Sorrows	(Unissued)
Quarter To Three	(Unissued)
Nivram	(Unissued)
Little B	(Unissued)
FBI	(Unissued)
Do You Wanna Dance	(Unissued)
Dim Dim The Lights	(Unissued)
My Blue Heaven	(Unissued)
Razzle Dazzle	(Unissued)
Roving Gambler	(Unissued)
Save My Soul	(Unissued)
When The Girl In Your Arms	(Unissued)
I Gotta Woman	(Unissued)
The Young Ones Medley:	(Unissued)
Lessons In Love	
Got A Funny Feeling	
The Young Ones	
We Say Yeah	

Lead Vocal:	**Cliff Richard**
Guitars:	**Hank Marvin/Bruce Welch**
Bass:	**Jet Harris**
Drums:	**Brian Bennett**
Producer:	**Norrie Paramor**
Engineers:	**Malcolm Addey/Ken Townsend**
Session hours:	**2nd House**

MARCH 13

At London's Savoy Hotel, Cliff receives an award from the Variety Club of Great Britain as 'Show Business Personality of the Year'.

MARCH

Along with Mike Berry and the Outlaws, Cliff and the Shadows perform at an historic event at the Eton College Missions Youth Club at Hackney Wick. The occasion is attended by Princess Margaret and the Earl of Snowdon, who are given a 15-minute ovation. Afterwards Cliff joins the Royal couple for tea, cakes and a chat. The Princess tells Cliff that she's going to see *The Young Ones* at the weekend, while the Earl of Snowdon starts to chat about his new Mini-Cooper. Cliff chats about his new purchase – a black cadillac – and promises that if he gets passed by their car he'll try not to pull a a face! Cliff says after the meeting, 'They're marvellously friendly people!' The occasion, some of which is

Cliff and the Shadows appearing before Princess Margaret.

recorded on film for posterity, features the Shadows playing 'Apache', while handclaps are provided by the Royal couple, Cliff, Arthur Muxlow (the Club's Vice-President), the Bishop of Bath and Wells and the Reverend W.S.Shergold, the Eton College Mission Club's President.

MARCH

Cliff and the Shadows meet Princess Margaret and Lord Snowdon at the Eton College Mission's Youth Club in Hamburg.

MARCH 25

Cliff withdraws from the Spastics Show at Wembley because of laryngitis. His recovery is aided by medicine recommended by Princess Margaret.

MARCH 30

It is announced that John Krish, documentary writer and director, is to direct Cliff's next film *Summer Holiday*, due to be filmed on location in Greece commencing in mid-May. The film was due to be undertaken by Sydney Furie, who directed *The Young Ones*, but he will continue working on a film starring Jess Conrad, *The Boys*, the music for which has been written by the Shadows.

APRIL

Cliff writes an article for the April issue of *Hit Parade* magazine.

4 APRIL

ABBEY ROAD
Studio session

For You For Me (7)	*Holiday Carnival EP*
I'm Walking The Blues (6)	*32 Minutes And 17 Seconds*

Lead Vocal:	**Cliff Richard**
Guitars:	**Hank Marvin/Bruce Welch**
Bass:	**Jet Harris**
Drums:	**Brian Bennett**
Producer:	**Norrie Paramor**
Engineer:	**Malcolm Addey**
Recorded in:	**Studio 2**
Session hours:	**7.00pm-10.30pm**

5 APRIL

ABBEY ROAD
Studio session

Summer Holiday	*(Unissued)*

Lead Vocal:	**Cliff Richard**
Guitars:	**Hank Marvin/Bruce Welch**
Bass:	**Jet Harris**
Drums:	**Brian Bennett**
Producer:	**Norrie Paramor**
Engineer:	**Malcolm Addey**
Recorded in:	**Studio 2**
Session hours:	**7.00pm-10.30pm**

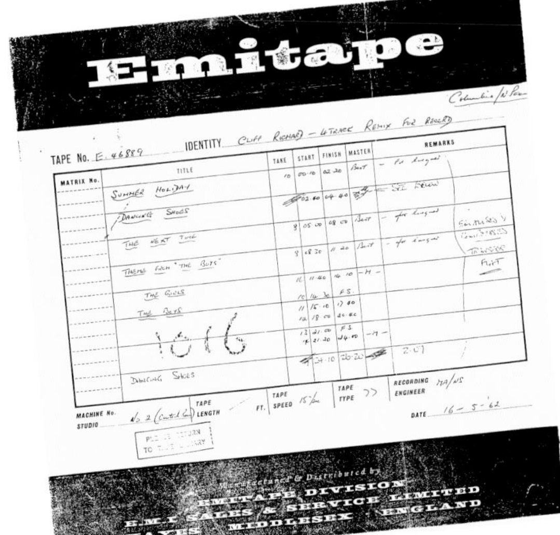

APRIL 6

A copy of the film *The Young Ones* is sent to Princess Margaret at Clarence House.

APRIL

'Cliff Richard No.1' EP is released.

12 APRIL

ABBEY ROAD
Studio session

Dancing Shoes	*(Unissued)*

Lead Vocal:	**Cliff Richard**
Guitars:	**Hank Marvin/Bruce Welch**
Bass:	**Jet Harris**
Drums:	**Brian Bennett**
Producer:	**Norrie Paramor**
Engineer:	**Malcolm Addey**
Recorded in:	**Studio 2**
Session hours:	**7.00pm-10.30pm**

APRIL 13

The Shadows become the first British group to win a Gold Disc, and Cliff receives one for 'The Young Ones'.
Both Gold Discs are presented to the artists during a tele-recording of the top weekend television pop music programme *Thank Your Lucky Stars.*

APRIL 13

Cliff's producer Norrie Paramor notches up a second hit for himself with 'The Theme from "Z" Cars'. It is Norrie's wife, Joan, who is responsible for persuading him to release it. On the subject of 'The Young Ones', Norrie says 'There's been a good deal of discussion about the backing for 'The Young Ones'. Some people said that when I dubbed on the strings it "made" the record. I don't agree. They add to the effect by all means, and they probably make it sound much nicer.'

APRIL 15

Dressed in a black tuxedo and white frilled shirt, Cliff headlines the annual *NME* Poll Winners' Concert at Wembley, which features among others Adam Faith, Helen Shapiro and Billy Fury. The awards are presented by Brenda Lee and Johnny Burnette. Cliff and the Shadows open with 'Do You Wanna Dance', followed by 'Razzle Dazzle', a selection of numbers from *The Young Ones* including the title track, 'Lessons in Love' and 'Got A Funny Feeling', concluding with 'We Say Yeah'. This is Jet Harris' final appearance with the Shadows.

APRIL 16

The *NME* Tenth Anniversary Book is published and inevitably includes articles on Cliff.
Cliff pays tribute to the Shadows:
'Hank Marvin is one of the nicest people you could ever wish to meet, and it's virtually impossible to get annoyed or mad with him. Nothing ever seems to bother him and he takes life in his stride without ever a grumble or a moan.'
'Bruce Welch is terribly reliable and he's a bit of a taskmaster in as much as he keeps the boys at it during rehearsals until everything is perfect. You see, perfection is Bruce's aim and he spares nothing to achieve his goal. His attitude has won the respect of all of us.'
Jet Harris is a quiet, shy person who's not in the least bit moody. He's a very deep, serious-thinking fellow, but you just can't help liking him. He has a wonderfully dry sense of humour and is without question the greatest animal lover you ever saw.'
'Brian Bennett is very honest. When a thing is bad, he'll have no hesitation in saying so. Similarly, if something impresses him, he really lets you know it. When Tony Meehan left the Shadows we immediately thought of Brian for a replacement. We thought he could do it, but we never realised he'd do it so well.'
Cliff also comments on the Shadows' debut album:
'As far as I'm concerned, this is the best LP ever recorded in Britain. I just love it and I play it at every available opportunity.'
In the same publication, Russ Conway talks about a couple of stunts pulled by Cliff. The first was during the London Palladium run:
'Cliff and the cast, which included Des O' Connor, Joan Regan, Edmund Hockridge and Billy Dainty, bought a pile of balloons, blew them all up and put them in my dressing room. Did I say pile of balloons? There were hundreds of them – all colours and all shapes and sizes. From floor to ceiling the room was packed tight with balloons – and when I arrived at the theatre, I just couldn't get in to make-up. It took half an hour before the room was anything like habitable. On another occasion Joan Regan was the victim of a glorious stunt instigated by Cliff. He enlisted the aid of a couple of friends, went off down the road a couple of hours before the show was due to start and bought a big pile of junk. They bought it all back to the theatre and had us sign "Best Wishes" labels which they fixed to the assortment – I recall there were such things as an ancient TV set that didn't work, an old fire and an enormous enamel basin with a hole in it! Then they dumped the lot in Joan's dressing room. When she opened the door she almost collapsed with laughter. That'll give you some idea of Cliff's fine sense of humour.'

APRIL 22

As Jet Harris leaves the Shadows to pursue a solo career, he is replaced by ex-Krew Kat bass guitarist Brian 'Licorice' Locking, who makes his debut behind Cliff at Blackpool. During the same show, rhythm guitarist Bruce Welch collapses with a septic throat and is replaced for a week by guitarist-songwriter Peter Carter of the original Checkmates.

APRIL 24

Cliff has dinner with the head of EMI, Sir Joseph Lockwood.

APRIL 27

Stanley Black is appointed musical director for Cliff's next film *Summer Holiday*. The supporting cast is to include Melvyn Hayes, Richard O' Sullivan and Teddy Green, with the Shadows having featured roles.

1 MAY

ABBEY ROAD
Studio session

Take Special Care (30)	*Cliff Richard*
I'll Be Waiting	*(Unissued)*

Lead Vocal:	**Cliff Richard**
Guitars:	**Hank Marvin/Bruce Welch**
Bass:	**Jet Harris**
Drums:	**Brian Bennett**
Producer:	**Norrie Paramor**
Engineer:	**Malcolm Addey**
Recorded in:	**Studio 2**
Session hours:	**7.00pm-10.00pm**

MAY 2

TV producer Jack Good reckons that Jet Harris will be a serious threat to Cliff Richard as a solo singer.

MAY 4

Cliff's 17th single, 'I'm Looking Out The Window'/'Do You

Wanna Dance', is released. One review says, 'Cliff Richard's most brilliant performance to date'. Comedian Norman Vaughan reveals that his first real break was acting as compere on Cliff's package show.

MAY 5

Cliff and the Shadows appear on TV's *Thank Your Lucky Stars* along with Joe Brown, Eden Kane and 14-year old newcomer Candy Sparling. DJ Pete Murray presents Cliff with a Gold Disc for 'The Young Ones' and the Shadows with one for 'Apache'.

5 MAY

ABBEY ROAD
Film soundtrack recordings for Summer Holiday

Dancing Shoes (4)	*B-side*
Summer Holiday (11)	*A-side*

Lead Vocal:	**Cliff Richard**
Guitars:	**Hank Marvin/Bruce Welch**
Bass:	**Brian Locking**
Drums:	**Brian Bennett**
Producer:	**Norrie Paramor**
Engineer:	**Malcolm Addey**
Recorded in:	**Studio 2**
Session hours:	**7.00pm-10.45pm**

These two tracks are listed as remakes on the EMI session sheets.

MAY 6

Having been recently honoured by the Songwriters' Guild for services to the music industry, Cliff appears at their 'Our Friends the Stars' charity show at London's Victoria Palace with the Shadows, Max Bygraves, Danny Williams, Eden Kane and the John Barry Seven.

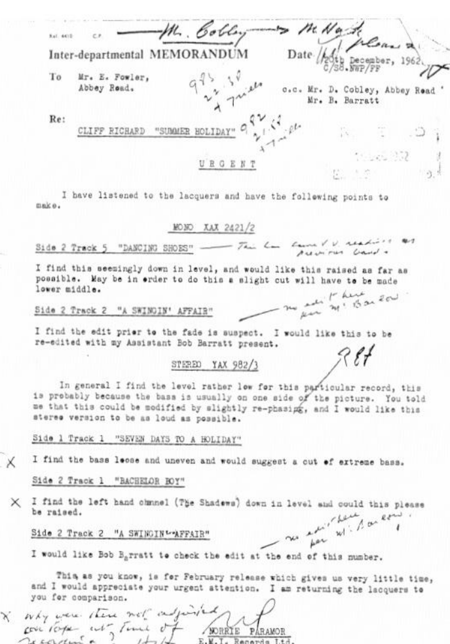

Inter-departmental MEMORANDUM Date 20th December, 1962.
C/S8.NWP/PF

To Mr. E. Fowler, Abbey Road.

c.c. Mr. D. Cobley, Abbey Road
Mr. B. Barratt

Re: CLIFF RICHARD "SUMMER HOLIDAY"

URGENT

I have listened to the lacquers and have the following points to make.

MONO XAX 2421/2

Side 2 Track 5 "DANCING SHOES"

I find this seemingly down in level, and would like this raised as far as possible. May be in order to do this a slight cut will have to be made lower middle.

Side 2 Track 2 "A SWINGIN' AFFAIR"

I find the edit prior to the fade is suspect. I would like this to be re-edited with my Assistant Bob Barratt present.

STEREO YAX 982/3

In general I find the level rather low for this particular record, this is probably because the bass is usually on one side of the picture. You told me that this could be modified by slightly re-phasing, and I would like this stereo version to be as loud as possible.

Side 1 Track 1 "SEVEN DAYS TO A HOLIDAY"

I find the bass loose and uneven and would suggest a cut of extreme bass.

Side 2 Track 1 "BACHELOR BOY"

I find the left hand channel (The Shadows) down in level and could this please be raised.

Side 2 Track 2 "A SWINGIN' AFFAIR"

I would like Bob Barratt to check the edit at the end of this number.

This, as you know, is for February release which gives us very little time, and I would appreciate your urgent attention. I am returning the lacquers to you for comparison.

NORRIE PARAMOR
E.M.I. Records Ltd.

MAY

'Hits From The Young Ones' EP is released.

MAY 10

Cliff's 17th single, 'I'm Looking Out The Window'/'Do You Wanna Dance' enters the top 10 as a double-sided hit.

10 MAY

ABBEY ROAD
Studio session

The Next Time (sp)	*A-side*

Lead Vocal:	**Cliff Richard**
Guitars:	**Hank Marvin/Bruce Welch**
Bass:	**Brian Locking**
Drums:	**Brian Bennett**
Piano/Organ:	**Norrie Paramor**
Producer:	**Norrie Paramor**
Engineer:	**Malcolm Addey**
Recorded in:	**Studio 2**
Session hours:	**7.00pm-10.30pm**

MAY 11

Charlie Chaplin's 17 year-old daughter Geraldine is one of many girls tested for the role of Cliff's girl-friend in *Summer Holiday*. It is announced that Peter Yates, until recently working on *The Guns Of Navarone*, is to direct the film.

MAY 14

Along with the Shadows and Norman Vaughan, Cliff appears in a cabaret show for a civic reception for Leyton Orient Football Club.

MAY 14/18

Summer Holiday begins to take shape at a gymnasium in Paddington. Cliff's co-star is American actress Laurie Peters who appeared in the Broadway production of *Sound Of Music* and the film *Mr Hobbs Takes A Holiday*, and recently married actor Jon Voight. The story revolves around a group of young mechanics who do up a London Transport double-decker bus and take it across Europe. En route they encounter a girl trio whose car breaks down on their way to a show in Athens, and a young boy stowaway who turns out to be a girl – all of whom end up on the bus. The stowaway is a young starlet desperate to get away from her clinging mother, who ends up chasing the bus across Europe in her car. Despite a few hairy situations, all ends happily with Don (Cliff) and Barbara (co-star Laurie Peters) falling in love. To make the part more realistic, Cliff practises driving a double-decker bus around London: 'I found it unexpectedly easy really; the only thing that fooled me was the length, which I found difficult to manage. Three double-decker buses are already in Europe waiting for us – there's only one bus actually featured in the film, but rather than cart it all round the Continent we've got three dotted about in various places and we shall use them as we come to them!'

17 MAY

ABBEY ROAD
Studio session

Les Girls	*Summer Holiday*
Round And Round	*Summer Holiday*
When My Dreamboat Comes Home	*32 Minutes And 17 Seconds*
Blueberry Hill	*32 Minutes And 17 Seconds*
It'll Be Me	*A-side*

Lead Vocal:	**Cliff Richard**
Guitars:	**Hank Marvin/Bruce Welch**
Bass:	**Brian Locking**
Drums:	**Brian Bennett**
Piano:	
Producer:	**Norrie Paramor**
Engineer:	**Malcolm Addey**
Recorded in:	**Studio 2**
Session hours:	**2.30pm-5.30pm (Shadows)/7.00pm-11.00pm**

MAY 18

Cliff and the Shadows team up with agent Leslie Grade and one of the world's biggest publishers, Aberbach Music, to form a record producing firm which they call Shad-Rich. As well as Leslie Grade, other directors are Aberbach US executive Freddie Bienstock and Cliff and the Shadows personal manager, Peter Gormley.

On the same day Cliff comments on Elvis Presley's new single 'Good Luck Charm': 'When I first heard it I didn't like it very much, but I found on hearing it a second time I enjoyed it immensely. It's slightly reminiscent of 'Teddy Bear' I think, but I rate it fifty times better than 'Rock-A-Hula-Baby', which I reckon was just about the worst record Elvis has made.'

MAY 19/20

Cliff and the Shadows fly to France for the weekend, to watch Ray Charles in concert at the Paris Olympia, and end up on their feet yelling and shouting enthusiastically. Shadow Bruce Welch says, 'We were screaming right along with the rest of them! It must have been quite a new experience for Cliff to be one of the screamers.'

MAY 25

It is announced that Cliff's management hope he will star in a modern version of an old pantomime at the London Palladium during the next winter season. Also a South African tour – intended to take place in October or November – is set up by the Grade Organisation. Kenya's political leader Tom Mboya is promised that Cliff will headline a charity show to aid the country's underprivileged children.

MAY 27

Cliff, the entire cast and film crew fly to Greece to commence shooting *Summer Holiday*.

JUNE 1

Cliff and the Shadows appoint their former drummer, Tony Meehan, as artists' and repertoire chief to take charge of all the recording activities for their newly-formed company Shad-Rich. Since leaving the Shadows, Tony has been working on finding new British talent for Decca Records as well as drumming on records for Jet Harris, John Leyton, Billy Fury and the Vernons Girls among others. Tony comments, 'I do not expect to record any numbers for Shad-Rich until all the initial complications are ironed out and the organisation is running smoothly. This is not expected to be until late summer.'

JUNE

'Cliff Richard No.2' EP is released.

JUNE 2

Columbia label manager Norrie Paramor flies to Greece for talks with Cliff.

JUNE 3

Norrie is in Greece when the whole cast is given a couple of days off from the gruelling 6am-8pm 7-days a week routine. A huge party was laid on.the highlight of which was when Cliff and the boys decided to re-create the "We've Got A Show" routine from *The Young Ones*. They were all a trifle rusty on the words and choreography except Cliff, who was the only one who was able to remember all his lyrics and steps without fault!'

JUNE 4

Cliff and most of the film cast hire a cabin cruiser to sail to the Greek isle of Hydra.

JUNE 9

Cliff's mother and sisters Jacqueline and Joan fly to Greece for a two-week holiday.

JUNE 16

The Shadows fly to Greece to join Cliff and film their part in *Summer Holiday*.

12 JULY

ABBEY ROAD
Studio session

A Forever Kind Of Love (11)	*Forever Kind Of Love EP*
Razzle Dazzle (sp)	*Cliff Richard*
Reelin' And Rockin' (3)	*Cliff Richard*

Lead Vocal:	**Cliff Richard**
Guitars:	**Hank Marvin/Bruce Welch**
Bass:	**Brian Locking**
Drums:	**Brian Bennett**
	The Norrie Paramor Orchestra
Producer:	**Norrie Paramor**
Engineer:	**Peter Bown**
Recorded in:	**Studio 2**
Session hours:	**7.00pm-10.45pm**

Razzle Dazzle is an edit of takes 1 and 4.

~~MONO/STEREO~~ REMIX FROM 4 TRACK TO MONO RECORDING SHEET

Sheet: 1 of: Class: "POP" Overall Title — Date of Session 24-7-62 — Job No: POG/2EMS

ARTISTIC INFORMATION — Artist(s) and/or cast: CLIFF RICHARD AND THE SHADOWS; Conductor: —; Orchestra: —; Accompaniment: —; Art. Dept. Rep.: BOB BARRATT

COSTING INFORMATION — Materials used: x; Session booked time: 10 – 1pm; Session actual: 10 – 1-15pm; Set-up/playback: ½; Order number: —; Company: COLUMBIA; Control room: 1/1A; Engineers: M.A. RL

Titles and Matrix Nos.	Author/Composer/Publisher	Reel Numbers	False Starts	Take No.	Take Details From	To	Dur.	M	Remarks
TAKE SPECIAL CARE		E47520		33	COMPLETE			(M)	ALL THESE EQUALISED AND COMPRESSED TRANSFER FLAT
A FOREVER KIND OF LOVE				15	— " —			*	
RAZZLE DAZZLE				6	— " —			(M)	
REELIN + A'ROCKIN				4	— " —			(M)	
THE GIRLS				16	— " —			(M)	
SWEET DREAMS				13	— " —			(M)	
ALL DAY				9	— " —			(M)	

* FOR PLAYBACK LACQUER ONLY

JULY 20

Cliff reminisces over his first four years at the top of the show business tree:

'Sometimes I think my mother will wake me up one morning and I'll find myself back to being just plain Harry Rodger Webb, an ordinary clerk.

I mean, I'm 22 years old now and when I realise that I can't even remember my 14th birthday it gets pretty frightening... another of my big ambitions is to follow in Jet's footsteps and become a serious actor. Cary Grant is my idol and as I get a bit older I'd like to try and model myself on him.'

20 JULY

ABBEY ROAD
Studio session

Wonderful To Be Young (14)	*Forever Kind of Love EP*

Lead Vocal:	**Cliff Richard**
Guitars:	**Hank Marvin/Bruce Welch**
Bass:	**Brian Locking**
Drums:	**Brian Bennett**
Producer:	**Norrie Paramor**
Engineers:	**Malcolm Addey/Peter Vince**
Recorded in:	**Studio 2**
Session hours:	**7.00pm-10.30pm**

AUGUST 3

American TV host Ed Sullivan in an interview about UK singers comments: '...I think someone like Cliff Richard shouldn't try to put on an Oxford accent when singing a rock'n'roll song. I know he doesn't and I think his act is all the better for it.'

11 AUGUST

ABBEY ROAD
Studio session

Wonderful To Be Young (28)	*A-side (US)*

Lead Vocal:	**Cliff Richard**
Guitars:	**Hank Marvin/Bruce Welch**
Bass:	**Brian Locking**
Drums:	**Brian Bennett**
Piano:	**Max Harris**
Vocals:	**Mike Sammes Singers-1pm-3pm**
Producer:	**Norrie Paramor**
Engineer:	**Malcolm Addey**
Recorded in:	**Studio 1**
Session hours:	**1.00pm-4.45pm**

26 AUGUST

Abbey Road

Film soundtrack recordings for Summer Holiday

Yugoslav Wedding	*Summer Holiday*
Let Us Take You For A Ride	*Summer Holiday*
Stranger In Town (4)	*Summer Holiday*
Swingin' Affair	*Summer Holiday*
All At Once (sp)	*Summer Holiday*

Lead Vocal:	**Cliff Richard**
	The Mike Sammes Singers
	The Stanley Black Orchestra

Producer:	**Norrie Paramor**
Engineers:	**Malcolm Addey/Richard Lush**
Recorded in:	**Studio 2**
Session hours:	**2.30pm-5.30pm/7.00pm-10.00pm**

All At Once is an edit of takes 6 and 7.

AUGUST 31

Ciff's 18th single 'It'll Be Me'/'Since I Lost You' is released. The 'A' side is a reworking of the old Jerry Lee Lewis rocker and the 'B' side is a song by Bruce Welch and Hank Marvin.

AUGUST

In Australia, Cliff tops the chart with 'The Young Ones' while 'Do You Wanna Dance' is at number 6. In Holland 'Do You Wanna Dance' is number 1, and in Norway 'I'm Looking Out The Window' is number 9.

SHADOWS AND TORNADOS MEET

Plus many other features and top news

LOVE ME b/w YOU'RE MY THRILL EVE BOSWELL on DECCA F 11509

new MUSICAL EXPRESS

WORLD'S LARGEST CIRCULATION OF ANY MUSIC PAPER —WEEKLY SALES EXCEED 200,000 (MEMBERS OF ABC)

EDEN KANE HOUSE TO LET DECCA

ELVIS and CLIFF FIGHT IT OUT

FRANK KELLY WITH THE HUNTERS fontana

'Send me the pillow'

c/w 'CEPT ME 267 242 TF

SEPTEMBER

EMI release Cliff's '32 Minutes and 17 Seconds' LP.

SEPTEMBER 8

Cliff appears on Billy Cotton's TV show.

OCTOBER

It's Wonderful To Be Young is released in the United States as Cliff flies to America to launch one of the biggest ever publicity campaigns to promote a British artist on the other side of the Atlantic...

OCTOBER

Cliff visits Elvis Presley's home Graceland in Memphis at the invitation of Elvis' father Vernon. The American singer is away at the time.

Theatre attendances for Cliff's American tour are low because of the effect of the Cuban Crisis.

During his stay in America Cliff meets Nat King Cole, Bobby Darin, Paul Anka and Sal Mineo.

OCTOBER 29

Cliff appears before the Queen on the Royal Variety Show with the Shadows, Helen Shapiro, Andy Stewart, Frank Ifield, Eartha Kitt, Johnny Dankworth and Cleo Laine.

Cliff sings 'The Young Ones', 'I'm On My Way' and 'Do You Wanna Dance'.

16 NOVEMBER

ABBEY ROAD

Film soundtrack recordings for Summer Holiday

Big News (sp)	*Summer Holiday*
Bachelor Boy (sp)	*B-side*

Lead Vocal:	**Cliff Richard**
Guitars:	**Hank Marvin/Bruce Welch**
Bass:	**Brian Locking**
Drums:	**Brian Bennett**
Producer:	**Norrie Paramor**
Engineer:	**Malcolm Addey**
Recorded in:	**Studio 2**
Session hours:	**7.00pm-11.00pm**

Big news is an edit of takes 12 and 13.
Bachelor Boy is an edit of takes 10 and 11.

22 NOVEMBER

ABBEY ROAD

Film Soundtrack Recording for Summer Holiday

Orlando's Mime-Part 1 (5)	*Summer Holiday*
Orlando's Mime-Part 2 (7)	*Summer Holiday*
Orlando's Mime-Part 3 (12)	*Summer Holiday*
Really Waltzing-Part 1 (5)	*Summer Holiday*
Really Waltzing-Part 2 (9)	*Summer Holiday*
Opening-Part 1 (6)	*Summer Holiday*
Opening-Part 2 (9)	*Summer Holiday*
Seven Days To A Holiday	*Summer Holiday*

Lead Vocal:	**Cliff Richard**
	The Stanley Black Orchestra
	The Mike Sammes Singers
Producer:	**Norrie Paramor**
Engineer:	**Malcolm Addey**
Recorded in:	**Studio 2**
Session hours:	**7.00pm-10.30pm**

NOVEMBER 30

The *New Musical Express* publishes the results of its 1962 readers' poll as follows:

World Musical Personality

1 Elvis Presley	19,083
2 Duane Eddy	9,825
3 Ray Charles	6,540
4 Cliff Richard	4,392

World Male Singer

1 Elvis Presley	24,243
2 Cliff Richard	7,803
3 Ray Charles	6,291

British Vocal Personality

1 Joe Brown	11,958
2 Cliff Richard	11,334
3 Frank Ifield	11,286

British Male Singer

1 Cliff Richard	18,006
2 Billy Fury	10,977
3 Frank Ifield	10,734

Best British Disc Of The Year

1 Frank Ifield	'I Remember You'
2 Tornadoes	'Telstar'
3 Cliff Richard	'The Young Ones'

SUMMER HOLIDAY

Warner Pathe, 1962. Running time: 109 minutes.
Cliff's fourth feature film.

Synopsis:
Four London Transport mechanics form a band named Don. They take an old bus and travel through five countries. The film depicts their adventures.

Cast:
Cliff Richard, Lauri Peters, Melvyn Hayes, Una Stubbs, Ron Moody, David Kossoff, The Shadows.

Credits:
Producer: Kenneth Harper. Director: Peter Yates. Choreographer: Herbert Ross. Original screenplay and story: Peter Myers and Ronald Cass. Musical score: Stanley Black. Photography: John Wilcox.

Songs:
'Seven Days To A Holiday', 'Summer Holiday', 'Let Us Take You For A Ride', 'Stranger In Town', 'Bachelor Boy', 'A Swingin' Affair', 'Really Waltzing', 'All At Once', 'Dancing Shoes', 'The Next Time', 'Big News' performed by Cliff Richard and The Shadows.
'Les Girls', 'Round And Round', 'Foot Tapper' performed by The Shadows. 'Orlando's Mime', 'Yugoslav Wedding' performed by the ABS Orchestra.

6 DECEMBER

ABBEY ROAD
Studio session

Carnival (sp)	*Holiday Carnival EP*
I'm In The Mood for Love(4)	*Love Songs EP*
Where The Four Winds Blow (2)	*Why Don't They Understand.*

Lead Vocal:	**Cliff Richard**
	The Norrie Paramor Orchestra
	The Mike Sammes Singers
Producer:	**Norrie Paramor**
Engineers:	**Malcolm Addey/Peter Vince**
Recorded in:	**Studio 2**
Session hours:	**7.00pm-9.45pm**

Carnival is an edit of takes 3 and 6.

DECEMBER 7

The Columbia label releases Cliff's 19th single 'The Next Time' backed with 'Bachelor Boy'. It's another chart topping smash for Cliff, and stays in the best seller lists for eighteen weeks. As one review says:
'It is a quiet lazily romantic number, with a most pleasing melody.'

10 DECEMBER

ABBEY ROAD
Film Soundtrack Recording for Summer Holiday

Foot Tapper	*Summer Holiday*

Guitars:	**Hank Marvin/Bruce Welch**
Bass:	**Brian Locking**
Drums:	**Brian Bennett**
Producer:	**Norrie Paramor**
Engineer:	**Malcolm Addey**
Recorded in:	
Session hours:	

12 DECEMBER

ABBEY ROAD
Studio session

I Found A Rose (4)	*Love Is Forever EP*
Moonlight Bay (3)	*Holiday Carnival EP*
Some Of These Days (4)	*Holiday Carnival EP*

Lead Vocal:	**Cliff Richard**
	The Norrie Paramor Orchestra
	The Mike Sammes Singers
Producer:	**Norrie Paramor**
Engineers:	**Malcolm Addey/Peter Vince**
Recorded in:	**Studio 2**
Session hours:	**7.00pm-9.30pm**

21 DECEMBER

ABBEY ROAD
Studio session

Perfidia (4)	*Cliff Richard*

Lead Vocal:	**Cliff Richard**
Guitars:	**Hank Marvin/Bruce Welch**
Bass:	**Brian Locking**
Drums:	**Brian Bennett**
Producer:	**Norrie Paramor**
Engineer:	**Malcolm Addey**
Recorded in:	**Studio 2**
Session hours:	**7.00pm-10.00pm**

DECEMBER

'The Next Time'/'Bachelor Boy' sells 250,000 copies in one week.

DECEMBER 24/25

Cliff relaxes at home.

DECEMBER 25

Cliff leads an ATV Christmas Day Show *Christmas Fare* which also features the Mike Cotton Jazzmen and Sheila Southern.

28 DECEMBER

ABBEY ROAD
Studio session

It's All In The Game (3)	*A-side*
From This Day On (8)	*(Unissued)*
I Only Have Eyes For You (6)	*Love Songs EP*

Lead Vocal:	**Cliff Richard**
	The Norrie Paramor Orchestra
	The Mike Sammes Singers
Producer:	**Norrie Paramor**
Engineer:	**Malcolm Addey**
Recorded in:	**Studio 2**
Session hours:	**2.30pm-5.30pm**

DECEMBER 29

Cliff flies to South Africa.

JANUARY-APRIL 1963

RADIO LUXEMBOURG STUDIOS, 38 HERTFORD STREET, LONDON
Radio Luxembourg Transcriptions

Bony Maronie	*(Unissued)*
What'd I Say	*(Unissued)*
Quarter To Three	*(Unissued)*
Razzle Dazzle	*(Unissued)*
Roseilea	*(Unissued)*
Move It	*(Unissued)*
Down The Line	*(Unissued)*
Reeling And Rocking	*(Unissued)*
I'm In Love Again	*(Unissued)*
Whole Lotta Shakin' Goin On	*(Unissued)*
Young Love	*(Unissued)*
I'm Looking Out The Window	*(Unissued)*
Sweeter Than You	*(Unissued)*
Willie Did The Cha Cha	*(Unissued)*
It's Only Make Believe	*(Unissued)*
Roving Gambler	*(Unissued)*
I Got A Woman	*(Unissued)*
Willie And The Hand Jive	*(Unissued)*
Donna	*(Unissued)*
My Babe	*(Unissued)*
Now's The Time To Fall In Love	*(Unissued)*
20 Flight Rock	*(Unissued)*
Dim, Dim The Lights	*(Unissued)*
When The Girl In Your Arms Is The Girl In Your Heart	*(Unissued)*
Do You Want To Dance	*(Unissued)*
Hang Up My Rock And Roll Shoes	*(Unissued)*
Save My Soul	*(Unissued)*
What'd I Say	*(Unissued)*
Good Golly Miss Molly	*(Unissued)*
Please Don't Tease	*(Unissued)*
Kansas City	*(Unissued)*
Me And My Shadows	*(Unissued)*
I'm Gonna Get You	*(Unissued)*
Where Is My Heart	*(Unissued)*
I Love You So	*(Unissued)*
Forty Days	*(Unissued)*
Me And My Shadows	*(Unissued)*

Lead Vocal:	**Cliff Richard**
Guitars:	**Hank Marvin/Bruce Welch**
Bass:	**Jet Harris**
Drums:	**Tony Meehan**

JANUARY 3

The first Number One of the New Year is 'The Next Time'/'Bachelor Boy', which stays on top until deposed by 'Dance On' from the Shadows!

A complete analysis of the *NME* Top 30 is published (operating on the usual system of 30 points for 1 week at number 1 down to 1 point for 1 week at number 30).

1 Elvis Presley	1,463
2 Cliff Richard	1,131
3 Frank Ifield	817
4 The Shadows	723
5 Acker Bilk	702
6 Billy Fury	701
7 Chubby Checker	656
8 Kenny Ball	611
9 Ray Charles	561
10 Del Shannon	555

Cliff is 122 points up on the 1961 table.

A letter to the British music papers from Louise Weinstock Jr. of West Lafayette, Indiana is published: 'I am a keen Cliff Richard fan. Many of my friends who have heard the seven Cliff albums which I possess agree that he is better than nine-tenths of our American singers. But the fact is that Cliff has not yet made a record with a really unusual or different sound, and the DJs are reluctant to play what amounts to a run-of-the-mill record by an artist who has had so many comparative flops here as Cliff. What Cliff needs is a disc with a new sound, maybe then he will become a star in America as well as Britain.'

JANUARY 4

Pop singer Kenny Lynch reveals that his favourite single is 'Bachelor Boy".

JANUARY 7

Along with other acts, Cliff's singles and albums now cost less due to a cut in purchase tax on records. A Cliff single is reduced by 8d to 6s 3d, and an album is to cost 30s 11d instead of 34s 4½d

JANUARY 10

Cliff's film *Summer Holiday* is premiered simultaneously in South Africa and London, and contains fifteen songs. Cliff, Melvyn Hayes, Teddy Green and Jeremy Bulloch portray a group of London Transport mechanics who 'do up' a double-decker bus and take it across Europe. The cast also includes Una Stubbs, Laurie Peters, Ron Moody and David Kossoff.

One critic says of *Summer Holiday*: 'I wouldn't have believed that such a first-class musical could have been made in this country – the film will provide all the amenities of a real holiday – with the exception of the tan.'

JANUARY 11

As the NME chart listed 'Bachelor Boy' and 'The Next Time' as entirely separate chart entries, Radio Luxembourg ran a competition on its *Friday Spectacular* inviting listeners to guess which side would go higher in the charts. There were 4000 entries.

JANUARY 16

Cliff and the Shadows begin a tour of South Africa, taking in Port Elizabeth, Johannesburg, Durban, Bulawayo and Salisbury in Rhodesia. Both South African and British newspapers cover the story of amazing fan scenes in Johannesburg and Cape Town.

JANUARY 17

Daily Express critic Leonard Mosley says, 'Cliff can't sing', predictably getting an angry response from thousands of fans.

JANUARY 18

Cliff admits that he thinks his girlfriend, Jackie Irving, looks like Sophia Loren.

JANUARY 21

The Radio Luxembourg show *ABC of the Stars* devotes the whole show to Cliff.

JANUARY 24

Elvis's film *Girls, Girls, Girls* has Elvis playing the part of a fisherman turned part-time entertainer. Despite featured songs like 'Return To Sender' and 'Because Of Love', the film is compared (inevitably) with *Summer Holiday*, and does not fare too well under the pens of the critics. As one reviewer puts it: 'I'm not praising Summer Holiday out of patriotism – it's simply a fact that it has far more freshness and zest than *Girls, Girls, Girls*!'

JANUARY 25

Danish newspapers reveal that Cliff sold more records than any other artist in Denmark during 1962.

JANUARY 28

Associated British-Pathe executive, Macgregor Scott, is in America discussing the screening of *Summer Holiday* in the United States. Most likely distributor is rumoured to be Paramount Pictures, who handled the North American release of *The Young Ones*.

FEBRUARY 6

In America *The Young Ones* is retitled *Wonderful To Be Young* and is reviewed rather cynically by the *San Fransisco Chronicle:* 'Richard has all the requisites for idolisation – big brown eyes, wavy hair, a pretty-boy face, a certain magnetism and an undistinguished voice!'

In Holland's *Muzick Expres* poll, Cliff beats Elvis, while the British press refer to North of England dancer Jackie Irving, as 'Cliff's new friend'.

FEBRUARY 8

Cliff's 20th single, 'Summer Holiday', is released and amongst the rave reviews is one from Keith Fordyce: 'Light-hearted, casual and happy, the mood of this most attractive song is contained in the line "We're going where the sun shines brightly". Top marks to all concerned, including composers Bruce Welch and Brian Bennett.'

FEBRUARY 8

Cliff sends a postcard to the *NME* depicting the Peninsular, which reads: 'Hello there from Africa. Weather great and tour fab. Everything and everyone swinging. This definitely must be the place! Regards, Cliff.'

FEBRUARY 10

Dedicated fans at Stockton queue all night for tickets to see a forthcoming Cliff and the Shadows concert.

FEBRUARY 10

Cliff buys a Chevrolet for his mother, Dorothy Webb.

FEBRUARY 11

Cliff makes an appearance at a charity concert for delinquent children in Nairobi, Kenya, which is organised by the Kenyan leader, Tom Mboya.

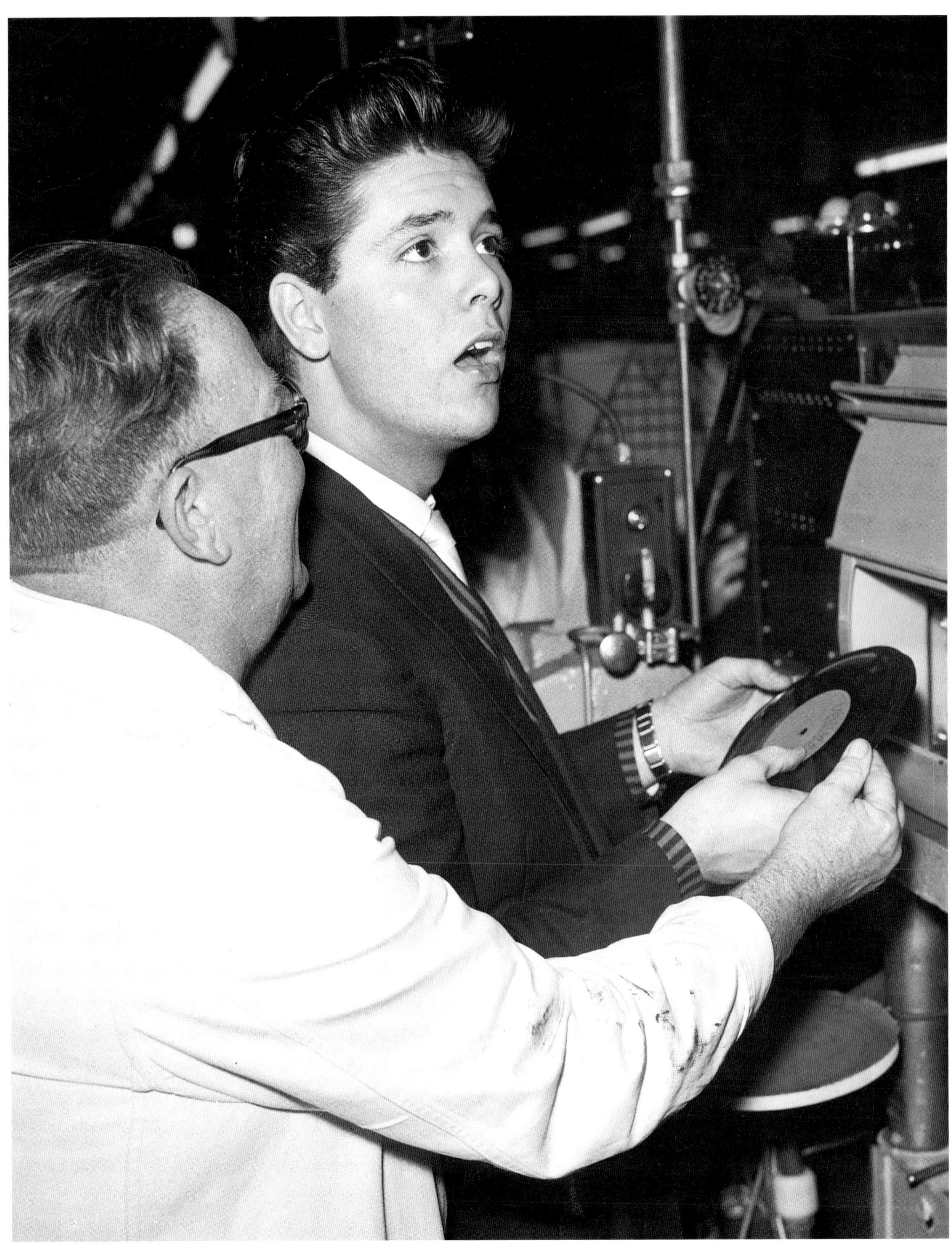

FEBRUARY 15

The single 'Summer Holiday' is officially released.

FEBRUARY 18, 19, 20

Cliff and the Shadows rehearse for the *Billy Cotton Band Show*.

FEBRUARY 20

Cliff talks to the press about his South African tour with the Shadows: 'The whole tour was quite fantastic and we did considerably more business than the last time we were there. The press were very kind to us; of the nineteen shows we played, we only had one bad review, and that was by a Johannesburg critic who thought the whole thing was ridiculous!'

Cliff also spoke about the previous week's *Daily Express* article: 'I agree that I'm not qualified to talk about it, but we did not go to Africa to delve into the racial question. We went there to entertain and perform, but if writers persist in asking me about it I have to make some comment – even if it's only to brush it aside because it's not my territory.'

FEBRUARY 20

Cliff has four titles in the Top 30:

9 'Summer Holiday'
16 'Bachelor Boy'
18 'The Next Time'
25 'Dancing Shoes'

He becomes the first artist to get four songs from one film (*Summer Holiday*) into the chart.

FEBRUARY 21

Cliff and the Shadows telerecord for the BBC TV programme *The Billy Cotton Band Show* to be transmitted on 24 February.

FEBRUARY 23

Cliff and the Shadows begin a 41-date 6-week tour of Britain at Cardiff's Sophia Gardens.

FEBRUARY 24

The Billy Cotton Band Show is transmitted on TV featuring Cliff and the Shadows, and Cliff and Billy Cotton together in top-hat and tails singing the Flanagan and Allen song 'Strollin'.

MARCH 1

It is announced that Cliff and the Shadows will star in their first BBC TV Spectacular in the spring, and they intend spending two weeks recording in Barcelona.

MARCH 1

Cliff is featured in an article in an American journal, *Newsweek,* in which he speaks of his success: 'I got my chance because teenagers have to have an idol, but the new teenagers coming up don't like to take what's left over. But I hope to grow with my audience.'

MARCH

Among the songs Cliff features in every performance of his 41-date British tour with the Shadows are: 'Do You Wanna Dance?', 'I Gotta Woman', 'Blueberry Hill' (featuring Hank Marvin on piano), 'The Next Time', 'Baby Face', 'Summer Holiday', 'Spanish Harlem', 'Love Hurts', 'Bachelor Boy', 'Dancing Shoes' and 'We Say Yeah'.

The tour also features the Trebletones, xylophone player/ comedian Alan Randall, vocalist Patsy Ann Noble, the Vernons Girls and Canadian compere Frank Berry.

MARCH

American singer Bobby Vee covers Cliff's 'Theme For A Dream' on his new album.

MARCH 7

Along with Frank Ifield and Judy Garland, Cliff and the Shadows tele-record in London for America's *Ed Sullivan Show*, and as they are appearing the same night at the ABC Cinema, Kingston-upon-Thames, they have to dash across London from ATV's Wood Green Empire.

MARCH 8

'Summer Holiday' tops the *New Musical Express* chart.

8 MARCH

ABBEY ROAD
Studio session

Lucky Lips (6)	*A-side*
I Wonder (9)	*B-side*

Lead Vocal:	**Cliff Richard**
Guitars:	**Hank Marvin/Bruce Welch**
Bass:	**Brian Locking**
Drums:	**Brian Bennett**
Producer:	**Norrie Paramor**
Engineer:	**Malcolm Addey**
Recorded in:	**Studio 2**
Session hours:	**7.00pm-10.45pm**

MARCH

Cliff and the Shadows' EP – 'Time For Cliff and the Shadows' – is released, containing 'So I've Been Told', ' I'm Walking The Blues', ' When My Dreamboat Comes Home', 'Blueberry Hill' and 'You Don't Know'.

Opposite: Cliff examines his latest record during a visit to EMI's record pressing plant.

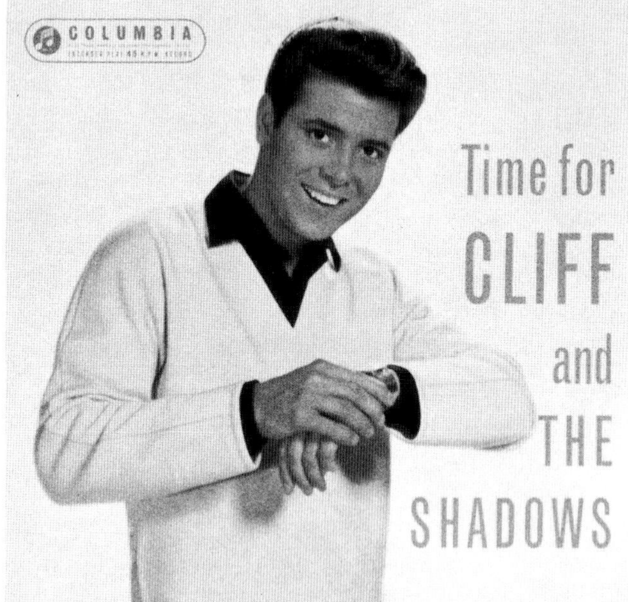

MARCH 14

It is announced that the film *Summer Holiday* will be launched in Canada at Easter, and is to be shown mainly at drive-in movies in Toronto and other major cities. Canadian reaction is to be used as a springboard for the American launch. To coincide with the film, Capitol Records announce that they will release the film soundtrack and relevant singles in Canada.

MARCH 15

Arthur Howes, the promoter of Cliff's tour, says: 'This is a record for any of the tours I have ever handled. Every ticket has been sold for every performance at every theatre!' At the same time, Cliff features in the charts of eight countries simultaneously:
'The Next Time' Number 2 in Israel
'The Next Time' Number 6 in France
'The Next Time' Number 10 in Norway
'The Next Time'/'Bachelor Boy' Number 1 in South Africa
'Bachelor Boy' Number 1 in Holland
'Bachelor Boy' Number 3 in Sweden
'Bachelor Boy' Number 5 in Hong Kong
'Bachelor Boy' Number 26 in Britain
'Summer Holiday' Number 1 in Britain

MARCH 22

It is announced that Cliff will undertake a new film, shooting for which is to commence at the end of his Blackpool summer season, resulting in the cancellation of proposed plans for an Australian tour.
Epic Records reveal that in future they will be releasing Cliff's records in the United States, while in Britain it is estimated that Cliff may well earn £6,000 composer's royalties for 'Bachelor Boy' which is to be included in a forthcoming Bachelors LP.

MARCH 22-28

Cliff appears at Leeds Odeon, Leicester De Montfort Hall, Ipswich Gaumont, Dover ABC, Hastings ABC and Southend Odeon.

MARCH 29

In the *NME* chart points table for the first quarter of 1963, Cliff has taken a strong lead and leads Elvis Presley for the first time since 1960.

1 Cliff Richard	584
2 Frank Ifield	322
3 Shadows	291
4 Tornados	275
5 Jet Harris and Tony Meehan	253
6 Elvis Presley	246
7 Beatles	235
8 Joe Brown	232
9 Bobby Vee	215
10 Springfields	210

Of Cliff's points 405 were amassed by 'The Next Time'/'Bachelor Boy' and the 'Summer Holiday' album overtook the consistently successful 'West Side Story' to lead the points table based on the album chart.

MARCH

America's 16 magazine reports that Cliff is becoming a big teenage favourite in the States through the film *Wonderful To Be Young*.

MARCH

Cliff and the Shadows say that their nickname for singer Dusty Springfield is 'The White Negress'.

APRIL 1

The 36-page April edition of *Hit Parade* magazine (price 2s.) features an article personally written by Cliff.

APRIL 6

Cliff is featured on the front cover of Pop Weekly with Laurie Peters, his *Summer Holiday* co-star, and the St. Bernard featured in the film. The magazine also publishes the results of a survey of over-25s as to their favourite artists. The results are as follows:

1 Frank Ifield
2 Cliff Richard
3 Acker Bilk
4 Shirley Bassey
5 The Shadows

APRIL

Cliff's current car is a cadillac, but a new sports car is ordered and on the way.

APRIL

In an interview, Cliff and the Shadows insist that during the summer season at Blackpool they are planning to go to the beach at 8 o'clock each morning 'for exercises and a good long run'.

10 APRIL

ABBEY ROAD
Studio session

Your Eyes Tell On You (10) *B-side*

Lead Vocal:	**Cliff Richard**
Guitars:	**Hank Marvin/Bruce Welch**
Bass:	**Brian Locking**
Drums:	**Brian Bennett**
Producer:	**Norrie Paramor**
Engineer:	**Malcolm Addey**
Recorded in:	**Studio 2**
Session hours:	**6.30pm-9.15pm**

APRIL

Franklyn Boyd, who played an important part in Cliff's early success, discovers a new singer, 16-year old Steve Marriott, who releases his first single 'Give Her My Regards'. Steve is eventually to lead the Small Faces and later form Humble Pie.

APRIL

Accidental meeting in the M1's Watford Gap Services of Cliff and the Shadows, the Beatles, Tommy Roe and Chris Montez.

APRIL

The Tornados go to watch Cliff and the Shadows on tour, who not only hope to reciprocate by going to see Billy Fury's ex-back-

Emitape

Remix from 4TRK

TAPE No. E49639 Z IDENTITY CLIFF RICHARD.

MATRIX No.	TITLE	TAKE	START	FINISH	MASTER	REMARKS
	YOUR EYES TELL ON YOU	RS10	00·10	02·40		
	PERFIDIA (21-DEC-62) IN ENGLISH	RS 4	02·50	05·00	M	
	I WONDER	RS 9	05·10	08·10	M	EQUALISED & COMPRESSED TRANSFER FUH

1318

MACHINE No. STUDIO 43 / 3 TAPE LENGTH FT. TAPE SPEED 15"/SEC TAPE TYPE 77 RECORDING ENGINEER MA / AB

PLEASE RETURN TO TAPE LIBRARY

STEREO

DATE 20.6.63.

E.M.I. TAPE LIMITED

ing group during their run of shows in Paris, but offer their advice on French audiences, sights to see and places to eat. On Cliff and the Shadows, the Tornados say, 'They're fantastically polished and present a wonderful act, but we wish people would not keep bringing up this question of rivalry. neither of us is trying to put the other out of business!'

APRIL 12

Cliff and the Shadows send autographed Easter eggs to fans in hospital.

In an interview, Cliff reveals that it's his ambition to have three number 1s in a row (his previous two singles both topped the chart – 'The Next Time'/'Bachelor Boy' and 'Summer Holiday'), but is not too optimistic about his chances: 'My last couple of releases were ready-made – in a sense they more or less selected themselves since they came straight from the film. Mind you, we would never have released 'Summer Holiday' as a single if it hadn't been featured in a film – frankly, we didn't think it was good enough to stand up on it's own!'

Cliff also speaks about his songwriting abilities: 'I've always enjoyed writing, but I've never really considered myself a great composer – normally I throw my numbers together very quickly. I get fed up with them after a while. I'm afraid I'm not like Bruce Welch, he can churn 'em out by the dozen!'

APRIL

At Bruce Welch's party guests include Cliff, the Beatles, Patsy Ann Noble and the Vernons Girls. Cliff and the Shadows do a mickey-take of the Beatles by singing 'Please Please Me' in exaggerated style – the Beatles reply with a deliberately out-of-tune send-up of Cliff and the Shadows. The two groups play guitars and sing together through the night in Bruce's kitchen, knocking out numbers by the Chiffons, Isley Brothers and Ray Charles. Cliff says of the Beatles: 'The greatest bunch of boys I've met since the Shadows!'

APRIL 13

'Bachelor Boy' enters the Australian charts.

APRIL

West end tailor Dougie Millings talks to the press about show-business fashion:

'I've been making Cliff's suits since he used to appear in the 2i's coffee bar, which is practically underneath my premises; that's how I sort of drifted into becoming a show-business tailor. Cliff, in fact, was the first big name I ever made suits for! He's got a very good figure from a tailor's point of view – regular measurements and no faults to cover up. If Cliff needs a suit for stage work, then the most popular material is Italian silk, but it's a bit expensive – about £40.'

APRIL 20

Kinematography Weekly reports that the film in which Cliff made his screen debut and sang 'Living Doll' – the drama *Serious Charge* – is on re-release and doing good business in cinemas around the country, now that its (then-newcomer) star is a superstar.

APRIL 21

Cliff and the Shadows appear at the *NME*'s Poll Winners' Concert at Wembley. Their set includes 'Bachelor Boy', 'Do You Wanna Dance', 'Summer Holiday' and 'Dancing Shoes'.

The subsequent review sums up the act by saying:

'It's difficult to find words to describe the annual shattering ovation given to the king of popland!'

APRIL 22

Cliff records his own Special for BBC.Television, to be screened in a few days tim Also appearing will be the Shadows and various other guest artists.

APRIL 27

R. Hodgetts of Edinburgh has a letter published in *Disc:*

'A lot is said and written about the wonderful artists such as Brenda Lee, Jerry Lee Lewis and Little Eva. Yet I feel the finest stage performance I have seen for some time was given by Cliff and the Shadows on their recent tour.'

APRIL 27

The Shadows earn their seventh Silver Disc for the single taken from *Summer Holiday* – 'Foot-Tapper', and Cliff's 21st single is released – 'Lucky Lips' written by the legendary American song-writing team of Lieber and Stoller, and previously released in the UK by Alma Cogan in March 1957 on the 'B' side of 'Whatever Lola Wants'!

APRIL 28

Cliff's BBC Television spectacular is screened on Sunday night. Included in the show are the new single, and tracks from the forthcoming 'Holiday Carnival' EP with Cliff and the Shadows which combines the Rooftop Singers' 'Walk Right In', with a folk medley comprising 'Greensleeves', 'All Through The Night' and 'Cockles And Mussels'.

Cliff also duets with comic actor Sid James and singer Millicent Martin on the show.

28 APRIL

EMI Studios Barcelona

Studio session

Perfidia (7)	*When In Spain*
Frenesi (5)	*When In Spain*
Tus Besos (23)	*When In Spain*
Amor, Amor, Amor (4)	*When In Spain*

Lead Vocal:	**Cliff Richard**
Guitars:	**Hank Marvin/Bruce Welch**
Bass:	**Brian Locking**
Drums:	**Brian Bennett**
	The Norrie Paramor Strings
Producer:	**Norrie Paramor**
Engineer:	**Malcolm Addey**
Session hours:	**6.00pm-9.00pm**

APRIL

'Lucky Lips' is reviewed – almost universally favourably – and as one record critic puts it:

'Lucky Lips' is not a new song. It has been tried on record before but never to the sort of success it is going to get from now on. Cliff takes the Lieber-Stoller shuffler and eases it onto your feet. Accompanied by the Shadows, he makes this a happy and extremely infectious release.

It'll take him high in the Top Ten once more. 'I Wonder' (the 'B' side), on which he is accompanied by the Norrie Paramor Strings, is a song written by Cliff and Hank Marvin. An attractive little Latin ballad.'

29 APRIL

EMI Studios Barcelona

Studio session

Solamente Una Vez (13)	*When In Spain*
Quizas, Quizas, Quizas (13)	*When In Spain*
Carnival (5)	*When In Spain*
Quien Sera (14)	*When In Spain*

Lead Vocal:	**Cliff Richard**
Guitars:	**Hank Marvin/Bruce Welch**
Bass:	**Brian Locking**
Drums:	**Brian Bennett**
	The Norrie Paramor Strings
Producer:	**Norrie Paramor**
Engineer:	**Malcolm Addey**
Session hours:	**7.00pm-10.00pm**

APRIL

A typical day for Cliff and the Shadows, based in Sitges, 23 miles from Barcelona:
9.00-1.00 Rehearsals in the music room at the hotel in Sitges.
1.00-4.00 Break
4.30 Bus to Barcelona (23 miles of bumpy roads with lots of steep climbs and hair-raising descents).
6.00-10.00 Recording
10.30 Bus back to the hotel, stopping at a transport cafe on the way.
1.00 Bed!
After work Cliff and the boys either relax in a small restaurant on the sea-front, where fish soup and asparagus is a definite favourite, or play the juke-box in Ricky's Bar. Cliff and the Shadows are given instruction in the art of bullfighting by an aged toreador using baby bulls, and are presented with diplomas stating that they have proved their mettle in the bull-ring. They are also talked into attending a real bull-fight, where despite initial apprehension Hank films all seven fights. Cliff is not wildly impressed: 'You certainly wouldn't call it a sport – I'm glad I went, but I wouldn't want to go to another!'

30 APRIL

EMI Studios Barcelona
Studio session

Te Quiero Dijeste (15)	*When In Spain*
Vaya Con Dios (9)	*When In Spain*
Me Lo Dijo Adela (7)	*When In Spain*

Lead Vocal:	**Cliff Richard**
Guitars:	**Hank Marvin/Bruce Welch**
Bass:	**Brian Locking**
Drums:	**Brian Bennett**
	The Norrie Paramor Strings
Producer:	**Norrie Paramor**
Engineer:	**Malcolm Addey**
Session hours:	**6.00pm-10.00pm**

1 MAY

EMI Studios Barcelona
Studio session

Maria No Mas (11)	*When In Spain*

Lead Vocal:	**Cliff Richard**
Guitars:	**Hank Marvin/Bruce Welch**
Bass:	**Brian Locking**
Drums:	**Brian Bennett**
	The Norrie Paramor Strings
Producer:	**Norrie Paramor**
Engineer:	**Malcolm Addey**
Session hours:	**7.00pm-10.00pm**

E 49710
TWO TRACK MONO
CLIFF RICHARD (3670 - 3CMS)
SHADOWS
1337
ORIGINAL
NOTE THIS TAPE IS NOT SUITABLE FOR TRANSFER.

MAY

Cliff's latest EP 'Holiday Carnival' is released, featuring 'Carnival', 'Moonlight Bay', 'Some Of These Days' and 'For You, For Me'.

MAY 11

Misses B. Davis and M. Richardson from Hampshire write to the music press: 'We wish to thank everybody connected with *Summer Holiday* for making such a wonderful film. Most people think we are mad because we have seen *Summer Holiday* fifteen times!'
Another letter on the subject of Cliff is published the same week: 'Recently, I purchased a good seat to see Cliff and the Shadows at a concert. I'd have done better to buy an LP! Why do the screamers go to these shows? Cliff and Co. tried, but it was five against the crowd. I thought it was gross bad manners on the part of the screaming three-quarters of the audience. My friends said, "Never again!", and I know what they mean.' (Mrs B. Ruston, Leeds)

MAY 12

BBC TV screen the Ivor Novello Awards, which include the Tornados, Matt Monro, Acker Bilk – and a clip of *Summer Holiday* as Cliff is unable to attend owing to a holiday in Spain.

MAY 14

Cliff and the Shadows broadcast from the Paris Olympia – topping the bill on the *Europe One* radio show.

MAY 18

J. Helm of Downes Place, London SE15 has the following letter published in the music press: 'Is Cliff Richard superhuman? Is he never off form? Does he ever muff his lines or forget the words oF a song? All his records are reviewed in such glowing terms. His every appearance on TV or radio is acclaimed as "brilliant". His films are guaranteed to be "the biggest thing on the British musical scene" practically before they are started. He is one of the best-dressed men. And now we are informed by his tailor that his figure is faultless! Frankly, I'm becoming a little bored with such perfection.'

MAY 18

In the Hong Kong charts Cliff's 'Summer Holiday' is No. 2 and 'Bachelor Boy' is No.6. In Norway 'Summer Holiday' is No.1, while in South Africa he has three in the Top Ten – 'Bachelor Boy' at No.3, 'Dancing Shoes' at No.4 and 'Summer Holiday' in the No.10 spot.

MAY

Cliff and the Shadows rehearse a routine for their forthcoming summer season, for which they promise 'an entirely new type of presentation'.

MAY 31

Prior to the public opening the following day, Cliff and the Shadows are the star attractions at the opening of Blackpool's £400,000 ABC Theatre before an invited audience of 2,000 and the Mayor of Blackpool.

MAY 31

Life With Cliff Richard is published – available from all good newsagents at 3s.6d a copy. It claims to 'paint a vivid portrait of the sincere, homely boy behind the glittering star legend…!'

JUNE 1

Cliff and the Shadows' opening night at Blackpool ABC. The show (seats from 6s.6d to 9s.6d) features colour film back-projection and includes a scene where Cliff, Hank and Bruce are in a speeded-up hair-raising race through London's traffic, only to end up crashing into the gates of Harrow School. The scenes range from Paris to Majorca, Hollywood, Lake Tahoe and Las Vegas, while the girls range from Cliff's *Young Ones* co-star Carole Gray to the girl with whom he is linked romantically by the press, Jackie Irving. Other artists appearing include Jim Dailey and Terry Wayne, and ventriloquist Arthur Worsley with his dummy Charlie Brown. As well as the usual numbers expected from him, Cliff also includes 'Moonlight Bay', Sophie Tucker's 'Some Of These Days', 'Strangers in Town' and 'Carnival'. Four hundred people attend the opening night supper party.

JUNE

Cliff's 'Hits From Summer Holiday' EP is released, featuring 'The Next Time', 'Summer Holiday', 'Dancing Shoes', and 'Bachelor Boy'.

JUNE 1

Disc magazine sounds out various artists on the subject of legendary singer Ray Charles. Cliff says: 'It was so great, I'm going again! I wasn't expecting the same from Ray on stage as on his records, but he doesn't lose one bit from appearing in person. When one realises that the man is blind, and he can't of course move around on stage but just sits at the piano, he is absolutely fantastic!'

JUNE

'Lucky Lips' peaks at No.4 in the *Record Retailer* chart and No. 3 in the *Disc* chart.

JUNE 7

Elstree Music publish *Cliff Richard and the Shadows Special Souvenir Album*, price 6s.

JUNE

Bruce Welch hosts a small party for Cliff in Blackpool. The Beatles are among the guests and Cliff, the Shadows and John, Paul, George and Ringo end up singing and playing together half the night.

JUNE

Cliff stays at Lytham St. Annes (5 miles south of Blackpool) for the summer season, and spends his spare time indulging in his favourite hobby – cine-photography. 'The Shadows and I are working on some comedy films with ourselves as the "stars" – you've never seen anything like it in your life! Also, I've had to move house once already; my address got out and I woke up one morning and found 150 fans outside. It wasn't that I minded, but it would have disturbed the neighbours if that had gone on all season, so I moved.'

JUNE

Cliff's mother and two of his sisters join him in Blackpool, and he now drives a new 160-mph Corvette which he exchanged for his red Thunderbird.

JUNE 14

In a letter to the music press, fan Jennifer Haines of Bournemouth writes:
'For goodness sake, Cliff fans, pull your socks up! Are you going to let Britain's King of Talent be beaten by a flash-in-the-pan group like the Beatles?'

JUNE 14

Stanley Matthews Jnr, son of legendary footballer Stanley Matthews, reveals that he's a big Cliff fan. Meanwhile, on the London Record label, similarly named Cliff Rivers releases his first British single.

JUNE 15

Producer of Cliff's forthcoming film, Kenneth Harper, announces that filming for the new movie will be based at ABC Studios in Elstree, with location shooting in Mexico and South America: Sidney Furie will direct. Peter Myers and Ronald Cass are signed to write the screenplay, as they have previously for *The Young Ones* and *Summer Holiday*.

JUNE 21

Cliff's 'Life Lines', first featured in the *New Musical Express* on November 14 1958, is the subject of a half-page in the June 21 issue and includes:
First public appearance: Youth Fellowship dance in Cheshunt, 1954.
Dislikes: Insincere people; putting on a false smile for photographers; smoking.
Favourite food: Indian curry and rice.
Favourite drink: Tizer with ice cream.
Favourite guitarists: Duane Eddy, Al Casey, Hank Marvin.
Favourite band: Glen Miller.
Favourite female singers: Connie Francis, Julie London, Helen Shapiro.
Favourite male singers: Elvis Presley, Rick Nelson, Ray Charles, the Beatles.
Hobbies: Collecting Elvis records; playing badminton.
Greatest ambition: To meet Elvis.
Musical education: Taught guitar by his father.
Former Job: Office clerk.
Educated: Stanley Park Road School, Carshalton. Cheshunt Secondary Modern.
Sisters: Donella, Jacqueline and Joan.

JUNE 22

Bill Edge from Howard Street, Salford 5, Lancashire writes to the music papers on the subject of Cliff's current single: 'I think that it is a crying shame that such a great artist as Cliff Richard should have to go on stage and sing a song ('Lucky Lips') which sounds like Elvis six years ago. I think that he should get some new songwriters. I could do better than this myself.'

JUNE 25

'Lucky Lips' is released in the US with 'The Next Time' on the 'B' side.

JUNE 28

The *NME* publish their points table for the first half of 1963 (30 points for a number 1 to 1 point for number 30).

1 Cliff Richard	877
2 The Beatles	577
3 Frank Ifield	548
4 The Shadows	522
5 Jet Harris and Tony Mehan	492

JUNE 29

Cliff announces the postponement of a projected Australasian tour the following February, and the intention of starting on the new film in November, followed by a British tour in March and April. A possible tour of Israel is also hinted at.

JUNE 29

Screenplay writers for the *Young Ones*, *Summer Holiday* and the forthcoming film, Peter Myers and Ronald Cass, chat to the press about Cliff. '...if Cliff had to give up singing, he could always make a living as a dancer...', '...he has a natural acting ability...', '...really, you can say he is part writer of some of the songs – but he doesn't get any of our royalties!', '...there is never any display of temperament...', Ronald Cass concludes the interview with the following tribute: 'I have a little boy of three – if he grows up to behave like Cliff, then I shall be happy.'

On the set of *Wonderful Life*.

JULY 1

From today, along with other EMI artists, Cliff's singles cost five pence more. His albums,too, go up from £1 10s 11d. to £1 12s 0d. and EPs are also affected, going up 8d to 10s.9d.

JULY 1

Cliff is deposed as 'Best Dressed Show Business Personality of the Year' when the British Federation of Clothing Manufacturers award the title to Adam Faith.

JULY

'Cliff's Hit Album' is announced, containing 14 tracks ranging from 'Move It' to 'Do You Wanna Dance?'.

JULY 5

Actress/singer Millicent Martin reveals that Cliff is her favourite TV personality.

JULY

Wink Martindale covers 'The Next Time' in the States, while Cliff's former manager Tito Burns announces that he's handling new Liverpool group, the Searchers, who have a Top 10 hit with 'Sweets For My Sweet'.

JULY 6

Other music papers adopt the *NME*'s chart system (30 points for a number 1 to 1 point for a number 30) to gauge artists' success in relation to each other. Disc's half-yearly analysis looked like this:

1 Cliff Richard	722
2 Beatles	583
3 The Shadows	538
4 Frank Ifield	535
5 Jet Harris and Tony Meehan	475
6 Gerry and the Pacemakers	450
7 Springfields	448
8 Billy Fury	392
9 Del Shannon	375
10 Roy Orbison	342

JULY

Cliff confesses that as an avid film fan he shows movies during the day just for friends at the ABC Blackpool. Some of the silver screen epics shown at the private viewings are Doris Day's *Calamity Jane*, Frank Sinatra's *Guys and Dolls* and Westerns *Shane*, *High Noon* and *The Magnificent Seven*. Cliff's all-time favourite, it seems, is *West Side Story*: 'I think it is the best film ever made – it has everything, a great story, fabulous songs and dancing that's out of this world.'

JULY 10

Cliff and the Shadows' producer, Norrie Paramor, talks about future recordings: 'I found, when I worked with the boys in Spain, that we can really get down to it and experiment a good deal more when the time factor is not so pressing, and it is so much easier on Cliff if we get together on the backing first. We can also come up with some new ideas – try out experiments with trumpets, strings and so forth. This has brought criticism from some quarters, but I am all for trying out something new.'

JULY 20

'Lucky Lips', coupled with 'The Next Time', is poised outside the American Top 100 at No.116 just a few days after its release.

JULY

Cliff's producer, Columbia A & R man Norrie Paramor, launches a search for new talent and starts by signing six Birmingham acts: Danny King and the Royals, Carl and the Cheetahs, Mike Sheridan and the Nightriders, The Rockin' Jaymen, Pat Wayne and Keith Powell and the Valets.

JULY 20

Frank Ifield's road manager, Fred Derry, talks to the British press about Cliff:

'During my ten years in show business, I have met plenty of big stars, and with some of them their heads are as big as their billing, but this is certainly not true of the biggest of them all. Cliff's phenomenal success has not spoiled him one bit – he is charming and completely unaffected. He treats everyone the same, from the humblest fan to the most influential person in the business. I don't know anyone who gets more presents from his admirers – they bombard him with knitted sweaters, ties and socks! Off-stage he likes nothing more than to relax with a book – he's a great reader of science-fiction space stories! He and the Shadows have a zany sense of humour – they sent a telegram to Frank Ifield when he opened in a Birmingham panto which read: "Just heard you're doing three matinees on Christmas Day!"'

JULY 20

'Lucky Lips' is No.1 in South Africa, No.3 in Israel and No.9 in Hong Kong, also in the Swedish Top Ten.

JULY 26

In a letter to the music papers, Ron Dennison writes from Ottawa, Canada: 'Cliff Richard has at last broken through in Canada! 'Bachelor Boy' was No.1 in most Canadian cities, including five unchallenged weeks here in Ottawa, and currently 'Summer Holiday' is the best-selling LP in the country. In fact, he is now so popular over here that several groups are modelling themselves on Cliff and the Shadows.'

JULY 27

Plans for top American TV host, Ed Sullivan, to record a show in Blackpool starring Cliff and the Shadows fall through, due to lack of suitable locations for filming.
'Cliff's Hit Album' is released. As one reviewer, Nigel Hunter, puts it: 'You can trace Cliff's pop progress as the album plays. The earlier items are noticeably simple and straightforward in content and accompaniment, but songs, performance and backings gain in depth and imagination as time goes by.'

JULY

The Shadows reveal that they are taking riding lessons – which they hint may give some clue as to what might be seen in Cliff's next film.

JULY

American magazine *16* runs the headline: 'Can Cliff Richard be the next Elvis?'

JULY 29

US composer Roy Bennett (who writes with Sid Tepper), flies to London with some new songs written with Cliff in mind: 'His very first Epic title, 'Lucky Lips', shows signs of breaking as a big hit, so we'd be delighted if he'd consider using more songs by us, remembering that he has featured our songs in the past – 'Travelling Light', 'When The Girl In Your Arms', 'The Young Ones' and ' 'D' In Love' amongst others.'

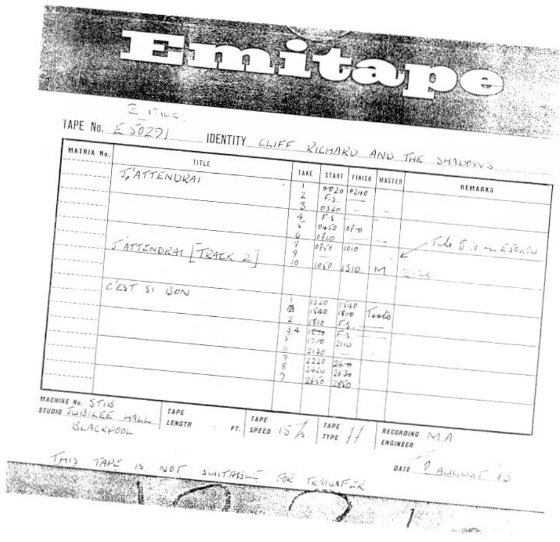

AUGUST 2

Cliff wins his first-ever American poll honour when he is voted 'Most Promising Singer' in a nation-wide ballot by the leading US teenage magazine *16*.

AUGUST 2

Cliff enters *Billboard*'s Hot 100 with 'Lucky Lips' – his first American hit since 'Living Doll'.

AUGUST

Cliff is reported as having taken up golf.

5 AUGUST

Jubilee Hall Blackpool
Studio session

Boum (10)	*When In France EP*
La Mer (8)	*When In France EP*
J'Attendrai	*(Unissued)*
C'est Si Bon (12)	*When In France EP*

Lead Vocal:	**Cliff Richard**
Guitars:	**Hank Marvin/Bruce Welch**
Bass:	**Brian Locking**
Drums:	**Brian Bennett**
Producer:	**Norrie Paramor**
Engineers:	**Malcolm Addey/Jimmy Johnson**
Session hours:	**mid-day-4.00pm**

6 AUGUST

Jubilee Hall Blackpool
Studio session

J'Attendrai (10)	*When In France EP*
Say You're Mine	*B-side*

Lead Vocal:	**Cliff Richard**
Guitars:	**Hank Marvin/Bruce Welch**
Bass:	**Brian Locking**
Drums:	**Brian Bennett**
Producer:	**Norrie Paramor**
Engineers:	**Malcolm Addey/Jimmy Johnson**
Session hours:	**mid-day-4.00pm**

AUGUST 9

'Lucky Lips' simultaneously tops the chart in six different countries: Norway, Israel, South Africa, Hong Kong, Sweden, and Holland. In America's *Billboard* chart, the same track climbs from No.95 to No.89.

9 AUGUST

JUBILEE HALL BLACKPOOL
Film soundtrack recordings for Wonderful Life

What've I Gotta Do (10)	*Wonderful Life*

Lead Vocal:	**Cliff Richard**
Guitar:	**Hank Marvin/Bruce Welch**
Bass:	**Brian Locking**
Drums:	**Brian Bennett**
Producer:	**Norrie Paramor**
Engineers:	**Malcolm Addey/Jimmy Johnson**
Session hours:	**mid-day-4.00pm**

AUGUST 10

During the 100th edition of ABC TV's *Thank Your Lucky Stars*, Cliff receives a Gold Disc for a million sales of 'Bachelor Boy'/'The Next Time'. Viewers see him singing, 'Your Eyes Tell On You' and the new single 'It's All In The Game'. Also appearing on the programme are Billy J. Kramer and the Dakotas, the Searchers and Brian Poole and the Tremeloes.

11 AUGUST

ABBEY ROAD
Studio session

Rotte Lippen Soll Man Küssen	*German A-side*

Lead Vocal:	**Cliff Richard**
Producer:	**Norrie Paramor**
Engineer:	**Malcolm Addey**
Recorded in:	**Studio 3**
Session hours:	**7.00pm-9.15pm**

Cliff's vocals were dubbed onto the existing track of Lucky Lips for this foreign release.

AUGUST 16

For his 22nd single, Cliff releases 'It's All In The Game', a song which Tommy Edwards took to the Number One spot in the British charts in 1958. The tune, originally entitled 'Melody In A Major', was written in 1912 by Chicago banker General Charles Gates Dawes, who later became Vice-President of the USA.. Cliff's version peaked at No. 2 during a three month stay in the Top Fifty.

AUGUST 16

'Lucky Lips' continues to climb the American Hot Hundred chart – a thirteen-place climb takes it to No.76.

AUGUST

In an interview with *Evening News* reporter James Green, Cliff admits that dancer Jackie Irving is his 'steady date'!

AUGUST 23

'Lucky Lips' rises to No.69 in the *Billboard* chart.

AUGUST 23

American TV host Ed Sullivan announces that he's booked Cliff for his coast-to-coast TV show in October.

AUGUST 23

Susan Goodall from Birmingham has an anti-gossip column letter published by the *NME*: 'I wish *NME*'s 'Alley Cat' would stop writing about Cliff Richard and Jackie Irving going steady. What if they are? I think it's about time that Cliff was given a little private life – he's only human, you know.'

AUGUST 30

In an *NME* feature:'Tribute to Cliff and the Shadows' fifth anniversary in show business', Cliff answers questions about his love-life and career:
Q. How do you envisage the next five years?

A. I think things will slow down tremendously…success is all very well, but it becomes pointless if one is unable to secure and solidify that position. From the recording point of view, there's very little else I can hope to do – apart from continuing to please the public to the best possible extent.

Q. When you started out as a rock and roller five years ago, did you plan to try and develop your career in this way?

A. No, I most certainly didn't. My attitude in those days was to live for the present, to exploit my latest record and to get as many bookings as I could.

Q. How do you feel about your film career? Do you think it might ultimately become the most important aspect of your career?

A. If by that you are suggesting that I might eventually give up touring, TV and recording in order to concentrate on films, the answer is definitely no!
Sooner or later I hope that I shall be able to make a film without any singing at all. My great ambition is to play Heathcliff in *Wuthering Heights.*

Q. Exactly four years ago, you declared that you had no intention of marrying before you were 27. Do you still feel the same way?

A. I've always thought I would marry at 27 simply because I regard it as the most suitable age for a man to marry. However, the situation doesn't arise at the moment because there are no prospects in view.

Q. Do you enjoy being a star or do you sometimes wish that you were just an ordinary bloke?

A. I very rarely have any complaints. I like the life very much indeed. You sometimes hear it said that it's a lonely life at the top, but I can assure you it isn't. It depends entirely on what you make of it yourself.

AUGUST 30

It is announced that *Summer Holiday* is to be released in America at the end of October.

AUGUST

Cliff tele-records a guest appearance for the ATV Midlands children's *Tingha and Tucker*, in which he is seen in a non-singing role as Uncle Cliff on Blackpool Beach.

SEPTEMBER 6

Esther L. M. Chamberlaine writes to the *NME* from Leighton Buzzard: 'Cliff Richard has had five years in show business – so what? The Everly Brothers have clocked up eight and they are the world's greatest. So why not a tribute to them – they deserve one.'

SEPTEMBER 7

Bobby Vee reveals that he is going to include Cliff's 'Theme For A Dream' on his next LP, and Pat Boone confesses that he prefers Cliff's new version of 'It's All In The Game' to the original.

SEPTEMBER 13

Cliff trots out his ten all-time favourite records:
1. 'Rock Around The Clock' – Bill Haley and the Comets.
''Rock Around The Clock' remains the most exciting side with the most authentic sound that rock and roll has ever produced.'
2 'Heartbreak Hotel' – Elvis Presley.
'It is to me the most dynamic Elvis Presley performance ever committed to wax.'
3 'Dum Dum' – Brenda Lee.
'Despite her many successes as a ballad singer, I happen to prefer Brenda as a rock and roll singer. She has a perfect rock voice.'
4 'Maria' – Andy Williams.
'Taken from Andy's MOON RIVER LP, this ballad has established itself in my mind as just about the most touching song based on someone's name ever written.'
5 'There's A Place' – the Kestrels.
'This group is outstanding among the comparatively few British vocal groups which simply sing instead of playing instruments as well.'
6 'My Colouring Book' – Andy Williams.
''My Colouring Book' may usually be considered more of a girl singer's number, after its US chart entries by both Kitty Kallen and Sandy Stewart, but I've chosen Andy William's again.'
7 'Drown In My Own Tears' – Ray Charles.
'When he turns to the blues, Ray Charles can tug at my heart-strings without fail. This fairly long track, taken from a 1959 concert, can be found on two LPs: 'Ray Charles In Person' or 'The Ray Charles Story (Vol 2)'
8 'Guess Who I Saw Today' – Nancy Wilson.
'She is neither a pop artist nor particularly commercial sounding in the "quality" field, but such a professional voice should be heard much, much more in Britain.'
9 'Woe Is Me' – Helen Shapiro.
'Having been recorded in Nashville, Tennessee, this could be thought of as an American side, I guess. Even so, as a British produced and British sung offering, 'Woe Is Me' rates as something for us to be conspicuously proud of.'
10 'FBI' – the Shadows.
'My favourite group! As soon as I heard this number on tape before release, I thought, "this has got to be a single!"'

SEPTEMBER 13

The Shadows are booked to top ATV's *Sunday Night at the London Palladium* for the second time in three months, thus delaying by a day their recording of the Ed Sullivan Show with Cliff.

SEPTEMBER 14

Newspapers report the liklihood of Robert Morley (who played Cliff's father in *The Young Ones*) appearing in the new film.

SEPTEMBER 20

Bruce Welch announces that he's leaving the Shadows due to health reasons, after visiting a Harley Street specialist who recommends a complete rest: 'It is terribly unfortunate and the last thing in the world I want to do, but if the doctor says it's the best thing, I have to listen to him.'
Cliff pays tribute to Bruce's contribution to Cliff and the Shadows' success story, 'It's going to be a terrible wrench for all of us after five years of close harmony, but you can't argue with your health. The main consolation is that we shall still be in close contact as Bruce will be looking after our publishing interests and continuing his songwriting.'

SEPTEMBER 22

Bruce Welch's 'farewell' TV appearance on *Sunday Night at the London Palladium.*

SEPTEMBER 24

Cliff speaks out about the way certain factions of the national press have been commenting on his relationship with dancer Jackie Irving: 'I get the impression they're trying to marry me off – they're certainly creating a romance where none exists. They must enjoy playing Cupid – or perhaps they're just short of news. It's true that I've taken Jackie out more than any other girl, but then being placed as I am, it's only natural that I should take out girls I know rather than those I don't know. Jackie and I have been thrown together professionally quite a lot and I've grown to know her pretty well. I enjoy her company very much, but I can assure you that we've never even discussed the possibility of marriage – except perhaps to the contrary. Jackie's a good pal and we're the best of friends, but the chances are that now the Blackpool season is over, I shan't see her again for a few months, and that hardly indicates romance, does it?'

SEPTEMBER 24

Having led the *NME* chart table by over 300 points from the Beatles at the year's half-way stage, Cliff's lead has now been narrowed down to 50 points. When asked if the prospect of being overhauled worries him, he replies: 'I'm not too woried about it because it's happened so often before. I actually won the points table on one occasion when Elvis was in the Army, but otherwise I've always been second to him. So I'm used to being runner-up, but if the Beatles win the points table, I'll have nothing but praise for them because they're a great group.'

SEPTEMBER 26

Cliff and the Shadows leave for a two-week tour of Israel – they are greeted there by enormous crowds.

SEPTEMBER

Rome record label boss, Francois Minchin, urges Norrie Paramor to record Cliff in Italian.

SEPTEMBER 29

Huge crowds bring traffic to a standstill as Cliff and the Shadows open their tour of Israel in Tel Aviv.

OCTOBER 1

Singer Heinz chooses his all-time Top 10, which includes Cliff's 'It's All In The Game': 'To my mind no Top 10 would be complete without Cliff being represented – and I sincerely believe this is one of his all-time best. It's a superb interpretation and a fine arrangement. I've long been an admirer of Cliff and this really does him credit.'

OCTOBER 5

Cliff telephones England from Israel and chats to Light Programme's *Saturday Club* compere, Brian Matthew, as part of the programme's fifth birthday celebrations.

OCTOBER

The ex-president of Cliff's Swedish fan club marries Spotniks member, Bob Lander.

OCTOBER

Cliff talks about 'My Own Taste in Music' in the October edition of *Hit Parade* (2s.).

OCTOBER 9

Cliff and the Shadows return from Israel, whereupon Peter Gormley comments on Bruce's resignation: 'When they get back from the French tour, Bruce will seek medical advice on whether his health will allow him to go to the Canary Islands to film there early in December.' Cliff raves in the press about the Israel tour: 'I honestly think it's the most enjoyable overseas tour we've ever done, although over there they show their appreciation by giving you the slow handclap!' Among the numbers in the acts, 'Bachelor Boy', 'Lucky Lips' and even 'Move It, and 'We Say Yeah' were included by huge demand.

13 OCTOBER

ABBEY ROAD
Studio session

Don't Talk To Him (11)	*A-side*

Lead Vocal:	**Cliff Richard**
Guitars:	**Hank Marvin/Bruce Welch**
Bass:	**Brian Locking**
Drums:	**Brian Bennett**
Producer:	**Norrie Paramor**
Engineer:	**Malcolm Addey**
Recorded in:	**Studio 3**
Session hours:	**7.00-10.30**

OCTOBER 15

Cliff and Peter Gormley fly to the States to record for the *Ed Sullivan Show*. Whilst in New York, Cliff buys records by John Hammond, Aretha Franklin, Nancy Wilson and Dakota Stanton, six slim-jim ties and two pairs of cufflinks. He also goes to see Dakota Stanton live in Grenwich Village, John Hammond at Folk City and *Lord Of The Flies*, about which he says, 'It's a weird film – but great!' During the flying visit, he also meets American hit-maker Mitch Miller, and Britain's Oliver star Georgia Brown.

OCTOBER

A company called J.B. Walker of Yorkshire advertises Cliff biros for 2s.6d. Cliff stationery for the same price (24 sheets of notepaper and 12 envelopes!) and a set of four pencils, also for 2s.6d. bearing the inscription, 'I Like Cliff!'

OCTOBER 18

Cliff's 'Lucky Lips' EP is released, containing the title track 'It's All In The Game', ' Your Eyes Tell On You' and 'I Wonder".

OCTOBER 18

Before leaving for a tour of France, Shadow Bruce Welch says he's now hopeful that, following more consultation with a specialist, he may be able to stay permanently with Cliff and the Shadows.

OCTOBER 19

A major announcement about Cliff's new film *Wonderful Life* discloses that it will be shot in the Canary Islands, commencing early in December. The musical score will include six pop songs, two Shadows instrumentals and nine production routines. Noted British actress Susan Hampshire is to play the leading lady, alongside Melvyn Hayes, Una Stubbs and Richard O'Sullivan.

Actors Dennis Price and Robert Morley are not now to appear on the film as first announced.

OCTOBER

Radio Luxembourg's Book Of Record Stars is published, and includes a six-page interview and photograph section devoted to Cliff. The article is headed 'Cliff says "Be yourself and be different!"' and contains advice on how to be popular, what kind of guys girls like and ways of doing something useful with your spare time: '...popularity isn't a matter of taking. It's a matter of giving and you win friends by offering your friendship, your help, not by standing around waiting for others to drop it into your lap...', '...maybe one reason for your seeming unpopularity is that you're in the wrong crowd...', '...one thing for sure, the girl who tries to win popularity by the necking route is heading for disaster. Boys who know that a chick is an easy "make" will take her out all night, but it won't be where anybody can see her...', 'all boys aren't angels, but most of them are looking for one.'

OCTOBER 19

Cliff's new co-star, Susan Hampshire, appears on BBC TV's *Juke Box Jury* with Dusty Springfield and 'Z Cars' actor Terence Edmond.

OCTOBER 30

Cliff and the Shadows pre-record *Thank Your Lucky Stars* for November.

NOVEMBER 1

Cliff's new single, his 23rd, 'Don't Talk To Him', is reviewed in the music press: 'Here's another facet of Cliff Richard's many talents. In sharp contrast to 'All In The Game' comes a haunting melody in slow cha-cha tempo, written by Bruce Welch and Cliff himself. Don't see how Cliff can go wrong here, 'cos it's ideal for dancing and makes easy-on-the-ear listening.

1 NOVEMBER

ABBEY ROAD

Film soundtrack recording for Wonderful Life

Do You Remember (16)	*Wonderful Life*
Walkin	*Wonderful Life*
Theme For Young Lovers	*Wonderful Life*

Lead Vocal:	**Cliff Richard**
Guitars:	**Hank Marvin/Bruce Welch**
Bass:	**Brian Locking**
Drums:	**Brian Bennett**
Producer:	**Norrie Paramor**
Engineer:	**Malcolm Addey**
Recorded in:	**Studio 3**
Session hours:	**7.00pm-10.45pm**

NOVEMBER 3

Cliff and the Shadows top the bill on *Sunday Night at the London Palladium*. It is Shadows' bass player 'Licorice' Locking's final live TV appearance with the Shadows, as he dramatically and suddenly announces his intention to leave the group to devote more time to being a Jehovah's Witness.

Cliff pays tribute to him: 'We shall certainly miss "Lick" terribly, he's been a good friend to all of us and I'm thankful that Bruce has decided to stay!'

5 NOVEMBER

ABBEY ROAD

Film soundtrack recordings for Wonderful Life

Wonderful Life (18)	*Wonderful Life*
On The Beach (11)	*A-side*

Lead Vocal:	**Cliff Richard**
Guitars:	**Hank Marvin/Bruce Welch**
Bass:	**Brian Locking**
Drums:	**Brian Bennett**
Producer:	**Norrie Paramor**
Engineer:	**Malcolm Addey**
Recorded in:	**Studio 3**
Session hours:	**7.00pm-10.45pm**

NOVEMBER

The press hint that Cliff may be joined on his Spring tour of Britain by Bob Miller and the Millermen, which would enable him to present full recording arrangements of ballads on stage. The suggestion apparently comes from Cliff after working with them on *Parade of the Pops*.

NOVEMBER 8

Cliff talks about his new single: 'Bruce brought me the melody and asked if I could think of a lyric – which I did. So this marks the birth of a new Rodgers and Hammerstein partnership!'

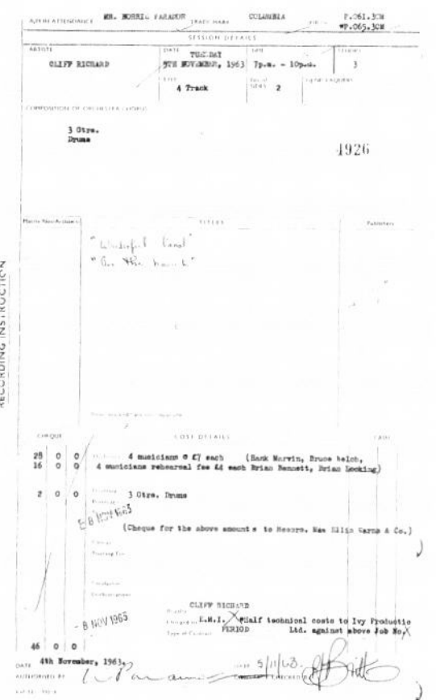

8 NOVEMBER

ABBEY ROAD
Studio session

Look Don't Touch	*(Unissued)*

Lead Vocal:	**Cliff Richard**
Guitars:	**Hank Marvin/Bruce Welch**
Bass:	**Brian Locking**
Drums:	**Brian Bennett**
Producer:	**Norrie Paramor**
Engineer:	**Malcolm Addey**
Recorded in:	**Studio 3**
Session hours:	**7.00pm-10.00pm**

NOVEMBER 8

NME reader C. A. Armstrong of Co. Durham, makes a prediction in the letters column of the paper: 'In five years' time, the Beatles will have settled down to steady jobs, Cliff Richard will still be getting world-wide hits (including America) and Elvis Presley will have made a non-singing film.'

NOVEMBER

Cliff and the Shadows send the Beatles a 'Good Luck' telegram before their appearance on the Royal Variety Show.

NOVEMBER 8

In America's *16* magazine, Cliff names Carole Gray as his favourite girl.

10 NOVEMBER

ABBEY ROAD
Film soundtrack recordings for Wonderful Life

A Matter Of Moments	*Wonderful Life*

Lead Vocal:	**Cliff Richard**
Guitars:	**Hank Marvin/Bruce Welch**
Bass:	**Brian Locking**
Drums:	**Brian Bennett**
Producer:	**Norrie Paramor**
Engineer:	**Malcolm Addey**
Recorded in:	**Studio 2**
Session hours:	**7.00pm-10.00pm**

Hank Marvin, John Rostill, Bruce Welch and Brian Bennett.

NOVEMBER 15

Cliff talks about the discovery by fans of his new £30,000 six-bedroom Tudor-style eleven-acre mansion in Upper Nazeing, Essex::

'We thought we could keep our new home secret, but now that it is known there is nothing we can do about it. Don't think I'm trying to hide from my fans, I'm not. Neighbours resented fans standing outside my last house and I don't blame them.'

The national papers also carry a story about a guard with dogs and a gun. Cliff comments:

That's a lot of rubbish, specially about the Alsatians. We've only got a poodle! It was just my chauffer's way of being funny, but on that day he had a bad scriptwriter.'

17 NOVEMBER

ABBEY ROAD
Studio session

I Only Came To Say Goodbye	*Angel EP*
Constantly (L'Edera)	*A-side*
I Only Know I Love You	*Foreign Release*

Lead Vocal:	**Cliff Richard**
	The Norrie Paramor Orchestra
Drums:	**Brian Bennett**
Producer:	**Norrie Paramor**
Engineer:	**Malcolm Addey**
Recorded in:	**Studio 2**
Session hours:	**7.00pm-10.15pm**

See May 1965 session for vocal overdub on Italian release of I Only Know I Love You.

23 NOVEMBER

ABBEY ROAD
Studio session

Watch What You Do With My Baby	*B-side*
I'm The Lonely One	*A-side*

Lead Vocal:	**Cliff Richard**
Guitar:	**Hank Marvin/Bruce Welch**
Bass:	**John Rostill**
Drums:	**Brian Bennett**
Piano:	**Norrie Paramor**
Producer:	**Norrie Paramor**
Engineer:	**Malcolm Addey**
Recorded in:	**Studio 2**
Session hours:	**7.00pm-10.30pm**

NOVEMBER 30

Cliff and the Shadows appear on *Thank Your Lucky Stars*.

NOVEMBER 31

Cliff conducts an interview from the snooker room of his house with pop writer Derek Johnson, who afterwards says: 'I experienced some difficulty in getting to the front door owing to the large number of fans who had congregated outside the house, and later in the day police had to be called to disperse crowds which had smashed down Cliff's fence.' During the interview, Cliff discusses the musical content of the forthcoming film *Wonderful Life*: 'I honestly think the pop songs are better than those in *Summer Holiday*. Bruce has written an absolutely fantastic ballad called 'In A Matter Of Moments'. I imagine it will be coupled with a light-hearted piece titled 'On The Beach' which I have written with Hank and Bruce.'

DECEMBER

Popic Figures of Nottingham advertise a life-like 5 ⁵/₈ inches high figurine of Cliff in Denby Pottery for 19s.6d.

DECEMBER 13

NME publish their poll results:

World's Most Outstanding Singer:
1 Cliff Richard
2 Elvis Presley

World's Outstanding Musical Personality:
1 Elvis Presley
2 Cliff Richard

British Male Singer:
1 Cliff Richard
2 Billy Fury

British Vocal Personality:
1 Joe Brown
2 Cliff Richard

DECEMBER

Radio Luxembourg *Top 20 Show* DJ, Barry Alldis, selects his favourite twenty records of 1963. Top of the list is Cliff's 'Bachelor Boy'.

DECEMBER 25

Cliff hosts an hour-long record show on the BBC Light Programme between 12.30 and 1.30pm. He also introduces the Shadows and plays some of his favourite records.

DECEMBER 25

Cliff and the Shadows (marking the debut of new Shadow, bass player John Rostill) star in an hour-long ATV Spectacular. The show is entitled *Sounds and Sweet Airs*.

Both the radio and TV shows were recorded before Cliff leaves for the Canary Isles, where he spends Christmas.

1964–1965

The Records 1964 – 1965
As Beatlemania began to develop into a phenomenon, Columbia released 'I'm The Lonely One' as the 1964 new year single, thereby getting off to a good start with the single reaching the top ten. At the same time, 'Don't Talk To Him', the smash hit from 1963 re-entered the chart for one week at No.50. For the follow up, an adaptation of the old Italian hit song 'L'Edera' was chosen, and did even better, appearing at No.3 as 'Constantly'. The next single 'On The Beach' was the lead and only single from the *Wonderful Life* soundtrack and, though still a strong release chartwise, it showed a slight decline when compared to its predecessors. The single 'I Could Easily Fall', taken from the cast recording of Cliff's pantomime ALADDIN AND HIS WONDERFUL LAMP, was already well on the way to becoming a hit before the show opened at the London Palladium just before Christmas 1964. Another track from the ALADDIN cast album 'This Was My Special Day' was issued as a theatre-only single not available through the usual record outlets, but only in the foyer of the London Palladium during the run of the pantomime. The single featured Cliff sharing vocals with other cast members – Audrey Bayley, Joan Palethorpe and Faye Fisher – and was given a regular Columbia catalogue number of DB 7435. But by far the big sellers of this period were those resulting from the first studio sessions in Nashville and New York. 'The Minute You're Gone' and 'Wind Me Up' reached No.1 and No.2 respectively. 'Angel'/'Razzle Dazzle' was another single like 'Gee Whiz It's You' and 'What'd I Say' that had been pressed in the United Kingdom for distribution overseas, but found its way briefly into UK record outlets.

The albums represented a mixed bag indeed. In the soundtrack division, WONDERFUL LIFE attained the best chart placing at No.2, not having such a wide appeal as SUMMER HOLIDAY, while the ALADDIN set did not do quite so well, only peaking at No.13. In the pop division CLIFF RICHARD consisted of left-overs from various sessions over a period of three years, and fared slightly better chartwise. MORE HITS BY CLIFF proved not to be quite as strong as CLIFF'S HIT ALBUM. It only reached the No.20 spot, and only for one week. Even worse was Cliff's last complete album of foreign language recordings. WHEN IN ROME failed to register on the chart at all, but the final album of the year, LOVE IS FOREVER, showed a considerable improvement by reaching No.19, although like MORE HITS only remained on the chart for one week.

No fewer than twelve EPs were released during this period following a by now predictable pattern of recycling material from albums. WONDERFUL LIFE NO.1 was the most successful of these despite the fact that the four tracks on the EP were also on the major hit album.

Although no further information could be found, an acetate of a track titled 'Taxi, Taxi, Take Me To Your Baby' thought to have been recorded during this period was auctioned at Sotheby's in 1988.

The Sessions 1964 – 1965
The first 1964 soundtrack session was done for *Wonderful Life* with one vital change in the recording procedure – whereas before the soundtrack sessions had been live ones, now first a basic track of the music would be taped and Cliff's vocals and back-up vocals would be dubbed in later. As the film called for plenty of songs, a slew of material was taped and fourteen songs eventually found their way onto the soundtrack album. The Stanley Black Orchestra and the Mike Sammes Singers swelled the ranks of the regulars.

In August, thirteen regular studio recordings were done, and all of these took place in New York and Nashville. Although not much is known about the sessions held in Nashville, it is certain that the Jordanaires – Elvis Presley's backing group – were called in for vocal support, being featured alongside a number of session musicians. Two new producers entered the studios with Cliff for the tracks recorded in Nashville and New York – Bob Morgan and Billy Sherrill. Later Sherrill was to build on his reputation through a string of solid hits by country artists like Tammy Wynette and impressive work with, among others, the British rock singer Elvis Costello. Of the material recorded, a great number of songs were of a very high quality indeed as proven by the three hit singles – 'On My Word', 'The Minute You're Gone' and 'Wind Me Up'. Plans were made to follow up the overall successful American recording sessions with some more at EMI's Studios in Milan during October, when the backing tracks for the WHEN IN ROME album was laid down. Cliff would not record his vocals until 1965. The taping of the songs for the ALADDIN pantomime cast album was done later that month at Abbey Road at a soundtrack session, with the musical score by the Shadows, and Cliff sharing vocals on a number of tracks with other cast members – Una Stubbs, Joan Palethorpe and Audrey Bayley were brought in for the sessions on the 16th. It is interesting to note that the first half on the session booked was for the Shadows only to record their instrumental tracks, while the songs featuring Cliff and other cast vocalists began at 7.00pm, and for

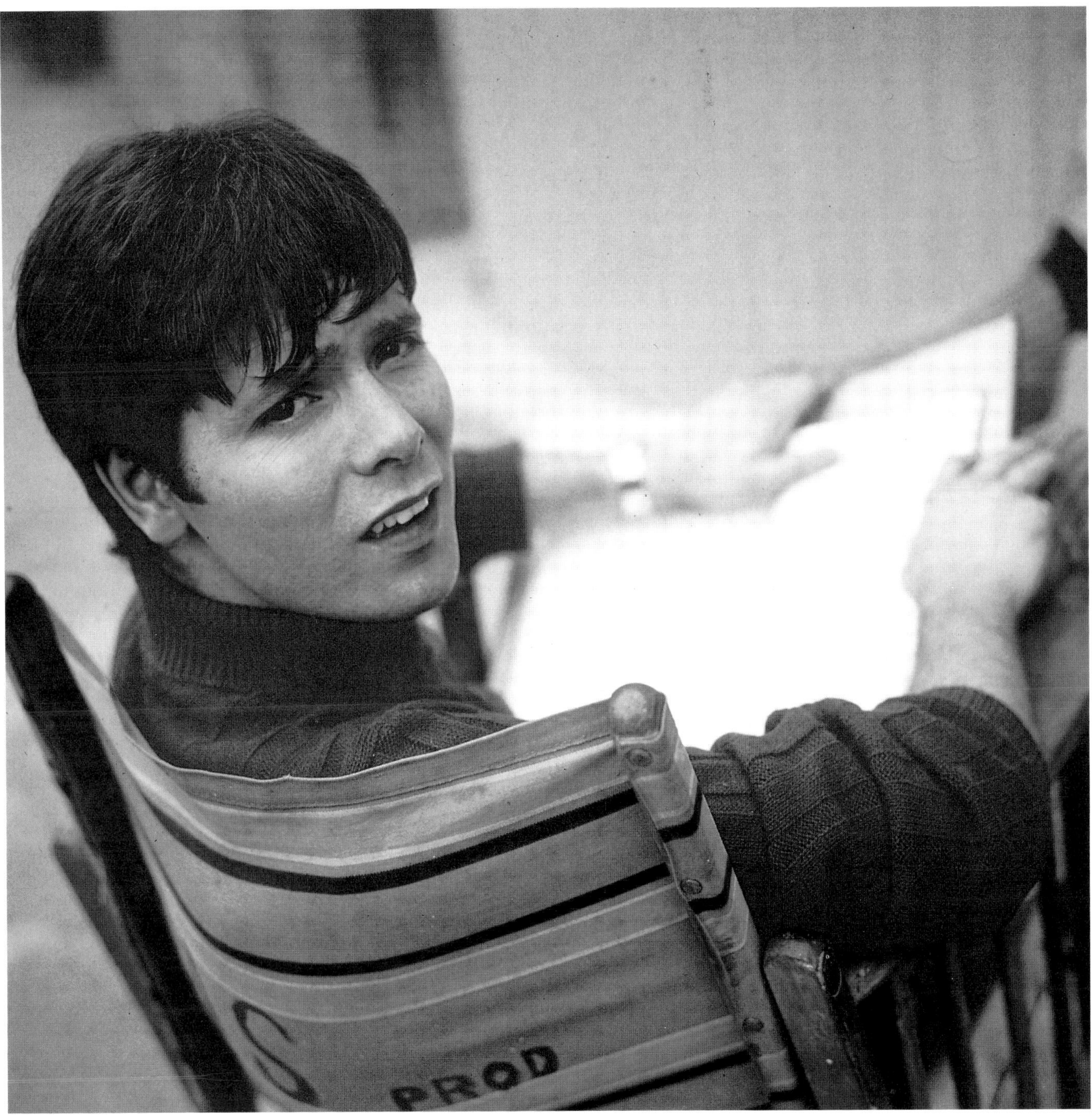

Relaxing during a break in filming.

the session on the 17th, the afternoon booking was to allow Norrie Paramor to lay down the orchestral tracks for the album. 1965 began with Cliff recording English versions of a number of WHEN IN SPAIN tracks. The original backing tracks were used on this session. For the sessions in May again a different studio was utilised, this time Estudios Valentim De Carvalho in Lisbon, which produced an unreleased song 'Deep Purple' that was recently discovered on a single-sided 7" Emidisc acetate lasting 2 minutes and 10 seconds. It is not known how many copies exist, but one was included in the Rock and Roll memorabilia Auction at Sotheby's on 28 August 1986. Over two further days Cliff put down his vocal on the existing backing tracks of the WHEN IN ROME album. There still remains an unissued track from these sessions. On the sessions for KINDA LATIN, three different orchestras were employed to provide a Latin-sounding setting for the material, which tended to a straight middle-of-the-road style of repertoire.

In all probability the last session of the year was set up to record a selection of Walt Disney songs. Four songs were taped and were treated as purely experimental recordings.

JANUARY

Cliff's Top Pops book is published, in which he writes about other artists:

Elvis Presley – Round the world, thousands copied him. Some simply grew Elvis sideburns, some styled their hair the Presley way and others sold their bicycles and put down a deposit on a guitar.

Adam Faith – Even a six-figure win on the pools wouldn't give you the satisfaction, adventure and the thrill of living that has come the way of Adam and me.

Billy Fury – Off-stage he doesn't strike one as furious at all. He talks quietly and laughs quietly – on-stage it's different.

Frank Sinatra – I spent an afternoon with him at Northwood, Middlesex, when he visited the British blind children. They flocked around him feeling for his hands. 'Oi, Sinarcher' cried one blind Cockney boy of six, 'come an' see the sandpit!'

The Everly Brothers – They produce a sound that is as ear-catching in Tokyo as it is in Tooting or Texas, and I see no reason why they should ever stop...!

JANUARY 3

NME publish the final chart points places for 1963 – 30 points for every week at number 1, down to 1 point for number 30.

1 Beatles	1,741
2 Cliff Richard	1,323
3 The Shadows	899
4 Gerry and the Pacemakers	894
5 Frank Ifield	838
6 Roy Orbison	772
7 Billy J. Kramer and the Dakotas	680
9 Billy Fury	623
10 Freddie and the Dreamers	584

JANUARY 3

In a survey by *Billboard* magazine, using the sales charts of 34 countries outside America, Cliff emerges as world champion with Elvis second and the Shadows and Frank Ifield third and fourth respectively.

JANUARY

Cliff reveals his hopes for the new year to reporter Alan Smith: 'I hope for a year of peace and prosperity for all mankind, and for the betterment of international relations and understanding. If in some small way the Shadows and I can help the spread of British goodwill abroad, then I shall be very happy.'

And on the music scene: 'I hope that the Beatles and their contemporaries go from strength to strength, because their achievements are acting as a tremendous shot in the arm to the music business as a whole.'

JANUARY 10

On the set of *Wonderful Life* Cliff talks about his acting career: 'I can't wait to get older – with a few wrinkles and some grey hairs I might get offered some full-length character roles.' He also gives a few tips on riding a camel: 'Don't imagine it's like riding a horse, that would be fatal. What you have to do is watch his droopy eyes, get ready for grunts and then hang on like grim death because it's rougher than a roller-coaster ride!'

JANUARY

Dave Clark of the Dave Clark Five includes Cliff's 'Do You Want To Dance' in his all-time Top 10. 'This is my personal choice. The old rocking-type tune is treated with a solid beat which all adds up to being first class to dance to.'

JANUARY

New York *Motion Picture Herald's* survey, using 2,300 British cinemas, puts Cliff as number 1 most popular film star in Britain for 1963, with Peter Sellers and Elvis Presley in second and third places respectively.

JANUARY 17

Bad weather in the Canaries delays the shooting of *Wonderful Life*.

JANUARY 24

One of the scenes in *Wonderful Life* is dubbed 'controversial' by some people on the set. The shot in question is the mickey-take of the beach scene between Sean Connery and Ursula Andress in the James Bond film *Dr No*. As 'Ursula', Susan Hampshire emerges from the waters of a tropical lagoon clad in a figure-revealing bikini, Cliff, as James Bond, is waiting on the beach and a passionate clinch ensues! Says Susan, 'After the kisses, I was going round bumping into furniture for hours.' Cliff comments: 'I kept telling the director I was ready for more and more takes!'

Cliff's 24th single is released, the 'A' side, 'I'm The Lonely One', is a song written by Viscounts member Gordon Mills. The 'B' side, 'Watch What You Do With My Baby', is a number from one of Elvis's songwriters Bill Giant.

JANUARY

Cliff buys a holiday home in Albufeira on the Atlantic coast of Portugal, where Frank Ifield, Shadow Bruce Welch and Cliff's manager Peter Gormley already have houses.

JANUARY

Among the reviews for Cliff's new single is one from Derek Johnson:

'This is the type of number that Cliff used to record years ago, but today it's well in keeping with teenage demand. A distinct

Rhythm and Blues flavour and a melody slightly reminiscent of 'What'd I Say'.'

JANUARY

Holidaying in the Canaries, Max Bygraves watches Cliff filming *Wonderful Life*.

JANUARY 31

Ralph G. Evans writes to the music press: 'Why did Cliff Richard and the Shadows have to sink so low and go all R & B on their latest record? On this disc, they lose all claim to originality.' 'It's All In The Game' starts to climb the American charts.

FEBRUARY

Cliff's 'When In France' EP is released, featuring 'La Mer', 'Boum', 'J'Attendrai' and 'C'est Si Bon!'.

FEBRUARY

Rave magazine is launched and includes a colour portrait of Cliff and a feature 'On location in the Canaries'.

FEBRUARY 7

The press reports that Cliff is not seeing dancer Jackie Irving any more.

FEBRUARY 11

On his return to Britain, 'I'm The Lonely One' enters the Top 20. Says Cliff: 'Actually, it wasn't originally planned as a single. I usually include a couple of rockers on my albums, and this song was cut with that in view, but the beat craze changed our plans!'

FEBRUARY 16

Cliff headlines at the London Palladium and among other songs sings, 'Maria' from West Side Story.

FEBRUARY

'It's All In The Game' peaks at No. 25 in US *Billboard* chart.

FEBRUARY 17

Talking to the press on board the former presidential yacht Potomac at Long Beach, California, Elvis Presley reveals, 'I like Cliff Richard's work.'

FEBRUARY

Cliff's former girl-friend, Jackie Irving, joins the Lionel Blair Dancers.

FEBRUARY/MARCH

Cliff and the Shadows shoot interior shots for *Wonderful Life* at Elstree Studios.

Hank, Bruce, Cliff, Brian and John.

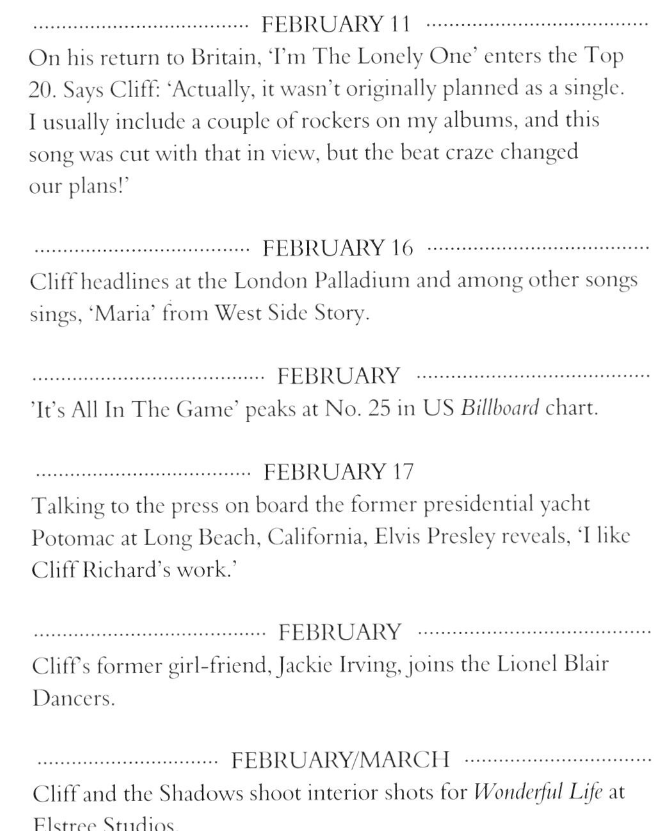

MARCH 6

In an interview, Shadow Hank Marvin says: 'We were very annoyed when we read some of the comments on our backing to Cliff's 'I'm The Lonely One'. A couple of writers suggested that we were simulating the Mersey sound. Frankly, I've never read such rubbish!'

MARCH

Beatles manager Brian Epstein declines an offer for his protegee, Cilla Black, to appear on Cliff's forthcoming tour.

MARCH

'Cliff Sings Don't Talk To Him' EP is released, featuring 'Don't Talk To Him', 'Say You're Mine', 'Who Are We To Say', 'Spanish Harlem' and 'Falling In Love With Love'.

MARCH 13

Interviewed on the Elstree set of *Wonderful Life*, Cliff says: 'This film has got to be twice as good as the last one to be half as good! People judge you by what they hold to be your personal best. People still say I've never made a record as good as 'Living Doll'.'

MARCH

For one scene of the film within *Wonderful Life* (entitled The Daughter of the Sheik) director Sidney Furie plans to take down the advertisements for the current film showing at the Warner Cinema in Leicester Square, and replace them with neons for a make-believe premiere.

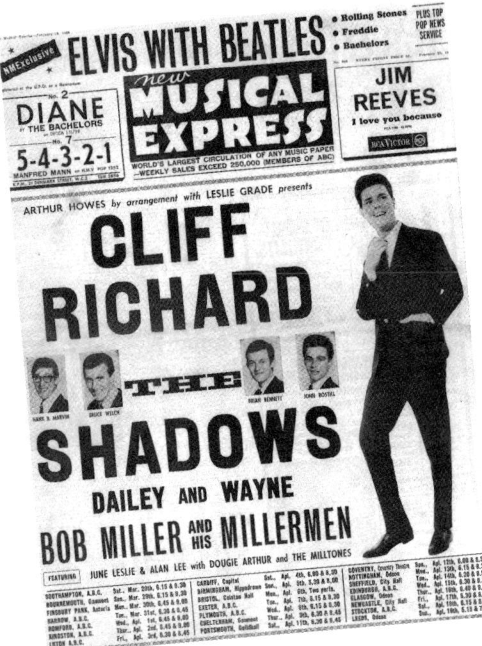

NMExclusive
ELVIS WITH BEATLES
• Rolling Stones
• Freddie
• Bachelors
PLUS TOP POP NEWS SERVICE
No. 2 DIANE by THE BACHELORS
No. 7 5-4-3-2-1 MANFRED MANN
new MUSICAL EXPRESS
WORLD'S LARGEST CIRCULATION OF ANY MUSIC PAPER —WEEKLY SALES EXCEED 250,000 (MEMBERS OF ABC)
JIM REEVES
I love you because
RCA VICTOR
ARTHUR HOWES by arrangement with LESLIE GRADE presents
CLIFF RICHARD
THE SHADOWS
DAILEY AND WAYNE
BOB MILLER AND HIS MILLERMEN
FEATURING JUNE LESLIE & ALAN LEE with DOUGIE ARTHUR and THE MILLTONES

MARCH

Police refuse permission to shoot the scenes for *Wonderful Life* in Leicester Square.

20 MARCH

ABBEY ROAD
Studio session

Zuviel Allein (I'm The Lonely One)	*German Release*
Sag 'No' Zu Ihm (Don't Talk To Him)	*German Release*

Lead Vocal:	**Cliff Richard**
Producer:	**Norrie Paramor**
Engineer:	**Malcolm Addey**
Recorded in:	**Studio 2**
Session hours:	**7.00pm-10.00pm**

Cliff's vocals were dubbed onto the existing tracks for these foreign releases.

MARCH

Cliff's latest American LP includes a version of 'Secret Love'.

26 MARCH

ABBEY ROAD
Studio session

True, True Lovin'	*B-side*
Just A Little Bit Too Late	*(Unissued)*

Lead Vocal:	**Cliff Richard**
Guitar:	**Hank Marvin/Bruce Welch**
Bass:	**John Rostill**
Drums:	**Brian Bennett**
Producer:	**Norrie Paramor**
Engineer:	**Malcolm Addey**
Recorded in:	**Studio 2**
Session hours:	**7.00pm-9.30pm**

MARCH 28

Cliff and the Shadows, augmented by Bob Miller and the Millermen, commence a 3-week British tour opening at the ABC Southampton.

MARCH 28

Cliff and the Shadows appear with the Hollies on the BBC Light Programme's *Saturday Club*.

MARCH

EMI chief Joseph Lockwood presents Cliff and the Shadows with a Gold Disc for one million worldwide sales of 'Lucky Lips'.

APRIL

On tour, Cliff opens his 35-minute act with 'I Wanna Know', followed by 'Come To Me', '24 Hours From Tulsa', 'Da-do-ron-ron', 'It's All In The Game', 'Maria', 'You Don't Know', 'Constantly', 'Bachelor Boy', 'Whole Lotta Shakin', ending with 'What'd I Say'.

APRIL 10

'I'm The Lonely One' enters America's *Billboard* magazine chart at number 92.

APRIL 10

Millie, riding high in the charts with 'My Boy Lollipop', names Cliff as her favourite singer.

APRIL 17

Cliff's new single 'Constantly' is reviewed. As one reviewer puts it: 'A captivating rock-a-ballad with an exotic Latin lift – this must rank as one of Cliff's best and most polished discs to date.'

22 APRIL

ABBEY ROAD

Film soundtrack recordings for Wonderful Life

In The Stars	*Wonderful Life*
A Little Imagination	*Wonderful Life*
Home	*Wonderful Life*
All Kinds Of People	*Wonderful Life*

Lead Vocal:	**Cliff Richard**
	The Stanley Black Orchestra
	The Mike Sammes Singers
Producer:	**Norrie Paramor**
Engineer:	**Malcolm Addey**
Recorded in:	**Studio 2**
Session hours:	**7.00pm-10.30pm**

APRIL 24

Cliff's 25th single 'Constantly' is released. Adapted from the Italian hit song 'L'Edera', it is backed with a composition written by Shadow Bruce Welch, 'True, True Lovin' '.

APRIL 24

Cliff's agent Leslie Grade reveals that he has turned down offers for the star to appear at prestigious cabaret venues The Sands and the Desert Inn in Las Vegas, the Beirut Casino, and the Australian Chevron Hilton.

APRIL 25

Cliff appears on *Thank Your Lucky Stars.*

CONSTANTLY
(L'EDERA)
Lyric by MICHAEL JULIEN
Music by S. SERACINI
Recorded on COLUMBIA by
CLIFF RICHARD
2/6

APRIL 26

Along with the Beatles, Rolling Stones, Manfred Mann, Gerry and the Pacemakers, the Dave Clark Five and other *NME* poll winners, Cliff and the Shadows appear at the annual concert staged by the music paper. Cliff sings Ray Charles' 'I Wanna Know', his hit from the previous Christmas 'Don't Talk To Him', 'Whole Lotta Shakin Goin On', 'Bachelor Boy' and 'I'm The Lonely One'.

MAY 1

Epic Records in America invite Cliff to record an album in the US without the Shadows.

MAY

It is announced that Cliff will visit Los Angeles in July to discuss starring in both a Hollywood musical and a Hollywood picture.

MAY 3

NME's poll concert is televised.

MAY 5

Cliff and the Shadows fly to Amsterdam to begin a continental tour.

MAY 8

Photoplay magazine features an exclusive article on Cliff: 'Is Cliff heading for marriage – his next step could be right up to the altar!'

MAY

Cliff's 'Palladium Successes' EP is released. The tracks are, 'I'm The Lonely One', 'Watch What You Do With My Baby', 'Perhaps, Perhaps, Perhaps' and 'Frenesi'.

Cliff and his *Wonderful Life* co-stars Una Stubbs and Melvyn Hayes.

MAY 12

Cliff records a programme for German TV in Munich.

20 MAY

ABBEY ROAD

Film soundtrack recordings for Wonderful Life

We Love A Movie (5)	*Wonderful Life*
Youth And Experience-Part 1 (2)	*Wonderful Life*
Youth And Experience-Part 2 (4)	*Wonderful Life*
Wonderful Life (18)	*(Unissued)*
A Girl In Every Port-Part 1 (2)	*Wonderful Life*
A Girl In Every Port-Part 2 (3)	*Wonderful Life*
A Girl In Every Port-Part 3	*Wonderful Life*

Lead Vocal:	**Cliff Richard**
	The Stanley Black Orchestra
Producer:	**Bob Barratt**
Engineers:	**Malcolm Addey/Alan Kane**
Recorded in:	**Studio 2**
Session hours:	**7.00pm-10.00pm**

On the EMI session sheets these are listed as backing tracks only.

MAY 22

Cliff is interviewed while he and the Shadows are playing at the Paris Olympia: 'It's really marvellous here in Paris; it's a fantastic city and the audience couldn't be bettered anywhere in the world. They have this admirable knack of remaining perfectly quiet during each number, then suddenly bursting into a volume of applause when it ends. In Belgium, Holland and Germany, we were playing different towns every day. Sometimes we'd have an afternoon show, then boat and train for a couple of hours and give an evening performance in another city miles away.' For the Paris show Cliff learns 'La Mer' and 'Boum' in French: 'That wasn't as tricky as 'Lucky Lips' and 'I'm The Lonely One', which I had to learn phonetically in German. I've also been singing a couple of Spanish songs on the tour, so altogether I've been working in four languages.'

26 MAY

ABBEY ROAD

Film soundtrack recordings for Wonderful Life

Youth And Experience (5)	*Wonderful Life*
A Girl In Every Port (sp)	*Wonderful Life*
We Love A Movie (5)	*Wonderful Life*

Vocals:	**Cliff Richard/Mike Sammes**
Producer:	**Norrie Paramor**
Engineers:	**Malcolm Addey/Richard Lush**
Recorded in:	**Studio 2**
Session hours:	**7.00pm-9.30pm**

This session was for the superimposition of vocals onto the 20 May backing tracks.

MAY 27

Two-week tour of Scandinavia begins.

MAY

In *Rave* magazine, astrologer Maurice Woodruff predicts that Cliff will fall in love.

END OF MAY

'Constantly' peaks at number 4 in the charts.

JUNE

Leslie Grade appoints sports writer Bob Ferrier as publicity agent for Cliff and the Shadows.

JUNE 12

The July edition of *Photoplay* features Cliff and Susan Hampshire on the front cover in a scene from *Wonderful Life*.

JUNE 12

In an interview with the *London Evening News*, Cliff says: 'People think I must be a millionaire. I'm not. Nowhere near it. I have to ask my accountant if I can afford it before making any really big purchase.'

JUNE 19

Cliff's new single 'On The Beach'/'A Matter Of Moments' is reviewed: ''On The Beach' is a medium-fast twister, and 'A Matter Of Moments' is one of Bruce Welch's best compositions.'

23 JUNE

ABBEY ROAD
Studio session

Twelfth Of Never (sp)	*A-side*
My Colouring Book (6)	*Love Is Forever EP*
Maria (sp)	*Look In My Eyes Maria EP*

Lead Vocal:	**Cliff Richard**
	The Cliff Richard Orchestra
	The Mike Sammes Singers-8pm-10.00pm only
Producer:	**Norrie Paramor**
Engineer:	**Malcolm Addey**
Recorded in:	**Studio 2**
Session hours:	**7.00pm-10.00pm**

Twelfth of Never is an edit of takes 3 and 4.
Maria is an edit of takes 7 and 8.

JUNE 26

Cliff's 26th single, 'On The Beach'/'A Matter Of Moments' is released.

JUNE 30

Cliff tele-records a Spectacular for the following day for ATV, featuring the Shadows and guest star Liza Minnelli.

JULY 1

ATV Spectacular is postponed owing to an ITV strike.

JULY

At the halfway mark in the *NME* annual points survey, Cliff is eleventh with fewer than half the points he had amassed by the same time the previous year.

1 Beatles	710
2 Bachelors	647
3 Dave Clark Five	529
4 Cilla Black	467
5 Hollies	458
6 Rolling Stones	448
7 Searchers	441
8 Gerry and the Pacemakers	412
9 Swinging Blue Jeans	391
10 Jim Reeves	352
11 Cliff Richard	344

Cliff with producers Bob Morgan and Norrie Paramor discussing possible titles for the forthcoming USA sessions.

JULY 2

Princess Alexandra and her husband, Angus Ogilvy, attend the premiere of *Wonderful Life* at the Leicester Square Empire in London. Proceeds of the event go to the National Association of Youth Clubs. Of the film, one critic says: 'No one will be able to say they haven't had their money's worth, there's everything in it but the kitchen sink.' And another comments: 'He (Cliff) improves with every picture he makes. Not only is his acting much more convincing, but he also displays considerable talent as a light comedian and impressionist.'

JULY

Plans for Cliff and the Shadows to write the music for – and star in – *Aladdin* at the London Palladium next Christmas are hinted at in the press. It is also rumoured that Robert Morley is likely to be cast as Abanazer.

JULY 12

Cliff guests on BBC 2's *The Best Of Both Worlds* with the Stanley Black Orchestra

JULY

Rave magazine reveals the location of Cliff's holiday home in Portugal and publishes pictures of Cliff and his sisters at their new home in Upper Nazeing, Essex.

JULY

'Wonderful Life' LP is released.

JULY 15

Cliff's postponed ATV Spectacular is screened, replacing the scheduled documentary about Beatlemania, 'Fans, fans, fans'.

17JULY

ABBEY ROAD
Studio session

Sway	*Cliff Richard*
It's Not For Me To Say (4)	*Cliff Richard*
The Song From Moulin Rouge (4)	*(Unissued)*
Look Homeward Angel (2)	*Love Is Forever*
(All Of A Sudden) My Heart Sings (sp)	*Love Is Forever*
Magic Is The Moonlight	*Cliff Richard*

Lead Vocal: **Cliff Richard**
The Norrie Paramor Orchestra
The Mike Sammes Singers

Producer: **Norrie Paramor**
Engineer: **Malcolm Addey**
Recorded in: **Studio 2**
Session hours: **7.00pm-9.45pm**

(All Of A Sudden) My Heart Sings is an edit of takes 5 and 7.

JULY

Go magazine publishes the book *Cliff and his Wonderful Life,* selling for 3s 6d .

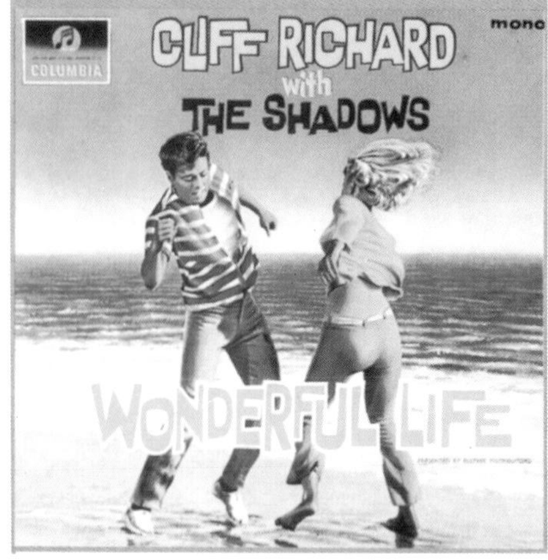

24 JULY

ABBEY ROAD
Studio session

Where Is Your Heart	*Look In My Eyes Maria EP*
Why Don't They Understand	*Why Don't They Understand EP*
House Without Windows	*Cliff Richard*
I'm Afraid To Go Home	*B-side*
If I Give My Heart To You	*Look In My Eyes Maria EP*

Lead Vocal: **Cliff Richard**
The Norrie Paramor Orchestra
The Mike Sammes Singers

Producer: **Norrie Paramor**
Engineer: **Malcolm Addey**
Recorded in: **Studio 2**
Session hours: **7.00pm-10.45pm**

JULY

As the film *Wonderful Life* is released in forty different cities, Cliff speaks about the picture: 'I've yet to see it properly – I've sat through it three or four times, but all I've seen is me and my mistakes!' He also comments on his recording career: 'We have been toying with the idea of releasing 'Maria' as a single, but we may just do a West Side Story EP on which it would be one of the tracks.'
In addition, Cliff reveals that he will be recording in New York and Nashville: 'I would also love to record in Chicago. That's the home of that great writer Curtis Mayfield, and that superb group the Impressions. Nothing would make me happier than to record a Mayfield song with the Impressions backing me!'

AUGUST

EMI release 'Wonderful Life No.1' EP, containing four tracks from the film.

19 AUGUST

COLUMBIA STUDIOS, NEW YORK
Studio session

Again	*Cliff Richard*
My Heart is An Open Book (8)	*Take Four EP*
Lies and Kisses (7)	*Take Four EP*

Lead Vocal: **Cliff Richard**
Orchestra conducted by **Stan Applebaum**

Producer: **Bob Morgan**
Engineer: **Frank Laico**
Recorded in: **Studio A**
Session hours: **7pm-10pm**

21 AUGUST

COLUMBIA STUDIOS, NEW YORK
Studio session

Everybody Needs Somebody To Love (15)	*Love Is Forever*
Through The Eye Of A Needle (8)	*Love Is Forever*
Look In My Eyes Maria (7)	*Look In My Eyes Maria EP*

Lead Vocal: **Cliff Richard**
Orchestra conducted by **Gary Sherman**

Producer: **Bob Morgan**
Engineer: **Frank Laico**
Recorded in: **Studio A**
Session hours: **7pm-10pm**

24 AUGUST

COLUMBIA STUDIOS, NASHVILLE
Studio session

I Don't Wanna Love You	*Cliff Richard*
Wind Me Up (Let Me Go)	*A-side*
Angel	*Cliff Richard*

Lead Vocal: **Cliff Richard**
Vocals: **The Jordanaires**

Producers: **Bob Morgan/Billy Sherrill**
Engineer: **Mort Thomason**
Recoreded in: **Studio B**
Session hours: **7pm-10pm**

25 AUGUST

COLUMBIA STUDIOS, NASHVILLE
Studio session

On My Word (8)	*A-Side*
Paradise Lost (11)	*Love is Forever*
Just Another Guy	*B-side*
The Minute You're Gone	*A-side*

Lead Vocal: **Cliff Richard**
Vocals: **The Jordanaires**

Producer: **Bob Morgan/ Billy Sherrill**
Engineer: **Mort Thomason**
Recorded in: **Studio B**
Session hours: **7pm-10pm**

AUGUST

During his stay in America, Cliff goes to see Barbra Streisand's *Funny Girl* on Broadway.
He also takes the opportunity of watching several live artists whom he has long admired, including Buddy Greco, Kay Starr and Della Reese.

WONDERFUL LIFE

Elstree Distributors, 1964. Running time: 113 minutes.
Cliff's fifth feature film.

Synopsis:
Johnnie (Cliff) and friends (The Shadows) entertain passengers on a luxury Mediterranean cruise but lose their jobs. They find themselves put to sea on a raft by an irritated ship's Captain. They reach land, which just happens to be the Canary Islands, and there they find themselves causing more than a minor disturbance in the filming of "Daughter Of A Sheik"

Cast:
Cliff Richard, Walter Slezak, Susan Hampshire, Derek Bond, Melvyn Hayes, Richard O'Sullivan, Una Stubbs, The Shadows.

Credits:
Producer: Kenneth Harper. Director: Sidney J Furie. Associate producer: Andrew Mitchell. Choreographer: Gillian Lynne. Original screenplay and story: Peter Myers and Ronald Cass. Background score, orchestrations, musical direction: Stanley Black. Photography: Ken Higgins.

Songs:
'Wonderful Life', 'A Girl In Every Port', 'Home', 'A Little Imagination', 'On The Beach', 'In The Stars', 'We Love A Movie', 'Do You Remember', 'What've I Gotta Do', 'All Kinds Of People', 'A Matter Of Moments', 'Youth And Experience' performed by Cliff Richard and The Shadows. 'Walkin'', 'Theme For Young Lovers' performed by The Shadows.

AUGUST 28

It is announced that Una Stubbs and Arthur Askey will appear with Cliff in Aladdin at the London Palladium later in the year.

Cliff flies to Portugal for a holiday on the Algarve.

SEPTEMBER

Cliff's 'A Forever Kind Of Love' EP is released.

SEPTEMBER 23

Cliff's 27th single, 'The Twelfth Of Never', is released and reviewed: 'Cliff reverts to his more romantic approach with his revival of the Johnny Mathis song – the captivating lilt is ideal for cheek-to-cheek dancing.'

SEPTEMBER 25

It is announced in the press that advance bookings for the London Palladium pantomime starring Cliff and the Shadows are the highest in the history of the theatre.

2/3 OCTOBER

EMI Studios, Milano

Studio session

O Mio Signore (The Questions) (4)	*See 13/14 May 1965*
Come Prima (For The First Time) (4)	*See 13/14 May 1965*
Concerto D'Automno (Autumn Concerto) (4)	*See 13/14 May 1965*
Arrivederci Roma (4)	*See 13/14 May 1965*
Legata Ad Un Granello Di Sabbia (3)	*See 13/14 May 1965*
Per Un Bacio D'Amor	*See 13/14 May 1965*
Che Cosa Del Mia Amore (5)	*See 13/14 May 1965*
Carina (5)	*See 13/14 May 1965*
Dicitencello Vuie (Just Say I Love Her)	*See 13/14 May 1965*
Nel Blu Dipinto /Di Blu (5)	*See 13/14 May 1965*
Dicitencello Vuie (Just Say I Love Her)	*See 13/14 May 1965*

	The Norrie Paramor Orchestra
Musical director:	**M. Di Ponti**
Producer:	**John Lee**
Engineer:	**Malcolm Addey**
Session hours:	

OCTOBER 9

Choosing his all-time Top 10 records for the *New Musical Express*, publicity-prone singer and one-time Elvis demo-disc stand-in P. J. Proby includes Cliff's 'Constantly'in his list, and adds the caustic comment:

'This is actually the first disc of Cliff Richard's that I've really liked – before that I quite honestly thought he was an atrocious singer!'

10 OCTOBER

Abbey Road

Studio session

Nur Mit Dir	
(On The Beach)	*German B-side*
Das Ist Die Frage Aller Fragen	
(Spanish Harlem)	*German A-side*

Lead Vocal:	**Cliff Richard**
Producer:	**Norrie Paramor**
Engineer:	
Recorded in:	**Studio 2**
Session hours:	**7.00pm-10.00pm**

Cliff's vocals were overdubbed on to the existing tracks for release in Germany.

15 OCTOBER

Abbey Road

Studio session

I'm In Love With You (5)	*B-side*
Evening Comes (3)	*Aladdin*
I Could Easily Fall In Love With You (7)	*A-side*
Havin' Fun	*Aladdin*

Lead Vocal:	**Cliff Richard**
Guitars:	**Hank Marvin/Bruce Welch**
Bass:	**John Rostill**
Drums:	**Brian Bennett**
Producer:	**Norrie Paramor**
Engineers:	**Malcolm Addey/Ken Scott**
Recorded in:	**Studio 2**
Session hours:	**2.30pm-6.00pm/7.00pm-11.00pm**

OCTOBER 16

NME publish a letter from an 'indignant Cliff fan' from Hull: 'How dare P. J. Proby call Cliff an atrocious singer! Until a few months ago, P. J. Proby was unknown, whereas Cliff is already world famous.'

16 OCTOBER

ABBEY ROAD
Studio session

Princess Instrumental	*Aladdin*
Genie With The Light Brown Lamp	*Aladdin*
Carnival Instrumental	*Aladdin*
Me Oh My	*Aladdin*
Widow Twankey Song (4)	*Aladdin*
I'm Feeling Oh So Lonely (4)	*Aladdin*
This Is My Special Day (11)	*A-side*

Lead Vocal:	**Cliff Richard**
Guitars:	**Hank Marvin/Bruce Welch**
Bass:	**John Rostill**
Drums:	**Brian Bennett**
	The Norrie Paramor Orchestra
Vocals:	**The Mike Sammes Singers**
	Una Stubbs/Joan Palethorpe/Audrey Bayley
Producer:	**Norrie Paramor**
Engineers:	**Malcolm Addey/Ken Scott**
Recorded in:	**Studio 2**
Session hours:	**2.30pm-5.30pm (Shadows)/7.00pm-10.00pm**

17 OCTOBER

ABBEY ROAD
Studio session

Emperor Theme (3)	*Aladdin*
Street Scene (6)	*Aladdin*
Dance Of The Warriors	*Aladdin*
The Dragon Dance (2)	*Aladdin*
Ballet-Part 1 (4)	*Aladdin*
Ballet-Part 2 (7)	*Aladdin*
Ballet-Part 3 (9)	*Aladdin*
Ballet-Part 4 (10)	*Aladdin*
There's Gotta Be A Way (5)	*Aladdin*
I've Said Too Many Things (4)	*Aladdin*
Make Everyday A Carnival Day (sp)	*Aladdin*

Lead Vocal:	**Cliff Richard**
	The Norrie Paramor Orchestra
	The Mike Sammes Singers
Producer:	**Norrie Paramor**
Engineers:	**Malcolm Addey/Ken Scott**
Recorded in:	**Studio 2**
Session hours:	**2.30pm-6.00pm/7.00pm-9.30pm**

These are orchestral tracks for the Aladdin LP
Make Everyday A carnival Day is an edit of takes 5 and 6

OCTOBER

Cliff tours Britain. He sings 'We Say Yeah' followed by 'A Matter Of Moments', 'Constantly', 'The Twelfth Of Never', 'Da-doo-ron-ron', '24 Hours From Tulsa','The Young Ones', 'Livin Doll', 'Lucky Lips' and 'Bachelor Boy', and 'What'd I Say'.

21 OCTOBER

ABBEY ROAD
Studio session

Friends (5)	*Aladdin*

Lead Vocal:	**Cliff Richard**
Guitars:	**Hank Marvin/Bruce Welch**
Bass:	**John Rostill**
Drums:	**Brian Bennett**
	The Norrie Paramor Orchestra
	The Mike Sammes Singers
Producer:	**Norrie Paramor**
Engineers:	**Malcolm Addey/Ken Scott**
Recorded in:	**Studio 3**
Session hours:	**2.30pm-3.30pm**

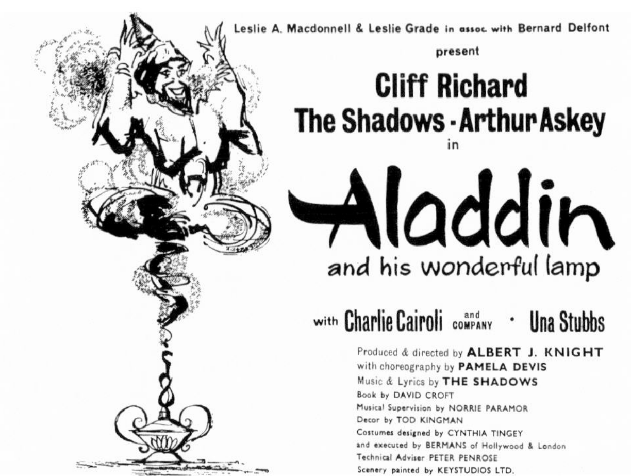

OCTOBER 30

On a fashion note, one critic reflects on Cliff's new short hair-cut in the era of the Beatle mop-top:
'It's a fascinating thought that at a time when most pop idols seem to be competing against each other to see who can grow the longest locks, one of our tip-top stars defies the trend by having his hair cut.'

OCTOBER

'Wonderful Life No.2' EP released.

NOVEMBER 2

Cliff and the Shadows perform at the Royal Variety Show in front of H.M. the Queen. Also appearing are Cilla Black, Brenda Lee, Kathy Kirby, Millicent Martin, Jimmy Tarbuck, David Jacobs, the Bachelors, Bob Newhart, Gracie Fields, Lena Horne, Morecambe and Wise and Toomy Cooper. Cliff sings 'Wonderful Life' accompanied by the entire London Palladium orchestra, conducted by Norrie Paramor, followed by 'The Twelfth Of Never', ending with a version of the Supremes' 'Where Did Our Love Go'.

NOVEMBER 20

Cliff and the Shadows' forthcoming LP 'Aladdin and his Wonderful Lamp' is reviewed.

NOVEMBER 27

Cliff's 28th single is released, both sides coming from the pantomime *Aladdin*: 'I Could Easily (Fall In Love With You)'/'I'm In Love With You'.

NOVEMBER 27

Cliff's agent Leslie Grade announces that Cliff and the Shadows are to star in a screen version of *Aladdin*: 'A complete new screenplay will be written and the film will have a very big budget. We haven't yet decided which company we will let make it; there have been many offers since I registered the title for film rights.'

NOVEMBER

In a popularity poll run by the *Muzik Expres*, which covers Holland, Belgium and parts of Germany, Cliff is voted top male singer with 39% of the votes, ahead of Sicilian-born Belgian singer Adamo with 17%, Elvis with 13% and Roy Orbison 7%.

NOVEMBER

Over £100,000 in advance booking money for *Aladdin* taken by the London Palladium.

DECEMBER

As leading lady in *Aladdin*, Una Stubbs talks about Cliff: 'Cliff is a marvellous person. I owe an awful lot to him – he gave me my first opportunity in show business. When I did my screen test for *Summer Holiday*, he told the producer that he thought I'd be right for the part.'

DECEMBER

In Michael Braun's newly published book on the Beatles, *Love Me Do*, he attributes this quote to John Lennon – 'We hate Cliff Richard's records.'

DECEMBER

Hits From 'Wonderful Life' EP released.

DECEMBER 11

The *NME* annual poll results are published:
World Male Singer

1	Elvis Presley	5,861

2 Roy Orbison	4,638
3 Cliff Richard	3,987

World Musical Personality

1 Elvis Presley	4,010
2 Roy Orbison	2,837
3 Cliff Richard	2,528

British Male Singer

1 Cliff Richard	6,269
2 Billy Fury	2,516
3 Mick Jagger	2,472

British Vocal Personality

1 Cliff Richard	5,785
2 John Lennon	4,613
3 Dusty Springfield	3,408

DECEMBER 22

Cliff and the Shadows open in *Aladdin* at the London Palladium with Una Stubbs and Arthur Askey. It is scheduled to run for 3½ months.

JANUARY 1

The *NME* annual points table for 1964 is published – 30 points for a number 1 down to 1 point for a number 30 record.

1 Beatles	1232
2 Bachelors	1035
3 Rolling Stones	1005
4 Jim Reeves	958
5 Roy Orbison	824
6 Searchers	749
7 Cliff Richard	747
8 Manfred Mann	676
9 Cilla Black	618
10 Hollies	610

Cliff reveals his New Year hopes for 1965: 'I trust that my next film is well-liked. It won't be a musical really, you see, as there's only about four songs in it. I don't think I want to undertake any tours this year. The panto doesn't finish until May 10th and we start filming soon after that. And on top of that I might possibly be making a film of *Aladdin* in 1965 too.'

JANUARY 12

Cliff sends a 'Good Luck' telegram to the Beatles for their London show.

JANUARY 13

Cliff's and Frank Ifield's private companies are taken over by Constellation Investments, bringing them £474,000. The *Daily Express* comments:
'Most of the money concerned is likely to go to the 24-year old pop singer Cliff Richard, which will almost certainly establish him as a millionaire.'

JANUARY 15

Twenty-one year old Freddy Self, former lead singer with Liverpool group the Trends and Cliff's understudy in *Aladdin*, releases a single 'Don't Cry'.

JANUARY 15

'I Could Easily Fall' chart in Britain, Sweden and Holland.

JANUARY

The Shadows' 35-minute film *Rhythm and Greens* goes on release, featuring Cliff as King Canute.

JANUARY

Actress Leslie Caron goes to see Cliff in *Aladdin* at the Palladium.

JANUARY 22

Cliff reveals that his current favourite single is Little Anthony and the Imperials' 'Goin' Out Of My Head'.

31 JANUARY

ABBEY ROAD
Studio session

You Belong To My Heart	*Cliff Richard*
May God Be With You	*(Unissued)*
Sweet And Gentle	*Take Four EP*
Kiss	*Cliff Richard*
Amor, Amor, Amor	*(Unissued)*

Lead Vocal: **Cliff Richard**

Producer: **Norrie Paramor**
Engineer: **Malcolm Addey**
Recorded in: **Studio 2**
Session hours: **5.45pm-7.25pm**

JANUARY

Cliff replies to press suggestions that he intends to retire and settle in Portugal:

'The truth is that sooner or later I do hope to retire from the business. Let's face it, that's the ultimateambition of most entertainers. We can't go on forever and the time must come when we have to quit. I would rather leave while I am at the top than wait for the public to turn its back on me'

FEBRUARY

Columbia release the 'Why Don't They Understand' EP

FEBRUARY

It is reported that Cliff Richard has formed his own film production company, Inter-State Films.

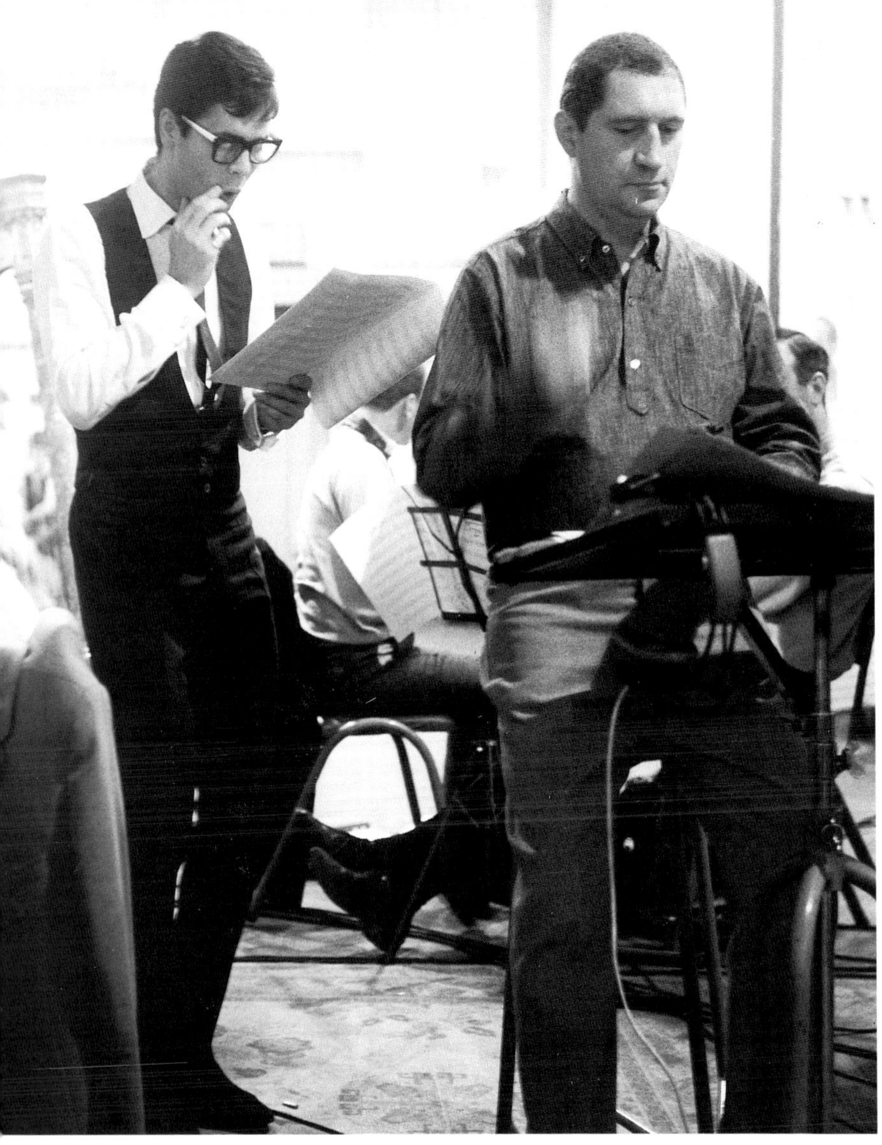

MARCH 14

On *Sunday Night at the London Palladium*, Cliff receives his *New Musical Express* trophy for being voted Top British Singer (for the sixth time).

MARCH 19

Norbert Langerbeins of Cologne writes to the music press, asking which is Cliff's favourite of all the songs he's recorded. Cliff replies: 'There's no doubt about my answer to this question – 'The Twelfth Of Never'. For years and years it was my favourite song ever since I heard it sung by Johnny Mathis, and I was really happy when I recorded it and it was issued as a single. An absolutely beautiful number!'

MARCH

Herman's Hermits record 'Travellin Light' (a 1959 hit for Cliff) for their new LP.

APRIL

Cliff's 'Havin' Fun' is in the Top 10 in Israel.

4 APRIL

ABBEY ROAD
Studio session

Whatcha' Gonna Do About It	*(Unissued)*
Just A Little Bit Too Late	*B-side*

Lead Vocal:	**Cliff Richard**
Guitars:	**Hank Marvin/Bruce Welch**
Bass:	**John Rostill**
Drums:	**Brian Bennett**
Producer:	**Norrie Paramor**
Engineer:	
Recorded in:	**Studio 2**
Session hours:	**2.30pm-5.30pm**

MARCH

'Hits from Aladdin and his Wonderful Lamp' EP released.

MARCH 5

Cliff's 29th single (recorded in Nashville), 'The Minute You're Gone'/'Just Another Guy' is released and reviewed: '"The Minute You're Gone" is unlike anything we've heard from Cliff before. The tune is catchy, simply constructed and easily memorised.'

MARCH 5

Edward Nunn of London N16 writes to the music press pointing out the facial similarity between Cliff and Dirk Bogarde.

MARCH

'I Could Easily Fall' is in the Top 10 in Israel, the Lebanon, Hong Kong, Finland and Holland. In Malaysia it's number 1 with 'Twelfth Of Never' at No. 3.

APRIL 9

In a retrospective look at the pantomime run, Cliff says: 'I haven't been bored once during the entire run. Each show has been interesting, mainly because something has happened at each performance.'

14 APRIL

ABBEY ROAD
Studio session

Boom Boom (That's How My Heart Beats)	*Take Four EP*

Lead Vocal: **Cliff Richard**

Producer: **Norrie Paramor**
Engineers:
Recorded in:
Session hours:

APRIL 15

Columbia release the LP 'Cliff Richard' which includes tracks recorded in London, New York, Nashville and Barcelona.

15 APRIL

ABBEY ROAD
Studio session

Es War Keine So Wunderbar Wie Du (I Could Easily Fall In Love)	*German A-side*
Es Könnte Schon Morgen Sein (The Minute You're Gone)	*German B-side*
It Could Already Be Tomorrow	*(Unissued)*
As Wonderful As You	*(Unissued)*

Lead Vocal: **Cliff Richard**

Producer: **Norrie Paramor**
Engineer:
Recorded in: **Studio 3**
Session hours: **7.00pm-10.00pm**

Cliff's vocals dubbed on to existing tracks for release in Germany.

APRIL 15

'The Minute You're Gone' knocks Unit Four Plus Two's 'Concrete And Clay' off the No.1 spot in the charts.

APRIL

Cliff and the Shadows tele-record three hour-long Spectaculars for ATV to be screened in June.

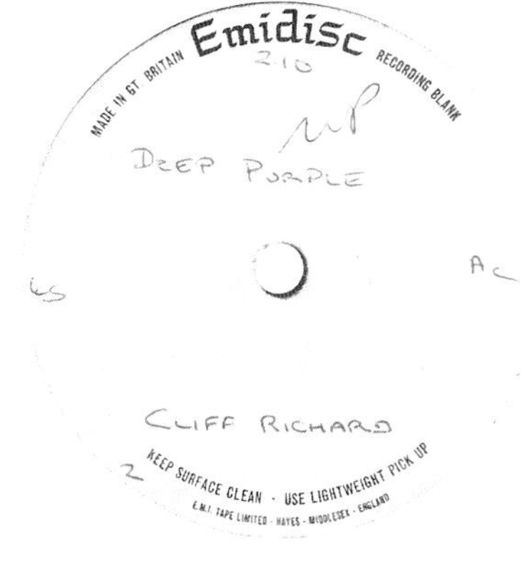

APRIL 21

In the *NME*, 'Alley-Cat' comments: 'In the next poll, Tom Jones could give Cliff Richard stiff opposition!'

APRIL 22

'The Minute You're Gone' is deposed at the top of the charts by the Beatles' 'Ticket To Ride'.

APRIL

Cliff holidays on the Norfolk Broads with the Young Crusaders group from Finchley.

APRIL 30

In reply to *NME*'s 'Alley-cat' comment the previous week, 'Alley-cat' fan writes: 'So "Alley-cat" thinks Cliff has to fear Tom Jones. Never! I saw Tom Jones on the Palladium when he "murdered" 'I Believe' – he's rough.'

10 MAY

ESTUDIOS VALENTIM DE CARVALHO, LISBON
Studio session

Someday (You'll Want Me To Love You) (9)	*Love Is Forever EP*
Have I Told you Lately That I Love You (7)	*Love Is Forever LP*
Look Before You Love (4)	*B-side*
Deep Purple (5)	*(Unissued)*
The Time In Between (7)	*A-side*
Into Each Life Some Rain Must Fall (9)	*Finders Keepers*

Lead Vocal: **Cliff RIchard**
Guitars: **Hank Marvin/Bruce Welch**
Bass: **John Rostill**
Drums: **Brian Bennett**

Producer: **Norrie Paramor**
Engineer: **Malcolm Addey**
Recorded in:
Session hours: **2.30pm-5.30pm/7.00pm-10.00pm**

13/14 MAY

ESTUDIOS VALENTIM DE CARVALHO, LISBON

Studio session

O Mio Signore (The Questions) (4)	*When In Rome*
Come Prima (For The First Time) (4)	*When In Rome*
Concerto D'Automno (Autumn Concerto) (4)	*When In Rome*
Casa Senza Finestre	*When In Rome*
Arrivederci Roma (4)	*When In Rome*
Legata Ad Un Granello Di Sabbia (3)	*When In Rome*
Per Un Bacio D'Amor	*When In Rome*
Che Cosa Del Mia Amore (5)	*When In Rome*
Carina (5)	*When In Rome*
Nel Blu Dipinto Di Blu (5)	*When In Rome*
Dicitencello Vuie (Just Say I Love Her)	*When In Rome*
Na Voce, 'Na Chitarra, E'o Poco 'E Lunu (8) (I Only Know I Love You)	*Italian Release*
Maria Ninguem (Maria's Her Name)	*When In Rome*
Non L'Ascoltare (Don't Talk To Him)	*When In Rome*
Tu, Tu Mi Piaci (True, True Lovin')	*Italian Release*

Lead Vocal: **Cliff Richard**

Producer: **John Lee**
Engineer: **Malcolm Addey**
Session hours:

The backing tracks of the original recordings were used on the following tracks: Casa Senza Finestre (House Without Windows)/ Maria Ninguem (Maria's Her Name)/ Non L'Ascoltare (Don't Talk To Him)/ Na Voce, 'Na Chitarra, E'oPoco 'E Lunu (I Only Know I Love You)/ Tu, Tu, Mi Piaci (True , True Lovin')

MAY 18

The *Daily Mirror* reports: 'Cliff Richard and Frank Ifield have made £256,000 profit on paper on the Stock Exchange in four months – last night Constellation shares went up to 10s. making Cliff's and Frank's shares worth £730,000.'

MAY

'Look In My Eyes Maria' EP released.

MAY

In an interview with *Disco* magazine, Cliff says that he does not know what happens to the greater part of his money: 'I leave it to the businessmen. All I've asked is that they tell me six months before I go broke so that I can get out.'

JUNE 4

Cliff's 30th single is released and reviewed – 'On My Word' (recorded in the US) and 'Just A Little Bit Too Late': 'It's set to a shuffle rhythm with a subtle Latin flavour, plus brass and chirping girls – Cliff sings in huskily appealing low register which contrasts effectively with the bounding beat.'

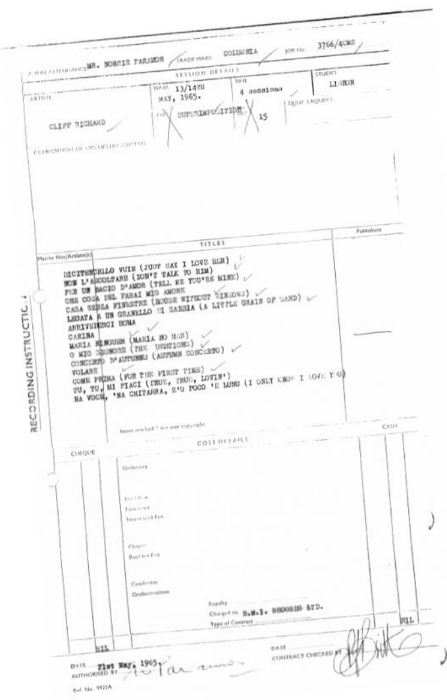

10 JUNE

ABBEY ROAD

Studio session

Long Ago	*Love Is Forever*
I'll Walk Alone	*Love Is Forever*
A Summer Place	*Love Is Forever*
My Foolish Heart	*Love Is Forever*

Lead Vocal: **Cliff Richard**
The Norrie Paramor Orchestra

Producer: **Norrie Paramor**
Engineer: **Malcolm Addey**
Recorded in: **Studio 2**
Session hours: **7.00pm-10.00pm**

JUNE 13

Cliff and the Shadows appear on *Sunday Night At The London Palladium.*

JUNE 18

Cliff admits that he actually buys the Beatles records but not the Rolling Stones, and of the current groups around he thinks the two likely to stay the course are the Beatles and the Searchers.

JUNE

The *NME* publish their points chart for the first six months of 1965 (30 points for a number 1 down to 1 point for the number 30 position):

1 Seekers	552
2 Sandie Shaw	481
3 Beatles	367
4 Cliff Richard	359

5 Rolling Stones	342
6 Animals	330
7 Kinks	317
8 Them	312
9 Marianne Faithfull	310
10 Herman's Hermits	309

JULY 8

Cliff and the Shadows fly to Scandinavia.

JULY 9

Cliff and the Shadows open their six-city tour with two dates in Copenhagen. Four thousand people, average age 15 years, attend the two appearances to hear Cliff sing numbers like 'Don't Talk To Him', 'Constantly', 'Angel', 'Bachelor Boy', 'Do You Wanna Dance?', 'On The Beach' and 'Hi Heel Sneakers'. The Shadows also do their own set, as do supporting Danish acts the Defenders and the Rocking Ghosts.

JULY

Cliff appears on the front cover of *Rave* magazine.

JULY

Cliff's Aladdin understudy, singer Freddie Self, changes his name to Freddie Ryder – chosen through a Radio Caroline competition.

JULY 16

Cliff at No.1 in Malaysia with 'The Minute You're Gone'.

JULY 23

Cliff is at No.2 in the Israeli chart with his version of 'Sway'.

JULY 25

In an interview with *Disc* magazine, Cliff reveals: 'I never eat lunch , apart from something like cheese and biscuits. I don't even have breakfast or a good meal when I get home in the evening – I've got to look after my weight.'

JULY 26

Cliff and the Shadows appear for half a week at Southend Odeon with Des O'Connor.

AUGUST

The music papers pose the question, 'Why has Cliff Richard never been on the TV show *Ready Steady Go*?'

AUGUST 6

Cliff and the Shadows fly out to Bahrain to begin a tour of Spain, France and Switzerland, taking in Vienna, Marseilles, Casablanca, Zurich and Geneva.

AUGUST 13

Cliff's 31st single is released: 'The Time In Between'/'Look Before You Love'. Derek Johnson of the *NME* writes: 'Back again with the Shadows after two American recorded singles, this is a

French song with a new English lyric which the Shadows were originally going to record.' Says Shadows Hank Marvin: 'We were thinking of cutting 'The Time In Between' but when Cliff heard it he was so enthusiastic about it that we passed it over to him.'

AUGUST

A plethora of artists are in the South of France at the same time as Cliff and the Shadows – Dionne Warwick, Francoise Hardy, Rolling Stone Keith Richard, and Paul McCartney's brother from the Scaffold group Mike McGear.

AUGUST

Columbia release Cliff's 'When In Rome' LP.

AUGUST

In an interview with *Disc* magazine, Cliff says: 'I would like to get married very much eventually... I've no one particular in mind at present. There's been a couple of false alarms which I wouldn't like to happen again.'

AUGUST

It is revealed that Cliff's next film will go into production on November 1. Cliff's manager, Peter Gormley, describes it as 'altogether more sophisticated than his last pictures'.

SEPTEMBER 2

Cliff performs at the ABC Northampton at a charity show in aid of a Milton Keynes church rebuilding fund.

MONO/STEREO

RECORDING SHEET

Sheet: 1 of: Class: Pop. Overall Title: 4T REMIX TO STEREO. Date of Session: 15TH OCT 65. Job No: 35013

ARTISTIC INFORMATION

Artiste(s) and/or cast: CLIFF RICHARDS
Conductor:
Orchestra:
Accompaniment:
Art. Dept. Rep.: MR. N. PARAMOR.

COSTING INFORMATION

Materials used: 1 x 77
Session booked time: 2:30-5:30
Session actual: 2:30 3:20
Set-up/playback: ½
Order number:
Company: COLUMBIA
Studio/control room: 65
Engineers: MA. PM.

Titles and Matrix Nos.	Author/Composer/Publisher	Reel Numbers	False Starts	Take No.	Take Details From	To	Dur.	M	Remarks
OUR DAY WILL COME.		57967	RS	1	COMPLETE		2:49	BEST.	(T4 57788.)
MEDITATION.		"	RS	1	"		3:08	BEST	(1 ")
QUIET NIGHTS		"	RS	1	"		3:32	BEST.	(T3
QUANDO QUANDO QUANDO.		"	RS	1	"		2:14	BEST.	(T3 57813)
ESO BESO.		"	RS	1			3:38	BEST	(T3 ")

SEPTEMBER 15

First of three ATV Cliff Richard and the Shadows specials shown on ITV.

SEPTEMBER 22

Second ATV Cliff and the Shadows special screened.
Cliff films US TV show for Ed Sullivan.

SEPTEMBER 24

Mary Langley of Barnsley has this letter published in the *NME:* 'Wasn't 'Time In Between' a waste of time? Please, Cliff, stop making lovey-dovey records. Don't you realise that most of your fans are adults now? I often hear records that I wish you'd made. Sorry, I know you don't really like critics but I see so many artists get to the top with trash, and I do so want you to show them that you're the best.'

SEPTEMBER 24-26

One-night stands in Britain.

SEPTEMBER 29

Third ATV Cliff and the Shadows special shown on ITV.

OCTOBER 1-3

One-night stands in Britain.

OCTOBER 1

Cliff is pictured by a hair-conscious press (in this year of the British beat boom) sporting a fringe.

4 OCTOBER

ABBEY ROAD
Studio session

The Girl From Ipanema (6)	*Kinda Latin*
Quiet Nights Of Quiet Stars (3)	*Kinda Latin*
Our Day Will Come (4)	*Kinda Latin*
Meditation (1)	*Kinda Latin*

Lead Vocal:	**Cliff Richard**
	The Bernard Ebbinghouse Orchestra
Producer:	**Norrie Paramor**
Engineer:	**Peter Bown**
Recorded in:	**Studio 2**
Session hours:	**7.00pm-9.30pm**

OCTOBER

Columbia release Cliff's 'Take Four' EP.

5 OCTOBER

ABBEY ROAD
Studio session

The Night	*B-side*

Lead Vocal:	**Cliff Richard**
Producer:	**Norrie Paramor**
Engineer:	
Recorded in:	**Studio 2**
Session hours:	

5 OCTOBER

ABBEY ROAD
Studio session

The Night	*B-side*

Lead Vocal: **Cliff Richard**

Producer: **Norrie Paramor**
Engineer:
Recorded in: **Studio 2**
Session hours:

7 OCTOBER

ABBEY ROAD
Studio session

Quando, Quando, Quando (3)	*Kinda Latin*
Eso Beso (3)	*Kinda Latin*
Fly Me To The Moon (6)	*Kinda Latin*
Blame It On The Bossa Nova (3)	*Kinda Latin*

Lead Vocal: **Cliff Richard**
The Reg Guest Orchestra

Producer: **Norrie Paramor**
Engineer: **Peter Bown**
Recorded in: **Studio 2**
Session hours: **7.00pm-10.15pm**

OCTOBER 10

Cliff Richard and the Shadows, confirming their status as truly international artists, fly across the Iron Curtain to Warsaw to play two historic concerts at the state-run Roma theatre in the Polish capital, the appearances having been organised by the Polish government.

OCTOBER 13

Cliff and the Shadows fly back to London.

OCTOBER 14

Cliff celebrates his 25th birthday in a typically jet-setting style as he and the Shadows fly to the Lebanon to play concerts in the capital Beirut.

OCTOBER 21

The BBC's Light Programme presents *The Cliff Richard Story*, a biographical radio documentary which is written and produced by Peter Noble.

22 OCTOBER

ABBEY ROAD
Studio session

Concrete And Clay (7)	*Kinda Latin*
Blowin' In The Wind (9)	*Kinda Latin*
One Note Samba (4)	*Kinda Latin*
Come Closer To Me (6)	*Kinda Latin*

Lead Vocal: **Cliff Richard**
The Les Reed Orchestra

Producer: **Norrie Paramor**
Engineer: **Peter Bown**
Recorded in: **Studio 3**
Session hours: **2.30pm-6.00pm**

OCTOBER

Cliff's 'Angel' in the Hong Kong Top 10.

27 OCTOBER

ABBEY ROAD
Studio session

Glaub Nur Mir (On My Word)	*German B-side*
Nur Bei Dir Bin Ich Zu Haus (Wind Me Up)	*German A-side*

Lead Vocal: **Cliff Richard**

Producer:
Engineer:
Recorded in: **Studio 2**
Session hours: **7.00pm-10.00pm**

Superimposition of German lyrics onto German backing tracks.

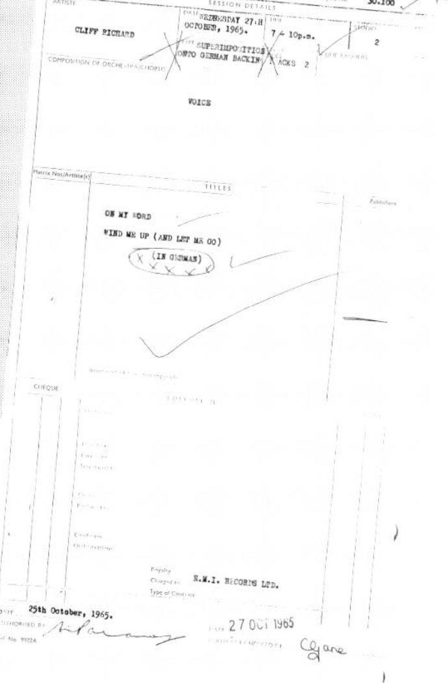

A/R IN ATTENDANCE MR. OTTO DEMLER
TRADE MARK COLUMBIA
JOB No. 30.100
ARTISTE CLIFF RICHARD
SESSION DETAILS
DATE WEDNESDAY 27TH OCTOBER, 1965.
TIME 7 – 10p.m.
STUDIO 2
SUPERIMPOSITION ONTO GERMAN BACKING TRACKS 2
COMPOSITION OF ORCHESTRA/CHORUS
VOICE
Matrix Nos/Artiste(s)
TITLES
ON MY WORD
WIND ME UP (AND LET ME GO)
(IN GERMAN)
Publishers
CHEQUE
Royalty Charged to E.M.I. RECORDS LTD.
Type of Contract
DATE 25th October, 1965.
AUTHORISED BY
DATE 27 OCT 1965

OCTOBER 28

Cliff and the Shadows become the first British artists to play at the French film industry's Gala Concert. It is staged at the Paris Marigny Theatre and they play in the presence of Princess Grace of Monaco. Cliff and the Shadows then go on to play a week of one-nighters in France.

OCTOBER

Ronnie Gabay of Jerusalem has a letter published in *NME* which

proclaims, amongst other things, that 'Cliff is still the most popular artist in Israel.'

OCTOBER 29

Rolling Stone guitarist Keith Richard reveals that he and singer Mick Jagger have written a song called 'Blue Turns To Grey' which Cliff Richard is going to record.

OCTOBER 29

Cliff's 32nd single 'Wind Me Up (Let Me Go)'/'The Night' is released. One reviewer says:
'It was recorded in Nashville, like his number 1 'The Minute You're Gone', though I don't think it'll be such a big hit as that. Slight suggestion of sweet corn.'

NOVEMBER 5

Cliff appears on ITV's *Thank Your Lucky Stars* with Newcastle R&B group the Animals, singer Ian Whitcomb and 'Moon River' hitmaker Danny Williams.

NOVEMBER 12

Following the mediocre receptions for 'Wind Me Up' by disc jockeys, record reviewers and the *Juke Box Jury* panel on television, Cliff replies to the critics both with another Top 20 chart entry and verbally:
'It just shows that you have to take adverse criticism with a pinch of salt. Frankly, I've given up worrying – it's impossible to please everyone all the time. Actually, it was Bruce Welch's brainwave to release 'Wind Me Up' as a single, and it was his suggestion that we released 'It's All In The Game' and 'The Twelfth Of Never' as singles.'
On the film front, Cliff comments:
'The last news to be announced was that we would make this film together and later start work on the screen adaptation of *Aladdin* some time in 1966. Now all that has changed and *Aladdin* is definitely going to be the next film. We have already returned the script three or four times for various alterations – for one thing, I wanted a bit more action and swashbuckling and less drama sequences.'

17 NOVEMBER

ABBEY ROAD
Studio session

I Love You The Way You Are	*(Unissued)*
I Still Send Her Flowers	*(Unissued)*
Close To Cathy	*Two A Penny*
Visions	*A-side*

Lead Vocal:	**Cliff Richard**
	The Bernard Ebbinghouse Orchestra
	The Mike Sammes Singers
Producer:	**Norrie Paramor**
Engineer:	**Malcolm Addey**
Recorded in:	**Studio 2**
Session hours:	**7.00pm-10.55pm**

RECORDING SHEET

Sheet: 1 of ... Class: Popular Overall Title: Mono Remix From 4 Track Date of Session: 1st Dec '65 Job No: 35,041 30,106

ARTISTIC INFORMATION — Artiste(s) and/or Cast: Cliff Richard; Conductor: ; Orchestra: ; Accompaniment: ; Art. Dept. Rep.: Mr N Paramor

COSTING INFORMATION — Materials Used: 1 x 7; Session Booked Time: 2.30 – 5.30; Session Actual: 2.30 – 4.45; Set-up/Playback: 2 / –; Order Number: ; Company: Columbia; Studio/Control Room: 65; Engineers: P.V. / M.B.

Titles and Matrix Nos.	Author/Composer/Publisher	Reel Numbers	False Starts	Take No.	From	To	Dur.	M	Remarks
Chim Chim Cheree *		E 58442 Mono		R.M. 1	Complete		3.14	Best	From Take 5
Sooner Or Later *				R.M. 1	Complete		2.19	Best	From Take 4
A Spoonful Of Sugar *				R.M. 1	Complete		2.55	Best	From Take 7
Zip-A-Dee-Doo-Dah *				R.M. 1	Complete		2.52	Best	From Take 4
Visions				R.M. 1	Complete		2.61	Best	From Take 3
Close To Cathy				R.M. 1	Complete		2.36	Best	From Take 4
I Still Send Her Flowers				R.M. 1	Complete		2.24	Best	From Take 4
I Love You The Way You Are				R.M. 1	Complete		2.14	Best	From Take 8

NOVEMBER

Cliff's 'Love Is Forever' LP is released.

18 NOVEMBER

ABBEY ROAD
Studio session

Sooner Or Later (4)	*(Unissued)*
A Spoonful Of Sugar (7)	*(Unissued)*
Zip-A-Dee-Doo-Dah (4)	*(Unissued)*
Chim Chim Cheree (5)	*(Unissued)*

Lead Vocal:	**Cliff Richard**
Orchestra	
Producer:	**Norrie Paramor**
Engineer:	**Malcolm Addey**
Recorded in:	**Studio 2**
Session hours:	**7.00pm-10.30pm**

LATE NOVEMBER

Various one-night stands around the country.

NOVEMBER 24

In an interview with the *Daily Express,* Cliff reveals: 'I now arrange my work to have weekends free for youth activities. All my closest friends are teachers.'

DECEMBER

Cliff reveals that neither he nor the Shadows have managerial contracts with Peter Gormley.

DECEMBER 3

Cliff talks to journalist Alan Smith about new recordings: 'One song we've just completed is called 'Kinda Latin' and another is 'Sing A Song Of Disney' with numbers from Disney films like 'Chim-Chim Cheree'. I used to write a lot, but just lately I haven't been able to get the inspiration. I think I've lost my contact. I don't do the same kind of songs I used to because I've had to change as the years have gone by. I can't stay for seven years what I was at 17. If I did, it would be bad for my career and bad for my ego.'

DECEMBER 4

Cliff and the Shadows headline a charity concert at his old school, Cheshunt Boys' School, with Mark Wynter, Unit Four Plus Two, Al Saxon and Elkie Brooks.

DECEMBER 10

The *NME* publish their 1965 poll results:

World Male Singer

1 Elvis Presley	6,002
2 Cliff Richard	4,848
3 Gene Pitney	3,526

World Music Personality

1 Elvis Presley	4,197
2 John Lennon	2,656
3 Bob Dylan	2,548
4 Cliff Richard	2,423

British Male Singer

1 Cliff Richard	6,599
2 Paul McCartney	2,892
3 Mick Jagger	2,736

British Vocal Personality

1 John Lennon	5,631
2 Cliff Richard	5,407
3 Mick Jagger	3,002

Best New Disc Of The Year

1 Rolling Stones	'Satisfaction'
2 Beatles	'Help'
3 Rolling Stones	'Get Off My Cloud'
4 Paul Mc Cartney	'Yesterday'
5 Cliff Richard	'The Minute You're Gone'

Cliff comments on his success in the *NME:*
I regard myself as a very fortunate person, for this is the eighth time you have bestowed poll honours on me – the first in 1958 was as "Best New Singer". I want you to know that I value it deeply.'

DECEMBER 25

Cliff Richard's Christmas Cheer is shown on BBC Television from 2.15 – 3.00pm. It stars Cliff, the Shadows and Frank Ifield.

DECEMBER 31

The *NME* Annual Points Championship results are published (30 points for a number 1, down to 1 point for a number 30):

1 Rolling Stones	836
2 Seekers	813
3 Beatles	760
4 Animals	656
5 Sandie Shaw	649
6 Cliff Richard	631
7 Ken Dodd	617
8 Yardbirds	607
9 Manfred Mann	569
10 Hollies	567

DECEMBER 31

G. J. Howard of Leicester has a letter published in the music press:
'Cliff Richard need not in any way feel surprised at being voted Top British Male Singer for the seventh year. For sheer professionalism there is no one who comes anywhere near him. Unless some miracle occurs during the next five years, he should still be on top for a long, long time.'

DECEMBER

In an interview with the London *Evening Standard*, Cliff reveals that two of his sisters have become Jehovah's Witnesses.

1966–1967

The Records 1966 – 1967

All the singles that were released in 1966 became top twenty hits. 'In The Country' taken from the CINDERELLA cast album was the one with the most impressive chart placing, but somehow the momentum was not maintained by the album. Given the quality of the previous single 'Time Drags By' from the FINDERS KEEPERS soundtrack it seems incredible that it did not reach higher than the No.10 spot. Of the four singles released the following year, no fewer than three reached the top ten. The single that did not do so well – 'I'll Come Running' – failed to reach the top twenty, stalling at No.26.

Two of the five albums released in this period did well and reached the top ten of the album charts. KINDA LATIN featured Latin flavoured material with songs like 'Blame It On The Bossa Nova', 'The Girl From Ipanema' and 'One Note Samba', a far cry not only from rock 'n' roll, but also from pop music as it was developing at that time. But the album sold well enough to reach No.9. The follow up album, the soundtrack of the film *Finders Keepers,* was even stronger than KINDA LATIN, and had a top ten single to spur interest. The album outdid all the others of this period by reaching the No.6 spot and staying on the chart for 18 weeks. DON'T STOP ME NOW was released next, but as there was no hit single to boost sales the album suffered chartwise whereas it could have been a smash album with its combination of some contemporary hits of the time and some rock 'n' roll standards. Sales of Cliff's first sacred album GOOD NEWS were not impressive, but considering the limited market for this kind of music the figures were still impressive enough.

The same trend was reflected in the sales of the CAROL SINGERS EP that featured Cliff singing carols accappella with a group of music teachers. None of the EPs released in this period notched up enough sales to make it to the EP or singles charts, even though some of the material on some of the EPs appeared only in that format.

The Sessions 1966 – 1967

Of the material selected for the April soundtrack session, 'Time Drags By' stands out as the one to take advantage of the multi-track system to good effect. For this, a basic track was laid down after which Cliff and the Shadows double-tracked their vocals eventually resulting in eight vocals on the record. Surprisingly, this did not become a major hit but it showed conclusively that Cliff was still a force to be reckoned with and could make records that were artistically significant. Work continued on FINDERS KEEPERS through to September with the Shadows providing musical and vocal backing joined by the Bernard Ebbinghouse Orchestra. It is unknown whether the sessions on 5 and 13 May were held at Abbey Road or Olympic Studios, or in fact at both, for Cliff and the Shadows to put down their tracks for the full length puppet feature *Thunderbirds Are Go!*

In October, a variety of material was taped for the DON'T STOP ME NOW album, the LA LA LA LA LA EP, and two well crafted pop songs for single release. The Bernard Ebbinghouse Orchestra was invited to provide musical accompaniment again as a result of their outstanding work on the previous sessions.

As had happened before with the *Aladdin* pantomime at the London Palladium, *Cinderella* necessitated cast sessions with all the material for the album being recorded through to November with, of course, the Shadows providing the score and musical accompaniment, and the Mike Sammes Singers adding some excellent vocal back-ups. Jackie Lee duetted with Cliff on 'Wouldn't It Be Nice' taped at one of the November sessions. The January/February sessions provided the remainder of the material needed to fill out the DON'T STOP ME NOW album. Some breathtaking rock performances were taped with musical backing from the Mike Leander Orchestra. The sessions in April and May were Cliff's first excursion into the gospel field, and provided all the tracks for the GOOD NEWS album. Sacred music had become very much a part of Cliff's life in the wake of his Christian conviction, so it was only natural for him to record this type of material.

After the July session that provided a number of songs for the TWO A PENNY soundtrack, Cliff did not enter the studio again until September when work was geared towards producing a Christmas EP. The tracks for CAROL SINGERS were done without any musical backing or orchestral arrangements, and were performed acappella with the Mastersingers, a Christian group of music teachers. All the tracks recorded on this session with the exception of 'The Holly And The Ivy' were spliced from several different takes to produce the finished masters. It is probable that this could have been the result of recording the selections in acappella. Although five of the tracks were released on the EP at the time, it would be a further twenty-three years before 'Twelve Days Of Christmas' and 'The Holly And The Ivy' would be issued. The two sessions on 27 and 28 September produced Italian and German versions of recent material.

Unfortunately the documentation filed at Abbey Road is rather misleading and it is unclear on which specific days the various-backing tracks and vocal tracks were recorded. From the session in October, 'All My Love' was chosen as an A-side in favour of 'I Only Live To Love You', although the latter was issued as a single in overseas countries.

For the last recordings of the year, and to have enough material for an album, Columbia simply recorded one of Cliff's live dates in Japan and, although there was some reshuffling as far as the Cliff classics went, the inclusion of some newer songs did not really offer anything new from a musical point of view. However, CLIFF IN JAPAN became a worldwide top seller appealing to the international audience the album was aimed at. 'Bachelor Boy' and 'It's All In The Game' were two extra tracks released only on the Japanese issue of the album.

17 JANUARY

ABBEY ROAD
Studio session

Blue Turns To Grey	*A-side*
Somebody Loses	*B-side*

Lead Vocal:	**Cliff Richard**
Guitars:	**Hank Marvin/Bruce Welch**
Bass:	**John Rostill**
Drums:	**Brian Bennett**
Producer:	**Norrie Paramor**
Engineers:	
Recorded in:	**Studio 2**
Session hours:	**7.00pm-11.15pm**

MARCH

It is reported that Cliff's next film may not be a movie version of the *Aladdin* pantomime after all, as several supporting artists are not available.

MARCH 22

Cliff appears on *Pop Inn* with Harry Secombe, Roy Orbison, Cilla Black and Crispian St Peters.

MARCH 26

Cliff and the Shadows appear on ABC TV's *Thank Your Lucky Stars* with Dusty Springfleld, Dave Dee, Dozy, Beaky, Mick and Tich, and Billy Joe Royal.

MARCH 28

Cliff and the Shadows top the bill on the BBC Light Programme's Monday lunch-time radio show.

APRIL 1

The *New Musical Express'* 'Alley-cat' – a column that is famous for rarely pulling its punches – makes the observation that Cliff and the Shadows looked decidedly dated on their appearance on *Thank Your Lucky Stars.*

APRIL 3

Cliff Richard and the Shadows appear at the *Daily Express* Record Star Show at the Empire Pool, Wembley, which is in aid of the Spastics Society.

APRIL

'When In Rome' EP is released.

APRIL

At the personal invitation of the Bishop of Coventry, Cliff takes part in a service at the Albert Hall, London, to mark the 25th Anniversary of the Abbey Christian Community.

APRIL

Cliff talks to the press:
On films: '*Aladdin* has now been postponed.'
On his new LP: 'Do you know what's given me the greatest kick in the preparation of the LP 'Kinda Latin'? It's the fact that the sleeve is going to feature a picture of my sister which I took myself.'
On holidays: 'I plan to go camping in Cornwall for a fortnight with the Crusader Union, and then I hope to have two or three weeks at my villa in Portugal.'
And on his future: 'It's perfectly true that I would like to take up teaching at some time in the future. After all, I have to be sensible and think ahead, because I can't expect to remain a star for the rest of my life. If I do eventually decide to retire, it's more likely to be in the region of five years' time.'

APRIL 8

BBC TV screens the *Stars Organisation for Spastics Special Star Show*, starring Cliff and the Shadows, Manfred Mann, the Fortunes, Sandie Shaw, Georgie Fame, Adam Faith, Wayne Fontana, Paul and Barry Ryan, Chris Andrews, Kenny Ball and Jackie Trent.

APRIL 15

Cliff's 1966 Christmas plans are revealed. He is to play Buttons in the Palladium production of *Cinderella*, scheduled to open a few days before Christmas and run until Easter 1967.

26 APRIL

ABBEY ROAD

Film soundtrack recordings for Finders Keepers

Oh Senorita (10)	*Finders Keepers*
Finders Keepers (1)	*Finders Keepers*
Time Drags By (4)	*A-side*

Lead Vocal:	**Cliff Richard**
Guitars:	**Hank Marvin/Bruce Welch**
Bass:	**John Rostill**
Drums:	**Brian Bennett**
Producer:	**Norrie Paramor**
Engineer:	**Malcolm Addey/Peter Vince/ Richard Lush**
Recorded in:	**Studio 2/3**
Session hours:	**2.30pm-5.30pm/7.00pm-12.30pm**

27 APRIL

ABBEY ROAD

Film Soundtrack recordings for Finders Keepers

My Way	*Finders Keepers*
Finders Keepers/My Way/Paella/Fiesta	*Finders Keepers*
This Day (6)	*(Unissued)*

Lead Vocal:	**Cliff Richard**
Guitars:	**Hank Marvin/Bruce Welch**
Bass:	**John Rostill**
Drums:	**Brian Bennett**
Producer:	**Norrie Paramor**
Engineers:	**Peter Vince/Richard Lush**
Recorded in:	**Studio 2**
Session hours:	**7.00pm-2.00am**

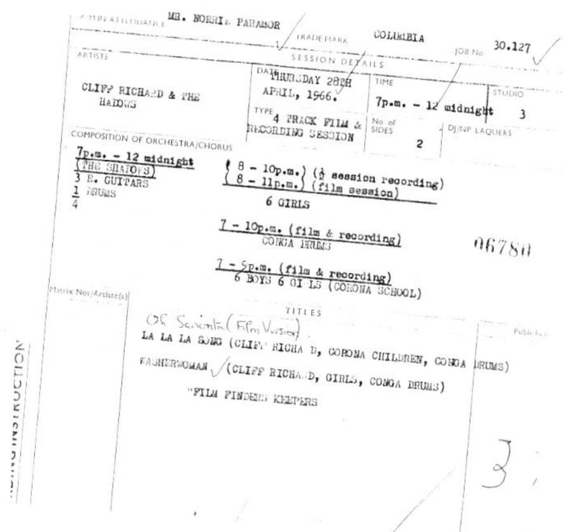

MR. NORRIE PARAMOR — TRADE MARK: COLUMBIA — JOB No. 30.127

ARTISTE: CLIFF RICHARD & THE SHADOWS

SESSION DETAILS — DATE: THURSDAY 28TH APRIL, 1966. — TIME: 7p.m. - 12 midnight — STUDIO: 3

TYPE: 4 TRACK FILM & RECORDING SESSION — No. of SIDES: 2 — DJ/NP LAQUERS

COMPOSITION OF ORCHESTRA/CHORUS

7p.m. - 12 midnight (THE SHADOWS)
3 E. GUITARS
1 DRUMS
4

8 - 10p.m. (½ session recording)
8 - 11p.m. (film session)
6 GIRLS

7 - 10p.m. (film & recording)
CONGA DRUMS

06780

7 - 5p.m. (film & recording)
6 BOYS 6 GIRLS (CORONA SCHOOL)

Matrix Nos/Artiste(s) — TITLES

Oh Senorita (Film Version)
LA LA LA SONG (CLIFF RICHARD, CORONA CHILDREN, CONGA DRUMS)
WASHERWOMAN (CLIFF RICHARD, GIRLS, CONGA DRUMS)
"FILM FINDERS KEEPERS

3

28 APRIL

ABBEY ROAD

Film soundtrack recordings for Finders Keepers

Washerwoman (2)	*Finders Keepers*
Oh Senorita (4)	*Film Version*
La La La Song (1)	*B-side*

Lead Vocal:	**Cliff Richard**
Guitars:	**Hank Marvin/Bruce Welch**
Bass:	**John Rostill**
Drums:	**Brian Bennett**
Conga Drums:	
Vocals:	**Corona Children**
Producer:	**Norrie Paramor**
Engineers:	**Peter Vince/Richard Lush**
Recorded in:	**Studio 3**
Session hours:	**2.30pm-6.00pm/7.00pm-midnight**

APRIL 30

Cliff and the Shadows feature in ABC TV's tenth anniversary programme *The ABC of ABC* with the Vernons Girls and Valerie Mountain.

30 APRIL

Abbey Road
Film soundtrack recordings for Finders Keepers

Paella	*Finders Keepers*
Fiesta	*Finders Keepers*

Lead Vocal:	**Cliff Richard**
Guitars:	**Hank Marvin/Bruce Welch**
Bass:	**John Rostill**
Drums:	**Brian Bennett**
Producer:	**Norrie Paramor**
Engineers:	
Recorded in:	**Studio 3**
Session hours:	**7.00pm-1.30am**

APRIL 30

Cliff and the Shadows appear at the *NME* Poll Winners' Concert. Among the other artists appearing are the Beatles, Rolling Stones, Walker Brothers., Small Faces, Yardbirds, Herman's Hermits and Roy Orbison. Cliff sings 'Blue Turns To Grey', 'The Minute You're Gone' and 'Bachelor Boy'.

MAY

It is reported that Cliff's former girl-friend, Jackie Irving, is currently seeing Adam Faith.

5 MAY

Abbey Road
Film soundtrack recordings for Thunderbirds Are Go

Shooting Star	*Thunderbirds Are Go EP*

Lead Vocal:	**Cliff Richard**
Guitars:	**Hank Marvin/Bruce Welch**
Bass:	**John Rostill**
Drums:	**Brian Bennett**
Producer:	**Norrie Paramor**
Engineers:	
Recorded in:	
Session hours:	

MAY 8

The first half of the *NME* poll concert featuring Cliff is screened.

MAY 9

Cliff and the Shadows co-star with Tom Jones and the Squires in a BBC 2-hour radio special, *Let the Good Times Roll!* Also featured are the Hollies, Lulu and compere Ray Orchard.

MAY

Cliff Richard Ltd is formed.

13 MAY

Abbey Road
Studio session

Yours	*German A-side*
Was Ist Dabei (The Time In Between)	*German B-side*

Lead Vocal:	**Cliff Richard**
Producer:	**Norrie Paramor**
Engineers:	**Peter Vince/Richard Lush**
Recorded in:	**Studio 3**
Session hours:	**7.00pm-10.00pm**

MAY 9-13

Final auditions to select supporting artists for Cliff's new film take place.

22 MAY

Abbey Road
Studio session

What Would I Do (For The Love Of A Girl)	*B-side*

Lead Vocal:	**Cliff Richard**
Guitars:	**Hank Marvin/Bruce Welch**
Bass:	**John Rostill**
Drums:	**Brian Bennett**
Producer:	**David Paramor/Norrie Paramor**
Engineers:	**Peter Vince/Richard Lush**
Recorded in:	**Studio 3**
Session hours:	**7.00pm-10.00pm**

MAY 27

Cliff's fifth film, *Finders Keepers*, starts production at Pinewood Studios. The picture is a light-hearted musical comedy about a nuclear bomb which is lost in the sea off the coast of Spain; the supporting cast includes the Shadows, and noted British character actors Robert Morley, Peggy Mount and Graham Stark. George Brown, who conceived the story, is the producer.

JUNE 3

Marlon Brando's girl-friend, 20-year-old South American actress Viviane Ventura, is named announced as Cliff's leading lady in *Finders Keepers*.

JUNE 3

In a letter to the music press, Mary Maynard of Richmond in Surrey says: 'Although I admire much of Cliff Richard's work, I can only deplore the proposed story for his next film. The lost nuclear bomb is hardly a suitable story for a "light-hearted musical comedy". Surely Mr Richard realises that this serious and dangerous situation is not fitting for any kind of frivolity. Nuclear bombings are no laughing matter.'

JUNE

It is announced that Terry Scott will appear at the London Palladium in Cliff and the Shadows' Christmas pantomime.

JUNE 4

Cliff and the Shadows appear on the 400th edition of the BBC's *Saturday Club* with Billy Fury and Marianne Faithfull.

4 JUNE

ABBEY ROAD

Film Soundtrack Recordings for Finders Keepers

Spanish Music	*Finders Keepers*
This Day	*Finders Keepers*

Lead Vocal:	**Cliff Richard**
Guitars:	**Hank Marvin/Bruce Welch**
Bass:	**John Rostill**
Drums:	**Brian Bennett**
Producer:	**Norrie Paramor**
Engineer:	
Recorded in:	**Studio 3**
Session hours:	**2.30pm-5.30pm (Shadows)/7.00pm-10.00pm**

JUNE 16

Cliff takes the stage at a Billy Graham Crusade meeting at London's Earls Court to sing 'It's No Secret' and announces that he is a Christian to an audience of 25,000. He also declares his intention to embark on a three-year divinity course when his pantomime finishes in April 1967.

JUNE 18

Cliff's mother, Dorothy, marries East End undertaker and their former chauffeur, Derek Bodkin. Says Cliff: 'I didn't know until this morning when they phoned me. I bought some wine and arrived for the celebrations after the ceremony.'

JUNE

Cliff talks to the press about various topics:

Finders Keepers:

'I think this is going to come out okay. We do about nine weeks in the studio and then go to the South Coast for some exteriors, and we have doubles in Spain doing other exteriors. I like all the songs in the picture, but think that 'This Day' and 'Time Drags By' are sort of stand-outs.'

On the set of *Finders Keepers*

His Christian activities:

'Someone suggested it is sissy to proclaim your Christian beliefs, but I don't think it is; I feel great all the time and know it is because of my beliefs. I've felt this way for two years now and it has relieved me of the petty jealousy one gets in show business and helped me to help others. I did a Billy Graham study course of about five weeks and found it stimulating; then I had a letter asking me if I would speak at a meeting. I was petrified. There was a desk in front of me and I put my arms on it as I spoke. Then, when I sang, I put my arms to my sides and had terrible pins and needles. I tried to raise my arms to emphasise the words in the song, but I couldn't, and at the end I walked off with my arms still pinned to my sides!'

Cliff also discussed the song he had performed at Earls Court, 'It's No Secret (What God Can Do)' and said that. although he liked Elvis Presley's version from the LP Peace in the Valley and was aware of versions by Pat Boone, Lonnie Donegan and Jo Stafford, he would not be recording it.

His mother's marriage:
'It's her life – I hope she and Derek (I can't call him Dad!) will be very happy. I'll be buying them a house as a wedding present and they'll be going to my place in Portugal. I'll also buy a house for my sisters if they want one, and one for my aunt and two teenage cousins who have been living with us. Then I'll probably sell the big house I have and get a flat.'

JUNE

The *Daily Express* reports that Cliff has given former Shadow Jet Harris a wedding present of a £700 guitar and amplifiers, so that he can get back into the music business.

JUNE 19

Granada TV announce that they plan to film a 45-minute Special focused on Soho's 2i's coffee bar, to be screened in September – the tenth anniversary of Tommy Steele being discovered there. Granada hope to include Cliff and the Shadows, songwriter Lionel Bart, Terry Dene, Wee Willie Harris and record producer Mickie Most.

JUNE 24

In the *NME*'s chart points table for the first half of the year, Cliff does not even figure in the Top 20.

JUNE

Cliff's nine-year-old 42,000-strong Fan Club announce they will be closing down the following April. Club secretary, 22-year-old Jan Vane, says: 'I am relinquishing the job and have already started winding up the Club's affairs.'

JUNE

Viviane Ventura, Cliff's leading lady in *Finders Keepers*, says: 'Cliff's so happy he makes me happy. When we have a romantic scene, we go into a corner to work things out. He is so open to suggestions and has so many good ideas himself that it's a joy to be in a picture with him – I'm a lucky girl.'

JULY 3

Cliff broadcasts the *Week's Good Cause* radio appeal on the BBC Home Service, on behalf of the organisation Westminster Homes for Elderly People.

JULY 15

'Visions', Cliff's 34th single, is reviewed: 'Cliff's at his most appealing in this subdued, wistful and sentimental number. Bernard Ebbinghouse's delicate accompaniment is unobtrusive, with a rippling guitar figure, softly chanting group and the suggestion of a Latin lilt.' The flip side is a Hank Marvin-Bruce Welch song, 'What Would I Do'.

JULY 21

'Visions' enters the charts.

JULY

Another delay is announced on the commencement of shooting for the film adaptation of *Aladdin*. The projected date for work to start is now spring 1967, which will mean postponement of plans for Cliff's divinity course.

JULY

Cliff sells his house, 'Rookswood', in Nazeing, Essex, for a reported £43,500.

AUGUST 5

Having previously been heralded in the press as Marlon Brando's girlfriend, it is revealed that Cliff's leading lady in *Finders Keepers*, Viviane Ventura, is engaged to Frank Duggan.

AUGUST

Pauline Harris from Stockton writes in *Fabulous 208* magazine's letters page: 'In my opinion 'Visions' is the best thing that Cliff has recorded for ages.' The magazine replies that the song was written by actor Paul Ferris (currently appearing in Harry Secombe's revue at the London Palladium) of the Paul Ferris-Nicky Henson songwriting team.

AUGUST13

Finders Keepers leading lady, Viviane Ventura, appears on BBC TV's *Juke Box Jury* with Simon Dee, actor Anthony Booth and singer Sheila Southern.

AUGUST 19

Cliff reveals that it is still one of his ambitions to film *Wuthering Heights*.

AUGUST 20

The papers publish news of Cliff buying a house for his mother at Highfield Drive, Broxbourne, another for his sisters nearby and a third for his aunt.

AUGUST

Cliff holidays in Portugal after finishing filming for *Finders Keepers*.

SEPTEMBER 2

A 'Cliff Crossword' compiled by D.R. Stanford of Birmingham is published in the *New Musical Express*.

SEPTEMBER

Daily Express columnist Judith Simons forecasts that Tom Jones will take over from Cliff as Britain's No.1 solo singing idol.

SEPTEMBER 10

Cliff talks to *Fabulous 208* magazine: 'I'm more ambitious now. The more success you have, the more you want. What's the use of feeling suicidal if you don't get what you want? Another way I've changed is that I have learned to take criticism. But you've got to be discerning about criticism – you must know what you've done wrong and be prepared for someone else to tell you about it.' And on his active interest in the Church: 'It's made so much difference to me. I'm a much happier person and I've never felt so refreshed before. My whole life has changed because of a healthier state of mind. I believe there's only one way to live and that is by the Bible. It's the only source which is completely reliable and I set my own life on this. If you've got a focal point in your life, you can't fail. The Church has been the biggest influence in my life. I think young people are a bit self-conscious about religion. I don't care what anybody thinks, I always go ahead and do the thing I think is right – regardless!'

SEPTEMBER 12

A Birmingham group called Finders Keepers release a single, 'Light', which is produced by Scott Walker. They insist that they didn't copy the name from Cliff's film.

19 SEPTEMBER

ABBEY ROAD
Studio session

Solitary Man (4)	*(Unissued)*
You Gotta Tell Me (15)	*(Unissued)*
I'll Be Back (3)	*Don't Stop Me Now*
Things We Said Today (8)	*(Unissued)*

Lead Vocal:	**Cliff Richard**
	The Bernard Ebbinghouse Orchestra
Producer:	**Norrie Paramor**
Engineers:	**Peter Vince/Richard Lush**
Recorded in:	**Studio 2**
Session hours:	**7.00pm-10.00pm**

20 SEPTEMBER

ABBEY ROAD
Studio session

Time (3)	*Sincerely Cliff*
Run To The Door (3)	*Finders Keepers*
It's All Over (7)	*(Unissued)*
Where Did The Summer Go (2)	*Finders Keepers*

Lead Vocal:	**Cliff Richard**
	The Bernard Ebbinghouse Orchestra
	The Mike Sammes Singers
Producer:	**Norrie Paramor**
Engineers:	**Peter Vince/Richard Lush**
Recorded in:	**Studio 2**
Session hours:	**7.00pm-10.00pm**

21 SEPTEMBER

ABBEY ROAD
Film soundtrack recordings for Thunderbirds Are Go/Studio session

Thunderbirds Theme	*Thunderbirds Are Go EP*
Zero X Theme	*Thunderbirds Are Go EP*
Lady Penelope	*Thunderbirds Are Go EP*
Never Knew What Love Could Do (5)	*La La La La La EP*
La La La La La (2)	*(Unissued)*
One Fine Day (3)	*(Unissued)*
I Saw Her Standing There (6)	*Don't Stop Me Now*

Lead Vocal:	**Cliff Richard**
Guitars:	**Hank Marvin/Bruce Welch**
Bass:	**John Rostill**
Drums:	**Brian Bennett**
Orchestra:	**Mike Leander**
Producer:	**Norrie Paramor**
Engineers:	**Peter Vince/Richard Lush**
Recorded in:	**Studio 2**
Session hours:	**2.30pm-5.45pm (Shadows)/7.00pm-10.15pm**

OCTOBER 4

Cliff appears on *Pop Inn* with Diana Dors and Herman's Hermits.

OCTOBER 7

One review of Cliff's 35th single, 'Time Drags By', says: 'This is an easygoing jog-trotter with a happy-go-lucky approach. The beat's pretty solid with tambourine and harmonica.'

OCTOBER 7

Paul McCartney raves about 'Time Drags By'.

OCTOBER 9

Cliff tops the bill and also comperes live the first *Sunday Night at the London Palladium* show of the 1966/67 season. He is presented with a petition organised by May Clifford of Islington and signed by 10,000 fans, begging him not to leave show business.

11 OCTOBER

ABBEY ROAD
Studio session

One Fine Day	*Don't Stop Me Now*
You Gotta Tell Me	*Don't Stop Me Now*
Things We Said Today	*La La La La La EP*
It's All Over	*A-side*
La La La La La	*La La La La La EP*
Solitary Man	*La La La La La EP*

Lead Vocal:	**Cliff Richard**
	The Bernard Ebbinghouse Orchestra
Vocals:	**Hank Marvin/Bruce Welch**
Producer:	**Norrie Paramor**
Engineers:	**Peter Vince/Richard Lush**
Recorded in:	**Studio 2**
Session hours:	

Cliff with Pippa Steele at the premiere of *Finders Keepers*

OCTOBER 14

Cliff celebrates his 26th birthday.

14 OCTOBER

ABBEY ROAD
Studio session

Why Wasn't I Born Rich (6)	*Cinderella*
Come (3)	*Cinderella*
Hey Doctor Man (5)	*Cinderella*

Lead Vocal:	**Cliff Richard**
Guitars:	**Hank Marvin/Bruce Welch**
Bass:	**John Rostill**
Drums:	**Brian Bennett**
Producer:	**Norrie Paramor**
Engineers:	**Peter Vince/Richard Lush**
Recorded in:	**Studio 2**
Session hours:	**2.30pm-6.00pm/7.00pm-12.15am**

RECORDING SHEET

Sheet: 1 of: Class: POP Overall Title: LP Date of Session: 14 Oct '66 Job No: 30165

ARTISTIC INFORMATION — COSTING INFORMATION 35070

Artiste(s) and/or cast: CLIFF RICHARD / SHADS

Art. Dept. Rep.: N PARAMOR

Materials used: — Session booked time: 7–10 Session actual: 7–12.15 Company: COL Studio/Control room: 2–2 Engineers: PV RL

Titles and Matrix Nos.	Author/Composer/Publisher	Reel Numbers	False Starts	Take No.	Take Details From	To	Dur.	M	Remarks
COME SUNDAY		E61788 4T	1	2	COMPLETE		2 20		
				3	—	–	2 20	Best	
HEY DOCTOR MAN		— —	1	2	—	–	2 04		
			3	4	—	–	3 03	~~Best~~	
— —		E61789 4T		5	—	–	3 03	Best	4T – 4T COPY

17 OCTOBER

ABBEY ROAD
Studio session

Autumn (6)	*Cinderella*
The Flyder And the Spy (9)	*Cinderella*
She Needs Him More Than Me (8)	*Cinderella*
Somewhere (5)	*(Unissued)*

Lead Vocal:	**Cliff Richard**
Guitars:	**Hank Marvin/Bruce Welch**
Bass:	**John Rostill**
Drums:	**Brian Bennett**
Producer:	**Norrie Paramor**
Engineers:	**Peter Vince/Richard Lush**
Recorded in:	**Studio 2**
Session hours:	**2.30pm-5.40pm (Shadows) /7.00pm-11.30pm**

19 OCTOBER

ABBEY ROAD
Studio session

Homeward Bound (8)	*Don't Stop Me Now*
Don't (5)	*Don't Stop Me Now*
Save The Last Dance For Me (2)	*Don't Stop Me Now*
Dizzy Miss Lizzy (1)	*Don't Stop Me Now*

Lead Vocal:	**Cliff Richard**
	The Mike Leander Orchestra
Vocals:	**The Breakaways**
Producer:	**Norrie Paramor/David Paramor**
Engineers:	**Peter Vince/Richard Lush**
Recorded in:	**Studio 2**
Session hours:	**7.00pm-10.15pm**

OCTOBER 22

Cliff joins the Archbishop of York and the Bishop of Coventry on stage at the Albert Hall to mark the 21st anniversary of the Lee Abbey evangelical training centre. Cliff, who sings two gospel songs at the event, says: 'As a Christian, I feel it is my duty to take every opportunity to profess I am a Christian and that I personally was saved by Jesus Christ.'

OCTOBER 24

In an interview with the *Sunday Mirror*, Cliff reveals that he has been invited to appear in Russia, Czechoslovakia, Yugoslavia and Bulgaria: 'The money just about covers expenses but, so what? I just love new, exciting experiences.'

OCTOBER 28

'Visions' is at No.5 in Poland.

OCTOBER 29

Cliff appears at a Christian meeting at the Liverpool Empire. He arrives with two clergymen, but needs a dozen bodyguards to control the fans. Cliff sings 'Sinner Man', a re-vamped version of Bob Dylan's 'Blowin' In The Wind' and 'It's No Secret' and talks to the audience from the stage: 'People do not realise how easy it is to become a Christian – and I hope that whether you are Christians or not your ears have been opened to Christianity.'

NOVEMBER

Cliff's 'La La La La La' EP is released and, along with the title track, includes Neil Diamond's 'Solitary Man', the Beatles' 'Things We Said Today' and 'Never Knew What Love Could Do'.

NOVEMBER 4

Columbia releases the 'Thuderbirds Are Go!' EP containing three Shadows tracks and a vocal ('Shooting Star') from Cliff. It is announced that a film of the same name in which puppet figures of Cliff and the Shadows perform to the sound-track will be premiered some time in December.

9 NOVEMBER

ABBEY ROAD
Studio session

The King's Place (2)	*Cinderella*
Peace And Quiet (5)	*(Unissued)*
Poverty (sp)	*Cinderella*

Lead Vocal:	**Cliff Richard**
Guitars:	**Hank Marvin/Bruce Welch**
Bass:	**John Rostill**
Drums:	**Brian Bennett**
	The Norrie Paramor Orchestra
Vocals:	**The Mike Sammes Singers**
Engineer:	**Norrie Paramor**
Engineers:	**Peter Vince/Richard Lush**
Recorded in:	**Studio 2**
Session hours:	**2.30pm-5.30pm**

Poverty is an edit of takes 9 and 10

10 NOVEMBER

ABBEY ROAD
Studio session

Das Glück Ist Rosarot	*German A-side*

Lead Vocal:	**Cliff Richard**
Producer:	**Norrie Paramor**
Engineers:	**Peter Vince/Richard Lush**
Recorded in:	**Studio 2**
Session hours:	**7.00pm-10.00pm**

NOVEMBER 11

It is announced that Cliff is unlikely to make any personal appearances during the next twelve months apart from one or two summer concerts.

Confirming his commitment to his Christian activity, it is also revealed that he will almost certainly have a leading dramatic role in a religious picture being made by an evangelical company, for which production is expected to begin in May.

In the film, Cliff will play an atheist who becomes converted to Christianity.

FINDERS KEEPERS

United Artists, 1966. Running time: 94 minutes.
Cliff's sixth feature film

Synopsis:
A group (Cliff and The Shadows) are booked into a hotel for the season but find the management cannot pay them. They become friendly with local people and hear how the traditional fiesta which surrounds the blessing of fishing boats is threatened by possible repercussions from a clutch of bombs which has been dropped in error by an American aircraft.

Cast:
Cliff Richard, The Shadows, Robert Morley, Peggy Mount, Viviane Ventura, Graham Stark, John Le Mesurier, Robert Hutton.

Credits:
Producer: George H Brown. Director: Sidney Hayers. Choreographer: Malcolm Clare. Original story: George H Brown. Screenplay: Michael Pertwee. Music and lyrics: The Shadows.

Songs:
'Finders Keepers', 'Time Drags By', 'Washerwoman', 'La La La Song', 'Oh Senorita', 'Fiesta', 'This Day', 'Paella', 'Run To The Door', 'Where Did The Summer Go', 'Into Each Life Some Rain Must Fall' performed by Cliff Richard and The Shadows. 'My Way', 'Spanish Music', 'Finders Keepers'/'My Way'/'Paella'/'Fiesta' performed by The Shadows.

11 NOVEMBER

ABBEY ROAD
Studio session

The Hunt (8)	*Cinderella*
Wouldn't It Be Nice (If Our Dreams Came True) (7)	*Cinderella*
Dare I Love Him Like I Do (5)	*Cinderella*

Lead Vocal:	**Cliff Richard**
	The Norrie Paramor Orchestra
Vocals:	**The Mike Sammes Singers**
Vocal Duet:	**Jackie Lee (Wouldn't It Be Nice)**
Vocal:	**Jackie Lee (Dare I Love Him)**
Producer:	**Norrie Paramor**
Engineers:	**Peter Vince/Richard Lush**
Recorded in:	**Studio 2**
Session hours:	**2.30pm-5.30pm**

NOVEMBER 13

The *Sunday Express* reports that Cliff is to be confirmed as a member of the Church of England, and that he has recently lunched with Canon Frederic Hood, Chancellor of St Paul's Cathedral.

Cliff's well-publicised religious beliefs are not new to the world of rock'n'roll; Pat Boone and Little Richard are just two American singers who similarly voiced their faith publicly, while in Britain Cliff's contemporary from the Fifties Terry Dene spent some years as a Jehova's Witness.

16 NOVEMBER

ABBEY ROAD
Studio session

Hey Doctor Man (6)	*Cinderella*
In The Country (4)	*A-side*
Peace And Quiet (5)	*Cinderella*
Welcome To Stoneybroke (4)	*Cinderella*

Lead Vocal:	**Cliff Richard**
Guitars:	**Hank Marvin/Bruce Welch**
Bass:	**John Rostill**
Drums:	**Brian Bennett**
	The Norrie Paramor Orchestra
Vocals:	**The Mike Sammes Singers**
Producer:	**Norrie Paramor**
Engineers:	**Peter Vince/Richard Lush**
Recorded in:	**Studio 3**
Session hours:	**7.00pm-midnight**

Cliff, his sister, Lady Penelope and Parker attend the premiere of *Thunderbirds Are Go!*

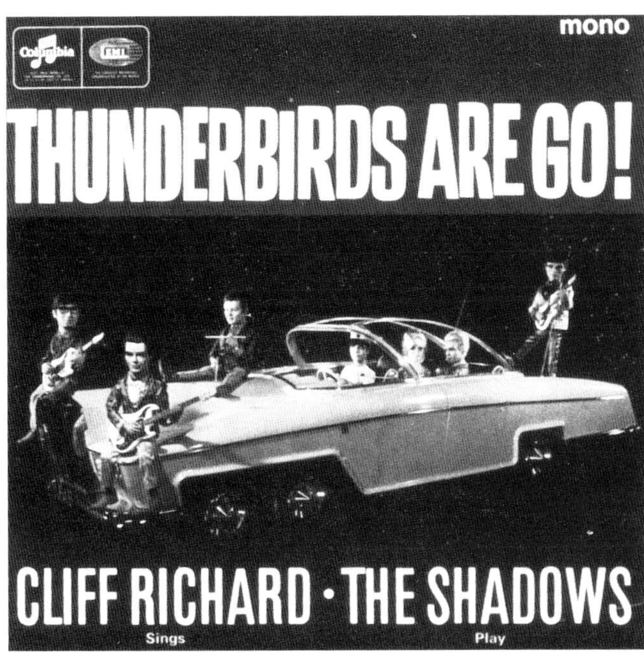

THUNDERBIRDS ARE GO!

United Artists, 1966. Running time: 90 minutes After the success of the THUNDERBIRDS TV series, Gerry and Sylvia Anderson produced this full length feature version for the cinema, and incorporated puppet replicas of Cliff and The Shadows, but it is not regarded as a major Cliff Richard film vehicle as are the others in this listing.

Character voices:
Sylvia Anderson, Ray Barrett, Alexander Divon, Peter Dyneley, Christine Finn, David Graham, Paul Maxwell, Neil McCallum, Bob Monkhouse, Shane Rimmer, Charles Tingwell, Jeremy Wilkin, Matt Zimmerman.

Songs:
'Shooting Star' performed by Cliff Richard and The Shadows
'Lady Penelope', 'Thunderbirds Theme', 'Zero X Theme' performed by The Shadows.

Credits:
Producer: Sylvia Anderson. Director: David Lane

19 NOVEMBER

ABBEY ROAD
Studio session

Peace And Quiet	*(Unissued)*
Why Wasn't I Born Rich	*Cinderella*

Lead Vocal:	**Cliff Richard**
	The Norrie Paramor Orchestra
Vocals:	**The Mike Sammes Singers**
Producer:	**Norrie Paramor**
Engineers:	**Peter Vince/Richard Lush**
Recorded in:	**Studio 2**
Session hours:	**2.30pm-5.30pm**

JANUARY 14

Cliff speaks out in an interview with *NME* 'I'm not being self-righteous, I just want to get out of this business because I feel I have to. When I leave depends on the results of my Religious Instruction 'O' level examination. Don't think I regard everybody in show business as sinful, I love the atmosphere and the life. If I didn't want to teach religious instruction in a secondary school, I'd stay in it till Doomsday. When I give up this life, it's not going to be a complete break; I don't think people realise that I'll still be making records. I just want to be an ordinary teacher in an ordinary secondary school. I don't care if some people do think I'm a phoney, they're entitled to their opinions.'

15 JANUARY

ABBEY ROAD
Studio session

Baby It's You (4)	*Don't Stop Me Now*
Don't Make Promises (3)	*Don't Stop Me Now*
Hang On To A Dream (4)	*Don't Stop Me Now*
Heartbeat (4)	*Don't Stop Me Now*

Lead Vocal:	**Cliff Richard**
Orchestra	
Producer:	**Norrie Paramor**
Engineers:	**Peter Vince/Richard Lush**
Recorded in:	**Studio 2**
Session hours:	**7.00pm-10.00pm**

JANUARY

EMI releasethe 'Cinderella' LP.

JANUARY

Cliff appears on the BBC Light Programme's *Five to Ten* religious programme: 'I've found I can mix both my Christian life and my show-biz life because I treat my show-biz life, as we are biblically told, as a job that we're going to give to God.'

JANUARY 21

In an in-depth article on the subject, 'Are films a jinx for pop stars?', journalist Derek Johnson comments: 'Most people regard *Finders Keepers* as Cliff Richard's worst film to date. This is an opinion that I do not share, but as I appear to be in the minority one can only say that it must be due to the hurried hotch-potch fashion in which it was put together. A pity, for Cliff had previously set an all-time high in the standard of British film musicals.'

JANUARY 28

Following the publicity surrounding his recent Christian activities, the 'Alley-cat' column of the *NME* suggests that Cliff should record a 'long-praying LP!'

JANUARY

Cliff's 'Blue Turns To Grey' is in the Polish Top 10.

JANUARY

Raymond Smith, from Dartford in Kent, writes to the music press on the subject of Cliffs beliefs: 'I have never really been a fan of Cliff Richard's, but I was thrilled to see how Cliff has stood out for what he believes to be right. I am sure he has not found it easy to stick to his Christian principles ... If becoming a religious instruction teacher is what he believes God wants him to do, then I hope nothing will stand in his way. He certainly seems to be a young person who knows where he is going and that is more than can be said for a lot of people nowadays.'

5 FEBRUARY

ABBEY ROAD
Studio session

Shout (8)	*Don't Stop Me Now*
My Babe (3)	*Don't Stop Me Now*
Good Golly Miss Molly (6)	*Don't Stop Me Now*
Move It (54)	*Don't Stop Me Now*

Lead Vocal:	**Cliff Richard**
Orchestra	
Producer:	**Norrie Paramor**
Engineers:	**Peter Vince/Richard Lush**
Recorded in:	**Studio 2**
Session hours:	**7.00pm-10.15pm**

FEBRUARY

The readers of the weekly pop music paper *Disc and Music Echo* vote Cliff Richard the 'best-dressed male star'. No mean feat in an era when beat groups were considered sartorial trend-setters.

MARCH 11

Cliff's 37th single, 'It's All Over', is released – a song originally recorded by the Everly Brothers and written by Don Everly. One reviewer says: 'One of those sentimental husky-voiced ballads that Cliff always handles with conviction . . . although I don't rate this as one of Cliff's best discs.' The 'B' side, 'Why Wasn't I Born Rich', is a Shadows' composition from the Cinderella pantomime.

MARCH 18

Miss P. Grossmith of Liverpool has a letter about Cliff published in the music press: 'If anyone is to be given credit for consistency, surely it must be Cliff Richard. His career began in 1957 before the Beatles, Stones and the Monkees were even thought of. Now, ten years later, Cliff is still chalking up hit after hit. I wonder if the Monkees will still be doing likewise in 1976?'

MARCH

Cliff speaks out about plans for a new, as yet untitled, film: 'The story will be about moral issues. Four songs will be featured, but the movie won't be a musical by any means. We don't intend to play up the comedy angle as we did with the H-Bomb in *Finders Keepers*. I particularly want to make a war story. I hope it will be a believable production showing how a group of young people can become easily involved in warfare, even though they do not want to be. The movie will not actually be about Vietnam, but it has been inspired by it and will project a similar situation.'

MARCH

In the Ivor Novello Awards, presented annually by the Songwriters' Guild of Great Britain, 'Time Drags By' – sung by Cliff in Finders Keepers- is runner-up to 'Born Free' in the 'Film Song of the Year' category.

APRIL 1

Cliff talks about his music: 'Ballads have been my stepping-stone. I like singing "raw" as I did at the start with numbers like 'Move It' – but if I hadn't changed, I couldn't have performed at all. Now I think it's time for a change again. I can't plug the Everly Brothers' LP enough, its fantastic. And I can't understand why the Evs. threw 'It's All Over' away on an LP. They should have released it as a single ages ago.' He goes on to talk about public reaction to his beliefs: 'The main reason I couldn't go on as I am now is simple enough; the public gets fed-up with a pop singer talking about religion. It's getting like that already. People are saying, "Oh no, not Cliff Richard spouting about religion again!" They're building up a resistance. If I become a teacher it means I shall have to go into a training school for at least three years. After that the novelty will have worn off and I don't think the children I teach would be distracted.'

APRIL

Cliff turns down an offer to head the *Sunday Night at the London Palladium* show as he says that with performances in *Cinderella* six nights a week Sunday is his only day off.

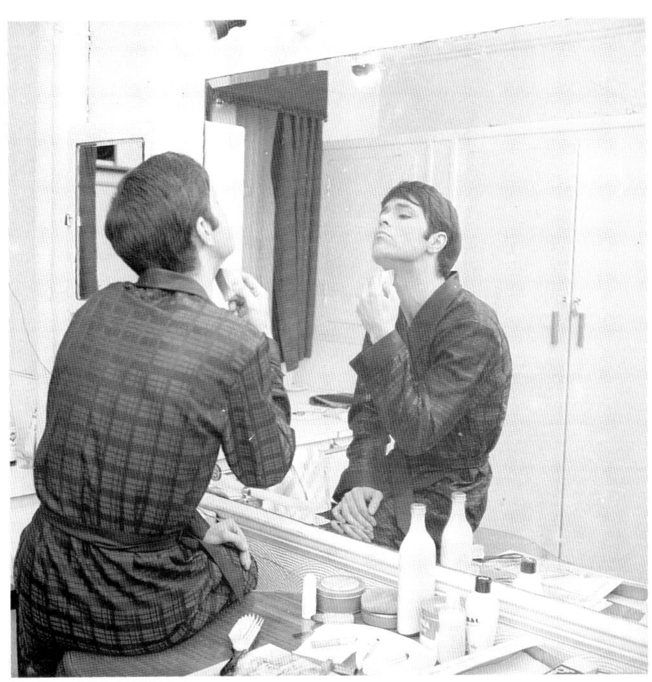

Relaxing backstage during the *Cinderella* pantomime run.

APRIL 8

'Don't Stop Me Now' LP is released.

APRIL

The national press report that Cliff and the Shadows are to split.

APRIL 22

Cliff's manager, Peter Gormley, answers the rumours that Cliff and the Shadows are going their separate ways: 'The misunderstanding has arisen because the Shadows will be touring abroad while Cliff is making his religious film – which starts shooting in

June and continues into July. They will get together again in September to work on the dramatic film inspired by the Vietnam war, and we are now planning another picture which will go into production early in 1968. This will be a musical spectacular in the pattern of Cliff and the Shadows' previous film successes. At the end of the year, they will make several TV appearances which will probably include a Christmas Day show and a short series of six half-hour programmes.'

24 APRIL

ABBEY ROAD
Studio session

I'll Come Running	*A-side*
I Get The Feeling	*B-side*
I'll Make It All Up To You	*Tracks And Grooves*
Our Storybook	*B-side*

Lead Vocal:	**Cliff Richard**
Orchestra	
Producer:	**Norrie Paramor**
Engineer:	
Recorded in:	**Studio**
Session hours:	

25 APRIL

ABBEY ROAD
Studio session

Bilder Von Dir (Visions)	*German B-side*
Ein Girl Wie Du (A Girl Like You)	*German A-side*

Lead Vocal:	**Cliff Richard**

APRIL 27

In an interview with *Disc and Music Echo*, Cliff says: 'When I quit I'll keep Cliff because I can't stand the name Harry, but I'll add "Webb" on the end because the "Richard" thing has got to go.'

27 APRIL

ABBEY ROAD
Studio session

We Shall Be Changed (2)	*Good News*
Mary What You Gonna Call That	
Pretty Little Baby (5)	*Good News*
Get On Board Little Children (3)	*Good News*
Go Where I Send Thee (3)	*Good News*

Lead Vocal:	**Cliff Richard**
Guitar:	**Hank Marvin/Bruce Welch**
Bass:	**John Rostill**
Drums:	**Brian Bennett**
Vocals:	
Producer:	**Norrie Paramor**
Engineers:	**Peter Vince/Mike Stone**
Recorded in:	**Studio 2**
Session hours:	**7.00pm-11.00pm**

28 APRIL

ABBEY ROAD
Studio session

All In The April Evening (3)	*(Unissued)*
Sweet Little Jesus Boy (2)	*B-side*
Were You There (3)	*(Unissued)*
What A Friend We Have In Jesus (2)	*Good News*
When I Survey The Wondrous Cross (4)	*Good News*

Lead Vocal:	**Cliff Richard**
	The Norrie Paramor Orchestra
Soprano Voice:	**Pat Clark**
Producer:	**Norrie Paramor**
Engineer:	**Peter Vince/Mike Stone**
Recorded in:	**Studio 2**
Session hours:	**7.00pm-10.00pm**

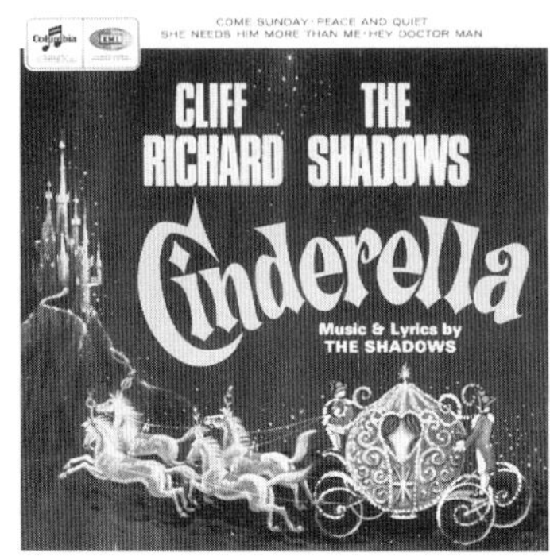

3 MAY

ABBEY ROAD
Studio session

Take My Hand, Precious Lord (4)	*Good News*
Just A Closer Walk With Thee (6)	*Good News*
Star Of Hope (2)	*(Unissued)*
It Is No Secret (sp)	*Good News*
May The Good Lord Bless And Keep You (sp)	*Good News*

Lead Vocal: **Cliff Richard**
The Bernard Ebbinghouse Orchestra

Producer: **Norrie Paramor**
Engineer: **Peter Vince/Mike Stone**
Recorded in: **Studio 2**
Session hours: **7.00pm-10.30pm**

It Is No Secret is an edit of takes 1 and 5.
May The Good Lord is an edit of takes 1 and 3.

MAY

An EP from 'Cinderella' is released.

4 MAY

ABBEY ROAD
Studio session

23rd Psalm (6)	*Good News*
The King Of Love My Shepherd Is (4)	*Good News*
There Is A Green Hill Far Away (4)	*(Unissued)*
Praise My Soul The King Of Heaven (3)	*(Unissued)*
All Glory Laud And Honour (2)	*Good News*

Lead Vocal: **Cliff Richard**
The Norrie Paramor Orchestra

Producer: **Norrie Paramor**
Engineer: **Peter Vince/Mike Stone**
Recorded in: **Studio 2**
Session hours: **7.00pm-10.15pm**

MAY 6

Cliff appears with Georgie Fame, the Troggs and the Searchers on the BBC Light Programme's 450th edition of *Saturday Club*. Cliff is backed on the show by the Mike Leander Orchestra.

MAY 7

Cliff appears at the *NME* Poll Winners' Concert at Wembley with the Beach Boys, Small Faces, Troggs, Move, Cat Stevens, Dusty Springfield, Georgie Fame, the Cream and comperes Jimmy Savile and Simon Dee. Cliff sings 'In the Country', 'It's All Over', 'Move It' and 'Shout'. His trophy for the Best British Male Vocalist is presented to him by John Maus of the Walker Brothers. Beatles manager Brian Epstein is seen in the audience enthusiastically applauding Cliff's act.

MAY 13

Cliff appears on BBC TV's *Juke Box Jury* with fellow panellists Anita Harris, Roy Hudd and actress Leila Tasha.

13 MAY

ABBEY ROAD
Studio session

Good News	*Good News*
Words	*(Unissued)*

Lead Vocal: **Cliff Richard**
The Norrie Paramor Orchestra

Producer: **Norrie Paramor**
Engineer: **Peter Vince/Mike Stone**
Recorded in: **Studio 2**
Session hours: **7.00pm-10.00pm**

MAY 24

Cliff stars in a one-hour ATV Spectacular.

1 JUNE

ABBEY ROAD
Studio session

The Day I Met Marie	*A-side*
Red Rubber Ball	*Two A Penny*
Put My Mind At Ease	*Tracks And Grooves*
I'd Just Be Fool Enough	*Tracks And Grooves*

Lead Vocal: **Cliff Richard**
The Mike Leander Orchestra

Producer: **Norrie Paramor**
Engineer: **Peter Vince**
Recorded in: **Studio**
Session hours:

JUNE 3

A disgruntled William Brown from Manchester writes to the British press:
'Let's have no more nonsense about Cliff Richard and Elvis Presley being the world's No. 1 singers -they should both listen to Frank Sinatra, who has been at the top for 25 years!'

JUNE 3

Cliff's 38th single is released – 'I'll Come Runnin''/'I Get The Feelin''. Both sides are Neil Diamond songs. One reviewer comments: '... it explodes into a pulsating chorus with blaring brass, chirping girls and Cliff in his most rhythmic mood.'

JUNE

Cliff (playing the part of an art student) films *Two a Penny* for evangelist Billy Graham, with all the proceeds going to charity. The film, with a £150,000 budget, includes three songs written by Cliff- who is also seen singing 'Twist and Shout' – and co-stars Avril Angers and Dora Bryan as Cliff's mother.

JUNE 18

Cliff (as an Anglican) chats with Cathy McGowan (Roman Catholic) and Hugh Lloyd (Methodist) about their beliefs in a religious discussion programme on the BBC Home Service.

JULY 1

The *NME* publish their half-yearly chart table based on the points system of 30 points for a week at number 1 to 1 point for a week at number30. The top five positions are:

1 Engelbert Humperdinck	554
2 Monkees	546
3 Tom Jones	453
4 Tremeloes	426
5 Jimi Hendrix	408

Cliff comes 18th with 248 points, equal with the Supremes.

I JULY

ABBEY ROAD

Film soundtrack recordings for Two A Penny

Two A Penny	*Two A Penny*
I'll Love You Forever Today	*A-side*
Twist And Shout	*Two A Penny*
Questions	*Two A Penny*

Lead Vocal: **Cliff Richard**
The Mike Leander Orchestra

Producer: **Norrie Paramor**
Engineer: **Peter Vince**
Recorded in: **Studio 2**
Session hours: **2.30pm-5.30pm**

JULY

Cliff's former Shadows bass player, Jet Harris, effects a comeback signing for Fontana Records, and has his new material produced by ex-Shadow Tony Meehan. Harris and Meehan had a string of hits together when they left the group in the early Sixties.

Mr. N. Paramor 55,094
Tape No. E65905 Z Identity Cliff Richard / Masterworks

Subject	Start	Finish		Remarks
Twelve Days Of Christmas				
Unto Us A Boy Is Born				
The Holly & The Ivy				V.B.C. EQ & LTD.

Tape Length 811 | Engineer Vince / Boys | Date 10. 9. 67 | Tape Speed 15 I.P.S.

IMPORTANT NOTICE TO PURCHASER

JULY 9

Cliff and Billy Graham appear on ABC TV's religious programme *Looking For An Answer.*

JULY

Cliff writes the three songs which he will feature in the film *Two A Penny* being made by Worldwide Productions for the Billy Graham organisation.

JULY 16

Cliff and self-confessed atheist, Paul Jones, take part in the BBC's controversial religious discussion programme *Looking For An Answer*. The programme includes scenes from Paul's film *Privilege* – some of which parody Christianity – and scenes from a Billy Graham religious film.

AUGUST 5

Cliff's 39th single is released – 'The Day I Met Marie'/'Our Story Book' and is described by one reviewer as 'a hauntingly tender ballad with a strong folk flavour . . . in the chorus it explodes into a jaunty martial beat with oom-pah trombones, tambourines and chanting girls.' The song is written by Hank Marvin and arranged by Mike Leander.

AUGUST12

Cliff flies to Portugal for a three-week holiday prior to beginning work with the Shadows on 'A musical with a war background'.

AUGUST 19

Jackie Irving, a former girl-friend of Cliff's, marries Adam Faith at Caxton Hall. Cliff's manager Peter Gormley is at the reception at Upper Court in Cobham, Surrey, along with Lionel Blair and TV producer Mike Mansfleld.

AUGUST 30

Cliff returns from holiday in Portugal.

SEPTEMBER 2

Strong rumours – that were to be repeated over the years – that

Cliff Richard and the Shadows will no longer work together are dispelled by the announcement that they will not only star together in a French TV spectacular, but also undertake major UK Television dates later in the year.

Their joint agent Michael Grade announces to the media: 'We are also working on plans for two or three big TV shows to be made in this country.'

10 SEPTEMBER

ABBEY ROAD
Studio session

It Came Upon A Midnight Clear (sp)	*(Unissued)*
In The Bleak Mid-Winter (sp)	*Carol Singers EP*
God Rest Ye Merry Gentlemen (sp)	*Carol Singers EP*
While Shepherds Watched (sp)	*Carol Singers EP*
Little Town Of Bethlehem (sp)	*Carol Singers EP*
Twelve Days Of Christmas (sp)	*We Should Be Together Christmas EP*
Unto Us A Boy Is Born (sp)	*Carol Singers EP*
The Holly And The Ivy (8)	*We Should Be Together Christmas EP*

Lead Vocal:	**Cliff Richard**
Vocals:	**The Mastersingers (John Horrex, George Pratt, Michael Warrington, Geoffrey Keating)**
Producer:	**Norrie Paramor**
Engineer:	**Peter Vince/John Barrett**
Recorded in:	**Studio 2**
Session hours:	**2.30pm-5.30pm/7.00pm-10.45pm**

SEPTEMBER 16

In an interview, Cliff recalls a conversation with John Lennon in which they were chatting about their favourite artists. 'I've always liked Ray Charles,' Cliff told John. 'Well, I used to until everyone else started liking him,' replied Lennon. Cliff says that he always remembered that odd attitude. 'When John Lennon told me that, I was shocked. I don't know if he still has the same views nowadays, but I thought it was dreadful that anyone should change their opinions just to be different from everyone else. I'm all in favour of non-conformists, but I certainly don't agree with people not conforming just to be different.'

SEPTEMBER

Cliff performs, 'The Day I Met Marie' on *Top Of The Pops*, hosted by Jimmy Savile, and is mobbed by fans. Cliff comments: 'I'm really surprised, I thought those days were over now.'

SEPTEMBER

Cliff reveals that when he made the film *Two A Penny*, Equity – the actors' union – would not allow him to work for nothing; they insisted on a payment of £40 a week.

SEPTEMBER

Cliff says of the Beatles and the Maharishi: 'I think they are searching along the wrong track – the Beatles have said they are searching for God. There's only one way to find him – that's through Jesus Christ.' On the subject of transcendental meditation, Cliff comments: 'Meditation, like an LSD trip, is only a temporary thing. Christianity is something which is with you all the time.'

SEPTEMBER 23

Cliff's manager Peter Gormley announces that the projected film is to be delayed until 1968. He denies that Cliff is to star in the film adaptation of Keith West and Mark Wirtz's 'Teenage Opera': 'We were asked if we were interested and we said we would be. In this case, though, I imagine that shooting would clash with Cliff's own film with the Shadows.'

SEPTEMBER 23

Melody Maker readers vote Cliff 'Top Male Singer', a title he regains from Tom Jones who captured the title from Cliff in 1966!

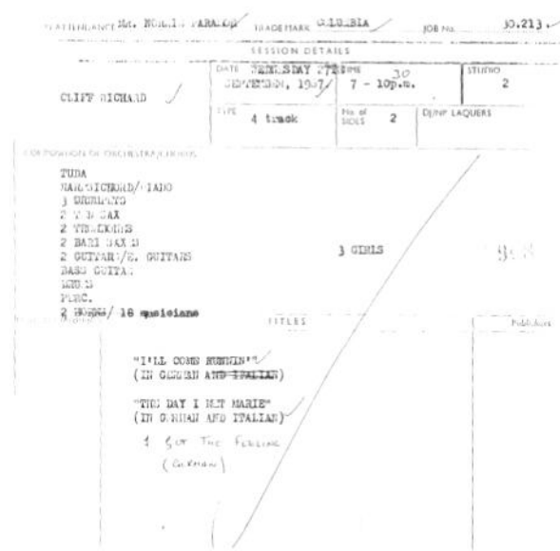

TRADEMARK JOB No.
SESSION DETAILS
CLIFF RICHARD
DATE 7 - 10p.m. STUDIO 2
TYPE 4 track No. of SIDES 2 DJ/NP LAQUERS
TUBA
PERC.
3 GIRLS
TITLES

27 SEPTEMBER

ABBEY ROAD
Studio session

Ich Kann Treu Sein (I'll Come Running)	*See 28 September*
Ein Sonntag Mit Marie (The Day I Met Marie)	*German B-side*
Imagina Un Giorno (The Day I Met Marie)	*See 28 September*
I Got The Feeling	*German Release*

Lead Vocal:	**Cliff Richard**
	The Bernard Ebbinghouse Orchestra
Producer:	**Norrie Paramor**
Engineer:	**Peter Vince**
Recorded in:	**Studio 2**
Session hours:	**7.00pm-10.30pm**

Some of the above titles are backing tracks only.

I think I recorded "I only live to love you" at the same time as "All my love" & we chose "All my love" for the single — Cliff

28 SEPTEMBER

ABBEY ROAD
Studio session

Es Ist Nicht Gut, Allein Zu Sein	*German A-side*
Mrs Emily Jones	*German B-side*
Ich Kann Treu Sein (I'll Come Running)	*German B-side*
Imagina Un Giorno (The Day I Met Marie)	*Italian A-side*
Oh, No, No (I Get The Feelin')	*Italian B-side*

Lead Vocal: **Cliff Richard**

Producer: **Norrie Paramor**
Engineer: **Peter Vince**
Recorded in: **Studio 2**
Session hours: **7.00pm-11.15pm**

5 OCTOBER

ABBEY ROAD
Studio session

All My Love	*A-side*
Don't Ask Me To Be Friends	*Tracks And Grooves*
I Only Live To Love You	*Foreign Release*

Lead Vocal: **Cliff Richard**
The Bernard Ebbinghouse Orchestra
Vocals: **The Mike Sammes Singers**

Producer: **Norrie Paramor**
Engineer: **Peter Vince**
Recorded in: **Studio 2**
Session hours: **7.00pm-10.15pm**

11 OCTOBER

ABBEY ROAD
Studio session

Cloudy	*Two A Penny*
The Letter	*(Unissued)*
The Girl Can't Help It	*Tracks And Grooves*
For Emily Whenever I May Find Her	*Sincerely Cliff*

Lead Vocal: **Cliff Richard**
The Mike Leander Orchestra
Vocals:

Producer: **Norrie Paramor**
Engineer: **Peter Vince**
Recorded in: **Studio 2**
Session hours: **7.00pm-10.00pm**

OCTOBER 14

On his 27th birthday, Cliff flies to Tokyo to star in two concerts and a television spectacular with Norrie Paramor conducting a Japanese orchestra.

OCTOBER

It is announced that Cliff is to be Britain's representative in the 1968 Eurovision Song Contest.

18 OCTOBER

SHIBUYA PUBLIC HALL, TOKYO, JAPAN
Live recordings

In The Country	*(Unissued)*
Dynamite	*Cliff In Japan*
Bachelor Boy	*Japanese Issue Only*
Finders Keepers	*Cliff In Japan*
On The Beach	*Cliff In Japan*
Evergreen Tree	*Cliff In Japan*
Visions	*Cliff In Japan*

What'd I Say	*Cliff In Japan*
Shout	*Cliff In Japan*
Twist And Shout	*Cliff In Japan*
Angel	*(Unissued)*
It's All In The Game	*Japanese Issue Only*
The Minute You're Gone	*Cliff In Japan*
The Day I Met Marie	*(Unissued)*
I'll Come Running	*Cliff In Japan*
The Next Time	*(Unissued)*
Spanish Harlem	*Cliff In Japan*
Move It	*Cliff In Japan*
Dizzy Miss Lizzy	*(Unissued)*
Hang On To A Dream	*Cliff In Japan*
Good Golly, Miss Molly	*(Unissued)*
La, La, La, La, La	*Cliff In Japan*
Living Doll	*Cliff In Japan*
Medley: Let's Make A Memory	*Cliff In Japan*
The Young Ones	*Cliff In Japan*
Lucky Lips	*Cliff In Japan*
Summer Holiday	*Cliff In Japan*
We Say Yeah	*Cliff In Japan*

Lead Vocal: **Cliff Richard**
The Norrie Paramor Orchestra

Producer: **Norrie Paramor**
Engineer:
Session hours;

OCTOBER

David Winter's book on Cliff – *New Singer, New Song* – is published.

OCTOBER 21

Cliff's 'Good News' album is released and includes 'The 23rd Psalm', 'When I Survey The Wondrous Cross', 'The King Of Love My Shepherd Is' and 'What A Friend We Have in Jesus'.

OCTOBER 29

The *Daily Mirror* reproduces part of an address given by Cliff to a congregation at Cuffley Free Church in Hertfordshire: 'People who sleep around make the most unhappy marriages – pre-marital sex is unhealthy to the mind.'

NOVEMBER 4

Cliff's 40th single 'All My Love'/'Sweet Little Jesus Boy' is released. One reviewer claims: 'The with-it set will probably regard it as a retrogressive step for Cliff Richard because he's abandoned the zestful, refreshing style of 'Marie' in favour of a sugary, sentimental ballad.'

NOVEMBER 25

Cliff talks about his sight problem:
'About a year ago, I got some contact lenses and I just couldn't wear them. Recently I was told that some German lenses were the best in the world, so last week I went to Germany and had them fitted there.
I find the strain affects my nose and makes me sneeze. I don't see people when I haven't got glasses or contact lenses – I just see vague blurs!'

NOVEMBER

Cliff and the Shadows announce the likelihood of a spring tour together, but reveal that not all the members of the group are keen to be in the new film, which is put back yet again – this time to June 1968.

DECEMBER 6

Cliff is confirmed as a member of the Church of England by the Bishop of Willesden, Graham Leonard, at St Paul'sChurch, Finchley, in North London.

DECEMBER 9

The *New Musical Express* poll results are published:

World Male Singer

1 Elvis Presley	4,632
2 Tom Jones	4,410
3 Cliff Richard	3,863

World Musical Personality

1 Elvis Presley	4,273
2 John Lennon	3,333
3 Cliff Richard	3,206

British Vocal Personality

1 Cliff Richard	4,700
2 John Lennon	4,019
3 Tom Jones	3,261

British Male Singer

1 Tom Jones	5,785
2 Cliff Richard	5,121
3 Engelbert Humperdinck	2,654

In the 'Best British Disc of the Year' category, Cliff's 'The Day I Met Marie' comes fourth behind three records that have since become acknowledged pop classics – Procol Harum's 'A Whiter Shade Of Pale', the Beatles' 'All You Need Is Love' and the Bee Gees' 'Massachusetts'.

DECEMBER

It is announced from his press office that Cliff is to star in a dramatic play to be recorded for ATV television in February, in which he plays the part of a young gang leader who plots to steal a famous jewel collection.
Cliff admits that he may not now start work on a new cinema film in the summer as was previously planned, as none of the scripts that have been submitted so far have been up to the required standard.

1968–1970

The Records 1968 – 1970

The Bill Martin and Phil Coulter composition 'Congratulations' was selected as the winning UK entry for the Eurovision Song Contest, and became Cliff's first No.1 single since 'The Minute You're Gone' had hit the top of the charts in 1965. Another three singles were released in 1968 but a slump in sales was illustrated by the fact that none of them reached the top twenty. However, all the singles released the following year brought Cliff back into that top twenty. 'Big Ship' packed enough commercial appeal to reach the No.8 spot, and 'Throw Down A Line' credited to Cliff and Hank eventually peaked at No.7. Somehow, 1970 turned out to be a mediocre year, although 'Goodbye Sam, Hello Samantha' was one of the more successful recordings and consequently reached higher on the charts than the other two singles released that year.

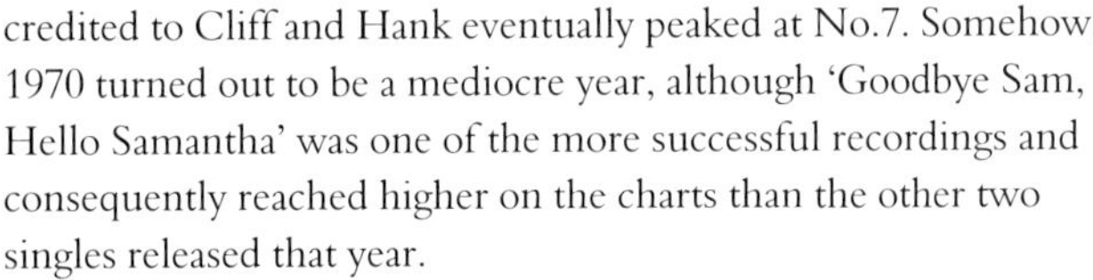

Sales of the albums released during this period followed the same mediocre pattern as the 1970 singles with a noticeable decline in chart placings, though the picture was definitely better as far as the new 'hits' compilation was concerned. THE BEST OF CLIFF was the only one to reach the top five of the album chart. None of the other albums climbed any higher than No.24, despite the fact that one of three budget priced albums featured new live recordings of Cliff's 1968 shows at London's Talk Of The Town. The full price albums didn't stir up much chart action either. After ESTABLISHED 1958, a tenth anniversary set that shared half the album with the Shadows, there was a Columbia demo for trade purposes pressed of the track 'Don't Forget To Catch Me' taken from the same album and given a PSR 316 number. A pair of religious albums ABOUT THAT MAN and HIS LAND simply went unnoticed. The fact that Cliff's final EP CONGRATULATIONS did not make the charts reflects a change in consumer habits. By this time budget price album sales had completely overtaken the sale of EP's.

The Sessions 1968 – 1970

During the February 1968 sessions, Cliff recorded all six prospective United Kingdom entries for the Eurovision Song Contest in preparation for their televising. Of these 'Congratulations' was chosen as the favourite and became the hit single of this period. The track was later re-recorded in no fewer than four foreign language versions at the April sessions.

For some reason or other the session on May 29 never really got off the ground, although it seems probable the session was set up to provide material suitable for the tenth anniversary album ESTABLISHED 1958. However that may be, the thread of the session was only taken up again in June and July when Cliff completed the tracks for his half of the album – a new batch of Shadows recordings made up the other half, and these were all taped at the same recording sessions.

The live recordings taped during this period were taken from the three shows recorded at London's Talk Of The Town between 30 May and 1 June. For the repertoire the basic formula of a mixture of old hits and covers was maintained. As far as the covers went, Cliff included a rousing rendition of 'Shout' which had been a top ten hit for Lulu, a knockout version of 'Ain't Nothing But A Houseparty' and a number of others.

Once more the Norrie Paramor Orchestra provided the musical accompaniment and arrangements, while the Breakaways were called on for vocal backing on most of the songs. For some reason these recordings were considered only suitable for release in the shape of a budget price album retailing at under £1. Sessions in November were held to record German language versions of recent album tracks.

For the Tyne Tees Television network series *Life With Johnny*, both the instrumental backing and vocals by Cliff and the Settlers were pre-recorded at the sessions over December 1968 to January 1969. The 22 songs taped were all featured in the six programmes of modern parables designed for religious broadcasting. The original plan to release a selection of these recordings as a soundtrack album was dropped along the way. It may well be that EMI felt its release might have had a limited appeal from a commercial point of view.

Besides the sessions aimed at producing new singles and album tracks for SINCERELY CLIFF and TRACKS 'N GROOVES, a variety of religious material was recorded. One single session in February 1970 provided all the items for ABOUT THAT MAN – a combination of songs and readings from the New Testament. However, there is no information filed relating to recording dates or studio locations for HIS LAND – the soundtrack for a film that Cliff made for the Billy Graham Organisation during a visit to Israel.

JANUARY 8-12

Cliff is featured on David Symonds' Radio 1 show every evening.

JANUARY

New Musical Express publish their 1967 points table (30 points for number 1, down to 1 point for number 30 etc). and Cliff comes 7th.

1 Engelbert Humperdinck	1218
2 Monkees	916
3 Tom Jones	890
4 Beatles	695
5 Tremeloes	633
6 Diana Ross & the Supremes	544
7 Cliff Richard	529
8 Dave Dee, Dozy, Beaky, Mick & Tich	489
9 Move	487
10 Traffic	479

The paper points out that not one of Cliff's releases has ever failed to make the *NME* chart, and that in this respect he has definitely taken over the title of 'King of Consistency' from 'the King' Elvis Presley.

JANUARY 13

Shadow Hank Marvin releases 'London's Not Too Far' – a song he originally wrote for Cliff.

JANUARY

Along with Sandie Shaw, Cliff attends the launch of Southern TV's pop series *New Release*.

JANUARY

Cliff sends Engelbert Humperdinck a 'Good Luck' telegram for the opening of his pantomime.

JANUARY 16

During their 'Talk Of The Town' season, Shadows drummer Brian Bennett is taken ill with appendicitis, resulting in Cliff sitting in on drums for one night only until the former Shadows drummer Tony Meehan takes over.

JANUARY 27

DJ Keith Skues selects his list of all-time Top 10 records which includes Cliff's 'Summer Holiday'.

JANUARY 28

In an interview with the *Sunday Times*, Cliff says:
'I've lived for years with people saying that I'm a poof, but I don't give a damn what they say. My best friends know me, and that's all that matters. Even before I became a Christian, I wasn't going to lay chicks just to prove myself...'

FEBRUARY

Cliff accepts an invitation to preach three sermons on the Christian faith and its relation to the world of show business at Notting Hill's Kensington Temple in May.
Cliff's involvement in Church matters is becoming an increasingly significant part of his life, as he lends his name not only to Christian-supported causes but gets involved musically and otherwise in the evangelical aspect of promoting his faith.

2 FEBRUARY

ABBEY ROAD
Studio session

Wonderful World	*Congratulations EP*
High And Dry	*B-side*
Do You Remember	*Congratulations EP*

Lead Vocal:	**Cliff Richard**
	The Bernard Ebbinghouse Orchestra
	The Norrie Paramor Orchestra
Bass Guitar:	**John Paul Jones (7.00pm-9.00pm only)**
Vocals:	**The Mike Sammes Singers (8.00pm-10.00pm only)**
	Hank Marvin/Bruce Welch (8.00pm-10.00pm only)
Producer:	**Norrie Paramor**
Engineer:	**Peter Vince**
Recorded in:	**Studio 2**
Session hours:	**7.00pm-10.30pm**

FEBRUARY

Cliff shoots the ATV play *A Matter Of Diamonds*.

3 FEBRUARY

ABBEY ROAD
Studio session

The Sound Of The Candyman's Trumpet	*Congratulations EP*
Shoom Llama Boom Boom	*(Unissued)*
Congratulations	*A-side*

Lead Vocal:	**Cliff Richard**
	The Norrie Paramor Orchestra
Bass Guitar:	**John Paul Jones**
Vocals:	**The Breakaways**
Producer:	**Norrie Paramor**
Engineer:	**Peter Vince**
Recorded in:	**Studio 2**
Session hours:	**8.00pm-11.30pm**

FEBRUARY

The results of the *Disc & Music Echo* poll are published.

Top Male Singer (British)
- 1 Tom Jones
- 2 Cliff Richard
- 3 Scott Walker (American)

Top Male Singer (World)
- 1 Scott Walker
- 2 Tom Jones
- 3 Cliff Richard

Mr Valentine – 1968
- 1 Scott Walker
- 2 Cliff Richard
- 3 Dave Clark

Best-Dressed Male Star
- 1 Cliff Richard
- 2 Tom Jones
- 3 Engelbert Humperdinck

Top TV Artist (Male)
- 1 Simon Dee
- 2 Tom Jones
- 3 Cliff Richard

11 FEBRUARY

ABBEY ROAD
Studio session

Little Rag Doll	*Congratulations EP*
Punch And Judy	*Sincerely Cliff*
Girl You'll Be A Woman Soon	*B-side*

Lead Vocal:	**Cliff Richard**
	The Mike Leander Orchestra
Producer:	**Norrie Paramor**
Engineer:	**Peter Vince**
Recorded in:	**Studio 2**
Session hours:	**7.00pm-10.30pm**

FEBRUARY 17

The six 'Eurovision Song Contest' contenders that Cliff is to sing in BBC TV's series *Cilla* are announced.

Congratulations by Bill Martin & Phil Coulter
Wonderful World by Guy Fletcher & Doug Flett
High & Dry by David & Jonathan
Do You Remember by Tommy Scott
Sound Of The Candyman's Trumpet by Tony Hazzard
Little Rag Doll by Mike Leander

Cliff in an unfamiliar role as he takes over from Brian Bennett during the Talk Of The Town season.

FEBRUARY 24

Lynne Grossmith from Liverpool has a letter about Cliff published in the music press: 'Many people fail to realise that Cliff was responsible for introducing pop into places like 'Talk Of The Town' that formerly would only have considered the Sinatras, Bennetts and Lena Hornes of the entertainment world.'

8 MARCH

ABBEY ROAD
Film soundtrack recordings for Two A Penny

Rattler	*Two A Penny*
Wake Up, Wake Up	*Two A Penny*
The Dreams I Dream	*Established 1958*
Lonely Girl	*Two A Penny*
And Me (I'm On The Outside Now)	*Two A Penny*
What's More (I Don't Need Her)	*B-side*
London's Not Too Far	*Sincerely Cliff*

Lead Vocal:	**Cliff Richard**
Guitars:	**Hank Marvin/Bruce Welch**
Bass:	**John Rostill**
Drums:	**Brian Bennett**
Vocals:	**The Breakaways**
	The Mike Leander Orchestra ('Two A Penny' tracks only)
Producer:	**Norrie Paramor**
Engineer:	**Peter Vince**
Recorded in:	**Studio 2**
Session hours:	**2.30pm-5.30pm/7.00pm-10.00pm**

MARCH 9

Cliff's sister Joan is given away by Cliff when she marries Colin Phipps at Hoddesdon, Hertfordshire.

MARCH 12

On the Cilla Black programme, viewers vote for 'the Song for Europe'. The winning number, to be sung by Cliff on the Eurovision Song Contest, is 'Congratulations', which polls 171,000 of the 250,000 votes.

15 MARCH

ABBEY ROAD
Studio session

Sternengold (All My Love) (8)	*German Release*
London Ist Nicht Weit (London's Not Too Far) (4)	*German B-side*

Lead Vocal:	**Cliff Richard**
	The Mike Leander Orchestra
Producer:	**Norrie Paramor**
Engineer:	**Peter Vince**
Recorded in:	**Studio 2**
Session hours:	**7.00pm-10.00pm**

MARCH 23

Cliff's 41st single, 'Congratulations', is released with 'High 'n' Dry' on the 'B' side. Reviewed as being 'in the same bubbling effervescent style as 'Puppet On A String' ' it is also written by the same songwriters – Bill Martin and Phil Coulter. The 'B' side is a Roger Cook and Roger Greenaway (David & Jonathan) song. The backing vocals on 'Congratulations' are by the Ladybirds.

MARCH

It is announced that Cliff is to star in three major continental gospel concerts with the Settlers, in aid of local charities.

MARCH 24

Cliff appears on Simon Dee's BBC TV show *Dee Time* with Adam Faith, Joe Brown, the Paper Dolls, the Easybeats and Lois Lane, but doesn't sing due to a sore throat.

MARCH

In *Disc and Music Echo*, Bob Farmer reviews and comments on Cliff's book *The Way I See It*: 'Cliff Richard, whether you think he's as nutty as a fruitcake or, as he really is, as nice as pie, is unquestionably doing a splendid job for his Saviour... he can communicate. The church's biggest failing in the present-day society is it's failure to communicate with the layman at large...' For his part, Cliff turns the teachings of Christ into amiable coffee-bar banter: 'He was a man like us... his mother was a woman, a human. His father is God. What a person! You really ought to get to know "him" and I must admit I still get knocked out when God answers my prayers.' Farmer goes on to say that, 'He writes – and talks – with the same enthusiasm as if he were a teenybopper raving about a pop-star, or a youngster boasting about his favourite football team. Cliff makes Christ a person to chat about easily and without embarrassment; the Church made him a forebidding figure, about who it is indecent to talk above a whisper.'

MARCH 25

Cliff takes part in a photo-session with stable-mate John Rowles to celebrate both his hit – 'If I Only Had Time' – and his 21st birthday.

APRIL 1

A Matter Of Diamonds, in which Cliff portrays a young crook, is shown on television.

APRIL 6

The Eurovision Song Contest is staged at London's Albert Hall and is screened in seventeen countries to 200 million viewers. Final placings are:

1 Spain Massiel	'La, La, La'
2 UK Cliff Richard	'Congratulations'
3 France Isabelle Aubert	'The Spring'

After coming runner-up to the Spanish winner, Cliff says: 'Of course I'm disappointed, but it was so close, I don't consider it any disgrace.'

APRIL

It is announced that fifty-six versions of 'Congratulations' are being released around the world and that Cliff has personally recorded the song for release in nearly every country in Europe. Co-writer Bill Martin comments: 'The ironic thing is that Germany, whose votes lost us the contest, have placed a 150,000 advance order!'

APRIL 6

Cliff's role in *A Matter Of Diamonds* is reviewed by David Hughes: 'Normally I never fail to feel embarrassed at the sight of a pop star attempting to become a serious actor, but Cliff has at last bridged the gap, and although 'Riley Walker' was not the most taxing of roles, he coped competently. But let this not be a signal for an avalanche of new pop stars to turn actors. Cliff has mildly embarrassed in at least four films before he found the conviction of his acting.

9 APRIL

ABBEY ROAD
Studio session

Man Gratuliert Mir (Congratulations)	*German A-side*

Lead Vocal:	**Cliff Richard**
Orchestra	
Producer:	**Norrie Paramor**
Engineer:	**Peter Vince**
Recorded in:	**Studio 2**
Session hours:	**7.30pm-9.45pm**

APRIL 13

Hollies drummer Bobby Elliott comments on Cliff's new single: 'I hate 'Congratulations' and I hate the whole atmosphere that surrounds the Eurovision Song Contest. This gives me a sickly feeling inside.'

APRIL

Singer John Rowles visits Cliff's personal clairvoyant, who tells him he will marry twice, have a son and own a house by the sea in the USA.

APRIL

Cliff holidays on the Norfolk Broads with the Crusader Union. The days are spent boating and the evenings are taken up with Bible classes and discussions. Someone suggests that as the Maharishi is to the Beatles, so Billy Graham is to Cliff. Cliff replies: 'The relationship is as wide apart as anything could be. I just admire what Billy Graham says and does – the Maharishi maintains he can do something for the Beatles. Billy Graham can't do anything for me in that way.'

APRIL

Cliff announces that he plans to star in a West End stage play for a seven-week season in the autumn.

APRIL

Cliff appears on an all-star Easter edition of BBC TV's *Top Of The Pops.* Top stars also appearing include the Hollies and Lulu.

23 APRIL

ABBEY ROAD
Studio session

Que Buena Suerte (Congratulations)	*Spanish A-side*
Ah Quelle Historie (Congratulations)	*French A-side*

Lead Vocal:	**Cliff Richard**
Producer:	**Norrie Paramor**
Engineer:	**Peter Vince**
Recorded in:	**Studio 1**
Session hours:	**7.00pm-10.00pm**

The April 9th orchestral track was used for this session.

APRIL 24

Cliff raves about the new Shadows single, 'Dear Old Mrs Bell': 'I think it's a great song – it's fantastic. The kind of record I'd buy.'

APRIL 25

Cliff flies to Sweden to start what is dubbed as a 'mini-Eurovangelism tour', taking in Stockholm, Rotterdam and Zagreb. His co-stars on the three-country tour are the Settlers, Cindy Kent, John Fyffe and Mike Jones.

APRIL

American versions of Cliff's 'Congratulations' are released by Perry Como and Bobby Vinton.

MAY 2

All over Europe, Cliff's Eurovision single 'Congratulations' is outselling the actual winner by Massiel.

3 MAY

ABBEY ROAD
Studio session

Il Mondo Et Tondo (Congratulations)	*Italian A-side*

Lead Vocal:	**Cliff Richard**
Producer:	**Norrie Paramor**
Engineer:	**Peter Vince**
Recorded in:	**Studio 2**
Session hours:	**7.00pm-9.15pm**

The April 9th orchestral track was used on this session.

MAY 4

Cliff appears on the BBC's 50th edition of the radio programme *Saturday Club* with the Bee Gees, the Hollies, the Tremeloes and the Seekers.

MAY 5

Cliff stars with the Bonzo Dog Doo-Dah Band and Lulu in ATV's *The Big Show*.

MAY 12

Cliff appears on the 16th *NME* Poll Winners' Concert at Wembley's Empire Pool in front of a 10,000 strong audience. He performs 'In The Country', 'Shout', 'The Day I Met Marie' and 'Congratulations'. He is presented with his award for 'Top British Vocal Personality' by American singer Robert Knight. The bill also includes Status Quo, Love Affair, Don Partridge, the Association, the Shadows, Amen Corner, the Herd, the Tremeloes, the Move, Dusty Springfield, Scott Walker, Dave Dee, Dozy, Beaky, Mick and Tich and the Rolling Stones.

MAY

'Congratulations' hits the top of the charts in Holland, Denmark, Belgium, Sweden and Norway, as it had the previous month in Great Britain. It also moves into the Top Ten charts in Spain, France, Germany and New Zealand.

MAY 12

Cliff's season at London's 'Talk Of The Town' nightclub opens. He includes in his set songs like 'Ain't Nothing But A Houseparty' and 'Girl, You'll Be A Woman Soon'. He tells the opening night audience, refering obliquely to his much-publicised religious activity:
'I'm not becoming a monk and I'm not becoming a nun either, and I have no stained glass windows in my E-type.'

MAY 18

Cliff announces that he wants to be the first British pop star on the 'Rock Revival Bandwagon':
'I don't think rock'n'roll ever died, it's always been around. The Beatles haved proved this with a lot of songs. I'd like to have 'Move It' out again – it would be good for me.'

Cliff also speaks out about his singular lack of success in the United States:
'It just won't happen for me there and I won't change my career to make it. There was a time when things were pro-British over there and anything that was big in the chart here, automatically got away. I was somehow left behind. We decided about five years ago that we couldn't gear our career to the States – yes, both the Shads and I are very tiny in America!'

In preparation for the Bratislava Song Festival, in which he is to appear in June, Cliff is given a lesson or two in the language by a Czechoslavakian actress, Olinka Berova.

29 MAY

ABBEY ROAD
Studio session

Girl On The Bus (3)	*Established 1958*
Don't Forget To Catch Me (1)	*(Unissued)*
What's Behind The Eyes Of Mary (1)	*(Unissued)*
The Average Life Of A Daily Man	*Established 1958*

Lead Vocal:	**Cliff Richard**
Guitars:	**Hank Marvin/Bruce Welch**
Bass:	**John Rostill**
Drums:	**Brian Bennett**
Producer:	**Norrie Paramor**
Engineers:	**Peter Vince**
Recorded in:	**Studio 2**
Session hours:	**2.30pm-5.00pm/7.00pm-10.00pm**

30 MAY

TALK OF THE TOWN, LONDON
Live recordings

Congratulations-Play On	*Live At The Talk Of The Town*
Shout	*Live At The Talk Of The Town*
All My Love	*Live At The Talk Of The Town*
Ain't Nothing But a Houseparty	*Live At The Talk Of The Town*
Something Good	*Live At The Talk Of The Town*
If Ever I Would Leave You	*Live At The Talk Of The Town*
Girl You'll Be A Woman Soon	*Live At The Talk Of The Town*
London's Not Too Far	*Live At The Talk Of The Town*
The Dreams I Dream	*Live At The Talk Of The Town*
The Day I Met Marie	*Live At The Talk Of The Town*
La La La La La	*Live At The Talk Of The Town*
A Taste Of Honey	*Live At The Talk Of The Town*
Lady Came From Baltimore	*Live At The Talk Of The Town*
When I'm 64	*Live At The Talk Of The Town*
What's More I Don't Need Her	*Live At The Talk Of The Town*
Medley: The Young Ones	*(Unissued)*
Lucky Lips	*(Unissued)*
Living Doll	*(Unissued)*
In The Country	*(Unissued)*
Congratulations	*Live At The Talk Of The Town*
Visions	*Live At The Talk Of The Town*
Congratulations-Play Off	*Live At The Talk Of The Town*

Lead Vocal: **Cliff Richard**
The Norrie Paramor Orchestra
Vocals: **The Breakaways**

Producer: **Norrie Paramor**
Engineers: **Peter Vince**
Session hours: **11.00pm-midnight**

Two more shows were recorded on the 31 May and 1 June with the same titles as recorded here.

RECORDING SHEET

Sheet: 1 of: 1 Class: Pop
Overall Title
ARTISTIC INFORMATION
Artiste(s) and/or cast: Cliff Richard & The Shadows
Conductor / Orchestra / Accompaniment / Art. Dept. Ref.: Mr. Norrie Paramor
Date of Session: 31st May '68 Job No: 36.00
COSTING INFORMATION
Materials used: 0 < 811
Session booked time: 2.30 – 5.30
Session actual: 2.30 – 6.00
Set-up/playback: 1½ / –
Company: Columbia
Studio/control room: 2/2
Engineers: P.V./M.S

Titles and Matrix Nos	Author/Composer/Publisher	Reel Numbers	False Starts	Take No.	Take Details From	To	Dur.	Remarks
Don't Forget To Catch Me		E 68819 4 Track (Cont.)		2	Complete		2.47	Best from take 1
What's Behind The Eyes Of Mary		E 68818 4 Track (Cont.)		3	Incomplete			Not wanted from take 2
Ooh La La		E 68819 4 Track (Cont.)	1	2	Complete		2.54	Best (fade)

31 MAY

ABBEY ROAD
Studio session

Don't Forget To Catch Me (2)	*Established 1958*
What's Behind The Eyes Of Mary	*(Unissued)*
Ooh La La (2)	*Established 1958*

Lead Vocal: **Cliff Richard**
Guitars: **Hank Marvin/Bruce Welch**
Bass: **John Rostill**
Drums: **Brian Bennett**

Producer: **Norrie Paramor**
Engineer: **Peter Vince**
Recorded in: **Studio 2**
Session hours: **2.30pm-6.00pm**

JUNE

'Congratulations' peaks at No.99 in the American *Billboard* Hot Hundred.

5 JUNE

ABBEY ROAD
Studio session

Somewhere By The Sea (4)	*Established 1958*
Here I Go Again Loving You (1)	*Established 1958*
Maggies Samba	*Established 1958*
Poem	*Established 1958*
The Magical Mrs Clamps	*Established 1958*

Lead Vocal:	**Cliff Richard**
Guitars:	**Hank Marvin/Bruce Welch**
Bass:	**John Rostill**
Drums:	**Brian Bennett**
Producer:	**Norrie Paramor**
Engineers:	**Peter Vince**
Recorded in:	**Studio 2**
Session hours:	**2.30pm-5.30pm**

JUNE

Cliff and the Shadows star in a 50-minute Redifussion TV Special *After Ten Fellas – Ten!* This is a look back over their ten years in show business

10 JUNE

ABBEY ROAD
Studio session

Not The Way That It Should Be	*Established 1958*

Lead Vocal:	**Cliff Richard**
Guitars:	**Hank Marvin/Bruce Welch**
Bass:	**John Rostill**
Drums:	**Brian Bennett**
Producer:	**Norrie Paramor**
Engineers:	**Peter Vince**
Recorded in:	**Studio 2**
Session hours:	**2.30pm-6.00pm**

JUNE 13-18

Along with Julie Driscoll and Brian Auger, Cliff is due to represent Britain in the Czechoslovakian Festival of Pop Songs – Bratislava, Lyra, '68. Gene Pitney represents the United States, Massiel represents Spain, and the Commonwealth is represented by the Easybeats. Due to an upset stomach, Cliff pulls out of the festival at the last minute.

As a result, rumours as to the reason for his absence are rife; one claims that he has been killed in a car crash and another that he is suffering from appendicitis.

JUNE 20

Cliff attends the premiere of Billy Graham's production *Two A Penny* in London. The film co-stars British actresses Dora Bryan and Avril Angers.

JUNE 21

Cliff's 42nd single, 'I'll Love You Forever Today'/'Girl, You'll Be A Woman Soon' is released. The 'A' side is featured in his film *Two A Penny*.

JUNE 22

Cliff appears as the star guest on BBC Television's *Billy Cotton Band Show*.

JUNE 22

Critic Alan Smith reviews *Two A Penny*:

'Attempted rape, the seduction of a young man by an older woman... drug trafficking... and Billy Graham with the word of God. In some respects it's the best film Cliff's ever made – as he says himself, he's no Sir Laurence, but at least he gets the chance to act in a serious and straightforward story. Rave versions by Cliff of 'Twist And Shout' plus three catchy numbers 'Two A Penny', 'Love You Forever Today' and 'Questions'.

JUNE 22

In *Disc* magazine, Penny Valentine reviews Cliff's new single, 'I'll Love You Forever Today':

'...probably the most boring song Cliff's ever recorded. It's a shame really, because with his nice inoffensive way of singing, he has usually managed to lift even the most trivial of songs to a slightly higher commercial plane. But it would take a coal-heaver to do anything with this one – and he's certainly not that.'

JUNE 28

Cliff's one-man television show, '*Cliff Richard at the Talk Of The Town*', is screened by BBC 2.

JUNE 29

In the *New Musical Express* half-yearly look at the chart points table, Cliff Richard is placed at joint 15th with the American group the Monkees.

JULY

'Congratulations' earns Cliff his first Gold Disc for five years.

1 JULY

ABBEY ROAD
Studio session

The Long Way Home	*(Unissued)*
What A Silly Thing To Do	*Tracks And Grooves*
Mr Nice	*B-side*
Baby I Could Be So Good At Loving You	*Sincerely Cliff*
Voyage To The Bottom Of The Bath	*Established 1958*
Banana Man	*Established 1958*

Lead Vocal:	**Cliff Richard**
	The Mike Leander Orchestra
Producer:	**Norrie Paramor**
Engineer:	**Peter Vince**
Recorded in:	**Studio 3**
Session hours:	**7.00pm-10.45pm**

TWO A PENNY

Worldwide Films, 1967. Running Time: 98 minutes.
Cliff's seventh feature film.

Synopsis:
Jamie Hopkins (Cliff), a young pedlar encounters Christain faith thanks to his girlfriend Carol.

Cast:
Cliff Richard, Dora Bryan, Ann Holloway, Avril Angers, Geoffrey Bayldon, Peter Barkworth, Nigel Goodwin, Billy Graham.

Credits:
Producer: Frank R Jacobson. Director: James F Collier.
Screenplay and original story: Stella Linden. Music composed and conducted by Mike Leander and also, Cliff Richard.

Songs:
'Two A Penny', 'I'll Love You Forever Today', 'Questions', 'Lonely Girl', 'And Me (I'm On The Outside Now)', 'Daybreak', 'Twist And Shout' performed by Cliff Richard.
'Long Is The Night', 'Celeste' (instrumentals)

Two A Penny premiere at the Prince Charles Cinema.

2 JULY

CHAPPELL STUDIOS
Studio session

As I Walk Into The Morning Of Your Life	*Tracks And Grooves*
In The Past	*Sincerely Cliff*
Marianne	*A-side*
Don't Let Tonight Ever End	*Tracks And Grooves*
What's Behind The Eyes Of Mary	*Established 1958*

Lead Vocal:	**Cliff Richard**
	The Mike Leander Orchestra
Producer:	**Norrie Paramor**
Engineer:	**Peter Vince**
Session hours:	**7.00pm-10.00pm**

JULY

Cliff's recording manager Norrie Paramor and his wife Joan celebrate their Silver Wedding, which is attended by Cliff's mother Dorothy and the Shadows.

1968 *July-September*

6 JULY

ABBEY ROAD
Studio session

Always	*Sincerely Cliff*
Occasional Rain	*B-side*

Lead Vocal: **Cliff Richard**
The Mike Leander Orchestra

Producer: **Norrie Paramor**
Engineer: **Peter Vince**
Recorded in: **Studio 2**
Session hours: **7.00pm-10.00pm**

RECORDING SHEET

[illegible]ereo MONO/STEREO Sheet: 1 of: 1 Class: Pop Overall Title: Mono Reductions & Stereo Remix
Date of Session: 8th July 68 Job No: 32019

ARTISTIC INFORMATION — Artiste(s) and/or cast: Cliff Richard — Art. Dept. Rep.: Mr Norrie Paramor

COSTING INFORMATION — Materials used: 2 x 811 — Session booked time: 10.00 – 1.00 — Session actual: 10.00 – 1.00 — Set-up/playback: ½ / – — Company: Columbia — Studio/control room: 53 — Engineers: PV. / Mb.

Titles and Matrix Nos.	Reel numbers	Take No.	Take details from	Dur.		Remarks
Occasional Rain	E 69167 Mono	RM 1	Complete	2·46	Best	From E 69446 – T 2
Always		RM 1	Complete	2·45	Best	– T's 3/4
What's Behind The Eyes Of Mary		RM 2	Complete	3·07	Best	– T 9
No Don't Stop De Underground		RM 1	Complete	2·40	Best	E 69159 – T 2
No Don't Stop De Underground	E 69168 ½ Stereo	RS 1	Complete	2·40	Best	
Occassional Rain		RS 1	Complete	2·48	Best	
Always		RS 1	Complete	2·45	Best	
What's Behind The Eyes Of Mary		RS 2	Complete	3·07	Best	
What A Silly Thing		RS 1	– " –	2·52	Best	
Baby I Could Be So Good At Loving You		RS 1	– " –	3·05	Best	
Mr. Nice		RS 1	– " –	2·15	Best	
The Long Way Home		RS 1	– " –	2·39	Best	
Somewhere By The Sea		RS 1		Edited	Best	

JULY 17

Cliff appears on BBC TV's *Juke Box Jury.*

JULY 22

Cliff flies to America for a six-week stay: five weeks on a private visit and one week with manager Peter Gormley for discussions with film companies.

JULY

John Rowles reveales that his hit 'If I Only Had Time' had previously been turned down by Cliff Richard and Engelbert Humperdinck.

AUGUST 10

It is reported that the Shadows will officially 'break up' at Christmas.

AUGUST 11

Tenth anniversary of Cliff's first official engagement – a 20-day season at Butlins Holiday Camp, Clacton.

AUGUST

In a interview, Shadow Hank Marvin talks about Cliff ten years on: 'He's much more mature of course, but he appears to be just as ambitious as he was then – perhaps more so. He's giving more and more of his time to helping others through his Crusader work and this is a change in him – taking time off when he could be earning money, to work for something that brings him no cash return. He was a young enthusiastic lad – and this he hasn't lost. He'd rave about some clothes he'd seen or a song, a film or a girl, it's still exactly the same. Before, he revelled in the first glories of fame, whereas now his natural enthusiasm is tempered with awareness.

AUGUST

Cliff and four friends holiday in the USA, taking in Sunset Strip, Disneyland, Santa Barbara, Las Vegas, San Francisco and Hollywood. While there, Cliff reflects that despite being on his fourth American label and having performed on seven Ed Sullivan shows, he still hasn't really cracked it in the States.

When asked about groupies, Cliff says: 'I didn't know you called them groupies, but thats a good word. There are a dozen or so girls who are always around – I see them everywhere. I couldn't say what the perfect girl is as far as hair colour and so on. I know I'd like her to be reserved, because I like to make the first move. A good dress sense is nice, and if she can cook corn on the cob...! I think American girls are more attractive on the whole because everyone looks so healthy here. English girls have that pasty look'.

AUGUST 31

Cliff announces that he will play gospel concerts with the Settlers folk group at Coventry Cathedral and London's Albert Hall later on in the year.

AUGUST

Billy Graham works on German and Japanese versions of Cliff's film *Two A Penny*.

AUGUST

On the subject of the Beatles, Cliff says:

'They felt they had to say clever things in front of the press, but when John Lennon, for example, came about with that quote about the Beatles being more popular than Jesus Christ, I regarded it as the height of childishness for a supposed adult cynic – I just feel the Beatles are too ready to rush on to new sounds...But as people, they've risen in my estimation because they try so hard to find something worthwhile out of life and when they find it's not the answer, they have the guts to say so – like with LSD and then with the Maharishi.
If only they gave Christianity the same gusto – boy, they'd find what they were seeking'.

SEPTEMBER

The *NME* adds a special tenth anniversary 'Cliff and the Shadows' supplement as a tribute to their decade in show business: '...he has won every major award Britain has to offer – World Male Singer, Top British Male Singer (on 8 occasions), Personality of the Year, Best Dressed Young Man, Artist who's the Greatest Credit to Show Business etc.'

SEPTEMBER

Cliff discusses his forthcoming 'A' level in religious instruction and the 'O' level he passed 3 years before: I was 25 – I went to Lewes in Sussex for a hush-hush exam. I was put into a room all alone and about five masters of the school took turns to watch that I didn't cheat! Imagine me cheating while doing a religious instruction exam!'

SEPTEMBER

Cliff continues to live in his Georgian house in Highgate with his friend, teacher Bill Latham (an ex-boyfriend of his sister Jacqueline) and Bill's mother. Cliff and Bill spend most Tuesday nights playing badminton at the church hall and discussing ways of making money for charity. On Sunday afternoons, Cliff is the assistant leader in the Crusaders Union – an inter-denominational religious group that teach boys of 8-18.

SEPTEMBER 14

Cliff's sister Jackie marries 19-year-old landscape gardener Peter Harrison at Hoddesdon Register Office.

SEPTEMBER 19

Cliff's 'Autumn Show' commences a 12 1/2-week run at the London Palladium. He is supported for the first two weeks by the Chris Barber Band, after which the Shadows take over on completion of their Danish tour.

SEPTEMBER 21

Cliff and the Shadows appear in a London Weekend TV Special *Cliff Richard at the Movies.*

SEPTEMBER 22

Cliff attends a Coventry 'Call to Mission' meeting.

SEPTEMBER

EMI release a special LP, 'Established 1958', to mark Cliff and the Shadows' tenth year in show business.

SEPTEMBER 28

The critics slate Cliff's London Palladium show, but not his performance. The general consensus of opinion is that Cliff's fans don't want to sit through acts by comedian Mike Yarwood, the Palladium Orchestra and Chris Barber's Traditional Jazz Band for two hours before the person they came to see even sings a note. Cliff includes, 'When I'm 64', 'Shout' and 'If Ever I Should Leave You'. One critic comments: 'It was a sad night – Cliff's return to the Palladium for his autumn season – sad, because it marked beyond all shadow of doubt that the era of Cliff, the teenage idol, has finally departed.

SEPTEMBER

Cliff's 43rd single is released – 'Marianne'/'Mr Nice'.

OCTOBER

Cliff is interviewed by Keith Skues for the BBC's *Saturday Club.*

10 OCTOBER

ABBEY ROAD
Studio session

Leave My Woman Alone	*B-side*
Will You Love Me Tomorrow	*Sincerely Cliff*
Bang Bang	*Tracks And Grooves*

Lead Vocal: **Cliff Richard**
The Norrie Paramor Orchestra

Producer: **Norrie Paramor**
Engineer: **Peter Vince**
Recorded in: **Studio 2**
Session hours: **2.00pm-5.00pm**

OCTOBER

Cliff performs at the London Palladium throughout October, while the press report that a weak supporting bill is not helping mediocre audience figures.

24 OCTOBER

ABBEY ROAD
Studio session

If I Do	*(Unissued)*
Note In A Bottle	*(Unissued)*
You Never Can Tell	*B-side*

Lead Vocal:	**Cliff Richard**
	The Norrie Paramor Orchestra
Producer:	**Norrie Paramor**
Engineer:	**Peter Vince**
Recorded in:	**Studio 1**
Session hours:	**2.00pm-4.45pm**

31 OCTOBER

ABBEY ROAD
Studio session

Wonderful World	*German B-side*
Marianne	*Hier Ist Cliff*
Geh Deinen Weg Nicht So Allein (The Dreams I Dream)	*Hier Ist Cliff*

Lead Vocal:	**Cliff Richard**
	The Norrie Paramor Orchestra
Producer:	**Norrie Paramor**
Engineer:	**Peter Vince**
Recorded in:	**Studio 2**
Session hours:	**2.00pm-5.00pm**

NOVEMBER

It is announced that Cliff and Anita Harris will star in ATV's *Bruce Forsyth Show* on Christmas Eve.

NOVEMBER 5

Cliff records for BBC's radio programme *Off The Record*, choosing and discussing eight of his favourite records.

NOVEMBER 9

It is revealed that Cliff is to star in his own mini-TV series for Tyne Tees in 1969 – six weekly religious shows with the Settlers, in which Cliff will not only perform alone and with the group but also in religious sketches.

NOVEMBER 16

Cliff's 44th single 'Don't Forget To Catch Me' is released and reviewed by journalist Penny Valentine: 'Presumably because he's celebrating his tenth anniversary in pop – though I hardly find this a good enough excuse – they have issued this track from Cliff's LP 'Established 1958'. I find it a bit pointless and sad. Lately, Cliff surprised me by coming up with some quite good records – 'Marianne' being one of the best – and it's a shame that this is reverting back to the corny, boring stuff of years gone by. A waste of time, talent and people's ears.'

20 NOVEMBER

ABBEY ROAD
Studio session

Twist Im Blut (Twist And Shout)	*Hier Ist Cliff*
Mr Niemand	*Hier Ist Cliff*
Die Liebe Ist Immer Nur Heut (I'll Love You Forever Today)	*Hier Ist Cliff*
Fragen (Questions)	*Hier Ist Cliff*

Lead Vocal:	**Cliff Richard**
	The Norrie Paramor Orchestra
Producer:	**Norrie Paramor**
Engineer:	**Peter Vince**
Recorded in:	**Studio 2**
Session hours:	**2.00pm-5.00pm**

NOVEMBER

Reviewer Derek Johnson goes into print with nothing but praise for Cliff's new single: 'I've got a feeling that this could give him his highest chart place since 'Congratulations''.On the same day, Cliff duets with French singer Mireille Mathieu on her British television show.

27 NOVEMBER

ABBEY ROAD
Studio session

Stell' Mich Deinen Eltern Vor (Not The Way That It Should Be)	*Hier Ist Cliff*
Deine Augen Träumen Mary (What's Behind The Eyes Of Mary)	*Hier Ist Cliff*
Ooh La La	*Hier Ist Cliff*

Lead Vocal:	**Cliff Richard**
	The Norrie Paramor Orchestra
Producer:	**Norrie Paramor**
Engineer:	**Peter Vince**
Recorded in:	**Studio 2**
Session hours:	**2.00pm-5.00pm**

Cliff appeared on TV with the Settlers as well as recording several tracks

28 NOVEMBER

ABBEY ROAD

Studio session

Zärtliche Sekunden	
(Don't Forget To Catch Me)	*German A-side*
Shoom Llama Boom Boom	*Hier Ist Cliff*
Story Ohne Happy-End	
(Girl On The Bus)	*Hier Ist Cliff*

Lead Vocal:	**Cliff Richard**
	The Norrie Paramor Orchestra
Producer:	**Norrie Paramor**
Engineer:	**Peter Vince**
Recorded in:	**Studio 2**
Session hours:	**2.00pm-5.00pm**

DECEMBER 1

Cliff introduces BBC Televison's long-running Sunday religious programme *Songs of Praise*, from the Holy Trinity Church in Manchester.

2/3 DECEMBER

ABBEY ROAD

Studio session

Love Is More Than Words	*(Unissued)*
Compassion Road	*(Unissued)*
No One Seems To Care	*(Unissued)*
Help	*(Unissued)*
That's What Love Is	*(Unissued)*

Lead Vocal:	**Cliff Richard**
	The Settlers (Cindy Kent, Mike Jones, John Fyffe, Geoffrey Srodzinski)
Producer:	**Norrie Paramor**
Engineer:	
Recorded in:	**Studio 3**
Session hours:	**2.00pm-5.00pm**

DECEMBER 4

Cliff takes part in the cutting of a 650lb-Christmas pudding for the Mental Health Trust at London's Carlton Towers Hotel.

RECORDING INSTRUCTIONS

A/M IN ATTENDANCE MR. N. PARAMOR TRADE MARK COLUMBIA JOB No. 36,007

ARTISTE	DATE	TIME	STUDIO
CLIFF RICHARD	28.11.68.	2. - 5.p.m.	2
	TYPE: 4 Track	No. of SIDES	DJ/NP LAQUERS

COMPOSITION OF ORCHESTRA/CHORUS

2 - 4.p.m.: 6 Violins, 2 Violas, 2 Celli, Trumpet
1 - 4.p.m.: 3 Boys (1 - 2.p.m. rehearsal)
3 - 5.p.m.: 1 Elec. Gtr.
2 - 5.p.m.: 2 Violins, Bass Gtr., Drums, Acc. Gtr./Elec., Elec. Gtr. (with trem)

8736

TITLES	Publishers
ZÄRTLICHE SEKUNDEN (Don't Forget to Catch Me) Marvin/Welch/Bennett/Hertha	Shadows
SHOOM LLAMA BOOM BOOM (Shoom Llama Boom Boom) Roker/Littlewood/Bradtke	Elizabethan
STORY OHNE HAPPY-END (Girl on the Bus) Rostill/Relin	Shadows

Items marked * are non copyright.

CHEQUE COST DETAILS CASH

DECEMBER 7

The *NME* Annual Poll results are published:

World Male Singer
1 Elvis Presley
2 Tom Jones
3 Cliff Richard

World Musical Personality
1 Elvis Presley
2 Jimi Hendrix
3 Cliff Richard

British Vocal Personality
1 Cliff Richard
2 Tom Jones
3 Paul McCartney

British Male Singer
1 Tom Jones
2 Cliff Richard
3 Scott Walker (American)

Cliff's 'Congratulations' is voted 4th best British Disc of the Year behind the Beatles' 'Hey Jude' (1), Mary Hopkin's 'Those Were The Days' (2) and the Rolling Stones' 'Jumping Jack Flash' (3).

DECEMBER 7

Disc and Music Echo publish a letter from Harry Morrison of Greenock, Renfrewshire: 'Having seen Cliff Richard, I am convinced he's going to reach the class and status of Frank Sinatra.

DECEMBER 14

Following the partial retirement of the Shadows, reports appear in the press that the Settlers will be Cliff's support group for many dates in 1969, as well as their recording a single together. Cliff says: 'I first saw them at a two-hour concert in London's Festival Hall and was immediately impressed. If it goes well, then obviously we'll record together much more.'

DECEMBER

BBC Radio Transcription

Sleigh Ride	*(Unissued)*
Santa Claus Is Coming To Town	*(Unissued)*
Winter Wonderland	*(Unissued)*
Jingle Bells	*(Unissued)*
White Christmas	*(Unissued)*
Good News	*(Unissued)*
Carnival	*(Unissued)*
Moonlight Bay	*(Unissued)*
Sweet Little Jesus Boy	*(Unissued)*
Mary What You Gonna Call That Pretty Little Baby?	*(Unissued)*
It Came Upon The Midnight Clear	*(Unissued)*
I Saw Three Ships	*(Unissued)*
Silent Night	*(Unissued)*
God Rest Ye Merry Gentlemen	*(Unissued)*

Lead Vocal **Cliff Richard**
The Norrie Paramor Orchestra
Vocals: **The Breakaways/The Mike Sammes Singers**

DATE UNKNOWN

BBC Radio Transcription

Move It	*(Unissued)*
Let It Be Me	*(Unissued)*
The Girl Can't Help It	*(Unissued)*
Great Balls Of Fire	*(Unissued)*
Lucille	*(Unissued)*
Jailhouse Rock	*(Unissued)*
Good Old Rock And Roll	*(Unissued)*
Do You Wanna Dance	*(Unissued)*
A Taste Of Honey	*(Unissued)*
The Day I Met Marie	*(Unissued)*
I Who Have Nothing	*(Unissued)*
I Saw The Light	

Lead Vocal: **Cliff Richard**
The Norrie Paramor Orchestra
Vocals: **The Ladybirds**

DECEMBER

Cliff rejects reports that his recent Palladium season had been a box office disappointment:
'I was told 90% of West End theatres would have liked to have done our business, but it was a bad time of year – there's no money and no people in November.'

DECEMBER

Cliff hits out at people's changing attitudes towards Christmas.

'Christmas is turning. People don't celebrate Christmas for the right reasons any more. To too many, Christmas is just a holiday – a booze-up time – although I've got nothing against boozing. They forget the fact that the only reason we celebrate is because it is Christ's birthday. They really don't know why they have these few days off from work.

There is so much apathy in the land towards religion that it must follow, in time, they will forget what everything's about. The only aspect of commerciality at Christmas of which I disapprove is the case of people who take advantage. The toymakers who up the price of toys at Christmas from 30 shillings to £2.00. That's sharp practice and deplorable.

DECEMBER

Following a gospel concert by Cliff at Manchester Palace with the Settlers, a critic in *The Guardian* newspaper writes that the concert was 'old-fashioned' and adds the hardly original comment 'The devil still has the best songs.'

DECEMBER 21

Cliff reveals his plans for 1969:
'I'm not letting up. I'm doing another film for the Billy Graham organisation, only this time it'll be on location in Israel and I'll play a guy adopted by a Jewish couple. I'll be recording again soon, but there's also the show I'm doing for Scottish TV in colour, which is being made with the Golden Rose of Montreux in mind and is a bit of technical genius in which there are marvellous camera angles and effects and things. It's called *Cliff in Scotland* and yes, I do wear a kilt!'

DECEMBER 25

Cliff sings 'Congratulations' on BBC Television's *Top of the Pops*. Also appearing are an all-star line-up of Manfred Mann, Esther and Abi Ofarim, Love Affair, Georgie Fame, the Beatles and the Rolling Stones.

DECEMBER 25

Cliff appears on the *Morecombe and Wise Christmas Show* on BBC TV with Lulu, Petula Clark, Nana Mouskouri, the Seekers and jazz legend Louis Armstrong.

DECEMBER 25

On BBC Radio 1, Cliff presents a Christmas Day special – an hour of his own favourite tracks from various seasonal Yuletide albums.

DECEMBER 27

Cliff flies off with friends for a four-day holiday.

JANUARY 4

In the *New Musical Express* 1968 points table based on chart positions during the year (30 points for 1 week at number 1, to 1 point for 1 week at number 30), Cliff appears in the 22nd position with 308 points between Hugo Montenegro and Otis Redding. Tom Jones heads the table with 708 points.

8 JANUARY

ABBEY ROAD
Studio session

Now I've Done It	*(Unissued)*
Where Is The Man	*(Unissued)*
You Held My Hand	*(Unissued)*
Forgive Me	*(Unissued)*
Johnny	*(Unissued)*
The Fellow Next To Me	*(Unissued)*
Don't Blame Me	*(Unissued)*
Johnny Wake Up To Reality	*(Unissued)*

Lead Vocal:	**Cliff Richard** **The Settlers (Cindy Kent, Mike Jones, John Fyffe, Geoffrey Srodzinski)**
Producer:	**Norrie Paramor**
Engineer:	
Recorded in:	**Studio 3**
Session hours:	**10.00pm-1.00am**

11 JANUARY

ABBEY ROAD
Studio session

Turn It Into Cash	*(Unissued)*
This Is My Kind Of Love	*(Unissued)*
I Will Arise And Go	*(Unissued)*
Celebrate	*(Unissued)*
Happy World	*(Unissued)*
Seeing Is Believing	*(Unissued)*
Till Winter Follows Spring	*(Unissued)*
Nowhere Man	*(Unissued)*

Lead Vocal:	**Cliff Richard** **The Settlers (Cindy Kent, Mike Jones, John Fyffe, Geoffrey Srodzinski)**
Producer:	**Norrie Paramor**
Engineer:	
Recorded in:	**Studio 3**
Session hours:	**2.30pm-5.30pm/7.00pm-10.00pm**

JANUARY 13-17

Cliff and the Norrie Paramor Orchestra are featured daily on Radio 1's *Dave Cash Programme*.

JANUARY 15-16

Cliff and the Settlers perform at London's Albert Hall in aid of the homeless starving refugees of Biafra. Tickets for the concerts

– advertised as 'A Gospel Folk-Beat-Blues Evening' – range from 3/6d to 19/6d.

31 JANUARY

IBC STUDIOS
Studio session

You'll Want Me	*Sincerely Cliff*
I'm Not Getting Married	*Sincerely Cliff*
Good Times (Better Times)	*A-side*

Lead Vocal:	**Cliff Richard**
	The Mike Vickers Orchestra
Producer:	**Norrie Paramor**
Engineer:	
Recorded in:	**Studio 3**
Session hours:	**7.00pm-10.00pm**

FEBRUARY 8

Cliff agrees to take part in a 12-minute colour film titled *Give Us This Day* – a short documentary about the John Groom Children's Homes in Kent. Cliff is to sing a song called 'Thank You' in the picture, which is to be available free of charge to schools, clubs and voluntary organisations.

FEBRUARY 19

Cliff appears on Cilla Black's TV show singing 'Good Times' and 'Don't Forget'.

FEBRUARY

The pop music paper, *Disc and Music Echo*, publishes the results of its annual poll.

Top Male Singer
1 Tom Jones
2 Scott Walker (American)
3 Cliff Richard

1 Scott Walker
2 Cliff Richard
3 Johnnie Walker (Radio DJ)

Top TV Artist / Male
1 Scott Walker
2 Cliff Richard
3 Simon Dee

Best Dressed Male Star
1 Cliff Richard
2 Scott Walker
3 Tom Jones

Cliff was voted 5th best male singer in the world behind Scott Walker, Tom Jones, Otis Redding and Elvis Presley.

FEBRUARY

Having been voted 'Best-Dressed Star', Cliff talks about fashion during rehearsals at West Finchley Methodist Church Hall: 'I've got nothing against outrageous clothing – in fact, if I'm invited to a party where they say 'informal clothes', I think it's a great excuse to wear something extravagant like a pink frilly shirt!' Cliff reveals that as well as sporting 50-guinea-plus suits from his Savile Row tailor, Robert Valentine, he also has some wilder gear like a jacket that's made out of 'Black Watch tartan material'.

21 FEBRUARY

ABBEY ROAD
Studio session

Releve Mon Defi (Questions)	*When In France LP*
Je Suis Formidable (Two A Penny)	*When In France LP*

Lead Vocal:	**Cliff Richard**
	The Norrie Paramor Orchestra
Producer:	**Norrie Paramor**
Engineer:	**Peter Vince**
Recorded in:	**Studio**
Session hours:	

FEBRUARY 22

Cliff's 45th single, 'Good Times (Better Times)'/'Occasional Rain', is released. One reviewer comments: 'A happy light-hearted and immensely danceable disc – though I don't rate the material as particularly memorable even though it was written by the joint talents of Jerry Lordan, Roger Cook and Roger Greenaway.' Another writes: 'Here's someone else who seems to simply float through recording sessions, pack his bag at the end of one 'take', smile 'thank you, fellas' and go home. Cliff's records are always simple, uncluttered, uncomplicated and as a result are often boring.'

FEBRUARY

Cliff spends ten days at EMI's Abbey Road Studios recording, 'Don't Forget To Catch Me' in Italian, German and French.

24 FEBRUARY

CHAPPELL STUDIOS
Studio session

Chi Lo Sà (On The Beach)	*Italian B-side*
Non Dimenticar Chi Ti Ama (Don't Forget To Catch Me)	*Italian A-side*

Lead Vocal: **Cliff Richard**
The Norrie Paramor Orchestra

Producer: **Norrie Paramor**
Engineer:
Session hours: **7.00pm-10.00pm**

24 MARCH

ABBEY ROAD
Studio session

Is There An Answer	*(Unissued)*
Small World	*(Unissued)*
The Carnivals Just For Me	*(Unissued)*
Can It Be True	*(Unissued)*

Lead Vocal: **Cliff Richard**
The Settlers (Cindy Kent, Mike Jones, John Fyffe, Geoffrey Srodzinski)

Producer: **Norrie Paramor**
Engineer:
Recorded in: **Studio 3**
Session hours:

FEBRUARY 27

Cliff appears on *Top of the Pops* with Sandie Shaw, Donald Peers, the Hollies, Cilla Black, Peter Sarstedt, Glenn Campbell and soul legend Marvin Gaye – and the show is hosted by radio disc jockey Stuart Henry.

MARCH 1

Cliff flies to Germany to make a guest appearance on the German equivalent of British television's popular *The Golden Shot* game show..

MARCH 3

Cliff flies to Romania for five days to play a guest spot in a televised song festival.

MARCH

Cliff appears on BBC TV's *Rolf Harris Show* which has been prerecorded.

MARCH 9-12

Cliff undertakes appearances in Italy.

MARCH 15

Earnest Fullman from Coventry has a letter about Cliff published in the press:
'Since his smash hit 'Congratulations', his records have been dull and wearing...buck up your ideas, Cliff, or you will be in the same boat as Elvis.'

MARCH 19

Cliff appears on *Top of the Pops* with the Tremeloes, Love Affair, Tony Blackburn, Marvin Gaye, the Hollies, Sandie Shaw and Peter Sarstedt. The show is hosted by veteran DJ and presenter Pete Murray.

MARCH 21-22

Cliff undertakes appearances in Holland.

MARCH 26

Cliff appears on Liberace's TV show.

APRIL 5

Discussing more rumours that he intends giving up the music business to pursue his religious activities, Cliff comments: 'I realise that if I quit, it would be like a rat deserting a sinking ship. There are other active Christians in show business, and it was partly due to some of them that I decided to stay in the business. There is nothing immoral or sordid about entertainment, providing you don't allow yourself to be carried away by the glamour and financial rewards. I am a hundred per cent Christian and everything I do is done with my religion in mind. I don't mean I have to walk around all day with God on my mind, but everything I do is motivated by my Christian beliefs. Unfortunately, even in religious activities, you find unscrupulous people. I was asked if I would talk to some young men and women in Scotland; at the time, I was busy filming and I told the person that if I could possibly make it, I would arrive. But he had big posters printed saying I was going to speak – naturally, he was selling tickets and making a lot of money out of it.'

APRIL

Cliff voices a concern about certain religious groups:
'Minority religious groups like the Jehovah's Witnesses and the Exclusive Brethren take things so literally they lose all the Bible's meaning – groups like the Exclusive Brethren really scare me. By cutting themselves off from the rest of the people, they are destroying the whole essence of Christianity, that of fellowship and spreading the gospel.'

APRIL 3

Cliff appears on *Top of the Pops* with the Hollies, the Marbles, the Beach Boys, Lulu, Joe South, Mary Hopkins, the Foundations and Marvin Gaye. The show is hosted by Alan Freeman.

APRIL 5

Cliff reveals that his first big thrill in his show business career was when he was impersonated on television by Benny Hill.

APRIL 8

In the *Daily Express*, Cliff complains that he's always had to be a 'larger-than-life' Cliff Richard in all his films. 'What I want is a tiny little nothing part opposite Albert Finney...no one takes me seriously. I have an unfortunate image.'

APRIL

Cliff talks on the subject of earnings, having revealed that he collects £15 in cash every Friday to see him through the week. 'Friday was always pay day for me and I think that unless you are paid in hard cash and actually see your money being spent, you can lose all sense of it's value. My father raised our whole family on £11 per week... If I thought my money could convert anyone to my beliefs, then I would give it all away. But money doesn't change anything. John Lennon could never be converted because of my money.'

APRIL

It is announced that later in the year, Cliff will speak at a Billy Graham religious crusade in the Holy Land.

APRIL 12

Cliff's first show-biz tailor, Dougie Millings, talks about his early days designing for Cliff: '...I made him a white sharkskin suit, with a black satin shirt and tie. He's kept coming back to me over the years and there was one time when he was in Glasgow and I was in London and we agreed to meet up at Carlisle, where I fitted him for a new suit on the station platform at midnight!'

18 APRIL

ABBEY ROAD

Studio session

Sam	*Sincerely Cliff*
So Long	*B-side*
Take Good Care Of Her	*Sincerely Cliff*

Lead Vocal:	**Cliff Richard**
Orchestra	
Producer:	**Norrie Paramor**
Engineer:	**Peter Vince**
Recorded in:	**Studio 2**
Session hours:	**7.00pm-10.00pm**

22 APRIL

ABBEY ROAD

Studio session

My Head Goes Around	*Tracks And Grooves*
Big Ship	*A-side*
When I Find You	*Sincerely Cliff*

Lead Vocal:	**Cliff Richard**
	Mike Vickers Orchestra
Producer:	**Norrie Paramor**
Engineer:	**Peter Vince**
Recorded in:	**Studio 2**
Session hours:	**7.00pm-10.00pm**

APRIL

Shadows guitarist Hank Marvin and Cliff are approached to do a tour of Japan, Hong Kong, Singapore and Australia in September

30 APRIL

ABBEY ROAD
Studio session

She's Leaving You	*B-side*
Time Flies	*B-side*
Take Action	*Sincerely Cliff*

Lead Vocal:	**Cliff Richard**
Producer:	**Norrie Paramor**
Engineers:	**Peter Vince/Richard Langham**
Recorded in:	**Studio 2**
Session hours:	**7.00pm-10.00pm**

APRIL

Scottish TV's *Cliff in Scotland* is entered for the Montreux Film Festival.

MAY

The Settlers release a new single, 'Love Is More Than Words', which Cliff has co-written.

2 MAY

ABBEY ROAD
Studio session

No Name No Fame	*(Unissued)*
Throw Down A Line	*A-side*
Early In The Morning	*Tracks And Grooves*

Lead Vocal:	**Cliff Richard**
Duet Vocals:	**Hank Marvin on Throw Down A Line/ The Mike Vickers Orchestra**
Producer:	**Norrie Paramor**
Engineer:	**Peter Vince**
Recorded in:	**Studio 2**
Session hours:	**7.00pm-10.00pm**

MAY 11

Cliff Richard closes the first half of the annual *New Musical Express* Poll Winners' Concert at London's Wembley Arena, where he appears along with American soul duo Bob and Earl, reggae star Desmond Dekker, novelty group the Scaffold, Marmalade, the Move, the Tremeloes, Lulu, Hank Marvin, Amen Corner, Love Sculpture and Peter Sarstedt.
The concert, attracting its usual capacity crowd, is compered by top disc jockeys Jimmy Savile and Tony Blackburn. For his appearance Cliff sings 'Move It', 'Good Times', 'La La La La La', and 'Congratulations'.

MAY 17

Cilla Black and Hank Marvin guest on BBC 1's Saturday night *Cliff Richard Show*.

MAY

The *NME* reviews Cliff's concert appearance: 'His voice is wild, screaming with soul. This is Cliff on his greatest form, literally destroying any contention that his religious beliefs make him tame and goody-goody. There is no doubt that Cliff Richard is a phenomenon of British pop...'

MAY

Estranged Bee-Gee Robin Gibb is invited to write a song for Cliff.

MAy

In Totteridge, Hertfordshire, singer Frank Ifield becomes a neighbour of Cliff's – as are Hank Marvin, Bruce Forsyth and Frankie Vaughan.

MAY 23

Cliff's 46th single 'Big Ship'/'She's Leaving You', is released and gets the thumbs up from the critics:
'Cliff Richard has never suffered the indignity of a chart failure...I have every confidence this will maintain his unbroken run of successes.' Another reviewer writes: 'I'd go so far as to say it's the best thing he's done. Raymond Froggatt wrote the song, which is a cross between a very stray immediate melody line and an almost gospel chorus.'

MAY 24

Cliff's former personal assistant Mike Conlin announces the release of a single ('200 Weeks') by a solo Australian vocalist whom he manages. The singer, Terry Britten, who was formerly with the Twilights, has already had four songs recorded by Cliff. On the same day, Cliff flies to the United States for discussions on his forthcoming film for Billy Graham, the follow-up to *Two A Penny*. Cliff is helping to write the music for the score.

May 26

Comedian Peter Kaye is praised by the press for his impersonation of Cliff on BBC TV.

JUNE

Cliff's 'Congratulations' wins him two Ivor Novello Awards, one for the most performed work and one for the 'International Song of the Year'.

JUNE 7

Cliff appears on Radio 1's *Pete's Saturday People* with the Flirtations and Raymond Froggatt.

JUNE 8

Cliff appears on *Top of the Pops* with Jethro Tull, Tommy Roe and Chicken Shack.

JUNE 9

Having appeared with Jethro Tull on the previous week's *Top of the Pops*, Cliff enthuses: 'I think Jethro Tull are fantastic. They have so much talent. But the term 'Underground' still baffles me – I think of it as meaning a group without a hit.'

JUNE 14

Cliff appears on *Top of the Pops* with the Ohio Express, Des O'Connor, Amen Corner, Edwin Hawkins Singers, Scott Walker and the Beatles. The show is hosted by Pete Murray.

JUNE 21

Singer Peter Sarstedt says of Cliff's current hit 'Big Ship': '...just another formula song. I don't know why he does that – I don't like any of his recent songs. With this, everything is arranged to sell with a huge 'S'.'

JUNE 28

Former Shadow Hank Marvin comments on Cliff's show business longevity: 'Much of the credit for Cliff's staying power must go to the way in which his career has been guided by Pete Gormley, his manager, who stays so much in the shadows. He has the knack of bringing out the best in his artists and building them up in a aura of prestige and stardom. Yet Peter himself hates personal publicity. He finds it all a bit of a drag; he never goes to premieres and things like that. His enjoyment is in having artists with a talent and doing his best for them.'

JULY 12

In the *NME* half-yearly chart table (30 points for a number 1, 1 point for number 30), Cliff is 28th with 190 points. Leaders are Fleetwood Mac with 479 points, followed by the Beatles with 389 and Herman's Hermits with 340.

29 JULY

ABBEY ROAD
Studio session

Reflections	*B-side*
Love, Truth And Emily Stone	*Tracks And Grooves*
With The Eyes Of A Child	*A-side*

Lead Vocal:	**Cliff Richard**
	The Mike Vickers Orchestra
Producer:	**Peter Vince**
Engineer:	
Recorded in:	**Studio 2**
Session hours:	**7.00pm-10.00pm**

AUGUST 23

The BBC announce plans for a TV series starring Cliff, to begin early in 1970, co-starring Hank Marvin and actress Una Stubbs.

AUGUST/SEPTEMBER

Cliff holidays in Portugal and then with the Crusader camp on Herm in the Channel Islands.

SEPTEMBER 4

Cliff is interviewed on BBC Radio 1's programme *Scene and Heard*. On the same day, Cliff and Hank appear on *Top of the Pops* along with Humble Pie.

SEPTEMBER 6

Cliff's new single (his 47th) is a duet with Hank Marvin, who wrote the 'A' side 'Throw Down A Line'. The 'B' side is 'Reflections'. Among the reviewers' comments: 'Cliff's back to blues...' 'The lyric is intense, almost bitter...' 'Cliff throws off years of boredom... it proves that Cliff has suddenly plonked himself right in the middle of the music scene of today...' 'A Number One'.

SEPTEMBER

On the subject of lyrics, Cliff comments: '...when I do forget lyrics, it's not usually new songs, but things like 'Livin' Doll'. I guess it's because I've sung it so many times, I don't bother to read the words and then my mind goes blank.'

SEPTEMBER 13

Cliff admits, 'Television still frightens me a little. *Top of the Pops* doesn't bother me because it's such a casual show. But I always have the feeling of all those unseen viewers.'

SEPTEMBER

It's rumoured that Cliff's next single may be another Hank Marvin song – 'Love Truth and Emily Stone'.

22 SEPTEMBER

ABBEY ROAD
Studio session

Abraham, Martin And John	*Tracks And Grooves*
You're Hearts Not In Your Love	*Tracks And Grooves*
Love Is Like A Crescendo	*(Unissued)*
Postmark Heaven	*(Unissued)*
Are You Only Fooling Me	*Tracks And Grooves*
When You Are There	*(Unissued)*

Lead Vocal:	**Cliff Richard**
Producer:	**Peter Vince**
Engineers:	
Recorded in:	**Studio 2**
Session hours:	**2.30pm-5.30pm/7.00pm-10.00pm**

SEPTEMBER 25

Jimmy Savile introduces *Top of the Pops* which includes Cliff and

Hank, Oliver, Fat Mattress, Bobby Gentry and Creedance Clearwater Revival.

SEPTEMBER 27

Radio 1 DJ David Symonds makes his feelings felt on 'Throw Down A Line': 'Cliff and Hank's record is very undignified. I think it falls between two kinds of thought and Cliff is basically at his best singing commercial pop-songs. This is out of character – he's a good clean cut lad. They're climbing on to a band-wagon and I don't think Cliff's personal commitments fit the scene.'

SEPTEMBER 29

Cliff guests on Pete Murray's *Open House* radio show for the BBC.

OCTOBER 14

Cliff is 29.

OCTOBER

The Shadows re-form to back Cliff on a Japanese tour. Hank Marvin, Brian Bennett and John Rostill add keyboard player Alan Hawkshaw to their line-up.Cliff comments on the Japanese fans: '...they don't understand the lyrics too well, and to them it's just a sound, so providing the melody is strong and simple, you're in with a chance.'

OCTOBER

KOREA
Live recordings

Shout	*Cliff Live In Korea*
Move It	*Cliff Live In Korea*
Its All In The Game	*Cliff Live In Korea*
Big Ship	*Cliff Live In Korea*
Good Times (Better Times)	*Cliff Live In Korea*
Throw Down A Line	*Cliff Live In Korea*
The Day I Met Marie	*Cliff Live In Korea*
La La La La La	*Cliff Live In Korea*
The Lady Came From Baltimore	*Cliff Live In Korea*
Ain't Nothing But A Houseparty	*Cliff Live In Korea*
The Young Ones	*Cliff Live In Korea*
Livng Doll	*Cliff Live In Korea*
In The Country	*Cliff Live In Korea*
Bachelor Boy	*Cliff Live In Korea*
Something Good	*Cliff Live In Korea*
If Ever I Would Leave You	*Cliff Live In Korea*
When I'm 64	*Cliff Live In Korea*
Early In The Morning	*Cliff Live In Korea*
Congradulations	*Cliff Live In Korea*
Visions	*Cliff Live In Korea*

Producer:
Engineer:
Session hours:

DATE UNKNOWN

LOCATION UNKNOWN
Studio session

(1)	
Ezekiel's Vision	*His Land*
(2)	
Hava Nagila	*His Land*
Dry Bones	*His Land*
(3)	
His Land	*His Land*
Jerusalem, Jerusalem	*His Land*
The New 23rd	*His Land*
His Land	*His Land*
Keep Me Where Love Is	*His Land*
(4)	
Over In Bethlehem	*His Land*
He's Everything To Me	*His Land*
Narration And Hallelujah Chorus	*His Land*
(5)	
Narration And Hallelujah Chorus	*His Land*

(1) Cliff Barrows with the Ralph Carmichael Orchestra
(2) Ralph Carmichael Orchestra and Chorus
(3) Cliff Richard
(4) Cliff Richard and Cliff Barrows
(5) Cliff Barrows, the Ralph Carmichael Orchestra and Chorus

Producer:
Engineer:
Session hours:

NOVEMBER 5

Cliff and the Shadows commence a short British tour, Marcie and the Cookies are also on the bill.

NOVEMBER

Several tour dates are cancelled, due to Cliff's laryngitis.

NOVEMBER 15

Cliff's 48th single, 'With The Eyes Of A Child'/'So Long' is released. The critics comment: '...an enchanting ballad with a philosophical lyric pleading for universal brotherhood...' '...a tender quasi-protest song with Cliff pleading for a more beautiful world in which kids can grow up'.

NOVEMBER

Cliff talks about actress Una Stubbs: 'She'd be my own personal Miss World. One of the most underestimated artists in the whole

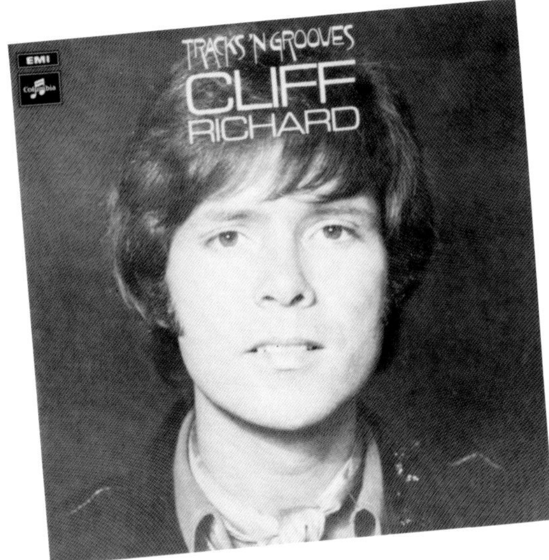

world too. We first met in *Summer Holiday*. She's a very experienced girl and the sort you can talk to quite easily and really open yourself up to her... a very wordly person.'

NOVEMBER 28

Cliff sings 'Throw Down A Line' and 'With The Eyes Of A Child' on French television.

DECEMBER

Cliff is tipped to top the list of Britain's 'Best Bespectacled Gentleman' poll the findings of which are being published by the Birmingham Opthalmic Council. He was third in 1965 and 11th in 1968. All his spectacles are supplied by Scruvers in London's Regent Street.

DECEMBER

Cliff tops the chart in Japan with a cover of Vanity Fayre's 'Early In The Morning'.

DECEMBER 20

It's announced by the Bromley Theatre Trust that Cliff will star in a stage version of a ten-year-old West End play *Five Finger Exercise*, and also – along with the Shadows – will do a stage musical version of Pinnochio for Christmas 1970.

DECEMBER 23

Cliff goes carol-singing with the Crusaders to raise money for Fegan's Homes, for which they collect about £20.00.

DECEMBER 24

Cliff attends the Christmas Eve Carol Service at his church in Finchley.

DECEMBER 24

Cliff appears on the *Cilla Black Show* which also stars Dusty Springfield and Kenny Everett, with a look-back at the music scene of 1969.

DECEMBER 24

Christmas With Cliff on Radio 1 and Radio 2. He features as disc jockey, playing an hour of his favourite records.

DECEMBER 25

Cliff stars in *Let's Go With Cliff* on Radio 4, in which his guests are Salena Jones, Los Paraguayos and the Norrie Paramor Orchestra.

DECEMBER 27

LWTV screens *The Young Ones*.

DECEMBER 31

Jimmy Savile introduces a 75-minute BBC 1 TV show *Pop Go The Sixties*, which includes Cliff and the Shadows performing their 1962 hit 'Bachelor Boy'. The show also includes Adam Faith, Helen Shapiro, the Rolling Stones, Sandie Shaw, the Tremeloes, the Who, the Bachelors, Lulu, Dusty Springfield and a film of the Beatles.

JANUARY

BBC 1's 13-week TV series, *It's Cliff Richard*, begins.

JANUARY

Talking at the BBC Theatre at Shepherd's Bush, Cliff says: 'I think my acting is the direction my career must improve in... I can't see my voice improving any more, and if I didn't have anything more to strive for, I might be in danger of getting stale.'

7 JANUARY

ADVISION
Studio session

The Joy Of Living — *A-side*

Lead Vocal:	**Cliff Richard**
	The Mike Vickers Orchestra
Vocals:	**Hank Marvin**
Producer:	**Norrie Paramor**
Engineer:	
Recorded in:	
Session hours:	

JANUARY

Cliff sticks up for the much criticised Kenny Rogers single, 'Ruby, Don't Take Your Love To Town', by replying to all the people who said it was a sick record: 'All those people who said that it sounded like a bunch of old women... it was a hard-hitting record, but hardly sick. There must have been lots of them who came back from a war and found themselves in that position. The record is a statement of true fact and as unpalatable as that may be, it cannot be sick and distasteful.'

JANUARY 10

The *NME* publish their annual chart table based on 30 points for a week at number 1 to 1 point for a week at number 30. Cliff is fifteenth in the table with 372 points between America's Isley Brothers and Peter Sarstedt. Table leaders are Fleetwood Mac with 728 points.

JANUARY

Comments appear in the press about comedy sketches spoiling Cliff's new series.

JANUARY 17

The *NME* publish the results of a points survey based on the Top 30 over the past decade:

1 Cliff Richard	7,913
2 Elvis Presley	6,438
3 Beatles	6,394
4 Shadows	3,790
5 Rolling Stones	3,126
6 Roy Orbison	3,103
7 Adam Faith	2,965
8 Hollies	2,863

21 JANUARY

CHAPPELL STUDIOS
Studio session

Lieben Kann Mann Einmal Nur	*German B-side*
Pentecost	*(Unissued)*
Kein Zug Nach Gretna Green	*German B-side*
Du Du Gelfäst Mir So	*German A-side*

Lead Vocal: **Cliff Richard**

Producer: **Norrie Paramor**
Engineer:
Session hours: **7.00pm-10.00pm**

JANUARY

On his TV show, Cliff does impressions of Tiny Tim and Ken Dodd.

JANUARY 24

The *NME* poll results are published:

British Male Singer

1 Tom Jones	5,332
2 Cliff Richard	4,667
3 Mick Jagger	2,378

British Vocal Personality

1 Cliff Richard	3,839
2 Tom Jones	3,695
3 John Lennon	1,776

World Male Singer

1 Elvis Presley	5,727
2 Tom Jones	3,816
3 Cliff Richard	2,925

Cliff is voted fourth most popular 'World Musical Personality' behind Elvis Presley (1), John Lennon (2) and Eric Clapton (3). Cliff and Hank's 'Throw Down A Line' is voted 5th best single of the year.

JANUARY

Korea votes Cliff their most popular star.

JANUARY

Cliff receives an award from the highly respected Songwriters' Guild of Great Britain for 'The Most Outstanding Service to Music in 1969'.

FEBRUARY 7

Cliff's 49th single, 'The Joy Of Living' (with Hank Marvin), also features Hank's 'Boogatoo' and Cliff's solo, 'Leave My Woman Alone'. The single is a cynical look at the modern age, where Britain is in danger of being turned into one huge motorway.

FEBRUARY 14

Disc and Music Echo publish their poll results:

Mr Valentine
1 Cliff Richard
2 Scott Walker
3 Johnnie Walker

Best-Dressed Male Star
1 Cliff Richard
2 Barry Gibb
3 Tom Jones

Top British Male Singer
1 Tom Jones
2 Cliff Richard
3 Scott Walker (American)

Top World Male Singer
1 Elvis Presley
2 Tom Jones
3 Cliff Richard

'Sincerely Cliff' is voted sixth-best LP, and Cliff and Hank's 'Throw Down A Line' is voted tenth-best single.

FEBRUARY 20

Cliff is featured on Dave Cash's Radio 1 show.

20 FEBRUARY

ABBEY ROAD
Studio session

The Birth Of John The Baptist And The Birth Of Jesus (Luke 1:5-38; 57-66;80. Luke 2: 1-20)	*About That Man*
Sweet Little Jesus Boy	*About That Man*
The Visit Of The Wise Men And The Escape To Egypt (Matthew 2:1-23)	*About That Man*
John The Baptist Points Out Jesus (John 1:19)	*About That Man*
Jesus Recruits His Helpers And Heals The Sick (Mark 1: 12-2: 12)	*About That Man*
Where Is That Man	*About That Man*
Jesus Addresses The Crowd On The Hillside (Matthew 5: 1-17; 21-28; 38-48. Matthew 6: 19-34. Matthew 7: 1-8; 13,14: 24-29)	*About That Man*
Can It Be True	*About That Man*
Jesus Is Betrayed And Arrested (Luke 22:1-6. John 13: 1-19, Luke 22: 33,34; 39-51; 54-62)	*About That Man*
The Trial Of Jesus,His Execution And Death (Luke 22: 66-71. John 18 28-19: 19. Luke 23: 39-46; 50	*About That Man*
The First Easter-The Empty Tomb (Luke 24: 1-12. John 20: 19-20. Luke 24: 44-48. Matthew 28: 18-20)	*About That Man*
Reflections	*About That Man*

Lead Vocal:	**Cliff Richard**
Guitar:	
Producer:	**Norrie Paramor**
Engineer:	**Richard Lush**
Recorded in:	**Studio 2**
Session hours:	**7.00pm-10.00pm**

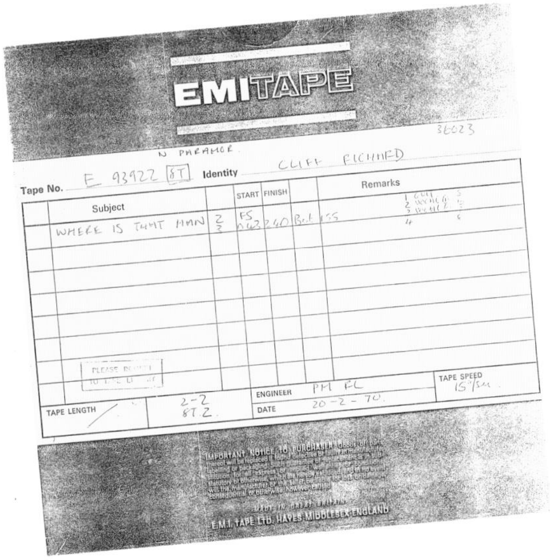

MARCH

Cliff attends a party at No.10 Downing Street given by the Prime Minister, Harold Wilson, in honour of West German Chancellor Willy Brandt. The gathering also includes singer Sandie Shaw and actress Una Stubbs.

12 MARCH

ABBEY ROAD
Studio session

Goodbye Sam Hello Samantha	*A-side*
I Ain't Got Time Anymore	*A-side*
Monday Comes Too Soon	*B-side*

Lead Vocal:	**Cliff Richard**
	The Mike Vickers Orchestra
Producer:	**Norrie Paramor**
Engineer:	
Recorded in:	**Studio 3**
Session hours:	**7.30pm-10.30pm**

MARCH

The final six songs for the 1970 Eurovision Song Contest are sung on Cliff's television series, and the winning song is revealed. Viewers vote Mary Hopkin's 'Knock, Knock Who's There?' into first place.

APRIL

A paperbook book, Cliff Richard-Questions, is published at the price of five shillings. In it Cliff sounds off on various topics:

Eurovision

The voting is right up the spout. Personally I think the only way to make any sense of the competition is to make it a bit more complicated. At the moment it's pretty obvious that many of the juries do not represent the tastes of their own countries anyway.

Girlfriends

I don't see how you can have a really close relationship with a girl unless you marry her. I doubt if it is possible – or very difficult - to have the sort of platonic relationship with a girl which two women may have or a man with a close male friend.

Racialism

No one race or skin colour is better than another in God's sight. Every individual has equal rights as a human being, and it's up to him to live with his neighbour be he black, yellow or white!

APRIL 6

Cliff appears at Batley Variety Club for a week of cabaret.

APRIL 11

It's announced that Cliff will sing and speak at a series of public meetings in London later in the year, to help launch a national campaign against the permissive society.

APRIL

BBC Radio presents *The Cliff Richard Story* with Robin Boyle.

APRIL

Cliff grows a beard in preparation for his starring role in the forthcoming stage play *Five Finger Exercise*.

MAY 3

A bearded Cliff appears at the *NME* Poll Winners' Concert, backed by the Candies. His act includes 'The Girl Can't Help It', 'Great Balls Of Fire' and 'Throw Down A Line'. Cliff's trophy is presented to him by singer Malcolm Roberts.

MAY 11

Five Finger Exercise opens at the Bromley New Theatre – Cliff takes eight curtain calls on the first night.

MAY 19

Cliff records a contribution for BBC TV's *Disney Show*.

MAY 30

Cliff releases his 50th single, a Mitch Murray-Peter Callarde-Geoff Stephens song, 'Goodbye Sam, Hello Samantha'. One critic says, 'Not a song of substance or durability, but one that's made for the charts.'

MAY

A party to celebrate his 50th single is attended by a host of stars including Radio 1's John Peel. Cliff says that his favourite of the fifty singles is 'The Day I Met Marie'.

1 JUNE

ABBEY ROAD
Studio session

The Old Accordion	*(Unissued)*
A Sad Song With A Happy Soul	*(Unissued)*
I Was Only Fooling Myself	*(Unissued)*

Lead Vocal:	**Cliff Richard**
Producer:	**Norrie Paramor**
Engineer:	
Recorded in:	**Studio 3**
Session hours:	**7.00pm-10.00pm**

JUNE 13

Cliff and Clodagh Rogers appear as guests in Roy Castle's BBC television show.

JUNE 13

Cliff makes a guest appearance at the Bratislava Song Festival in Czechoslovakia. Other guests include Paul and Barry Ryan.

29 JUNE

CHAPPELL STUDIOS
Studio session

Goodbye Sam Das Ist Die Liebe (Goodbye Sam, Hello Samantha)	*German A-side*

Lead Vocal:	**Cliff Richard**
Producer:	**Norrie Paramor**
Engineer:	
Session hours:	**7.00pm-10.00pm**

30 JUNE

ABBEY ROAD
Studio session

Indifference	*(Unissued)*
Rain Cloud	*(Unissued)*

Lead Vocal:	**Cliff Richard**
Producer:	**Norrie Paramor**
Engineer:	
Recorded in:	**Studio 2**
Session hours:	**7.00pm-10.00pm**

JULY

DJ Terry Wogan says that 'Goodbye Sam, Hello Samantha' is not one of Cliff's strongest: 'By anyone else it wouldn't have a chance.'

JULY 4

The *NME* publish their half-yearly points table (30 points for a week at number 1 to 1 point for a week at number 30). Cliff is 54th with 91 points between the Beach Boys and Joe Dolan. The Jackson Five are top of the table with 342 points.

JULY

Cliff flies to South Africa at the invitation of the Bishop of Natal to speak and sing in Durban at a series of youth meetings sponsored by Christian businessmen and aimed at the youth of the country.

JULY

Journalist Andy Gray answers the question of how Cliff has outlasted all his rivals: '...Friendliness... Cliff has always been so genuinely friendly with everyone. You never hear of him having a feud or a disagreement or being nasty to anyone. He never

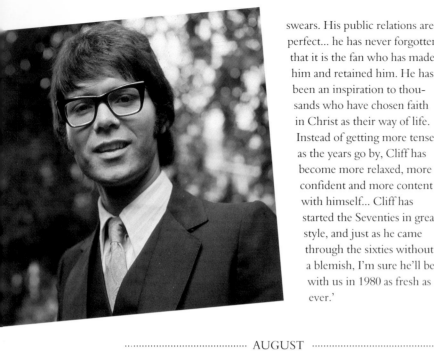

swears. His public relations are perfect... he has never forgotten that it is the fan who has made him and retained him. He has been an inspiration to thousands who have chosen faith in Christ as their way of life. Instead of getting more tense as the years go by, Cliff has become more relaxed, more confident and more content with himself... Cliff has started the Seventies in great style, and just as he came through the sixties without a blemish, I'm sure he'll be with us in 1980 as fresh as ever.'

AUGUST

Cliff is holidaying.

AUGUST 22

Cliff's 51st single, 'I Ain't Got Time Anymore'/'Monday Comes Too Soon', is released. The song is scored and arranged by Mike Vickers of Manfred Mann fame.

AUGUST 24

Cliff says: 'I personally respect John Lennon for what he's trying to do for peace. He's doing what he thinks is right, in the same way that I make no secret that I'm using my career to promote Christianity. But Lennon has become a laughing-stock among so many people.'

SEPTEMBER

Cliff is delayed for five hours at Copenhagen Airport, due to a bomb scare and the potential threat of a hijack.

SEPTEMBER

Cliff spends some leisure time at the cinema. Among the films he sees are *Rosemary's Baby*, *A Man Called Horse*, *The Wild Bunch* and *Bonnie And Clyde*.

SEPTEMBER 28

Cliff starts a four week season at London's 'Talk Of The Town'. His set includes, 'Move It', 'Jailhouse Rock', 'Great Balls Of Fire', 'Through The Eyes Of A Child' and 'I Who Have Nothing'. On stage, Cliff jokes about his religious convictions: 'I've heard it said that I've got stained-glass windows in my Mini, but that's ridiculous – they're in my Jenson!'

OCTOBER 4

Cliff appears in *Sing A New Song* with the Settlers for BBC TV's department of religious programmes.

OCTOBER 9

Cliff receives the National Viewers' and Listeners' Association annual award for an 'Outstanding Contribution to Religious Broadcasting and Light Entertainment'.

The award is presented by Malcolm Muggeridge, and Mrs Mary Whitehouse, (who founded the Association) tells Cliff: 'You really have made a nonsense of this thing about the generation gap.'

OCTOBER 14

Cliff celebrates his 30th birthday.

OCTOBER

Cliff considers buying a house in Weybridge, Surrey, on the same exclusive estate where fellow superstars of pop Tom Jones, Engelbert Humperdinck and Gilbert O'Sullivan already have properties.

NOVEMBER 7

Cliff appears on Radio Luxembourg discussing his future with Ken Evans.

NOVEMBER 8

Cliff is featured on Dave Lee Travis' Radio 1 show; the other guests are singer Cat Stevens and the former leader of Herman's Hermits, Peter Noone.

NOVEMBER 11-14

A two-week tour of Britain is entitled 'Cliff In Concert' on which Cliff is accompanied by Marvin, Welch and Farrar.

16 NOVEMBER

ABBEY ROAD
Studio session

Don't Move Away (3)	*B-side*
I Was Only Fooling Myself (4)	*B-side*
Sunny Honey Girl (4)	*A-side*

Lead Vocal:	**Cliff Richard**
Guitar:	
Bass:	
Drums:	
Piano:	
Organ:	
Acoustic Guitar:	
Strings	
Vocals:	**Olivia Newton-John (on Don't Move Away)**
Producer:	**Norrie Paramor**
Engineer:	**Peter Vince/Richard Lush**
Recorded in:	**Studio 2**
Session hours:	**7.00pm-10.00pm**

17 NOVEMBER

ABBEY ROAD
Studio session

Silvery Rain	*A-side*
Take A Look Around	*(Unissued)*

Lead Vocal: **Cliff Richard**

Producer: **Norrie Paramor**
Engineer: **Peter Vince/Richard Lush**
Recorded in: **Studio 3**
Session hours: **2.30pm-5.30pm**

NOVEMBER 18-21

More concerts on the 'Cliff In Concert' tour.

24 NOVEMBER

ABBEY ROAD
Studio session

Umbarella (Annabella Umbrella)	*Ich Träume Deine Träume*
Lass Uns Schnell Vergessen (Don't Ask Me To Be Friends)	*Ich Träume Deine Träume*
Das Girl Von Nebenan	*German B-side*
Du Fragst Mich Immer Wieder	*Ich Träume Deine Träume*
Wenn Du Lachst, Lacht Das Gluck (Sally Sunshine)	*German A-side*

Lead Vocal: **Cliff Richard**

Producer: **Norrie Paramor**
Engineer:
Recorded in: **Studio 2**
Session hours: **2.30pm-5.30pm/7.00pm-10.00pm**

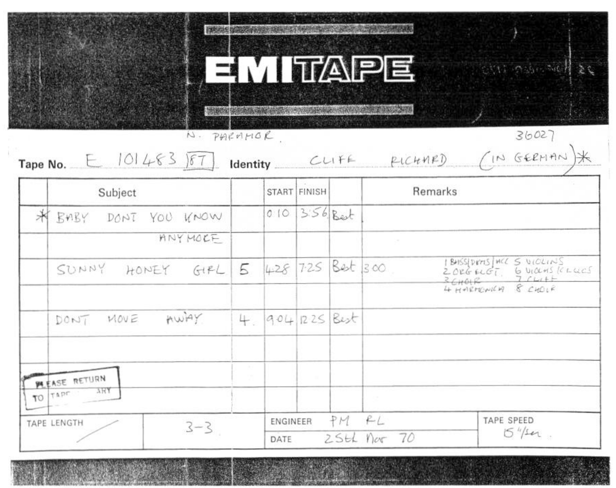

EMITAPE

N. PARAMOR. 36027

Tape No. E 101483 [8T] Identity CLIFF RICHARD (IN GERMAN) *

	Subject		START	FINISH		Remarks
*	BABY DONT YOU KNOW ANYMORE		0.10	3.56	Best	
	SUNNY HONEY GIRL	5	4.28	7.25	Best	3.00 — 1 BASS/DRMS/ACC 2 ORG & GT 3 CHOIR 4 HARMONICA 5 VIOLINS 6 VIOLAS/CELLOS 7 CLIFF 8 CHOIR
	DONT MOVE AWAY	4.	9.04	12.25	Best	

PLEASE RETURN TO TAPE [LIBR]ARY

TAPE LENGTH 3-3 | ENGINEER PM RL | DATE 25th Nov 70 | TAPE SPEED 15"/sec

25 NOVEMBER

ABBEY ROAD
Studio session

Ein Spiel Ohne Grenzen	*German B-side*
Concerto	*Ich Träume Deine Träume*
Neben Dir Wirds Keine Geben (Early In The Morning)	*Ich Träume Deine Träume*
Zum Heiraten Bin Ich Kein Typ (I'm Not Getting Married)	*Ich Träume Deine Träume*
Der Mann Neben Dir (Baby Don't You Know Anymore)	*Ich Träume Deine Träume*
Ich Träume Deine Träume	*German A-side*

Lead Vocal: **Cliff Richard**

Producer: **Norrie Paramor**
Engineer:
Recorded in: **Studio 2**
Session hours: **2.30pm-5.30pm/7.00pm-10.00pm**

NOVEMBER 28

Having been described in an interview as 'mechanically charming', Cliff retorts:
'I'm not going to pretend it didn't hurt me because it did – deeply. But what really stung was the realisation that here was somebody knocking me for trying to be pleasant and friendly.
If we really do live in a permissive society, then shouldn't it be the case that I should be allowed to be 'mechanically charming' if I want to be?
Shouldn't I be free too? The fact is, I'm only as human as the next person when it comes to criticism, and I don't mind admitting that I find it hard to take when I feel it's unjustified.'

DECEMBER 14-18

Cliff is featured on Terry Wogan's Radio 1 show with Billie Davis and the Casuals.

DECEMBER 17

BBC Television screens *The Young Ones* movie.

DECEMBER 24

BBC Television screen a Cliff Richard special with Cliff, Hank Marvin and Una Stubbs.

DECEMBER

It is reported that Cliff is to release a maxi-single. An early sign of the decline of the single in terms of record sales, maxi-singles were the music industry's response to a market moving more and more towards albums. It was really a repackaged and renamed version of the old EP (extended play) format , with three or four tracks instead of the usual two. Later attempts to rescue the doomed single have included the 12" single and CD singles.

1971 – 1974

The Records 1971 – 1974

The decline in chart placings continued throughout this period with some singles barely nudging the top twenty and others not even doing that. Of the more successful ones, 'Sunny Honey Girl' enjoyed moderate sales sending the single to a top twenty position. The next two singles just did not have enough impact to score big on the charts, although the follow-up 'Sing A Song Of Freedom' became the most successful, reaching the No.13 spot and spending more weeks on the chart than any of the previous 1971 singles. 1972 turned out to be another poor year chart-wise, with only 'Living In Harmony' showing enough promise to chart, as the previous one 'Jesus' failed to appeal to a mass audience. A worse fate lay in store for the last single of the year – 'Brand New Song' simply went unnoticed and became the first ever Cliff single not to reach the charts, and the first one produced without Norrie Paramor's guidance. However, the following year did show an improvement, with Cliff again representing Britain in the Eurovision Song Contest. 'Power To All Our Friends' became his biggest hit since 'Congratulations' in 1968, but the two other singles that were released in 1973 were hardly hit records. 'Hangin' On', the only single in 1974, fared slightly better, peaking at No.13. On the album front, matters were not improved. None of the albums reached any higher than the top 40. The soundtrack album from *Take Me High* did only slightly better than THE BEST OF CLIFF VOL.2, but considerably worse than previous soundtrack albums, a fate that was to befall the film at the box-office as well.

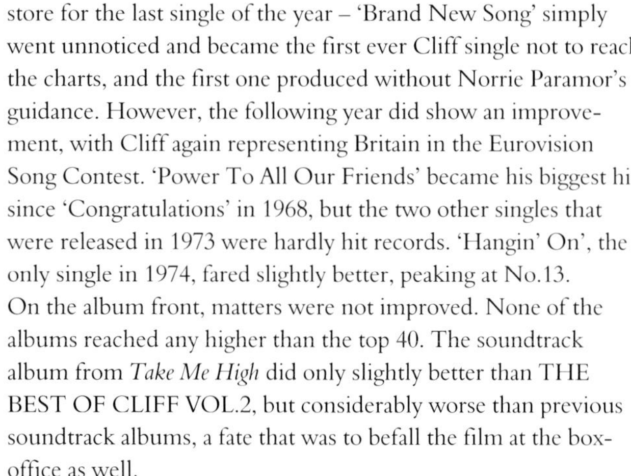

There was also an EMI promotional demo issued in October 1974 to radio stations combining 'Nothing To Remind Me' and 'The Leaving' taken from the 31ST OF FEBRUARY STREET album.

The Sessions 1971 – 1974

The February 1971 sessions show a continuation of the line that started in March 1970 with its emphasis on the recording of A and B side material, but surprisingly no album tracks were taped during this time. Besides all the recording activity, 1972 was the year that saw Cliff return to Japan for live work, and from this tour EMI put together an album of live recordings released in the Far East only as LIVE IN JAPAN. As for the musicians backing Cliff, his old pals from the Shadows, Bruce Welch and Hank Marvin appeared with their new partner John Farrar as Marvin, Welch and Farrar. Brian Bennett, another Shadow regular, played drums and was a natural choice as musical director. Alan Hawkshaw was brought in to provide the piano work, and vocal backing came from Olivia Newton-John and Pat Carroll. For the repertoire of the show, a basic set-up was followed with a string of hit material interspersed with some new songs.

Plans were made to follow-up these live recordings with more sessions at Abbey Road. These sessions produced the single 'A Brand New Song' and two tracks for the 31ST OF FEBRUARY STREET album. David MacKay took over as supervisor of the recording sessions from this point, and given the presence of a different producer the radical change in sound perhaps did not come as a total surprise. More A and B side recordings were taped at the next few sessions and, as happened before with 'Congratulations', Cliff's 1972 Eurovision Song 'Power To All Our Friends' had to be recorded in a number of foreign languages for the respective territories.

The last feature film Cliff made was shot in 1973 necessitating soundtrack sessions, although these did not yield any hit songs. It is known that Cliff put down his vocals at the September recording dates on some of the tracks after the backing tracks had been completed as far back as May. During this same period the incidental music for the film was also recorded.

For the September 1973 sessions, the Morgan Studios were chosen. The band assembled for the sessions featured a number of musicians that would work with Cliff through to the eighties, people like Terry Britten, Alan Tarney, and Trevor Spencer. Using the same procedure as on the debut CLIFF album, a specially invited audience was assembled at Morgan Studios for a live recording that would provide all the material for the HELP IT ALONG album. A session on the 26th was held to add strings to the live tracks.

Cliff returned to Abbey Road to complete tracks for the 31ST OF FEBRUARY STREET album early in 1974. Perhaps as an acknowledgement of the changes that had taken place in the music scene, it was decided to include material of a more contemporary nature, and generally the songs that make up the album are of a high standard, with some being especially impressive in an attempt to produce a concept album.

Cliff and Debbie Watling, his co-star in *Take Me High*

Following the success of the LIVE IN JAPAN album it seemed the obvious thing to do was to record another live set, aimed again at the Japanese and Far East audiences only. At least two complete shows were recorded by EMI, but of these only items selected for release on the JAPAN TOUR double album were filed with Abbey Road, although these tapes do contain four unissued tracks – 'Living In Harmony', 'Nothing To Remind Me', 'The Next Time' and 'Wind Me Up'. It is not known why these four were omitted from the album, and one can only assume the reasons were likely to have been over-running of the duration of the album, or technical problems that may have arisen during recording.

JANUARY 2

NME publish their chart table for 1970 based on 30 points for a week at number 1 to 1 point for a week at number 30. Cliff comes 40th with 230 points, between the Beach Boys and Hot Legs. The chart leader is Elvis Presley with 799 points.

JANUARY 2

Cliff's BBC TV series makes it debut – co-starring Una Stubbs and Hank Marvin.

JANUARY

Impresario Leslie Grade announces that he is keen to produce a big-budget musical starring Cliff.

JANUARY 9

Cliff's 52nd single is released. 'Sunny Honey Girl' has two songs on the 'B' side – 'I Was Only Fooling Myself' and a duet with Olivia Newton-John 'Don't Move Away'. One reviewer says: 'It's likely to be one of Cliff's biggest hits for some time.' The 'A' side is a song jointly written by two songwriting teams – Roger Cook and Roger Greenaway teaming up with Johnny Goodison and Tony Hillier.

JANUARY 9

The second in the BBC TV series *It's Cliff Richard* features Marvin, Welch and Farrar.

JANUARY 16

It's Cliff Richard features the New Seekers. Cliff performs George Harrison's 'My Sweet Lord'.

JANUARY 18-22

Cliff is featured on Jimmy Young's Radio 1 show with the Rockin' Berries, the Symbols and the Barron Knights.

JANUARY 23

Elton John appears on *It's Cliff Richard*, singing 'Your Song'.

JANUARY

The *NME* poll results are published:

World Male Singer

1 Elvis Presley	5,702
2 Cliff Richard	3,697
3 Tom Jones	2,420

World Musical Personality

1 Elvis Presley	4,637
2 Cliff Richard	2,708
3 Andy Williams	1,789

Best TV/Radio Show

1 'Top Of The Pops'	11,237
2 'Disco 2'	2,116
3 'It's Cliff Richard'	1,816

British Vocal Personality

1 Cliff Richard	3,547
2 Tom Jones	2,385
3 Cilla Black	1,696

British Male Singer

1 Cliff Richard	4,998
2 Tom Jones	3,777
3 Paul Mccartney	1,536

Cliff's 'Goodbye Sam, Hello Samantha' is voted the 7th best British single of 1970, and *Tracks 'n' Grooves* the 8th best LP.

JANUARY 24

Cliff provides the commentary for 'Lollipop Tree', a section on 'The World About Us.' He talks about a home for 800 children at the foot of the Himalayas.

12 FEBRUARY

CHAPPELL STUDIOS
Studio session

Pigeon	*B-side*
Annabella Umbrella	*B-side*

Lead Vocal: **Cliff Richard**

Producer: **Norrie Paramor**
Engineer:
Session hours: **7.00pm-10.00pm**

FEBRUARY 20

In Cliff's TV show, Clodagh Rogers performs the six final numbers in 'A Song for Europe'. Producer Michael Hurll makes public his problems with the usual voting system due to the current postal strike. The winning song is 'Jack In The Box'.

MARCH

At the invitation of the Reverend Patrick Goodland, Cliff appears at the Stanmore Baptist Church in North London. The sermon is replaced by Cliff answering questions on his religious views from his close friend, Bill Latham, who is also Educational Officer of the Evangelical Alliance Relief Fund. The topics range from 'Did Una Stubbs wear a wig?' through to 'Drug taking and suicides in show business' and 'Cliff possibly being seen as a "Jeckyl and Hyde" figure.' Cliff says during the interview that his Christian views are not a gimmick: 'With 99% of the population, a gimmick is something instantly commercial. This does not describe Christianity. I could have found a better gimmick.'

MARCH

BBC 1 and Cliff's management negotiate for another TV series.

MARCH

Cliff buys a house in Essex for the Christian Arts Centre.

5 MARCH

CHAPPELL STUDIOS
Studio session

'Cause I Believe In Loving	*(Unissued)*
I Who Have Nothing	*(Unissued)*

Lead Vocal:	**Cliff Richard**
Producer:	**Norrie Paramor**
Engineer:	
Session hours:	**7.00pm-10.00pm**

MARCH 6

Cliff duets with Petula Clark on his TV show.

Derek Harvey from Headington, Oxford, attacks Cliff's TV show in a letter to the press: 'The comedy content is embarrassing – Cliff's versions of other people's hits always sound like inferior covers... compare his programmes with those of Andy Williams, Petula Clark or Des O'Connor.'

20 MARCH

ABBEY ROAD
Studio session

Flying Machine	*A-side*

Lead Vocal:	**Cliff Richard**
	The Norrie Paramor Orchestra
Producer:	**Norrie Paramor**
Engineer:	
Recorded in:	**Studio 3**
Session hours:	**2.30pm-5.30pm**

MARCH 26

Cliff kicks of a European tour in Holland before appearing in Denmark, Germany, Austria, Switzerland and Belgium.

APRIL

Cliff's 53rd single, 'Silvery Rain' (written by Hank Marvin), is described by reviewer Derek Johnson as 'one of the least commercial and uncharacteristic he has ever recorded'. Backed by 'Annabella Umbrella' and 'Time Flies', it is a social comment on the problems of pesticides and poisons. Cliff replies to the critics:

'There's no reason why a song shouldn't have something to say and still have an infectious beat – pop is an art form. You have to make complete use of it.'

APRIL 3

Derek Harvey's letter evokes a reply from those in agreement and those who disagree. Lesley Short from Havant, replies: 'I thought the Cliff Richard shows knocked them for six. I find his family very entertaining, which is more than I can say for the Andy Williams production.' 'Senior Citizen' from Croydon, Surrey, writes: 'Cliff at thirty still seems to cling to his Harry Wharton of Greyfriars nice-chap image – the show is so juvenile it might as well switch slots with *Doctor Who*.'

APRIL 11

Cliff is featured on the *Dave Lee Travis Show* on Radio 1, with Dave Edmunds, Rockpile and Seals and Croft.

APRIL 17

Northern cabaret dates are announced for Cliff in June.

28 APRIL

ABBEY ROAD
Studio session

Mr Cloud	*B-side*

Lead Vocal:	**Cliff Richard**
Producer:	**Norrie Paramor**
Engineer:	
Recorded in:	
Session hours:	

MAY 10-29

Cliff appears in the play *The Potting Shed* at the Bromley New Theatre.

MAY

Plans are announced for Cliff's next film, *Xanadu*, which is to be shot entirely on location in Newcastle. The story is by Alan Plater, who wrote *The Virgin and the Gypsy*, with Peter Hammond of *Spring and Port Wine* fame directing. Producer Andrew Mitchell comments, 'This will not be a sugar-sweet out-and-out musical. Basically it's the tale of a romance between two young people in an industrial city.'

JUNE

At the Dickie Valentine Memorial Concert, Cliff duets with Petula Clark.

2 JUNE

ABBEY ROAD
Studio session

La Ballade De Baltimore	*French A-side*
L'Amandier Sauvage	*French B-side*

Lead Vocal:	**Cliff Richard**
Producer:	**Norrie Paramor**
Engineer:	
Recorded in:	**Studio 2**
Session hours:	**2.30pm-5.30pm/7.00pm-10.00pm**

JUNE 26

Cliff's 54th single 'Flying Machine' is released. One reviewer writes: '...days from now... we shall all have joined the butcher's boys and milk roundsmen in whistling it's happy tune'.

JUNE

It is announced that shooting for Cliff's sixth film, *Xanadu*, will start in mid-September.

JULY 5

In the 1970/71 Ivor Novello Awards, Cliff receives an award for 'Outstanding Service to British Music'.

JULY 26-30

Cliff is featured on Radio 1's Tony Brandon show with Middle Of The Road, Christie and the Searchers.

AUGUST 7

The BBC announces that the new Cliff series will start around Christmas. Hank Marvin will still be resident and the time will extend to 45 minutes.

AUGUST

'Flying Machine' becomes Cliff's first-ever single not to make the Top 30.

AUGUST

Cliff spends an evening watching the New Seekers at London's 'Talk Of The Town'.

23 AUGUST

ABBEY ROAD
Studio session

Kleine Taube (You're My Pigeon)	*German B-side*

Lead Vocal:	**Cliff Richard**
Producer:	**Norrie Paramor**
Engineer:	
Recorded in:	**Studio 2**
Session hours:	**2.30pm-5.30pm/7.00pm-10.00pm**

24 AUGUST

ABBEY ROAD
Studio session

Sing A Song Of Freedom	*A-side*
A Thousand Conversations	*B-side*

Lead Vocal:	**Cliff Richard**
Producer:	**Norrie Paramor**
Engineer:	
Recorded in:	**Studio 2**
Session hours:	**2.30pm-5.30pm/7.00pm-10.00pm**

AUGUST 30

BBC 1 screen *Getaway with Cliff*, a 50 minute programme featuring Olivia Newton-John, Hank Marvin, Bruce Welch and John Farrar.

AUGUST

The shooting of *Xanadu* is postponed until the spring because of possible 'adverse weather conditions'.

SEPTEMBER

Cliff's 'Flying Machine' tops the chart in Denmark.
It is announced that Cliff will undertake several British dates at the end of the year.

9 SEPTEMBER

ABBEY ROAD
Studio session

The Old Accordion	*B-side*

Lead Vocal:	**Cliff Richard**
Producer:	**Norrie Paramor**
Engineer:	
Recorded in:	**Studio 1**
Session hours:	**9.30pm-10.00pm**

OCTOBER

Cliff's 'Flying Machine' tops the Malaysian charts.

OCTOBER 11-NOVEMBER 2

Cliff headlines a three-week show at the London Palladium supported by Marvin, Welch and Farrar and Olivia Newton-John.

OCTOBER 14

Cliff celebrates his 31st birthday.

OCTOBER 30

'Sing A Song Of Freedom'/'A Thousand Conversations' is Cliff's 55th single. One reviewer comments: 'Cliff plays it safe by treading the well-worn path to freedom.'

NOVEMBER 1-5

Cliff is featured on Dave Lee Travis's Radio 1 show with Peter Noone, Marmalade, the Drifters and Richard Barnes.

NOVEMBER 6

Jimmy Tarbuck and Cliff appear in Cilla Black's new BBC 1 series *Cilla*.

NOVEMBER

Impresario Leslie Grade and theatre chief Louis Benjamin announce that Cliff's Palladium show has broken box-office records.

THE DOME, BRIGHTON
MONDAY, 22 NOV., 1971
at 9 p.m.
CLIFF RICHARD
ROW
E 41
STALLS CIRCLE £1.25
(GROUND FLOOR)
Tickets cannot be accepted for exchange or refund. Latecomers will not have access to their seats until a suitable interval.
TO BE RETAINED

NOVEMBER

'Sing A Song Of Freedom' is banned in South Africa because of political repressiveness.

NOVEMBER/DECEMBER

Cliff undertakes several British dates supported by Marvin, Welch and Farrar and Olivia Newton-John.

DECEMBER

Commenting on Christmas, Cliff says: 'I think it's foolish for people to moan about it being too commercial because it's treated in a non-religious way. You have to remember that the majority of the people don't believe in Christ, and Christmas is about Christianity. It certainly doesn't worry me that it's commercial – because I don't celebrate it in a commercial way. It is without a doubt the birth of the Messiah – and the only way to enjoy Christmas is to thoroughly believe in it. That's why so many people only enjoy it at one level.'

14 DECEMBER

ABBEY ROAD
Studio session

Jesus — *A-side*

Lead Vocal: **Cliff Richard**

Producer: **Norrie Paramor**
Engineer:
Recorded in: **Studio 2**
Session hours: **7.00pm-10.00pm**

DECEMBER 24

BBC 1 screens a *Cliff Christmas Eve Special.*

JANUARY

Cliff begins a new 13-week BBC TV series *It's Cliff Richard*. The Flirtations and Olivia Newton-John are resident but not Hank Marvin, and the critics seem to think that it lacks his humour. Una Stubbs is prevented from appearing in the first show because she is expecting a baby – Dandy Nichols appears in her place. The series is produced by Michael Hurll.

JANUARY/FEBRUARY

Among Cliff's guests on *It's Cliff Richard* are Elton John, Labi Siffre and the New Seekers, who sing the six songs for Eurovision on the series.

JANUARY 22

Brian Wright from South Nutfield, Surrey, has a letter published in the music press: 'What has happened to Cliff? I've watched his show every week since it started, and I'm appalled at the utter rubbish I see and hear. Surely someone with Cliff's talent could do without the so-called comedy? Even the audience sounds false. If he goes on with such a shocking show, Cliff will lose a lot of fans, I'm sure.'

JANUARY 22

The *NME* poll results are published:

World Male Singer

1 Elvis Presley	4,748
2 Cliff Richard	1,645
3 Tom Jones/Rod Stewart	1,027

World Musical Personality

1 Elvis Presley	3,698
2 Cliff Richard	1,363
3 Rod Stewart	1,010

British Male Singer

1 Cliff Richard	3,883
2 Tom Jones	1,989
3 Rod Stewart	1,806

British Vocal Personality

1 Cliff Richard	2,864
2 Rod Stewart	2,177
3 Cilla Black	1,758

Best TV/Radio Show

1 *Top of the Pops*	5,577
2 *Old Grey Whistle Test*	1,816
3 *It's Cliff Richard*	905

JANUARY 5

Cliff's stablemate, Labi Siffre, reveals that unlike Cliff he is not a devout Christian: 'I went to a monastic institution, but I'm anti-religion. I find it degrading. I think it's time we all believed in ourselves rather than something of which we have no proof.'

FEBRUARY 26

Cliff's 56th single, 'Jesus'/'Mr Cloud', is released. Reviewer Danny Holloway write: 'This is Cliff singing to his main man, asking him to come back to earth and save us from the scum and filfth we live in. The song isn't exactly heavyweight, but that won't stop the mums and vicars from buying it.'

FEBRUARY

Cliff presents a series for BBC Radio 1 and 2, *Music for Sunday* on which he plays records by other Christian artists and some of his own.

MARCH

Roy Wood, of the newly-formed Electric Light Orchestra and late of the Move, talks about writing songs for Cliff: '...the thing is, when you write material for the ELO, or the Move or whatever, you do occasionally get ideas that could never be used for those bands... why not give songs to other artists, Cliff Richard and people like that?'

MARCH 11

Cliff gives a religious concert for Tear Fund at Manchester's new Century Hall.

MARCH 25

The Metropolitan Police promote a national young people's 'Help the Police' competition, and are helped by the support of Olivia Newton-John, Cliff Richard and DJs Tony Blackburn and Emperor Rosko.

APRIL 14-15

Cliff appears in a gospel concert at the Philharmonic Hall in Liverpool.

APRIL 14

The *Sun* newspaper presents Cliff with it's award for 'Top Male Pop Personality' for the third year running.

28 APRIL

ABBEY ROAD
Studio session

Empty Chairs	*B-side*
Run For Shelter	*(Unissued)*

Lead Vocal:	**Cliff Richard**
Guitars:	
Bass:	
Drums:	
Piano:	
Vocals:	**John Farrar/Pat Farrar**
Producer:	**Norrie Paramor**
Engineer:	
Recorded in:	**Studio 3**
Session hours:	**2.30pm-5.30pm/7.00pm-10.00pm**

APRIL-SEPTEMBER

Cliff undertakes a lot of work abroad, touring dozens of countries in Europe, the Middle East and the Far East.

MAY

Radio 1 broadcasts the one hundred best-selling records of the last decade. Cliff's only placing is 'The Young Ones' at number 7.

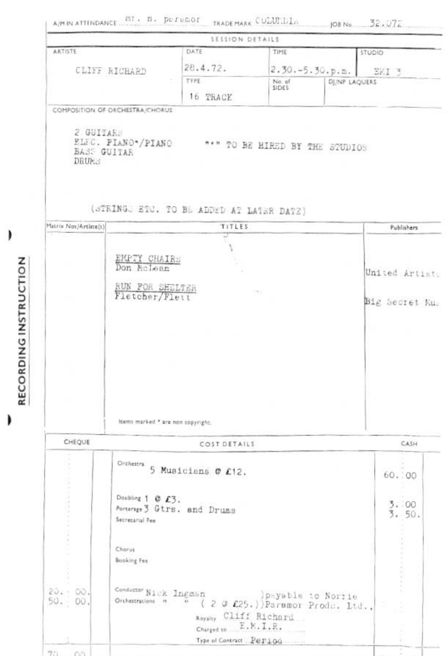

RECORDING INSTRUCTION

A/M IN ATTENDANCE Mr. N. Paramor TRADE MARK COLUMBIA JOB No. 32.072

SESSION DETAILS

ARTISTE	DATE	TIME	STUDIO
CLIFF RICHARD	28.4.72.	2.30.-5.30.p.m.	EMI 3
	TYPE: 16 TRACK	No. of SIDES	DJ/NP LAQUERS

COMPOSITION OF ORCHESTRA/CHORUS

2 GUITARS
ELEC. PIANO*/PIANO — "*" TO BE HIRED BY THE STUDIOS
BASS GUITAR
DRUMS

(STRINGS ETC. TO BE ADDED AT LATER DATE)

Matrix Nos/Artiste(s)	TITLES	Publishers
	EMPTY CHAIRS Don McLean	United Artists
	RUN FOR SHELTER Fletcher/Flett	Big Secret Mu.

Items marked * are non copyright.

CHEQUE	COST DETAILS	CASH
	Orchestra 5 Musicians @ £12.	60. 00
	Doubling 1 @ £3.	3. 00
	Porterage 3 Gtrs. and Drums	3. 50.
	Secretarial Fee	
	Chorus	
	Booking Fee	
20. 00.	Conductor Nick Ingman)payable to Norrie	
50. 00.	Orchestrations " " (2 @ £25.))Paramor Prods. Ltd.,	
	Royalty Cliff Richard	
	Charged to E.M.I.R.	
	Type of Contract Period	
70. 00.		66. 50.

MAY 27

An autumn tour of Britain for Cliff is announced.

MAY 27

The New Musical Express prints the following apology: 'We regret if we caused any distress to anyone by the suggestion made in this column that Cliff Richard was involved in the termination of the engagement between Olivia Newton-John and Bruce Welch.'

JUNE

Elvis Presley's legendary vocal backing group, the Jordanaires, express a keenness to record with Cliff.

JULY

Cliff's 57th single is released, 'Living In Harmony'/'Empty Chairs'. Reviewer Danny Holloway writes: 'Cliff is back with Norrie Paramor, who assisted his success in the beginning. The song is well-performed, although the subject matter is slightly trite. Cliff seems to force himself to keep up with the trends and I sometimes wonder why he bothers.'

4 JULY

ABBEY ROAD
Studio session

Living In Harmony	*A-side*

Lead Vocal:	**Cliff Richard**
Guitars:	
Bass:	
Drums:	
Keyboards:	
Percussion:	
Vocals:	
Strings	
Producer:	**Norrie Paramor**
Engineer:	
Recorded in:	**Studio 3**
Session hours:	**2.30pm-5.30pm**

SEPTEMBER 2

BBC 2 TV screens *The Case*, a comedy thriller which includes eight songs. Produced by Michael Hurll, it stars Cliff, Olivia Newton-John and Tim Brooke-Taylor.

22/23 SEPTEMBER

KOSEI NENKIN HALL, TOKYO JAPAN
Live Recordings

Can't Let You Go	*Live In Japan*
Have A Little Talk With Myself	*Live In Japan*
Sunny Honey Girl	*Live In Japan*
The Minute You're Gone	*Live In Japan*
Flying Machine	*Live In Japan*
The Day I Met Marie	*Live In Japan*
Silvery Rain	*Live In Japan*
My Way	*Live In Japan*
Move It	*Live In Japan*
Sing A Song Of Freedom	*Live In Japan*
Living In Harmony	*Live In Japan*
Walk On By/The Look Of Love	*Live In Japan*
Early In The Morning	*Live In Japan*
Goodbye Sam Hello Samantha	*Live In Japan*
Hit Medley:	*Live In Japan*
Living Doll	
Bachelor Boy	
The Young Ones	
Congratulations	*Live In Japan*
Rock Medley:	*Live In Japan*
The Girl Can't Help It	
Great Balls Of Fire Lucille	
Jailhouse Rock	
Good Old Rock And Roll	
Do You Wanna Dance.	

Lead Vocal:	**Cliff Richard**
Guitar:	**Hank Marvin**
Bass:	**John Farrar**
Drums:	**Brian Bennett**
Piano:	**Alan Hawkshaw**
Vocals:	**Olivia Newton-John/Pat Caroll**
Producer:	
Engineer:	
Session hours:	

MONO/STEREO RECORDING SHEET

Sheet: 1 of: 1 Class: POPULAR Overall Title 8T → STEREO Date of Session 24.10.72 Job No: —

ARTISTIC INFORMATION — ARTISTE(S) AND/OR CAST: CLIFF RICHARD – LIVE IN JAPAN; ART. DEPT. REP. P. GORMLEY

COSTING INFORMATION — MATERIALS USED: 3 × 816 ¼"; SESSION BOOKED TIME: 10-1 / 2.30-5.30; SESSION ACTUAL: 10-1 / 2.30-5.30; STUDIO/CONTROL ROOM: 4; ENGINEERS: PV JK

TITLES and MATRIX Nos.	REEL NUMBERS	TAKE DETAILS
(OPENING INSTRUMENTAL) BACKSCRATCHER	E107407 Z	1st PERF 2nd Night
CAN'T LET YOU GO		
HAVE A LITTLE TALK WITH MYSELF		
SUNNY HONEY GIRL		
THE MINUTE YOUR GONE		
FLYING MACHINE		
THE DAY I MET MARIE		
SILVERY RAIN		
MY WAY		
MOVE IT	E107408 Z	1st Night
LIVING IN HARMONY		2nd Night
WALK ON BY/LOOK OF LOVE		
EARLY IN THE MORNING		
GOODBYE SAM		
LIVING DOLL		
BACHELOR BOY		
THE YOUNG ONES		
CONGRATULATIONS		
THE GIRL CAN'T HELP IT	E107409 Z	
GREAT BALLS OF FIRE		
LUCILLE		
JAILHOUSE ROCK		
GOOD OLD ROCK N' ROLL		
DO YOU WANNA DANCE		
SING A SONG OF FREEDOM		1st Night

11 OCTOBER

ABBEY ROAD
Studio session

A Brand New Song	*A-side*
The Singer	*31st Of February Street*
Going Away	*31st Of February Street*

Lead Vocal:	**Cliff Richard**
Producer:	**David MacKay**
Engineer:	**Peter Vince**
Recorded in:	**Studio 3**
Session hours:	**10.00pm-1.00am**

OCTOBER 18-DECEMBER 6

Backed by the Brian Bennett Orchestra, Cliff undertakes a 23-venue, 26-date tour of Britain.

NOVEMBER 6

The New Seekers, Vera Lynn, Henry Hall, Gilbert O'Sullivan, Lulu and Cliff appear in a BBC 2 TV Special *50 Years of Music* to mark the 50th anniversary of broadcasting in Britain.

NOVEMBER

Reviewer Michael Parsons writes of Cliff's concert at Croydon: 'For an artist to stay at the top for as long as Cliff Richard has, he must adapt to the changing whims of his fans... no one can doubt his showmanship and finesse – even if his attempts at humour did fall on barren ground – nor the exuberant liveliness with which he injects his act. But there was something lacking... but the masses appeared to go home well-satisfied, so he's obviously lost nothing over the last fourteen years as far as they are concerned.'

DECEMBER 2

Cliff's 58th single, 'A Brand New Song'/'The Old Accordion', is released and becomes Cliff's first 45 not to chart when it fails to reach the Top 50. Cliff tells the *Melody Maker*: 'I really can't understand why, I played it to my mother and she was sure it would be a hit.'

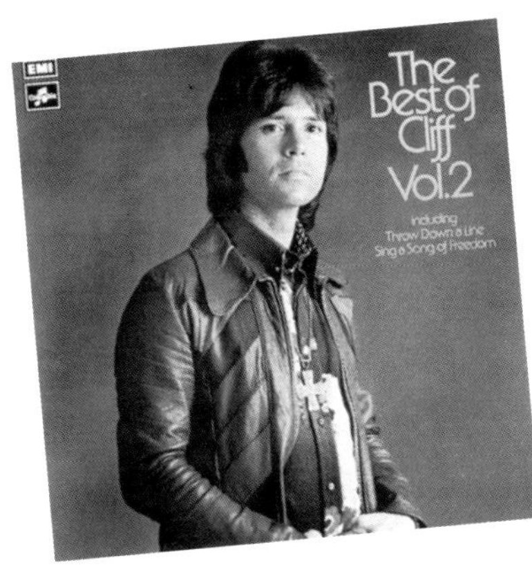

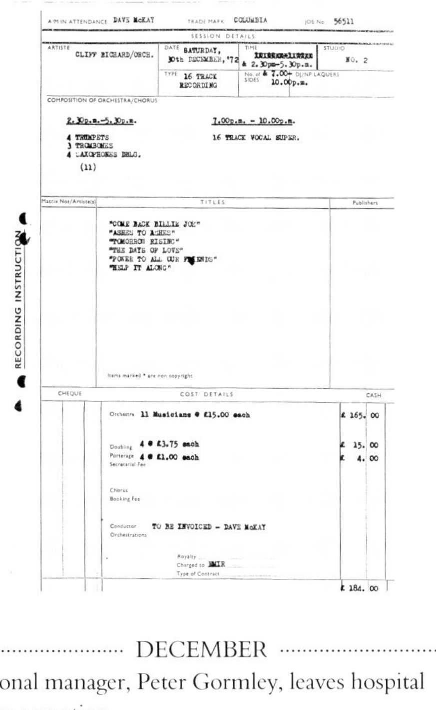

A/M IN ATTENDANCE DAVE McKAY TRADE MARK COLUMBIA JOB No 56511

SESSION DETAILS

ARTISTE: CLIFF RICHARD/ORCH.
DATE: SATURDAY, 30th DECEMBER, '72
TIME: & 2.30pm-5.30p.m. & 7.00-10.00p.m.
STUDIO: NO. 2
TYPE: 16 TRACK RECORDING
No. of SIDES
DJ/NP LAQUERS

COMPOSITION OF ORCHESTRA/CHORUS

2.30p.m.-5.30p.m.
4 TRUMPETS
3 TROMBONES
4 SAXOPHONES DBLG.
(11)

7.00p.m. - 10.00p.m.
16 TRACK VOCAL SUPER.

RECORDING INSTRUCTION

Matrix Nos/Artiste(s)	TITLES	Publishers
	"COME BACK BILLIE JOE" "ASHES TO ASHES" "TOMORROW RISING" "THE DAYS OF LOVE" "POWER TO ALL OUR FRIENDS" "HELP IT ALONG" Items marked * are non copyright	

CHEQUE	COST DETAILS	CASH
	Orchestra 11 Musicians @ £15.00 each	£ 165. 00
	Doubling 4 @ £3.75 each	£ 15. 00
	Porterage 4 @ £1.00 each	£ 4. 00
	Secretarial Fee	
	Chorus	
	Booking Fee	
	Conductor TO BE INVOICED - DAVE McKAY	
	Orchestrations	
	Royalty	
	Charged to EMIR	
	Type of Contract	
		£ 184. 00

DECEMBER

Cliff's personal manager, Peter Gormley, leaves hospital following an operation.

DECEMBER 6

Cliff appears in a special concert with Dana, Gordon Giltrap, the Settlers, Larry Norman, the Brian Bennett Sound and Roy Castle to help raise money for the Arts Centre Group.

DECEMBER 11-23

Cliff appears at the Batley Variety Club, Yorkshire.

27 DECEMBER

ABBEY ROAD
Studio session

Ashes To Ashes	*B-side*
The Days Of Love	*B-side*
Come Back Billie Jo	*B-side*

Lead Vocal:	**Cliff Richard**
Guitar:	**Terry Britten/Kevin Peek**
Bass:	**Alan Tarney**
Drums:	**Trevor Spencer**
Keyboards:	
Percussion:	**Barrie Guard**
Acoustic Guitar:	
Vocals:	
Producer:	**David MacKay**
Engineer:	**Peter Vince**
Recorded in:	**Studio 2**
Session hours:	**2.30pm-5.30pm/7.00pm-10.00pm**

28 DECEMBER

ABBEY ROAD
Studio session

Help It Along	*A-side*
Power To All Our Friends	*A-side*
Tomorrow Rising	*B-side*

Lead Vocal:	**Cliff Richard**
Guitar:	**Terry Britten/Kevin Peek**
Bass:	**Alan Tarney**
Drums:	**Trevor Spencer**
Keyboards:	
Percussion:	**Barrie Guard**
Acoustic Guitar:	
Vocals:	
Producer:	**David MacKay**
Engineer	**Peter Vince**
Recorded in:	**Studio 2**
Session hours:	

DECEMBER

Agent Arthur Howes announces that Cliff's tour was the biggest and most successful yet.

JANUARY 2

BRT TIV in Belgium shows *Cliff in Scotland*. Songs included are 'Hail Caledonia'. 'Skye Boat Song', 'Courting In The Kitchen', 'Let's Have A Ceilidh', 'Bonnie Mary Of Argyll' and 'Scotland The Brave'.

JANUARY 6

Sire announce that they now issue Cliff's products in America.

JANUARY

Cliff appears over six weeks on Cilla Black's BBC1 TV series, performing songs for the Eurovision Song Contest. The songs are 'Come Back Billie Joe', 'Ashes To Ashes', 'Tomorrow Rising', 'The Days Of Love', 'Power To All Our Friends' and 'Help It Along'.'Power To All Our Friends' was finally chosen as the British entry in the Contest.

JANUARY 13

Cliff is interviewed over the British Forces Broadcasting Service by Brian Cullingford.

JANUARY 19

Cliff appears on BBC 2's *They Sold A Million.*

JANUARY

Cliff begins a three week cabaret season at the Talk Of The Town in London.

JANUARY 27

The *NME* publish their 1972/73 readers poll:
Male Singer

1 Rod Stewart
2 Gilbert O'Sullivan
3 David Bowie
4 Cliff Richard
5 Marc Bolan

Cliff comes 7th in the World Male Singer section behind Elvis Presley, Rod Stewart, Alice Cooper, Robert Plant, Neil Young and John Lennon.

FEBRUARY 25

Cliff appears in an eight-week series of contemporary Christian and general music concerts being held at St Paul's Cathedral.

FEBRUARY

In an interview, Cliff says: 'Mary Whitehouse is ten years ahead of her time... the cinema medium is being wasted. Morally something has got to be done about it. There's a need for censorship.'

MARCH 3

Reviewing Cliff's 'Talk Of The Town' set, critic James Johnson writes: 'It's an easy enough task these days to make Cliff Richard seem slightly ridiculous. So easy in fact, it's hardly worthwhile. In between numbers he thankfully kept the chat to a minimum, even when he was telling us a little bit about Jesus... which sounded rather incongruous over the clink of champagne glasses...'

MARCH 9

Cliff's 59th single, 'Power To All Our Friends', is released. This winning song for Europe is coupled with 'Come Back Billie Joe', 'This I suppose,' said a reviewer, 'is what happens when cardboard radicalism meets sickening sentimentality at the Eurovision Song Contest', going on to describe the record as 'A hideous cringing piece of complacent mediocrity'.

21 MARCH

ABBEY ROAD
Studio session

Gut, Dass Es Freunde Gibt (Power To All Our Friends)	*German A-side*

Lead Vocal:	**Cliff Richard**
Producer:	**David MacKay**
Engineer:	**Peter Vince**
Recorded in:	**Studio 2**
Session hours:	**7.00pm-10.00pm**

The original backing track was used for these foreign versions.

23 MARCH

Abbey Road
Studio session

Il Faut Chanter La Vie (Power To All Our Friends)	*French A-side*
Todo El Poder A Los Amigos (Power To All Our Friends)	*Spanish A-side*

Lead Vocal: **Cliff Richard**

Producer: **David MacKay**
Engineer: **Peter Vince**
Recorded in: **Studio 3**
Session hours: **2.30pm-5.30pm**

APRIL

'Power To All Our Friends' becomes Cliff's first top 10 single since 'Goodbye Sam, Hello Samantha' in 1970.

APRIL 1

In an interview with the *News Of The World,* Cliff reveals: 'In the past two or three years I've not dated many girls at all, I don't know whether the inclination has gone or not... at the moment there's no one I want to date... I've not gone out saying to myself "I'll find a virgin." If I fall in love with a girl, it wouldn't matter how promiscuous she'd been; it wouldn't worry me. That's because the fantastic thing about Christianity is it doesn't matter what you were, but what you're going to be as a Christian.'

APRIL 2

Cliff is the subject of *My Top Twelve* on the Brian Matthews Radio 1 programme.

APRIL 7

Singing 'Power To All Our Friends', Cliff represents the United Kingdom in the Eurovision Song Contest, which is held at the Nouveau Theatre, Luxembourg; over 300 million people from 32 countries watch the competition.

APRIL

Having come third in the Eurovision Song Contest, Cliff says of the winning, 'Tu te reconnaitras (Wonderful Dream)', by Luxembourg's Anne-Marie David: 'I just don't like the winning song... no, it's not sour grapes!'

APRIL 12-MAY 8

Cliff appears in concerts across Australia as part of an evangelistic crusade under the banner of 'Help, Hope and Hallelujah'. His backing group is the Strangers, John Farrar's old group re-formed and including John and his wife Pat. Cliff's set includes 'Sing A Song Of Freedom', 'How Great Thou Art', 'Day By Day', 'Silvery Rain', 'Everything Is Beautiful' and 'Jesus Loves You'.

MAY 4

It is announced that Cliff is to make his first feature film since *Finders Keepers* in 1966. Shooting is due to start in Birmingham on June 4 for the musical tentatively titled *Hot Property*.

26 MAY

Abbey Road
Film soundtrack recordings for Take Me High

Winning (1)	*Take Me High*
Take Me High (3)	*See 18 September*
Its Only Money (2)	*Take Me High*
Life (2)	*See 27 May*
Midnight Blue	*Take Me High*
Driving	*Take Me High*
Driving (instrumental)	*Take Me High*

Lead Vocal: **Cliff Richard**

Producer: **David MacKay**
Engineer: **Tony Clark/Mike Jarrett**
Recorded in: **Studio 3**
Session hours: **10.00am-1.30pm/2.30pm-6.30pm/7.30pm-10.45pm**

27 MAY

Abbey Road
Film soundtrack recordings for Take Me High

Brumburger Duet (5)	*See 28 May*
The Game (3)	*See 28 May*
The Anti Brotherhood Of Man (1)	*See 28 May*
Life (7)	*Take Me High*

Lead Vocal: **Cliff Richard**

Producer: **David MacKay**
Engineer: **Tony Clark/Mike Jarrett**
Recorded in: **Studio 3**
Session hours: **10.00am-1.30pm/2.30pm-6.00pm**

28 MAY

ABBEY ROAD
Film soundtrack recordings for Take Me High

The Anti Brotherhood Of Man (1)	*Take Me High*
The Game (3)	*Take Me High*
The Word Is Love	*Take Me High*
Brumburger Duet (5)	*Take Me High*

Lead Vocal:	**Cliff Richard**
Producer:	**David MacKay**
Engineer:	**Tony Clark/Mike Jarrett**
Recorded in:	**Studio 3**
Session hours:	**10.00am-1.15pm/2.00pm-6.30pm/ 7.30pm-3.30am**

MAY

'Power To All Our Friends' tops the chart in Holland.

JUNE

Cliff's 60th single is released: 'Help It Along'/'The Days Of Love'/'Tomorrow Rising'/'Ashes To Ashes.'

JUNE/JULY

Cliff on location in Birmingham, shooting his new film re-titled *Take Me High*. His co-stars include Debbie Watling, George Cole and Anthony Andrews.

AUGUST 8

Cliff announces that he will appear on the bill of the 'Spiritual Re-emphasis' concert at Wembley with Johnny Cash and Billy Graham.

AUGUST

It is revealed that Cliff is to play Bottom in a version of *A Midsummer Night's Dream*.

16 AUGUST

ABBEY ROAD
Studio session

Sweet Loving Ways	*(Unissued)*

Lead Vocal:	**Cliff Richard**
Guitars:	
Bass:	
Drums:	
Piano:	
Producer:	**David MacKay**
Engineer:	
Recorded in:	**Studio 3**
Session hours:	**10.00am-1.00pm**

AUGUST 27-SEPTEMBER 1

Johnny Cash, Parchment, Judy McKenzie and Cliff are among the musical contributors to the Spree (Spiritual Re-emphasis) gathering at Earls Court, London, for a teach-in.

SEPTEMBER 1

Cliff appears at Wembley Stadium, London, with country super-star Johnny Cash and the world's best-known evangelist, Billy Graham.

3 SEPTEMBER

ABBEY ROAD
Film soundtrack recordings for Take Me High

Why (1)	*Take Me High*
Brumburger Finale (1)	*Take Me High*
Join The Band (1)	*Take Me High*
Hover (9)	*Take Me High*
Magnificent Women (3)	*Film Only*
Fox Hunt (2)	*Film Only*

Lead Vocal:	**Cliff Richard**
Duet Vocals:	**Anthony Andrews on Why**
Guitar:	
Steel Guitar:	
Bass:	
Drums:	
Saxophone:	
Strings:	
Producer:	**David MacKay**
Engineer:	**Tony Clark/Mike Jarrett**
Recorded in:	**Studio 3**
Session hours:	**10.00-1.30pm/2.30pm-5.30pm**

MONO/STEREO — RECORDING SHEET

Sheet: 1 of: 1 Class: Pop Overall Title: 16T Record Dolby Date of Session: 4th Sept '73 Job No: 56579

ARTISTIC INFORMATION — Artiste(s) and/or Cast: Cliff Richard; Art. Dept. Rep.: Dave MacKay

COSTING INFORMATION — Materials used: 1 x 2" 815; Session booked time: 10.00-13.00; Session actual: 10.00-14.00; Set-up/playback: 1/2 hr.; Studio/control room: 3-3; Engineers: AC-MJ

Titles and Matrix Nos.	Reel Numbers	False Starts	Take No.	Take Details	Remarks
Ginnette	2610-16T Dolby	1, 3	2 BD, 4	Complete	Best
Parlez-Moi D'Amour	"		1	"	Best
Woman Magnificent	2609-16T Dolby Cont.		3	"	Best Super sax (9) piano (10)
Hover	"		9	"	Best Super sax (9) (11) harpsichord (10)
Tim Meets Flaxman	2610-16T Cont.	2,3 / 6-9	4, 5, 10	"	Super congas (12); Best
Midnight Blue	1740-16T Cont.		10	"	Best Super perc. (13) gtr. (14) rhythm section (1) (13) flute (8)

4 SEPTEMBER

ABBEY ROAD

Film soundtrack recordings for Take Me High

Ginnette (4)	*Film Only*
Parlez Moi D'Amour (1)	*Film Only*
Tim Meets Flaxman (10)	*Film Only*

Producer: **David MacKay**
Engineer: **Tony Clark/Mike Jarrett**
Recorded in: **Studio 3**
Session hours: **10.00-2.00pm**

SEPTEMBER 8

Reporter Nick Kent writes on attending the Cliff Richard/Johnny Cash Wembley festival: 'You see, the real success behind commercial Christianity is that it has to be moronic. Sure it can be a little pretentious, and it has to contain that neatly-packed bland message – basically, however, it simply needs to appeal to just that sort of mentality which comes from brainless submission to the Almighty... looking like he'd just come out of rigorous training for the John Denver "Wimp of the Week" sweepstakes, Cliff bounced around, flashing his teeth and oozing good humour...'

18 SEPTEMBER

ABBEY ROAD

Film soundtrack recordings for Take Me High

Take Me High (3)	*Take Me High*

Lead Vocal: **Cliff Richard**

Producer: **David MacKay**
Engineer: **Tony Clark/Mike Jarrett**
Recorded in: **Studio 3**
Session hours: **10.00-2.00pm**

24/25/26 SEPTEMBER

MORGAN STUDIOS

Live Studio session

Mr Businessman	*Help It Along*
Reflections	*(Unissued)*
Amazing Grace	*Help It Along*
Jesus Is My Kind Of People	*Live At Spree*
Higher Ground	*Help It Along*
Sing A Song Of Freedom	*Help It Along*
Day By Day	*Help It Along*
I've Got Confidence	*(Unissued)*
Jesus Loves You	*Help It Along*
Silvery Rain	*Help It Along*
One Fine Day	*(Unissued)*
Fire And Rain	*Help It Along*
Yesterday, Today, Forever	*Help It Along*
Jesus	*Help It Along*
Streets Of London	*(Unissued)*
Celestial Houses	*B-side*
Chaser	*(Unissued)*

Lead Vocal: **Cliff Richard**
Guitars: **Terry Britten/Kevin Peek**
Bass: **Alan Tarney**
Drums: **Trevor Spencer**
Keyboards: **Cliff Hall**
Percussion: **Barrie Guard**
Orchestra conducted by **Barrie Guard (26th only)**

Producer: **David MacKay**
Engineer: **Roger Quested**
Recorded in: **Studio 3**
Session hours: **24: 10.00am-1.00pm/2.30pm-5.30pm/7.00pm-10.00pm**
25: 10.00am-1.00pm/2.30pm-5.30pm
26: 10.00am-1.00pm/2.30pm-5.30pm (Orchestra only)

NOVEMBER

Cliff's new film *Take Me High* is premiered in London. The music and lyrics are by Australian songwriter/producer Tony Cole, and the picture co-stars Debbie Watling, Moyra Fraser, George Cole, Hugh Griffith and Anthony Andrews. Cliff plays the part of a young merchant banker, Tim Matthews, who ends up running a restaurant with his new-found girlfriend Sarah (Debbie Watling). The selling point of the establishment is their creation of the 'Brumburger', a hybrid of the abbreviation for Birmingham and a hamburger. The director is David Askey, producer is Kenneth Harper and the screenplay is by Charles Renfold.

NOVEMBER 26

Cliff's former bass player, ex-Shadow John Rostill, is found dead in his recording studio.

Still from the film *Take Me High*

28 NOVEMBER

MORGAN STUDIOS
Studio session

Pour Tojours Ce Jour (I'll Love You Forever Today)	*When In France LP*

Lead Vocal: **Cliff Richard**

Producer: **David MacKay**
Engineer:
Session hours:

DECEMBER

Cliff's 61st single is released – 'Take Me High'/'Celestial Houses'.

JANUARY 1

At Southall, Cliff plays in his first football match for twenty years for the Buzz All Stars XI v Choralerna: Buzz being a British Christian youth monthly journal and Choralerna a Swedish Christian choir.

TAKE ME HIGH

Anglo EMI, 1973. Running time: 90 minutes
Cliff's eighth feature film.

Synopsis:
Tim Matthews (Cliff), a rich, somwhat ruthless and ambitious young city gent works for a London merchant bank and expects an assignment to New York. Instead, he finds himself sent to Birmingham. Later he finds himself involved with a French restaurant owner, Sarah. They open a Brumburger establishment, Brumburger being a new form of hamburger.

Cast:
Cliff Richard, Debbie Watling, George Cole, Hugh Griffith, Anthony Andrews, Richard Wattis, Ronald Hines.

Credits:
Producer: Kenneth Harper. Director: David Askey. Screenplay: Charles Penfold. Musical score: Tony Cole. Photography: Norman Warwick.

Songs:
'It's Only Money', 'Midnight Blue', 'Life', 'Driving', 'The Game', 'Take Me High', 'The Anti-Brotherhood Of Man', 'Winning', 'Join The Band', 'The World Is Love', 'Brumburger' performed by Cliff Richard. 'Why' performed by Cliff Richard and Anthony Andrews. 'Brumburger Duet' performed by Cliff Richard and Debbie Watling. 'Hover', 'Driving' (instrumentals)

11 FEBRUARY

ABBEY ROAD
Studio session

Give Me Back That Old Familiar Feeling (5)	*See 12 February*
You And Me (2)	*See 12 February*
You And Me Hangin' On (2)	*See 13 February*
Nothing To Remind Me	*31st Of February Street*

Lead Vocal:	**Cliff Richard**
Guitar:	**Terry Britten**
Acoustic Guitar:	**Kevin Peek**
Bass:	**Alan Tarney**
Drums:	**Trevor Spencer**
Keyboards:	**Cliff Hall**
Keyboards:	**Dave Macrae**
Steel Guitar:	**Gordon Huntley**
Percussion:	**Barrie Guard**
Percussion:	**Trevor Spencer**
Vocals:	**Anna Peacock/JeanHawker/ Cliff/Terry Britten/Alan Tarney/ David Mackay**
Orchestra conducted by	**Barrie Guard**

Producer:	**David MacKay**
Engineer:	**Tony Clark/Mike Jarrett**
Recorded in:	**Studio 3**
Session hours:	**10.30am-1.30pm/2.30pm-6.00pm**

BREAK 13.30 - 14.30

MONO/STEREO — RECORDING SHEET
Sheet: 1 of: 1 Class: POP Overall Title: 16T DOLBY RECORDING Date of Session: 11th Feb '74 Job No: 57193P

ARTISTIC INFORMATION — ARTISTE(S) AND/OR CAST: CLIFF RICHARD — ART. DEPT. REP.: DAVE MACKAY

COSTING INFORMATION — MATERIALS USED: 1 x 2" 816 — SESSION BOOKED TIME: 10.30-17.30 — SESSION ACTUAL: 10.30-18.00 — SET-UP/PLAYBACK: 1/2 HR — STUDIO/CONTROL ROOM: 3-3 — ENGINEERS: AC-MJ

TITLES and MATRIX Nos	REEL NUMBERS	FALSE STARTS	TAKE No	TAKE DETAILS	REMARKS
Give Me Back That Old Familiar Feeling	4260 16T Dolby	1,2 / 4	3 / 5	COMPLETE	BEST
You And Me		1	2		BEST Super Vocal (16) Acc Gtr. (10) Vocal (15) Elec. Gtr (6)
Hangin' On		1 / 3	2 / 4 BD / 5 / 6		BEST Super [illegible] (9) Acc gtr. (10)

BREAK 13.30 - 14.30

MONO/STEREO — RECORDING SHEET
Sheet: 1 of: 2 Class: POP Overall Title: 16T DOLBY RECORDING + SUPER Date of Session: 13th Feb '74 Job No: 57193P

ARTISTIC INFORMATION — ARTISTE(S) AND/OR CAST: CLIFF RICHARD — ART. DEPT. REP.: DAVE MACKAY

COSTING INFORMATION — MATERIALS USED: 2 x 2" 815 — SESSION BOOKED TIME: 10.30-10.30 — SESSION ACTUAL: 10.30-10.30 — SET-UP/PLAYBACK: 1/2 HR — STUDIO/CONTROL ROOM: 2-2 — ENGINEERS: AC-MJ

TITLES and MATRIX Nos	REEL NUMBERS	FALSE STARTS	TAKE No	TAKE DETAILS	REMARKS
The Leaving	4297 16T Dolby cont.	1 / 6	2 / 3 / 4 BD / 5 / 7	COMPLETE	BEST
Long Lonely Time	4298 16T Dolby	1 / 4,5 / 7	2 / 3 BD / 6 / 8		BEST
Love Is Here	16T Dolby	1,2 / 4,5	3 / 6		BEST
There You Go Again	4299 16T Dolby	1,2 / 4 / 7	3 / 5 BD / 8		BEST
Fireside Song	429A 16T Dolby cont.		3		BEST Super (4) shakes (13) vibes (14) gtr.
You	4297 16T Dolby cont.		3		BEST Super perc (11) (12) gtr (8)

1 x 1/4" 816 USED FOR TAPE ECHO

12 FEBRUARY

ABBEY ROAD
Studio session

Fireside Song (sp)	*31st Of February Street*
Night At The Whirl (2)	*(Unissued)*
Travellin' Light (11)	*31st Of February Street*
You Will Never Know (8)	*See 14 February*
Our Love Could Be So Real (17)	*See 14 February*
You (3)	*See 13 February*
Give Me Back That Old Familiar Feeling (5)	*31st Of February Street*
You And Me (2)	*(Unissued)*

Guitar:	**Terry Britten**
Acoustic Guitar:	**Kevin Peek**
Bass:	**Alan Tarney**
Drums:	**Trevor Spencer**
Keyboards:	**Cliff Hall/Dave Macrae**
Steel Guitar:	**Gordon Huntley**
Percussion:	**Barrie Guard/Trevor Spencer**
Saxophone:	**Bob Bertles**
Vocals:	**Anna Peacock/Jean Hawker/Cliff/Terry Britten/Alan Tarney/ David Mackay**
Orchestra conducted by	**Barrie Guard**

Producer:	**David MacKay**
Engineer:	**Tony Clark/Mike Jarrett**
Recorded in:	**Studio 2**
Session hours:	**10.30am-1.30pm/ 2.30pm-6.00pm/ 7.00pm-10.30pm**

13 FEBRUARY

ABBEY ROAD
Studio session

The Leaving (7)	*31st Of February Street*
Long Long Time (8)	*See 14 February*
Love Is Here (6)	*See 14 February*
There You Go Again (8)	*See 14 February*
You Keep Me Hangin' On (6)	*A-side*
You (3)	*(Unissued)*

Lead Vocal:	**Cliff Richard**
Guitar:	**Terry Britten**
	Kevin Peek
Bass:	**Alan Tarney**
Drums:	**Trevor Spencer**
Keyboards:	**Cliff Hall/Dave Macrae**
Steel Guitar:	**Gordon Huntley**
Percussion:	**Barrie Guard**
	Trevor Spencer
Vocals:	**Anna Peacock**
	Jean Hawker
	Cliff
	Terry Britten
	Alan Tarney
	David Mackay
Orchestra conducted by	**Barrie Guard**
Producer:	**David MacKay**
Engineer:	**Tony Clark**
Recorded in:	**Studio 2**
Session hours:	**10.30am-1.30pm/ 2.30pm-5.30pm/ 7.00pm-10.00pm**

14 FEBRUARY

ABBEY ROAD
Studio session

Long Long Time (8)	*31st Of February Street*
Love Is Here (6)	*B-side*
There You Go Again (8)	*31st Of February Street*
You Will Never Know (8)	*31st Of February Street*
Our Love Could Be So Real (17)	*31st Of February Street*

Lead Vocal:	**Cliff Richard**
Producer:	**David MacKay**
Engineer:	**Tony Clark/Mike Jarrett**
Recorded in:	**Studio 2**
Session hours:	**10.30am-1.30pm/ 2.30pm-5.30pm**

25 FEBRUARY

ABBEY ROAD
Studio session

No Matter What (6)	*31st Of February Street*
31st Of February Street (Opening) (8)	*31st Of February Street*
31st Of February Street (Closing) (2)	*31st Of February Street*

Lead Vocal:	**Cliff Richard**
Guitar:	**Terry Britten**
Acoustic Guitar:	**Kevin Peek**
Bass:	**Alan Tarney**
Drums:	**Trevor Spencer**
Keyboards:	**Cliff Hall/Dave Macrae**
Steel Guitar:	**Gordon Huntley**
Percussion:	**Barrie Guard/Trevor Spencer**
Vocals:	**Anna Peacock/JeanHawker/ Cliff/Terry Britten/ Alan Tarney/ David Mackay**
Orchestra conducted by	**Barrie Guard**
Producer:	**David MacKay**
Engineer:	**Tony Clark**
Recorded in:	**Studio 2**
Session hours:	**10.30am-5.30pm**

MARCH 2

The London Palladium announces that Cliff will headline a season at their theatre in the Spring.

MARCH

Cliff is awarded the Silver Clef trophy for outstanding services to the music industry at the second annual Music Therapy Committee lunch. The award is presented by the Duchess of Gloucester.

MARCH 23

On the Transatlantic label, the group Stray release a version of Cliff's 1958 hit 'Move It'. This was originally intended to be released the previous November, to coincide with the fifteenth anniversary of Cliff's chart debut.

APRIL 3

Backed by the Barrie Guard Orchestra, Cliff begins a season at the London Palladium supported by Australian singer Pat Carroll, who formerly sang in a duo with Olivia Newton-John. Cliff's set includes 'Constantly', 'Take Me High', 'In The Country', 'Dancing Shoes', Do You Wanna Dance' and a duet with Pat Carroll – 'You Got What It Takes'.

APRIL

Rolf Harris deputises for three nights at the Palladium, as Cliff is ill with throat and chest problems.

MAY 4

Cliff's 62nd single, 'You Keep Me Hanging On'/'Love Is Here' is released. Reviewer Charlie Gillett comments: 'One of the best things about this is you'd never guess it was Cliff. Another is that the song is a winner all by itself.

MAY 4

Cliff appears on BBC TV's *Mike Yarwood Show* singing 'You Keep Me Hanging On'.

MAY 9

On the *Nana Mouskouri Show* on BBC TV, Cliff sings 'Constantly' and 'Give Me Back That Old Familiar Feeling', before duetting with Nana on 'I Believe In Music'.

MAY

In Cheshunt, Cliff appears as Bottom in his old school's production of Shakespeare's *A Midsummer Night's Dream*.

JUNE

Cliff's 'Help It Along' album is released, in aid of Tear Fund.

JUNE 17

Cliff chats on Radio 2's *Pause For Thought*.

20 JUNE

MORGAN STUDIOS
Studio session

Honky Tonk Angel	*A-side*

Lead Vocal:	**Cliff Richard**
Guitars:	**Terry Britten**
Bass:	**Alan Tarney**
Drums:	**Trevor Spencer**
Piano:	**Dave Macrae**
Producer:	**Hank Marvin/Bruce Welch/John Farrar**
Engineer:	**Roger Quested**
Session hours:	**11.00am-1.00pm/2.00pm-6.00pm**

RECORDING SHEET — Job No. 2600SP

ARTISTIC INFORMATION — Artist: CLIFF RICHARD — JAPAN TOUR '74
Location: CONTROL TWO — Engineers: PV. JB — Producer: CLIFF
COSTING INFORMATION — Session Booked Time: 10 — 10 — Remixing: 10.30 — 1.30 — Copying: 3.00 — 6.30
Materials Used: 6 × 816 (¼") 4 × 7" SPOOLS

REEL NOS.	TITLES	TAKE DETAILS	REMARKS
8622 Z CONT'	DONT MEET THE BAND	COMPLETE	[BEST] REMIXED FROM 8057-16T
	ROCK MEDLEY	COMPLETE	[BEST] REMIXED FROM 8059-16T
	HIGHER GROUND	COMPLETE	[BEST] — " —
	SING A SONG OF FREEDOM (PLAYOUT)	COMPLETE	[BEST] — " —
	VISIONS (LINK)	COMPLETE	[BEST] — " —
	POWER TO ALL OUR FRIENDS	COMPLETE	[BEST] — " —
	— " — PLAY OFF	COMPLETE	[BEST] — " —
8623 Z	GUITAR MAN	COMPLETE	[BEST] REMIXED FROM 8057-16T

24 JUNE

MORGAN STUDIOS
Studio session

Es Gehoren Zwei Zum Glucklichsein (Hangin' On)	*German A-side*
Liebesleid (Love Is Here)	*German B-side*

Lead Vocal:	**Cliff Richard**
Producer:	**David MacKay**
Engineers:	**Roger Quested**
Session hours:	**10.30am-1.30pm (Strings)/2.30pm-6.00pm (Vocals)**

JULY 9

The International Cliff Richard Movement gathers members together at the United Reformed Church, Crouch End, London. Cliff gives a short concert and answers members' questions. Two films, *Love Never Gives Up* and *A Day In The Life Of Cliff Richard*, are shown.

AUGUST/SEPTEMBER

BBC TV screens a new *It's Cliff Richard* series.

AUGUST 3

Ex-New Seeker, Lyn Paul, guests on Cliff's BBC TV show.

AUGUST 28

Cliff appears in a special concert at the New Gallery, Regent Street, London for the Crusaders.

SEPTEMBER 4

Cliff lends his support to the Romsey Abbey appeal, at which he meets and chats to Lady Mountbatten.

SEPTEMBER

A list of venues for Cliff's forthcoming tour is published, on which he will be accompanied by a 20-piece orchestra.

RECORDING SHEET ①-② — Job No. 2600SP

ARTISTIC INFORMATION — Artist: CLIFF RICHARD — [JAPAN TOUR '74]
Location: CONTROLROOM TWO — Engineers: PV. JB — Producer: CLIFF
COSTING INFORMATION — Session Booked Time: 10 — 10 — Remixing: 10 — 10.30 — Playback: 10.30 — 11.00
Materials Used: 2 × 816 (¼")

REEL NOS.	TITLES	TAKE DETAILS	REMARKS
8620 Z CONT'	HANGING ON	COMPLETE	[BEST] REMIXED FROM 8057-16T
	MAKE IT EASY ON YOURSELF / THE SUN AINT GONNA SHINE ANYMORE	COMPLETE	[BEST] — " —
	GET BACK	COMPLETE	[BEST] — " —
	FIRESIDE SONG	COMPLETE	[BEST] REMIXED FROM 8055-16T
	TRAVELLING LIGHT	COMPLETE	[BEST] — " —
	GIVE ME BACK THAT OLD FAMILIAR FEELING	COMPLETE	[BEST] — " —
	EARLY IN THE MORNING	COMPLETE	[BEST] — " —
8621 Z	TAKE ME HIGH	COMPLETE	[BEST] — " —
	HIT MEDLEY	COMPLETE	[BEST] — " —
	CONSTANTLY	COMPLETE	[BEST] REMIXED FROM 8056-16T

7/8 OCTOBER

SHINJUKU KOSEINENKIN TOKYO JAPAN
Live Recordings

Winning	*Japan Tour*
Do You Wanna Dance	*Japan Tour*
(You Keep Me) Hangin' On	*Japan Tour*
Make It Easy On Yourself	*Japan Tour*
The Sun Ain't Gonna Shine Anymore	*Japan Tour*
Living In Harmony	*(Unissued)*
Get Back	*Japan Tour*
Fireside Song	*Japan Tour*
Travelling Light	*Japan Tour*
Give Me Back That Old	
Familiar Feeling	*Japan Tour*
Early In The Morning	*Japan Tour*
Take Me High	*Japan Tour*
Hit Medley:	*Japan Tour*
Congratulations	
In The Country	
Dancing Shoes	
The Day I Met Marie	
On The Beach	
Sing A Song Of Freedom.	*Japan Tour*
Constantly	*Japan Tour*
Nothing To Remind Me	*(Unissued)*
You've Lost That Lovin' Feelin	*Japan Tour*
Gospel Medley:	*Japan Tour*
Jesus	
Amazing Grace	
Jesus Is My Kind Of People	*Japan Tour*
Don't Talk To Him	*Japan Tour*
Bachelor Boy	*Japan Tour*
Don't Meet The Band	*Japan Tour*
Rock Medley:	*Japan Tour*
His Latest Flame	
Chantilly Lace	
Bonie Moronie	
Do You Wanna Dance	
Crocodile Rock	
Do You Wanna Dance.	*Japan Tour*
Higher Ground	*Japan Tour*
Sing A Song Of Freedom	*Japan Tour*
Visions	*Japan Tour*
Power To All Our Friends	*Japan Tour*
The Next Time	*(Unissued)*
Wind Me Up	*(Unissued)*

CLIFF RICHARD
FAR EAST CONCERT TOUR - OCTOBER 1974
REEL ONE [8054 16T]
1 Overture
No VG.
2 Winning
3 Do You Wanna Dance ?
4 Hanging On
5 Make It Easy On Yourself / The Sun Ain't Gonna Shine Anymore
6 Harmony (LIVING IN HARMONY)
No VG
7 Get Back
REEL TWO [8055 - 16T]
8 Fireside Song

Lead Vocal:	**Cliff Richard**
Guitars:	**Brian Lewes/Kevin Peek**
Bass:	**Alan Tarney**
Drums:	**Trevor Spencer**
Piano:	**Cliff Hall**
Vocals:	**Bruce Welch**
	The Barrie Guard Orchestra

Producer:
Engineer:
Session hours:

OCTOBER 23-NOVEMBER 1

Cliff undertakes a series of gospel dates.

OCTOBER 27

Cliff and the Shadows reunite especially for a charity concert at the London Palladium in aid of the dependants of the late Colin Charman, who used to produce *Top of the Pops*. Cliff sings 'Willie And The Hand Jive', 'Bachelor Boy', 'Don't Talk To Him', 'A Matter Of Moments' and 'Power To All Our Friends'. Also on the bill are Cilla Black, Dana, the Two Ronnies, Bruce Forsyth, Dick Emery, Harry Secombe, the Young Generation and the Ronnie Hazlehurst Orchestra.

OCTOBER

The Daily Express reports that local Tory parties in Scotland using Cliff's 'Sing A Song Of Freedom' as their anthem have been told to pay performing rights.

NOVEMBER 19

Cliff opens a Christian bookshop in Sutton.

NOVEMBER

As a result of the concert with Cliff on October 27, the Shadows are invited to sing the United Kingdom's six Eurovision song possibilities for 1975.

NOVEMBER

In an article in the *Daily Mirror* newspaper, Cliff makes the astonishin claim that it was God that was responsible for curing his slipped disc.

UNITED KINGDOM TOUR

NOVEMBER 7
Odeon Theatre, Birmingham

NOVEMBER 8
Colston Hall, Bristol

NOVEMBER 9
Central Hall, Chatham

NOVEMBER 13
Double Diamond Club, Caerphilly

NOVEMBER 14
Double Diamond Club, Caerphilly

NOVEMBER 15
Double Diamond Club, Caerphilly

NOVEMBER 16
Double Diamond Club, Caerphilly

NOVEMBER 20
New Theatre, Oxford

NOVEMBER 21
New Theatre, Oxford

NOVEMBER 22
New Theatre, Southport

NOVEMBER 23
New Theatre, Southport

NOVEMBER 27
Guildhall, Portsmouth

NOVEMBER 28
Fairfield Hall, Croydon

NOVEMBER 29
Congress Theatre, Eastbourne

NOVEMBER 30
Winter Gardens, Bournemouth

DECEMBER 4
City Hall, Sheffield

DECEMBER 5
De Montfort Hall, Leicester

DECEMBER 6
Talk of the Midlands, Derby

DECEMBER 7
City Hall, St. Albans

DECEMBER 11
Free Trade Hall, Manchester

DECEMBER 12
Town Hall, Leeds

DECEMBER 13
Empire Theatre, Sunderland

DECEMBER 14
City Hall, Hull

1975–1977

The Records 1975 – 1977

Both the singles for 1975 – 'It's Only Me You've Left Behind' and 'Honky Tonk Angel' – failed to chart at all. However, 1976 showed an improved quality of songs that began to be reflected in the chart. The most successful of these, 'Devil Woman' reached No.9 and 'Miss You Nights' No.15, although matters were not improved by the follow-up singles through to 1977. Only 'I Can't Ask For Anymore Than You' culled from the September 1975 sessions and 'My Kinda Life' from the EVERY FACE TELLS A STORY album made it into the top twenty.

The picture was definitely better as far as the albums were concerned. Of the three released in this period, all reached the top ten and sales figures showed considerable improvement compared to the immediately preceding years. I'M NEARLY FAMOUS proved to be a total turnaround for Cliff's recording career that, through sheer outstanding artistic triumph, took an unprecedented upswing. The next album EVERY FACE TELLS A STORY was in fact another strong one, but 40 GOLDEN GREATS was even stronger becoming Cliff's first No.1 album since SUMMER HOLIDAY had hit the top of the album charts in 1963. Although the TV advertised album contained all previously released material, it has proven to be a consistent seller over the years.

Promotional items provided two items of interest for 1977. The EVERY FACE TELLS A STORY EP (EMI PSR 410) contained selected tracks from the album and was issued to record stores only, as was the 40 GOLDEN GREATS double EP (EMI PSR 414/415) that featured edited highlights of all 40 tracks.

The Sessions 1975 – 1977

For the September 1975 sessions at Abbey Road, three songs had been channelled to Cliff through Bruce Welch, who was producer for 'Devil Woman', 'I Can't Ask For Anymore Than You' and 'Miss You Nights'. Collectively these singles showed that Cliff had not only caught up with the contemporary scene, but was breaking new ground as well. Perhaps none of this could have been accomplished without the talented musicians backing Cliff. Men like Terry Britten, Graham Todd, Alan Tarney, and Clem Cattini were all experienced pros making them ideal for bringing out Cliff's talents. Apart from this great line-up of band members and the technical expertise of producer and engineer, there was Tony Rivers who did all the vocal arrangements superbly. But perhaps the most important fact was that Cliff was being offered quality song material again, thanks largely to Bruce. The decision to follow up these magnificent sessions in December was seen as a desire to make an album in the same vein with the same musicians and technical crew in attendance. Many of the sessions at this time were for the overdubs of various instruments, that also included strings which were added onto all the tracks. The songs recorded were further explorations of the material taped in September that met with great critical acclaim hailed as 'the renaissance of Cliff Richard'. Even the more serious music press gave the I'M NEARLY FAMOUS album jubilant reviews. Remixing sessions that ran from December through to March were done at Abbey Road with Bruce being assisted by Tony Clark and John Barrett. The material offered for recording at the album sessions for EVERY FACE TELLS A STORY was again of a high standard. Of these 'Dream Maker', 'You Got Me Wondering' and 'Don't Turn The Light Out' were in a class of their own. The sessions lasted five days through to September 1976 providing all the tracks needed for the album, and were completed under more or less identical conditions to the I'M NEARLY FAMOUS sessions with the same musicians and technical crew. Various overdubs were added from September through to early October 1976, followed by remixing sessions through to December. A series of sessions in January 1977 was geared towards producing a new inspirational album. The band was virtually the same as the one used during this period with the addition of Bryn Haworth on guitar and Stuart Calver joining Tony Rivers and John Perry on backing vocals. The session on the 19th also produced the children singing part of 'Why Should The Devil Have All The Good Music'. Cliff was credited as producer on all the tracks that made up the SMALL CORNERS album. Overdubs were added at Abbey Road during January and remixing sessions ran from February through to July. In November the BBC Radio Transcription Unit recorded two concerts at the Fairfield Hall in Croydon for later radio broadcast. Of the material broadcast, emphasis was placed on Cliff's current repetoire, including songs such as 'Miss You Nights', 'Devil Woman', and 'My Kind Of Life' with only a few oldies featured.

JANUARY

Cliff rehearses with Swedish Christian choir Choralerna.

JANUARY 18-22

Cliff appears with Choralerna in Manchester, Newcastle and Leicester.

JANUARY 25

'The Name of Jesus' concert at London's Albert Hall features Choralerna and Malcolm and Alwyn. Cliff sings.

27 JANUARY

Abbey Road
Studio session

Love Enough	*See 7 February*
It's Only Me You've Left Behind	*See 7 February*

Producer:	**Hank Marvin/Bruce Welch/John Farrar**
Engineer:	
Recorded in:	**Studio 3/2**
Session hours:	**10.00am-1.00pm/7.00pm-10.00pm**

29 JANUARY

Abbey Road
Studio session

You're The One	*See 7 February*

Producer:	**Hank Marvin/Bruce Welch/John Farrar**
Engineer:	
Recorded in:	**Studio 2**
Session hours:	**10.00am-1.00pm/7.00pm-10.00pm**

JANUARY

The *NME* publish their 1974 chart points survey, based on 30 points for 1 week at number 1, to 1 point for 1 week at number 30. In his lowest ever showing in the table, Cliff comes 129th (sandwiched between Medicine Head and Donny Osmond) with 43 points. The table is headed by the Bay City Rollers, Alvin Stardust and Mud.

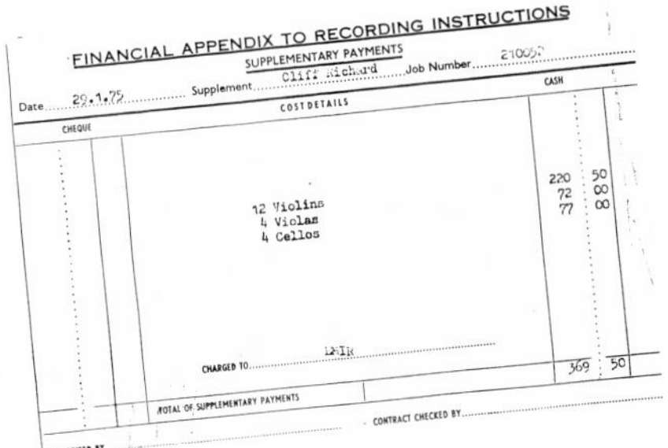
FINANCIAL APPENDIX TO RECORDING INSTRUCTIONS
SUPPLEMENTARY PAYMENTS
Date 29.1.75 Supplement Cliff Richard Job Number 21005?
COST DETAILS — CHEQUE — CASH
12 Violins 220 50
4 Violas 72 00
4 Cellos 77 00
CHARGED TO ... 369 50
TOTAL OF SUPPLEMENTARY PAYMENTS
CONTRACT CHECKED BY
AUTHORISED BY

7 FEBRUARY

Abbey Road
Studio session

It's Only Me You've Left Behind	*A-side*
Love Enough	*B-side*
You're The One	*B-side*

Lead Vocal:	**Cliff Richard**
Producer:	**Hank Marvin/Bruce Welch/John Farrar**
Engineer:	
Recorded in:	**Studio 2**
Session hours:	**2.30pm-10.00pm**

FEBRUARY 21

Cliff lunches with John Lang, the head of BBC Religious Programmes.

MARCH

Cliff's 63rd single is released: 'It's Only Me You've Left Behind'/'You're The One'. Both songs were produced by Marvin, Welch and Farrar, and despite being above average material failed to make any impact on the chart.

APRIL

Cliff promotes his new single in Austria.

APRIL 9

Cliff is interviewed on the Bay City Rollers' Granada TV Show *Shang-A-Lang*.

APRIL 19

Sally James interviews Cliff on LWT's *Saturday Scene*. During the programme, the original version of 'Travellin' Light' is played, whereupon Cliff mentions that there is a better version on his new album 'The 31st Of February Street'.

19 APRIL

Empire Pool, Wembley
Live recording for Echo

Love Never Gives Up	*Dick Saunders' 10th Annual Rally*
Why Me Lord	*(Unissued)*
Didn't He	*(Unissued)*

Producer:	
Engineer:	
Session hours:	

APRIL 19

Cliff attends the 'Way To Life' rally at Wembley's Empire Pool. With evangelist Dick Saunders and Bill Latham also on the platform. Cliff talks about his Christian conversion and his faith. He sings 'Love Never Gives Up', 'Why Me Lord' and 'Didn't He'.

APRIL

Sunday – BBC Radio 4's religious current affairs magazine programme – broadcasts part of the previous week's 'Way To Life' Christian rally.

APRIL 30

Cliff goes to the theatre to see *Joseph and the Amazing Technicolour Dreamcoat*.

MAY

Cliff receives a presentation from the World Record Club to mark the sale of 40,000 copies of the six-record boxed set 'The Cliff Richard Story'.

29 MAY

ABBEY ROAD
Studio session

(Wouldn't You Know It)
Got Myself A Girl — *See 4 July*

Guitar:	**Terry Britten**
Bass:	**Alan Tarney**
Drums:	**Clem Cattini**
Keyboards:	**Graham Todd**
String arrangements by	**Richard Hewson**
Vocals:	**Tony Rivers**
	John Perry
	A. Harding
Producer:	**Hank Marvin/Bruce Welch/ John Farrar**
Engineer:	**Tony Clark**
Recorded in:	**Studio 2**
Session hours:	**2.30pm-5.30pm**
	7.00pm-10.00pm

JUNE 5

Cliff headlines a special charity concert at Manchester's Free Trade Hall, promoted by Piccadilly Radio, with all proceeds going to the dependents of two Manchester policemen who died on duty – Sgt. Williams and PC Rodgers. Sgt. Williams had died after rioting which took place outside Granada's TV studios.

JULY

Helen Moon of Cromer writes to the BBC's *Jim'll Fix It* show to ask Jimmy Saville if she could meet her hero, Cliff, with the Shadows. Cliff sings 'Run Billy Run' and gives Helen a signed copy of 'The 31st of February Street' album.

4 JULY

ABBEY ROAD
Studio session

(Wouldn't You Know It)
Got Myself A Girl — *B-side*

Lead Vocal:	**Cliff Richard**
Producer:	**Hank Marvin/Bruce Welch/John Farrar**
Engineer:	
Recorded in:	**Studio 2**
Session hours:	**2.30pm-10.00pm**

JULY 22

Cliff attends a Variety Club lunch at London's Savoy Hotel in honour of singer Vera Lynn.

AUGUST

It's announced that Cliff is off to Moscow to record an album of Russian songs.

SEPTEMBER 6

The first of a new BBC TV series *It's Cliff and Friends* is screened. Guests include Su Shiffrin and David Copperfield and the producer is Phil Bishop. Cliff sings, 'All You Need Is Love', 'Good On The Sally Army', 'All I Wanna Do', 'I've Got Time' and 'Love Train'.

8 SEPTEMBER

ABBEY ROAD
Studio session

Devil Woman (3) — *See 9 September*
I Can't Ask For Anymore Than You (5) — *See 9 September*

Guitar:	**Terry Britten**
Bass:	**Alan Tarney**
Drums:	**Clem Cattini**
Keyboards:	**Graham Todd**
Producer:	**Bruce Welch**
Engineers:	**Tony Clark**
	John Barrett
Recorded in:	**Studio 2**
Session hours:	**2.30pm-6.15pm**
	7.00pm-10.30pm

RECORDING SHEET — Job No. 21013 P

ARTISTIC INFORMATION — Artist: CLIFF RICHARD — Date: 9 9 1975 — Location: STUDIO TWO — Engineers: AC JB — Producer: BRUCE

COSTING INFORMATION — Session Booked Time: 1.30–5.30 / 7.00–10.00

REEL NOS.	TITLES	False Starts	Take Nos.	TAKE DETAILS	DUR	REMARKS
	DEVIL WOMAN		3	COMPLETE		BEST OVERDUB VOCAL
	I CAN'T ASK FOR ANYMORE THAN YOU		5	COMPLETE		BEST OVERDUB VOCAL
	MISS YOU NIGHTS		1	COMPLETE		
			5	COMPLETE		
			7	COMPLETE		
			8	COMPLETE		
			11	COMPLETE		BEST

9 SEPTEMBER

ABBEY ROAD

Studio session

Miss You Nights (11)	*See 11 September*
Devil Woman (3)	*I'm Nearly Famous*
I Can't Ask For Anymore Than You (5)	*I'm Nearly Famous*

Lead Vocal: **Cliff Richard**
Guitar: **Terry Britten**
Bass: **Alan Tarney**
Drums: **Clem Cattini**
Keyboards: **Graham Todd**

Producer: **Bruce Welch**
Engineers: **Tony Clark/John Barrett**
Recorded in: **Studio 2**
Session hours: **3.00pm-5.45pm/7.00pm-10.00pm**

SEPTEMBER

Cliff's 64th single, 'Honky Tonk Angel'/'Wouldn't You Know It' is released, but does not make the charts.

11 SEPTEMBER

ABBEY ROAD

Studio session

Miss You Nights (11) — *I'm Nearly Famous*

Lead Vocal: **Cliff Richard**
Producer: **Bruce Welch**
Engineers: **Peter Vince/John Barrett**
Recorded in: **Studio 2**
Session hours: **2.30pm – 5.30pm/6.30pm-10.46pm**

Vocals added to Miss You Nights

SEPTEMBER 20

On ITV's *Supersonic*, Cliff sings 'Honky Tonk Angel' and 'Let's Have A Party'.

OCTOBER 3

A clip of Cliff is shown on Yorkshire TV's *Pop Quest*, hosted by Stevi Merike.

OCTOBER 14

Noel Edmonds records Cliff's 35th birthday on his Radio 1 breakfast show and plays 'Please Don't Tease'.

OCTOBER

Alvin Stardust releases his version of Cliff's 'Move It' as a single.

OCTOBER

On ITV's *Today* programme, Cliff is interviewed by Sandra Harris and declares that he had no idea that a 'honky tonk angel' (the title of his current single) was a prostitute until somebody told him while he was in America. He reveals that he heard the song on an old country album a couple of years previously, liked it and recorded it. Cliff says that he had not wanted to upset anybody, and if DJs didn't want to play it he wouldn't particularly mind. He admits that he hadn't heard of American bars called 'honky tonks' or the Rolling Stones 'Honky Tonk Women'.

OCTOBER

On the subject of Cliff's opinions on 'Honky Tonk Angel', critic Xavier Webster writes: 'It's hypocrisy to put prostitutes outside the cosy Christian circle, but cashing in on it is something else again.'

OCTOBER

Still on the subject of 'Honky Tonk Angel', Cliff says: 'I hope it's a flop. I never want to hear it again and I hope most of the public never hear it. I knew honky-tonks were something to do with bars, but I completely misconstrued the meaning. Okay, some people might say I'm naive – obviously it's very embarrassing for me. Now I know what I've been singing about, I've taken steps to do all I can to make it a flop. I hope no one buys it... If the record is a hit and I'm asked to sing it, I will refuse unless the words are changed.'

RECORDING SHEET — Job No. 21013P

ARTISTIC INFORMATION — Artist: CLIFF RICHARD — Date: 3 12 1975 — Location: STUDIO THREE — Engineers: AC JB — Producer: BRUCE WELCH

REEL NOS.	TITLES	False Starts	Take Nos.	TAKE DETAILS	DUR	REMARKS
	IT'S NO USE PRETENDING (REMAKE)			COMPLETE		BEST
	LOVERS		2	COMPLETE		
			5	COMPLETE		
			6	COMPLETE		BEST
	JUNIOR COWBOY		1	COMPLETE		
			3	COMPLETE		
			4	COMPLETE		
			5	COMPLETE		
			9	COMPLETE		
			11	COMPLETE		
			12	COMPLETE		
	EVEN IF THE MYSTERY		2	COMPLETE		
			3	COMPLETE		
			4	COMPLETE		

NOVEMBER

Cliff appears on Capital, London's commercial radio station with DJ Roger Scott in a nostalgia show reliving 1959. Cliff's second hit, 'High Class Baby', is played.

1 DECEMBER

ABBEY ROAD
Studio session

I Wish You'd Change Your Mind (4)	*(Unissued)*
You've Got To Give Me All Your Lovin' (1)	*See 11 December*
If You Walked Away (6)	*(Unissued)*
Alright It's Alright (3)	*See 10 December*

Guitar:	**Terry Britten**
Bass:	**Alan Tarney**
Drums:	**Clem Cattini**
Keyboards:	**Graham Todd**
String arrangements by	**Richard Hewson**
Vocals:	**Tony Rivers/John Perry/ A. Harding**
Producer:	**Bruce Welch**
Engineers:	**Tony Clark**
Recorded in:	**Studio 3**
Session hours:	**2.30pm-5.45pm/ 6.30pm-7.30pm**

2 DECEMBER

ABBEY ROAD
Studio session

If You Walked Away (5)	*See 8 December*
Every Face Tells A Story (3)	*(Unissued)*
I'm Nearly Famous (2)	*See 11 December*
It's No Use Pretending (1)	*(Unissued)*

Guitar:	**Terry Britten**
Bass:	**Alan Tarney**
Drums:	**Clem Cattini**
Keyboards:	**Graham Todd**
String arrangements by	**Richard Hewson**
Vocals:	**Tony Rivers/ John Perry/ A. Harding**
Producer:	**Bruce Welch**
Engineer:	**Tony Clark**
Recorded in:	**Studio 3**
Session hours:	**2.30pm-6.00pm/ 7.00pm-10.15pm**

DECEMBER 3

Cliff records a *Christmas Day Special* produced by David Winter for BBC Radio.

3 DECEMBER

ABBEY ROAD
Studio session

It's No Use Pretending (4)	*(Unissued)*
Lovers (6)	*(Unissued)*
Junior Cowboy (11)	*See 8 December*
Such Is The Mystery (4)	*See 10 December*

Guitar:	**Terry Britten**
Bass:	**Alan Tarney**
Drums:	**Clem Cattini**
Keyboards:	**Graham Todd**
String arrangements by:	**Richard Hewson**
Vocals:	**Tony Rivers/John Perry/ A. Harding**
Producer:	**Bruce Welch**
Engineer:	**Tony Clark**
Recorded in:	**Studio 3**
Session hours:	**2.30pm-5.30pm/ 6.30pm-10.15pm**

DECEMBER 4

Cliff begins recording for a series of *Gospel Road* for BBC Radio 1 and Radio 2.

4 DECEMBER

ABBEY ROAD
Studio session

I Wish You'd Change Your Mind (6)	*See 12 December*
Lovers (8)	*See 8 December*

Guitar:	**Terry Britten**
Bass:	**Alan Tarney**
Drums:	**Clem Cattini**
Keyboards:	**Graham Todd**
String arrangements by:	**Richard Hewson**
Vocals:	**Tony Rivers/John Perry/A. Harding**
Producer:	**Bruce Welch**
Engineer:	**Tony Clark**
Recorded in:	**Studio 3**
Session hours:	**2.30pm-6.00pm/6.45pm-9.00pm**

8 DECEMBER

ABBEY ROAD
Studio session

If You Walked Away (5)	*I'm Nearly Famous*
Junior Cowboy (11)	*B- side*
Lovers (8)	*I'm Nearly Famous*

Lead Vocal:	**Cliff Richard**
Producer:	**Bruce Welch**
Engineers:	**Tony Clark/John Barrett**
Recorded in:	**Studio 3**
Session hours:	**2.30pm-5.15pm/7.15pm-11.30pm**

Vocals added to the above tracks

RECORDING SHEET

Job No. 21013F

ARTISTIC INFORMATION — COSTING INFORMATION

Dolby	Artist	Date	Session Booked Time	Materials Used
24T / 16T / 8T / 4T / 2T / Mono / Quad	CLIFF RICHARD	5.12.1975	2.30 – 5.30/7.00 –	1 x 7" Spool
		Location: STUDIO THREE	Recording/SI: 1.30 – 5.30/7.00 – 11.00	
		Engineers: AC . JB	Remixing	
		Producer: BRUCE WELCH	Copying: 11.00 – 11.30	
			Playback / Editing	

Reel Nos.	Titles	False Starts	Take Nos.	Take Details From	To	Dur.	Remarks
11952-D24T CONT'	JUNIOR COWBOY		11	COMPLETE		2'42	(M) OVERDUB GTR'S TRES 13 11/1 17
11983 D24T CONT'	LOVERS		8	COMPLETE		3'00	(M) OVERDUB SLIDE GTR TRK 17
— —	IF YOU WALKED AWAY		5	COMPLETE		3'03	(M) OVERDUB GTR TR 17 TR 13
— —	I WISH YOU'D CHANGE YOUR MIND AND ...		6	COMPLETE		3'00	(M) OVERDUB GTR TR 17
11952-D24T CONT'	IT'S NO USE PRETENDING		4	COMPLETE		4'35	(M) OVERDUB GTR TR 14 TR 11/12
	1 x 7½ IPS TAPE COPY TAKEN OF :- SUCH IS THE MYSTERY / LOVERS / IF YOU WALKED AWAY						

Ref. No 9864A — Abbey Road

10 DECEMBER

ABBEY ROAD
Studio session

It's No Use Pretending (6)	*See 11 December*
Such Is The Mystery (4)	*I'm Nearly Famous*
Alright It's Alright (3)	*I'm Nearly Famous*

Lead Vocal:	**Cliff Richard**
Guitar:	**Terry Britten**
Bass:	**Alan Tarney**
Drums:	**Clem Cattini**
Keyboards:	**Graham Todd**
String arrangements by:	**Richard Hewson**
Vocals:	**Tony Rivers/ John Perry/A. Harding**
Producer:	**Bruce Welch**
Engineer:	**Tony Clark/John Barrett**
Recorded in:	**Studio 3**
Session hours:	**2.15pm-5.45pm/6.30pm-midnight**

11 DECEMBER

ABBEY ROAD
Studio session

Miss You Nights (6)	*(Unissued)*
It's No Use Pretending (6)	*I'm Nearly Famous*
I'm Nearly Famous (2)	*I'm Nearly Famous*
You've Got To Give Me All Your Loving (1)	*I'm Nearly Famous*

Lead Vocal:	**Cliff Richard**
Producer:	**Bruce Welch**
Engineer:	**Tony Clark/John Barrett**
Recorded in:	**Studio 3**
Session hours:	**mid-day-1.15pm/2.30pm-6.15pm/ 7.00pm-9.30pm**

Miss You Nights was a remake for ITV
The remaining tracks were for vocal overdubs only

12 DECEMBER

ABBEY ROAD
Studio session

I Wish You'd Change Your Mind (6) *I'm Nearly Famous*

Lead Vocal:	**Cliff Richard**
Producer:	**Bruce Welch**
Engineers:	**Tony Clark/John Barrett**
Recorded in:	**Studio 3**
Session hours:	**2.30pm-6.00pm/7.00pm-12.30pm**

DECEMBER 27

BBC1 TV screens *Cliff and Friends.*

JANUARY

Cliff bans Aj Nebber from singing 'Dear Auntie Vera' on his TV show. The song is about a girl who asks an agony columnist how she can get a bigger bust.

JANUARY

BBC Radio's 1 and 2 run a new series of *Gospel Road*, in which ex-Settler Cindy Kent reviews new records while Cliff contributes his own material and introduces songs by other people.

JANUARY 31

EMI release 'The Music and Life of Cliff Richard', a six casette box set. The tracks, including the occasional Shadows number, are linked by Cliff's thoughts and memories.

DISC

FEBRUARY

EMI release 'Miss You Nights'/'Love Is Enough'. This is Cliff's 65th single and is produced by former Shadow Bruce Welch.

FEBRUARY 14

Cliff appears on ITV's *Supersonic*, singing 'Miss You Nights'.

FEBRUARY 28

Cliff enters the charts with 'Miss You Nights' – his first appearance on the singles chart since July 1974.

MARCH

Cliff's intended visit to the Soviet Union is postponed.

MARCH

Rocket Records release 'Miss You Nights' in the United States.

25 MARCH

ABBEY ROAD
Studio session

Love On (3) *See 26 March*

Guitar:	**Terry Britten**
Bass:	**Alan Tarney**
Drums:	**Clem Cattini**
Keyboards:	**Graham Todd**
String arrangements by :	**Richard Hewson**
Vocals:	**Tony Rivers/John Perry/A. Harding**
Producer:	**Bruce Welch**
Engineer:	**Tony Clark**
Recorded in:	**Studio 3**
Session hours:	**10.00pm-1.45am**

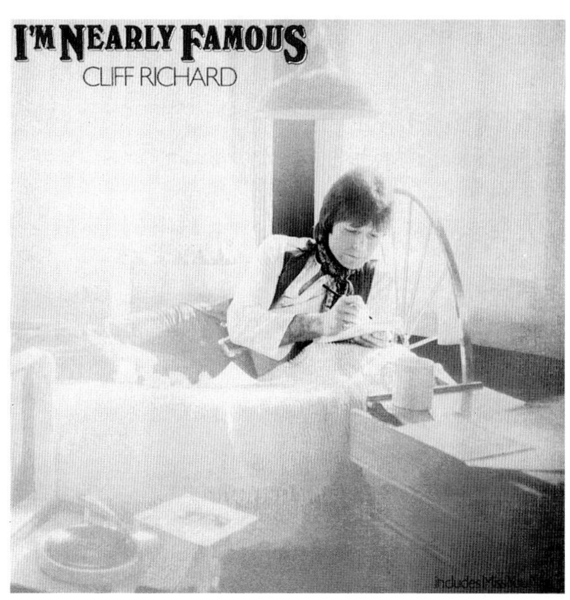

26 MARCH

ABBEY ROAD
Studio session

Love On (3) *B-side*

Lead Vocal:	**Cliff Richard**
Producer:	**Bruce Welch**
Engineer:	**Tony Clark/John Barrett**
Recorded in:	**No 2 Control Room**
Session hours:	**3.00pm-5.30pm**

APRIL 15

Religious organisation Scope stages two charity concerts featuring Cliff and Larry Norman at Birmingham's Odeon Theatre. The concerts are in aid of the National Institute for the Healing of Addictions – an organisation subscribed to by the Who's Pete Townsend. Eric Clapton is among the celebrities to be cured by treatment offered by the Institute.

APRIL 23

Cliff's 66th single, 'Devil Woman'/'Love On', is released. One reviewer, Bob Edmonds, asks: 'Has Cliff been caught out again? He cut a previous single, 'Honky Tonk Angel', without apparently knowing what it was about. This time someone may have forgotten to tell him what the words "devil" and "woman" mean. You see, Cliffie, a "devil" is a naughty person and a "woman" is more or less a person of the opposite sex. Now, is it right for an upstanding young man to sing about naughtiness and sex? Isn't this just setting a bad example to his followers?'

APRIL 26

Cliff records for Dutch television's *Eddy Go Round* show, which is to be transmitted in June.

MAY 3

Radio Luxembourg broadcastys a preview of Cliff's new album 'I'm Nearly Famous'.

MAY 17

Cliff records *Insight* for Radio 1 with producer Tim Blackmore.

MAY 20

Cliff is interviewed at Radio 210 in Reading – the latest ILR station to go on the air.

MAY

A Hong Kong newspaper prints a bizarre piece of editorial under the heading 'Cliff Richard Circus is Coming To Town': 'Clifford Richard Hong Kong's golden boy and Great Britains answer to "Black Oak Arkansas" is expected for concert dates in Hong Kong sometime in June according to L'artiste's recording Labelle, EMI. Clifford the controversial heavy metal gun of rock, known for his bizarre stage regalia and electic cynicism is rumoured to be bringing with him 1,500 watt strobe lights, the Bolshoi Ballet and a herd of performing elephants.'

MAY 30

Radio 1's *Insight* programme is transmitted, sub-titled 'Showmanship in Pop'. It features Alice Cooper, Rick Wakeman, Marc Bolan and Cliff.

JUNE 13

On *Insight* Cliff and former Shadow Bruce Welch survey their 18-year association.

JUNE

Among the celebrities seen sporting Cliff's 'I'm Nearly Famous' badges are guitarists Jimmy Page, Jeff Beck, Eric Clapton and Pete Townsend.

JUNE 19

Cliff appears on ITV's *Supersonic*, singing 'Honky Tonk Angel'.

JUNE 26

Cliff appears on ITV's *Supersonic* singing 'Let's Have A Party'.

'Devil Woman' picks up heavy 'FM' air-play on San Franciscan radio stations.

JULY 24

BBC2 screens *Cliff In Concert*.

JULY 31

Cliff's 67th single, 'I Can't Ask For Anything More Than You'/'Junior Cowboy' is released. Reviewer Charles Shaar Murray writes: 'Cliff's record is a startling performance, sung almost entirely in a pubescent/feminine soul falsetto; it earns one's respect for the technique and execution, but... let's just say that he's gonna seem very weird doing it on *Top Of The Pops*.'

JULY/AUGUST

Cliff is in America promoting 'I'm Nearly Famous'

RECORDING SHEET

Job No. 95667P

ARTISTIC INFORMATION — Artist: CLIFF RICHARD

Date: 6/9/1976 · Location: No 2 · Engineers: AC JB · Producer: BRUCE WELCH

COSTING INFORMATION — Session Booked Time: 10 — 10 · Recording/SI: 10 — 2.00/3.00 — 7.00, 8.00 — 10.00 · Copying · Playback 10 — 1045 · Editing · Materials Used: 3 X815/2

REEL NOS.	TITLES	False Starts	Take Nos.	TAKE DETAILS	DUR.	REMARKS
14903-D24T	LAY BACK AND SMILE		1	COMPLETE	4'07	
			2	COMPLETE	4'00	
— —			3	COMPLETE	4'00	BEST
	GIVE ME LOVE YOUR WAY		1	COMPLETE	3'17	
14904-D24T			2	COMPLETE	3'30	
	TOO LATE TO SAY GOODBYE	1-3	4	COMPLETE	3'15	BEST
	PART OF ME		1	COMPLETE	3'43	BEST
	DON'T TURN OUT THE LIGHT		2	COMPLETE	3'42	
			1	BREAKDOWN @ END	3'13	
14905-D24T			2	COMPLETE	3'41	
			3	COMPLETE	3'37	BEST
		4-6	7	COMPLETE	3'41	

Elton John presents Bruce and Cliff with awards for 'I'm Nearly Famous'

AUGUST

In America,'Devil Woman' enters the *Cashbox* and *Billboard* charts to give Cliff his third-ever hit Stateside and his first since 'It's All In The Game' in 1964.

SEPTEMBER 6

Cliff is interviewed for BBC Television's *Nationwide* and also on Thames Television.

6 SEPTEMBER

ABBEY ROAD

Studio session

Lay Back And Smile (Try A Smile) (3)	*See 14 September*
Give Me Love Your Way	*(Unissued)*
Too Late To Say Goodbye (4)	*(Unissued)*
Part Of Me (1)	*(Unissued)*
Don't Turn Out The Light (3)	*(Unissued)*

Guitars:	**Terry Britten**
Bass:	**Alan Tarney**
Drums:	**Brian Bennett**
Keyboards:	**Graham Todd**
Percussion:	**Brian Bennett/Frank Ricotti**
Vocals:	**Cliff/Tony Rivers/John Perry**
Strings arranged by	**Richard Hewson**
Producer:	**Bruce Welch**
Engineer:	**Tony Clark/John Barrett**
Recorded in:	**Studio 2**
Session hours:	**10.00am-2.00pm/3.00pm-7.00pm/8.00pm-10.00pm**

7 SEPTEMBER

ABBEY ROAD
Studio session

Don't Turn Out The Light (3)	*See 14 September*
Give Me Love Your Way (14)	*See 15 September*
Spider Man (8)	*See 15 September*
When Two Worlds Drift Apart (5)	*See 13 September*

Guitars:	**Terry Britten**
Bass:	**Alan Tarney**
Drums:	**Brian Bennett**
Keyboards:	**Graham Todd**
Percussion:	**Brian Bennett/Frank Ricotti**
Vocals:	**Cliff/Tony Rivers/John Perry**
Strings arranged by:	**Richard Hewson**
Producer:	**Bruce Welch**
Engineer:	**Tony Clark/Mike Jarrett/Allan Rouse**
Recorded in:	**Studio 2**
Session hours:	**11.00am-2.45pm/3.45pm-6.30pm/7.30pm-midnight**

8 SEPTEMBER

ABBEY ROAD
Studio session

Joseph (7)	*See 15 September*
It'll Be Me Babe (3)	*See 15 September*
Dream Maker	*(Unissued)*

Guitars:	**Terry Britten**
Bass:	**Alan Tarney**
Drums:	**Brian Bennett**
Keyboards:	**Graham Todd**
Percussion:	**Brian Bennett** **Frank Ricotti**
Vocals:	**Cliff/Tony Rivers/John Perry**
Strings arranged by	**Richard Hewson**
Producer:	**Bruce Welch**
Engineers:	**Peter Vince/Tony Clark/Mike Jarrett/Allan Rouse**
Recorded in:	**Studio 2**
Session hours:	**11.00am-1.15pm/2.15pm-6.15pm/7.00pm-10.00pm**

SEPTEMBER 9

The *Guardian* newspaper publishes a letter from Brian Green of Epping in Essex: 'Sir, they got Cliff Richard – we got the Foxbat. At that rate of exchange, send them Jethro Tull and you could disband NATO.'

9 SEPTEMBER

ABBEY ROAD
Studio session

Dream Maker (5)	*(Unissued)*
Must Be Love (13)	*See 17 September*

Guitars:	**Terry Britten**
Bass:	**Alan Tarney**
Drums:	**Brian Bennett**
Keyboards:	**Graham Todd**
Percussion:	**Brian Bennett/Frank Ricotti**
Vocals:	**Cliff/Tony Rivers/John Perry**
Strings arranged by:	**Richard Hewson**
Producer:	**Bruce Welch**
Engineer:	**Tony Clark/Hayden Bendall**
Recorded in:	**Studio 2**
Session hours:	**10.30am-1.30pm/2.30pm-6.00pm/7.00pm-10.30pm**

10 SEPTEMBER

ABBEY ROAD
Studio session

You Got Me Wondering (3)	*See 13 September*
Every Face Tells A Story (9)	*See 14 September*
Part Of Me	*(Unissued)*

Guitars:	**Terry Britten**
Bass:	**Alan Tarney**
Drums:	**Brian Bennett**
Keyboards:	**Graham Todd**
Percussion:	**Brian Bennett/Frank Ricotti**
Vocals:	**Cliff/Tony Rivers/John Perry**
Strings arranged by:	**Richard Hewson**
Producer:	**Bruce Welch**
Engineer:	**Tony Clark**
Recorded in:	**Studio 2**
Session hours:	**10.30am-1.00pm/2.00pm-7.00pm/7.30pm-10.30pm**

13 SEPTEMBER

ABBEY ROAD
Studio session

You Got Me Wondering (3)	*Every Face Tells A Story*
When Two Worlds Drift Apart (5)	*B-side*

Lead Vocal:	**Cliff Richard**
Producer:	**Bruce Welch**
Engineer:	**Tony Clark/Allan Rouse**
Recorded in:	**Studio 2**
Session hours:	**2.30pm-6.00pm/7.00pm-10.30pm**

14 SEPTEMBER

ABBEY ROAD
Studio session

Every Face Tells A Story (9)	*(Unissued)*
Don't Turn The Light Out (3)	*Every Face Tells A Story*
Try A Smile (3)	*Every Face Tells A Story*

Lead Vocal:	**Cliff Richard**
Producer:	**Bruce Welch**
Engineer:	**Tony Clark/Allan Rouse**
Recorded in:	**Studio 2**
Session hours:	**10.00am-1.45pm/2.30pm-6.15pm/7.15pm-10.00pm**

15 SEPTEMBER

ABBEY ROAD
Studio session

Spider Man (8)	*Every Face Tells A Story*
It'll Be Me Babe (3)	*Every Face Tells A Story*
Joseph (7)	*Small Corners*
Give Me Love Your Way (14)	*Every Face Tells A Story*

Lead Vocal:	**Cliff Richard**
Producer:	**Bruce Welch**
Engineer:	**Tony Clark/Mike Jarrett**
Recorded in:	**Studio 2**
Session hours:	**2.30pm-6.00pm/7.00pm-11.00pm**

17 SEPTEMBER

ABBEY ROAD
Studio session

No One Waits (4)	*B-side*
Must Be Love (13)	*Every Face Tells A Story*

Lead Vocal:	**Cliff Richard**
Guitars:	**Terry Britten**
Bass:	**Alan Tarney**
Drums:	**Brian Bennett**
Keyboards:	**Graham Todd**
Percussion:	**Brian Bennett** **Frank Ricotti**
Vocals:	**Cliff/Tony Rivers** **John Perry**
Strings arranged by:	**Richard Hewson**
Producer:	**Bruce Welch**
Engineer:	**Tony Clark** **Allan Rouse**
Recorded in:	**Studio 2**
Session hours:	**10.00am-1.45pm** **2.30pm-6.30pm** **7.30pm-11.00pm**

18 SEPTEMBER

ABBEY ROAD
Studio session

Mr Dream Maker (2)	*Every Face Tells A Story*
Every Face Tells A Story (7)	*Every Face Tells A Story*

Lead Vocal:	**Cliff Richard**
Guitars:	**Terry Britten**
Bass:	**Alan Tarney**
Drums:	**Brian Bennett**
Keyboards:	**Graham Todd**
Percussion:	**Brian Bennett** **Frank Ricotti**
Vocals:	**Cliff/Tony Rivers/** **John Perry**
Strings arranged by:	**Richard Hewson**
Producer:	**Bruce Welch**
Engineer:	**Tony Clark** **Allan Rouse**
Recorded in:	**Studio 2**
Session hours:	**10.00am-2.15pm** **2.45pm-4.30pm** **6.30pm-10.00pm**

22 SEPTEMBER

ABBEY ROAD
Studio session

That's Why I Love You (5)	*B-side*
Nothing Left To Say (3)	*B-side*

Lead Vocal:	**Cliff Richard**
Guitars:	**Terry Britten**
Bass:	**Alan Tarney**
Drums:	**Brian Bennett**
Keyboards:	**Graham Todd**
Percussion:	**Brian Bennett/Frank Ricotti**
Vocals:	**Cliff/Tony Rivers/John Perry**
Strings arranged by:	**Richard Hewson**
Producer:	**Bruce Welch**
Engineer:	**Peter Vince/Hayden Bendall**
Recorded in:	**Studio 2**
Session hours:	**10.00am-1.30pm/2.30pm-** **6.30pm/7.00pm-10.30pm**

24 SEPTEMBER

ABBEY ROAD
Studio session

Up In The World (7)	*Every Face Tells A Story*

Lead Vocal:	**Cliff Richard**
Guitars:	**Terry Britten**
Bass:	**Alan Tarney**
Drums:	**Brian Bennett**
Keyboards:	**Graham Todd**
Percussion:	**Brian Bennett/Frank Ricotti**
Vocals:	**Cliff/Tony Rivers/John Perry**
Strings arranged by:	**Richard Hewson**
Producer:	**Bruce Welch**
Engineer:	**Tony Clark**
Recorded in:	**Studio 2**
Session hours:	**10.00am-11.30pm**

OCTOBER

His single 'Devil Woman' becomes Cliff Richard's biggest-ever hit on the other side of the Atlantic, making both the No.6 position in the *Billboard* chart and the No. 5 spot in the rival *Cashbox* chart.

OCTOBER 1

Cliff kicks off a gospel tour in aid of Tear Fund, the British overseas relief and development organisation.

Cliff answers questions from the press

OCTOBER 22-LATE NOVEMBER

Cliff gives a string of British pop concerts.

OCTOBER 31

BBC TV screens *The Young Ones*.

NOVEMBER 5

Talking to Sandy Harrod of the *Croydon Advertiser* before a Tear Fund concert, Cliff explains that the fund was set up eight or nine years ago to provide money for Third World projects. Talking about his August tour of the Soviet Union, Cliff says: 'I suppose they chose me because I'm fairly middle-of-the-road,' and of his revived recording career: 'I've broken out of the poly-thene bag...' At Cliff's Tear Fund concerts, songs performed include 'Devil Woman', 'Miss You Nights', and 'Willie And The Hand Jive'.

NOVEMBER

It's announced that Cliff intends ' to have another go' at the Eurovision Song Contest.

NOVEMBER

Cliff reveals that he is to visit India – his birthplace.

NOVEMBER 14

The *Sunday People* newspaper prints an article by Peter Bishop, questioning the prolific use of four-letter words in the pop paper *New Musical Express* under the heading: 'Should we Fling this Filth at our Pop Kids?' The article complains that in one recent *NME* article, the four-letter word for sexual relations appeared no fewer than seven times. Alongside the banner headline the Sunday People prints a picture of Cliff who 'refuses to have the *NME* in the house'.

NOVEMBER 22

Cliff performs at London's Royal Albert Hall with the Brian Bennett Band.

NOVEMBER

Cliff Richard's 68th single, 'Hey Mr Dream Maker'/'No One Waits' is released.

DECEMBER

In India, Cliff meets Mother Teresa of Calcutta and her missionaries of charity. He visits the homes for the destitute and dying.

DECEMBER 7/8

Cliff gives two performances at the Kalamandir Auditorium, New Delhi, India..

DECEMBER

Cliff visits Tear Fund projects in Bangladesh.

DECEMBER 30

On Belgian TV's *Adamo Special*, Cliff sings 'Power To All Our Friends', 'Honky Tonk Angel' and duets with Adamo on 'Living Doll'.

DECEMBER 31

BBC1's *A Jubilee of Music* is screened, featuring Vera Lynn, Lulu, Acker Bilk and Cliff.

JANUARY 1

The *NME* jokingly award Cliff 'The First Annual Mary Whitehouse Seal of Good Housekeeping Award' for refusing to have *NME* in the house.

JANUARY

In the *NME* 1976 singles chart table (30 points for 1 week at number 1, 1 point for 1 week at number 30) Cliff is placed 28th with 229 points, between Diana Ross and Hot Chocolate. Abba come top with 995 points, followed by Rod Stewart. In the album yearly chart, 'I'm Nearly Famous' comes 45th.

JANUARY 8

Cliff appears on BBC TV's *Multi-Coloured Swap Shop* with Noel Edmonds.

10 JANUARY

ABBEY ROAD
Studio session

My Kinda Life — *A-side*

Lead Vocal: **Cliff Richard**
Guitars: **Mo Witham**
Bass: **Alan Jones**
Drums: **Roger Pope**
Keyboards: **Alan Hawkshaw**
Vocals: **Cliff/Tony Rivers/John Perry**

Producer: **Bruce Welch**
Engineer: **Tony Clark**
Recorded in: **Studio 2**
Session hours:

17 JANUARY

ABBEY ROAD
Studio session

Goin' Home (3) — *See 2 February*
Up In Canada (2) — *See 2 February*
I've Got News For You (1) — *See 26 January*
Why Should The Devil
Have All The Good Music (3) — *See 31 January*

Guitar: **Terry Britten/Bryn Haworth**
Bass: **Alan Tarney**
Drums: **Brian Bennett**
Percussion: **Brian Bennett**
Keyboards: **Graham Todd**
Vocals: **Tony Rivers/John Perry**
Stuart Calver

Producer: **Cliff Richard**
Engineers: **Tony Clark**
Hayden Bendall
Recorded in: **Studio 3**
Session hours: **10.00am-1.30pm**
2.30pm-8.00pm

18 JANAURY

ABBEY ROAD
Studio session

Why Me Lord (3) — *See 27 January*
Yes He Lives (1) — *See 27 January*
You Can't Get To Heaven.... (6) — *See 31 January*
When I Survey The Wondrous Cross — *See 4 February*

Guitar: **Terry Britten**
Bryn Haworth
Bass: **Alan Tarney**
Drums: **Brian Bennett**
Percussion: **Brian Bennett**
Keyboards: **Graham Todd**
Vocals: **Tony Rivers**
John Perry
Stuart Calver

Producer: **Cliff Richard**
Engineer: **Tony Clark**
Hayden Bendall
Allan Rouse
Recorded in: **Studio 3**
Session hours: **10.00am-1.30pm**
2.00pm-6.00pm
7.00pm-11.00pm

19 JANUARY

ABBEY ROAD
Studio session

I Wish We'd All Been Ready	*See 27 January*
Hey Watcha Say (3)	*See 31 January*
Good On The Sally Army (2)	*See 31 January*
I Love (3)	*See 3 June*

Guitar: **Terry Britten/Bryn Haworth**
Bass: **Alan Tarney**
Drums: **Brian Bennett**
Percussion: **Brian Bennett**
Vocals: **Tony Rivers/John Perry/Stuart Calver**

Producer: **Cliff Richard**
Engineer: **Tony Clark/Hayden Bendall**
Recorded in: **Studio 3**
Session hours: **11.00am-1.30pm/2.30pm-5.30pm/7.00pm-10.00pm**

26 JANUARY

ABBEY ROAD
Studio session

I've Got News For You (1)	*Small Corners*

Lead Vocal: **Cliff Richard**

Producer: **Cliff Richard**
Engineer: **Tony Clark/Hayden Bendall**
Recorded in: **Studio 2**
Session hours: **2.30pm-6.30pm/7.00pm-10.00pm**

27 JANUARY

ABBEY ROAD
Studio session

Why Me Lord (3)	*Small Corners*
Yes He Lives (1)	*Small Corners*
I Wish We'd All Been Ready (4)	*Small Corners*

Lead Vocal: **Cliff Richard**

Producer: **Cliff Richard**
Engineer: **Tony Clark/Hayden Bendall**
Recorded in: **Studio 2**
Session hours: **2.30pm-6.30pm/7.00pm-9.00pm**

31 JANUARY

ABBEY ROAD
Studio session

Good On The Sally Army (2)	*Small Corners*
Why Should The Devil... (3)	*Small Corners*
Hey Watcha Say (3)	*Small Corners*
You Can't Get To Heaven... (6)	*(Unissued)*

Lead Vocal: **Cliff Richard**

Producer: **Cliff Richard**
Engineer: **Tony Clark/Hayden Bendall**
Recorded in: **Studio 3**
Session hours: **2.30pm-6.00pm/7.00pm-10.15pm**

2 FEBRUARY

ABBEY ROAD
Studio session

Goin' Home (3)	*Small Corners*
Up In Canada (2)	*Small Corners*

Lead Vocal: **Cliff Richard**

Producer: **Cliff Richard**
Engineer: **Tony Clark/Hayden Bendall**
Recorded in: **Studio 3**
Session hours: **2.30pm-6.15pm/7.00pm-11.00pm**

ARTIST CLIFF RICHARD
TAPE BOX No. 16960 D24T
TITLE NEWS FOR YOU
JOB No. 95727P
1 Bass
2 Bass DIT
3 Bass Drum
4 Snare
5–6 Kit
7–8 PIANO
9 Elec Gtr.
10 Elec Gtr
11 Elec Gtr
12 CLAVINET
13 CLAVINET
14 Elec Gtr SOLO
15 Elec Gtr SOLO HARM
17 Tambourine
19 Vox BEST
20 B.Vs – "I got news"
22 B.Vs "start to live again"
23 B.Vs
REMARKS
(22) la la la's at END

4 FEBRUARY

ABBEY ROAD
Studio session

When I Survey The Wondrous Cross — *Small Corners*

Lead Vocal:	**Cliff Richard**
Producer:	**Cliff Richard**
Engineer:	**Tony Clark/Hayden Bendall**
Recorded in:	**Studio 2**
Session hours:	**2.30pm-6.30pm/7.00pm-00.30am**

FEBRUARY 10

For World Records 25th Anniversary, Cliff Richard is their guest of honour.

FEBRUARY 26

ITV's *Supersonic* features Cliff, Guys 'n' Dolls, Racing Cars, Golden Earring and Dennis Weaver.

MARCH 6

The Cliff Richard Movement magazine *Dynamite* reports that Cliff's Tear Fund concerts in 1976 raised over £37,000, the money providing six vehicles for Argentina, the Yemen Arab Republic, Nigeria, Haiti and Burundi, as well as a generator for a hospital in India, a rural development centre in Kenya and a nutritional training centre in Zaire.

MARCH

EMI release Cliff's 69th single, 'My Kinda Life'/'Nothing Left For Me To Say' and reviewer Steve Clark writes: 'It's twelve years if it's a day since Cliff exchanged his quiff and leather jacket for all things wholesome, and to hear him sing a song eulogising the life of a guitar picker is about as convincing as Margaret Thatcher telling us how she'll put things right before you can say "Sir Keith Joseph". The rock 'n' roll backing is not exactly stuffed with raunch.'

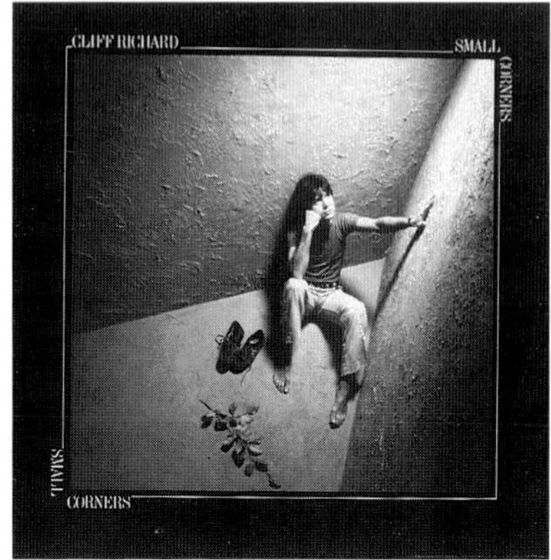

MARCH

Cliff attends a dinner party at Elton John's house. Former *Ready Steady Go* compere Cathy McGowan is also present.

30 MARCH

ABBEY ROAD
Studio session

Imagine Love — *B-side*

Lead Vocal:	**Cliff Richard**
Guitars:	**Terry Britten**
Bass:	**Alan Tarney**
Keyboards:	**Alan Hawkshaw**
Drums:	**Trevor Spencer**
Producer:	**Bruce Welch**
Engineer:	**Tony Clark**
Recorded in:	**Studio 2**
Session hours:	**10.00am-5.30pm**

MARCH 31-APRIL 10

Cliff spends 2 weeks in South Africa.

APRIL

Journalist Monty Smith writes of Cliff: 'Besides being a neat riposte to America's apparent indifference, the 'I'm Nearly Famous' album had an entirely deserved regenerative effect on Cliff's career. He was hardly at a make or break point but, give the lad credit, he could easily have gone the way of most main-stream performers at that stage – to the great cabaret club in the West End.'

APRIL

Cliff appears on *Top of the Pops* singing 'My Kinda Life'.

APRIL

'My Kind Of Life' reaches No.15 on the British charts and spends a total of eight weeks in the Top Twenty.

MAY 2-25

Cliff tours Australasia.

MAY 7

ITV's *All You Need Is Love* looks at the early days of rock 'n' roll. Cliff is featured, along with Elvis Presley, Bill Haley, Jerry Lee Lewis, Carl Perkins, Chuck Berry, Chubby Checker, Gene Vincent, Tommy Steele, Terry Dene, Little Richard and Lonnie Donegan.

MAY 29

London Weekend Television screens Cliff's 1966-made film *Finders Keepers*.

3 JUNE

ABBEY ROAD
Studio session

I Love (3)	*Small Corners*

Lead Vocal:	**Cliff Richard**
Producer:	**Cliff Richard**
Engineer:	**Tony Clark/Hayden Bendall**
Recorded in:	**Studio 3**
Session hours:	**10.00am-1.15pm**

JUNE 6

As part of the Queen's Silver Jubilee celebrations, Cliff speaks at a youth rally in Windsor Great Park.

JUNE

On the subject of the new punk rock explosion, Cliff comments: 'I don't like what punk rockers do – especially to themselves... some like Tom Robinson and Elvis Costello are great, but most of them are lousy and I find it all a bit repulsive that people should want to look so ugly. The punks think they own the pop scene, but they forget they're just leasing it from us... What we've got going now is the first generation of forty year olds who dig rock 'n' roll. When I was eighteen, people of forty hated rock. Now, when we're sixty... it may sound ridiculous, but I'm going to love rock, the music will still be our music.'

JUNE 13-27

Cliff undertakes a promotional visit to the USA.

JUNE 27

EMI release Cliff's 70th single, 'When Two Worlds Drift Apart'/'That's Why I Love You'.

JUNE 29

Cliff records 'When Two Worlds Drift Apart' for *Top of the Pops.*

JULY 2

Cliff guests on ITV's *Saturday Scene.*

11 JULY

ABBEY ROAD
Studio session

Can't Take The Hurt Anymore	*A-side*
Needing A Friend	*B-side*
Mobile Alabama School Leaving	
Hullaballoo	*(Unissued)*

Lead Vocal:	**Cliff Richard**
Guitars:	**Terry Britten/Tim Renwicks/Alan Parker/ Alan Tarney/Duncan Mackay**
Bass:	**Alan Tarney/Alan Jones**
Drums:	**Brian Bennett/Trevor Spencer**
Percussion:	**Brian Bennett/Trevor Spencer**
Keyboards:	**Graham Todd/Alan Tarney**
Vocals:	**Tony Rivers/John Perry/Stuart Calver/ Alan Tarney/Cliff**
String arrangements by :	**Richard Hewson**
Producer:	**Bruce Welch**
Engineer:	**Tony Clark**
Recorded in:	**Studio 3**
Session hours:	

JULY 20

Cliff attends a reception at Buckingham Palace.

AUGUST 2-16

Cliff holidays in Portugal.

AUGUST

The *Sunday Mirror* asks celebrities who they'd like to be stranded with on a desert island. Frankie Howerd chooses Mary Whitehouse, newscaster Reginald Bosanquet chooses Muppet Miss Piggy, and Cliff selects actress Farrah Fawcett-Majors... 'so that she can give me tennis lessons.'

AUGUST 17

The London news station LBC on *Newsbea,t* and the BBC World Service, both interview Cliff.

SEPTEMBER

Hodder & Stoughton publish Cliff's own book *Which One's Cliff?* Written by Cliff in conjunction with Bill Latham, the book deals with not only his career in the music business but also his Christian beliefs.

SEPTEMBER 9-24

Cliff tours Europe.

SEPTEMBER

In *The Sunday Times* colour supplement, journalist Gordon Burn writes of Cliff: 'Just because he's 37, well-preserved and not ashamed to admit being celibate for the past twelve years, doesn't necessarily mean a thing.'

SEPTEMBER 28

On his Radio 1 show, Dave Lee Travis talks to Cliff for an hour and plays tracks.

OCTOBER 1

Along with Robert Morley, Cliff appears on Michael Parkinson's BBC1 chat show.

OCTOBER 7

Cliff kicks off his 1977 gospel tour at the Redworth Leisure Centre.

OCTOBER 7-22

Touring England on the gospel tour.
At EMI's sales conference dinner, singer Roger Chapman makes loud and rude comments about Cliff's self-imposed twelve-year celibacy.

OCTOBER 14

Cliff's 37th birthday is spent playing at the Manchester Free Trade Hall.

OCTOBER 18

To celebrate the Queen's Silver Jubilee and the centenary of the invention of the gramaphone, the British Phonographic Institution, in its Britannia Awards, names Cliff 'Best British Male Artist'. Queen's 'Bohemian Rhapsody' is 'Best British Pop Single' and Julie Covington and Graham Parker tie for 'Most Outstanding New British Recording Artist'.
Cliff gives a gospel show in Rotterdam.

OCTOBER 28

The Songwriter's Guild of Great Britain presents Cliff with the Gold Badge Award.

NOVEMBER 9-DECEMBER 12

Cliff on tour in England and Scotland.

NOVEMBER

Cliff is interviewed by presenter Sally James on ATV's Saturday morning children's programme *Tiswas,* before becoming involved in the messy slapstick routine treatment that's synonymous with the show. EMI Records issue 'Small Corners', an album of religious songs.

NOVEMBER

Miss Margica Caraghin writes a rather over the top letter to the music press from Galati, Romania:
'What could be more beautiful and more wonderful than to celebrate Cliff Richard today when he celebrates his birthday. How wonderful it is Cliff Richard's birthday! Let's be next to him my friends, from all over the world! Let's be next to him as we have always been, so he should feel the warmth of our endless and burning love for him. The English nation celebrates him, and at the same time the entire world, the entire musical world, celebrates him since Cliff belongs to the entire musical world, loving him and appreciating him...'
History does not record whether this was written with effusive gushing sincerity or was the work of a wag!

NOVEMBER

Cliff is photographed with Tony James and Bob Andrews from Generation X.

NOVEMBER

Journalist Bob Woffinden writes of Cliff: 'He's still neat, deferential and responsible; he still hasn't moved on to higher things... in fact, Richard might be capable of much more yet, but he's so determinedly inoffensive that we're never likely to find out what.'

NOVEMBER 12

Cliff appears on the Saturday morning TV show *Tiswas.*

NOVEMBER 21

Cliff is interviewed by the press from 11am to 6pm.

24/25 NOVEMBER

FAIRFIELD HALLS, CROYDON
Live Recordings for BBC Radio

I'm Nearly Famous	*(Unissued)*
My Kinda Life	*(Unissued)*
Every Face Tells A Story	*(Unissued)*
When Two Worlds Drift Apart	*(Unissued)*
Summer Holiday	*(Unissued)*
Living Doll	*(Unissued)*
Bachelor Boy	*(Unissued)*
Please Don't Tease	*(Unissued)*
Give Me Love Your Way	*(Unissued)*
Try A Smile	*(Unissued)*
Up In The World	*(Unissued)*
Yes He Lives	*(Unissued)*
Miss You Nights	*(Unissued)*
You've Got To Give Me All Your Lovin'	*(Unissued)*
Move It	*(Unissued)*
Devil Woman	*(Unissued)*

Lead Vocal: **Cliff Richard**

NOVEMBER 26

It is announced that Cliff and the Shadows will play together for the first time in ten years at a series of reunion concerts at the London Palladium. The shows are due to take place in February/March 1978, and recorded for.future release.

DECEMBER

Cliff attends the Record Industry Ball at London's famous Dorchester Hotel.

DECEMBER 17

Cliff appears on BBC TV's live *Swap Shop Christmas Show.* They screen the video of 'My Kinda Life' and Cliff takes one of his belts as a 'swap'.

1978–1980

The Records 1978 – 1980

In 1978 both singles and album chart placings were disappointing, as illustrated by the fact that not one single reached the top 40. Even if 'Green Light' and 'Hot Shot', released the following year, sold slightly better, their peaking at No.57 and 46 respectively hardly made them hit records. However, the one that did make it to the top of the charts became Cliff's first No.1 since 1968 and his biggest selling single with sales just under 3 million worldwide. 'We Don't Talk Anymore' stayed on the charts for 14 weeks. All the singles that were released in 1980 reached the top twenty, with 'Carrie' achieving the most impressive chart placing at No.4, followed by 'Dreamin' at No.8, and 'Suddenly', a duet with Olivia Newton-John from the film soundtrack of *Xanadu*, peaked at No.15.

Sales of the 1979 live album were considerably better than the two released in 1978. THANK YOU VERY MUCH contained the recordings made of the 20th Anniversary reunion concerts at the London Palladium with the Shadows. For the repertoire of the shows, the basic set-up as used before was followed – namely a string of hits interspersed with some new songs. The old hits were mainly drawn from sixties repertoire while, for new material, naturally the recent hit 'Devil Woman' was chosen as well as 'Miss You Nights', 'The song I haven't left out of any of my concerts since the first time I recorded it in 1975'. The follow-up album ROCK 'N' ROLL JUVENILE, outdid all the other albums of this period by reaching the No.3 spot and staying on the chart for 22 weeks. It had two top 5 singles to spur interest 'Carrie' and 'We Don't Talk Anymore'. The successor, I'M NO HERO, released in 1980, turned out to be another big seller and, although this time there were no hit singles to boost sales, the album did very well by reaching No.4 and staying on the charts for 11 weeks. There was another album scheduled for release prior to this one. CLIFF – THE EARLY YEARS was a compilation of all the early hits but for reasons unknown, its February release was cancelled.

The Sessions 1978 – 1980

For the January 1978 sessions that ran through to April, Bruce Welch again landed himself the job of producer, this time for the GREEN LIGHT album. The band was virtually identical to the one used on SMALL CORNERS and EVERY FACE TELLS A STORY, and again featured Shadows drummer Brian Bennett. A couple of intriguing items from these sessions was the new version of Cliff's 1960 hit 'Please Don't Tease' that turned up on the B-side of 'Please Remember Me', but somehow never quite matched the greatness of the original recording, and the working title of 'Count Me Out' was simply called 'New Song'. Overdubs were added from January through to May, while remixing was done from March to July and, in all probability, strings were likely to have been added during the sessions held in June. It should be noted here that some of the tracks listed as unissued would only be backing tracks. However, a vocal track for 'Ships That Pass In The Night' was taped and probably still exists. To collect sufficient material for an album, EMI recorded three shows, at the London Palladium, one on 3rd March, and two on the 4th, when Cliff and the Shadows were reunited on stage for the first time in ten years, recreating the special magic of their twenty-year musical history. (Although three shows were recorded only the information listed was logged with Abbey Road.) Bruce Welch supervised all aspects of the recording and technical work as producer, and although it is not clear how directly Cliff was involved with repair work on these recordings, it is certain that Bruce conducted a string of overdubbing and mixing sessions at Abbey Road, doing a lot of work on the tapes during October and November to make the resulting THANK YOU VERY MUCH album a very impressive item. Stereo remixing sessions were carried out in December and ran through to January 1979. Although Bruce was responsible for all the work on the album, Hank Marvin did assist in the overdubbing of the Shadows tracks. It is thought that all the shows taped were done so in their entirety, which would suggest that there are a number of songs that remain unreleased, and probably unmixed. If this is the case, those tracks would include 'Walk Don't Run', 'Little B', 'Let Me Be The One', 'Wonderful Land', 'FBI' (Shadows), 'Yes He Lives', 'Every Face Tells A Story', 'Up In The World', 'Up In Canada', 'Melting Into One','The Minute You're Gone', 'Bachelor Boy' (Cliff). It should be noted, though, that a selection of these were featured in the video version of the show, for which remixing was carried out separately at sessions from 1 December through to mid January.The tracks remixed for the video are 'FBI', 'Let Me Be The One', 'Yes He Lives' and 'Up In Canada'. The April 1978 sessions produced two additional tracks for the GREEN LIGHT album with the same crew and band in attendance as for January.

For the sessions that produced the ROCK 'N' ROLL JUVE-

NILE material, the Pathe Marconi studio was chosen. Two different recording occasions in July 1978 and again in January 1979 were needed to complete the tracks. Rough mixes of some of the tracks were produced on 17 February for, in all probability, Cliff or Bruce to take away. The band featured the usual regulars, while new musicians including Herbie Flowers and Tristan Fry from Sky, and Peter Skellen, a singer-songwriter who had a top ten hit with 'You're A Lady', were brought in to help out. Producer credits were shared between Cliff and Terry Britten. He was the songwriter-musician who had worked on a number of Cliff's recording sessions, and of course had penned 'Miss You Nights' and 'Devil Woman'. Overdubbing was carried out at Abbey Road between January and April with remixing running from April through to October, with a backing track of 'Hot Shot' being taped on the 30th for BBC's *Top Of The Pops.* Plans were made to follow up these overall successful sessions with another at RG Jones Recording Studios in Wimbledon. This took place in May. Bruce Welch had already selected the song, and of course produced the Alan Tarney composition 'We Don't Talk Anymore' as Cliff's best selling single of his career. In December the BBC Radio Transcription Unit taped three concerts at the Odeon Hammersmith, for broadcast at a later date. For whatever reason, the session that produced the 'Suddenly' track, duetted with Olivia Newton-John, appears to have been recorded in a garage located in Los Angeles. Obviously the acoustics in this improvised studio presented serious problems with traffic noise levels outside. Compounding the technical problems was the recording method used of Cliff and Olivia taping their vocals simultaneously onto a pre-recorded backing track. It is thought Olivia returned at a later date to re-record her vocal due to her track containing the noise levels as mentioned. The track was produced by John Farrar who played on the backing along with other musicians David McDaniel, Ed Greene, Michael Boddicker and Richard Hewson.

The songs Cliff was to record at the Riverside Studios at his final session of 1980 provided the material for the I'M NO HERO album.

On 14th October the BBC filmed Cliff's 40th Birthday concert at the Apollo Victoria in London. The show will form part of the forthcoming four-part series on Cliff to be shown in 1981.

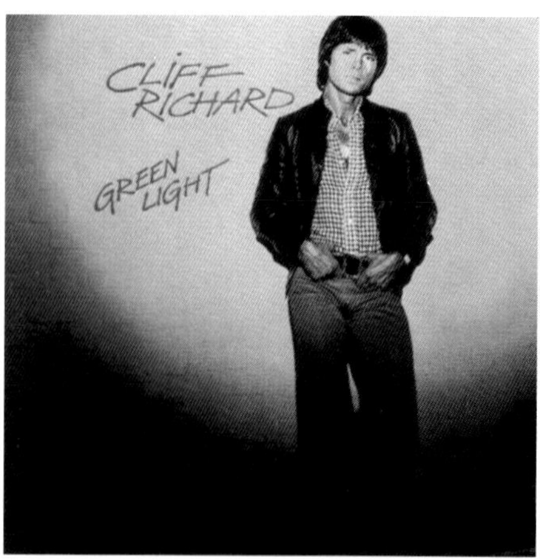

9 JANUARY

ABBEY ROAD
Studio session

Under Lock And Key (2)	*(Unissued)*
Ease Along (3)	*See 7 February*

Guitar: **Terry Britten/Tim Renwick/Alan Parker/ Alan Tarney**
Bass: **Alan Tarney/Alan Jones**
Drums: **Brian Bennett/Trevor Spencer**
Percussion: **Brian Bennett/Trevor Spencer**
Keyboards: **Graham Todd/Alan Tarney/Duncan Mackay**
Vocals: **Tony Rivers/John Perry/Stuart Calver/ Alan Tarney/Cliff**
String arrangements by **Richard Hewson**

Producer: **Bruce Welch**
Engineers: **Tony Clark/Hayden Bendall**
Recorded in: **Studio 3**
Session hours: **10.00am-1.30pm**
2.00pm-6.45pm

10 JANUARY

ABBEY ROAD
Studio session

Please Remember Me (2)	*See 7 February*
Ships That Pass In The Night (1)	*See 19 February*

Guitar: **Terry Britten/Tim Renwick/Alan Parker/ Alan Tarney**
Bass: **Alan Tarney/Alan Jones**
Drums: **Brian Bennett/Trevor Spencer**
Percussion: **Brian Bennett/Trevor Spencer**
Keyboards: **Graham Todd/Alan Tarney/Duncan Mackay**
Vocals: **Tony Rivers/John Perry/Stuart Calver/ Alan Tarney/Cliff**
String arrangements by **Richard Hewson**

Producer: **Bruce Welch**
Engineers: **Tony Clark/Hayden Bendall**
Recorded in: **Studio 3**
Session hours: **10.30am-1.30pm**
2.00pm-6.30pm

11 JANUARY

ABBEY ROAD
Studio session

Free My Soul (4)	*Green Light*
Muddy Water (2)	*See 11 February*

Lead Vocal: **Cliff Richard**
Guitar: **Terry Britten/Tim Renwick/Alan Parker/ Alan Tarney**
Bass: **Alan Tarney/Alan Jones**
Drums: **Brian Bennett/Trevor Spencer**
Percussion: **Brian Bennett/Trevor Spencer**
Keyboards: **Graham Todd/Alan Tarney/Duncan Mackay**
Vocals: **Tony Rivers/John Perry/Stuart Calver/ Alan Tarney/Cliff**
String arrangements by **Richard Hewson**

Producer: **Bruce Welch**
Engineers: **Tony Clark/Hayden Bendall**
Recorded in: **Studio 3**
Session hours: **10.30am-1.30pm/2.00pm-7.00pm**

JANUARY

Cliff releases his 71st single, 'Yes He Lives'/'Good On The Sally Army'. Both songs are taken from the 'Small Corners' LP.

12 JANUARY

ABBEY ROAD
Studio session

Never Even Thought (1)	*See 19 February*
Do What You Gotta Do (1)	*See 19 February*

Guitar:	**Terry Britten/Tim Renwick/ Alan Parker/Alan Tarney**
Bass:	**Alan Tarney/Alan Jones**
Drums:	**Brian Bennett/Trevor Spencer**
Percussion:	**Brian Bennett/Trevor Spencer**
Keyboards:	**Graham Todd/Alan Tarney/ Duncan Mackay**
Vocals:	**Tony Rivers John Perry Stuart Calver Alan Tarney Cliff**
String arrangements by	**Richard Hewson**
Producer:	**Bruce Welch**
Engineers:	**Tony Clark Hayden Bendall**
Recorded in:	**Studio 3**
Session hours:	**10.30am-1.30pm 2.00pm-6.30pm**

13 JANUARY

ABBEY ROAD
Studio session

While She's Young (3)	*See 15 March*

Guitar:	**Terry Britten/Tim Renwick/ Alan Parker/Alan Tarney**
Bass:	**Alan Tarney/Alan Jones**
Drums:	**Brian Bennett/Trevor Spencer**
Percussion:	**Brian Bennett/Trevor Spencer**
Keyboards:	**Graham Todd/Alan Tarney/ Duncan Mackay**
Vocals:	**Tony Rivers John Perry Stuart Calver Alan Tarney Cliff**
String arrangements by	**Richard Hewson**
Producer:	**Bruce Welch**
Engineers:	**Tony Clark/ Hayden Bendall**
Recorded in:	**Studio 3**
Session hours:	**10.30am-4.00pm**

14 JANUARY

ABBEY ROAD
Studio session

Gettin' The Feelin' (1)	*See 11 February*
Please Don't Tease (5)	*See 10 February*
Start All Over Again	*See 15 March*

Guitar:	**Terry Britten/Tim Renwick/Alan Parker/Alan Tarney**
Bass:	**Alan Tarney/Alan Jones**
Drums:	**Brian Bennett/Trevor Spencer**
Percussion:	**Brian Bennett/Trevor Spencer**
Keyboards:	**Graham Todd/Alan Tarney/Duncan Mackay**
Vocals:	**Tony Rivers John Perry Stuart Calver Alan Tarney Cliff**
String arrangements by	**Richard Hewson**
Producer:	**Bruce Welch**
Engineers:	**Tony Clark/Hayden Bendall**
Recorded in:	**Studio 3**
Session hours:	**2.00pm-7.00pm**

15 JANUARY

ABBEY ROAD
Studio session

Count Me Out (2)	*See 25 April*

Guitar:	**Terry Britten/Tim Renwick/Alan Parker/Alan Tarney**
Bass:	**Alan Tarney/Alan Jones**
Drums:	**Brian Bennett/Trevor Spencer**
Percussion:	**Brian Bennett/Trevor Spencer**
Keyboards:	**Graham Todd/Alan Tarney/Duncan Mackay**
Vocals:	**Tony Rivers John Perry Stuart Calver Alan Tarney Cliff**
String arrangements by	**Richard Hewson**
Producer:	**Bruce Welch**
Engineers:	**Tony Clark Hayden Bendall**
Recorded in:	**Studio 3**
Session hours:	**3.00pm-9.00pm**

27 JANUARY

ABBEY ROAD
Studio session

Under Lock And Key (3) — *See 21 February*

Guitar:	**Terry Britten/Tim Renwick/ Alan Parker/Alan Tarney**
Bass:	**Alan Tarney/Alan Jones**
Drums:	**Brian Bennett/Trevor Spencer**
Percussion:	**Brian Bennett/Trevor Spencer**
Keyboards:	**Graham Todd/Alan Tarney/ Duncan Mackay**
Vocals:	**Tony Rivers/John Perry/Stuart Calver/Alan Tarney/Cliff**
String arrangements by:	**Richard Hewson**
Producer:	**Bruce Welch**
Engineers:	**Tony Clark/Hayden Bendall**
Recorded in:	**Studio 3**
Session hours:	**10.00am-5.30pm**

Job No. 95948 P
RECORDING SHEET
ARTISTIC INFORMATION — Artist: CLIFF RICHARD
Date 27-1-1978 Location Studio 3 Engineers A.C. H.B. Producer Bruce Welch
COSTING INFORMATION — Session Booked Time 10:00 - 17:30 Recording/St 10:30 -
Materials Used: 1x Ampex G.M. 2"
TITLES: UNDER LOCK + KEY (REMAKE); NEW SONG; FREE MY SOUL; NEVER EVEN THOUGHT
Take Nos.: 1-3
REMARKS: 3 BEST BASS O/D; Harpsichord O/Ds

JANUARY 31

Along with Roy Castle and his wife Fiona, Cliff takes part in a Booksellers' Convention at Wembley. Among the songs he sings are 'Every Face Tells A Story', 'When I Survey The Wondrous Cross' and 'Why Should The Devil Have All The Good Music'. The last two songs are featured on Cliff's current album of religious songs 'Small Corners'.

FEBRUARY 4

Singer Ian Dury says of Cliff's new single:
'The work of a great entertainer in his prime. Stevie Wonder and John Coltrane have both done music about Jesus as well. Every time Cliff comes on, time stands still to this very day... some say he lives in Hendon.'

7 FEBRUARY

ABBEY ROAD
Studio session

Ease Along (3)	*Green Light*
Please Remember Me (2)	*Green Light*

Lead Vocal:	**Cliff Richard**
Producer:	**Bruce Welch**
Engineers:	**Tony Clark/Hayden Bendall**
Recorded in:	**Studio 3**
Session hours:	**10.30am-2.00pm/2.30pm-5.00pm/ 5.30pm-10.00pm**

10 FEBRUARY

ABBEY ROAD
Studio session

Please Don't Tease (5) — *Green Light*

Lead Vocal:	**Cliff Richard**
Producer:	**Bruce Welch**
Engineers:	**Tony Clark/Hayden Bendall**
Recorded in:	**Studio 3**
Session hours:	**10.30am-2.00pm/2.30pm-11.30pm**

11 FEBRUARY

ABBEY ROAD
Studio session

Gettin' The Feelin' (1)	*(Unissued)*
Muddy Water (2)	*(Unissued)*

Producer:	**Bruce Welch**
Engineers:	**Tony Clark/Hayden Bendall**
Recorded in:	**Studio 3**
Session hours:	**2.30pm-midnight**

FEBRUARY 15

Cliff sings two songs from his 'Small Corners' album on BBC TV's *Pebble Mill At One.*

FEBRUARY 16

The Arts Centre Group stage a special concert at Croydon featuring Cliff, Roy Castle, Dana and Neil Reid.

Hank and Cliff share a joke during rehearsals for their reunion concert

19 FEBRUARY

ABBEY ROAD
Studio session

Ships That Passed In The Night (1)	*(Unissued)*
Never Even Thought (1)	*Green Light*
Do What You Gotta Do (1)	*(Unissued)*

Lead Vocal: **Cliff Richard**

Producer: **Bruce Welch**
Engineers: **Tony Clark/Hayden Bendall**
Recorded in: **Studio 3**
Session hours: **2.00pm-10.30pm**

21 FEBRUARY

ABBEY ROAD
Studio session

Under Lock And Key (3) *Green Light*

Lead Vocal: **Cliff Richard**

Producer: **Bruce Welch**
Engineers: **Tony Clark/Hayden Bendall**
Recorded in: **Studio 3**
Session hours: **10.30am-1.30pm/2.00pm-6.45pm/7.00pm-11.30pm**

FEBRUARY 27-MARCH 11

Cliff and the Shadows reunite to play a two week 20th Anniversary Show at the London Palladium.

MARCH 2

Mike Read interviews Cliff at the London Palladium for Radio Luxembourg.

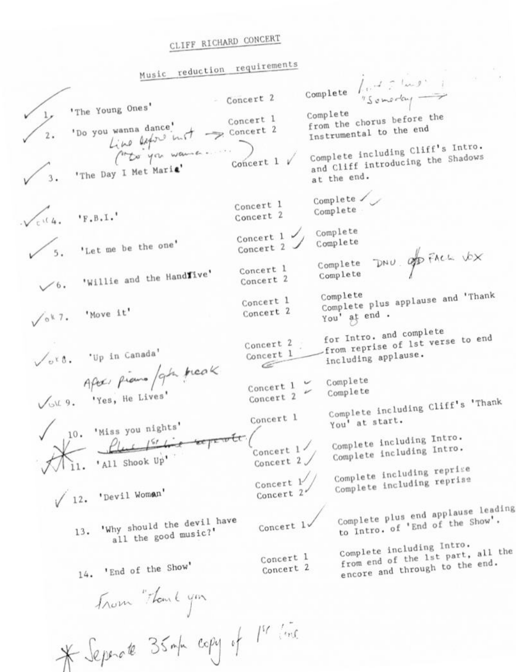

CLIFF RICHARD CONCERT

Music reduction requirements

1.	'The Young Ones'	Concert 2	Complete
2.	'Do you wanna dance'	Concert 1 Concert 2	Complete from the chorus before the Instrumental to the end
3.	'The Day I Met Marie'	Concert 1	Complete including Cliff's Intro. and Cliff introducing the Shadows at the end.
4.	'F.B.I.'	Concert 1 Concert 2	Complete Complete
5.	'Let me be the one'	Concert 1 Concert 2	Complete Complete
6.	'Willie and the HandJive'	Concert 1 Concert 2	Complete Complete
7.	'Move it'	Concert 1 Concert 2	Complete Complete plus applause and 'Thank You' at end .
8.	'Up in Canada'	Concert 2 Concert 1	for Intro. and complete from reprise of 1st verse to end including applause.
9.	'Yes, He Lives'	Concert 1 Concert 2	Complete Complete
10.	'Miss you nights'	Concert 1	Complete including Cliff's 'Thank You' at start.
11.	'All Shook Up'	Concert 1 Concert 2	Complete including Intro. Complete including Intro.
12.	'Devil Woman'	Concert 1 Concert 2	Complete including reprise Complete including reprise
13.	'Why should the devil have all the good music?'	Concert 1	Complete plus end applause leading to Intro. of 'End of the Show'.
14.	'End of the Show'	Concert 1 Concert 2	Complete including Intro. from end of the 1st part, all the encore and through to the end.

3 MARCH

LONDON PALLADIUM

Live recordings

Shadoogie	*Thank You Very Much*

Guitars:	**Hank Marvin/Bruce Welch**
Bass:	**Alan Jones**
Drums:	**Brian Bennett**
Keyboards:	**Cliff Hall**
Producer:	**Bruce Welch**
Engineer:	**Tony Clark**
Session hours:	**8.45pm show**

4 MARCH

LONDON PALLADIUM

Live recordings

Apache	*Thank You Very Much*
Atlantis	*Thank You Very Much*
Miss You Nights	*Thank You Very Much*
All Shook Up	*Thank You Very Much*
Move It	*Thank You Very Much*
Willie And The Hand Jive	*Thank You Very Much*
Devil Woman	*Thank You Very Much*

Guitars:	**Hank Marvin/Bruce Welch**
Bass:	**Alan Jones**
Drums:	**Brian Bennett**
Keyboards:	**Cliff Hall**
Lead Vocal:	**Cliff Richard**
Guitar:	**Terry Britten/Dave Christopher/ Graham Murray**
Bass:	**Mo Foster**
Keyboards:	**Graham Todd**
Drums:	**Graham Jarvis/Clem Cattini**
Vocals:	**Tony Rivers/Stuart Calver/John Perry**
Producer:	**Bruce Welch**
Engineer:	**Tony Clark**
Session hours:	**6.15pm show**

4 MARCH

LONDON PALLADIUM

Live recordings

The Young Ones	*Thank You Very Much*
Do You Wanna Dance	*Thank You Very Much*
The Day I Met Marie	*Thank You Very Much*
Nivram	*Thank You Very Much*
Please Don't Tease	*Thank You Very Much*
Yes He Lives	*(Unissued)*
Up In Canada	*(Unissued)*
Why Should The Devil	*Thank You Very Much*
End Of The Show	*Thank You Very Much*

Guitars:	**Hank Marvin/Bruce Welch**
Bass:	**Alan Jones**
Drums:	**Brian Bennett**
Keyboards:	**Cliff Hall**
Lead Vocal:	**Cliff Richard**
Guitar:	**Terry Britten/Dave Christopher/ Graham Murray**
Bass:	**Mo Foster**
Keyboards:	**Graham Todd**
Drums:	**Graham Jarvis/Clem Cattini**
Vocals:	**Tony Rivers/Stuart Calver/John Perry**
Producer:	**Bruce Welch**
Engineer:	**Tony Clark**
Session hours:	**8.45pm show**

MARCH 6

EMI Records host a special honourary dinner for Cliff at 'Rags' restaurant in London.

MARCH 7

Cliff dines with Elton John.

15 MARCH

ABBEY ROAD
Studio session

While She's Young (3)	*Green Light*
Start All Over Again	*Green Light*

Lead Vocal:	**Cliff Richard**
Producer:	**Bruce Welch**
Engineers:	**Tony Clark/Hayden Bendall**
Recorded in:	**Studio 3**
Session hours:	**2.30pm-6.30pm/ 7.30pm-11.30pm**

APRIL

EMI France release 'Why Should The Devil Have All The Good Music' and 'Hey Watcha Say'.

17 APRIL

ABBEY ROAD
Studio session

Searching For A Green Light (1)	*See 25 April*

Guitar:	**Terry Britten/Tim Renwick/ Alan Parker/Alan Tarney**
Bass:	**Alan Tarney/Alan Jones**
Drums:	**Brian Bennett/Trevor Spencer**
Percussion:	**Brian Bennett/Trevor Spencer**
Keyboards:	**Graham Todd/Alan Tarney/ Duncan Mackay**
Vocals:	**Tony Rivers John Perry Stuart Calver Alan Tarney Cliff**
String arrangements by	**Richard Hewson**
Producer:	**Bruce Welch**
Engineer:	**Tony Clark**
Recorded in:	**Studio 3**
Session hours:	**2.30pm-11.00pm**

Cliff Richard and the Shadows – Thank You Very Much!

18 APRIL

ABBEY ROAD
Studio session

She's A Gypsy (1) — *See 25 April*

Guitar:	**Terry Britten/Tim Renwick/Alan Parker/ Alan Tarney**
Bass:	**Alan Tarney/Alan Jones**
Drums:	**Brian Bennett/Trevor Spencer**
Percussion:	**Brian Bennett/Trevor Spencer**
Keyboards:	**Graham Todd/Alan Tarney/Duncan Mackay**
Vocals:	**Tony Rivers/John Perry/Stuart Calver/ Alan Tarney/Cliff**
String arrangements by:	**Richard Hewson**
Producer:	**Bruce Welch**
Engineer:	**Tony Clark**
Recorded in:	**Studio 3**
Session hours:	**11.30am-midnight**

25 APRIL

ABBEY ROAD
Studio session

Count Me Out (2)	*Green Light*
Green Light (1)	*Green Light*
She's A Gypsy (1)	*Green Light*

Lead Vocal:	**Cliff Richard**
Producer:	**Bruce Welch**
Engineers:	**Peter Vince/Hayden Bendall**
Recorded in:	**Studio 3**
Session hours:	**2.00pm-6.00pm 6.30pm-11.30pm**

JUNE 27

Cliff attends the opening of the Arts Centre's new headquarters in Short Street, London, near the Old Vic.

JUNE 20

Cliff attends a Music Therapy Committee lunch.

JULY

Cliff's 72nd single is released: 'Please Remember Me'/'Please Don't Tease'. The 'A' side is a song written by American singer/composer Dave Loggins and comes from Cliff's forthcoming album 'Green Light'; the 'B' side is an updated version of Cliff's 1960 hit.

18-20 JULY

PATHE MARCONI, PARIS
Studio session

Walking In The Light	*See 18 April*
Monday Thru Friday	*See 10 February*
Doing Fine	*See 18 April*
Sci-Fi	*See 18 April*
You Know That I Love You	*See 17 March*
Fallin' In Luv'	*See 30 June*

Guitars:	**Terry Britten**
Bass:	**Herbie Flowers**
Drums	**Graham Jarvis**
Keyboards:	**Bill Livesy**
Percussion:	**Tristan Fry**
Melotron:	**Peter Skellern**
Slide Guitar:	**Bryn Haworth**
Saxophone:	**Martin Dobson**
Brass:	**Mel Collins/Martin Drover/Chris Mercer**
Vocals:	**Cliff Richard/Terry Britten/Madelaine Bell**
Producer:	**Cliff Richard/Terry Britten**
Engineers:	**Tony Clark/Hayden Bendall**

SUMMER

Cliff visits South Africa, Australia and Hong Kong.

SEPTEMBER 1

Cliff meets pensioners in Weybridge, Surrey, to present them with budgerigars.

SEPTEMBER 2

Cliff joins evangelist Dick Saunders on stage and sings 'Up In Canada', 'Lord, I Love You' and 'When I Survey The Wondrous Cross'.

SEPTEMBER

Interviewed by *Dynamite* magazine, Cliff feels that although the Rolling Stones make great records, their lyrics are ridiculous.

UNITED KINGDOM TOUR

NOVEMBER 1
Gaumont Theatre, Southampton

NOVEMBER 3/4
Odeon Theatre, Birmingham

NOVEMBER 8/9
Usher Hall, Edinburgh

NOVEMBER 10/11
Town Hall, Middlesbrough

NOVEMBER 15/16
City Hall, Sheffield

NOVEMBER 17
New Theatre, Oxford

NOVEMBER 18
Centre, Brighton

NOVEMBER 22
De Montfort Hall, Leicester

NOVEMBER 23
Colston Hall, Bristol

NOVEMBER 24/25
Winter Gardens, Bournemouth

NOVEMBER 29/30
Fairfield Hall, Croydon

DECEMBER 1/2
Cliffs Pavilion, Southend

DECEMBER 6/7
Apollo Theatre, Manchester

DECEMBER 8/9
Opera House, Blackpool

DECEMBER 11
Royal Albert Hall, London

THE BRIGHTON CENTRE
SATURDAY, 18th NOVEMBER, 1978
at 7.30 p.m.
CLIFF RICHARD
ROW
BB 29
STALLS (MAIN HALL)
Including VAT £1.50
Tickets cannot be accepted for exchange or refund. Neither the Council nor their Officers accept any responsibility for any loss or damage (howsoever sustained or caused) to any property whatsoever brought on to these premises.

SEPTEMBER 21

On German TV's *Star Parade*, Cliff sings 'Please Remember Me' and 'Lucky Lips'.

OCTOBER 1

BBC Radio 1 broadcasts the first in a five part series entitled *Twenty Golden Years*. Narrated by Tim Rice, the series traces Cliff Richard's successful career in show business through interviews and music.

OCTOBER 9/10

Under the banner of 'Help, Hope & Hallelujah', Cliff gives two concerts to celebrate the tenth anniversary of Tear Fund. His songs include 'Such Is The Mystery', 'Song For Sarah', 'Yes He Lives', 'Up In Canada', 'You Can't Get To Heaven By Living Like Hell', 'Yesterday Today Forever' and 'Why Should The Devil Have All The Good Music'.

OCTOBER 10

Hilversum Radio in Holland broadcasts the Albert Hall concert.

OCTOBER

Tear Fund's tenth anniversary and the ninth anniversary of Cliff's involvement. Since his initial donation of two gospel concerts in 1969, Cliff has undertaken an annual concert tour, membership of its board, narration of three promotional trips and visits to the Fund's projects in Sudan, Nepal and Bangladesh.

OCTOBER

Of the Tear Fund concerts, Cliff says: 'You know, it never fails to encourage me when I think that at this very moment, somewhere in the world a Christian is using an x-ray unit or a Land-Rover or even a building paid for by one of these concerts.'

OCTOBER 30

On an Australian TV show, *Australian Music to the World,* Cliff sings 'Devil Woman'. A clip filmed at Cliff's home in Weybridge, in which he chats about John Farrar and Olivia Newton-John, is also shown.

NOVEMBER 6

Cliff attends a party in London's Belgrave Square for the launch of the first *Guiness Book of British Hit Singles* along with Elton John, Bob Geldof, Vera Lynn, Hank Marvin, the Drifters, Billy Idol, Paul Jones, Mike D'Abo and Russ Conway, amongst others. A photograph of all present is taken for the cover of the second *Guiness Book of British Hit Singles.*

NOVEMBER

Cliff's 73rd single is released: 'Can't Take The Hurt Anymore'/'Needing A Friend'.

JANUARY 1

KBS TV in Korea screens *The Young Ones.*

7-12 JANUARY

PATHÉ MARCONI, PARIS
Studio session

Hot Shot	*See 17 February*
Carrie	*See 2 February*
Language Of Love	*See 27 January*
Cities May Fall	*See 27 January*
My Luck Won't Change	*See 17 February*
Rock And Roll Juvenile	*(Unissued)*

Guitars:	**Terry Britten**
Bass:	**Herbie Flowers**
Drums:	**Graham Jarvis**
Keyboards:	**Bill Livesy**
Percussion:	**Tristan Fry**
Melotron:	**Peter Skellern**
Slide Guitar:	**Bryn Haworth**
Saxophone:	**Martin Dobson**
Brass:	**Mel Colins/Martin Drover/Chris Mercer**
Vocals:	**Cliff Richard/Terry Britten/Madelaine Bell**
Producer:	**Cliff Richard/Terry Britten**
Engineers:	**Tony Clark/Hayden Bendall**

JANUARY

The UK Scripture Union launches a series of cassettes which feature Cliff reading from the scriptures.

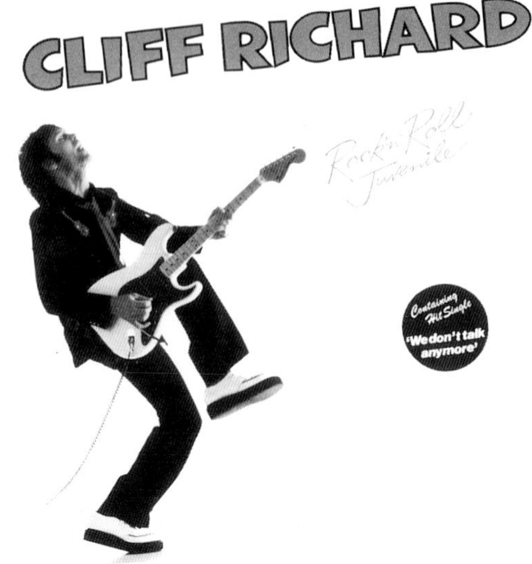

24 JANUARY

ABBEY ROAD
Studio session

Rock And Roll Juvenile (4) — *Rock And Roll Juvenile*

Lead Vocal: **Cliff Richard**
Guitars: **Terry Britten**
Bass: **Herbie Flowers**
Drums: **Graham Jarvis**
Keyboards: **Bill Livesy**
Percussion: **Tristan Fry**
Melotron: **Peter Skellern**
Slide Guitar: **Bryn Haworth**
Saxophone: **Martin Dobson**
Brass: **Mel Colins**
Martin Drover
Chris Mercer
Vocals: **Cliff Richard**
Terry Britten
Madelaine Bell

Producer: **Cliff Richard/Terry Britten**
Engineers: **Tony Clark/Hayden Bendall**
Recorded in: **Studio 3**
Session hours: **mid-day-2.15pm**
3.15pm-10.00pm

27 JANUARY

ABBEY ROAD
Studio session

Language Of Love — *Rock And Roll Juvenile*
Cities May Fall — *Rock And Roll Juvenile*

Lead Vocal: **Cliff Richard**

Producer: **Cliff Richard**
Terry Britten
Engineers: **Tony Clark**
Hayden Bendall
Recorded in: **Studio 3**
Session hours: **10.00am-2.00pm**
2.30pm-6.00pm
6.30pm-10.00pm

FEBRUARY 1

At a special lunch at Claridges Hotel in London, EMI Records present Cliff with a gold clock and a gold replica of the key to their headquarters in Manchester Square, to celebrate their twenty-one-year partnership.

2 FEBRUARY

ABBEY ROAD
Studio session

Carrie — *A-side*

Lead Vocal: **Cliff Richard**

Producer: **Cliff Richard/Terry Britten**
Engineers: **Tony Clark/Hayden Bendall**
Recorded in: **Studio 3**
Session hours: **11.00am-10.00pm**

10 FEBRUARY

ABBEY ROAD
Studio session

Monday Thru Friday — *Rock And Roll Juvenile*

Lead Vocal: **Cliff Richard**

Producer: **Cliff Richard/Terry Britten**
Engineers: **Tony Clark/Hayden Bendall**
Recorded in: **Studio 3**
Session hours: **mid-day-7.00pm/8.00pm-midnight**

FEBRUARY 13

At the Music Week Awards, Cliff and the Shadows receive an award for twenty-one years as major British recording artists.

17 FEBRUARY

ABBEY ROAD
Studio session

Hot Shot — *Rock And Roll Juvenile*
My Luck Won't Change — *Rock And Roll Juvenile*

Lead Vocal: **Cliff Richard**

Producer: **Cliff Richard/Terry Britten**
Engineers: **Tony Clark/Hayden Bendall**
Recorded in: **Studio 3**
Session hours: **mid-day-7.00pm**

FEBRUARY 27

Cliff lunches at New Scotland Yard.

MARCH

'Green Light'/'Imagine Love' becomes Cliff's 74th British single. Written by Alan Tarney, it is produced by Bruce Welch.

17 MARCH

ABBEY ROAD
Studio session

You Know That I Love You	*Rock And Roll Juvenile*

Lead Vocal:	**Cliff Richard**
Producer:	**Cliff Richard/Terry Britten**
Engineers:	**Tony Clark**
Recorded in:	**Studio 3**
Session hours:	**mid-day-11.30pm**

18 APRIL

ABBEY ROAD
Studio session

Walking In The Light	*B-side*
Doing Fine	*Rock And Roll Juvenile*
Sci	*Rock And Roll Juvenile*

Lead Vocal:	**Cliff Richard**
Producer:	**Cliff Richard/Terry Britten**
Engineers:	**Tony Clark**
Recorded in:	**Studio 3**
Session hours:	**10.30am-1.30pm/2.30pm-7.00pm/ 8.00pm-00.30am**

APRIL 20

At St. Alban's Cathedral, Cliff takes part in a special youth festival.

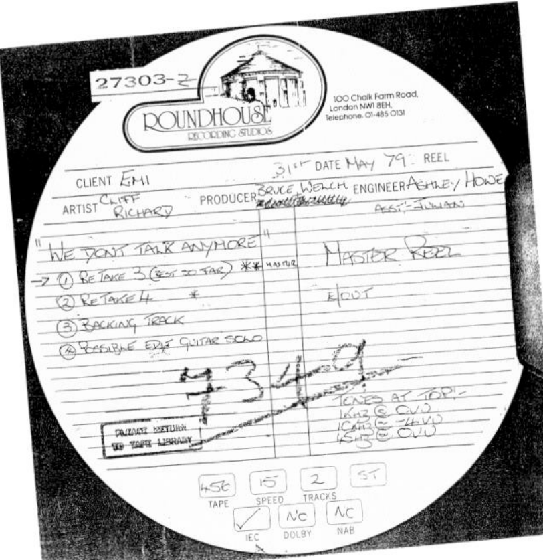

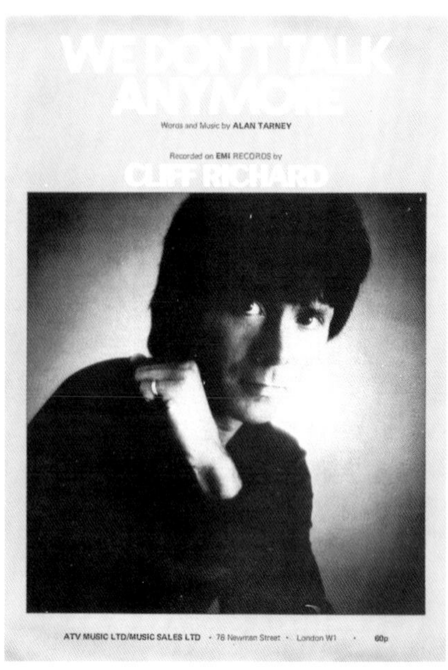

MAY 1

Cliff is present at the Local Radio Awards at Grosvenor House Hotel, London. This is an event organised by *Radio & Record News*.

29 MAY

RG JONES
Studio session

We Don't Talk Anymore (3)	*A-side*

Lead Vocal:	**Cliff Richard**
Guitars:	**Alan Tarney**
Keyboards:	**Alan Tarney**
Bass:	**Alan Tarney**
Drums:	**Trevor Spencer**
Backing Vocals:	**Alan Tarney**
Producer:	**Bruce Welch**
Engineer:	**Tony Clark**
Session hours:	

MAY 31/JUNE 1

Cliff records for Dutch TV.

JUNE 10

Cliff talks of his Christian faith at a Liverpool Theatre chat show.

JUNE 12

Cliff takes part in more Bible readings for the Scripture Union cassettes. On the same day, to celebrate the fiftieth anniversary of the Dutch Youth Hostel Organisation, he appears on Dutch TV's

Auro Gala Special singing 'Miss You Nights' and 'When Two Worlds Drift Apart'.
Cliff attends the European Baptist Congress at the Brighton Centre, Sussex. He talks about the work of Tear Fund and his visit to the Soviet Union, as well as singing nine songs.

30 JUNE

ABBEY ROAD
Studio session

Fallin' In Luv' — *Rock And Roll Juvenile*

Lead Vocal:	**Cliff Richard**
Producer:	**Cliff Richard/Terry Britten**
Engineers:	**Tony Clark**
Recorded in:	**Studio 3**
Session hours:	**10.30am-12.30pm**

JULY 5

At a Variety Club of Great Britain lunch, Cliff is guest of honour in celebration of his twenty-one years in show business. The function is attended by the Duke of Kent, the Shadows and Joan Collins amongst others.

JULY

Cliff's 75th single is released: 'We Don't Talk Anymore' and 'Count Me Out'. The 'A' side is written by Alan Tarney and produced by Bruce Welch. The Terry Britten-Bruce Welch 'B' side is taken from the 'Green Light' album.The single, which made the Number One spot, stayed in the charts for 14 weeks.

26 AUGUST

ODELL, BEDFORDSHIRE
Live Recording

Yes He Lives

Lead Vocal:	**Cliff Richard**
Guitars:	**Snowy White/Mart Jenner**
Keyboards:	**Mike Moran/Derek Beauchemin**
Bass:	**George Ford**
Drums:	**Graham Jarvis**
Backing Vocals:	**Tony Rivers/John Perry/Stuart Calver**
Producers:	**Doug Hopkins/Tony Tew**
Engineer:	**Tim Summerhayes**
Session hours:	

Rock'n'Roll Juvenile!

AUGUST 25

Eleven years and 124 days since he last topped the chart with 'Congratulations', Cliff gets to Number One with 'We Don't Talk Anymore', deposing Bob Geldof's Boomtown Rats with 'I Don't Like Mondays'.

AUGUST 25

An historic moment as Cliff becomes the second singer who discarded the surname Webb to top the chart in the same year – Cliff's real name being Harry Webb. The other is Gary Numan (Gary Webb) who topped the charts in July with 'Are Friends Electric' and also September with 'Cars'.

AUGUST

Cliff launches his own gospel label Patch Records in association with EMI. The first release is a Cliff produced album by Garth Hewitt, which is launched at the Greenbelt Festival in Hertfordshire.

AUGUST 26

Cliff appears at the Greenbelt Christian Music Festival, where he sings for 90 minutes backed by George Ford, Graham Jarvis, Mart Jenner, Snowy White, Mike Moran, Tony Rivers, Stu Calver and John Perry. He is also interviewed by poet and writer Steve Turner about his faith.

AUGUST 27

BBC Radio 1 broadcast a special programme on Greenbelt.

SEPTEMBER 5

Cliff is a guest on Capital Radio's *Roger Scott Show* in London.

SEPTEMBER 18

Cliff attends a Filey Christian Holiday Crusade meeting, where he participates in discussions and signs books.

SEPTEMBER

Cliff's original producer Norrie Paramor dies.

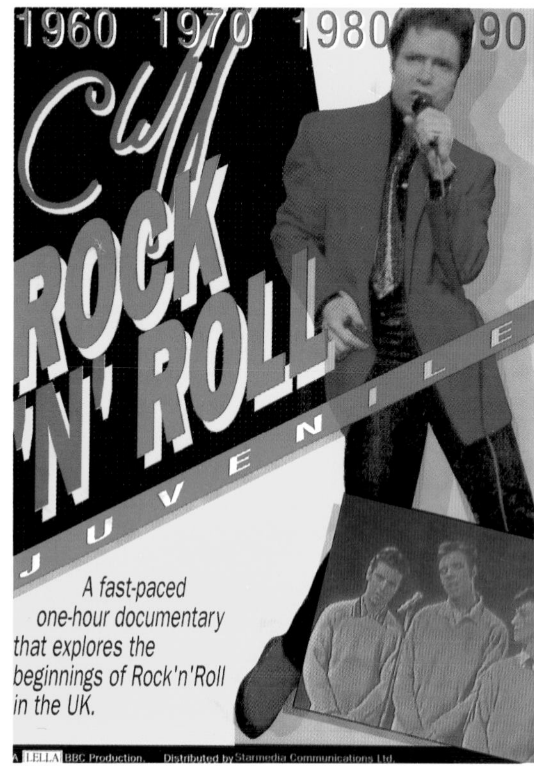

SEPTEMBER 19

On Manchester's local Piccadilly Radio, Cliff is the guest of DJ Roger Day.

SEPTEMBER 22

Cliff takes part in 'Hosannah '79', an anti-racist festival held in Birmingham.

SEPTEMBER 22

After one month at No.1, 'We Don't Talk Anymore' is knocked off the top of the chart by Gary Numan's 'Cars'.

26 OCTOBER

ABBEY ROAD
Studio session

Moving In — *B-side*

Lead Vocal:	**Cliff Richard**
Keyboards:	**Graham Todd/Adrian Lee**
Guitars:	**Mart Jenner**
Drums:	**Clem Cattini**
Bass:	**George Ford**
Producer:	**Cliff Richard**
Engineer:	
Recorded in:	**Studio 3**
Session hours:	**10.00am-10.00pm**

NOVEMBER

Cliff's 76th single is released: 'Hot Shot'/'Walking In The Light'. Produced by Cliff and Terry Britten, the 'A' side is taken from the 'Rock'n'Roll Juvenile' album, being one of seven tracks where Terry Britten collaborated with Scots singer/songwriter B. A. Robertson.

NOVEMBER 17

'We Don't Talk Anymore' becomes Cliff's fourth single to enter the American Top 40, the others being 'Living Doll' (1959), 'It's All In The Game' (1964), and 'Devil Woman' (1976).

DECEMBER 2

In Camberley, Surrey, Cliff takes part in a concert in aid of the International Year of the Child.

13/14/15 DECEMBER

HAMMERSMITH ODEON, LONDON

Live Recordings for BBCRadio

Rock And Roll Juvenile	*(Unissued)*
If You Walked Away	*(Unissued)*
I'm Nearly Famous	*(Unissued)*
Hot Shot	*(Unissued)*
Why Should The Devil Have	
All The Good Music	*(Unissued)*
Sci-Fi	*(Unissued)*
Carrie	*(Unissued)*
My Luck Won't Change	*(Unissued)*
Green Light	*(Unissued)*
Miss You Nights	*(Unissued)*
Do You Wanna Dance	*(Unissued)*
Monday Thru Friday	*(Unissued)*
Devil Woman	*(Unissued)*
We Don't Talk Anymore	*(Unissued)*

Lead Vocal:	**Cliff Richard**
Guitar:	**Terry Britten/Mart Jenner**
Bass:	**George Ford**
Drums:	**Graham Jarvis**
Synthesisers:	**Adrian Lee**
Keyboards:	**Graham Todd**
Vocals:	**Tony Rivers/Stuart Calver/John Perry**

DECEMBER 16

Following a spectacular torchlight procession from London's Trafalgar Square, along the Mall to Buckingham Palace, Cliff leads a crowd of tens of thousands, young and old, as he sings carols, accompanying himself on guitar. He performs from a specially constructed stage facing Buckingham Palace.

The Queen and Prince Charles join in the carols from the balcony of the Palace, and later Cliff is received in the Royal residence after the celebrations, which are to mark the end of the Year of the Child.

DECEMBER 18

Cliff sings at a special concert in aid of the International Year of the Child.

DECEMBER 23

Cliff turns DJ for two hours on BBC Radio 1's *Star Special* when he plays his favourite records.

DECEMBER 26

On BBC Radio 2's *Two Sides Of Cliff*, Cliff plays records by himself and the Shadows.

DECEMBER

'We Don't Talk Anymore' breaks into the American Top 10, finally peaking at number 7.

DECEMBER

Record Collector magazine prints out the going rate for some of Cliff's old records:

'32 Minutes And 17 Seconds ' LP – £12
'Serious Charge' EP – £10
'Expresso Bongo' EP – £10

JANUARY 7

Cliff is interviewed by Mike Douglas on his USA TV show about his OBE and his American career.

JANUARY 8

On USA TV's *Dinah Shore Show*, Cliff chats about his childhood, his OBE and American girls.

FEBRUARY

Cliff's 77th single is released: 'Carrie'/'Moving In'.

Cliff and Olivia during the making of the 'Suddenly' video.

FEBRUARY 6

Cliff appears at a special tribute concert to Norrie Paramor, his long-time friend and producer who died the previous year. Backed by the Ron Goodwin Orchestra and Tony Rivers, John Perry and Stu Calver, Cliff sings six numbers which are closely associated with Norrie: 'Bachelor Boy', 'Constantly', 'The Day I Met Marie', 'Congratulations', 'The Young Ones' and 'Summer Holiday'.

FEBRUARY 7

Cliff attends a 'Christians in Sport' dinner in London.

FEBRUARY 10

Cliff takes part in an evangelist meeting in Cambridge with Dr Billy Graham, and in the evening speaks at Great St Mary's, the University Church.

FEBRUARY 20

In an article in the *Daily Star*, Cliff says: 'Sex outside marriage is wrong... I believe that people who are promiscuous do find it much more difficult to have a stable relationship, and that is what marriage is. Marriage is a special thing, and quite simply I haven't found the right girl yet. I've only been in love twice and it was a long time ago'.

FEBRUARY 27

In the National Pop and Rock Awards organised by Radio 1, *Nationwide* and the *Daily Mirror*, Cliff receives the *Nationwide* Golden Award as 'Best Family Entertainer'.

MARCH

ITV's *Pop Gospel* series begins, during which Cliff appears in two programmes.

MARCH

LOS ANGELES
Studio session

Suddenly	*A-side*
Lead Vocal:	**Cliff Richard**
Guitar and Synthesiser:	**John Farrar**
Bass:	**David McDaniel**
Drums:	**Ed Greene**
Vocoder:	**Michael Boddicker**
Strings arranged and conducted by:	**Richard Hewson**
Vocals:	**Cliff/Olivia Newton-John**
Producer:	**John Farrar**
Engineer:	**David J. Holman**
Session hours:	

MARCH

'Carrie' enters the British Top 10, peaking at number 4 to become Cliff's 43rd Top 10 hit single in Britain.

SPRING

Cliff is voted 'Top Pop Star' by the viewers of Noel Edmonds' Saturday morning TV show *Swap Shop*.

SPRING

Cliff wins the TV Times award for 'The Most Exciting Male Singer On Television'.

MARCH

Cliff goes on a business trip to America.
'Carrie' enters the Top Ten, peaking at No.3.

MARCH 27

Cliff appears in front of 5,500 people at London's Albert Hall at the 'Sing Good News' event, honouring the top writers in a contest organised by the Bible Society. Cliff sings 'Why Should The Devil Have All The Good Music' and 'When I Survey The Wondrous Cross'.

APRIL 5

'Carrie' enters the American charts to become Cliff's fifth big Stateside hit.

APRIL 15

Cliff records for the *Pop Gospel* show in Manchester.

APRIL 16

During Capital Radio's 'Help A London Child' campaign, listener Kim Kayne beats off other bidders with a £1,400 pledge to the charity in exchange for lunch with Cliff. The lunch – in Cliff's office in Upper Harley Street – consists of melon, fillet steak with Spanish sauce, green beans with ham, new potatoes, aubergines, salad, strawberry shortcake, champagne, wine and coffee.

MAY

'Carrie' reaches the American Top 40.

JUNE/JULY

Cliff rehearses for his forthcoming Gospel Tour.

12 MAY-27 JUNE

RIVERSIDE STUDIOS
Studio sessions

Take Another Look	*I'm No Hero*
Anything I Can Do	*I'm No Hero*
A Little In Love	*A-side*
Here (So Doggone Blue)	*I'm No Hero*
Give A Little Bit More	*I'm No Hero*
In The Night	*I'm No Hero*
I'm No Hero)	*I'm No Hero*
Dreamin'	*A-side*
A Heart Will Break	*I'm No Hero*
Everyman	*I'm No Hero*
Dynamite'	*B-side*
Hold On	*B-side*

Lead Vocal: **Cliff Richard**
Bass Guitars: **Alan Tarney**
Synthesiser: **Michael Boddicker/Nick Glennie-Smith**
Drums: **Trevor Spencer**

Producer: **Alan Tarney**
Engineer: **Ashley Howe**

8 JULY

RIVERSIDE STUDIOS
Studio session

Keep On Looking	*B-side*

Lead Vocal: **Cliff Richard**

Producer:
Engineer:

JULY 18

July gospel tour begins.

JULY 23

On Mike Read's Radio 1 *Breakfast Show*, Cliff expresses his gratitude to all his fans before going to Buckingham Palace to collect his OBE from the Queen. As Cliff and his mother Dorothy arrive at Buckingham Palace in his Rolls-Royce, the crowd sings 'Congratulations'. In the white and gold Buckingham Palace ballroom, before being presented to the Queen, Cliff – dressed in sober black suit with red tie, red rose and bright red trainer shoes – explains the reason for his eccentric garb: 'I haven't got any morning dress, so I thought I would wear something colourful! I've been to the Palace before and I knew there was a lot of red about the place. I have always been a very firm Royalist and have followed the Royal family since I was a kid.' Two hours later at 12.30 Cliff leaves Buckingham Palace for a champagne lunch.

SUMMER

Cliff appears in Germany with his new group, now known as the Sky Band, and includes in his set 'The Rock That Doesn't Roll', 'The Twelfth Of Never', 'The Minute You're Gone', 'Sci-Fi', 'Devil Woman' and 'Green Light'.

AUGUST

'Dreamin''/'Dynamite' becomes Cliff's 78th single. The 'B' side is a new version of the 21-year-old 'B' side to 'Travellin' Light', which became a hit in it's own right.

SEPTEMBER 1,8,15

Cliff contributes to BBC World Service *Reflections*, in which he selects and reads Biblical texts.

SEPTEMBER

'Dreamin' climbs into the British Top 10, peaking at number 8 to become Cliff's 44th single to make the British Top 10.

SEPTEMBER

A lunchtime press launch is held in London's West End to promote Happy Christmas From Cliff, a slim volume published by Hodder & Stoughton. It contains many seasonal colour photo-

A day at Riverside Recordings
◁ Arrived ... got stuck straight in.
Alan suggests how to sing the song.... ▽
◁ did it my way!!
Should have listened to Alan. △
◁ End of the day – A little play.
Actually all day!

graphs of Cliff at home and abroad, as well as puzzles, quizzes and accounts of Christmas around the world.

SEPTEMBER 23

Cliff is a guest on Radio 2's *John Dunn Show*.

OCTOBER

Cliff takes part in a television show to raise money for charity.

OCTOBER 14

Cliff commences a five night stand at London's Apollo Theatre, where the crowd sing 'Happy Birthday' to him on the opening night. Numbers in the set include 'Move It', 'Carrie', 'Miss You Nights', 'Give A Little Bit More', 'Everyman', 'The Young Ones', 'Living Doll' and 'A Little In Love'.

The show on the 14th is also filmed and recorded by BBC Television for broadcast at a later date.

14 OCTOBER

APOLLO VICTORIA, LONDON

Live recordings for BBC Television

My Kinda Life	*(Unissued)*
Sci-Fi	*(Unissued)*
Devil Woman	*(Unissued)*
'D' In Love	*(Unissued)*
The Young Ones	*(Unissued)*
Learning How To Rock And Roll	*(Unissued)*
Dynamite	*(Unissued)*
Daddy's Home	*(Unissued)*
Do You Wanna Dance	*(Unissued)*
Dream	*(Unissued)*
A Heart Will Break	*(Unissued)*
Such Is The Mystery	*(Unissued)*

Lead Vocal: **Cliff Richard**

OCTOBER 27

Noel Edmonds chats to Cliff on BBC TV's Saturday morning show *Swap Shop*.

OCTOBER

EMI Records release Cliff Richard's 79th single, 'Suddenly', on which he sings with Olivia Newton-John. The 'B' side is performed by Olivia alone: 'You Made Me Love You'. The song eventually reaches the No.15 position, spending a total of seven weeks in the British charts.

DECEMBER 13

On BBC Television's *Michael Parkinson Show*, Cliff sings Elvis's 'Heartbreak Hotel' and at the end of the programme 'All The Way' with the other guests.

Cliff Richard – 40 Today!

CHRISTMAS

Top London store Selfridges invite Cliff and several other major celebrities to design their own shop window. Cliff's window is on the traditional religious theme – 'Christmas Through The Eyes Of A Child'.

1981–1983

The Records 1981 – 1983

The singles released in 1981 were obvious choices for release. The live single 'Daddy's Home' became the biggest hit of the year reaching the No.2 spot, and was a cover of an original by Shep and the Limelights, featured on Cliff's jukebox at his home. The next single 'The Only Way Out', released in 1982, only peaked at No.10 in spite of the heavy airplay it was guaranteed as a follow-up to 'Daddy's Home'. Of the next two singles, 'Where Do We Go From Here' failed to appeal to a mass audience, although the next one, 'Little Town', became a Christmas hit just outside the top ten. The first single of 1983, 'She Means Nothing To Me', was a breathtaking rock performance with Phil Everly that caught listeners' imaginations and eventually peaked at No.9. The track had a lot of people sit up straight expecting more of the same. Unfortunately for those people, the next single was a ballad, but a superior one from the catalogue of Buddy Holly. 'True Love Ways' did even better than the previous single, reaching No.8. Another three singles followed; of these 'Never Say Die' and 'Please Don't Fall In Love' were the hits. During this same period 'Move It', 'Living Doll', 'Travellin' Light' and 'Please Don't Tease' were reissued with their original Columbia catalogue numbers, as part of the twelve Cliff classic singles that were repackaged into a boxed set with new picture sleeves. To promote this set, a singles sampler simply called CLIFF was issued to retail outlets. Judged by the chart placings, this period album-wise was very successful for Cliff and EMI. However, a substantial part of the sales were taken up by the 1981 TV advertised compilation album LOVE SONGS that featured all previously released material. Coming hot on the heels of this one, WIRED FOR SOUND stormed up the charts to reach the No.4 spot and had a top five single to spur interest. Like its predecessor, NOW YOU SEE ME, NOW YOU DON'T reached the same position on the album chart the following year, and did slightly better than the DRESSED FOR THE OCCASION and SILVER albums in 1983.

The Sessions 1981 – 1983

For 1981 plans had been made to shoot a four-part documentary television series. The project was given the working and final title of *Cliff*. For inclusion, the BBC simultaneously filmed and taped concerts at the Manchester Apollo and the Hammersmith Odeon. Cliff had some new songs in his repertoire, and of these 'Daddy's Home', 'Shakin' All Over' and 'Stood Up' were licensed for record release, but only the first two titles were issued. More filming and live recordings were made on 2 April, when Cliff appeared in concert at the Savoy Theatre in New York but none of this material would be made available commercially. More recording dates were planned for the end of May, and ran through to July. These sessions, at Gallery Studios, produced a total of ten tracks, all for the WIRED FOR SOUND album. Alan Tarney took over as producer, becoming responsible for all the technical and instrumental backing work. Since Alan had worked as a musician during Cliff's recent recording sessions and had witnessed his work at some of the peak periods of his career, he was only too aware of Cliff's unique talent and what was necessary to bring that talent out to the full. In this respect the partnership of Cliff and Alan was ideal. While Alan's backing work was proficient enough, the sessions still featured a number of musicians for additional accompaniment; these included Graham Jarvis and Trevor Spencer on drums, and John Clarke and Nick Glennie-Smith on guitar and keyboard work.

For the next sessions in September, Cliff returned to Abbey Road. From these, two tracks for the NOW YOU SEE ME, NOW YOU DON'T album were taped with the remaining tracks being put down at Strawberry Studios during sessions that ran through to January 1982. Apart from the album tracks the rest of the material recorded – all in the inspirational genre – included some fine 'A' and 'B' side material. Of these, the reworking of 'Little Town of Bethlehem' as 'Little Town' featured one of the most outstanding arrangements. It is not known if the four unreleased tracks from these sessions are incomplete or finished takes. In October, BBC Television filmed and recorded another live concert at the Apollo Victoria. From a rock point of view, the highlight session of this period was the recording of 'She Means Nothing To Me', taped at Eden Studios in October 1982 during a Phil Everly session. The track featured musicians who had not worked with Cliff before, people like Stuart Colman, Mickey Gee and Mark Knopfler. This was the kind of material that made Cliff, Phil and the band rock the plaster off the ceiling, and it seems a shame that the song never became a regular item in Cliff's live repertoire. Another duet 'I'll Mend Your Broken Heart' was also taped, which was later released on the album PHIL EVERLY. More recordings were planned for Cliff's concert at the Royal Albert Hall in November. For this engagement, the repertoire had undergone some changes to include more recent material and, of the songs performed, all but four were chosen for record release as the DRESSED FOR THE OCCASION album. For the first time, Cliff was accompanied by the London Philharmonic Orchestra, while some members of Cliff's studio band and backing vocalists helped out.

The songs Cliff was to record in the Strawberry Studios during May and June 1983 were to be included on the SILVER 25TH commemorative album. However, during these sessions interest was not limited exclusively to new material, and some different approaches to classic rock 'n roll material were tried out. Of these 'Teddy Bear', 'Lucille' and a new reworked version of 'Move It' were outstanding. These and seven others represented the material for the ROCK 'N ROLL SILVER album that became the companion to SILVER, and released only as a limited edition two-album box set. Overdubbing of strings was carried out in July and August at Henry Wood Hall, with final mixing being done at Townhouse Studios in late August.

A final session in August produced the single 'Baby You're Dynamite', also featured on the SILVER album.

JANUARY

'A Little In Love' is in the American charts, peaking at No.17.

JANUARY

Cliff undertakes a promotional visit to the United States for his forthcoming March tour.

JANUARY 4

Cliff appears on the *John Kelly Show* on Los Angeles TV.

JANUARY 5

Cliff appears on the *John Davison Show* on Los Angeles TV.

JANUARY 6

Cliff appears on US TV in the *Dionne Warwick Solid Gold Show* in Los Angeles.

JANUARY 7

Cliff appears on the *Merv Griffin Show* on Los Angeles TV.

JANUARY 10

Cliff in Ontario, Canada

JANUARY 11

Cliff travels to New York.

JANUARY 12

Cliff in New York. At home his 80th single, 'A Little In Love'/'Keep On Looking', is released.

JANUARY

Cliff flies to London on Concorde from Kennedy Airport, NY.

JANUARY 16

Cliff has a meeting with Billy Graham at the Royal Albert Hall, London. On the same day he attends the twenty-fifth birthday celebrations of the major British evangelical magazine Crusade, where he talks about his recent American trip, his forthcoming concerts and the death of John Lennon.

JANUARY 18-21

Cliff rehearses for his gospel tour.

JANUARY 22

Cliff's manager, Peter Gormley, meets with Dave Clark who is laying the foundations for his musical *Time.*

JANUARY 22-FEBRUARY 7

Cliff undertakes several gospel tour dates.

JANUARY 27

Cliff films a video for 'A Little In Love' at Farningham in Kent with producer David Mallett.

JANUARY

New York journalist David Fructs describes Cliff as 'looking like a hip seminary student in an unassuming cardigan sweater, aviator glasses and brown suede sneakers'.

FEBRUARY 3

BBC producer Norman Stone films Cliff at home.

6 FEBRUARY

APOLLO, MANCHESTER
Live recordings for BBC Television

Why Should The Devil Have All The Good Music	*(Unissued)*
Better Than I Know Myself	*(Unissued)*
Son Of Thunder	*(Unissued)*
You Can't Get To Heaven By Living Like Hell	*(Unissued)*
Fools Wisdom	*(Unissued)*
Take Me Where I Wanna Go	*(Unissued)*
Under The Influence	*(Unissued)*
I Wish We'd All Been Ready	*(Unissued)*
Lost In A Lonely World	*(Unissued)*
The Rock That Doesn't Roll	*(Unissued)*

Lead Vocal: **Cliff Richard**

FEBRUARY

Cliff is interviewed after his gospel concert at Sheffield by German magazine *Bravo*.

FEBRUARY 9

Cliff records for *Top Of The Pops* and the *Kenny Everett Show* at Riverside Studios, London. Musicians are Alan Tarney, Trevor Spencer, Mart Jenner and Mark Griffiths.

FEBRUARY 10

Cliff sings with a choir of 400 girls to raise money for St Brendan's School, Clevedon, Bristol. The school's headmaster, John Davey, had been Cliff's teacher who helped him to pass his 'O' level in religious studies in 1965.

FEBRUARY 14

Cliff attends a Crusaders meeting at Central Hall, Westminster, London.

FEBRUARY 15

Cliff attends a 'Christians in Sport' dinner in Watford.

FEBRUARY 16-22

Cliff rehearses at Shepperton Studios.

FEBRUARY 17

Cliff records for Kenny Everett's TV Show.

FEBRUARY 24

At London's Cafe Royal, Cliff receives the *Daily Mirror* Readers' Award as 'Outstanding Musical Personality of the Year', which is presented to him by Una Stubbs.

FEBRUARY 26

Cliff goes to see the premiere of the film about Agatha Christie.

FEBRUARY 27

Cliff flies from Heathrow Airport, bound for Canada and the United States on a month-long tour.

MARCH

While rehearsing in Hollywood, a tour truck loaded with equipment and instruments worth £40,000 is stolen.

MARCH

Cliff's first UK video is released: *The Young Ones*, retailing at £28.30.

MARCH 20

BBC TV screens *Cliff In London* – excerpts from Cliff's autumn concerts at the Apollo.

MARCH 31

Cliff's mother Dorothy and Bill Latham fly to New York City to join Cliff.

2 APRIL

SAVOY THEATRE, NEW YORK
Live recordings for BBC Television

Travellin' Light	*(Unissued)*
Move It	*(Unissued)*
Devil Woman	*(Unissued)*
Give A Little Bit More	*(Unissued)*
Green Light	*(Unissued)*
Monday Thru Friday	*(Unissued)*
I'm Nearly Famous	*(Unissued)*
We Don't Talk Anymore	*(Unissued)*
Miss You Nights	*(Unissued)*
Thank You Very Much	*(Unissued)*

Lead Vocal: **Cliff Richard**

APRIL 20

Cliff flies back to England, arriving Heathrow's Terminal 3.

APRIL 27-30

Cliff rehearses at Shepperton Studios for his 'Rock Special'.

1 MAY

HAMMERSMITH ODEON
Live recordings for BBCTelevision

Rock And Roll Juvenile	*(Unissued)*
Daddy's Home	*A-side*
Stood Up	*(Unissued)*
Move It	*(Unissued)*
Shakin' All Over	*B-side*
Gee Whiz It's You	*(Unissued)*
Whole Lotta Shakin' Goin' On	*(Unissued)*
Blue Suede Shoes	*(Unissued)*
Great Balls Of Fire	*(Unissued)*
Lucille	*(Unissued)*
When Will I Be Loved	*(Unissued)*
Teddy Bear	*(Unissued)*
Long Tall Sally	*(Unissued)*
Rip It Up	*(Unissued)*

Lead Vocal:	**Cliff Richard**
Keyboards:	**Graham Todd**
Drums :	**Graham Jarvis**
Guitar:	**John Clark**
Bass :	**Mark Griffiths**
Vocals:	**Tony Rivers**

MAY 1

Cliff stars in a 'Rock Special' at the Hammersmith Odeon, which is filmed by BBC producer Norman Stone to go out on television at a later date. Live songs from the concert are later inter-cut with reminiscences by a variety of Cliff's friends and show business colleagues such as Adam Faith, Marty Wilde and the Shadows.

MAY

Phil Everly of the Everly Brothers comments that Cliff was one of the very few artists who ranked just below Elvis Presley in the rock 'n' roll pantheon.

MAY

'Give A Little Bit More' is released as a single in America and reaches number 39 in the charts. Although Cliff is thought of as having no following in the USA whatsoever, he has actually enjoyed a dozen or so chart entries, from as early as 1959 when 'Living Doll' got to number 30 in the *Billboard* list. His biggest American hit was 'Devil Woman' which got to No. 6 in 1976, rivalled closely by 'We Don't Talk Anymore' which hit No. 7 in 1979.

MAY 3

The BBC films Cliff, backed by the Fantoms, at London's Hard Rock Cafe.
Cliff is voted No.1 in the 'Top Pop Star' category in the *Sunday Telegraph* Readers' Poll.

David Bryce and Cliff at the mixing desk.

MAY 21-23

Cliff filming on location for EMI.

27 MAY-9 JULY

GALLERY STUDIOS

Studio sessions

Wired For Sound	*A-side*
Once In A While	*Wired For Sound*
Better Than I Know Myself	*Wired For Sound*
Oh No, Don't Let Go	*Wired For Sound*
'Cos I Love That Rock And Roll	*Wired For Sound*
Broken Doll	*Wired For Sound*
Lost In A Lonely World	*Wired For Sound*
Summer Rain	*Wired For Sound*
Young Love	*Wired For Sound*
Say You Don't Mind	*Wired For Sound*

Lead Vocal:	**Cliff Richard**
All Instruments:	**Alan Tarney**
Guitar:	**John Clark (Lost In A Lonely World)**
Drums:	**Graham Jarvis/Trevor Spencer**
Piano:	**Michael Boddicker (Young Love)**
Vocals:	**Cliff/Alan Tarney**
Producer:	**Alan Tarney**
Engineers:	**Michael Boddicker/Ian Litle**

JUNE

Cliff's 'Love Songs' album is released and becomes his fifth to get to Number One in the LP charts.

JUNE 13

Cliff attends the opening of a new hair-dressing salon in Surrey.

JUNE 30

Cliff guests on Michael Aspel's Capital Radio show.

JULY 8

Cliff appears on Radio London

JULY 10

Cliff is interviewed on the Weybridge Hospital Radio Station, Radio Wey.

JULY 23

The 'Wired For Sound' video is shot in Milton Keynes.

JULY 24

Cliff has a barbecue at home.

JULY 27

Cliff flies to Portugal for a two-week holiday.

AUGUST 11

Cliff flies from Portugal to South Africa to continue his holiday.

USA / CANADIAN TOUR

MARCH 3
Paramount Theatre, Seattle

MARCH 4
Royal Theatre, Victoria

MARCH 5
Q.E. Theatre

MARCH 7
Jubilee Auditorium, Calgary

MARCH 8
Jubilee Auditorium, Edmonton

MARCH 9/10
Centre of the Arts, Regina

MARCH 11/12
Centennial Auditorium, Winnipeg

MARCH 15
Guthrie Theatre, Minneapolis

MARCH 17
Chester Fritz Auditorium, Grand Forks

MARCH 19
Ft. Williams Gardens

MARCH 20
The Gardens, Sault St. Marie

MARCH 21
Arena, Sudbury

MARCH 23
National Arts Centre, Ottawa

MARCH 24
Hamilton Place, Hamilton

MARCH 27
Circle In The Square, Kitchener

MARCH 26
Arena, Kingston

MARCH 28
Alumni Hall, London

MARCH 30
O'Keefe Centre, Toronto

MARCH 31
St. Dennis Theatre, Montreal

APRIL 2
Savoy, New York

APRIL 3
Emerald City, Philadelphia

APRIL 4
Painters Mill, Baltimore

APRIL 6
Front Row, Cleveland

APRIL 7
Palace,Cincinnatti

APRIL 8
Palace Theatre, Columbus

APRIL 9
Park West, Chicago

APRIL 10
PAC Centre, Milwaukee

APRIL 12
Uptown Theatre, Kansas City

APRIL 14
Rainbow Theatre, Denver

APRIL 15
Kingsbury Hall, Salt Lake City

APRIL 17
Foxwarfield, San Fransisco

APRIL 18
Santa Monica Civic Auditorium, Los Angeles

Songs featured on the tour:
'Son Of Thunder'/'Monday Thru Friday'/'Dreamin'/'When Two Worlds Drift Apart'/'Green Light'/'Move It'/'Heartbreak Hotel'/'Why Should The Devil Have All The Good Music'/'Hey Mr Dream Maker'/'Carrie'/'Miss You Nights'/'A Little In Love'/'Everyman'/'Sci-Fi'/'Summer Rain'/'Devil Woman'/'The Rock That Doesn't Roll'/'Give A Little Bit More'/'A Heart Will Break'/'We Don't Talk Anymore'/'Thank You Very Much'/'Take Another Look'/'Do You Wanna Dance'/'My Luck Won't Change'

Publicity shot from the 'Wired For Sound' video

AUGUST 15-22

Cliff in Mauritius.

AUGUST 15

After five weeks a Number One,Cliff's 'Love Songs'LP is knocked off the top of the charts by The Official BBC Album of the Royal Wedding.

AUGUST 17

Cliff's 81st single, 'Wired For Sound'/'Hold On' is released and becomes his 6th single to peak at number 4 in the charts.

AUGUST 23-27

Cliff rehearses at Shepperton Studios.

AUGUST 28

Cliff flies to Amsterdam for one concert.

AUGUST 30

Cliff appears at the Greenbelt Christian Festival in Hertfordshire.

SEPTEMBER 1 & 2

Cliff undertakes two gospel shows at London's Wembley Conference Centre.

SEPTEMBER 1

Get It Together screen the 'Wired For Sound' video.

9-11 SEPTEMBER

ABBEY ROAD
Studio session

Son Of Thunder	*Now You See Me Now You Don't*
Take Me To The Leader	*(Unissued)*

Lead and Backing Vocals:	**Cliff Richard**
Guitar:	**Mart Jenner**
Keyboards/Synthesizers:	**Craig Pruess**
Bass:	**Paul Westwood**
OBX Synthesizer:	**Dave Cooke**
Drums:	**Graham Jarvis**
Electronic Percussion/Sequencers:	**Craig Pruess**

Producers:	**Cliff Richard/Craig Pruess**
Engineers:	**John Walker/Tony Richards**
Recorded in:	**Studio 3**
Session hours:	**9- 11.00am-9.00pm** **10- 11.00am-10.30pm** **11- 11.00am-10.00pm**

SEPTEMBER 10

Cliff sings 'Wired For Sound' on *Top Of The Pops.*

SEPTEMBER 12-20

Cliff spends a week in Wales.

SEPTEMBER 14

'Wired For Sound'/'Hold On' is released in America, but doesn't get higher thanNo.77.

21/22 SEPTEMBER

ABBEY ROAD
Studio session

The Water Is Wide	*Now You See Me Now You Don't*

Lead and Backing Vocals:	**Cliff Richard**
Guitar:	**Mart Jenner**
Bass:	**Mo Foster**
Keyboards:	**Peter Skellern**
Drums:	**Andy Pask**
Keyboards/Synthesizers:	**Craig Pruess**

Producers:	**Cliff Richard/Craig Pruess**
Engineers:	**John Walker/Tony Richards**
Recorded in:	**Studio 2**
Session hours:	**21- 11.00am-11.00pm** **22- 11.00am-11.00pm**

SEPTEMBER 26-OCTOBER 10

Cliff spends two weeks in New York and Los Angeles.

OCTOBER 13

Cliff dines with Rick Parfitt, guitarist with rock group Status Quo.

OCTOBER 14

Cliff's 41st birthday.

OCTOBER 15

Cliff records for *Musik Laden* on German TV.

OCTOBER 20

The video for 'Daddy's Home' is shot at Ewarts Studio in Wandsworth. Cliff's brief is to look unshaven and wear tight jeans, a white T-shirt and black leather jacket.

OCTOBER 24

At Addlestone Police Station in Surrey, Cliff presents awards to local children.

NOVEMBER 4

'Service for the Blind' interview Cliff.

NOVEMBER 23

Cliff appears on the bill of the Royal Variety Performance at Drury Lane, London.

NOVEMBER 23

BBC Television screen the first of a four-part series entitled *Cliff,* which looks at Cliff's twenty-three years in show business. Aspects covered include his gospel and orthodox concerts, religion, life on the road, his charity work and interviews with business and personal friends including Olivia Newton-John, Adam Faith, Marty Wilde and disc jockeys Kenny Everett, Dave Lee Travis and Mike Read.
Cliff's friend and religous advisor, Bill Latham, discusses the gospel tours and reveals that they made £50,000-£60,000 a year for Tear Fund. Religious broadcaster David Winter talks about Cliff's conversion to Christianity.

NOVEMBER

Cliff and one of Britain's top lady tennis players, Sue Barker, become friends and start spending a lot of time in each other's company.

NOVEMBER 28

Cliff's 82nd single, 'Daddy's Home', is a song which has long been one of his favourites – the original by Shep and the Limelites featuring on Cliff's Bell-Ami jukebox at his home. The 'B' side is the old Johnny Kidd song 'Shakin' All Over'. 'Daddy's Home' becomes Cliff's 9th single to come to rest at the number 2 spot in the charts.

NOVEMBER 28

Sally James interviews Cliff on the Saturday morning TV programme *Tiswas.*

NOVEMBER 30

Cliff undertakes a book-signing session at London's Heathrow Airport (Terminal 1).

NOVEMBER 30

BBC 2 screen the second part of the series *Cliff* which looks at the religious side of his career.

DECEMBER 7

BBC 2 transmit the third part of of the series *Cliff,* which includes footage filmed at his concerts in America.

DECEMBER 14

The fourth and final part of the series *Cliff* is shown, featuring the concert recorded the previous October at the Apollo, Victoria, in London.

DECEMBER 22

Cliff records for BBC TV's *Pop Quiz.*

DECEMBER 23

Cliff flies to Miami to spend Christmas in Florida.

JANUARY 2

Cliff arrives back in England from Miami.

4-15 JANUARY

STRAWBERRY STUDIOS
Studio sessions

The Only Way Out	*A-side*
Thief In The Night	*Now You See Me Now You Don't*
Where Do We Go From Here	*A-side*
Little Town	*See 25/26 March*
It Has To Be You, It Has To Be Me	*Now You See Me Now You Don't*
Discovering	*B-side*
You, Me And Jesus	*B-side*
Under The Influence	*B-side*
Closer To You	*(Unissued)*
Now That You Know Me	*(Unissued)*
Take Me Where I Wanna Go	*(Unissued)*

Lead and Backing Vocals:	**Cliff Richard**
Guitar:	**Mart Jenner/Bill Roberts/John Clark**
Bass:	**Mark Griffiths/Paul Westwood**
Fretless Bass:	**Mo Foster**
Bass:	**Andy Pask**
Drums:	**Graham Jarvis/Andy Pask**
Keyboards:	**Graham Todd/Craig Pruess**
OBX Synthesiser:	**Dave Cooke**
Piano:	**Peter Skellern**
Percussion/Sequencer:	**Craig Pruess**
Auto Harp:	**Craig Pruess**
Harmonium/Sleigh Bells:	**Craig Pruess**
Saxophone:	**Mel Collins**
Violin:	**Paul Hart (on Little Town)**
Backing Vocals:	**Cliff/Tony Rivers/Nigel Perrin**
Producers:	**Cliff Richard/Craig Pruess**
Engineer:	**John Walker/Steve Cook**

JANUARY 21

Cliff is interviewed on the telephone by eight Australian newspapers and nine Australian radio stations over a period of fourteen hours.

FEBRUARY 1-6

Cliff appears at Blazers night club in Windsor, Berkshire.

FEBRUARY 10

Cliff departs for a world tour with ever-present tour manager, David Bryce, and commences with appearances in Bangkok, Singapore and Hong Kong.

FEBRUARY 22-MARCH 13

Cliff's trek continues with Australian appearances in Perth, Adelaide, Melbourne, Brisbane, Sydney, and in Christchurch and Auckland, New Zealand..

MARCH 17-19

Cliff appears in Los Angeles and New York.

MARCH 22

Cliff arrives back in England.

25/26 MARCH

Abbey Road
Studio session

Little Town	*A-side*

Tympani/Chimes:	**Dave Arnold**
Trumpets:	**John Wilbraham/Crispian Steele-Perkins/Paul Cosh/Ted Hobart/Michael Laird/Gerry Ruddock/Mark Emney/Simon Ferguson**
French Horns:	**Jeff Bryant/John Pigneevy/Chris Larkin/John Rooke/Robin Davies/Philip Eastop**
Bass Trombones:	**Geoff Perkins/Steve Saunders**
Tenor Trombones:	**John Iveson/Dave Purser/Michael Hext/David Whitson/Paul Beer/Roger Brenner**
Double Basses:	**Ian Anderson/Michael Brittain/Chris Laurence**
Orchestra conducted by	**Martyn Ford**
Producers:	**Cliff Richard/Craig Pruess**
Engineer:	**John Kurlander**

29 MARCH-2/5 APRIL

Strawberry Studios
Studio sessions

First Date	*Now You See Me Now You Don't*
Now You See Me, Now You Don't	*Now You See Me Now You Don't*
The Rock That Doesn't Roll	*(Unissued)*
Be In My Heart	*Now You See Me Now You Don't*

Lead and Backing Vocals:	**Cliff Richard**
Guitar:	**Mart Jenner/John Clark**
Bass:	**Andy Pask**
Drums:	**Graham Jarvis**
Percussion/Sequencer:	**Craig Pruess**
Saxophone:	**Mel Collins**
Harmonium:	**Craig Pruess**
Orchestra conducted by	**Martyn Ford**
Backing Vocals:	**Cliff/Tony Rivers/The Mike Sammes Singers-Be In My Heart only**
Producers:	**Cliff Richard/Craig Pruess**
Engineer:	**Keith Bessey/Steve Cook**

MARCH 31

Weetabix hold a press conference in the Derby & Queensbury Room at London's Cafe Royal with Cliff, who is spearheading a campaign with them to raise money for underprivileged children.

APRIL 4

Cliff visits Cranleigh School in Surrey.

APRIL 10

Cliff assists in Capital Radio's 'Help a London Child'.

APRIL 18

Cliff attends the 'Christians in Sport' dinner in Watford.

APRIL 21

Cliff is interviewed by *Family* magazine, the *Surrey Herald* and the Guildford Church magazine prior to attending the TV Times awards at Thames TV's Teddington Studios.

APRIL 29-MAY 2

Cliff visits Northern Ireland.

MAY 9-15

Cliff and Bill Latham visit Kenya on behalf of Tear Fund.

MAY 27

Photographer Brian Aris takes new shots of Cliff at his Holborn Studios in London.

SOUTH EAST ASIA AND AUSTRALIAN TOUR

FEBRUARY 3/4
Singapore

FEBRUARY 6/7
Bangkok

FEBRUARY 9/10/11
Hong Kong

FEBRUARY 13/14/15
Manila

FEBRUARY 18/19/20/21
Melbourne

FEBRUARY 23/24
Canberra

FEBRUARY 26/27
Brisbane

MARCH 1/2/3/4
Sydney

MARCH 7
Adelaide

MARCH 8/9
Adelaide

MARCH 12/13
Perth

JUNE

ABBEY ROAD
Studio session

Love And A Helping Hand	*B-side*

Lead Vocal: **Cliff Richard**
Keyboards: **Craig Pruess**

Producer: **Craig Pruess**
Engineer: **Keith Bessey**

JUNE 9

At Wokingham in Berkshire, Cliff opens a new Dr Barnardo's children's home.

JUNE 13

Radio 2's Nick Page interviews Cliff at home.

JUNE 15

Cliff watches Sue Barker play in a tennis tournament at Eastbourne.

JUNE 19

Cliff sees Andrew Lloyd Webber's musical *Cats*.

JULY 5

EMI release Cliff's 83rd single, 'The Only Way Out'/'Under The Influence' which reaches No.10 in the charts.

JULY 5-31

Cliff flies out to the States and begins a tour which will cover the USA and Canada.

AUGUST 5-27

Cliff flies out to Bermuda for a holiday. Also on holiday with him are Bill Latham and both their mothers..

SEPTEMBER 6

Cliff's 84th single 'Where Do We Go From Here'/'Discovering', is released but only reaches No. 60 – Cliff's lowest ever chart placing.

SEPTEMBER 8

'Where Do We Go From Here' video is shot in London.

SEPTEMBER 14-15

Cliff is interviewed by Capital Radio, British Forces Network, Radio 1's *Talkabout*, Radio 1's Andy Peebles and Guildford Hospital Radio.

SEPTEMBER 1982-JANUARY 1983

RIVERSIDE STUDIOS

Studio session for DJM

Drifting	*A-side*
Jesus Call Your Lambs	*Sheila Walsh LP*

Lead Vocal:	**Cliff Richard**
Guitar:	**John Clark**
Acoustic Guitar:	**Rick Fenn**
Synthesisers/Piano/Brass/Percussion:	**Craig Pruess**
Vocals:	**Sheila Walsh/Cliff Richard**
Producer:	**Cliff Richard/Craig Pruess**
Engineer:	**Keith Bessey**
Session hours:	

Cliff and Phil Everly at Eden Studios recording 'She Means Nothing To Me'.

SEPTEMBER 27

EMI film Cliff for a Christmas record token commercial.

5 OCTOBER

EDEN STUDIOS, LONDON
Studio session for Capitol

She Means Nothing To Me	*A-side*
I'll Mend Your Broken Heart	*Phil Everly LP*

Lead Vocal:	**Cliff Richard**
Lead Guitars:	**John David/Mark Knopfler/ Billy Bremner**
Acoustic Guitars:	**Billy Bremner**
Tremolo Guitar:	**Billy Bremner**
Reverse Lead Guitar:	**Stuart Colman**
Rhythm Guitars:	**Mark Knopfler/Mickey Gee**
Bass:	**Stuart Colman**
Drums:	**Terry Williams**
Piano:	**Pete Wingfield**
Percussion:	**Stuart Colman/Rod Houison**
Backing Vocals:	**Cliff Richard/Phil Everly**
Producer:	**Stuart Colman**
Engineer:	**Rod Houison**
Session hours:	**10.00am-9.00pm**

OCTOBER 9-NOVEMBER 2

Cliff tours Europe and Scandinavia.

NOVEMBER 7

Cliff attends the 'Christmas in Sport' dinner in Liverpool.

NOVEMBER 15

EMI release Cliff's 85th single, 'Little Town'/'Love And A Helping Hand'/'You, Me And Jesus'.

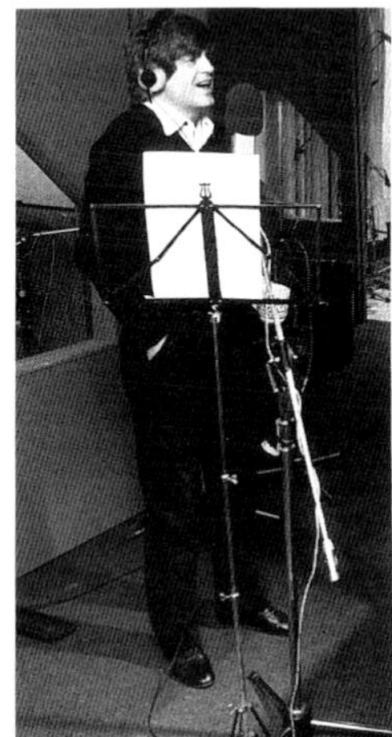

NOVEMBER 23

Cliff performs at the Royal Albert Hall, London with the Royal Philharmonic Orchestra.

23 NOVEMBER

ROYAL ALBERT HALL
Live recordings

Green Light	*Dressed For The Ocassion*
We Don't Talk Anymore	*Dressed For The Ocassion*
True Love Ways	*Dressed For The Ocassion*
Softly As I Leave You	*Dressed For The Ocassion*
Carrie	*Dressed For The Ocassion*
Miss You Nights	*Dressed For The Ocassion*
Galadriel	*Dressed For The Ocassion*
Maybe Someday	*Dressed For The Ocassion*
Thief In The Night	*Dressed For The Ocassion*
Up In The World	*Dressed For The Ocassion*
Treasure Of Love	*Dressed For The Ocassion*
Devil Woman/Reprise	*Dressed For The Ocassion)*
Discovering	*(Unissued)*
You, Me And Jesus	*(Unissued)*
Daddy's Home	*(Unissued)*
Little Town	*(Unissued)*

Lead Vocal:	**Cliff Richard**
The London Philharmonic Orchestra conducted by:	**Richard Hewson**
Synthesiser:	**David Cooke**
Bass:	**Mark Griffiths**
Drums:	**Graham Jarvis**
Piano:	**Steve Gray**
Vocals:	**Tony Rivers/Tony Harding/ Stuart Calver/John Perry**
Producer:	**Cliff Richard/Richard Hewson**
Engineers:	**John Kurlander**
Session hours:	

Recorded on Pumacrest Mobile by **Doug Hopkins**
Mixed at Strawberry Studios South by **Keith Bessey**

NOVEMBER 27

Noel Edmonds chats to Cliff on his live TV show.

DECEMBER 1

Phil Everly and Cliff have photographs taken together.

DECEMBER

'Little Town' peaks at the No.11 position in the charts, and spends a total of seven weeks in the Top Twenty.

DECEMBER 23

Cliff sings 'Little Town' on *Top Of The Pops*.

DECEMBER 23

Cliff attends the Arts Centre Group carol service.

JANUARY 13

The film *Cliff in Kenya* is premiered at the BAFTA cinema in London's Piccadilly.

JANUARY 15-16

Cliff takes part in a tennis tournament in Holland.

JANUARY 20-26

Cliff appears at Blazers night club in Windsor, Berkshire.

JANUARY 28

As part of the Weetabix appeal, Cliff presents a cheque to the children of the Great Ormond Street Hospital in London.

FEBRUARY 19

Cliff's 86th single 'She Means Nothing To Me', on which Cliff duets with Phil Everly, is released. The 'B' side, 'A Man And A Woman', features Phil Everly only. The single is produced by Stuart Colman

MARCH

'She Means Nothing To Me' peaks at No.9.

7-12 MARCH

ABBEY ROAD
Studio session

Back In Vaudeville	*Foreign B-side*

Producer:	**Bruce Welch**
Engineer:	
Recorded in:	**The Penthouse Studio**
Session hours:	

21/22/23 MARCH

AIR RECORDING STUDIOS, LONDON
Studio session

Please Don't Fall In Love	*A-side*
Too Close Too Heaven	*B-side*
How To Handle A Woman	*(Unissued)*

Lead Vocal:	**Cliff Richard**
Guitar:	**Ray Russell/Alan Parker**
Bass:	**Frank McDonald**
Drums:	**Graham Jarvis**
Percussion:	**Ray Cooper/Tony Carr**
Keyboards:	**Mike Batt**
Vocals:	**Mike Batt/Cliff Richard**
Producer:	**Mike Batt**
Engineer:	**Steve Churchyard**
Recorded in:	**Studio 2**
Session hours:	**21- 10.00am-6.00pm** **22- 11.00am-2.00am** **23- 2.00pm-1.30am**

Strings were recorded at C.T.S. Wembley, possibly on the 21st and Engineered by **Dick Lewsey**.

MARCH 24

At St Martin-in-the-Fields church in London, Cliff attends a memorial service for comedian Arthur Askey.

APRIL 9-29

Cliff on a European and Scandinavian gospel tour taking in Lisbon, Barcelona, Stuttgart, Hamburg, Essen, Malmo, Gothenburg, Rotterdam, Antwerp and Brussels.

UNITED KINGDOM TOUR

NOVEMBER 2/3/4
Apollo, Glasgow

NOVEMBER 5/6/7
Playhouse, Edinburgh

NOVEMBER 11/12/13/14
Apollo, Manchester

NOVEMBER 18/19/20/21
Centre, Brighton

NOVEMBER 25/26
Odeon, Birmingham

NOVEMBER 27/28
Odeon, Birmingham

DECEMBER 2/3/4/5
Hammersmith Odeon, London

DECEMBER 9/10/11/12
Winter Gardens, Bournemouth

DECEMBER 16/17/18/19
Coliseum, St. Austell

The Band:
Guitar: John Clark/Mart Jenner
Bass: Mark Griffiths
Keyboards: Alan Park/Dave Cooke
Drums: Graham Jarvis
Vocals: Tony Rivers/Stu Calver/John Perry

THE BRIGHTON CENTRE
SATURDAY, 21st NOVEMBER, 1981
at 8.00 p.m.
SAVILE ARTIS 4 RESENTS
CLIFF RICHA D in Concert
G 31 WEST BALCONY £4.50
Skyline RESTAURANT (Magnificent Sea View) Open two hours prior to most performances Reservations: Telephone 203130

Neither the Council or their officers accept any responsibility for any loss or damage (howsoever caused or sustained) to any property whatsoever brought on to these premises.
Tickets cannot be exchanged or refunded.

The taking of unauthorised photographs during an artiste's live performance is a breach of the Copyright Act 1956. Cameras being used in defiance of this regulation will be removed to the cloakroom for the duration of the performance. The Management may also exercise the right to expose film if so requested by the artiste.

APRIL

EMI release Cliff's 87th single, 'True Love Ways'/'Galadriel'. 'True Love Ways' had previously been a hit for Buddy Holly in 1960 and for Peter and Gordon in 1965.

MAY

Cliff's 88th single is released. The A-side, 'Drifting', is a duet with Sheila Walsh. The B-side is by Sheila Walsh only.

9-18 MAY

STRAWBERRY STUDIOS SOUTH
Studio sessions

Makin' History	*Rock And Roll Silver*
Move It	*Rock And Roll Silver*
Donna	*Rock And Roll Silver*
Teddy Bear	*Rock And Roll Silver*
It'll Be Me	*Rock And Roll Silver*
Lucille	*Rock And Roll Silver*
Little Bitty Pretty One	*Rock And Roll Silver*
Never Be Anyone Else But You	*Rock And Roll Silver*
Be Bop A Lula	*Rock And Roll Silver*
Tutti Frutti	*Rock And Roll Silver*

Lead Vocal:	**Cliff Richard**
Guitar:	**John Clark/Mart Jenner**
Bass:	**Mark Griffiths**
Keyboards:	**Dave Cooke/Alan Park**
Drums:	**Graham Jarvis**
Vocals:	**Cliff/Tony Rivers/Stu Calver/John Perry**
Producer:	**Craig Pruess**
Engineer:	**Keith Bessey**

19 MAY-3 JUNE-16 JUNE

STRAWBERRY STUDIOS SOUTH
Studio sessions

Silver's Home Tonight	*Silver*
Hold On	*Silver*
Front Page	*Silver*
Ocean Deep	*Silver*
Locked Inside Your Prison	*Silver*
The Golden Days Are Over	*Silver*
Love Stealer	*Silver*

Lead Vocal:	**Cliff Richard**
Guitar:	**John Clark/Mart Jenner**
Bass:	**Mark Griffiths**
Drums:	**Graham Jarvis**
Keyboards:	**Craig Pruess/Alan Park**
Sax:	**Mel Collins**
Synthesizers:	**Craig Pruess**
Orchestra conducted by:	**Martyn Ford**
Vocals:	**Cliff/Tony Rivers/Stu Calver/ John Perry**
Producer:	**Craig Pruess**
Engineer:	**Keith Bessey**

Strings were recorded at Henry Wood Hall during July/August. Mixed at The Townhouse Studios July/August.

21/22 MAY

MAYFAIR RECORDING STUDIOS
Studio session

Never Say Die (Give A Little Bit More)	*A-side*

Lead Vocal:	**Cliff Richard**
Guitars:	**Terry Britten**
Bass:	**Mark Griffiths**
Drums:	**Graham Jarvis**
Keyboards:	**Michael Boddicker**
Saxophone:	**Ronnie Asprey**
Trumpet:	**Martin Drover**
Vocals:	**Terry Britten**
Producer:	**Terry Britten**
Engineers:	**John Hudson**
Recorded in:	**Studio 1**
Session hours:	**21- 10.20am-10.30pm 22- 10.30am-9.30pm**

Overdubs and mixing were carried out on 28/29 May, 7/21 June and 22 July.

JUNE 6

Lord Snowdon photographs Cliff at a 4-hour session in London.

JUNE 7

Cliff records for BBC TV's *Pop Quiz*.

JUNE 11

Cliff records for *Time Of Your Life* at BBC TV centre with Noel Edmonds and Una Stubbs.

JUNE 23

Cliff attends the retirement party for a Baptist minister in Walton-on-Thames, Surrey.

JUNE 27

Radio 1 broadcaster and music journalist Paul Gambaccini takes part in a 'rock seminar' with Cliff at the Arts Centre Group in London.

JULY 1

BBC TV screen *Time Of Your Life*.

JULY 2-3

Cliff watches the tennis finals at Wimbledon.

JULY 18

Cliff goes to Holland for an international conference with Billy Graham.

JULY 19

Cliff records the video for 'Never Say Die (Give A Little Bit More)'.

AUGUST

ABBEY ROAD
Studio session

Baby You're Dynamite	*A-side*

Lead Vocal:	**Cliff Richard**
Guitar:	**Nigel Jenkins**
Bass:	**Alan Jones**
Drums:	**Brian Bennett**
Keyboards:	**Guy Fletcher**
Vocals:	**Cliff/Guy Fletcher**
Producer:	**Bruce Welch**
Engineer:	**Peter Vince**
Recorded in:	**Studio 2**
Session hours:	

AUGUST 3-24

Cliff holidays in Portugal.

AUGUST 22

Cliff's 89th single, 'Never Say Die (Give A Little Bit More)' is released. The 'B' side is Cliff's version of the Little Richard/Everly Brothers classic 'Lucille'.

AUGUST 27

Cliff appears at the Greenbelt Christian Festival.

SEPTEMBER 8

Cliff sends a congratulatory telegram to the Shadows at a 'Silver Luncheon' to celebrate their 25 years in the business and the publication of their autobiography with Mike Read.

SEPTEMBER 14-23

Cliff in Los Angeles and Salt Lake City.

OCTOBER 10

Cliff co-hosts the Radio 1 *Breakfast Show* live from Mike Read's house in Weybridge, Surrey.

OCTOBER 14

Cliff's 43rd birthday.

OCTOBER 25

Cliff attends a charity lunch at London's Dorchester Hotel in the presence of Princess Anne, in aid of the Bone Marrow Unit at Westminster Hospital.

OCTOBER 27

Cliff records for TV's *Pebble Mill at One*.

NOVEMBER 1

Cliff attends the 'Tin Pan Alley Ball' at London's Royal Lancaster Hotel.

NOVEMBER 5

Olivia Newton-John and her sister are guests of Cliff's at his Apollo concert.

NOVEMBER 7

EMI release Cliff's 90th single, 'Please Don't Fall In Love'/'Too Close Too Heaven', which climbs to No. 7 in the charts.

NOVEMBER 7

Princess Alexandra and Angus Ogilvy watch Cliff at the Apollo.

NOVEMBER 11

After his show at the Apollo, Cliff dines with Princess Anne and Tim Rice.

NOVEMBER 13

Cliff watches the Benson & Hedges tennis final at Wembley.

NOVEMBER 17

TV AM film Cliff at David Lloyd's Tennis Centre.

DECEMBER 8

Cliff attends a Variety Club lunch at London's Hilton Hotel.

DECEMBER 19

Cliff's own pro-celebrity tennis tournament is staged at the Conference Centre, Brighton. Participants are Cliff, Hank Marvin, actor Trevor Eve, Mike Read, Sue Barker, Sue Mappin, Jo Durie and Ann Hobbs. The round-robin tournament is won by Trevor Eve and Anne Hobbs.

DECEMBER 20

Cliff attends the Arts Centre Group carol service at All Souls' Church in Langham Place, London.

THE CLIFF RICHARD SILVER TOUR

OCTOBER 5/6/7/8
Apollo, Oxford

OCTOBER 11/12
Apollo, Glasgow

OCTOBER 14/15
Playhouse, Edinburgh

OCTOBER 19/20/21/22
Apollo, Manchester

OCTOBER 26/27/28/29
Odeon, Birmingham

NOVEMBER 3 – DECEMBER 3 (excluding Sundays)
Apollo, Victoria, London

1984–1987

The Records 1984 – 1987

Given the quality of the three singles released, 1984 surprisingly turned out to be a very poor year for Cliff on the singles chart. The duet with Janet Jackson on 'Two To The Power' definitely showed promise, but the single failed to register at all and, although neither of the other two singles were big hits, they still did considerably better than this one. While suffering from the same defect, two of the singles released the following year just did not have enough impact to score big on the charts. However, the public was not slow to pick up on 'She's So Beautiful' sending this, the first single from *Time – The Musical*, to a top twenty position and staying on the chart for nine weeks. Two of the four singles in 1986 reached the top three. Of these the new comic version of 'Living Doll' with The Young Ones repeated its 1959 success of reaching the pinnacle of the charts, while 'All I Ask Of You', duetted with Sarah Brightman, peaked at No.3. Another duet, this time with Elton John on 'Slow Rivers', did not do as well. Two tracks, 'My Pretty One' and 'Some People', culled from the ALWAYS GUARANTEED album, were selected for single release and became Cliff's two top ten hits in a row for 1987. Even though one more single was lifted from the album, 'Remember Me' failed to repeat the success of the previous two, only achieving moderate success at No.35.

The same fate befell the 1984 album THE ROCK CONNECTION and, despite containing some fine newly recorded material, the album consisted of mainly previously released tracks from ROCK 'N ROLL SILVER, and consequently sales and chart action were disappointing, but perhaps the album was only released as EMI may have been impatient to get new product out.

However, ALWAYS GUARANTEED released in September 1987 became Cliff's most successful studio album. A compilation album ROCK ON WITH CLIFF RICHARD put out in 1987 by EMI's Music For Pleasure mid-price label featured an alternate take of 'Dynamite'. This version is much faster than the original single and has an altogether more frantic feel about it. It is uncertain which 1959 session this version comes from. There are two, one on 9 March, and the other on 25 July, and both appear to be complete takes.

The Sessions 1984 – 1987

The material recorded at the first two sessions of this period were in the duet category. 'Two To The Power' was taped at Advision Studios with Janet Jackson, and 'Slow Rivers' with Elton John was done at SOL Studios during the recording of his FIRE ON ICE album.

Although the June/July sessions belong to material that started out as a TV project, only six new recordings were put on tape. Of these the reworking of 'Willie And The Hand Jive' is an outstanding arrangement of the 1959 hit, and of the new material 'Heart User' is instilled with all the fire and electricity of a fifties performance. Producer credits were shared between Cliff and engineer Keith Bessey, and in the same vein as ROCK 'N' ROLL SILVER, the band was trimmed down to a basic rock line-up. However, as these sessions had not produced enough material for an album, it was decided to add the Phil Everly duet remixed, together with 'Dynamite' and a further six songs from ROCK 'N ROLL SILVER for release as THE ROCK CONNECTION.

No studio sessions took place again until December when, in preparation for his leading role in the West End musical *Time,* plans were put into action for Cliff to record at the Roundhouse Studios where he put down the vocals to 'She's So Beautiful'. Stevie Wonder produced, arranged and played on the track that became the first featured single. Material recorded during the next sessions in June and August was also tied in to the musical and provided another two A-sides.

The first sessions for 1986 took place in January at the Master Rock Studios with Stuart Colman producing a special remake of Cliff's 1959 hit 'Living Doll' for Comic Relief. Vocals for the track were laid down by Cliff and the alternative comedy team of *The Young Ones* in only 20 minutes, although mixing took up to six weeks. Of the musicians for this session, there was a change personnel-wise, but only on this occasion – Tim Renwick on guitar, Howard Tibble on drums, Stuart Colman on bass and Pete Wingfield on keyboard. Of the old Shadows crew, Hank Marvin was in the studio to recreate his original 1959 guitar solo.

Because of Cliff's total involvement with *Time*, recording sessions over this period became correspondingly more difficult to schedule. A session in August took Cliff back to Abbey Road to duet with Sarah Brightman on 'All I Ask Of You' with Andrew Lloyd Webber producing, and sessions at RG Jones Studios running from 13 October produced all the tracks for the ALWAYS GUARANTEED album. Alan Tarney provided the technical and musical expertise by playing all instrumentation on the backing tracks as well as supervising production of the sessions. One new talent brought in for the recording of 'Under Your Spell' was Chris Eaton who helped out on additional keyboard work, but only on this track.

JANUARY 7-8

Cliff watches an indoor tennis tournament from a private box at London's Royal Albert Hall.

JANUARY 15-18

Cliff holidays in Portugal.

JANUARY 24-FEBRUARY 10

Cliff is in the Far East and America for two weeks.

FEBRUARY 21-23

Cliff holidays in Portugal.

FEBRUARY 29

Cliff appears live on BBC Radio 4's *Woman's Hour.*

MARCH 13-17

Cliff goes to Scandinavia for a promotional visit.

MARCH 19

EMI release Cliff's 91st single, 'Baby You're Dynamite'/'Ocean Deep', which peaks at number 27 in the charts. It is subsequently 'flipped', with the 'B' side 'Ocean Deep' becoming the 'A' side which then re-enteres the chart and peaks at number 72.

MARCH 30

Cliff records for Terry Wogan's BBC TV show.

APRIL 1-15

Cliff and Bill Latham go to Haiti, where they visit Port-au-Prince and La Gonave. During the visit, Cliff is moved to write a song about La Gonave.

APRIL 26

Cliff sees Andrew Lloyd Webber's musical *Starlight Express.*

26 APRIL

ADVISION
Studio session for A & M

Two To The Power	*A-side*
Lead Vocal:	**Janet Jackson/Cliff Richard**
Producer:	**Giogio Moroder**
Engineer:	
Session hours:	**7.00pm-10.00pm**

MAY 9

Cliff attends a service at Westminster Abbey for 'Christian Heritage Year'.

MAY 10

Cliff is filmed in Switzerland for the Golden Rose of Montreux festival.

15 MAY

THE 'SOL' STUDIOS
Studio session for Rocket

Slow Rivers	*A-side*
Lead Vocal:	**Cliff Richard**
Piano:	**Elton John**
Guitars:	**Davey Johnstone**
Bass:	**Paul Westwood**
Keyboards:	**Fred Mandell**
Drums:	**Charlie Morgan**
Vocals:	**Elton John/Cliff Richard**
Backing Vocals:	**Kiki Dee**
Strings arranged and conducted:	**James Newton Howard**
Producer:	**Gus Dudgeon**
Engineer:	**Stuart Epps**
Session hours:	**8.00pm-10.00pm**

Strings recorded at CTS, Wembley

JUNE 2

Cliff takes part in a charity concert for the Elmbridge Hospice appeal in Surrey.

JUNE 11

Cliff records for BBC Television's *Rock Gospel Show*.

JUNE 13

Cliff attends 'Mission to London', a Christian evening at Queen's Park Rangers football ground in west London. Throughout the Eighties, Cliff's Christian activities were to take up as much of his professional career as a public performer as were his 'secular', non-religious appearances.

JUNE 16-21

Cliff spends five days in Portugal.

CLIFF RICHARD and the SHADOWS – TOGETHER

JULY 2
Wembley Arena, London

JULY 3
Wembley Arena, London

JULY 4
Wembley Arena, London

JULY 5
Wembley Arena, London

JULY 7
National Exhibition Centre, Birmingham

JULY 8
National Exhibition Centre, Birmingham

JULY 9
National Exhibition Centre, Birmingham

JULY 10
National Exhibition Centre, Birmingham

JULY 11
National Exhibition Centre, Birmingham

Songs featured on the tour:
'Move It'/'Don't Talk To Him'/'Please Don't Tease'/'It's All In The Game'/'Lucky Lips'/'Wonderful Land'/'Cavatina'/'FBI'/'Living Doll'/'Bachelor Boy'/'Summer Holiday'/'The Young Ones'/'I Love You'/'The Day I Met Marie'/'The Twelfth Of Never'/'Congratulations'/'Let Me Be The One'/'Power To All Our Friends'/'On The Beach'/'I Could Easily Fall'/'Do You Wanna Dance'/'We Don't Talk Anymore'/'Visions'

24 JUNE

GALLERY STUDIOS
Studio session

La Gonave	*The Rock Connection*
Small World	*B-side*
I Will Follow You	*B-side*
Tiny Planet	*Its A Small World*

Lead Vocal: **Cliff Richard**

Producer: **Cliff Richard/Craig Pruess**
Engineer: **Keith Bessey**
Session hours:

30 JULY-3 AUGUST

STRAWBERRY STUDIOS SOUTH
Studio session

Learning How To Rock And Roll	*The Rock Connection*
Heart User	*The Rock Connection*
Willie And The Hand Jive	*The Rock Connection*
Lovers And Friends	*The Rock Connection*
Over You	*The Rock Connection*
Shooting From The Heart	*The Rock Connection*

Lead Vocal: **Cliff Richard**

Producer: **Cliff Richard/Keith Bessey**
Engineer: **Keith Bessey**
Session hours:

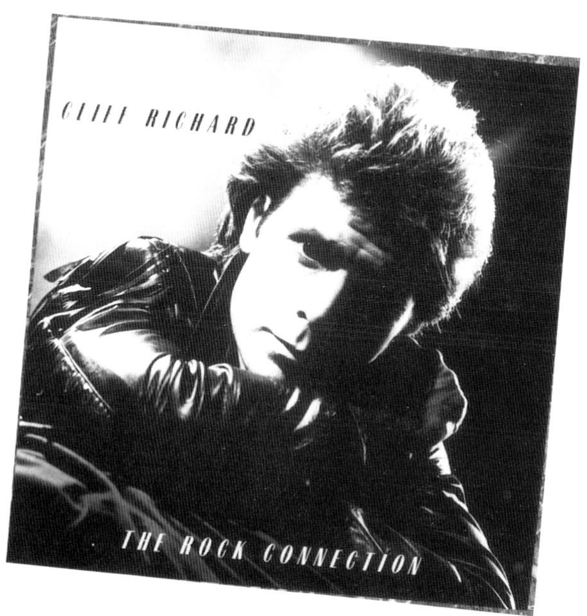

AUGUST 2-23

Cliff holidays in Portugal.

AUGUST 28

Cliff and Dave Clark meet to discuss the musical *Time*.

SEPTEMBER 1-29

Cliff undertakes a British gospel tour.

SEPTEMBER 7

TVS film Cliff at the David Lloyd Tennis Centre.

SEPTEMBER

EMI release Cliff's 92nd single, 'Two To The Power' with Janet Jackson. The 'B' side, 'Rock 'n' Roll', features Janet Jackson only.

OCTOBER 8-13

Cliff in concert at Blazers night club, Windsor, Berkshire.

OCTOBER 14

Cliff leaves for Australia on his 44th birthday.

THE 'ROCK CONNECTION' TOUR
Australia and New Zealand

OCTOBER 20
Amphitheatre, Darwin

OCTOBER 25/26
Entertainment Centre, Perth

OCTOBER 30
The Showgrounds, Cairns

OCTOBER 31
The Showgrounds, Townsville

NOVEMBER 2
The Showground, Mackay

NOVEMBER 3
Musicbowl, Rockhampton

NOVEMBER 5/6
Festival Hall, Brisbane

NOVEMBER 9/10
Entertainment Centre, Sydney

NOVEMBER 12/13
Bruce Stadium, Canberra

NOVEMBER 14/15
Entertainment Centre, Melbourne

NOVEMBER 16
Entertainment Centre, Melbourne

NOVEMBER 18/19/20/21
Apollo Stadium, Adelaide

NOVEMBER 24
Mount Smart, Auckland

NOVEMBER 26/27
Michael Fowler Centre, Wellington

Songs featured on the tour:
'Learning How To Rock And Roll'/'The Young Ones'/'Dreamin''/'Never Say Die'/'Donna'/'The Only Way Out'/'Love Stealer'/'Locked Inside Your Prison'/'Shooting From The Heart'/'Miss You Nights'/'Heart User'/'Galadriel'/'Devil Woman'/'Move It'/'Daddy's Home'/'Be-Bop-A-Lula'/'Lucille'/'Under The Gun'/'Lovers And Friends'/'The Golden Days Are Over'/'Ocean Deep'/'Thief In The Night'/'Wired For Sound'/'Living Doll'/'Summer Holiday'/'Bachelor Boy'/'We Don't Talk Anymore'

The band:
Guitars: John Clark/Mart Jenner
Bass: Mark Griffiths
Drums: Graham Jarvis
Keyboards: Alan Park/Dave Cooke
Vocals: Tony River/Stu Calver/John Perry

OCTOBER 22

Cliff's 93rd single, 'Shooting From The Heart'/'Small World' is released, but only reaches No. 51 in the charts.

DECEMBER 8

Cliff attends the Silver Wedding party of Shadows drummer Brian Bennett and his wife Margaret, at their home in Hertfordshire.

DECEMBER 9

Cliff records at the BBC TV Centre for a *Rock Gospel Show* Christmas special.

DECEMBER 10

Cliff records for Mike Yarwood's Christmas show.

DECEMBER 15

The second pro-celebrity tennis tournament organised by Cliff takes place at the Brighton Conference Centre. The eight players are Cliff, Hank Marvin, Mike Yarwood, Terry Wogan, Annabel Croft, Sarah Gomer, Julie Salmon and Sue Mappin.

DECEMBER

Cliff attends the Arts Centre Group Carol Service at All Soul's Church, Langham Place, in London.

20/21 DECEMBER

ROUNDHOUSE STUDIOS
Studio session

She's So Beautiful	*A-side*

Lead Vocal: **Cliff Richard**

Producer: **Stevie Wonder**
Engineer:
Session hours:

All instruments played by Stevie Wonder and recorded at Wonderland Studios, Los Angeles.

DECEMBER 26-JANUARY 14

Cliff and Bill Latham fly to South Africa for 3 weeks.

JANUARY 14

Cliff returns from South Africa.

JANUARY 21

Cliff's 94th single is released: 'Heart User'/'I Will Follow You'. It peaks at No. 46.

JANUARY 25

Cliff appears live on pop TV programme *The Tube*, singing 'Lovers and Friends', 'Lucille' and 'Heart User'.

FEBRUARY 1

Cliff is interviewed for Radio 1's *History of Pop*, *Newsbeat*, Gloria Hunniford on Radio 2, Capital Radio's Roger Scott and Radio Luxembourg.

FEBRUARY 2

Cliff appears on Michael Aspel's TV show *Aspel and Friends*.

FEBRUARY 9

Cliff appears on BBC TV's *Saturday Superstore*.

FEBRUARY 11

Cliff attends a reception at 10 Downing Street, the official London residence of Prime Minister Margaret Thatcher.

FEBRUARY 17-18

Cliff records at the BBC TV Centre for an Easter special.

FEBRUARY 19-28

Cliff holidays in Portugal.

MARCH 17-25

Cliff holidays in Portugal.

MARCH 30

Cliff, along with many other celebrities, attends broadcaster/journalist Paul Gambaccini's birthday party in North London.

APRIL 16

At the David Lloyd Tennis Centre, Cliff participates in a Pro-Am tournament.

APRIL 30

Cliff films in Bath for *Jim'll Fix It.*

MAY 1

Along with Alvin Stardust, Andrew Lloyd Webber, Mike McCartney, Bobby Davro and Dave Lee Travis, Cliff attends the launch of the Waddington's board game 'Mike Read's Pop Quiz' at Stringfellows night club in London.

MAY 5

Cliff takes part in LWT's *40 Years of Peace* at London's Palace Theatre.

MAY 16

Cliff is given a demonstration of the latest laser lights available.

MAY 19-28

Cliff holidays in Portugal.

BBC Wales uses David Lloyd's Tennis Centre to shoot a health film Don't Break Your Heart in which Cliff takes part.

MAY 30

Along with Lonnie Donegan, Vera Lynn, Hank Marvin, David Cassidy and Bob Geldof, Cliff attends a *Guiness Book of Hit Singles* presentation by Norris McWhirter at a lunch at the Savoy Hotel for the book's authors Tim and Jo Rice, Paul Gambaccini and Mike Read.

JUNE 8

Cliff sends a wedding congratulations telegram to Nick Beggs of the pop group Kajagoogoo and his wife Boo.
Cliff plays in Bernard Cribbins' pro-celebrity tennis tournament at Foxhills, Surrey

Rick Parfitt and Cliff backstage at the Live Aid concert.

10/11 JUNE

GALLERY STUDIOS
Studio session

It's In Every One Of Us — *A-side*

Lead Vocal:	**Cliff Richard**
Guitars:	**John Clark**
Bass:	**Andy Pask**
Drums:	**Graham Jarvis**
Keyboards:	**Craig Pruess**
Strings:	**Martin Loveday/Gavyn Wright**
Producer:	**Keith Bessey/Craig Pruess**
Engineer:	**Keith Bessey**

JUNE 17-21

Ken Russell produces Cliff's 'She's So Beautiful' video in the Lake District.

JUNE 25

Cliff dines at the House of Commons.

JUNE 30

Cliff attends a 'Christians in Sport' service.

JULY 1

Cliff opens the new Addlestone District Health Centre in Surrey.

JULY 9-27

Cliff undertakes a gospel tour of Britain and the Channel Islands, which is cut short due to a throat infection.

JULY 16

While playing in Guernsey, Cliff and Bill Latham spend a day on the island of Herm renewing their friendship with Major and Mrs Wood and their family, as they had camped on the island with the Crusaders in the late Sixties.

JULY 29-AUGUST 3

Cliff spends a few days in the USA.

AUGUST 5-22

Cliff holidays in Portugal.

AUGUST 23-25

Cliff spends two days in Norway filming for a TV gala.

25 AUGUST

MARCUS STUDIOS LONDON

Studio session

Born To Rock And Roll *A-side*

Lead Vocal:	**Cliff Richard**
Guitars:	**Billy Squire**
Bass:	**Jerry Hay/John Edwards**
Drums:	**Graham Jarvis**
Keyboards:	**Dave Stewart/Paul Wickens**
Vocals:	**Billy Squire/Stuart Mather**
Producer:	**Peter Collins**
Engineer:	**Chris Porter**
Session hours:	**mid-day-8.00pm**

Mixed at Sarm Studios on 29 August-2 September

AUGUST 31

Cliff attends a Polish Youth Conference in Warsaw.

SEPTEMBER 2

EMI release Cliff's 95th single, 'She's So Beautiful'/'She's So Beautiful', the 'B' side being a different mix. The single reaches No. 17 in the charts.

SEPTEMBER 6-13

Cliff does Continental television, press and radio promotion for his latest record releases in Germany, Belgium, Holland and Denmark.

SEPTEMBER 16

In Birmingham, Cliff attends the launch of the publication *You, Me and Jesus,Vvolume 2.*

SEPTEMBER 23-25

Cliff spends three daysat Bisham Abbey Sports Centre in connection with the 'Cliff Richard Tennis Hunt'.

SEPTEMBER 28

Cliff appears on BBC TV's *Saturday Superstore.*

NOVEMBER 5-DECEMBER 14

Cliff undertakes many concerts in England and Scotland.

NOVEMBER 7

Cliff meets singer Van Morrison at London's Hammersmith Odeon.

NOVEMBER 25

EMI release Cliff's 96th single, 'It's In Every One Of Us'/'Alone'. This is the first time that a Cliff single has had a wholly instrumental 'B' side. It's Cliff's second single to be released from the musical *Time* and it peaks at No. 45.

DECEMBER 1

Cliff appears on BBC TV's *Pebble Mill at One.*

DECEMBER 19

Cliff opens a new X-ray unit at Weybridge Hospital in Surrey.

DECEMBER 21

Cliff appears on BBC TV's *Saturday Superstore.*

DECEMBER 21

Cliff's third annual pro-celebrity tennis tournament at the Brighton Conference Centre. Players are Cliff, Hank Marvin, Shakin' Stevens, Mike Read, Annabel Croft, Anne Hobbs, Virginia Wade and Sara Gomer.

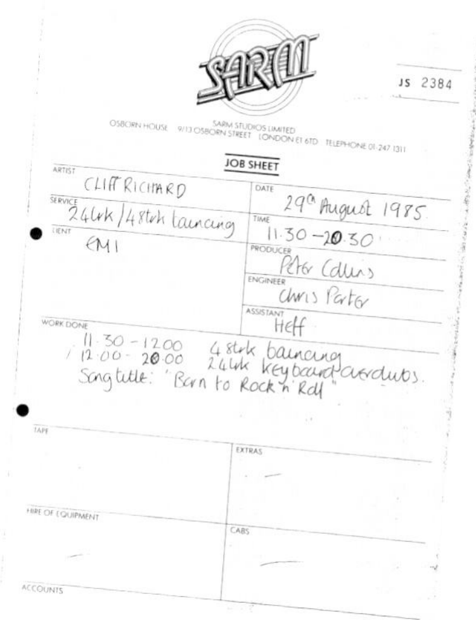

SARM

JS 2384

SARM STUDIOS LIMITED
OSBORN HOUSE 9/13 OSBORN STREET LONDON E1 6TD TELEPHONE 01-247 1311

JOB SHEET

ARTIST: CLIFF RICHARD	DATE: 29th August 1985
SERVICE: 24trk/48trk bouncing	TIME: 11.30-20.30
CLIENT: EMI	PRODUCER: Peter Collins
	ENGINEER: Chris Porter
	ASSISTANT: Heff

WORK DONE
11.30-12.00 48trk bouncing
12.00-20.00 24trk keyboard overdubs
Song title: "Born to Rock n' Roll"

TAPE	EXTRAS
HIRE OF EQUIPMENT	CABS
ACCOUNTS	

THE 'ROCK CONNECTION' TOUR
Europe

SEPTEMBER 30
Deutsches Museum, Munich

OCTOBER 1
Sportshalle, Graz

OCTOBER 2
Sportshalle, Vienna

OCTOBER 4
Grugahalle, Essen

OCTOBER 5
Forest National, Brussels

OCTOBER 7
Ahoy, Rotterdam

OCTOBER 8
Munsterlandhalle, Munster

OCTOBER 9
Stadthalle, Bremen

OCTOBER 10
Herninghalle, Herning

OCTOBER 11
Vejlby-Risskov Halle, Aarhus

OCTOBER 13
Concert House, Stockholm

OCTOBER 15
Ice Hall, Helsinki

OCTOBER 17
Drammen Hall, Oslo

OCTOBER 18/19/20
Falkoner Theatre, Copenhagen

OCTOBER 21
Aalborg Hall, Aalborg

OCTOBER 23
CCH, Hamburg

OCTOBER 24
CCH, Hamburg

OCTOBER 25
Jahrhunderthalle, Frankfurt

OCTOBER 26
Jahrhunderthalle, Frankfurt

OCTOBER 28
Sporthalle, Cologne

OCTOBER 29
Stadion Sporthalle, Hanover

Songs featured on the tour:
'Wired For Sound'/'Heart User'/'Move It'/'Please Don't Fall In Love'/'Never Say Die'/'A Heart Will Break'/'Yesterday, Today, Forever Under The Gun'/'Free My Soul'/'Take Me Back'/'Miss You Nights'/'Dreamin''/'Daddy's Home'/'Devil Woman'/'It's No Use Pretending'/'Sci-Fi'/'We Don't Talk Anymore'/'You Know That I Love You'/'Hey Mr Dream Maker'/'It Must Be Love'/'Carrie'/'Ease Along'/'Walking In The Light'/'She's So Beautiful'/'It's In Every One Of Us'

Recording 'Living Doll' with the Young Ones...'Get Down'

JANUARY 10

Cliff attends the funeral of his drummer – Graham Jarvis, at Beckenham Crematorium, Elmers End, London SE20.

JANUARY 11

Cliff flies from Heathrow for a holiday in Miami.

JANUARY 18

Departs from Miami.

JANUARY 19

Arrives Heathrow.

JANUARY 23/24

Cliff begins dance lessons at Pineapple Studios in London.

JANUARY 24

Attends Arts Centre Group (ACG) Dinner.

JANUARY 26

Attends ACG Supper Party.

JANUARY 27

Interviewed by the Sunday Express at London's Portman Hotel.

JANUARY 28

Dance lessons at Pineapple Studios.

29 JANUARY

MASTER ROCK STUDIOS

Studio session for WEA

Living Doll	*A-side*
Lead Vocal:	**Cliff Richard**
Guitar:	**Hank Marvin**
Guitar:	**Tim Renwick**
Bass:	**Stuart Colman**
Drums:	**Howard Tibble**
Keyboards:	**Pete Wingfield**
Vocals:	**Cliff and The Young Ones (Nigel Planer/Rik Mayall/Adrian Edmonson/Christopher Ryan)**
Producer:	**Stuart Colman**
Engineer:	**Carb Kanelle/Damien Asker-Brown**
Session hours:	**7.00pm-10.00pm**

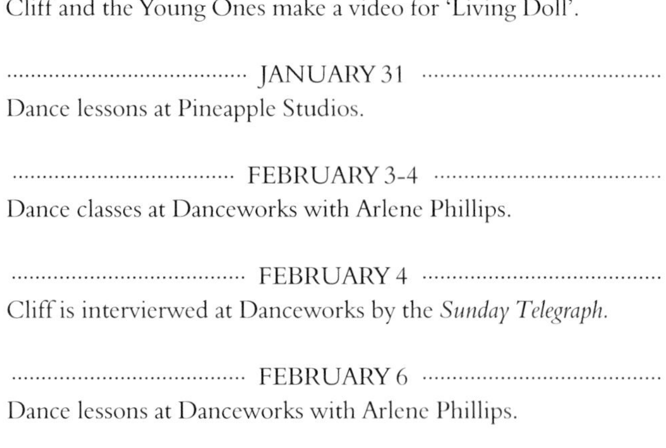

JANUARY 30

Cliff and the Young Ones make a video for 'Living Doll'.

JANUARY 31

Dance lessons at Pineapple Studios.

FEBRUARY 3-4

Dance classes at Danceworks with Arlene Phillips.

FEBRUARY 4

Cliff is intervierwed at Danceworks by the *Sunday Telegraph.*

FEBRUARY 6

Dance lessons at Danceworks with Arlene Phillips.

FEBRUARY 8

Cliff attends the musical *Guys and Dolls* in London and has dinner with Lulu afterwards.

FEBRUARY 9

Cliff records 'She's So Beautiful' for the *TV Times Awards Television Show.*

FEBRUARY 10

Attends the BPI (British Phonographic Industry) Awards Dinner at London's Grosvenor House Hotel.

FEBRUARY 14

Attends *TV Times* Awards at Thames TV Studios at Teddington Lock, Middlesex..

FEBRUARY 20

Interviewed by the *Observer*, and records 'It's In Every One Of Us' for transmission on the TV Show *Aspel and Friends.*

FEBRUARY 21

Undertakes a photosession for the *Observer.*

FEBRUARY 22

'It's In Every One Of Us' is transmitted on the TV Show *Aspel and Friends.*
Cliff attends a Crusader Rally.

FEBRUARY 26

Cliff is interviewed by DJ Richard Skinner. Cliff sings 'She's So Beautiful' on the *TV Times Awards Show.*

MARCH

Cliff's 97th single – 'Living Doll' (with the Young Ones) is released by EMI.

MARCH 1

Cliff attends Westminster Chapel, London.

MARCH 5

Appears on *Reporting London* for Thames TV.

MARCH 20

Cliff sends telegram to the newly opened Princess Alice Hospice in Esher, Surrey.

MARCH 22

Cliff appears on BBC TV's *Saturday Superstore* to talk about the Comic Relief single 'Living Doll'.

MARCH 25

Interviewed by David Wigg of the *Daily Express.*

MARCH 27

Previews for the musical *Time* at London's Dominion Theatre.

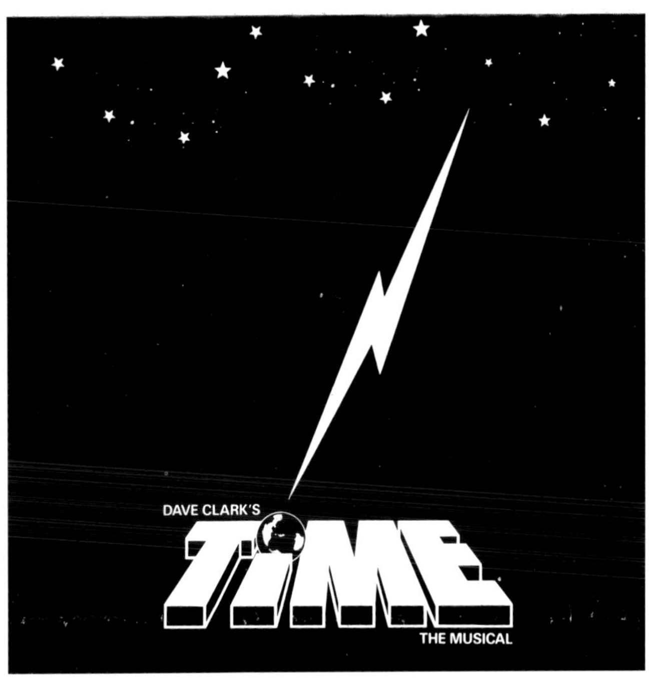

APRIL

SHAFTSBURY AVENUE, LONDON
Live recording for WEA

Living Doll — *Uterrly, Utterly Live*

Vocals: **Cliff Richard/Nigel Planer/Rik Mayall/Adrian Edmonson/Christopher Ryan**

APRIL

'Living Doll' becomes Cliff's 11th number one, nearly 27 years after it first topped the charts.

APRIL 1

Interviewed by BBC News, followed by a press launch for the Sport Aid appeal.

APRIL 7

Royal preview of *Time* at the Dominion Theatre, in the presence of the Duchess of Kent. Proceeds of the evening going to Cancer Research.

APRIL 9

Time opens at the Dominion with Cliff playing the part of Chris Wilder 'Rock Star'.

APRIL 19

Cliff presents the NVALA Award to Blue Peter at the BBC 'local' church,All Souls Church, Langham Place, W1, near the front door of Broadcasting House..

APRIL 20

Cliff and Bill Latham attend a Centenary service at St Pauls, Finchley.

APRIL 21

Interviewed for Australia's Channel 10 Programme.

APRIL 22

Interviewed with Dave Clark for *Good Morning America*, live on the American NBC network.
Interviewed by Gloria Hunniford for Radio Two and Kid Jensen for Capital Radio.

APRIL 23

Records an introduction for the Sport Aid video at Molinaire Studios, London.

APRIL 30

Opens a home for the mentally handicapped at Paddington.

MAY

'Born To Rock And Roll'/'Law Of The Universe' becomes Cliff's 98th single, and the third single to be released from the musical *Time*.

MAY 1

The video of 'Living Doll' is shown in Sweden on Oppen Rida.

MAY 2

Cliff and Bill Latham attend the funeral of Bill's mother Mamie at Leatherhead Crematorium.

MAY 10

'Living Doll' hits No.1 in Australia and spends several weeks at the top.

MAY 13

Interviewed by Piccadilly Radio.

MAY 15

Interviewed by Radio Leicester.

MAY 18

Attends All Souls Church, Langham Place, London, W1.

MAY 20

Cliff has pictures taken with potential young tennis stars at the Dominion Theatre to publicise his new project – 'Search For A Star'.

MAY 25

Cliff does a Sport Aid workout for two hours, between three and five in the afternoon.

MAY 27

Interviewed by BBC World Service.

MAY 28

Interviewed by Ian Robertson for Radio Hallam.

MAY 29

Makes a prize presentation for EMI Record Tokens.

JUNE 1

Attends Supper Party at ACG.

JUNE 8

Cliff hosts a party at his home for the entire cast of the Dave Clark musical *Time*.

JUNE 10

The 'Time' album is released in Australia.

JUNE 11

Interviewed by Mike Hughes for TV Radio Extra, Australia.

JUNE 12

Interviewed by Jane Noakes for BBC Radio Scotland.

JUNE 13

Cliff and David Bryce have a session listening to new songs at their office in Esher.

JUNE 14

Time producer Dave Clark denounced as 'Rubbish' the rumour that the musical is to be axed.

JUNE 20

Cliff presents the Pro-Celebrity Tennis Trophy at the Royal Albert Hall, after his performance in *Time*.

JUNE 24

Interviewed by Radio 2 W S in Sydney, Australia.

JUNE 26

Attends the matinee of David Essex's new musical *Mutiny*, based on the story *Mutiny On The Bounty*.

JUNE 27

Attends the tennis at Wimbledon.

JUNE 29

Attends a 'Christians In Sport' service at Mill Mead.

JUNE 30

Attends the tennis at Wimbledon.

JULY 2

Attends the tennis at Wimbledon.

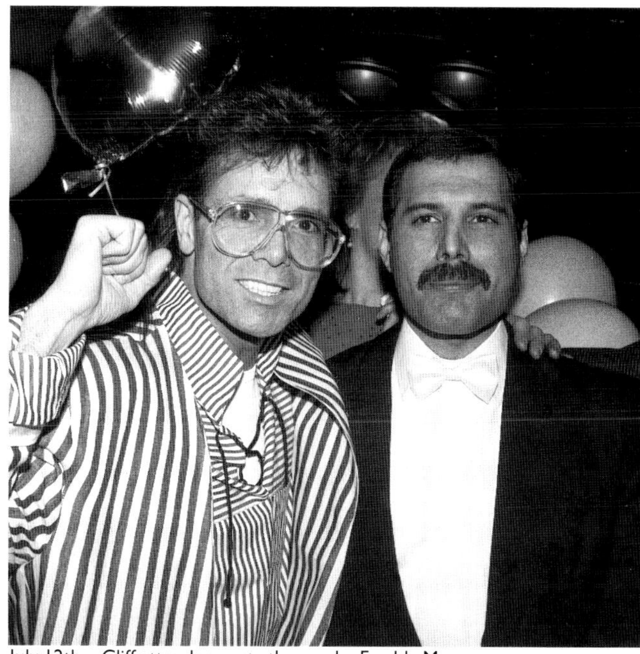

July 12th – Cliff attends a party thrown by Freddy Mercury

JULY 4

Interviewed by Marianne Collicutt for the local magazine *The Informer* and attends the tennis at Wimbledon.

JULY 6

Attends the tennis at Wimbledon.

JULY 7

Interviewed by 5 D M Sydney, Australia.

JULY 8

Cliff plays tennis at Wimbledon.

JULY 12

Attends party thrown by Queen's Freddie Mercury.

JULY 15

Interviewed by Simon Cummings for County Sound Radio, Guildford.

JULY 18

Attends Davis Cup tennis at Wimbledon.

JULY 28

Receives a Sport Aid cheque presentation from leading fan club member Janet Johnson.

JULY 29

Cliff dines with Cindy Kent, former singer with The Settlers, with whom he's performed many times in the past.

6 AUGUST

ABBEY ROAD
Studio session for Polydor

All I Ask Of You	*A-side*
Only You	*B-side*

Vocals:	**Cliff/Sarah Brightman**
Producer:	**Andrew Lloyd Webber**
Engineer:	
Recorded in:	**Studios 1 (basic track) and 3 (overdubs)**

AUGUST 11

Cliff dines with former Kajagoogoo bassist Nick Beggs.

AUGUST 19

Has photograph taken for a British Rail Promotion.

Cliff hands over *Time* to David Cassidy

AUGUST 25

Cliff's Golf GTI acquaplanes on the M4 as he's travelling from the David Lloyd Tennis Centre at Heston to perform at the Dominion – he escapes with a bruised leg and a sore back. Here is how the newspapers reported it:
Daily Express – 'Cliff's miracle crash escape'
Daily Mail – 'Cliff Richard's crash escape'
Star – 'Cliff Richard walks out of car wreck'
Daily Mirror – 'Cliff Richard in motorway pile-up'
Sun – 'Cliff Richard in miracle M4 car escape'

7 SEPTEMBER

Studio session

Live-in World	*A-side*

Vocals:	**Cliff Richard/ The Young Ones/ Robin Gibb/Holly Johnson/ Hazel O'Connor/Kim Wilde/Steve Harley**
Producer:	
Engineer:	
Session hours:	

13 OCTOBER-NOVEMBER

RG JONES
Studio session

One Night	*Always Guaranteed*
Once Upon A Time	*Always Guaranteed*
Some People	*A-side*
Forever	*Always Guaranteed*
Two Hearts	*Always Guaranteed*
Under Your Spell	*Always Guaranteed*
This Time Now	*Always Guaranteed*
My Pretty One	*A-side*
Remember Me	*A-side*
Always Guaranteed	*Always Guaranteed*

Lead Vocal:	**Cliff Richard**
Guitars/Bass/Keyboards/ Drum Programming:	**Alan Tarney**
Additional Keyboards:	**Chris Eaton (on Under Your Spell)**
Producer:	**Alan Tarney**
Engineers:	**Gerry Kitchingham/Ben Robbins**
Session hours:	

SEPTEMBER 2

Attends matinee of Andrew Lloyd Webber's musical *Cats*.

SEPTEMBER 22/23/24

Cliff is at Bisham Abbey with aspiring young tennis players on his 'Search For A Star' tennis project.

SEPTEMBER 25

Interviewed by New Zealand radio.
'All I Ask Of You' by Cliff and Sarah Brightman is released. The follow up to 'Phantom Of The Opera' – the title track from Andrew Lloyd Webber's new musical. The single, written by Andrew Lloyd Webber and Charles Hart, features The Royal Philharmonic Orchestra.

OCTOBER 2

Cliff pre-records an interview for TV-AM.

OCTOBER 10

Interviewed by Stan Rofe for 3 D B Melbourne.

OCTOBER 11

Appears on BBC TV's *Saturday Superstore*.

OCTOBER 14

Cliff's birthday.

OCTOBER 15

Interviewed by John Dunn for Radio Two, Sue Jamieson for LBC, Matthew Bannister and Paul Cook for Capital Radio.

OCTOBER 16

Interviewed for Canberra Radio, Australia.
Sir Laurence Olivier, represented in *Time* by a hologram, comes to see the show for the first time and receives a standing ovation.

OCTOBER 19

Records *Cliff From The Hip* television show from London's Hippodrome, where two numbers are recorded – 'Leather Jackets' by Elton John and 'Slow Rivers' by Elton and Cliff.

OCTOBER 23

Attends Thames TV 'Sports Personality of the Year' award.

OCTOBER 24

Interviewed by Bob Holness for LBC.

OCTOBER 28

Attends American Express Tennis Presentation at the Haymarket.

OCTOBER 29

Attends the launch of Mike Read's book – *The Cliff Richard File* – at the Italian Restaurant in London's Old Compton Street which used to be the 2 I's Coffee bar back in the late 50s/early 60s, where the likes of Cliff, Adam Faith and Tommy Steele began their careers. The restauranters kindly consented to it being turned back into the 2i's, complete with name over the door, for the launch.

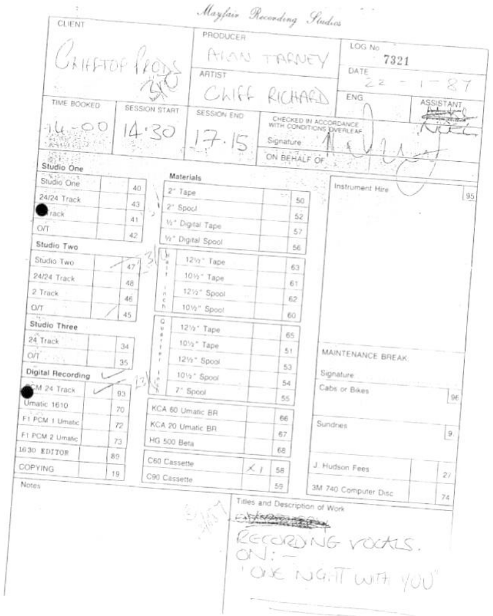
Mayfair Recording Studios
CLIENT: CHIEFTOP PRODS
PRODUCER: ALAN TARNEY
LOG No 7321
DATE 22-1-87
ARTIST: CLIFF RICHARD
TIME BOOKED 14-00 · SESSION START 14·30 · SESSION END 17.15
Titles and Description of Work: RECORDING VOCALS. ON:– 'ONE NIGHT WITH YOU'

NOVEMBER 16

Cliff records the television special *Cliff From The Hip* at the London Hippodrome. Originally planned to be filmed without an audience, it also features Marti Webb, Billy Ocean, Five Star and the Shadows, as well as the pre-recording of Elton John. In the end there is an audience, comprising mainly members of Cliff's fan club.

NOVEMBER 27

Attends the Westminster City Council's Anti-Drugs Lunch at the Rock Garden, where he signs a 'Say No To Drugs Plaque' along with Rolling Stone Bill Wyman, Julian Lennon, Hazel O'Connor, John Entwhistle of the Who, Dire Straits and Sheila Ferguson from the Three Degrees. Afterwards he lunches with the Princess of Wales, who also attends.

DECEMBER 3

Records Breakfast Time TV from the Dominion.

DECEMBER 8

Opens the Tear Fund Christmas Sale at St Peters Church, Vere Street, London – which sells work from the Third World countries Thailand, Haiti, India and Bangladesh.

DECEMBER 10

Records for Noel Edmonds TV Show.

DECEMBER 13

Cliff meets the winners of the 'Beautiful Britain Christmas Cards' competition.

DECEMBER 14

Records for the ACG Carol Concert for BBC Radio Two, to be transmitted over the Christmas period, along with Roy Castle, Dana, Alvin Stardust and the London Community Gospel Choir at Wembley Conference Centre.

DECEMBER

HMV and Virgin stores stock The Young Ones jigsaw puzzles (stills from the video) at £3.99.

DECEMBER 21

Cliff's annual Pro-Celebrity Tennis Tournament at the Brighton Conference centre includes Peter Cook, Ronnie Corbett and Hank Marvin.

DECEMBER 29

Attends a party for the cast of *Time* at the Dominion.

JANUARY 12

Cliff attends the birthday party of actor Anthony Andrews.

JANUARY 16

Cliff records 'Jim'll Fix It' at the Dominion.

JANUARY 19

Cliff appears on 'Wogan' in the costume he wears as Chris Wilderin *Time*, complete with hair extensions.

FEBRUARY 4

Records for BBC Radio 2's *Good Morning Sunday* show with Roger Royle at the Dominion.

FEBRUARY 5

Cliff views a house in Abinger Hammer, Surrey with a possible view to buying.

FEBRUARY 6

Interviewed for *Jam* Magazine.

FEBRUARY 12

Cliff views a property in Pyrford, Surrey.

FEBRUARY 18

Cliff attends the matinee of *Phantom Of The Opera.*

MARCH 4

Cliff presents awards to the Metropolitan Police competition winners, the event being covered by Thames News.

MARCH 6

Re-views the house in Pyrford, Surrey.
Interviewed by TV-AM and Swansea Sound at the Dominion.

MARCH 18

Interviewed by the Radio Academy.

MARCH 25

Interviewed for TV's *Breakfast Time* with former Partridge Family singer David Cassidy, who is to take over Cliff's role in *Time* when he leaves.

MARCH 26

Shoots 'Crusader' video for Greenleaf.

MARCH 28

Attends photocall at the Dominion with David Cassidy.

MARCH 31

Attends reception for Rank at Atheneum.

APRIL 6

Interviewed about Elvis Presley by BBC TV and interviewed with David Cassidy for Thames News.

APRIL 10

Presents Butlins Prize Presentation at the Dominion.

APRIL 13

David Cassidy takes over Cliff's role of Chris Wilder in *Time*.

APRIL 22

Cliff goes on holiday.

APRIL 29

Returns home from holiday.

APRIL

STUDIO UNKNOWN

Studio sessions

Love Ya	*B-side*
Under The Gun	*B-side*
One Time Lover Man	*B-side*
Another Christmas Day	*B-side*
Yesterday, Today Forever	*B-side*
Wild Geese	*B-side*
Reunion Of The Heart	*B-side*

Lead Vocal: **Cliff Richard**
Producer:
Engineer:
Session hours:

APRIL 30

Holds press launch of his Pro-Celebrity Tennis Sponsorship at the Pinafore Room, Savoy Hotel, London.

MAY 1

Undertakes a two-hour sitting for Madame Tussauds. Attends 'Power For Living' dinner at the Berkeley Hotel, London.

MAY 7

Video for nex single 'My Pretty One' shot at Albert Wharf, London, SW11.

MAY 9

Presents Art Group prizes locally, at Hersham Village Hall.

MAY 10

Flies to Portugal.

MAY 28

Returns to Britain.

MAY 31

Starts tour rehearsals at Wimbledon Theatre and attends Laurence Olivier's birthday celebration at the National Theatre.

JUNE 2

Interviewed by Just 17, Capital Radio and Syndicated Radio.

JUNE 3

Interviewed by *The Sun* and by Steve Jones for LBC.

JUNE 4

Interviewed by *Smash Hits magazine.*

JUNE 5

Interviewed by Radio 4 at Wimbledon Theatre and by Piers Morgan for the *South London News.*

'BEYOND TIME' – UK GOSPEL TOUR

JUNE 9
Newcastle.

JUNE 10/11/12/13
Edinburgh.

JUNE 16/17
Brighton.

JUNE 19/20
Wembley.

JUNE 25/26/27
National Exhibition Centre, Birmingham

Songs featured on the tour:
'I'm Alive'/'She's So Beautiful'/'Such Is The Mystery'/'Under The Gun'/'Money'/'Mr Businessman'/'All I Want'/'A World Of Difference'/'All By Myself'/'Little Town'/'Another Christmas Day'/'Yesterday, Today, Forever'/'His Love Covers Our Sins'/'Wild Geese'/'When I Survey The Wondrous Cross'/'Yes He Lives'/'Where Do We Go From Here'/'Reunion Of The Heart'/'I Will Follow You'/'My Pretty One'/'Walking In The Light'/'It's In Every One Of Us'/'Where You Are'/'I Wish We'd All Been Ready'/'Brave New World'/'Share A Dream'

JUNE 8

Cliff's next single – 'My Pretty One' is released with 'Love Ya' on the 'B' side, and a third track 'Under The Gun' appearing on the 12"version.

Cliff performs a concert at the Wimbledon Theatre, prior to his Gospel Tour – the proceeds of the evening going to the Cliff Richard Charitable Trust, with the monies then being divided 50% to the Tear Fund, and 50% distributed to other British charities.

JUNE 9

Records the *Roxy* TV Show in Newcastle.

JUNE 13

Cliff presents the awards to the winners of the'Search For A Star' project which he promoted.

JUNE 14

Dines at Alton Towers, Stoke on Trent, prior to taking part in the *It's A Royal Knockout* television special, organised by Prince Edward, on the following day.

JUNE 15

Participates in *It's A Royal Knockout* with Prince Edward, the Duchess of York and a host of other celebrities.

JUNE 17

Interviewed by *London Daily News* and by TV-AM.

Views another house in St Georges Hill, Weybridge.

JUNE 20

Records 'It's Wicked' TV Show from Hyde Park.

JUNE 22

Appears on 'Wogan', hosted by Sue Lawley.

JUNE 23

Appears on TV's *Get Fresh* from Carlisle.

JUNE 24

Pre-records *Top Of The Pops*, singing Alan Tarney's 'My Pretty One'.

JUNE 25

Records for BBC TV's *Midlands Today* at the National Exhibition Centre, Birmingham.

JUNE 30

Presents awards for Readers Digest.

JULY 3

Records for *The Edna Everage TV Show*.

JULY 5

Attends the tennis finals at Wimbledon.

JULY 7

Sings 'Some People' for *Hold Tight* Television show from the Alton Towers theme park.

JULY 8

Flies to Berlin to appear on German television.

JULY 9

Sings 'My Pretty One' on German television.

JULY 10

Flies to Dusseldorf.

JULY 12

Attends ACG Supper Party.

JULY 18

Attends a reunion of the cast of *Summer Holiday* at London's Churchill Hotel.

JULY 20

Appears on a local show from a school nearby his home, St Maur's Convent.

JULY 22

Television rehearsals in Germany for the *Wunsch Konzert* programme.

JULY 23

Sings 'My Pretty One' live on *Wunsch Konzert.*

JULY 26

Cliff performs three songs on Television South's *Summertime Special* from Bournemouth – 'Summer Holiday'/'Some People' and 'My Pretty One'.

JULY 30

Interviewed by Australian Radio.

JULY 31-AUGUST 15

Holiday in Brindisi.

AUGUST 1

Summertime Special is transmitted.

AUGUST 17

Cliff's new single – 'Some People' is released with 'One Time Lover Man' on the 'B' side and 'Reunion Of The Heart' on the 12" version.

AUGUST 17-23

Cliff moves house.

AUGUST 24

Undertakes photosession at London's Garrick Theatre.

AUGUST 25

Appears on TV show *The Roxy* from Newcastle.

AUGUST 27

Launches his new album from the boat 'The Hispanola' moored at Victoria Embankment.

SEPTEMBER 1-2

Performs on German television.

SEPTEMBER 2

Flies back to the UK.

SEPTEMBER 3

Interviewed by Radio One and by John Sachs for London's Capital Radio.
Pre-records *Top Of The Pops*, singing 'Some People'.

SEPTEMBER 4

Departs for Germany.

SEPTEMBER 5

Sings on German television and is interviewed by the press for a UNICEF Gala.

SEPTEMBER 6

Returns from Germany.

SEPTEMBER 7

Attends EMI World Conference at Brighton.

SEPTEMBER 9

Sings on Norwegian TV in Oslo.

SEPTEMBER 10

Interviewed by Norwegian radio.
Departs for Copenhagen and undertakes various interviews with the Danish media.

SEPTEMBER 12

Performs on Danish TV in Copenhagen.

SEPTEMBER 13

Returns from Copenhagen.

SEPTEMBER 14

Cliff's new album – 'Always Guaranteed' – is released.

SEPTEMBER 15

Shoots the video for his next single 'Remember Me'.

SEPTEMBER 16

Pre-records 'Remember Me' for the next edition of *Top Of The Pops* – as he is going to be out of the country on a European Tour when it is broadcast.

SEPTEMBER 17

Cliff pre-records an interview for the *Sunday, Sunday* television programme with the show's presenter and interviewer Gloria Hunniford.

SEPTEMBER 18

Pre-records *This Is Your Life* message.

SEPTEMBER 24-28

Wimbledon show.

SEPTEMBER 29

Flies to Holland.

SEPTEMBER 30

Interviewed by Dutch press and television.

OCTOBER 4

Cliff sends a telegram to the Shadows, wishing them luck for the opening date of their tour at Caesar's Palace, Luton.

OCTOBER 14

Cliff performs live on a German Television programme in Baden Baden.

OCTOBER 16

Sings live on *Rockline* from Cologne.

OCTOBER 19

Cliff's new single – 'Remember Me' is released, with 'Another Christmas Day' on the 'B' side and 'Brave New World' appearing as a bonus track on the 12"version.

NOVEMBER 11-12

Flies to the UK then back to Europe.

DECEMBER 3

Flies back to the UK.

DECEMBER 7

Attends EMI Dinner.

DECEMBER 18

Attends the ACG's Christmas Celebration Service at All Souls Church, Langham Place, London.

DECEMBER 19

Cliff's annual Pro-Celebrity Tennis Tournament is held at Brighton's Conference Centre.
Taking part with Cliff are footballer Emlyn Hughes, singer Elton John, comedian Mike Yarwood, and tennis stars Annabel Croft, Sara Gomer,.Sue Barker, and Virginia Wade.

DECEMBER 30

Cliff records a contribution for the annual BBC Variety Club Awards ceremony.

ALWAYS GUARANTEED TOUR

OCTOBER 1
Berlin

OCTOBER 2
Stadthalle, Wolfsburg

OCTOBER 4/5
CCH, Hamburg

OCTOBER 6
Kuppelsaal, Hanover

OCTOBER 8
Stadthalle, Bremen

OCTOBER 9
Grugahalle, Essen

OCTOBER 10
Forest National, Brussels

OCTOBER 12-13
De Doelen, Rotterdam

OCTOBER 15
Halle Munsterland, Munster

OCTOBER 17
Sporthalle, Cologne

OCTOBER 18
Mozartsaal, Mannheim

OCTOBER 19
Stadthalle, Karlsruhe

OCTOBER 20
Saarlandhalle, Saarbrucken

OCTOBER 22
Siegerlandhalle, Siegen

OCTOBER 24
Festhalle, Frankfurt

OCTOBER 25
Hallen Stadion, Zurich

OCTOBER 26
Stadthalle, Freiburg

OCTOBER 28
Oberschwabenhalle, Ravensburg

OCTOBER 29-30
Deutsches Museum, Munich

OCTOBER 31
Stadthalle, Vienna

NOVEMBER 2-3
Hall Spodek, Katowice

NOVEMBER 4-6
Sporthall, Budapest

NOVEMBER 8
Hala Tivoli, Ljubliana

NOVEMBER 9
Dom Sportova, Zagreb

NOVEMBER 10
Hala Pionir, Belgrade

NOVEMBER 13
Carl Diem Hall, Wurzburg.

NOVEMBER 14
Eissporthalle, Kassel.

NOVEMBER 15
Stadthalle, Osnabruck.

NOVEMBER 18
Grieghall, Bergen.

NOVEMBER 19
Drammens Hall, Oslo

NOVEMBER 20
Liseberg Hall, Gothenburg.

NOVEMBER 21
Solna Hall, Stockholm.

NOVEMBER 23
Ice Hall, Helsinki.

NOVEMBER 25-26
Valby Hall, Copenhagen.

NOVEMBER 27
Aalborg Hall, Aalborg.

NOVEMBER 28
Skive Hall, Skive.

NOVEMBER 30
Herning Hall, Herning.

DECEMBER 1-2
Vejlby Risskov Hall, Aarhus.

DECEMBER 8-12
National Exhibition Centre, Birmingham.

Songs featured on the tour:
'I'm Alive'/'We Don't Talk Anymore'/'Daddy's Home'/'All The Time You Need'/'Money'/'Mr Businessman'/'Devil Woman'/'All By Myself'/'Wouldn't You Know It (Got Myself A Girl)'/'Spanish Harlem'/'Living Doll'/'The Young Ones'/'Move It'/'Lucky Lips'/'One Night'/'Under Your Spell'/'This Time Now'/'Always Guaranteed'/'Two Hearts'/'Some People'/'Forever'/'My Pretty One'/'Remember Me'/'Miss You Nights'/'UFO Thief In The Night'/'I Wish We'd All Been Ready'/'Share A Dream'/'Little Town'

The Band:
Guitars: John Clark/Steve Lauri
Bass: Mark Griffiths
Drums: Adrian Sheppard
Keyboards: Paul Moessl/Alan Park
Vocals: Rosemarie Ford/Mick Mullins/Peter Howarth

1988–1990

The Records 1988 – 1990

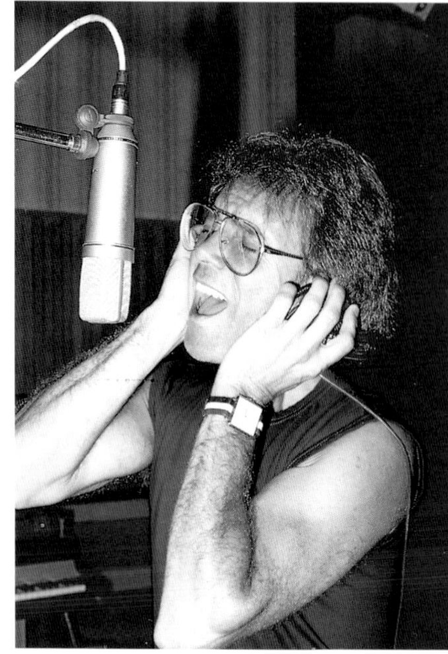

This was to become one of Cliff's most successful periods. Of the two singles released in 1988, 'Mistletoe And Wine' became a massive Christmas hit and the biggest selling single of that year, staying at the No.1 spot over the festive season. The follow-up single was the beautiful ballad 'The Best Of Me', making Cliff the first British artist to release 100 singles and it occupied the No.2 spot on the singles chart in the spring of 1989. The third top three single in a row was with 'I Just Don't Have The Heart' produced by hit-makers Stock, Aitken and Waterman. However, it should be noted that the correct title should have been 'Just Don't Have The Heart', but has always appeared on labels and sleeves as 'I Just Don't Have The Heart.' Although neither of the last two singles of the year were big hits they still managed to achieve top twenty positions. Given the quality and excellent choice of singles released in 1990, it seems incredible that 'Silhouettes' and 'From A Distance' didn't reach any higher on the charts than the No.10 and 11 positions respectively. Of course the Christmas single 'Saviour's Day' was the biggest seller of the year, repeating the success of 'Mistletoe And Wine' by reaching the No.1 spot, although this time only remaining at the top for one week.

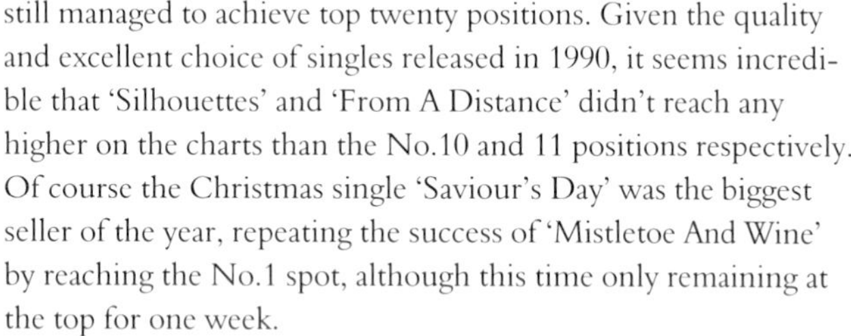

Sales of the albums during this period reached the level of the singles. PRIVATE COLLECTION featured the very best recordings from 1979-1988, occupying the No.1 spot on the album chart as Cliff's 30th year ended. Although the next one, STRONGER, was released to jubilant reviews, perhaps it lost out somewhat to the fact that four hit singles were culled from the album. Of course, the FROM A DISTANCE – THE EVENT double album resulted in exceptional sales figures largely due to the memento aspect of Cliff's two great evenings at Wembley Stadium – not only for those who were there, but for those who weren't and realised what they had missed.

The Sessions 1988 – 1990

The June 1988 sessions at RG Jones were set up to record the 'Mistletoe And Wine' Christmas single with two days of additional recording held in July. These sessions introduced Paul Moessl as Cliff's musical director. A third series of sessions was held in August to produce a new B-side and the first material for the STRONGER album. 'Share A Dream' featured Aswad playing all the instruments and providing backing vocals as well as producing the track.

Cliff's vocal for 'I Just Don't Have The Heart', the dance track produced by Stock, Aitken and Waterman, was done at the PWL Studio on 8 and 9 February, after the backing track had been recorded during the previous two weeks, although mixing and remixing sessions continued through to August when backing vocals and additional accompaniment were possibly added to the basic rhythm track. A definite disadvantage of this procedure was Cliff's absence when this work was done, but final mixes would be submitted to Cliff for his approval. It is interesting to note that this track was given the working titles of 'Harry' and 'Harry II'. In all probability, the two titles were used to identify differences to the backing track. During a session on 5 February at Black Barn Studios in Ripley, Cliff provided vocal harmonies to the charity recording of 'Everybody's Got A Crisis In Their Life' proceeds of which were donated to the Leukaemia Research Fund at Great Ormond Street Children's Hospital and the Queen Elizabeth Hospital For Children. Produced by Jim Cozens and David Croft, the record which featured contributions from other artists never found distribution by a major label. Sessions running through February and March at RG Jones were taken up with more and final work for the STRONGER album. As had happened with ALWAYS GUARANTEED, Alan Tarney was responsible for most of the instumental work with Cliff's live band appearing on only four of the tracks. The repertoire still represented good quality material, making the results of these sessions outstanding. Recordings like 'Stronger Than That', 'The Best Of Me', 'Lean On You' and 'Joanna', though perhaps not being sensational, still made great music.

The Stones Mobile Recording Unit was installed in the grounds at Wembley Stadium to record the 'Event' concerts on 16 and 17 June. Engineered by Mick McKenna and Keith Bessey both shows were taped in their entirety providing an enormous amount of material to select from for the FROM A DISTANCE – THE EVENT album. In this respect, some crucial decisions had to be made on the tracks to include and those to omit. For the five and a half hour shows, Cliff worked with the original *Oh Boy!* team of the Dallas Boys and the Vernons Girls; was reunited with the Shadows; duetted with Aswad and the Kalin Twins; and rocked with Jet Harris and Tony Meehan on 'Move It'; as well as being backed by his regular live band on his own set. The mixing of the tracks for the album took place at RG Jones Studios, Sarm West and PWL.

The next studio sessions took place in December with Cliff visiting the PWL studios again, this time to take part in the recording of 'Do They Know It's Christmas' for Band Aid II, a

project designed to raise money for famine in Ethiopia. The track, produced by Stock, Aitken and Waterman, was taped over two days on the 3rd and 4th with Cliff and various other artists contributing vocals.

More live recordings were done in June 1990 at the concert in aid of the Nordoff-Robbins Music Therapy Centre. Cliff was again reunited with the Shadows for a 45-minute set and, although broadcast live in its entirety on Radio One, only 'On The Beach' and 'Do You Wanna Dance' were used on KNEBWORTH – THE ALBUM. There was no time for repair work to be done as it was planned to have the album in the shops right on the heels of all the media hullabaloo.

A series of remixes of 'We Don't Talk Anymore' was carried out in July and August by Ian Curnow and Phil Harding at the PWL Studios. Several different versions were produced including a 7", 12" and a master mix as well as a PA version, which is likely to have been the one used during the 'From A Distance' tour. It is unknown to what extent Cliff was involved with the remixing and, as a number of remixes were completed, it is difficult to identify with any certainty which mixes have been released. Cliff returned to RG Jones for his only other studio sessions for 1990. These provided a new B-side for 'From A Distance' and the song Cliff had selected for his Christmas single. 'Saviour's Day' was laid down in three days during July with guitar overdubs by John Clarke being added on the 20th and vocal backings on the 21st. With Cliff taking care of production, final mixing of the tracks was done over two days assisted by Gerry Kitchingham, Paul Moessl and Ben Robbins.

JANUARY 4

Cliff departs for Australia.

JANUARY 6

Arrives in Sydney.

JANUARY 9

Flies from Sydney to Melbourne.

JANUARY 10

Cliff participates in Paul McNamee's celebrity Charity Tennis Tournament.

JANUARY 17

Attends the Gospel Music festival in Melbourne.

JANUARY 18

Flies from Melbourne to Sydney.

JANUARY 25

Participates in the Bicentennial TV Gala in Sydney.

JANUARY 28

Conducts a press day in Auckland.

JANUARY 29-FEBRUARY 1

Rehearses for the tour at the Logan Campbell Centre, Auckland, New Zealand.

FEBRUARY 1

Cliff's new single – 'Two Hearts' is released with 'Yesterday, Today, Forever' on the 'B' side and 'Wild Geese' being the bonus 12" track.

FEBRUARY 15

Conducts Press Day in Sydney, then flies to Perth.

MARCH 26

Flies from Australia.

MARCH 27

Arrives in the UK.

APRIL 7

Cliff attends the Ivor Novello Awards.

APRIL 13

Cliff is interviewed by Michael Parkinson for a Yorkshire Television programme.

APRIL 14

Attends a benefit evening for the musical *Time.*

APRIL 19

Flies to Israel.

ALWAYS GUARANTEED WORLD TOUR
NEW ZEALAND/AUSTRALIA

FEBRUARY 2/3/4
Logan Campbell Centre, Auckland.

FEBRUARY 6/7/8/9
Michael Fowler Centre, Wellington.

FEBRUARY 10
Town Hall, Christchurch.

FEBRUARY 11
Town Hall, Christchurch.

FEBRUARY 12/13/14
Town Hall, Christchurch.

FEBRUARY 16/17
Entertainment Centre, Perth.

FEBRUARY 20/21/22/23
Apollo Stadium, Adelaide.

FEBRUARY 26/27
Entertainment Centre, Brisbane.

MARCH 1/2
Entertainment Centre, Sydney.

MARCH 5
Velodrome, Launceston.

MARCH 6
KGV Stadium, Hobart.

MARCH 9/10/11
Entertainment Centre, Melbourne.

MARCH 12
Bruce Stadium, Canberra.

MARCH 13
Bruce Stadium, Canberra.

MARCH 17
Dean Park, Townsville.

MARCH 19
Amphitheatre, Darwin.

APRIL 22

Flies from Israel to Portugal.

APRIL 30

Returns from Portugal.

MAY 3

Interviewed by the Norwegian Press.

MAY 3-5

Rehearses at the Gallery.

MAY 7

Flies to Oslo for press and television interviews.

MAY 23

Flies to the UK.

JUNE 1

Cliff opens a new channel at County Sound Radio, and then hosts a Cliff Fun Day at Beckenham Tennis Centre.

JUNE 2

Cliff sings 'When I Survey The Wondrous Cross' for a BBC Schools television programme from Ealing.

6-10 JUNE and 12-13 JULY

RG JONES
Studio sessions

Mistletoe And Wine *A-side*

Lead Vocal: **Cliff Richard**
Keyboards/Synths/Drum Programming: **Paul Moessl**
Bass: **Mark Griffiths**
Strings arranged and conducted by: **Paul Moessl/Jack Rothstein**
Horns arranged by: **Barry Castle**
Backing Vocals: **Peter Howarth/Mick Mullins/ Keith Murrell/Sonia Morgan**

Producer: **Cliff Richard**
Engineer: **Gerry Kitchingham/Ben Robbins**
Session hours:

Strings were probably overdubbed during the July sessions.

JUNE 13

Royal Charity Tennis.

JUNE 14

Flies to Madrid.

ALWAYS GUARANTEED WORLD TOUR
EUROPE

MAY 8
Skedsmo Hall, Oslo.

MAY 9
Valby Hall, Copenhagen.

MAY 10
Fyns Forum, Odense.

MAY 11/12
Sporthalle, Cologne.

MAY 13
Ahoy, Rotterdam.

MAY 14
Eberthalle, Ludwigshafen.

MAY 15
Schleyerhalle, Stuttgart.

MAY 16
Frankenhalle, Nurenburg.

MAY 17
Philipshalle, Dusseldorf.

MAY 18
CCH, Hamburg.

MAY 21
Ostseehalle, Kiel.

MAY 22
Fyns Forum, Odense

Songs featured on the tour:
'Born To Rock And Roll'/'A Little In Love'/'Daddy's Home'/'All The Time You Need'/'Marmaduke'/'Under The Gun'/'Devil Woman'/'All By Myself'/'Living Doll'/'The Young Ones'/'Spanish Harlem'/'Lucky Lips'/'Move It'/'Summer Holiday'/'I Could Easily Fall'/'In The Country'/'Visions'/'Always Guaranteed'/'My Pretty One'/'Two Hearts'/'Some People'/'Remember Me'/'Miss You Nights'/'UFO'/'Thief In The Night'/'I Wish We'd All Been Ready'/'Share A Dream'/'We Don't Talk Anymore'/'Wired For Sound'

The Band:
Guitars: John Clark/Steve Lauri
Bass: Mark Griffiths
Drums: Peter May

Cliff scores again with another gold disc

JUNE 15

Records for Spanish TV programme *S'Abado Noche*. Returns to the UK.

JUNE 22

Flies to Copenhagen.

JUNE 23

Performs on Copenhagen TV Special. Returns to Britain on the same day.

JUNE 28

Interviewed by Mike Read for Singapore Airlines programme.

JULY 2

Attends Semi-finals day at Wimbledon.

JULY 5

Attends a press launch and conference at the National Exhibition Centre, Birmingham.

JULY 6

Interviewed for *Woman* magazine.

JULY 15

Participates in a video cameo for 'On The Beach' at home.

JULY 25

Undertakes a photo session for his new album.

JULY 28

Films a TV advertisement for his new album.

JULY 31-AUGUST 20

Cliff goes to Portugal for a holiday.

AUGUST

RG JONES
Studio session

All The Time You Need — *B-side*
Marmaduke — *B-side*

Lead Vocal: **Cliff Richard**
Guitars: **John Clark/Steve Laurie**
Bass: **Mark Griffiths**
Drums: **Henry Spinetti**
Piano: **Alan Park**
Synths: **Paul Moessl**
Vocals: **Mick Mullins/Peter Howarth/Keith Murrell**

Producer: **Cliff Richard**
Engineer: **Gerry Kitchingham/Ben Robbins**
Session hours;

AUGUST 18

Publication of 'Single-Minded'.

AUGUST 22

Interviewed for UK Radio Stations:
Clyde, Red Dragon, Forth, Downtown, BRMB, Piccadilly, Radio City, Hallam, Southern Sound, Metro and a BBC Special.

AUGUST 23

Interviewed by Anne Robinson for Radio Two, by Radio Radio, Jeff Graham for Radio Luxembourg and Mark Smith for LBC.

29-31 AUGUST

BATTERY STUDIOS
Studios sessions

Share A Dream	*Stronger*
Lead Vocal:	**Cliff Richard**
All instruments and backing Vocals:	**Aswad**
Producer:	**Aswad**
Engineer:	**Godwin Logie**
Recorded in:	**'The Lighthouse' Studio**

A family snapshot, Cliff with his mother and sister

SEPTEMBER 1

Interviewed by *Sunday Express Magazine.* Dines with the group Aswad.

SEPTEMBER 2

Book signing at Selfridges Store, then Bentalls in Kingston.

SEPTEMBER 5

Attends EMI's Regional Press Day.

SEPTEMBER 6

Attends European Press Day at the Theatre Royal.

SEPTEMBER 7

Rehearses for his new video at Albert Wharf Studios in Battersea.

SEPTEMBER 8

Shoots video.

SEPTEMBER 9-23

Rehearses for tour at Pinewood Studios.

SEPTEMBER 22

Cliff presents 'Search For A Star' tennis awards at Bisham Abbey.

NOVEMBER 1

Records a TV Special with Terry Wogan.

NOVEMBER 16

Terry Wogan's TV Show transmitted.

NOVEMBER 21

Cliff sings two songs at the Royal Command Performance.

CLIFF RICHARD – 30TH ANNIVERSARY TOUR

SEPTEMBER 25/26/27
R.D.S., Dublin.

SEPTEMBER 29/30/OCTOBER 1
King's Hall, Belfast.

OCTOBER 4
Hammersmith Odeon, London.

OCTOBER 5/6/7/8
Hammersmith Odeon, London.

OCTOBER 11/12/13/14
City Hall, Sheffield.

OCTOBER 19/20/21/22
Playhouse, Edinburgh.

OCTOBER 26/27/28/29
Apollo, Manchester.

NOVEMBER 2/3/4/5
Newport Centre, Newport.

NOVEMBER 9/10/11/12
Coliseum, St Austell.

NOVEMBER 16/17/18/19
International Centre, Bournemouth

NOVEMBER 23/24/25/26
Empire, Liverpool.

NOVEMBER 30/DECEMBER 1/2/3
Conference Centre, Brighton.

DECEMBER 7/8/9/10
National Exhibition Centre, Birmingham.

Songs featured on the tour:
'Born To Rock And Roll'/'Move It'/'Daddy's Home'/'All The Time You Need'/'Devil Woman'/'All By Myself'/'We Don't Talk Anymore'/'Another Tear Falls'/'Some People'/'Marmaduke'/'Under The Gun'/'Ocean Deep'/'Living Doll'/'The Young Ones'/'Bachelor Boy'/'In The Country'/'Visions'/'All Shook Up'/'The Minute You're Gone'/'I Wish You'd Change Your Mind'/'Carrie'/'True Love Ways'/'My Pretty One'/'Miss You Nights'/'Thief In The Night'/'UFO'/'Get It Right Next Time'/'Blue Suede Shoes'/'Great Balls Of Fire'/'Lucille'/'Long Tall Sally'/'Rip It Up'/'It'll Be Me'/'Mistletoe And Wine'

The Band:
Guitars: John Clark/Steve Lauri
Bass: Mark Griffiths
Drums: Henry Spinetti
Keyboards: Paul Moessl/Alan Park
Vocals: Mick Mullins/Peter Howarth/Keith Murrell

NOVEMBER 25

Cliff opens a new indoor tennis centre at Warrington.

NOVEMBER 27

Cliff records the *Jimmy Tarbuck Show* and performs 'Mistletoe And Wine'.

NOVEMBER 28

Cliff's new single – 'Mistletoe And Wine' is released, with 'Marmaduke' on the 'B' side and 'Little Town' being the bonus track on the 12".

DECEMBER 6

Pre-records 'Mistletoe And Wine' for *Top Of The Pops* and the Des O'Connor Show.

DECEMBER 10

'Mistletoe And Wine' goes to Number One in the singles chart.

DECEMBER 13

Appears at the Hammersmith Odeon for G.O.S.H.(Great Ormond Street Hospital)

DECEMBER 16

Attends the ACG Christmas Celebrations at All Souls Church, Langham Place, London.

DECEMBER 17

Cliff's Pro-Celebrity Tennis Tournament at Brighton Conference Centre, with Anne Hobbs, Aled Jones, Jo Durie, Jimmy Tarbuck, Annabel Croft, Mike Read and Virginia Wade.

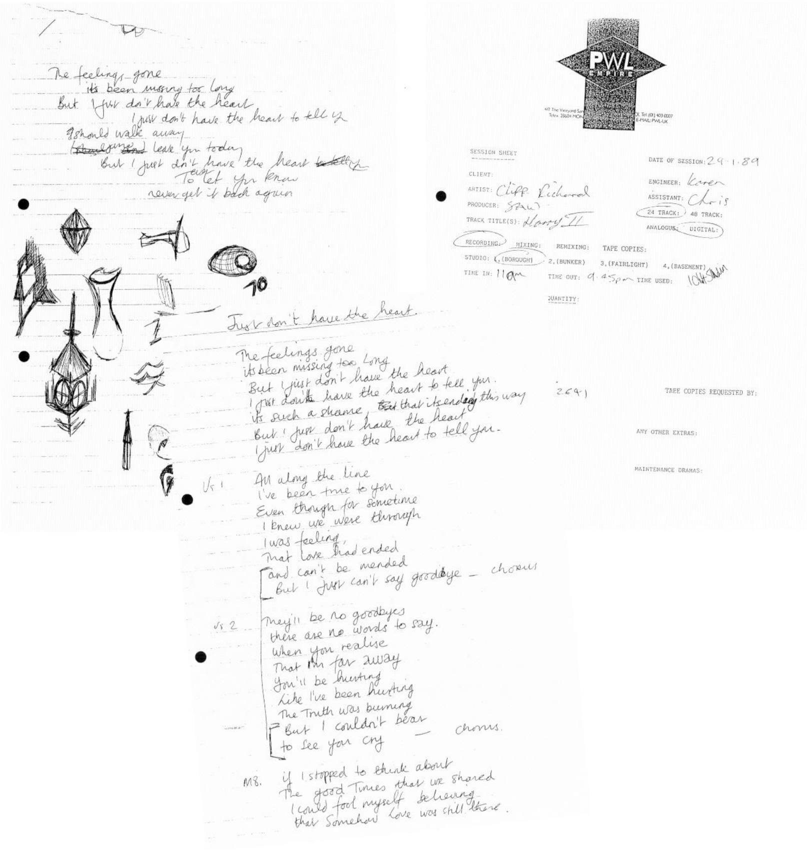

DECEMBER 20

Performs in the 'Save The Children' concert at London's Royal Albert Hall.

DECEMBER 27

Flies to Perth in Australia.

DECEMBER 27-JANUARY 5

Cliff sees in the New Year in Perth.

JANUARY 6

Cliff flies to Sydney.

JANUARY 11

Attends Tear Fund meeting in Sydney.

JANUARY 12

Cliff flies to Melbourne.

JANUARY 13

Attends Arts Group meeting in Melbourne.

JANUARY 14

Attends Tear Fund meeting in Melbourne.

JANUARY 15

Cliff plays in pro-celebrity tennis tournament in Melbourne.

JANUARY 19

Cliff flies to New Zealand.

JANUARY 20

Cliff dines with executives.of EMI Records' New Zealand division.

JANUARY 21

Attends Tear Fund meeting in Auckland.

JANUARY 22

Attends Tear Fund meeting in Wellington.

JANUARY 23

Cliff flies to Singapore.

JANUARY 27

Leaves Singapore and flies to Britain.

JANUARY 28

Arrives in Britain.

2 FEBRUARY

UNKNOWN LOCATION

Live recording

Burn On	*The Kendrick Collection*
Fighter	*The Kendrick Collection*
Shine Jesus Shine	*The Kendrick Collection*

Vocals: **Cliff Richard**
The All Souls Orchestra

Producer: **Burt Rhodes**
Engineer: **Graham McHutchon**

20 JANUARY-7 FEBRUARY

PWL STUDIOS

Studio session

Harry (working title of Just Don't Have The Heart) — *A-side*

Keyboards: **Mike Stock/Matt Aitken**
Drums: **A. Linn**

Producer: **Stock/Aitken/Waterman**
Engineers: **Karen Hewitt/Yoyo**
Recorded in: **Studios 1 (Borough) and 2 (The Bunker)**

5 FEBRUARY

BLACK BARN STUDIOS, RIPLEY
Studio sessions

Everybody's Got A Crises In Their Life *A-side*

Keyboards: **Rick Wakeman/Mike Smith**
Bass: **John Wetton**
Acoustic Guitars: **Justin Hayward/Jim Cozens**
Electric Guitar: **David Croft**
Lead Vocal: **Simon Cummings**
Vocal Harmonies: **Cliff Richard**
Backing Vocals: **Alvin Stardust/Ann Bryson/Justin Hayward/ Ian Herron/Adam Fenton/Tank James/ Marietta Parfitt/Mike Smith/Diane Solomon/ Stephanie De Sykes/Carl Wayne/JohnWetton/ Joanne Zorian/Jill Croft/Julie Morgan**

Producers: **Jim Cozens/David Croft**
Engineer: **Robin Black**
Assistant Engineer: **Matthew Oliver**
Session hours:

FEBRUARY 6

Interviewed by Italian television.

FEBRUARY 7

Cliff hosts photocall for the press at Wembley Stadium and meets with producers Stock, Aitken and Waterman.

FEBRUARY 8

Cliff and the Shadows attend a music therapy tribute lunch.

8/9 FEBRUARY

PWL STUDIOS
Studio session

Harry
(working title of Just Don't Have The Heart) *A-side*

Lead Vocals: **Cliff Richard**
Vocals: **Mae McKenna/Miriam Stockley**

Producer: **Stock/Aitken/Waterman**
Engineers: **Karen Hewitt/Yoyo**
Recorded in: **Studios 1 (Borough)**

FEBRUARY 13

Cliff attends the BPI Awards.

FEBRUARY 14

Cliff sees the musical *Brigadoon*.

FEBRUARY 19

Cliff attends the Rainbow Project at the House of Lords.

20 FEBRUARY

THE TOWNHOUSE
Studio session

Whenever God Shines His Light *A-side*

Lead Vocals: **Van Morrison**
Duet vocals: **Cliff Richard**

Producer:
Engineers:
Recorded in:

FEBRUARY 23

Cliff flies to San Remo.

FEBRUARY 24

Undertakes promotion in Italy.

FEBRUARY 25

Performs at the San Remo Festival, which is televised.

FEBRUARY 26

Appears on television in San Remo.

MARCH 10

Flies to Rome.

MARCH 11

Appears on Rome TV show – *Europa Europa.*

MARCH 12

Flies to Britain.

27 FEBRUARY-9, 13-17, 22-23 MARCH

RG Jones
Studio sessions

Stronger Than That	*A-side*
Who's In Love	*Stronger*
Clear Blue Skies	*Stronger*
Lean On You	*A-side*
Keep Me Warm	*Stronger*
Everybody Knows	*Stronger*
Forever You Will Be Mine	*Stronger*
Better Day	*Stronger*
Hey Mister	*B-side*
Wide Open Space	*B-side*
The Best Of Me	*A-side*
Joanna	*B-side*
Lindsay Jane	*B-side*

Lead Vocal:	**Cliff Richard**
Drums/Keyboards/Guitars:	**Alan Tarney**
Guitars:	**John Clark**
Bass:	**Mark Griffiths**
Drum Programming:	**Paul Moessl**
Sax:	**Dave Bishop**
Vocals:	**Mick Mullins/Keith Murrel/ Sonia Morgan**
Producer:	**Alan Tarney/Cliff Richard**
Engineers:	**Gerry Kitchingham/Ben Robbins**

MARCH 21

Cliff flies to the Dutch capital Amsterdam to record a television appearance.

MARCH 25

Flies to Portugal.

MARCH 31

Flies to Germany.

APRIL 1

Returns to Britain.

APRIL 3

2,000 fans are invited to the London Palladium, where Cliff and Mike Read present six of Cliff's new recordings for the fans to select their favourites-
(This was the order of popularity:)
1. Stronger Than That
2. Best Of Me
3. Just Don't Have The Heart
4. Joanna
5. Lean On You
6. Forever You'll Be Mine

Among other songs, Cliff also sings 'Bachelor Boy' as a tribute to a devoted fan called Julie, who always attended Cliff's concerts in a wheelchair, and had recently died.

APRIL 3

Records for BBC's *On The Waterfront.*

APRIL 4

Attends the Ivor Novello Awards at the Grosvenor House.

APRIL 5

Attends the UK Press Day at EMI from 12-6pm and then sees the preview of Andrew Lloyd Webber's *Aspects Of Love* at the Prince of Wales Theatre, London.

APRIL 7

Flies to Budapest.

APRIL 9

Returns to Britain.

APRIL 11-17

Cliff rehearses for his new tour.

APRIL 11

Attends church meeting in Plaistow, East London.

APRIL 13

Cliff sees the new musical *Metropolis* at Piccadilly Theatre, London.

APRIL 14

Sends telegram to Lulu at the Cafe Royal, where a 25-Year Tribute Lunch is being thrown in her honour.

APRIL 18-22

Caesar's Palace, Luton.

APRIL 19

Advance discussions with the authorities regarding Cliff receiving the freedom of the City of London.

APRIL 25-29

Cliff plays a week at Savvas Club in Usk, South Wales.

Geoff Capes proves he is 'stronger', taken during the press launch for 'Stronger'

APRIL 26

Cliff records a video message for the Barron Knights.

APRIL 29

Attends Spastics Society 'Silver Mile' Appeal in Cardiff.

MAY 1

Video Shoot.

MAY 2

Cliff starts a series of dates at Blazers Club, Windsor.

MAY 4

Interviewed for a Radio One special and interviewed and videoed by Mike Read, discussing all his singles to date.
Blazers, Windsor.

MAY 5

Blazers, Windsor.
Interviewed by Graham Blackstock for the *Evening Standard* and by Alistair McIver for the *European* newspaper.

MAY 6

Blazers, Windsor.

MAY 7

Cliff opens a new studio at Hospital Radio Wey in Weybridge.

MAY 12

Cliff finishes his run at Blazers, Windsor.

MAY 12

Records for *Rockline* with Tim Blackmore.

MAY 14

Appears on BBC TV's *Going Live* to assist with the SOS Presentations.

MAY 17

Cliff meets at his office with singer/arranger Tony Rivers and former Shadows Jet Harris and Tony Meehan.

MAY 19

Interviewed by Frank Bough for SKY satellite television.

MAY 30

Cliff releases his 100th single – 'Best Of Me' which eventually reaches No.2..
Attends Billy Graham dinner at London's Guildhall.

MAY 31

Interviewed by Radio Veronica, Holland.

JUNE 2

Cliff guests on Radio 1's *Singled Out* programme, reviewing the new releases.

JUNE 5-9

Dance rehearsals at Pineapple Studio.

JUNE 14

Records for LWT's *Friday Live*.

THE EVENT
June 16 & 17
Wembley Stadium, London

Facts and Figures about The Event

14 cameras were used to film the event shooting 41 miles of film. There were 120 technicians.
1,510,000 watts of lighting used.
The stage was 400 feet long, 15 feet high and 150 feet deep.
Programme sales beat all other records for any event at Wembley Stadium.
The weight suspended over the stage was approximately 14 tons.
90 artists took part in the show.
3,484 meals were served to the various staff and crew prior to the show.
215,000 watts of sound weighing 24 tons.
Over 10 miles of cable and 156 microphones were used.
In the recording of the event over 60,000 feet of 48-track digital tape was used.

Live recordings

Oh Boy Medley:

Whole Lotta Shakin' Goin' On	*From A Distance*
Bird Dog	*From A Distance*
Let's Have A Party	*From A Distance*
It's My Party	*From A Distance*
C'Mon Everybody	*From A Distance*
Whole Lotta Shakin' Goin' On	*From A Distance*
Zing Went The Strings Of My Heart	*From A Distance*
Always	*From A Distance*
When	*From A Distance*
The Glory Of Love	*From A Distance*
Hoots Mon	*From A Distance*
Don't Look Now	*From A Distance*
The Girl Can't Help It	*From A Distance*
Sea Cruise	*From A Distance*
Medley:	
Book Of Love	*From A Distance*
Blue Moon	*From A Distance*
Do You Wanna Dance	*From A Distance*
Chantilly Lace	*From A Distance*
At the Hop	*From A Distance*
Rock And Roll Is Here To Stay	*From A Distance*

Lead Vocal: **Cliff Richard**
Vocals: **The Dallas Boys/ The Vernon Girls/ The Kalin Twins/The *Oh Boy* Band**

The Young Ones	*From A Distance*
In The Country	*From A Distance*
Bachelor Boy	*(Unissued)*
Willie And The Hand Jive	*(Unissued)*
Living Doll	*(Unissued)*
Please Don't Tease	*(Unissued)*
Dynamite	*(Unissued)*
It'll Be Me	*(Unissued)*

Lead Vocal: **Cliff Richard**
Guitars: **Hank Marvin/Bruce Welch**
Bass: **Mark Griffiths**
Drums: **Brian Bennett**
Keyboards: **Cliff Hall**
Saxophone: **Ray Beavis**

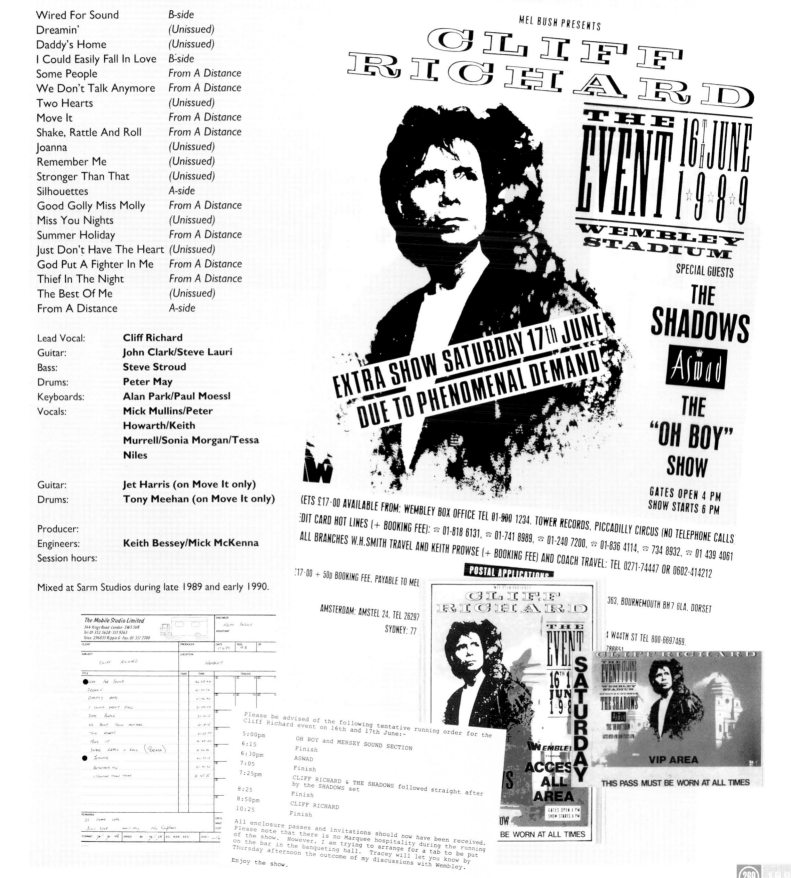

Wired For Sound	*B-side*
Dreamin'	*(Unissued)*
Daddy's Home	*(Unissued)*
I Could Easily Fall In Love	*B-side*
Some People	*From A Distance*
We Don't Talk Anymore	*From A Distance*
Two Hearts	*(Unissued)*
Move It	*From A Distance*
Shake, Rattle And Roll	*From A Distance*
Joanna	*(Unissued)*
Remember Me	*(Unissued)*
Stronger Than That	*(Unissued)*
Silhouettes	*A-side*
Good Golly Miss Molly	*From A Distance*
Miss You Nights	*(Unissued)*
Summer Holiday	*From A Distance*
Just Don't Have The Heart	*(Unissued)*
God Put A Fighter In Me	*From A Distance*
Thief In The Night	*From A Distance*
The Best Of Me	*(Unissued)*
From A Distance	*A-side*

Lead Vocal:	**Cliff Richard**
Guitar:	**John Clark/Steve Lauri**
Bass:	**Steve Stroud**
Drums:	**Peter May**
Keyboards:	**Alan Park/Paul Moessl**
Vocals:	**Mick Mullins/Peter Howarth/Keith Murrell/Sonia Morgan/Tessa Niles**

Guitar:	**Jet Harris (on Move It only)**
Drums:	**Tony Meehan (on Move It only)**

Producer:	
Engineers:	**Keith Bessey/Mick McKenna**
Session hours:	

Mixed at Sarm Studios during late 1989 and early 1990.

MEL BUSH PRESENTS
CLIFF RICHARD
THE EVENT
16TH JUNE 1989
WEMBLEY STADIUM
SPECIAL GUESTS
THE SHADOWS
ASWAD
THE "OH BOY" SHOW
GATES OPEN 4 PM
SHOW STARTS 6 PM
EXTRA SHOW SATURDAY 17th JUNE
DUE TO PHENOMENAL DEMAND
ETS £17·00 AVAILABLE FROM: WEMBLEY BOX OFFICE TEL 01-900 1234. TOWER RECORDS, PICCADILLY CIRCUS (NO TELEPHONE CALLS
EDIT CARD HOT LINES (+ BOOKING FEE): 01-818 6131, 01-741 8989, 01-240 7200, 01-836 4114, 734 8932, 01 439 4061
ALL BRANCHES W.H.SMITH TRAVEL AND KEITH PROWSE (+ BOOKING FEE) AND COACH TRAVEL: TEL 0271-74447 OR 0602-414212
POSTAL APPLICATIONS
17·00 + 50p BOOKING FEE, PAYABLE TO MEL
363, BOURNEMOUTH BH7 6LA, DORSET
AMSTERDAM: AMSTEL 24, TEL 26297
SYDNEY: 77
W 44TH ST TEL 800-6697469.

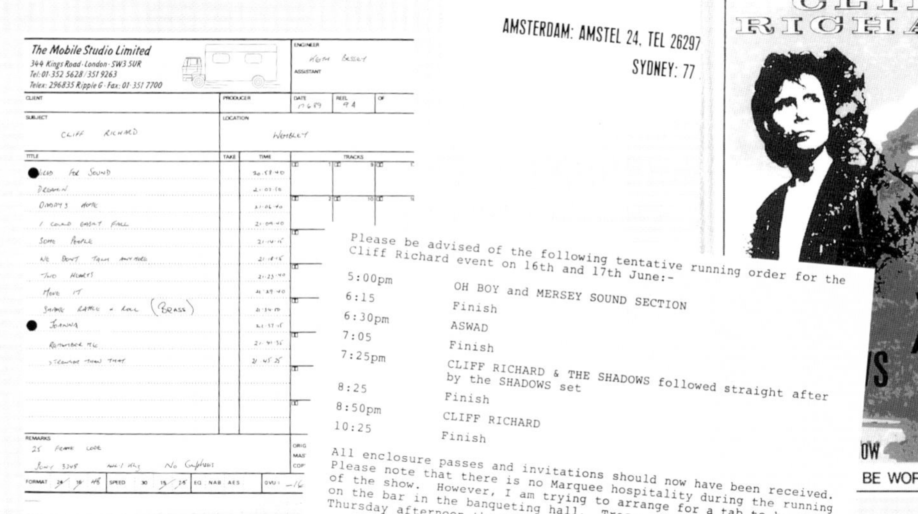

Please be advised of the following tentative running order for the Cliff Richard event on 16th and 17th June:-

5:00pm	OH BOY and MERSEY SOUND SECTION
6:15	Finish
6:30pm	ASWAD
7:05	Finish
7:25pm	CLIFF RICHARD & THE SHADOWS followed straight after by the SHADOWS set
8:25	Finish
8:50pm	CLIFF RICHARD
10:25	Finish

All enclosure passes and invitations should now have been received. Please note that there is no Marquee hospitality during the running of the show. However, I am trying to arrange for a tab to be put on the bar in the banqueting hall. Tracey will let you know by Thursday afternoon the outcome of my discussions with Wembley.

Enjoy the show.

13 JUNE-1 JULY

JFM STUDIOS TWICKENHAM
Studio session

Where You Are — *Songs of Life music from Mission '89*

Lead vocal: **Cliff Richard**
Piano: **Dave Cooke**

Producer: **Dave Cooke**
Engineers: **Wally Duguid/David Hofer**
Session hours:

JUNE 19

Cliff plays in a tennis tournament for the British Deaf Association at the David Lloyd Centre, Raynes Park, in the presence of the Princess of Wales. Also taking part are Ivan Lendl, Michael Chang, Stefan Edberg, Peter Fleming, John Lloyd, Mike Read, Jeffrey Archer and Bruce Forsyth.

JUNE 21

Watches Billy Graham at Crystal Palace.

JUNE 22-24

Flies to Holland to play in a tennis tournament.

JUNE 26

Watches Billy Graham at Earls Court.

JUNE 29

Reads lesson for the Wishing Well Appeal Thanksgiving Service at Westminster Abbey.

JUNE 30

Attends the tennis championships at Wimbledon.

JULY 1

Watches Billy Graham at Earls Court.

JULY 3

Attends the tennis at Wimbledon.

JULY 4

Billy Graham lunches with Cliff at home.

5-9 JULY

GERMANY
Studio session

Miss You Nights — *Special A-side*

Choir:

Producer:
Engineer:

The above details are the only information available about this recording that was featured in the A Distance Box Set. It is unclear if Cliff recorded a new vocal for this track.

JULY 5-9

Cliff goes to Germany to perform at the 8th Ard-Wunsch Konzert live from Bonn's prestigious Beethoven Hall. The event is part of festivities celebrating the 2,000th anniversary of the city of Bonn.

JULY 9

Attends the men's finals at Wimbledon, where he sees Boris Becker beat Stefan Edberg.

JULY 10-18

Cliff in rehearsal for the Gospel Tour.

JULY 12

At London's Guildhall, Cliff receives the 'Freedom Of The City Of London'. As a free man he can now drive any sheep he owns over London Bridge without payment and can be hanged with a silk cord instead of a rope (should the need arise). He becomes the first person from the world of popular music to have the honour bestowed on him.

JULY 31

Cliff hosts a barbecue at home for all the staff from his office.

AUGUST 8-29

Cliff on holiday.

AUGUST 14

Cliff's 101st single is released – 'I Just Don't Have The Heart' written by Stock, Aiken and Waterman. The single eventually reaches No. 3.

SEPTEMBER

JFM STUDIOS TWICKENHAM
Studio session

Where You Are	*B-side*
Lead Vocal:	**Cliff Richard**
Producer:	**Dave Cooke**
Engineer:	
Session hours:	

SEPTEMBER 1

Cliff shoots the video for 'I Just Don't Have The Heart' at K Stage, Shepperton Studios.

SEPTEMBER 2

Cliff presents prizes at the St. Georges Hill Tennis Club Junior Tournament.

SEPTEMBER 8

Cliff rehearses and records 'I Just Don't Have The Heart' for the *Sue Lawley Show* – to be screened the following day.

SEPTEMBER 9

Flies to Yugoslavia for the release of his 'Sasha' album.

SEPTEMBER 10

Returns to the UK.

SEPTEMBER 12

Appears on Roy Castle's *Record Breakers* and in the evening sees a preview of the West End show *Miss Saigon*.

SEPTEMBER 14

Flies to Paris to perform 'I Just Don't Have The Heart' on French television, where he gives interviews and dines with executives from EMI, France.

SEPTEMBER 17-27

Cliff in Europe.

SEPTEMBER 27

Flies to the USA, where he stays until October 6.

OCTOBER 4

Cliff's 102nd solo single – 'Lean On You' is released. It eventually reaches No.17.

OCTOBER 9

Cliff records for the TV show *Motormouth*.

OCTOBER 12

Cliff sings 'Lean On You' on *Top Of The Pops* and records an interview for the Steve Wright show on Radio One.

OCTOBER 13

Flies to Germany to undertake television and recordings.

OCTOBER 15

Returns to UK.

OCTOBER 18

Records for the *Des O'Connor Show*, as well as doing interviews for TV Times and Central Television.

OCTOBER 19

Flies to Austria to appear on television.

OCTOBER 20

Flies to Denmark to perform on television. His contribution to *Record Breakers* is transmitted.

OCTOBER 21

His recording for *Motormouth* is transmitted.

OCTOBER 23

He performs on Dutch television, and the album 'Stronger' is launched in Paris.

OCTOBER 24

Flies to Spain.

OCTOBER 25

Performs on Spanish TV and his recording for the *Des O'Connor Show* is transmitted.

OCTOBER 30

The album 'Stronger' is launched at the Trocadero in Piccadilly.

OCTOBER 31

Flies to Sweden to appear on TV in Gothenburg.

NOVEMBER 1

Performs on Swedish television.

NOVEMBER 2

Performs on French television, in Paris.
Flies to Singapore.

NOVEMBER 3-5

Cliff spends three days in Singapore.

CLIENT: PWL ?
DATE: 3/12/89
ARTIST: BAND AID 2
TIME FROM: 10AM TO: 02.00am
TITLE: DO THEY KNOW ITS XMAS
REEL NO.S: X242 A216
PRODUCER: S/A/W
EXT. MUSICIANS: !!!
ENGINEER: KAREN/YOYO
M.U. SERIAL NO:
ASSISTANTS: JULIAN CHRIS BARRY
24/48 TRACK: DIGITAL X242 A216
TIME SPENT: RECORDING DRUMS + KEYBOARDS + VOCALS

PWL EMPIRE

CLIENT:
DATE:
ARTIST:
TIME FROM: TO:
TITLE:
REEL NO.S:
PRODUCER:
EXT. MUSICIANS:
ENGINEER:
M.U. SERIAL NO:
ASSISTANTS:
24/48 TRACK:
TIME SPENT:

NOVEMBER 6

Flies to Japan.

NOVEMBER 7-11

Cliff spends five days in Japan.

NOVEMBER 12

Returns to the UK.

NOVEMBER 15

Sees Neil Diamond performing at Wembley Arena.

NOVEMBER 17

Rehearses dancing at Pineapple Studios.

NOVEMBER 18

Appears on Belgian television.

NOVEMBER 19

Returns to the UK.

NOVEMBER 20

At the Thames TV Sports Personality Luncheon Cliff presents veteran tennis star Fred Perry with his award.

NOVEMBER 22

Records LWT's New Year's Eve show at the London Palladium.

NOVEMBER 23

Cliff attends *Back To The Future II* premiere at the Empire, Leicester Square.

NOVEMBER 25

Sings 'Lean On You' and 'Mistletoe And Wine' on the *Late, Late TV Show* in Dublin.

NOVEMBER 28

Appears on French TV – *Sacre Soiree.*

NOVEMBER 29

Appears on French TV and is interviewed by the press.

NOVEMBER 30

Appears on French TV and is interviewed by the press and radio.

DECEMBER

JFM Studios Twickenham
Studio session

The Winner — *B-side*

Lead Vocal: **Cliff Richard**

Producer: **Dave Cooke**
Engineer:
Session hours:

DECEMBER 1

Cliff attends a performance of *A Little Light Music.*

DECEMBER 2

Cliff attends the Princess Alice Hospice Christmas event at Guildford, at which he sings 'Mistletoe And Wine'.

3/4 DECEMBER

PWL Studios
Studio session for

Do They Know It's Christmas — *A-side*

Keyboards: **Mike Stock/Matt Aitken**
Guitar: **Matt Aitken/Chris Rea**
Drums: **A. Linn/Luke Goss**

Producer: **Stock/Aitken/Waterman**
Engineers: **Karen Hewitt/Yoyo**
Recorded in: **Studio 1/4**
Session hours: **3rd-10.00am-2.00am**
4th-11.00am-8.30pm

DECEMBER 4

Cliff and Van Morrison shoot a video at Shepperton Studios for their duet 'Whenever God Shines His Light'.

DECEMBER 7

Cliff sings 'Move It' at the memorial concert for disc jockey

Roger Scott at EMI's Abbey Road Studios, and records 'My Top Ten' for Radio One. Later in the day Cliff switches on the Christmas lights at Weybridge, Surrey.

DECEMBER 8

Cliff and Van Morrison perform 'Whenever God Shines His Light' on Terry Wogan's TV show.

DECEMBER 9

'Whenever God Shines His Light' enters the singles chart, eventually coming to rest at number 20. They perform the song on German TV's *Wetten Das.*

DECEMBER 14

Cliff and Van Morrison perform the single on *Top Of The Pops*. Cliff records for *Sunday, Sunday*, on which he sings 'Mistletoe And Wine'.

DECEMBER 15

Cliff attends the ACG Christmas celebration at All Souls Church in Langham Place – where he and Van Morrison perform 'Whenever God Shines His Light'.

DECEMBER 16

Cliff's Pro-Celebrity Tennis Tournament at Brighton. Players include Roy Castle, Mike Read, Jason Donovan, Clare Wood, Virginia Wade, Anne Hobbs, Jo Durie, and Cliff.

DECEMBER 17

Cliff receives the TV Times Award at Teddington Studios.

DECEMBER 19

Cliff sings 'Mistletoe And Wine' for the Save The Children Concert at the Royal Albert Hall.

1990

RG Jones
Studio session

To A Friend	*A-side*

Vocals: **Alexander Mezek/Cliff Richard**

Producer:
Engineer:
Session hours:

JANUARY 2

Cliff rehearses for the video of 'Stronger Than That' at Weybridge.
Transmission of the TV Times Awards.

JANUARY 3

Cliff rehearses for video.

JANUARY 4

Video shoot at Shepperton Studios for 'Stronger Than That'.

JANUARY 5-6

Rehearsals start for Australasian Tour.

JANUARY 8-13

Rehearsals for Australasian Tour.

JANUARY 14

The launch of charity single 'Everybody's Got A Crisis In Their Life' by County Sound disc jockey Simon Cummings. Written by Jim Cozens it features, among others – Cliff Richard, Rick Wakeman, Justin Hayward, Alvin Stardust, Stephanie De Sykes, Carl Wayne, Mike Smith (ex Dave Clark Five) and bass player John Wetton.

JANUARY 15-17

Cliff continues rehearsals for his Australian tour.

JANUARY 18

Interviewed by the Australian press.
Rehearsals continue.

JANUARY 19

Rehearsals.
Cliff sees Eric Clapton at the Royal Albert Hall.

JANUARY 20

Rehearsals.

JANUARY 25

Cliff flies to Melbourne to begin Australasian Tour.

JANUARY 27-28

Dance rehearsals at Melbourne.

JANUARY 29

Flies from Melbourne to Sydney.

JANUARY 30

Cliff holds a press conference in Sydney.

JANUARY 31

Flies from Sydney to Wellington.

FEBRUARY 12

Cliff's 103rd single – 'Stronger Than That' (an Alan Tarney song) is released in Britain, eventually peaking at No.14.

FEBRUARY 28

Flies from New Zealand to Australia.

STRONGER TOUR

FEBRUARY 3-9
Michael Fowler Centre, Wellington.

FEBRUARY 12-17
Logan Campbell Centre, Auckland.

FEBRUARY 20-23
Town Hall, Christchurch.

FEBRUARY 25-27
Dunedin.

MARCH 3/4
Entertainment Centre, Perth.

MARCH 7-10
Apollo Stadium, Adelaide.

MARCH 13/14
Entertainment Centre, Melbourne.

MARCH 17
KGV Stadium, Hobart.

MARCH 18
Velodrome, Launceston.

MARCH 21-22
Entertainment Centre, Sydney.

MARCH 24-25
Bruce Stadium, Canberra.

MARCH 27-28
Festival Hall, Brisbane.

MARCH 31
Amphitheatre, Darwin.

Songs featured on the tour:
'Best Of Me'/'Green Light'/'Dreamin''/'Please Don't Tease'/'Daddy's Home'/'Keep Me Warm'/'Lean On You'/'We Don't Talk Anymore'/'My Pretty One'/'Carrie'/'Shake, Rattle And Roll'/'Silhouettes'/'I Just Don't Have The Heart'/'Stronger Than That'/'Joanna'/'Everybody Knows'/'It'll Be Me'/'Good Golly Miss Molly'/'The Young Ones'/'Summer Holiday'/'Living Doll'/'Anyone Who Had A Heart'/'Devil Woman'/'Miss You Nights'/'Fighter'/'Thief In The Night'/'Share A Dream'/'From A Distance'

MARCH 1

Arrives in Perth.

APRIL 1

Flies from Tasmania to UK via Singapore.

APRIL 6

Cliff attends 'Search For A Star' launch to find and encourage young tennis players at Cottenham Park, Merton.

APRIL 19

A Finnish TV crew interview Cliff at his office.
Cliff opens the First Floor Theatre in Westminster.

APRIL 20

Cliff meets with Shadows Brian Bennett and Bruce Welch at his Esher office.

APRIL 23

Cliff attends a Phil Collins concert at the Royal Albert Hall.

APRIL 25

Cliff rehearses with dancers at Pineapple Studio for his forthcoming Scandinavian/European Tour.

APRIL 26

Rehearses at Bray Studios.

APRIL27

Cliff attends the ballet at Wimbledon Theatre.

STRONGER OVER EUROPE

MAY 5
Fyens Forum, Odense.

MAY 6
Vejlby Riiskov Hallen, Aarhus.

MAY 7
Cirkelhallen, Herning.

MAY 9/10/11
Valby Hallen, Copenhagen.

MAY 15
Kuppelshal, Hanover.

MAY 16
Munsterlandhalle, Munster.

MAY 17
Kiev.

MAY 19
Forest National, Brussels.

MAY 20
Ahoy, Rotterdam.

MAY 22
Philipshalle Dusseldorf.

MAY 29

Schleyerhalle, Stuttgart.

MAY 30
Festhalle, Frankfurt.

MAY 31
Deutsches Museum, Munich.

JUNE 1
Sportshalle, Vienna.

JUNE 3
Linz.

JUNE 5
Hallen Stadion, Zurich.

JUNE 7
Paris.

Songs featured on the tour:
'Best Of Me'/'Green Light'/'Dreamin''/'Please Don't Tease'/'Daddy's Home'/'Keep Me Warm'/'Lean On You'/'Sea Cruise'/'We Don't Talk Anymore'/'My Pretty One'/'Carrie'/'Shake, Rattle And Roll'/'Silhouettes'/'I Just Don't Have The Heart'/'Stronger Than That'/'Joanna'/'Everybody Knows'/'Some People'/'It'll Be Me'/'Good Golly Miss Molly'/'The Young Ones'/'Summer Holiday'/'Living Doll'/'Anyone Who Had A Heart'/'Devil Woman'/'Miss You Nights'/'Fighter'/'Thief In The Night'/'Share A Dream'/'From A Distance'

The band:
Guitars: John Clark/Steve Lauri
Bass: Mark Griffiths
Drums: Peter May
Keyboards: Paul Moessl/Alan Park
Sax: Ray Beavis
Vocals: Keith Murrell/Mick Mullins/Peter Howarth

MAY 1

Flies to Helsinki.

MAY 12

Returns to the UK.

MAY 14

Flies to Hamburg.

MAY 23

Flies from Dusseldorf to Britain.for a break in the tour.

JUNE 6

Cliff attends the French Open Tennis in Paris.

JUNE 8

Flies from Paris to the UK.

JUNE 10

Cliff attends the Beckenham Tennis Finals.

JUNE 12

Attends DJ Mike Read's musical *Young Apollo,* about the poet Rupert Brooke, premiered at the Thorndike Theatre, Leatherhead, Surrey..

JUNE 16

Cliff plays Celebrity Tennis at the David Lloyd Centre, Raynes Park, Middlesex..

JUNE 17

Attends the finals of the Stella Artois Tournament at London's Queens Club.

JUNE 20

Attends the Sevenoaks Summer Festival.

JUNE 22

Cliff plays in a charity tennis tournament at London's Royal Albert Hall.

JUNE 26-27

Cliff rehearses with the Shadows for the Knebworth Nordoff Robbins Concert.

JUNE 28

Cliff rehearses for the Toyota Gala Dinner at the Grosvenor House Hotel in London, in the Presence of Her.Royal.Highness. The Princess Royal.

JUNE 30

Cliff and the Shadows perform at Knebworth alongside the likes of Tears For Fears, Pink Floyd, Status Quo, Elton John, Paul McCartney and Robert Plant, in aid of the Nordoff Robbins Music Therapy Clinic.

30 JUNE

KNEBWORTH

Live recordings for Polydor

Move It	*(Unissued)*
Summer Holiday	*(Unissued)*
The Young Ones	*(Unissued)*
On The Beach	*(Knebworth-The Album)*
Living Doll	*(Unissued)*
Good Golly Miss Molly	*(Unissued)*
Bachelor Boy	*(Unissued)*
Fall In Love With You	*(Unissued)*
Do You Wanna Dance	*(Knebworth-The Album)*
In The Country	*(Unissued)*
It'll Be Me	*(Unissued)*
Shake, Rattle And Roll	*(Unissued)*
We Don't Talk Anymore	*(Unissued)*

Lead Vocal:	**Cliff Richard**
Guitars:	**Hank Marvin/Bruce Welch**
Bass:	**Mark Griffiths**
Drums:	**Brian Bennett**
Keyboards:	**Cliff Hall**
Synths:	**Paul Moessl**
Brass:	**Ray Beavis/Dick Hanson/Chris Gower/John Earle**
Vocals:	**Hank Marvin/Bruce Welch/Mick Mullins/Pete Howarth/Keith Murrell**

Producer:	
Engineers:	
Session hours:	**3.30pm-4.15pm**

The entire show was broadcast 'live' on BBC Radio One but only two tracks were used on KNEBWORTH-THE ALBUM.

Cliff's 1990 tour — a record-breaker

Due to overwhelming ticket demand, seven new dates have been added to Cliff Richard's UK and Irish tour. Cliff will now undertake a series of 28 dates beginning with a record-breaking 12 nights at Birmingham's N.E.C. in November.

The format of these concerts, inspired by last year's Wembley Stadium success, will see Cliff and his band opening the first half with an 'Oh Boy' section — a collection of classic rock and roll songs from the '50s and '60s. The second half will concentrate on the more recent highlights from this artist's spectacular career.

When Cliff Richard — The Event took place over two nights at Wembley Stadium before capacity crowds totalling 144 thousand people on June 16 and 17 last year, many of the highlights were recorded and form the basis of From A Distance (The Event), a double album to be released, via EMI, on November 5.

'FROM A DISTANCE' TOUR

NOVEMBER 1
National Exhibition Centre, Birmingham

NOVEMBER 2
National Exhibition Centre, Birmingham.

NOVEMBER 3
National Exhibition Centre, Birmingham.

NOVEMBER 5
National Exhibition Centre, Birmingham.

NOVEMBER 6
National Exhibition Centre, Birmingham.

NOVEMBER 7
National Exhibition Centre, Birmingham.

NOVEMBER 9
National Exhibition Centre, Birmingham.

NOVEMBER 10
National Exhibition Centre, Birmingham.

NOVEMBER 11
National Exhibition Centre, Birmingham.

NOVEMBER 13
National Exhibition Centre, Birmingham.

NOVEMBER 14
National Exhibition Centre, Birmingham.

NOVEMBER 15
National Exhibition Centre, Birmingham.

NOVEMBER 17
Exhibition Centre, Aberdeen.

NOVEMBER 18
Exhibition Centre, Aberdeen.

NOVEMBER 19
Exhibition Centre, Aberdeen.

NOVEMBER 20
Exhibition Centre, Aberdeen.

NOVEMBER 21
Exhibition Centre, Aberdeen.

NOVEMBER 22
Exhibition Centre, Aberdeen.

NOVEMBER 28
National Exhibition Centre, Birmingham.

NOVEMBER 29
National Exhibition Centre, Birmingham.

DECEMBER 2
Wembley Arena.

DECEMBER 3
Wembley Arena.

DECEMBER 4
Wembley Arena.

DECEMBER 7
Wembley Arena.

DECEMBER 8
Wembley Arena.

DECEMBER 10
Wembley Arena.

DECEMBER 11
Wembley Arena.

DECEMBER 12
Wembley Arena.

DECEMBER 14
The Point, Dublin.

DECEMBER 15
The Point, Dublin.

DECEMBER 18
King's Hall, Belfast.

DECEMBER 19
King's Hall, Belfast.

DECEMBER 28
Wembley Arena.

DECEMBER 29
Wembley Arena.

DECEMBER 30
Wembley Arena.

JANUARY 1
Wembley Arena.

JANUARY 2
Wembley Arena.

JANUARY 3
Wembley Arena.

JANUARY 5
Wembley Arena.

JANUARY 6
Wembley Arena.

JANUARY 7
Wembley Arena.

Songs featured on the tour:
'Move It'/'Oh Boy Medley'/'Zing Went The Strings Of My Heart'/'Always'/'When'/'Silhouettes'/'Shake, Rattle And Roll'/'Why Do Fools Fall In Love'/'Willie And The Hand Jive'/'Hoots Mon'/'Don't Look Now'/'The Girl Can't Help It'/'Sea Cruise'/'Daddy's Home'/'Rock Medley'/'Always Guaranteed'/'Stronger'/'Some People'/'Carrie'/'I Just Don't Have The Heart'/'Miss You Nights'/'Devil Woman'/'We Don't Talk Anymore'/'Best Of Me'/'Fighter'/'Thief In The Night'/'Mistletoe And Wine'/'Little Town'/'From A Distance'/'Saviours Day'

The band:
Guitar/Vocals: John Clark
Bass/Vocals: Steve Stroud
Drums/Vocals: Peter May
Keyboards/Vocals: Paul Moessl/Bob Noble
Sax: Dave Bishop/Jamie Talbot
Trombone: Peter Beechill
Trumpet: Steve Sidwell

The dancers:
Robin Cleaver/Alex Worrall/Carol Wadsworth/Dawn Jalland/Chantelle/Charles Shirvell/Drew Millar/Frazer Hurrell/Benji/Steve Agyei

JULY 2

Cliff helps with the St Peter's Hospital Scanner Appeal at the local Foxhills Golf and Tennis Club.

JULY 4

Cliff attends the tennis at Wimbledon.

JULY 10

Cliff attends the Hampton Court Flower Festival.

JULY 12

Interviewed by Hong Kong Radio.

JULY 13

Interviewed by German television.

16-18 & 20-23 JULY

RG JONES
Studio session

Lindsay Jane II	*B-side*
Saviours Day	*A-side*

Lead Vocal:	**Cliff Richard**
Guitar:	**John Clark**
Keyboards/Synths/Drum Programming:	**Paul Moessl**
Vocals:	**Cliff/Pete Howarth/Keith Murrell/ Mick Mullins/Tessa Niles**
Producer:	**Cliff Richard/Paul Moessl**
Engineers:	**Gerry Kitchingham/Ben Robbins**

JULY 19

Cliff performs on the bill at the Palladium for a show to celebrate the Queen Mother's 90th Birthday.

JULY 27

Cliff records for a Billy Graham video at Bray Studios.

JULY 29-31

Band auditions at Bray Studios.

AUGUST 2

Routines with manager Barrie Guard and records for BBC TV's *What's That Noise.*

AUGUST 4

Cliff flies to Portugal for a holiday.

AUGUST 13

Cliff's 104th solo single – 'Silhouettes' – is released. It climbs to No. 10 in the charts.

AUGUST 25

Cliff returns to the UK.

AUGUST 28

Cliff attends the L.T.A. Pro-Celebrity Wheelchair Tennis tournament at Bishops Park.

SEPTEMBER 3

Cliff rehearses at Bray Studios and records piece for BBC TV's *8.15 from Manchester.*

SEPTEMBER 4

Rehearsals.

SEPTEMBER 7

Radio and TV Disc Jockey Anne Nightingale interviews Cliff at Bray Studios.

SEPTEMBER 8

Cliff flies to Berlin for a Charity event.

SEPTEMBER 9

Returns to the UK.

SEPTEMBER 10

Rehearsals for N.E.C. Concerts begin.
Cliff opens a trade exhibition at Olympia.

SEPTEMBER 11-14

Rehearsals.

SEPTEMBER 14

Cliff is interviewed during rehearsals at Bray Studios for Sky Television.

SEPTEMBER 15

Rehearsals.

SEPTEMBER 17

Cliff opens at Savvas Club in Usk, South Wales for a week's cabaret engagement.

SEPTEMBER 18

Savvas.
BBC TV's *What's That Noise* transmitted.

SEPTEMBER 19-20

Savvas.

SEPTEMBER 21

Savvas.
Interviewed by the Sunday Telegraph.

SEPTEMBER 22

Savvas.

SEPTEMBER 25

Cliff shoots 'Saviours Day' video at Durdle Dor in Dorset.

OCTOBER 1

Cliff's 105th single – 'From A Distance' is released. It eventually climbs to No. 11.

OCTOBER 2-6

Cliff rehearses with dancers.

OCTOBER 6

Cliff appears on *Going Live* singing 'From A Distance'.

OCTOBER 8

Rehearsals and Cliff interviewed by the *Daily Express.*

OCTOBER 9

Rehearsals.

OCTOBER 10

After rehearsals Cliff is interviewed by David Jensen for London's Capital Radio.

OCTOBER 11

Rehearsals.

OCTOBER 12

Rehearsals.
Interviewed by Simon Mayo for Radio One and Graham Dene for Capital Gold.

OCTOBER 13

Cliff is interviewed by County Sound Radio on the eve of his 50th birthday, which he celebrates with a party at home for his friends. As midnight strikes he pronounces that he doesn't feel any different!

OCTOBER 15-16

Rehearses at Pineapple Studios.

OCTOBER 17

Rehearses at Bray Studios.

OCTOBER 20

Cliff flown to Frankfurt and back in a private jet to record for a German TV show *Flitterabend.*

OCTOBER 21-27

Rehearsals.

NOVEMBER 5

'From A Distance-The Event' album released.

NOVEMBER 7

A belated 50th birthday party is thrown for Cliff.

NOVEMBER 9

The *TV Times* do a photosession with Cliff for their Christmas edition.

NOVEMBER 12

Cliff performs the ceremonial 'switching on' of the Oxford Street Christmas lights in London.

NOVEMBER 18

Interviewed by the Scottish media.

NOVEMBER 23

Appears on BBC TV's *Children In Need.*

NOVEMBER 26

Cliff's 106th solo single – 'Saviours Day' is released. It eventually hits the No. 1 spot.
Cliff performs 'Saviours Day' – his 'Christmas record' for 1990 - on Terry Wogan's television show.

NOVEMBER 27

Cliff records 'Saviours Day' for Des O'Connor's TV show and for TV's *Motormouth* and is interviewed by David Wigg for the *Sunday Express.*

DECEMBER 1

Motormouth recording is transmitted.

DECEMBER 6

Cliff sings 'Saviours Day' on *Top Of The Pops.*

DECEMBER 8

During the concert Cliff links up with Granada Television for a tribute to the long-running 'soap' *Coronation Street* – one of his favourite television programmes.

DECEMBER 10

Cliff records for TV-AM's Christmas Day show.

DECEMBER 12

Des O'Connor show is transmitted.

DECEMBER 13

Cliff records for Gloria Hunniford's TV show *Sunday, Sunday.*

DECEMBER 16

Cliff's Pro-Celebrity Tennis Tournament is played at Brighton. Taking part with Cliff are Sara Gomer, actor Jeremy Irons, Clare Wood, magician Paul Daniels, Jo Durie, Bruce Forsyth and Virginia Wade.

DECEMBER 22

Cliff appears on *Going Live's* TV Christmas Special.

DECEMBER 23

Cliff takes part in the ACG celebration at Riverside Studios.

1991—1995

The Records 1991 – 1995

The Simon May & Mike Read composition 'More To Life' taken from the BBC TV drama series "Trainer" was selected for the first single release of 1991. It was also the first for ten months hitting the shops in September, and not stirring up much chart action by only reaching No.26. 'We Should Be Together' was the follow-up Christmas single reaching No.10 on the charts, and although it had been tipped to repeat the success of the previous seasonal hits, it should be remembered that this was the year in which Freddie Mercury died, and after that dramatic event, Queen's 'Bhoemian Rhapsody' was the Christmas No.1. 'We Should Be Together' was released in various different formats, and probably the most exciting of these was 'The Christmas EP' which featured two previously unreleased seasonal tracks from 1967. They were 'Twelve Days Of Christmas' and 'The Holly And The Ivy'.

The last single of the year; 'This New Year' almost went unnoticed by only reaching No.30. In 1992 only one single was released, 'I Still Believe In You' which sailed into the charts to peak at No.6. March 1993 saw the release of 'Peace In Our Time' which reached a high of No. 8 in the charts, and although there will undoubtedly be more singles between the compilation of this chronicle being completed and publication, the information here is accurate up to April 1993.

On the album front there was the release of two compilation albums with a difference - TOGETHER WITH CLIFF RICHARD marked Cliff's first ever traditional Christmas album with a selection of seasonal standards, previously released hits, and of course, the Christmas and New Year singles which boosted it's sales to reach No.10 on the album chart. For this one EMI issued a special promo CD with excerpts that included a seasonal message from Cliff.

The collection entitled MY KINDA LIFE was a selection of new versions of songs that had been remixed and re-recorded, and released in France only.

Most ambitiously, THE CLIFF RICHARD CD COLLECTION was a series of two-for-one CDs, EMI in one release restoring all of the extensive Cliff Richard back catalogue to the shelves of record stores. This was complemented at the end of 1994 by another 'greatest hits' collection, this time entitled THE HIT LIST, a double-CD which compiled 37 tracks from 'Move It' to 'Green Light'.

The Sessions 1991 – 1995

For New Year's Day 1991, BBC Radio One were at Wembley Arena for a live broadcast of the entire "From A Distance" concert. In June Cliff once again worked alongside Bruce Welch, who produced two tracks for CLIFF RICHARD-THE ALBUM as well as the B-side to the 'Peace In Our Time' single. More sessions followed later that same month, this time at RG Jones when Cliff over three days cut the 'More To Life' track that would be heard over the titles and credits of a new BBC-TV drama called *Trainer*. On the sessions running from 24 June through July work was geared towards producing enough material for a Christmas album. It is known that Cliff was in the studios from May 20 through to May 31, probably working on the Christmas album. Ten songs of Cliff's own interpretations of Yuletide standards were recorded. Among these were 'White Christmas', 'Silent Night', 'O Come All Ye Faithful', 'Have Yourself A Merry Little Christmas' and 'Scarlet Ribbons'. The latter track was later remixed for 12" and CD release. There were, of course, some new songs, and amongst these 'We Should Be Together' and 'This New Year' were released as the seasonal singles. The next RG Jones sessions took place in February when Cliff re-recorded new vocals for 'Carrie' and French lyrics for "When Two Worlds Drift Apart'. Additional work on the backing tracks was carried out over four days in April for what would later be released in France as 1992 versions of songs drawn from his seventies and eighties material. Work resumed at RG Jones in May when Cliff cut more material for CLIFF RICHARD-THE ALBUM. Plans were made to follow these sessions in July for the recording of 'This Is Our Country', a song written by Chris Eaton and scheduled for release as a single to commemorate the fortieth anniversary of the Queen's reign. Sessions at The Hit factory in September and Nomis Studios in November completed work on the album which was mixed at RG Jones during January 1993. As had happened with the "From A Distance" tour, BBC Radio arranged for a complete taping of the "Access All Areas" concert at Wembley Arena in November. Highlights of this recording would be edited for Radio Two broadcast in December 1992. June 1993 saw Cliff duetting in the studio with country legend Tammy Wynette on 'This Love' as part of Tammy's 25th Anniversary album, and in September 1994 he teamed up with Phil Everly for a reprise of two Everly Brothers hits, 'When Will I Be Loved' and 'All I Have To Do Is Dream'.

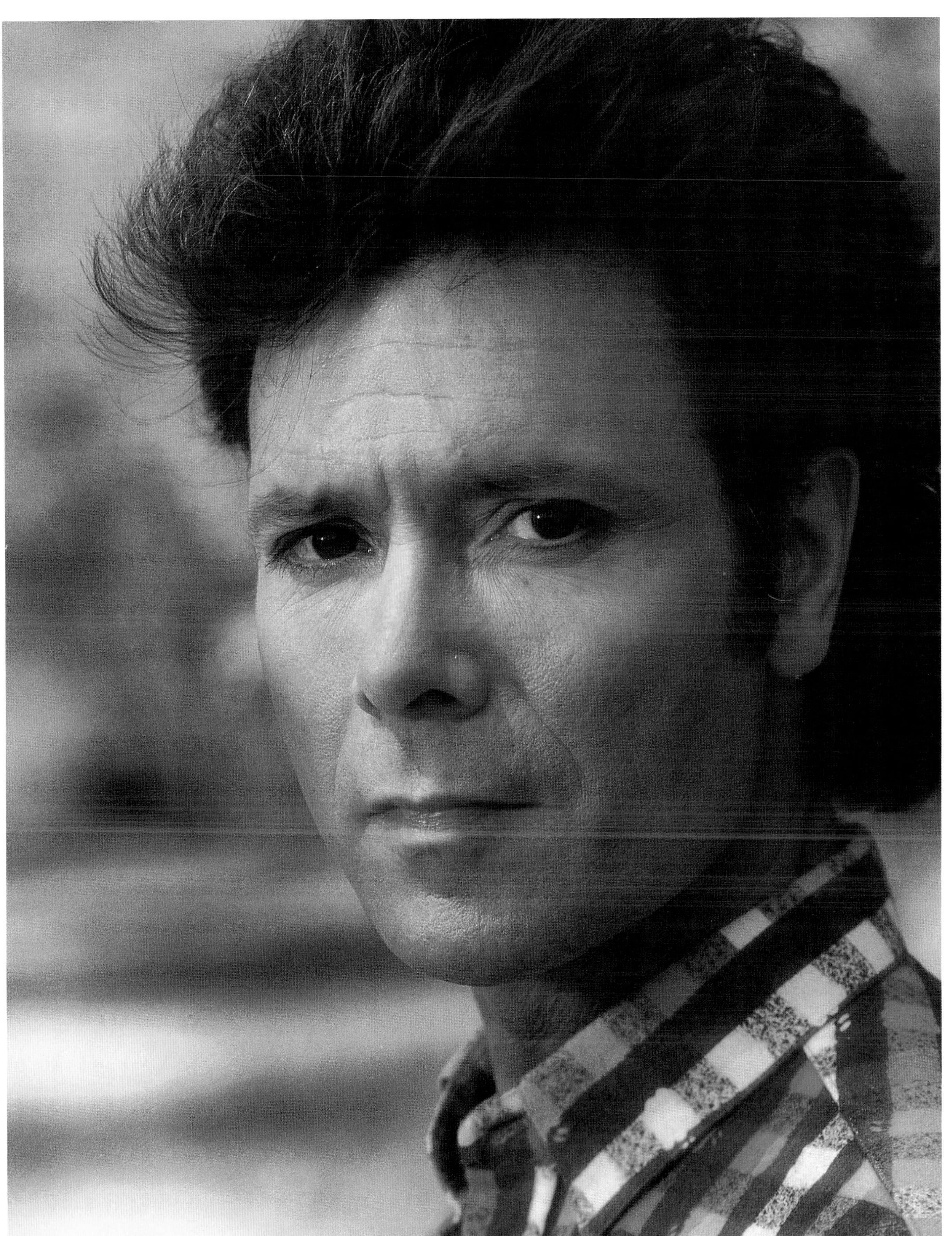

I JANUARY

WEMBLEY ARENA, LONDON
BBC Radio Transcription

Move It	*(Unissued)*
Oh Boy Medley:	*(Unissued)*
Oh Boy	*(Unissued)*
Whole Lotta Shaking Goin On	*(Unissued)*
Bird Dog	*(Unissued)*
Let's Have A Party	*(Unissued)*
It's My Party	*(Unissued)*
C'Mon Everybody	*(Unissued)*
Whole Lotta Shakin Goin On	*(Unissued)*
Zing Went The Strings Of My Heart	*(Unissued)*
Always	*(Unissued)*
When	*(Unissued)*
Silhouettes	*(Unissued)*
Shake, Rattle And Roll	*(Unissued)*
Why Do Fools Fall In Love	*(Unissued)*
Willie And The Hand Jive	*(Unissued)*
Hoots Mon	*(Unissued)*
Don't Look Now	*(Unissued)*
The Girl Can't Help It	*(Unissued)*
Sea Cruise	*(Unissued)*
Daddy's Home	*(Unissued)*
Medley:	
Book Of Love	*(Unissued)*
Blue Moon	*(Unissued)*
Do You Wanna Dance	*(Unissued)*
Chantilly Lace	*(Unissued)*
At the Hop	*(Unissued)*
Rock And Roll Is Here To Stay	*(Unissued)*
Always Guaranteed	*(Unissued)*
Stronger	*(Unissued)*
Some People	*(Unissued)*
Carrie	*(Unissued)*
I Just Don't Have The Heart	*(Unissued)*
Miss You Nights	*(Unissued)*
Devil Woman	*(Unissued)*
We Don't Talk Anymore	*(Unissued)*
Best Of Me	*(Unissued)*
Fighter/Thief In The Night	*(Unissued)*
Mistletoe And Wine	*(Unissued)*
Little Town	*(Unissued)*
From A Distance	*(Unissued)*
Saviours Day	*(Unissued)*

Lead Vocal:	**Cliff Richard**
Guitar/Vocals:	**John Clark**
Keyboards/Vocals:	**Paul Moessl/Bob Noble**
Bass/Vocals:	**Steve Stroud**
Drums/Vocals:	**Peter May**
Saxophone:	**Dave Bishop/Jamie Talbot**
Trombone:	**Peter Beechill**
Trumpet:	**Steve Sidwell**

The entire show was broadcast 'live' on BBC Radio One.

JANUARY 4

Cliff opens Harrods Sale at 9am. In return, Chairman Mohammed Al Fayed donates £50,000 to the *Daily Express* Children of Chernobyl Appeal.

JANUARY 7

Cliff attends a charity night for the Children of Chernobyl, which raises £70,000 for the charity. Guests include Cilla Black, Una Stubbs, Esther Rantzen, Hayley Mills, Andrew Lloyd Webber and Daily Express editor Sir Nicholas Lloyd – the latter presenting Cliff with a painting by Russian artist Andrei Pakhomov.

JANUARY 10

Begins routining for Gospel Tour.

JANUARY 12

Flies to the U.S.A for a holiday in Florida.

JANUARY 26

Cliff flies to Toronto, Canada.

JANUARY 29

Flies from Toronto to Heathrow.

FEBRUARY 1

Cliff plays in a charity tennis tournament in Manchester.

FEBRUARY 22

Prepares for his Gospel Tour and has a production meeting for his forthcoming tour.

FEBRUARY 23-27

Gospel Tour preparations.

FEBRUARY 28

Gospel Tour rehearsals start.

FEBRUARY 29

Gospel Tour rehearsals.

MARCH 2-12

Gospel Tour rehearsals at Bray.

MARCH 24

Cliff attends a party thrown by Elton John.

APRIL 5

Cliff dines with director Frank Dunlop to discuss *Wuthering Heights.*

APRIL 7-12

Cliff holiday's at his house in Wales.

APRIL 13

Appears on German TV show *Wetten das in Berlin.*

AN EVENING WITH CLIFF RICHARD GOSPEL TOUR

MARCH 13
Temple Park Centre, South Shields.

MARCH 14
The Sands Centre, Carlisle.

MARCH 15
Opera House, Blackpool.

MARCH 16
Free Trade Hall, Manchester.

MARCH 20
Cornwall Coliseum, St Austell.

MARCH 21
The Plaza, Exeter.

MARCH 22
Newport Centre, Newport.

MARCH 23
Apollo Theatre, Oxford.

MARCH 27
Assembly Rooms, Derby.

MARCH 28
Arts Centre, University of Warwick, Coventry.

MARCH 29
Congress Theatre, Eastbourne.

MARCH 30
Royal Albert Hall, London.

Songs featured on the tour:
'All Shook Up'/'Move It'/'Better Than I Know Myself'/'Saviours Day'/'The Only Way Out'/'From A Distance'/'Where You Are'/'Discovering'/'Yesterday, Today, Forever'/'Lost In A Lonely World'/'When I Survey The Wondrous Cross'/'Flesh And Blood'/'Make Me New'/'Shine Jesus Shine'

APRIL 19

Records for German television at home.

APRIL 24

Plays in Pro-Celebrity Tennis Tournament at Woking.

MAY 2

Cliff attends the Ivor Novello Awards Lunch.

MAY 8

Cliff attends a reception at No. 10 Downing Street.

MAY 12

Cliff rehearses with dancers for 'We Don't Talk Anymore' for the World Music Awards in Monte Carlo.

MAY 14-15

World Music Awards in Monte Carlo.

MAY 16

Returns to the UK.

MAY 18

Cliff attends the wedding of Warren Bennett (the son of Shadow's drummer Brian Bennett) at St John The Baptist Church in Aldenham, Hertfordshire.

MAY 23

Cliff attends an Everly Brothers concert at the Royal Albert Hall.

MAY 25

Cliff watches Billy Graham at Edinburgh.

JUNE 3

Cliff interviewed by Tim Rice at EMI's Abbey Road Studios.

JUNE 4

Cliff watches Billy Graham at Glasgow.

JUNE 5

Cliff dines with Helen Shapiro.

7-8 JUNE

WESTSIDE STUDIOS
Studio sessions

I Need Love	*Cliff Richard-The Album*
Somebody Loves You	*B-side*
Little Mistreater	*Cliff Richard-The Album*

Lead Vocal:	**Cliff Richard**
Keyboards:	**Paul Moesll/Steve Piggott**
Bass:	**Steve Piggott**
Saxaphones:	**Snake Davis**
Producers:	**Bruce Welch/Cliff Richard**
Engineer:	**Keith Bessey**
Session hours:	

10-13 JUNE

RG JONES
Studio sessions

More To Life	*A-side*

Lead Vocal:	**Cliff Richard**
Programming and Keyboards:	**Paul Moessl**
Guitars:	**Paul Dunne/John Clark**
Bass:	**Steve Stroud**
Drums and Percussion:	**Peter May**
Strings:	**Andrew Greasley**
Backing Vocals:	**Cliff Richard**
Producers:	**Cliff Richard**
	Paul Moessl
Engineer:	**Gerry Kitchingham**
Assistant Engineers:	**Andrew Greasley**
	Ben Robbins
Session hours:	

JUNE 13

Attends a Christians in Sport dinner in Swindon, Wiltshire.

Ben Robbins, engineer, at RG Jones Studios

JUNE 15

World Music Awards screened on ITV.

JUNE 16

Cliff attends the final of the Stella Artois Tennis Tournament at Queens Club in London.

JUNE 21

Cliff plays pro-celebrity tennis at the Royal Albert Hall, along with Frank Bruno, Michael Aspel, Terry Wogan, Mats Wilander, John Lloyd and Stefan Edberg, to raise money for Muscular Dystrophy.

24 JUNE – JULY

RG JONES
Studio sessions

Silent Night	*Together With Cliff Richard (27-7-91)*
Have Yourself A Merry Little Christmas	*Together With Cliff Richard*
Venite (O Come All Ye Faithful)	*Together With Cliff Richard (20-7-91)*
Scarlet Ribbons	*B-side (23-7-91)*
Christmas Alphabet	*Together With Cliff Richard (23-7-91)*
We Should Be Together	*A-side (19-7-91)*
Christmas Never Comes	*Together With Cliff Richard*
The Christmas Song (Merry Christmas To You)	*Together With Cliff Richard*
This New Year	*A-side*
White Christmas	*Together With Cliff Richard*

Lead Vocal:	**Cliff Richard**
Keyboards and Drum Programming:	**Paul Moessl**
Drums and Percussion:	**Peter May/Frank Ricotti**
Guitars:	**John Clark/Paul Dunne**
Bass:	**Steve Stroud/Mark Griffiths**
Brass:	**Dave Bishop/Derek Watkins**
Strings:	**Andrew Greasley/Dave Cunliffe**
Backing Vocals:	**Cliff Richard/Tony Rivers/Anthony Thompson/Mick Clark/Tessa Niles/Peter Howarth**
Additional Vocals:	**Mae McKenna/Sonia Morgan/Mick Mullins/Keith Murrell/Nigel Perrin/Miriam Stockley**
Producers:	**Cliff Richard/Paul Moessl**
Engineers:	**Gerry Kitchingham/Ben Robbins/Andrew Greasley**
Session hours:	

JULY 3/5/7

Cliff attends the tennis at Wimbledon. Sees Michael Stich beat Boris Becker in the men's final on the 7th.

CLIFF RICHARD

WE SHOULD BE TOGETHER

Christmas E.P.

CLIFF RICHARD

Features Special Engraved AUTOGRAPH etched onto disc

THIS NEW YEAR

TITLE TOGETHER FOR CHRISTMAS
ARTIST CLIFF RICHARD
PRODUCER PAUL – CLIFF
ENGINEER GERRY KITCHINGHAM
RGJONES RECORDING STUDIOS
SYNC BOX SBX-80
BPM 90
NOTES: Telephone effects at intro to be run live with percussion

JULY 10
Attends the Hampton Court Flower Festival.

JULY 14
Sees Bonnie Raitt in concert.

JULY 18
Goes to the Royal Tournament in the evening.

JULY 19
Goes to Sandown Park to see the TV series *Trainer* being filmed, as Cliff has recorded the title song.

JULY 21
Cliff attends the Federation Tennis Cup at Nottingham and appears on the *Radio One Roadshow* with Mike Read broadcasting from the site. Cliff sits with the Princess of Wales for the Opening Ceremony.

JULY 23
Cliff plays tennis at the Federation Cup Children's Day at Nottingham.

AUGUST 4
Leaves for holiday in Portugal.

AUGUST 25
Returns to the UK.

AUGUST 28
Cliff attends Mike Read's new musical *Oscar* about Oscar Wilde, at Chilston Park Country House Hotel in Kent.

SEPTEMBER 1
Cliff takes part in Gloria Hunniford's Charity Tennis Tournament in Sevenoaks, Kent.

SEPTEMBER 2
Cliff's 107th solo single – 'More To Life' is released. Written by Simon May and Mike Read it is the theme song for the new ITV series *Trainer*. It reaches No. 21.

SEPTEMBER 4
Cliff pre-records 'More To Life' for *Top Of The Pops.*

SEPTEMBER 5
Peter Lewry & Nigel Goodall's book of Cliff's Recording Sessions is published – *The Complete Recording Sessions 1958-1990*
Cliff rehearses for his video in Birmingham.

SEPTEMBER 6
Cliff rehearses for video of 'I Love You' in Birmingham.

7 SEPTEMBER

PEBBLE MILL TV STUDIOS
Live recordings for television/video

I Love You	*B-side*

SEPTEMBER 7

Shoots video of 'I Love You' in front of his audience.

SEPTEMBER 13

Cliff is taken by helicopter to a dinner with the managing director of EMI at Maidstone, Kent.

SEPTEMBER 16

Cliff opens at Savvas Club in Usk, South Wales.

SEPTEMBER 17-21

Continues week-long booking at Savvas Club, Usk..

SEPTEMBER 22-27

Rehearsals for Australasian Tour at Bray Studios.

SEPTEMBER 28

Interviewed by Mike Read at home for a Radio Two Christmas Special.

SEPTEMBER 29-OCTOBER 4

Rehearsals for Australasian Tour at Bray Studios.

OCTOBER 7

Cliff flies to Australia.

OCTOBER 12

Flies from Australia to New Zealand.

OCTOBER 13

Rehearses in Auckland.

NOVEMBER 4

Flies from Auckland to Perth.

NOVEMBER 5-6

Rehearses in Perth.

NOVEMBER 7

Holds press conference in Perth.

NOVEMBER 8

Rehearses in Perth.

NOVEMBER 18

Cliff's Christmas album is released in the UK.

NOVEMBER 25

Cliff's 108th solo single – 'We Should Be Together' is released.

DECEMBER 2

The tour complete, Cliff flies home.

DECEMBER 12

Cliff performs 'We Should Be Together' on *Top Of The Pops* and on the Des O'Connor TV show.

AUSTRALIA/NEW ZEALAND TOUR

OCTOBER 14-19
Logan Campbell Centre, Auckland.

OCTOBER 21-27
Michael Fowler Centre, Wellington.

OCTOBER 28-NOVEMBER 3
Town Hall, Christchurch.

NOVEMBER 9-10
Entertainment Centre, Perth.

NOVEMBER 13-14
Apollo Stadium, Adelaide.

NOVEMBER 16
Velodrome, Launceston.

NOVEMBER 17
KGV Stadium, Hobart.

NOVEMBER 19-21
Entertainment Centre, Melbourne.

NOVEMBER 23-24
Bruce Stadium, Canberra.

NOVEMBER 27-28
Festival Hall, Brisbane.

NOVEMBER 30-DECEMBER 1
Entertainment Centre, Sydney.

Songs featured on the tour:
'Move It'/'Living Doll'/'I Could Easily Fall'/'Summer Holiday'/'Bachelor Boy'/'Shine On'/'It's All In The Game'/'Silhouettes'/'All Shook Up'/'That's Alright'/'Lord I Love You'/'Free'/'Daddy's Home'/'Please Don't Tease'/'On The Beach'/'From A Distance'/'Wired For Sound'/'Scarlett Ribbons'/'Miss You Nights'/'Devil Woman'/'Silvery Rain'/'Joy Of Living'/'Some People'/'Best Of Me'/'We Don't Talk Anymore'/'We Should Be Together'/'Mistletoe And Wine'/'Little Town'/ 'Saviours Day'

DECEMBER 14

Cliff's Pro-Celebrity Tennis Tournament at the Brighton Centre. Players include Des O'Connor, Amanda Barrie, Mike Read, Alvin Stardust, Bill Roache, Clare Wood, Virginia Wade, Jo Durie and Sara Gomer.

Cliff with long-term manager David Bryce.

DECEMBER 17

Cliff performs in the recording of the TV special *Joy To The World* at the Royal Albert Hall. Pre-records for Simon Mayo's Radio One show, Sky News, Capital Radio and Radio Luxembourg.

DECEMBER 19

Cliff interviewed by County Sound Radio.

DECEMBER 20

Cliff records a message for the Searchers to congratulate them on 30 years in the music business. In the evening Cliff takes part in the ACG Christmas celebrations.

DECEMBER 21

Radio Two Christmas Special transmitted.

JANUARY 1

Records *Top Of The Pops*, singing his new single 'This New Year' – a Chris Eaton song.

JANUARY 3

Attends the 'Saltmine' event at the Royal Albert Hall.

JANUARY 14

Cliff undertakes a sitting for Rock Circus at Madame Tussaud's.

JANUARY 16

Cliff records a piece for the *Week's Good Cause* appeal for P.H.A.B. at Broadcasting House, London.

JANUARY 18

Departs for his first skiing holiday in Lech, Austria.

JANUARY 25

Returns to the UK.

JANUARY 28

Meets with Christian writer Steve Turner who is to undertake a biography on Cliff, to be published in the Spring of 1993. Cliff attends the opening of Jack Good's musical *Good Rockin' Tonight* in which Cliff is played by Timothy Whitnall. His former colleagues from the Jack Good days, Marty Wilde and Joe Brown, are also in the audience.

JANUARY 30

Records an interview on video for the Searchers and talks to James Whitbourn for BBC *Prayer For The Day*. Interviewed by County Sound Radio.

FEBRUARY 1

Flies to Ostend to perform three songs on Belgian Television – 'Some People', 'Miss You Nights' and 'This New Year'.

1-2 FEBRUARY

RG Jones
studio sessions

Carrie	*My Kinda Life*
Remember	*B-side*

Lead Vocal: **Cliff Richard**

Producers: **Cliff Richard/Paul Moessl**
Engineers: **Gerry Kitchingham/Ben Robbins**

New vocals were cut for the above two tracks. See also session dated 20-23 April

FEBRUARY 5

Records television interview for 'No Smoking Day' followed by an interview with Kingston Hospital Radio.

FEBRUARY 11

BBC TV/Radio 2 undertake a promotional shoot at Cliff's Office.

FEBRUARY 12

Cliff visits Kingston School, Manor Hospital in Epsom and Beacon School in Banstead.

FEBRUARY 13

Attends the film premiere of *Star Trek VI – The Undiscovered Country*. Also in the audience are Boy George, Eric Idle and Jim Davidson.

FEBRUARY 15

Cliff performs 'This New Year' on German television.

FEBRUARY 18

Takes part in a photoshoot for Dr Barnados in Dorking.

FEBRUARY 20

Lunches at the House of Commons and stays for 'Question Time' and sees *Phantom Of The Opera* in the evening.

FEBRUARY 23

Six-part Radio 2 series on Cliff begins.

FEBRUARY 25

The All England Tennis Club at Wimbledon is the very appropriate venue for the launch of Cliff's 1992 Tennis Trail.
The sponsors of the event are Direct Line Insurance, and the project director is Sue Mappin. The well-publicised launch is attended by Sue Barker, Annabelle Croft, Gloria Hunniford, Debbie McGhee, Angela Rippon, Paul Daniels, Roy Castle and Mike Read amongst others.

FEBRUARY 28

Appears on Terry Wogan's television show, on which he surprises the audience by doing an impromptu performance with the Scots group Wet, Wet, Wet.

MARCH 6

Belgian TV interview Cliff at his office where he later meets up with singer/songwriter B.A. Robertson.

MARCH 10

Sees *Carmen Jones* at the Old Vic.

MARCH 12

Cliff attends a photocall at the Savoy Hotel in London for the 'Spectacles Wearer of the Year award'.
Flies to Paris to have dinner with EMI executives.

MARCH 15

Records for Bruce Forsyth's TV show at BBC Television Centre.

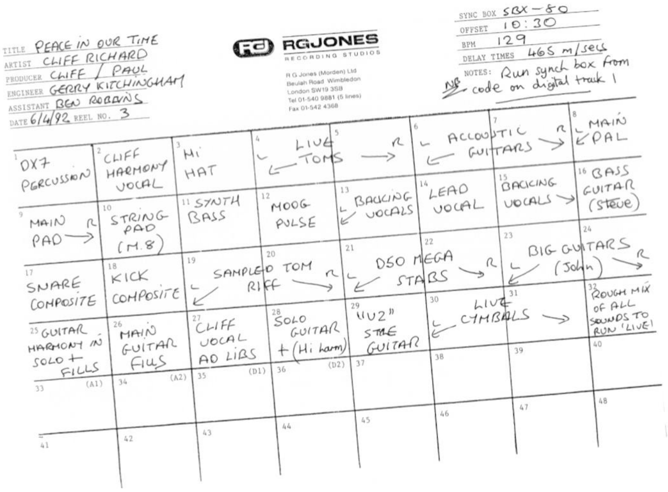

MARCH 19

Cliff dines with actor David Suchet – best known as television's Hercule Poirot.

MARCH 20

Attends Wet, Wet, Wet concert at Wembley Arena and is invited by the group to sing with them on 'Goodnight Girl'.

MARCH 21

Attends the Bishop Wand School event in Staines, Middlesex, before going on to the Silver Wedding of his friends Gerald and Anona Coates.

MARCH 22

Cliff presents a BAFTA Award for the Best Original Film Music at the Grosvenor House Hotel – the winner was the much-acclaimed *Cyrano De Bergerac.*

MARCH 24

Cliff goes to Lech in Austria for a second skiing holiday.

MARCH 31

Returns to the UK.

20-23 APRIL

RG Jones
Studio sessions

Born To Rock And Roll	*My Kinda Life*
Devil Woman	*My Kinda Life*
Carrie	*My Kinda Life*
Thru Friday	*My Kinda Life*
Hot Shot	*My Kinda Life*
Language Of Love	*My Kinda Life*
Lucille	*My Kinda Life*
Lean On You	*My Kinda Life*
My Kinda Life	*My Kinda Life*
Remember	*My Kinda Life*
Two Hearts	*My Kinda Life*
Never Even Thought	*My Kinda Life*

Additional Drums & Keyboards: **Paul Moesll**
Additional Guitars: **John Clark**

Producers: **Cliff Richard/Paul Moessl**
Engineers: **Gerry Kitchingham/Ben Robbins**
Session hours:

25-31 MAY/8 JUNE

RG Jones
Studio sessions

Human Work Of Art	*Cliff Richard-The Album (11-7-92)*
Peace In Our Time	*A-side*
Bulange Downpour	*B-side (19-7-92)*
There's No Power In Pity	*B-side (16-7-92)*
Love Is The Strongest Emotion	*Cliff Richard-The Album (7-7-92)*
Handle My Heart (With Love)	*Cliff Richard-The Album (29-5-92)*
Ragged	*B-side (26-5-92)*
Love's Salvation	*Cliff Richard-The Album (8-6-92)*
Only Angel	*Cliff Richard-The Album (8-7-92)*
You Move Heaven	*Cliff Richard-The Album (10-6-92)*
Hold Us Together	*Cliff Richard-The Album (25-5-92)*
Never Let Go	*Cliff Richard-The Album (28-5-92)*
Brother To Brother	*Cliff Richard-The Album (6-7-92)*

Lead Vocal: **Cliff Richard**
Keyboards/Drum Programming: **Paul Moessl**
Guitars: **John Clark**
Bass: **Steve Stroud**
Drums/Percussion: **Peter May**
Additional Percussion: **Gary Wallis (on Handle My Heart)**
Strings arranged by **Richard Hewson/Paul Moessl**
Strings conducted by **Richard Hewson**
Additional strings: **Andrew Greasley (on Hold Us Together)**
Brass section: **Dave Bishop, Pete Beachill, Jamie Talbot/Simon Gardener**
Backing vocals: **Cliff Ricahrd/Tessa Niles/ Keith Murrell/JudithWalmsley/ Peter Howarth**
Additional backing vocals: **The London Community Gospel Choir (on Peace In Our Time)**
Featured vocalist: **Judith Walmsley (on Love is The Strongest Emotion)**

Producers: **Paul Moessl/Cliff Richard**
Engineers: **Gerry Kitchingham/Ben Robbins**

The dates in brackets show the actual date, where known, that Cliff overdubbed his vocal to the basic track.

APRIL 4

Cliff attends the Jack Good rock'n'roll musical *Good Rocking Tonight* once again.

APRIL 5

Cliff attends Mike Read's *Poetry In Motion*, which is based on – and features – the work of poet Sir John Betjeman, at the Richmond Theatre.

APRIL 10

Cliff goes to the ballet at Sadlers Wells.

APRIL 12

Attends the *Jesus Christ Superstar* Anniversary Concert at the Palace Theatre in London.

APRIL 13

Cliff records a video for *The Word*, on which he faces questions on a variety of subjects from teenagers.

APRIL 14

Undertakes photosession for the *Sunday Times.*

APRIL 15

Interviewed by French TV and press at his office.

APRIL 22

Interviewed for Australian Radio.

APRIL 25

Cliff and Bill Latham fly to Uganda for Tear Fund. A documentary is filmed during their stay.

MAY 1

Returns to the UK.

MAY 5

Cliff presents the Webb Ivory Fund Raising Awards.

MAY 8

Flies to Copenhagen to perform 'Some People', 'We Don't Talk Anymore' and 'She's So Beautiful' on Danish television.

MAY 9

Returns to the UK.

MAY 11

Cliff's French album – 'My Kinda Life' is released. Records for Gloria Hunniford's TV Show, the whole programme being devoted to Cliff. Among those taking part are Paul Jones, Peter Waterman, John Foster and Mike Read. Cliff sings 'Move It' and 'My Kinda Life'.

MAY 12

Gloria Hunniford Show transmitted. Cliff flies to Monte Carlo to take part in the presentation of the World Music Awards with Olivia Newton John.

MAY 14

World Music Awards recorded.

MAY 15

Cliff returns to the UK.

MAY 16-17

Cliff takes part in the Tennis Trail at Swansea.

MAY 18

Cliff participates in a charity go-kart competition, organised by his office.

MAY 20

Cliff meets with Hank Marvin at Radlett.

MAY 21

Takes part in Crusader video. Interviewed by the *Sunday Express* and Radio Two for *Volunteers Week*.

MAY 22

Flies to Paris to sing 'Lucille' on French TV.

MAY 23

Returns to the UK.

MAY 28

Meets Children In Need auction winner Molly Baig at RG Jones Studios.

JUNE 2-5

Cliff flies to Paris to promote his album and for the French Open Tennis Tournament.

JUNE 5

Returns to the UK.

JUNE 6

Attends the tennis at Beckenham.
The World Music Awards are transmitted.

JUNE 7

Attends the tennis at Beckenham.

JUNE 9

Interviewed for *First Night,* Midlands TV, about the N.E.C. and his tour. Dines with veteran tennis commentator Dan Maskell at a tribute dinner.

JUNE 11

Has photograph with Joanna Lumley at the Theatre Royal for the Variety Club.

JUNE 13

Attends the tennis at Queens Club.

JUNE 14

Spends the day on the Tennis Trail at Warrington, where he is interviewed by John Motson.

JUNE 18

Cliff attends Mike Read's musical *Oscar* at the Old Fire Station, Oxford.

JUNE 19

Cliff interviewed at home by Alan Titchmarsh.

JUNE 22

Cliff rehearses for Royal Albert Hall show at Sadlers Wells.

JUNE 23

Cliff takes part in a special tribute evening for the late Sammy Davis Jnr at the Royal Albert Hall.

JUNE 25

Takes part in a 'Crusader' video at his office then attends a Wimbledon players meeting at Putney.

JUNE 28

Cliff sings 'Move It' on the roof of BBC's Broadcasting House to open 'National Music Day'.

JUNE 29-JULY 5

Attends the tennis at Wimbledon. Sees the Ladies' and Men's finals.

JULY 8

Cliff goes to the preview of the International Flower Show at Hampton Court.

JULY 10

Bill Latham interviews Cliff about his faith at Yeldall Manor.

JULY 16

Cliff has 'Joy To The World' photograph taken with Gloria Hunniford, is interviewed for *Surrey County Magazine*, records 'Joy To The World' video message and a piece for Age Concern.

JULY 18-19

Cliff with the Tennis Trail in Devon.

JULY 20

Cliff unveils his new waxwork at Rock Circus.

JULY 22

Cliff attends the Trailblazer Assessment Day at Wimbledon.

JULY 27

Cliff leaves for a holiday in Portugal.

AUGUST 17

Returns to the UK.

AUGUST 19

Cliff joins his band and backing singers for tour rehearsals at Bray Studios.

AUGUST 20-22

Tour rehearsals at Bray Studios.

AUGUST 22

Records flexi-disc for tour programme at Bray Studios.

AUGUST 24

Starts a week of appearances at Savvas Club in Usk, South Wales.

AUGUST 25

Savvas Club, Usk, South Wales.

AUGUST 26

Savvas Club, Usk, South Wales.
Undertakes a photosession.

AUGUST 27

Savvas Club, Usk, South Wales.
Undertales a photosession.

AUGUST 28-29

Savvas Club, Usk, South Wales.

AUGUST 30

Attends a party given by Roy Castle.

SEPTEMBER 10-13

Rehearses with band and backing singers for forthcoming tour.

SEPTEMBER 14-27

Full scale rehearsals at Docklands.

14 SEPTEMBER

THE HIT FACTORY
Studio sessions

I Still Believe In You	*A-side*
Lead vocal:	**Cliff Richard**
Piano:	**Dave Arch**
Guitars:	**John Clark**
Bass:	**Steve Stroud**
Strings arranged by	**Richard Hewson/Paul Moessl**
Strings conducted by	**Richard Hewson**
Producers:	**Paul Moessl**
Engineers:	**Mike Ross-Trevor**

SEPTEMBER 18

Interview about Helen Shapiro for TV's *The Human Factor.*

SEPTEMBER 25

Interviewed at Docklands for a Drug Prevention Campaign video.

OCTOBER 11

The Variety Club throw a tribute lunch for Cliff at Birmingham.

Cliff soars above the sea of syrup

Pop

Cliff Richard: NEC Birmingham

by SPENCER BRIGHT

A GIANT image of Cliff Richard flickers on to a plain gauze backdrop. It moves and shrinks until suddenly it becomes the real thing.

Cliff appears alone, strumming Move It on his acoustic guitar. In an instant, he has blown away the bombast of his last over-produced tour.

Although some fancy footwork and snazzy effects will come later, here is the essence of Cliff. Like him or loathe him, his considerable talent shines through.

For the first 50 minutes he goes through the familiar Cliff rock 'n' roll act. He does his best to look risque in a waistcoat, black drainpipe trousers and trainers. A few numbers in, off comes the waistcoat to reveal a fetching, loose satin shirt with a Mondrian design.

Hero

He punches the air, does some formation dancing and gradually builds the crescendo as more members of his backing group traipse on.

Cliff is indisputably Britain's best-loved pop-rock star. In a 37-date tour through the UK and Ireland, 320,000 people will see him and it's unlikely many will be disappointed.

The tour travels through his career from the young buck of Young Ones to impersonating his hero Elvis in That's All Right (Mama).

Of course, as Cliff informs us, his real hero isn't Elvis, but Jesus. And there is no doubt that ever-so gradually he is injecting his religious message into his shows.

'As a Christian it amazes me that people still turn away from something that is free,' is his way of introducing the devotional Free. As you would expect, it is heartfelt.

The second rockier, special effects-filled half of the show has Cliff on a raised platform behind the gauze with images of a multitude of people, then the heavenly stars, convincingly projected in a 3-D effect around him as he sings From A Distance.

But however carefully controlled the climate in a Cliff concert, there's always a rough edge. Tonight it's a new song, Little Miss Treater, which sees him raunchy and funky. This is offset by a sunny back-projection of Cliff, his band and a pretty, blonde female backing singer in a tug-of-war scene.

As always, Christmas comes early in a Cliff show — in December, Silent Night and Mistletoe And Wine will make sense, but at the start of October, they are a little unseasonal.

Cliff mocks himself a little, alluding to his status as an all-round family entertainer. It's true, of course — he is.

Sometimes that can be cloying and sentimental, but there's no denying his ability to captivate and charm.

Still rocking along with Cliff: Sentimental but so captivating

ACCESS ALL AREAS TOUR

OCTOBER 1/2/3
National Exhibition Centre, Birmingham.

OCTOBER 5/6/7
National Exhibition Centre, Birmingham.

OCTOBER 9/10/11
National Exhibition Centre, Birmingham.

OCTOBER 13/14/15
National Exhibition Centre, Birmingham.

OCTOBER 17/18
National Exhibition Centre, Birmingham.

OCTOBER 22/23/24/25
Arena, Sheffield.

OCTOBER 27
Arena, Sheffield.

OCTOBER 29/30/31
S.E.C.C., Glasgow.

NOVEMBER 2/3/4
Wembley Arena.

NOVEMBER 10/11/12
Wembley Arena.

NOVEMBER 14/15/16
Wembley Arena.

NOVEMBER 18/19/20
Wembley Arena.

NOVEMBER 27/28/29
Wembley Arena.

Still tugging the heart-strings

POP / Tony Parsons reviews the boyish 52-year-old Cliff Richard at Wembley

YOU don't expect hecklers at a **Cliff Richard** concert. But pop's favourite bachelor boy had just finished a stirring version of *Move It* when some uncouth rowdy started shouting from near the front.

"I know that voice," Cliff said reassuringly. "It's a gentleman called Doug. Every time he shouts out he raises money for charity."

Warm applause. Good old Cliff. Even his hecklers have haloes. What a guy. Thirty-four years in the business and he can still fill **Wembley Arena**, he can still shake his skinny rump all night long and he still doesn't look like he shaves. His distinguishing features may be his cleanliness and his longevity but, in an industry that is overpopulated with dirty one-hit wonders, it certainly makes a change.

And you can't tell me that Cliff has never touched your heart. I don't believe you. This boyish 52-year-old — possibly the only boyish 52-year-old on the planet — has released so much stuff that there's something there for everyone. Those early Elvis impersonations are OK — *Living Doll, Please Don't Tease, On the Beach* — but personally I favour Cliff's later work — *Wired for Sound, Mistletoe and Wine, We Don't Talk Any More*, the gloriously mawkish *Daddy's Home* and the classic *Devil Woman.*

Even stuff that should be unbearably corny brought a lump to my throat. Cliff's weepy ballad, *Miss You Nights*, has the line, "Looking windward for my compass" but this man is such a consummate craftsman that he makes the line somehow credible. What's so strange, you ask yourself, about looking windward for your compass?

He played for nearly three hours and it was mostly all hits. Incredible. This man will be around when Nirvana are history. Cliff has seen them come and seen them go. All of them. Sometimes he took time to give us a little historical perspective.

"Rock 'n' roll in its infancy was very simple," Cliff explained. "Then high technology came in and swept everything aside." But mostly he sang songs that you knew all the words to and danced like a dervish with his pants on fire.

Cliff gave us a couple of raps about Jesus but he doesn't ram his Christianity down anyone's throat. There were just as many speeches about Elvis. Ultimately Cliff Richard is one of the great English rockers. As he duck-walked during *That's All Right Mama* or bounced around the stage doing stuff from *Access All Areas*, his next album, time and time again he made me think of pop's other Peter Pan. Yes, Cliff kept reminding me of Mick Jagger. I wonder, could they possible be related?

"As far as I'm concerned," said Cliff, "there's only one art form. Rock 'n' roll!"

And amen to that.

DECEMBER 7/8
King's Hall, Belfast.

DECEMBER 10/11/12
The Point, Dublin

Songs featured on the tour:
'Move It'/'Living Doll'/'The Young Ones'/'Summer Holiday'/'Love On'/'It's All In The Game'/'Silhouettes'/'That's Alright'/'Free'/'Daddy's Home'/'Please Don't Tease'/'On The Beach'/'From A Distance'/'Monday Thru Friday'/'Some People'/'Little Mistreater'/'Devil Woman'/'Miss You Nights'/'Willie And The Hand Jive'/'Love Is The Strongest Emotion'/'Silvery Rain'/'I Still Believe In You'/'We Don't Talk Anymore'/'Silent Night-Mistletoe And Wine'/'Human Work Of Art'/'Handle My Heart'/'Wired For Sound'/'My Kinda Life'/'Peace In Our Time'/'When Two Worlds Drift Apart

The band:
Guitars: John Clark
Bass: Steve Stroud
Drums: Peter May
Keyboards: Paul Moessl/Bob Noble
Brass: Dave Bishop/Simon Gardner
Vocals: Judith Walmsley/Gillian Jackson/Steve Bayliss/
Stephen Butler

MOVE IT
LIVIN DOLL
YOUNG ONES
SUMMER HOLIDAY
LOVE ON
ALL IN THE GAMI
SILHOUETTES
THATS OK MAMA
FREE
DADDY'S HOME
PLEASE DON'T T
ON THE BEACH

FROM A DISTANCE
MONDAY TO FRIDAY
SOME PEOPLE

MISS TREATER

DEVIL WOMAN
MISS U NIGHTS
WILLIE

LOVE IS
SILVERY RAIN
WHEN TWO WORLDS
WE DON'T TALK
SILENT NIGHT
MISTLETOE

HUMAN WORK OF ART
HANDLE MY HEART
WIRED FOR SOUND
play off
Intros
MY KINDA LIFE

PEACE IN OUR TIME
play off

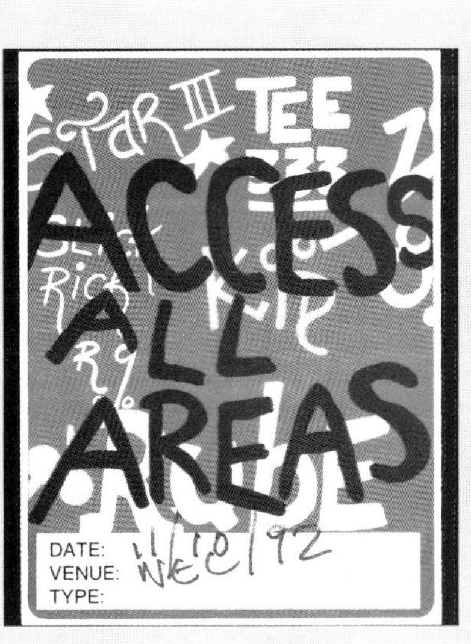

LATE OCTOBER

NOMIS STUDIOS
Studio session

Healing Love	*Cliff Richard-The Album (17-11-92)*

Lead Vocal:	**Cliff Richard**
Guitar Programming:	**Nik Kershaw**
Keyboards:	**Richard Cottle**
Backing Vocals:	**Cliff Richard/Nik Kershaw**
Producers:	**Cliff Richard/ Nik Kershaw/Paul Moessl**
Engineers:	**Stuart Bruce**

NOVEMBER

WEMBLEY ARENA
BBC Radio Transcription

Move It	
Living Doll	*(Unissued)*
The Young Ones	*(Unissued)*
It's All In The Game	*(Unissued)*
That's All Right	*(Unissued)*
Free	*(Unissued)*
Daddy's Home	*(Unissued)*
Please Don't Tease	*(Unissued)*
On The Beach	*(Unissued)*
From A Distance	*(Unissued)*
Some People	*(Unissued)*
Miss You Nights	*(Unissued)*
Willie And The Hand Jive	*(Unissued)*
I Still Believe In You	*(Unissued)*
We Don't Talk Anymore	*(Unissued)*
Wired For Sound	*(Unissued)*
Silent Night/Mistletoe And Wine	*(Unissued)*
My Kinda Life	*(Unissued)*
Peace In Our Time	*(Unissued)*

Lead Vocal:	**Cliff Richard**
Guitar:	**John Clark**
Keyboards/Vocals:	**Paul Moessl/Bob Noble**
Bass:	**Steve Stroud**
Drums:	**Peter May**
Saxophone:	**Dave Bishop**
Brass:	**Simon Gardner**
Vocals:	**Stephen Butler/Judith Walmsley/ Gillian Jackson/Steve Bayliss**

NOVEMBER 3

Shoots a video for 'I Still Believe In You'.

NOVEMBER 12

Interviewed by Daily Express journalist David Wigg.

NOVEMBER 16

Interviewed for *Good Morning Sunday* Christmas Show.

NOVEMBER 19

All monies from the show on the 19th go to the NSPCC.

NOVEMBER 23

Cliff's new single 'I Still Believe In You' released. The CD single includes 'Ocean Deep' and the French adaptation of 'When Two Worlds Drift Apart' ('Remember').

27/28 NOVEMBER

WEMBLEY ARENA
BBC Radio Transcription

Living Doll	*B-side*
That's All Right	*B-side*

Lead Vocal/Guitar:	**Cliff Richard**
Producer:	**Keith Bessey**

DECEMBER 1

Cliff appears on Pebble Mill to sing his new single.

DECEMBER 3

Cliff pre-records for Wogan's TV show, singing his new single.

DECEMBER 4

Interviewed for Ulster TV.
The Wogan TV show transmitted.

DECEMBER 15

Cliff appears on Simon Bates Radio 1 show live and takes part in 'Joy To The World' at the Royal Albert Hall – to be transmitted at Christmas.

DECEMBER 19

Cliff's own Tennis Tournament celebrates its 10th birthday at the National Indoor Arena at Birmingham. Players include Cliff, Frank Bruno, Roy Castle, Mike Read, Virginia Wade, Gloria Hunniford, Clare Wood and Jo Durie. Michael Ball also attends – joining in the songs after the tournament.

JANUARY 30-FEBRUARY 6

Cliff goes skiing in Lech, Austria.

MARCH 15

Cliff's new single – 'Peace In Our Time' – is released. The CD single also includes 'That's Alright Mama' and 'Living Doll' both

AN EVENING WITH CLIFF RICHARD GOSPEL TOUR

MARCH 30
The Point, Dublin.

MARCH 31/APRIL 1
Dundonald International Ice Bowl, Belfast.

APRIL 2
Scottish Exhibition Centre, Glasgow.

APRIL 3
Exhibition and Conference Centre, Aberdeen.

APRIL 7
International Conference Centre, Harrogate.

APRIL 8
Royal Centre, Nottingham.

APRIL 9
Kings Park Centre, Northampton.

APRIL 10
Symphony Hall, Birmingham.

APRIL 14
The Pavilions, Plymouth.

APRIL 15
International Centre, Bournemouth.

APRIL 16
Centre, Brighton.

APRIL 19
Hammersmith Apollo, London.

Songs featured on the tour:
'The Only Way Out'/'His Love Covers Our Sins'/'Healing Love'/'Peace In Our Time'/'There's No Power In Pity'/'I'm In Love With My TV'/'Where You Are'/'Why Should The Devil Have All The Good Music'/'Saviours Day'/'Free'/'Better Than I Know Myself'/'Song For Sarah'/'From A Distance'

The band:
Guitar: John Clark
Bass: Steve Stroud
Drums: Peter May
Keyboards: Paul Moessl/Dave Cooke

recorded during the 'Access All Areas' Tour. The single eventually reaches the number 8 spot.

MARCH 23-26

Cliff rehearses for the Gospel Tour.

APRIL 5

PMI release a double video – 'Access All Areas-The Tour 1992'. Filmed during Cliff's Wembley Arena concerts that took place in November 1992.

APRIL 19

'Cliff Richard-The Album' is released by EMI.

APRIL30

'Cliff Richard-The Album' enters the British charts at No. 1. In the music video charts of the same week the 'Access All Areas' double video is also at No. 1.

MAY 4

Filming at home for Celador Productions with Rex Bloomstein.

MAY 6

Tennis assessment day at Wimbledon indoor tennis centre.

MAY 7

Cliff, Tim Rice and director Frank Dunlop meet at London's Langham Hilton to discuss the Heathcliff project.

MAY 10

Tennis Trail begins at Solihull – runs until 16th.

MAY 11

Video shoot at the Rainbow Theatre in Finsbury Park, London, for the single 'Human Work Of Art'.

MAY 16

Cliff sings 'Human Work Of Art' on Bruce Forsyth's tv show *Bruce's Guest Night*.

MAY 17

Cliff flies to Holland.
The Tennis Trail commences in Newcastle – runs until 23rd.

MAY 18

Cliff sings 'Peace In Our Time' live on the Dutch television show *Staatsloteris*, as well as being interviewed by the local media.

MAY 19

Returns to London.

MAY 20

Filming at Cliff's office for tv documentary.
Cliff performs in a charity cabaret at Banqueting House attended by the Princess of Wales.

MAY 21

Cliff opens a new independent local radio station at Slough.

MAY 22

Cliff performs 'Human Work Of Art' on the German tv show *Flitterabend*.

MAY 23

Cliff dines with Alvin Stardust and his wife Julie.

MAY 24

The Tennis Trail commences in Sheffield and runs until the 30th May.

MAY 25

Cliff, John Farmer, Tim Rice and director Frank Dunlop meet to discuss *Heathcliff*.

MAY 27

John Farmer and Tim Rice work on *Heathcliff* at Tim's house in Barnes.
Cliff undertakes a charity presentation to British Airways.
Meets with Nigel Goodwin of the A.C.G.

MAY 28

Cliff opens a home for the homeless at Guildford.

MAY 30

Cliff flies to Hamburg.
Cilla Black's show is transmitted with Cliff singing 'Human Work Of Art'.

MAY 31

Cliff performs 'Human Work Of Art' on German tv.

JUNE 1

The single 'Human Work Of Art' is released.
Cliff flies to Frankfurt from Hamburg and back to London while his charity and religious affairs manager Bill Latham meets with Princess Catherine of Yugoslavia.

JUNE 3

Cliff and the writers meet to discuss *Heathcliff*.

JUNE 6

Cliff attends the Beckenham Tennis Tournament.

JUNE 3

Cliff's pro-celebrity Tennis Tournament box office opens as he flies to Portugal for a short holiday until the 12th.
Bruce Forsyth's tv show *Bruce's Guest Night* is transmitted on which Cliff sings 'Human Work Of Art'.

JUNE 13

Cliff attends the final of the Stella Artois Tennis Tournament at Queens.

JUNE 14

The Tennis Trail commences at Bodmin and runs for three days.

JUNE 15

Cliff routines for Michael Ball's tv show.

JUNE 17

Cliff attends the Webb Ivory awards at London's Grosvenor House.
Tennis Trail commences in Birmingham and runs until the 20th.

JUNE 18

Cliff sings with the All Souls orchestra on their 21st anniversary at the Royal Albert Hall.

JUNE 20

Cliff records for the Michael Ball tv show and duets with Michael Ball, backed by an orchestra, although Cliff is unable to play guitar due to a broken bone in his left hand which had been injured in May.

JUNE 21

Cliff attends Wimbledon.

JUNE 22

Cliff dines with Frank Allen of the Searchers.

JUNE 23

Cliff sits in the Royal box at Wimbledon.

JUNE 24-25

Photo shoot at his home in Weybridge.

JUNE 26

Cliff attends Wimbledon.

JUNE 28

Cliff meets with Tammy Wynette at his home before recording part of their duet 'This Love' at R.G. Jones Studio. The track is to be part of an album project to commemorate Tammy's 25th anniversary in the business, with her duetting with various singers. The album is to be released in the States late in 1994 with

'This Love' scheduled to be a UK release for 1995. Tammy commented 'Recording with Cliff was a breathtaking experience. Cliff is truly one of the greatest voices I have ever heard and include the memory of that day as one of the highlights of my 28-year career.'

JUNE 29

Cliff is interviewed for the BBC World Service; meets Princess Margarita of Romania and five children from Chernobyl.

JUNE 30

Cliff and Tammy Wynette record at R.G.Jones This session included Tammy's vocal.

JULY 1

Cliff records a book of Bible stories. Backing vocals and saxophone for 'This Love' are recorded at R.G.Jones.

JULY 2

Cliff attends Wimbledon.

JULY 4

Cliff attends Wimbledon final.

JULY 5

Cliff plays in pro-am Tennis Tournament at Queens Club in London. Cliff is partnered by Ken Rosewall – twice Wimbledon's mens doubles winner.

JULY 6

Cliff attends a preview of the Hampton Court flower show and checks the final mixes of 'This Love'. The track 'Healing Love' is re-mixed sightly at Abbey Road Studios.

JULY 9

Cliff records with Hank Marvin at Brian Bennett's studio in Radlett.

JULY 12

Tennis Trail commences at Warrington – runs until the 18th.

JULY 14

Cliff sees the musical *City of Angels*.

JULY 15

'An Evening with Cliff Richard' at Glastonbury Abbey with Cliff and Bill Latham.

JULY 19

Cliff takes part in a phone interview direct to South Africa, with Radio 702 in Johannesburg.
'An Evening with Cliff Richard' at Byfleet with Cliff and Bill Latham.

JULY 20

Cliff flies to Portugal for a four-week holiday until August 28th.

JULY 29

The *Michael Ball Show*, featuring Cliff, is transmitted.

AUGUST 29

Cliff performs at the 20th anniversary of the Greenbelt Festival.

SEPTEMBER 3

Dines with *Heathcliff* director Frank Dunlop.

SEPTEMBER 4

Records at Central Hall Westminster for Tear Fund's 'Songs of Praise'.

SEPTEMBER 7

Cliff opens a new David Lloyd Tennis Club in Glasgow.

SEPTEMBER 9

Cliff films tv commercial for Australia.

SEPTEMBER 10

Cliff plays tennis at London's Vanderbilt Club and is interviewed for BFBS and Anglia Television.

SEPTEMBER 15

Cliff records for Cilla Black's television anniversary special. Cliff and Cilla sing a duet and he also performs 'Never Let Go'.

SEPTEMBER 19

Cliff plays pro-celebrity tennis at Match Point in Manchester.

SEPTEMBER 20

The single 'Never Let Go' is released.

SEPTEMBER 21

Cliff flies to Milan.

SEPTEMBER 22

Interviewed by Italian magazines, radio and tv in Milan and undertakes a photo session.

SEPTEMBER 23

Cliff flies from Milan to Paris.

SEPTEMBER 24

Cliff performs on the *Dorothee* show, on which he sings 'Peace In Our Time' and duets on 'Bachelor Boy'.

SEPTEMBER 25

Cliff records tv's in Paris before flying back to London.

SEPTEMBER 26

Takes part in the Michael Ball charity show at London's Dominion Theatre in which they duet on an Everly Brothers medley.
Cilla Black's tv show is transmitted – Cliff performs 'Never Let Go'.

SEPTEMBER 28

Video shoot for 'Never Let Go' at Black Island Studios in London.

SEPTEMBER 29

Interviewed by Radio One and Capital Radio.
Attends Redhill church mission meeting.

SEPTEMBER 30

Cliff Richard's Favourite Bible Stories is published, containing 42 stories selected by Cliff.

OCTOBER 1

Interview with the Israeli media.

OCTOBER 2

Equipment loaded in to Shepperton Studios for the tour rehearsals.

OCTOBER 4

Rehearsals commence – until the 12th.

EUROPE '93

OCTOBER 30
Seiden Sticken, Bielefeld

OCTOBER 31
Kuppelsaal, Hannwer

NOVEMBER 2
I.C.C., Berlin

NOVEMBER 3
Alte Oper, Frankfurt

NOVEMBER 4
Philipshalle, Dusseldorf

NOVEMBER 6
Zenith, Paris

NOVEMBER 7
Ahoy, Rotterdam

NOVEMBER 8
Stadthalle, Bremen

NOVEMBER 11
Festhalle, Bern

NOVEMBER 12
Sedlmayrhalle, Munich

NOVEMBER 14
Austria Centre, Vienna

NOVEMBER 15
Oberfrankenhalle, Bayreuth

NOVEMBER 17
C.C.H., Hamburg

NOVEMBER 18/19
Valby Hallen, Copenhagen

NOVEMBER 20
Idraettens Hos, Vejle

NOVEMBER 21
Aalborg

NOVEMBER 24
Skiverhallen, Skive

NOVEMBER 25
Fins Forum, Odense

NOVEMBER 26
Circle Hall, Herning

NOVEMBER 28
Forest National, Brussels

OCTOBER 5

Children in Need tv interview at Shepperton.

OCTOBER 13

Records greeting for Anne Diamond and Nick Ross's programme.

OCTOBER 15

Cliff and his entourage fly to Bahrain.

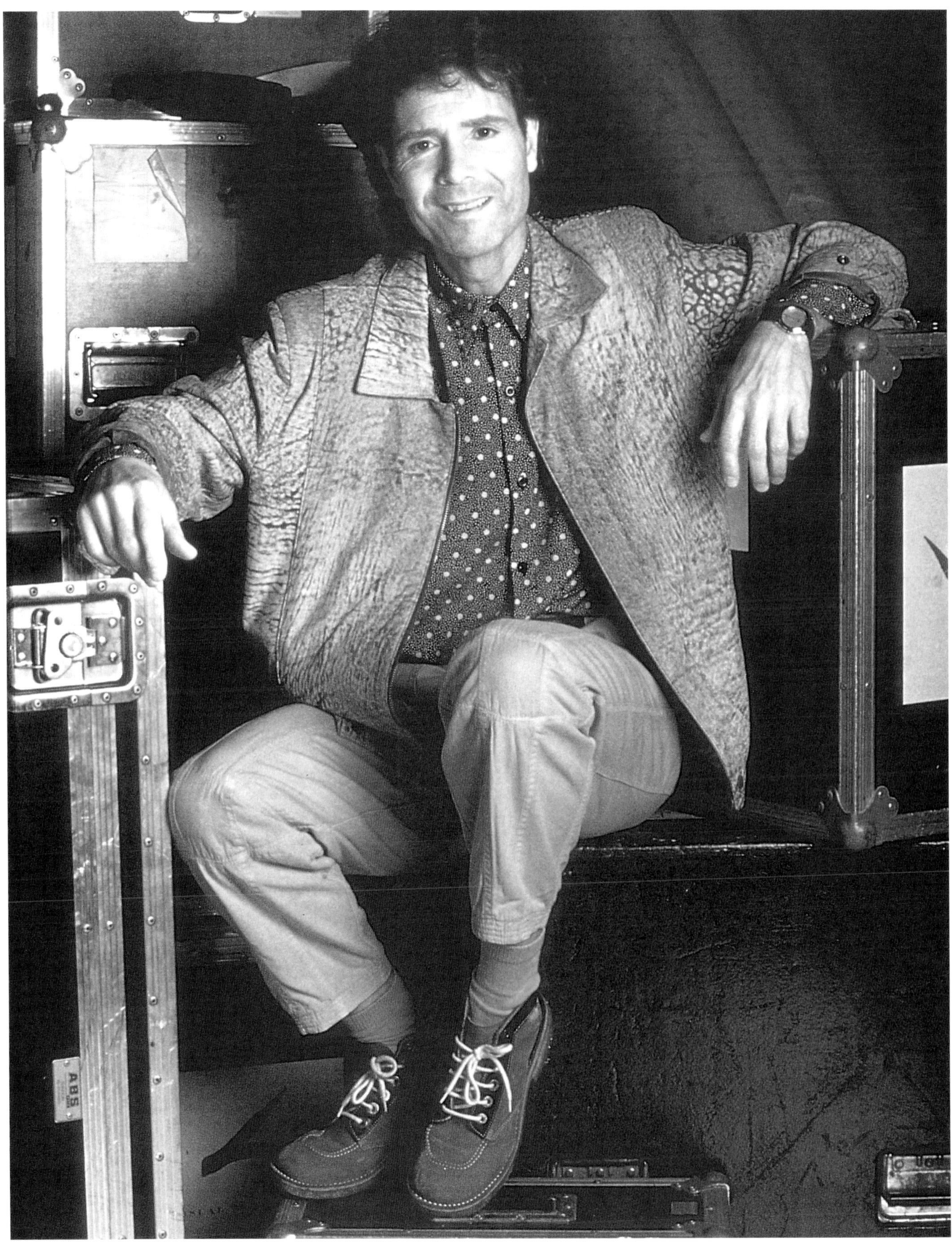

OCTOBER 16

Bahrain Diplomat Hotel.
At the Cliff Richard Fan Club convention in Torrence, California, Ian Samwell is officially presented with a platinum disc for sales of 'Move It' – Cliff's first single that Ian had written 35 years earlier.

OCTOBER 18

Abu Dhabi – Marine Club

OCTOBER 20

Dubai – Dubai Hotel

OCTOBER 21

Dubai – Leisureland Ice

OCTOBER 22

Dubai

OCTOBER 23

Cliff returns to London.

OCTOBER 24

Rehearsals at Pinewood Studios until the 28th.

OCTOBER 27

Filmed for 'Smile for Life'.
Phone interviews with the Danish media.

OCTOBER 28

Heathcliff meeting with Tim Rice, John Farmer and Frank Dunlop.

OCTOBER 29

Cliff flies to Germany.
Cliff Richard – the Complete Chronicle is published by Hamlyn.

OCTOBER 31

Tear Fund's *Songs of Praise* is transmitted.

NOVEMBER 2

Berlin – I.C.C. and press conference.

NOVEMBER 14

'The Story So Far' video released.

NOVEMBER 29

Cliff returns to London.

DECEMBER 2

Cliff is interviewed by phone on the Gloria Hunniford show on BBC Radio Two.
Takes part in a go-karting evening for the Red Cross in the presence of the Princess of Wales.

DECEMBER 2

Interviews with Anglia TV and the Young Telegraph.

DECEMBER 6

The single 'Healing Love' is released.

DECEMBER 7

Cliff records 'Healing Love' and 'Human Work of Art' for the Pebble Mill tv programme.
Pre-records for the *Des o'Connor Show* at Teddington.

DECEMBER 8

Top of the Pops and interviews for *The Money Programme*.

DECEMBER 9

Interviewed by Ray Coleman for *Billboard* magazine.

DECEMBER 10

Interviewed by Capital Radio, Radio One Radio Clyde, Chiltern Radio, Signal Radio, Radio City, Hallam Radio, BRMB, Metro Radio & Invicta Radio.

DECEMBER 11

Performs for *Songs of Praise* at Wembley Conference Centre.

DECEMBER 12

Cliff flies to New York.

DECEMBER 14

Cliff returns to London.

DECEMBER 15

Phone interview with Kingston fm.

DECEMBER 16

Sings 'Saviours Day' on a Recording for *Joy to the World* tv extravaganza.

DECEMBER 17

Christmas shopping.

DECEMBER 18

Cliff's pro-celebrity Tennis Tournament at Birmingham – players include Jasper Carrot.

DECEMBER 19

Cliff performs at Jasper Carrot's *Turning Point* charity event at the NEC in Birmingham.

DECEMBER 21

Cliff's christmas carols at home.

DECEMBER 22

BBC2 repeat *Songs of Praise* featuring Cliff.
The Des o'Connor Show featuring Cliff is transmitted.

DECEMBER 24

Joy to the World is transmitted.
The South Bank Show, dedicated to Cliff, is transmitted.

DECEMBER 25

Christmas Presence, featuring Cliff, is transmitted on BBC 1.

DECEMBER 27

Cliff flies to Portugal for a holiday until 7th January.
The Concert is transmitted by Carlton TV.

JANUARY 1

Cliff on holiday at his house in Portugal until the 7th.

JANUARY 18

Cliff attends an EMI logo design meeting before going on to a Variety Club lunch at Kings Hospital, Dulwich.

JANUARY 19

Cliff sees the musical *Miss Saigon*.

FEBRUARY 5

Cliff flies to Lech in Austria for a skiing holiday until the 12th.

FEBRUARY 14

Cliff is awarded the mens 'head of the year' award by the National Hairdressers Federation, beating the singer/impressionist Joe Longthorne and footballer Glen Hoddle. An award also goes to Cliff's personal hairdresser Paul Chandler of the Paul Merton salon.

FEBRUARY 17

Cliff attends a meeting to discuss the brochure for his next tour.

FEBRUARY 21

The Old Hall in London's Lincolns Inn Fields is the venue for the London press launch for *Heathcliff*. Cliff tells the journalists that the 1939 portrayal of Heathcliff by Laurence Olivier was his favourite.

FEBRUARY 22

Heathcliff launch at the NEC Birmingham and Sheffield.

FEBRUARY 23

Heathcliff launch at Aberdeen and Glasgow.

FEBRUARY 24

Heathcliff box office opens.
Cliff plays tennis at Wimbledon's All-England Club.

FEBRUARY 28

Kiri Te Kanawa dines with Cliff at his home.

MARCH 1

Cliff attends a charity event for Romanian Aid.

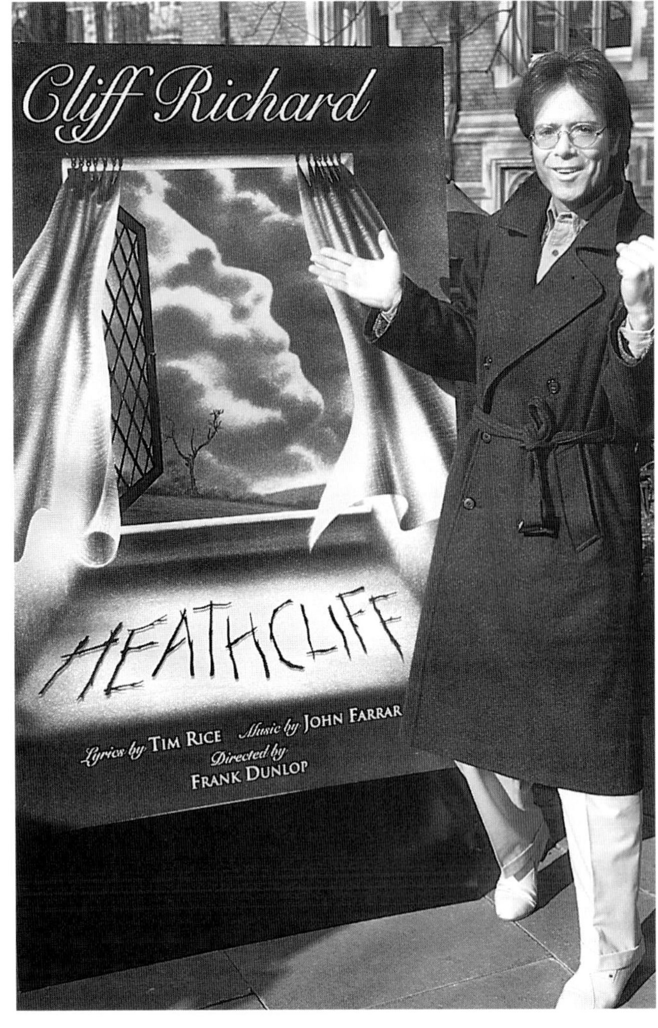

MARCH 8

Cliff interviewed by Belgian radio.
Michael Ball and Cathy McGowan dine with Cliff at his home.

MARCH 10

Cliff plays tennis with Buster Mottram at the All-England Lawn Tennis Club and is afterwards interviewed by his opponent for his programme in the evening.
Cliff attends Kiri Te Kanawa's concert at the Royal Albert Hall.

MARCH 11

Cliff attends a charity photo call for the local White Lodge Centre.

MARCH 13

Cliff dines with Gloria Hunniford.

MARCH 14

Heathcliff meeting with Tim Rice and Frank Dunlop.
Cliff flies to Haworth in Yorkshire to visit the home of Emily Bronte – the authoress of 'Wuthering Heights' the book on which his projected musical *Heathcliff* is based.

MARCH 15

Director Frank Dunlop and Cliff's schoolteacher Jay Norris accompany him on his visit to Haworth Parsonage, where they are shown the sofa on which Emily Bronte is said to have died. They explore the surrounding countryside, taking in a 3-mile walk to Top Withens and the ruined farmhouse that is said to have inspired her.
Sky TV film the visit, during which Jay Norris said of Cliff: 'I thought he was too nice for the showbusiness rat-race'.

MARCH 17

Cliff interviewed by writer Hunter Davies.

MARCH 18

Cliff plays tennis with a journalist from the *Sun* newspaper and is interviewed by his opponent.

MARCH 19

All day *Heathcliff* meeting with Tim Rice and John Farrow.

MARCH 20

Cliff attends a reception at the prime minister's London residence – 10 Downing Street – for Michael Ball's favourite charity for research into ovarian cancer.

MARCH 21

Cliff records at the Penthouse Suite in EMI's Abbey Road studio. Cliff's Tennis Trail at Southampton for three days.

MARCH 22

Cliff, Tim Rice and John Farrow have publicity shots taken at Abbey Road.

MARCH 23

Cliff attends a meeting for potential back projections for *Heathcliff*.

MARCH 24

Recording with John Farrow.

ARTIST Cliff Richard / Phil Everly
PRODUCER Cliff Richard
ENGINEER Gerry Kitchingham
ASSISTANT John Brant
DATE 10/9/94 REEL NO. 1

RGJONES RECORDING STUDIOS
R G Jones (Morden) Ltd
Beulah Road Wimbledon
London SW19 3SB
Tel 01-540 9881 (5 lines)
Fax 01-542 4368

SYNC BOX No code recorded
OFFSET —
BPM —
DELAY TIMES
NOTES: Transfered from 24 track analogue to 32 track digital

1	2 Snare	3 — Toms	4 —	5 — Cymbals	6 —	7 bass gtr	8 Electric gtr (1)
9 Electric gtr (2)	10 Acc gtr (1)	11 Intro gtr (overdub)	12 Lead vocal (Cliff)	13 Lead vocal (Phil)	14 Backing vocals (1)	15 Rhodes El pno	16
17 Backing vocals (2)	18 CP70 synth	19 Acc gtr (2)	20 — crowd	21 —	22 — Ambience	23 —	24
25	26	27	28	29	30	31	32
33 (A1)	34 (A2)	35 (D1)	36 (D2)	37	38	39	40
41	42	43	44	45	46	47	48

MARCH 25

Recording with John Farrow and Tessa Niles.

MARCH 26-28

Recording.

MARCH 29

Cliff is interviewed for a tribute to the Morecambe & Wise tv show.

APRIL 3

Cliff flies to Lech in Austria for another skiing holiday until the 9th April.

APRIL 13

Cliff drives to Dover en route to Portugal.

APRIL 14

Drives to Portugal for a holiday until 27th.

APRIL 14-15

Heathcliff auditions at the Old Vic.

Skiing in Austria with author Mike Read (left) and friend Charles Haswel.

APRIL 18

The Tennis Trail at Sheffield until the 22nd.

APRIL 25

Tennis Trail at Wrexham until May lst.

APRIL 28

Heathcliff auditions at the Old Vic.

APRIL 30

Cliff takes part in the Tennis Trail extravaganza day at Wrexham, North Wales.
Attends an evening performance of the musical *Copacabana* in Manchester.

MAY 2

Phone interview with Seattle USA's *Goldmine* magazine.

MAY 4

Cliff is photographed for his calendar.

MAY 5

Cliff attends a memorial service for tv producer Gordon Elsbury.

MAY 9

Tennis Trail at Swansea for several days .

MAY 11

Tennis Trail at Norwich until 15th.

MAY 13

The postponement of *Heathcliff* is announced.

MAY 14

The *Morecambe & Wise Show*, featuring Cliff, is transmitted by BBC television.

MAY 16

Tennis Trail at Welwyn until 20th.
Brian Conley dines with Cliff at home.

MAY 17

Cliff takes part in a live telephone interview with BBC Radio Two.

MAY 23

Tennis Trail at Liverpool until 29th.

MAY 24

Records for Cilla Black's *Surprise Surprise*.

MAY 25

At London's Grosvenor House Hotel Cliff presents Tim Rice with his Ivor Novello award for outstanding contribution to British music.

MAY 30

Cliff interviewed by Gloria Hunniford for Radio Two on the postponement of *Heathcliff*.

JUNE 2

Cliff filmed for EMI's centenary video.

JUNE 5

Cliff attends the Beckenham tennis finals.
Surprise Surprise featuring Cliff is transmitted.

JUNE 6

Tennis Trail at Sunderland until 12th.

JUNE 7

Cliff interviewed for a television programme on the history of the London Palladium.

JUNE 12

Attends the final of the Stella Artois tennis tournament at London's Queens Club.

JUNE 13

Cliff presents a Children In Need prize.
Tennis Trail at Bodmin until 17th.

JUNE 18

Cliff sees Torville & Dean at Wembley.

JUNE 19

Cliff plays in a pro-celebrity tennis match at London's Hurlingham Club.

JUNE 20

Cliff at Wimbledon for the start of the tennis fortnight.

JUNE 21-24

Wimbledon.

JUNE 25

Cliff entertains his family at home.

JUNE 27-JULY 1

Wimbledon.

JULY 3

Cliff attends the Wimbledon men's finals.

JULY 4

Cliff takes part in a pro-celebrity tennis tournament at Queens Club, London, partnering Ken Rosewall and later John Newcombe. After Rosewall is taken ill Cliff and John Newcombe lose in the final to Andrew Castle and Alan Cunningham, which is televised by Sky TV.

JULY 5

Cliff attends the Hampton Court Flower Show preview.
The Tennis Trail begins at Solihull and runs until the 8th.

JULY 10

The Tennis Trail begins at Westway and runs until the 17th.

JULY 14

Jonathan Dawson interviews Cliff about his garden for a feature in the *Mail On Saturday* magazine.
Cliff performs for 250 people in the Byfleet village hall to raise money for repairs to the local church. Among the songs performed are 'Living Doll'; 'Silhouettes'; 'On The Beach'; 'Daddy's Home' and 'Summer Holiday' with special Byfleet lyrics.

JULY 16

Cliff's summer party at home.

JULY 19

Cliff appears at Liverpool Empire with Bucks Fizz, The Drifters, Sir John Mills, Joe Brown, The Merseybeats, Kenny Ball, Gerry Marsden and the cast of *Brookside* for Roy Castle's *Train of Hope* concert.

JULY 25

Cliff undertakes a photo session.

JULY 26

Cliff flies to his home in Portugal for a holiday until August 19th.

AUGUST 6

Daily Mail article published under the headline : 'rock follies in Cliff's garden.'

AUGUST 11

Re-mastering of the Hit List album.

AUGUST 19

Re-mastering at Metropolis Studios in Chiswick.

AUGUST 23

Cliff interviewed by David Wigg about his sports idols, and interviewed at Brooklands for *Top Gear* about the Jensen Interceptor.

SEPTEMBER 1

Cliff films at home for Gloria Hunniford's tv show.

Cliff at the Sparks Tennis event, flanked by Anneka Rice (left) and Kiri Te Kanawa, July 1994

SEPTEMBER 5

Filming at Bray Studios.

SEPTEMBER 6

Cliff records for Children in Need.

SEPTEMBER 7

Re-mixing at R G Jones Studio for 'When Will I Be Loved' and 'All I Have To Do Is Dream'.

SEPTEMBER 8

Cliff and Bill Latham attend Roy Castle's funeral, the entertainer having died after a long battle against cancer.

SEPTEMBER 9-12

Cliff at R G Jones Studio.

SEPTEMBER 13

Cliff is a guest at the Dorincourt Centre for the Disabled at Leatherhead.

SEPTEMBER 15

Mastering 'When Will I Be Loved' and 'All I Have To Do Is Dream' at Metropolis Studios.

SEPTEMBER 22

Cliff is interviewed by the *Daily Express*, the *Daily Mirror*, BBC World Service and cable television.

SEPTEMBER 23

Recording at R G Jones Studio.

SEPTEMBER 26

Cliff flies to Glasgow to be interviewed live on Scottish tv by Billy Sloan.

SEPTEMBER 27

Cliff is interviewed by *Bella* magazine, *Mojo* magazine, the *Independent* and is photographed for the *Sunday Mirror* magazine.

SEPTEMBER 28

Cliff voices German tv and radio commercials.

SEPTEMBER 29

Cliff is interviewed by BFBS, IRN, Mercia Gold radio, the *Independent Citizen*, the *Guardian Gazette* and the *Evening Standard*.

SEPTEMBER 30

Cliff flies to Eurodisney for a short break until October 3rd.

OCTOBER 2

Cliff featured on the BBC2 programme *Top Gear – The Car and the Stars*.

OCTOBER 3

The 'Hit List' double cd and video is released. The cd charts at number 3 in the first week, and the video at number 2. The album soon goes platinum.

OCTOBER 4

Cliff opens two London based childrens homes – in Paddington and Ladbroke Grove.

OCTOBER 5

At R G Jones the applause is removed from 'All I Have To Do Is Dream'.

OCTOBER 6

Cliff is interviewed by *Woman's Journal* and later opens a new indoor tennis centre at St George's College, Weybridge.

OCTOBER 7

Cliff flies to Portugal for a holiday until the 14th.

OCTOBER 15

Tour rehearsals begin at Bray Studios until the 21st.

OCTOBER 17

Cliff shoots the tv advertisement for the Hit List Tour.

OCTOBER 18

Cliff attends the premiere for the new Disney film *The Lion King* at the Odeon Leicester Square.

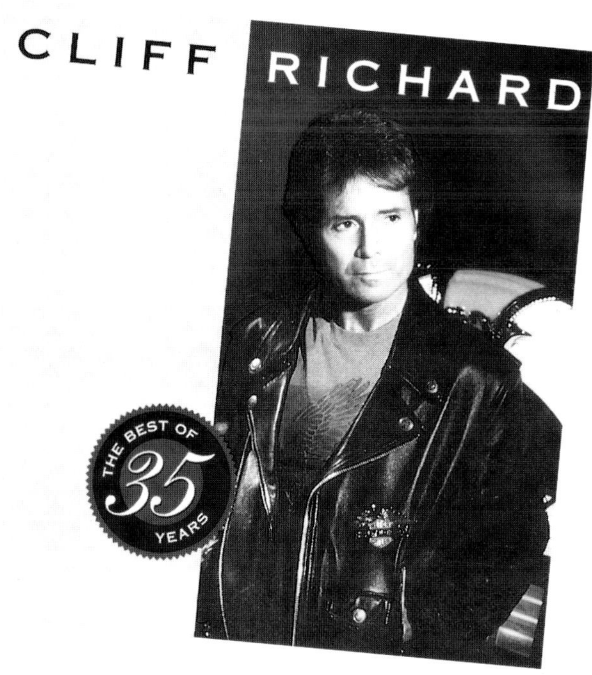

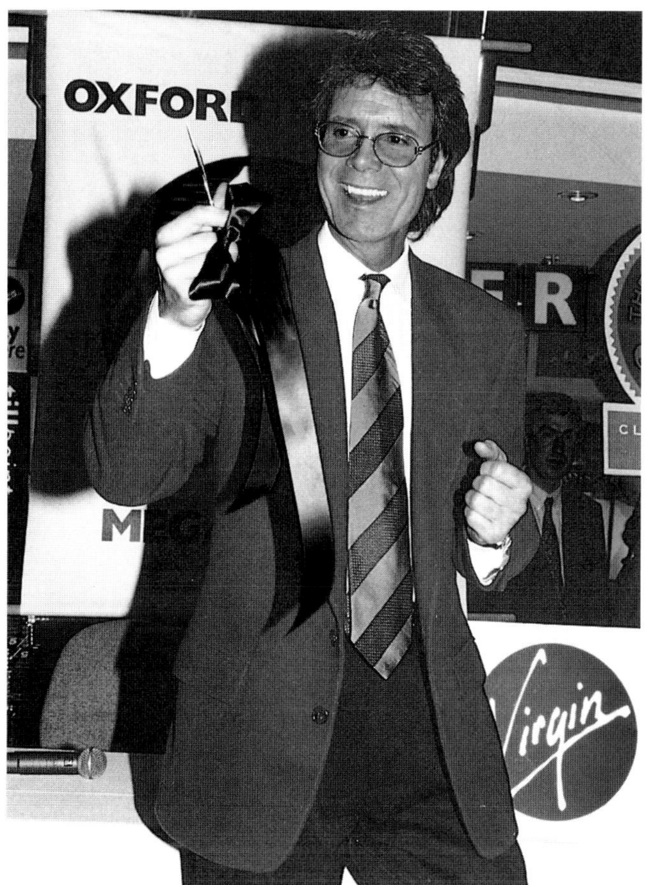

Opening the new singles department at the Virgin Megastore.

OCTOBER 22

Cliff performs in driving rain before the rugby league final at Wembley Stadium.

OCTOBER 24

Cliff plays tennis at David Lloyd's Tennis Club at Raynes Park.

OCTOBER 25

Cliff dines with choreographer neighbour Peter Gordeno.

OCTOBER 26

Phone interview with the Danish media.

OCTOBER 28

Cliff films for *Power for Living*.

OCTOBER 31

Cliff dines at the Groucho Club with Tim Rice and Frank Dunlop.

NOVEMBER 1

Cliff is interviewed for Radio Two by Brian Matthew.

NOVEMBER 2

Cliff is interviewed for Radio Five.

With Phil Everly, Sheffield Arena, December 1994.

NOVEMBER 3

Cliff shoots tv promos at Docklands during rehearsals for the tour.

NOVEMBER 7

The video 'Christmas with Cliff Richard' is released, featuring Cliff in concert at Chichester's Festival Theatre on 12th December 1980.

NOVEMBER 9

Cliff appears on Pebble Mill tv show where he presents former Shadow Hank Marvin with a gold disc for the album 'Heartbeat', before performing 'Travelling Light' and 'Living Doll' together.

NOVEMBER 10

Cliff switches on the christmas lights at Birmingham.

NOVEMBER 13

Cliff is interviewed by Gordon Giltrap for *Guitarist* magazine.

NOVEMBER 15

Appears on *Good Morning* with Anne Diamond and Nick Owen.

NOVEMBER 16

Cliff opens the Birmingham Indoor Tennis Centre and plays a match with wheelchair and able-bodied players.
Cliff is interviewed by Pebble Mill for a documentary on tv theme writer Simon May.

NOVEMBER 18

Hit List Tour begins at Wembley.

NOVEMBER 22

Hit List Tour at Wembley.
Backstage Sir Colin Southgate from EMI presents Cliff with a platinum disc for the Hit List album.

NOVEMBER 24

Phone interview with the *Radio Times*.

NOVEMBER 28

'All I Have To Do Is Dream' – a duet with Phil Everly – is released. 'Miss You Nights' is on the 'b' side.

NOVEMBER 29

Live interview with Mick Brown for Capital Radio.

With old Shadows partner Hank Marvin at Birmingham Tennis Tournament.

NOVEMBER 30

Cliff attends a thanksgiving service at All Souls Church for Roy Castle. Broadcast on Radio Two, the service includes Cliff singing 'When I Survey The Wondrous Cross'.

DECEMBER

Cliff's comments during an interview that in an ideal world mothers should stay at home and bring up their children, is met by a howl of protest from some sections of the media.

DECEMBER 3

Records for Budapest tv.

DECEMBER 12

Cliff spends the day christmas shopping at Harrods.

DECEMBER 17

Cliff's pro-celebrity Tennis Tournament at Birmingham includes Mr Motivator, guitarist Hank Marvin, comedian/singer Brian Conley, and tennis stars Chris Bailey, Jeremy Bates, Virginia Wade and Jo Durie.

Channel Four transmit the second half of the Hit List Tour, which had been filmed at Sheffield.

DECEMBER 20

The Pebble Mill documentary on Simon May with a contribution from Cliff is transmitted.

DECEMBER 21

Cliff's latest release 'All I Have To Do Is Dream', a duet with Phil Everly, is heard playing in the background of Cliff's favourite television programme, the long-running soap opera set in the north of England, *Coronation Street.*

DECEMBER 28

Cliff flies to Portugal for a break until the 6th of January.

JANUARY 10

Cliff records 'We Being Many' with Helen Shapiro at R G Jones.

JANUARY 16

Tennis Trail at Norwich until the 20th.

Cliff interviews tennis champion Martina Navratilova on the ITV show *This Morning.*

JANUARY 30

Tennis Trail at Corby until 3rd February.

HIT LIST TOUR – UK

NOVEMBER 18/20/22/23/25/26/27/29/30
Wembley Arena

DECEMBER 3/4/6
Glasgow

DECEMBER 8/9/10
Aberdeen

DECEMBER 13/14/15/16
Sheffield

DECEMBER 19/20
Belfast

DECEMBER 21/22
Dublin

HIT LIST TOUR – THE FAR EAST

JANUARY 23/24
QE2 Stadium, Hong Kong

JANUARY 25/26
Singapore

JANUARY 28/29/30/31
Town Hall, Christchurch

FEBRUARY 2/3
Supertop, Auckland

FEBRUARY 4
Bowl of Brooklands, Aew Plymouth

FEBRUARY 9
Entertainment Centre, Brisbane

FEBRUARY 11/12
Entertainment Centre, Newcastle

FEBRUARY 14/15
Flinders Park, Melbourne

FEBRUARY 17/18
Bruce Indoor Stadium, Canberra

FEBRUARY 20/21/22
Entertainment Centre, Sydney

FEBRUARY 24/25
Entertainment Centre, Adelaide

FEBRUARY 28 / MARCH 1
Entertainment Centre, Perth

HIT LIST TOUR – SOUTH AFRICA

APRIL 11
Greenpoint Stadium

APRIL 13
St George's Park, Port Elizabeth

APRIL 15
King's Park Stadium, Durban

APRIL 17
Ellis Park Stadium, Johannesburg

APRIL 19
Springbok Park, Bloemfontein

APRIL 21
Loftus Versueld, Pretoria

Songs featured on the tour:
'Move It'/'Living Doll'/'Travelin' Light'/'A Voice In The Wilderness'/'Fall In Love With You'/'Please Don't Tease'/'Nine Times Out of Ten'/'I Love You'/'Theme For a Dream'/'Gee Whiz It's You'/'A Girl Like You'/'When The Girl In Your Arms Is The Girl In Your Heart'/'The Young Ones'/'Do You Wanna Dance'/'It'll Be Me'/'The Next Time'/'Bachelor Boy'/'Summer Holiday'/'Lucky Lips'/'It's All In The Game'/'Don't Talk to Him'/'Constantly'/'The Minute You're Gone'/'Wind Me Up (Let Me Go)'/'Congratulations'/'Power To All Our Friends'/'We Don't Talk Anymore'/'Carrie'/'Wired For Sound'/'Daddy's Home'/'Some People'/'Mistletoe & Wine'/'Miss you Nights'/'Green Light'

FEBRUARY 6

Flies to Australia.
Tennis Trail at Portsmouth until 11th February.

FEBRUARY 27

Tennis Trail begins at Liverpool until 3rd March.

MARCH 6

Tennis Trail at Nottingham until 11th March.

MARCH 20

Tennis Trail at Aberdeen until 25th March.

MARCH 25

Cliff flies to Lech, Austria, for a skiing holiday until 3rd April.

MARCH 27

Tennis Trail at Sheffield until 31st.

APRIL 24

Tennis Trail at Caernarvon until 29th April.

CLIFF RICHARD - DISCOGRAPHY 1958 – 1995

UK SINGLES

Move It/Schoolboy Crush
DB 4178 August 1958

High Class Baby/My Feet Hit The Ground
DB 4203 November 1958

Livin' Lovin' Doll/Steady With You
DB 4249 January 1959

Mean Streak/Never Mind
DB 4290 April 1959
(Also released on 78 rpm)

Living Doll/Apron Strings
DB 4306 July 1959

Travellin' Light/Dynamite
DB 4351 October 1959

A Voice In The Wilderness/Don't Be Mad At Me
DB 4398 January 1960
(First seven 45s also released on 78 rpm)

Fall In Love With You/Willie And The Hand Jive
DB 4431 March 1960

Please Don't Tease/Where Is My Heart?
DB 4479 June 1960

Nine Times Out Of Ten/Thinking Of Our Love
DB 4506 September 1960

I Love You/'D'In Love
DB 4547 November 1960

Theme For A Dream/Mumblin' Mosie
DB 4593 February 1961

Gee Whiz It's You/I Cannot Find A True Love
DC 756 March 1961

A Girl Like You/Now's The Time To Fall In Love
DB 4667 June 1961

When The Girl In Your Arms (Is The Girl In Your Heart)/Got A Funny Feeling
DB 4716 October 1961

What'd I Say/Blue Moon
DC 758 1961

The Young Ones/We Say Yeah
DB 4761 January 1962

I'm Looking Out The Window/Do You Wanna Dance
DB 4828 May 1962

It'll Be Me/Since I Lost You
DB 4886 August 1962

The Next Time/Bachelor Boy
DB 4950 November 1962

Summer Holiday/Dancing Shoes
DB 4977 February 1963

Lucky Lips/I Wonder
DB 7034 May 1963
It's All In The Game/Your Eyes Tell On You
DB 7089 August 1963

Don't Talk To Him/Say You're Mine
DB 7150 November 1963

I'm The Lonely One/Watch What You Do With My Baby
DB 7203 January 1964

Constantly/True True Lovin'
DB 7272 April 1964

On The Beach/A Matter Of Moments
DB 7305 June 1964

The Twelfth Of Never/I'm Afraid To Go Home
DB 7372 October 1964

I Could Easily Fall (In Love With You)/I'm In Love With You
DB 7420 December 1964

This Was My Special Day/I'm Feeling Oh So Lonely
DB 7435 December 1964

The Minute You're Gone/Just Another Guy
DB 7496 March 1965

Angel/Razzle Dazzle
DC 762 May 1965

On My Word/Just A Little Bit Too Late
DB 7596 June 1965

The Time In Between/Look Before You Love
DB 7660 August 1965

Wind Me Up/The Night
DB 7745 October 1965

Blue Turns To Grey/Somebody Loses
DB 7866 March 1966

Visions/What Would I Do (For The Love Of A Girl)
DB 7968 July 1966

Time Drags By/The La La La Song
DB 8017 October 1966

In The Country/Finders Keepers
DB 8094 December 1966

It's All Over/Why Wasn't I Born Rich?
DB 8150 March 1967

I'll Come Running/I Get The Feelin'
DB 8210 June 1967

The Day I Met Marie/Our Story Book
DB 8245 August 1967

All My Love/Sweet Little Jesus Boy
DB 8293 November 1967

Congratulations/High'n'Dry
DB 8376 March 1968

I'll Love You Forever Today/Girl You'll Be A Woman Soon
DB 8437 June 1968

Marianne/Mr Nice
DB 8476 September 1968

Don't Forget To Catch Me/What's More (I Don't Need Her)
DB 8503 November 1968

Good Times (Better Times)/Occasional Rain
DB 8548 February 1969

Big Ship/She's Leaving You
DB 8581 May 1969

Throw Down A Line (with Hank Marvin)/Reflections
DB 8615 September 1969

With The Eyes Of A Child/So Long
DB 8648 November 1969

The Joy Of Living (with Hank Marvin)/Leave My Woman Alone/Boogatoo (Hank Marvin)
DB 8657 February 1970

Goodbye Sam Hello Samantha/You Can Never Tell
DB 8685 June 1970

I Ain't Got Time Anymore/Monday Comes Too Soon
DB 8708 August 1970

Sunny Honey Girl/Don't Move Away (with Olivia Newton-John)/I Was Only Fooling Myself
DB 8747 January 1971

Silvery Rain/Annabella Umbrella/Time Flies
DB 8774 April 1971

Flying Machine/Pigeon
DB 8797 July 1971

Sing A Song Of Freedom/A Thousand Conversations
DB 8836 November 1971

Jesus/Mr Cloud
DB 8864 March 1972

Living In Harmony/Empty Chairs
DB 8917 August 1972

A Brand New Song/The Old Accordion
DB 8957 December 1972

Power To All Our Friends/Come Back Billie Jo
EMI 2012 March 1973

Help It Along/Tomorrow Rising/The Days Of Love/Ashes To Ashes
EMI 2022 May 1973

Take Me High/Celestial Houses
EMI 2088 November 1973

(You Keep Me) Hangin' On/Love Is Here
EMI 2150 March 1975

It's Only Me You've Left Behind/You're The One
EMI 2279 March 1975

Honky Tonk Angel /(Wouldn't You Know It) Got Myself A Girl
EMI 2344 September 1975

Miss You Nights/Love Enough
EMI 2376 February 1976

Devil Woman/Love On (Shine On)
EMI 2485 May 1976

I Can't Ask For Anything More Than You/Junior Cowboy
EMI 2499 August 1976

Hey Mr Dream Maker/No One Waits
EMI 2559 November 1976
My Kinda Life/Nothing Left For Me To Say
EMI 2584 February 1977

When Two Worlds Drift Apart/That's Why I Love You
EMI 2663 June 1977

Yes! He Lives/Good On The Sally Army
EMI 2730 January 1978

Please Remember Me/Please Don't Tease
EMI 2832 July 1978

Can't Take The Hurt Anymore/Needing A Friend
EMI 2885 November 1978

Green Light/Imagine Love
EMI 2920 March 1979

We Don't Talk Anymore/Count Me Out
EMI 2675 July 1979

Hot Shot/Walking In The Light
EMI 5003 November 1979

Carrie/Moving In
EMI 5006 February 1980

Dreamin'/Dynamite
EMI 5095 August 1980

Suddenly (with Olivia Newton-John)/You Made Me Love You (Olivia Newton-John)
JET 7002 October 1980

A Little In Love/Keep On Looking
EMI 5123 January 1981

Wired For Sound/Hold On
EMI 5221 August 1981

Daddy's Home/Shakin' All Over
EMI 5251 November 1981

The Only Way Out/Under The Influence
EMI 5318 July 1982

Where Do We Go From Here?/Discovering
EMI 5341 September 1982

Little Town/Love And A Helping Hand/You, Me And Jesus
EMI 5348 November 1982

She Means Nothing To Me (with Phil Everly)/A Man And A Woman (Phil Everly)
Capitol CL 276 January 1983

True Love Ways/Galadriel
EMI 5385 April 1983

Drifting (with Sheila Walsh)/It's Lonely When The Lights Go Out (Sheila Walsh)
DJM SHEIL 1 May 1983

Drifting (with Sheila Walsh)/It's Lonely When The Lights Go Out (Sheila Walsh)
DJM SHEIL 100 - picture disc May 1983

Never Say Die/Lucille
EMI 5415 August 1983

Never Say Die/Lucille
EMI 12EMI 5415 - 12" single August 1983

Please Don't Fall In Love/Too Close To Heaven
EMI 5437 November 1983

Baby You're Dynamite/Ocean Deep
EMI 5457 March 1984

Baby You're Dynamite/Ocean Deep/Baby You're Dynamite (extended mix)
12EMI 5457 12" single March 1984

Ocean Deep/Baby You're Dynamite
EMI 5457 May 1984

Two To The Power (with Janet Jackson)/Rock And Roll (Janet Jackson)
A & M AM 210 September 1984

Two To The Power (with Janet Jackson)/Rock And Roll/Don't Mess Up This Good Thing (Janet Jackson)
A & M AMX 210 - 12" single Sept. 1984

Shooting From The Heart/Small World
Rich 1 October 1984

Shooting From The Heart/Small World
RICHP 1 - picture disc November 1984

Heart User/I Will Follow You
Rich 2 January 1985

Heart User/I Will Follow You/Heart User (extended mix)
EMI 12 Rich 2 - 12" single January 1985

She's So Beautiful/She's So Beautiful (inst)
EMI 5531 September 1985

She's So Beautiful/She's So Beautiful (extended mix)
12EMI 5531 12" single September 1985

It's In Every One Of Us/Alone (instrumental)/It's In Everyone Of Us (choral version)
EMI 5537 November 1985

It's In Every One Of Us/It's In Every One Of Us (instrumental)/Alone
EMI 12EMI 5537 - 12" single Nov. 1985

Living Doll (with The Young Ones)/Happy
WEA YZ65 March 1986

Living Doll (with The Young Ones)/Happy/Disco Funk Get Up Get Down
WEA YZ65T - 12" single March 1986

Born To Rock And Roll/Law Of The Universe
EMI 5545 May 1986

Born To Rock And Roll/Law Of The Universe
EMI 12EMI 5545 - 12" single May 1986

All I Ask Of You (with Sarah Brightman)/Phantom Of The Opera Overture
Polydor POPSX 802 - September 1986

All I Ask Of You (with Sarah Brightman)/Phantom Of The Opera Overture/Only You
Polydor POPSX 802 - 12" single
September 1986

Slow Rivers (with Elton John)/Billy And The Kids (Elton John)
Rocket EJS 13 November 1986

Slow Rivers (with Elton John)/Billy And The Kids/Lord Of The Flies (Elton John)
Rocket EJS 13-12 - 12" single Nov. 1986

My Pretty One/Love Ya/Under The Gun
EM 4 June 1987

My Pretty One/Love Ya/Under The Gun
12EM 4 - 12" single June 1987

My Pretty One/Love Ya
EMG 4 - gatefold sleeve June 1987

My Pretty One/Love Ya/Under The Gun
12EMP 4 - 12" single with poster

Some People/One Time Lover Man
EM 18 - August 1987

Some People/One Time Lover Man/Reunion Of The Heart
12EM 18 - 12" single August 1987

Some People/One Time Lover Man
EMG 18 - gatefold sleeve August 1987

Some People/One Time Lover Man
EMP 18 - picture disc August 1987

Remember Me/Another Christmas Day
EM 31 October 1987

Remember Me/Another Christmas Day/Brave New World
12EM 31 - 12" single October 1987

Remember Me/Another Christmas Day/Brave New World
CDEM 31 - CD single October 1987

Remember Me/Another Christmas Day/Brave New World
12EMP 31 - special 12" single Oct. 1987

Two Hearts/Yesterday, Today, Forever
EM 42 February 1988

Two Hearts/Yesterday, Today, Forever/Wild Geese
12 EM 42 - 12" single February 1988

Two Hearts/Yesterday, Today, Forever/Wild Geese
12 EMG 42 - 12" gatefold single with Valentine's card
February 1988

Mistletoe And Wine/Marmaduke
EM 78 November 1988

Mistletoe And Wine/Marmaduke/Little Town
12EM 78 - 12" single November 1988

Mistletoe And Wine/Marmaduke/Little Town/La Gonave
CDEM 78 - CD single with Christmas card
November 1988

Mistletoe And Wine/Marmaduke/Little Town
12EMX 78 - 12" single with advent calendar
November 1988

Mistletoe And Wine/Marmaduke
EMP 78 - 7" poster bag with calendar
November 1988

Mistletoe And Wine/Maramaduke/True Love Ways
EMS 78 - Special 7" December 1988

The Best Of Me/Move It/Lindsay Jane
EM 92 May 1989

The Best Of Me/Move It/Lindsay Jane/High Class Baby
12EM 92 - 12" single May 1989

I Just Don't Have The Heart/Wide Open Space
EM 101 August 1989

I Just Don't Have The Heart/Wide Open Space/I Just Don't Have The Heart (inst)
12EM 101 - 12" single August 1989

I Just Don't Have The Heart/Wide Open Space/I Just Don't Have The Heart (inst)
12EMP 101 - 12" single Aug.1989

I Just Don't Have The Heart/Wide Open Space/I Just Don't Have The Heart (instrumental)
CDEM 101 - CD single August 1989

I Just Don't Have The Heart/Wide Open Space/I Just Don't Have The Heart (instrumental)
TCEM 101 - cassette single August 1989

Lean On You/Hey Mister
EM 105 October 1989

Lean On You/Hey Mister/Lean On You (extended mix)
12EM 105 - 12" single October 1989

Lean On You/Hey Mister/Lean On You (extended mix)
EMPD 105 - 7" picture disc October 1989

Lean On You/Hey Mister/Lean On You (extended mix)
CDEM 105 - CD single October 1989

Lean On You/Hey Mister/Lean On You (extended mix)
TCEM 105 - cassette single October 1989

Whenever God Shines His Light (single version)/I'd Love To Write Another Song (Van Morrison)/Whenever God Shines His Light (album version)
POLYDOR VAN52 December 1989

Stronger Than That/Joanna
EM 129 February 1990

Stronger Than That/Joanna/Stronger Than That (extended mix)
12EM 129 - 12" single February 1990

Stronger Than That/Joanna
12EMP 129 - 12" poster bag February 1990

Stronger Than That/Joanna
CDEM 129 - CD single February 1990

Stronger Than That/Joanna
TCEM 129 - cassette single February 1990

Stronger Than That/Joanna
EMS 129 - postcard pack February 1990

Silhouettes/The Winner
EM 152 August 1990

Silhouettes/The Winner
EMS 152 - special package including free print August 1990

Silhouettes/The Winner/All The Time You Need
12EM 152 - 12" single August 1990
Silhouettes/The Winner/All The Time You Need
CDEM 152 - CD single August 1990
Silhouettes/The Winner/All The Time You Need
TCEM 152 - cassette single August 1990

From A Distance/Lindsay Jane II
EM 155 October 1990

From A Distance/I Could Easily Fall (In Love With You)
EMPD 155 - limited edition 7" picture disc featuring alternative B-side October 1990

From A Distance/Lindsay Jane II/Wired For Sound
12EMP 155 - 12" single poster bag
October 1990

From A Distance/Lindsay Jane II/Wired For Sound
CDEM 155 - CD single October 1990

From A Distance/Lindsay Jane II
TCEM 155 - cassette single October 1990

Saviour's Day/The Oh Boy Medley
XMAS 90 November 1990

Saviour's Day/The Oh Boy Medley
XMASP 90 - Decade pack includes five photos from five decades
November 1990

Saviour's Day/The Oh Boy Medley/Where Are You
12XMAS 90 - 12" single November 1990

Saviour's Day/The Oh Boy Medley
TCXMAS 90 - cassette single Nov.1990

Saviour's Day/The Oh Boy Medley/Where Are You
CDXMAS 90 - CD single November 1990

More To Life/Mo's Theme (instrumental)
EM 205 September 1991

More To Life/Mo's Theme (instrumental)
TCEM 205 - cassette single Sept.1991

More To Life/Mo's Theme (instrumental)
CDEM 205 - CD single September 1991

We Should Be Together/Miss You Nights (Live Version)
TCXMAS 91 - cassette single Nov.1991

We Should Be Together/Miss You Nights (live version)/Mistletoe And Wine
CDXMAS 91 - CD single November 1991

We Should Be Together/Miss You Nights (live version)
XMASG 91 - 7" souvenir edition in gatefold sleeve November 1991

We Should Be Together/Mistletoe And Wine/Twelve Days Of Christmas/The Holly And The Ivy
XMAS 91 - Christmas EP inserts into 7" gatefold sleeve
December 1991

This New Year (Edit)/Scarlet Ribbons
EMS 218 - features special engraved autograph etched onto disc
December 1991
This New Year/Scarlet Ribbons (12" remix)/We Don't Talk Anymore (remix 1991)
12EMP 218 - 12" single includes special free calendar poster
December 1991

This New Year/I Love You/Scarlet Ribbons (12" remix)/We Don't Talk Anymore (remix 1991)
CDEM 218 - CD single December 1991

This New Year/Scarlet Ribbons
TCEM 218 - cassette single Dec. 1991

I Still Believe In You/Bulange Downpour
EM 255 November 1992

I Still Believe In You/Bulange Downpour
TCEM 255 - cassette single Nov. 1992

I Still Believe In You/Bulange Downpour/There's No Power In Pity
CDEMS 255 - CD single November 1992

I Still Believe In You/Remember (When Two Worlds Drift Apart - French adaption)/Ocean Deep
CDEM 255 - second CD single to complete special set November 1992

Peace In Our Time/Somebody Loves You
EM 265 March 1993

Human Work Of Art/Ragged
EM 267 June 1993

Never Let Go/Congratulations
EM 281 September 1993

Healing Love/Carrie
EM 294 December 1993

All I Have To Do Is Dream/Miss You Nights
EM 360 November 1994

UK EPs

Serious Charge (Drifters)
Living Doll/No Turning Back/Mad About You/Chinchilla
SEG 7895 May 1959

Cliff No.1 (Drifters)
Apron Strings/My Babe/Down The Line/I Gotta Feeling/Baby I Don't Care/Jet Black
SEG 7903/ESG 7754 June 1959

Cliff No.2 (Drifters)
Donna/Move It/Ready Teddy/Too Much/Don't Bug Me Baby/Driftin'
SEG 7910/ESG 7769 July 1959

Expresso Bongo (Shadows)
Love/A Voice In The Wilderness/The Shrine On The Second Floor/Bongo Blues SEG 7971/ESG 7783 January 1960

Cliff Sings No.1
Here Comes Summer/I Gotta Know/Blue Suede Shoes/The Snake And The Bookworm
SEG 7979/ESG 7788 February 1960

Cliff Sings No.2
Twenty Flight Rock/Pointed Toe Shoes/Mean Woman Blues/I'm Walkin'
SEG 7987/ESG 7794 March 1960

Cliff Sings No.3
I'll String Along With you/Embraceable You/As Time Goes By/The Touch Of Your Lips
SEG 8005/ESG 7808 June 1960

Cliff Sings No.4
I Don't Know Why /Little Things Mean A Lot/Somewhere Along The Way/That's My Desire
SEG 8021/ESG 7816 September 1960

Cliff's Silver Discs
Please Don't Tease/Fall In Love With You/Nine Times Out Of Ten/Travellin' Light
SEG 8050 December 1960

Me And My Shadows No.1
I'm Gonna Get You/You And I/I Cannot Find A True Love/Evergreen Tree/She's Gone
SEG 8065/ESG 7837 February 1961

Me And My Shadows No.2
Left Out Again/You're Just The One To Do It/Lamp Of Love/Choppin' And Changin'/We Have It Made
SEG 8071/ESG 7841 March 1961

Me And My Shadows No.3
Tell Me/Gee Whiz It's You/I'm Willing To Learn/I Love You So/I Don't Know
SEG 8078/ESG 7843 April 1961

Listen To Cliff
What'd I Say/True Love Will Come To You/Blue Moon/Lover
SEG 8105/ESG 7858 October 1961

Dream
Dream/All I Do Is Dream Of You/I'll See You In My Dreams/When I Grow Too Old To Dream
SEG 8119/ESG 7867 November 1961

Listen To Cliff No.2
Unchained Melody/First Lesson In Love/Idle Gossip/Almost Like Being In Love/Beat Out Dat Rhythm On A Drum
SEG 8126/ESG 7870 December 1961

Cliff's Hit Parade
I Love You/Theme For A Dream/A Girl Like You/When The Girl In Your Arms (Is The Girl In Your Heart)
SEG 8133 February 1962

Cliff Richard No.1
Forty Days/Catch Me/How Wonderful To Know/Tough Enough
SEG 8151 April 1962

Hits From The Young Ones
The Young Ones/Got A Funny Feeling/Lessons In Love/We Say Yeah
SEG 8159 May 1962

Cliff Richard No.2
Fifty Tears For Every Kiss/The Night Is So Lonely/Poor Boy/Y'Arriva
SEG 8168 June 1962

Cliff's Hits
It'll Be Me/Since I Lost You/Do You Want To Dance/I'm Looking Out The Window
SEG 8203 November 1962

Time For Cliff And The Shadows
So I've Been Told/I'm Walking The Blues/When My Dreamboat Comes Home/Blueberry Hill/You Don't Know
SEG 8228/ESG 7887 March 1963

Holiday Carnival
Carnival/Moonlight Bay/Some Of These Days/For You For Me
SEG 8246/ESG 7892 May 1963

Hits From Summer Holiday
Summer Holiday/The Next Time/Dancing Shoes/Bachelor Boy
SEG 8250/ESG 7896 June 1963

More Hits From Summer Holiday
Seven Days To A Holiday/Stranger In Town/Really Waltzing/All At Once
SEG 8263/ESG 7898 September 1963

Cliff's Lucky Lips
It's All In The Game/Your Eyes Tell On You/Lucky Lips/I Wonder
SEG 8269 October 1963

Love Songs
I'm In The Mood For Love/Secret Love/Love Leters/I Only Have Eyes For You
SEG 8272/ESG 7900 November 1963

When In France
La Ber/Boum/J'Attendrai/C'est Si Bon
SEG 8290 February 1964

Cliff Sings Don't Talk To Him
Don't Talk To Him/Say You're Mine/Spanish Harlem/Who Are We To Say/Falling In Love With Love
SEG 8299 March 1964

Cliff's Palladium Successes
I'm The Lonely One/Watch What You Do With My Baby/Perhaps Perhaps Perhaps/Frenesi
SEG 8320 May 1964

Wonderful Life No.1
Wonderful Life/Do You Remember/What've I Gotta Do/Walkin' (Shadows)
SEG 8338/ESG 7902 August 1964

A Forever Kind Of Love
A Forever Kind Of Love/It's Wonderful To Be Young/Constantly/True True Lovin'
SEG 8347 September 1964

Wonderful Life No.2
A Matter Of Moments/Girl In Every Port/A Little Imagination/In The Stars
SEG 8354/ESG 7903 October 1964

Hits From Wonderful Life
On The Beach/We Love A Movie/Home/All Kinds Of People
SEG 8376/ESG7906 December 1964

Why Don't They Understand
Why Don't They Understand/Where The Four Winds Blow/The Twelfth Of Never/I'm Afraid To Go Home
SEG 8384 February 1965

Cliff's Hits From Aladdin And His Wonderful Lamp
Havin' Fun/Evening Comes/Friends/I Could Easily Fall (In Love With You)
SEG 8395 March 1965

Look In My Eyes Maria
Look In My Eyes Maria/Where Is Your Heart/Maria/If I Give My Heart To You
SEG 8405 May 1965

Angel
Angel/I Only Came To Say Goodbye/On My Word/The Minute You're Gone
SEG 8444 September 1965

Take Four
Boom Boom (That's How My Heart Sings)/My Heart Is An Open Book/Lies And Kisses/Sweet And Gentle
SEG 8450 October 1965

Wind me Up
Wind me Up/The Night/The Time In Between/Look Before You Love
SEG 8474 February 1966

Hits From When In Rome
Come Prima (For The First Time)/Nel Blu Di Pinto Di Blu (Volare)/Dicitencello Vuie (Just Say I Love Her)/Arrivederci Roma
SEG 8478 April 1966

Love Is Forever
My Colouring Book/Fly Me To The Moon/Someday/Everyone Needs Someone To Love
SEG 8488 April 1966

Thunderbirds Are Go
Shooting Star/Lady Penelope (Shadows)/Thunderbirds Theme (Shadows)/Zero X Theme (Shadows)
SEG 8510 December 1966

La La La La La
La La La La La/Solitary Man/Things We Said Today/Never Knew What Love Could Do
SEG 8517 December 1966

Cinderella
Come Sunday/Peace And Quiet/She Needs Him More Than Me/Hey Doctor Man
SEG 8527 May 1967

Carol Singers
God Rest Ye Merry Gentlemen/In The Bleak Midwinter/Unto Us A Boy Is Born/While Shepherds Watched/O Little Town Of Bethlehem
SEG 8533 November 1967

Congratulations
Congratulations/Wonderful World/Do You Remember/High And Dry/The Sound Of The Candyman's Trumpet/Little Rag Doll
SEG 8540 April 1968

Christmas EP
We Should Be Together/Mistletoe And Wine/Twelve Days Of Christmas/The Holly And The Ivy
XMAS 91 December 1991

UK Albums

Cliff
Apron Strings/My Babe/Down The Line/I Got A Feeling/Jet Black (Drifters)/Baby I Don't Care/Donna/Move It/Ready Teddy/Too Much/Don't Bug Me Baby/Driftin' (Drifters)/That'll Be The Day/Be Bop A Lula (Drifters)/Danny/Whole Lotta Shakin' Goin' On
Mono SX 1147 April 1959

Cliff Sings
Blue Suede Shoes/The Snake And The Bookworm/I Gotta Know/Here Comes Summer/I'll String Along With You/Embraceable You/As Time Goes By/The Touch Of Your Lips/Twenty Flight Rock/Pointed Toe Shoes/Mean Woman Blues/I'm Walking/I Don't Know Why/Little Things Mean A Lot/Somewhere Along The Way/That's My Desire
Mono SX 1192 November 1959

Me And My Shadows
I'm Gonna Get You/You And I/I Cannot Find A True Love/Evergreen Tree/She's Gone/Left Out Again/You're Just The One To Do It/Lamp Of Love/Choppin' And Changin'/We Have It Made/Tell Me/Gee Whiz It's You/I Love You So/I'm Willing To Learn/I Don't Know/Working After School
Mono SX 1261 Stereo SCX 3330 Oct.1960

Listen To Cliff
What'd I Say/Blue Moon/True Love Will Come To You/Lover/Unchained Melody/Idle Gossip/First Lesson In Love/Almost Like Being In Love/Beat Out Dat Rhythm On A Drum/Memories LingerOn/Temptation/I Live For You/Sentimental Journey/I Want You To Know/We Kiss In A Shadow/It's You
Mono SX 1320 Stereo SCX 3375 May1961

21 Today
Happy Birthday To You/Forty Days/Catch Me/How Wonderful To Know/Tough Enough/Fifty Tears For Every Kiss/The Night Is So Lonely/Poor Boy/Y'Arriva/Outsider/Tea For Two/To Prove My Love For You/Without You/A Mighty Lonely Man/My Blue Heaven/Shame On You
Mono SX 1368 Stereo SCX 3409 Oct 1961

The Young Ones
Friday Night/Got A Funny Feeling/Peace Pipe (Shadows)/Nothing's Impossible/The Young Ones/All For One/Lessons In Love/No One For Me But Nicki/What Do You Know We've Got A Show - Vaudeville Routine/When The Girl In Your Arms (Is The Girl In Your Heart)/Just Dance/Just Dance-Mood Mambo/The Savage (Shadows)/We Say Yeah
Mono SX 1384 Stereo SCX 3397
December 1961

32 Minutes And 17 Seconds With Cliff Richard
It'll be Me/So I've Been Told/How Long Is Forever/I'm Walking/The Blues/Turn Around/Blueberry Hill/Let's Make A Memory/When My Dreamboat Comes Home/I'm On My Way/Spanish Harlem/You Don't Know/Falling In Love With Love/Who Are We To Say/I Wake Up Cryin'
Mono SX 1431 Stereo SCX 3436 Oct.1962

Summer Holiday
Seven Days To A Holiday/Summer Holiday/Let Us Take You For A Ride/Les Girls (Shadows)/Round And Round (Shadows)/Foot Tapper (Shadows)/Stranger In Town/Orlando's Mime/Bachelor Boy/A Swingin' Affair/Really Waltzing/All At Once/Dancing Shoes/Yugoslav Wedding/The Next Time/Big News
Mono SX 1472 Stereo SCX 3462 Jan.1963

Cliff's Hit Album
Move It/Living Doll/Travellin' Light/A Voice In The Wilderness/Fall In Love With You/Please Don't Tease/Nine Times Out Of Ten/I Love You/Theme For A Dream/A Girl Like You/When The Girl In Your Arms/The Young Ones/I'm Looking Out The Window/Do You Wanna Dance
Mono SX 1512 Stereo SCX 1512 July 1963

When In Spain
Perfidia/Amor, Amor, Amor//Frenesi/Solamente Una Vez/Vaya Con Dios/Me Lo Dijo Adela/Maria No Mas/Tus Besos/Quizás, Quizás, Quizás/Te Quiero Dijiste/Canción De Orfeo/Quien Sera
Mono SX 1541 Stereo SCX 3488
September 1963

Wonderful Life
Wonderful Life/A Girl In Every Port/Walkin' (Shadows)/Home/A Little Imagination/On The Beach/In The Stars/We Love A Movie/Do You Remember/What've I Gotta Do/Theme For Young Lovers (Shadows)/All Kinds Of People/A Matter Of Moments/Youth And Experience
Mono SX 1628 Stereo SCX 3515 July 1964

Aladdin And His Wonderful Lamp
Emperor Theme (Orchestra)/Chinese Street Scene (Orchestra)/Me Oh My (Shadows)/I Could Easily Fall (In Love With You)/Little Princess (Shadows)/This Was My Special Day/I'm In Love With You/There's Gotta Be A Way/Ballet: (Rubies, Emeralds, Sapphires, Diamonds) (Orchestra)/Dance Of The Warriors(Orchestra)/ Friends/Dragon Dance (Orchestra)/Genie With The Light Brown Lamp (Shadows)/Make Ev'ry Day A Carnival Day/Widow Twankey's Song (Orchestra)/I'm Feeling Oh So Lonely (Orchestra)/I've Said Too Many Things/Evening Comes/Havin' Fun
Mono SX 1676 StereoSCX 3522 Dec.1964

Cliff Richard
Angel/Sway/I Only Came To Say Goodbye/Take Special Care/Magic Is The Moonlight/House Without Windows/Razzle Dazzle/I Don't Wanna Love You/It's Not For Me To Say/You Belong To My Heart/Again/ Perfidia/Kiss/Reelin'n'Rockin'
Mono SX 1709 Stereo SCX 3456 April1965

More Hits By Cliff
It'll Be Me/The Next Time/Bachelor Boy/Summer Holiday/Dancing Shoes/Lucky Lips/It's All In The Game/Don't Talk To Him/I'm The Lonely One/Constantly/On The Beach/A Matter Of Moments/The Twelfth Of Never/I Could Easily Fall (In Love With You)/
Mono SX 1737 Stereo SCX 3555 July 1965

When In Rome
Come Prima/Nel Blu Dipinto Di Blu/Concerto D'Autumno/O Mio Signore/Maria Ninguem/Non L'Ascoltare/Dicitencello Vuie/Arrivederci Roma/Carina/Legata Ad Un Granello Di Sabbia/Casa Senza Finestre/Che Cosa Del Farai Mio Amour/Per Un Bacio D'Amore
Mono SX 1762 August 1965

Love Is Forever
Everyone Needs Someone To Love/Long Ago (And Far Away)/All Of A Sudden (My Heart Sings)/Have I Told You Lately That I Love You/Fly Me To The Moon/A Summer Place/I Found A Rose/My Foolish Heart/Through The Eye Of A Needle/My Colouring Book/I Walk Alone/Someday (You'll Want Me To Want You)/Paradise Lost/Look Homeward Angel
Mono SX 1769 Stereo SCX 3569
November 1965

Kinda Latin
Blame It On The Bossa Nova/Blowing In The Wind/Quiet Nights Of Quiet Stars/Eso Beso/The Girl From Ipanema/One Note Samba/Fly Me To The Moon/Our Day Will Come/Quando, Quando, Quando/Come Closer To Me/Meditation/Concrete & Clay
Mono SX 6039 Stereo SCX 6039 May 1966

Finders Keepers
Finders Keepers/Time Drags By/Washerwoman/La La La Song/My Way (Shadows)/Oh Senorita/Spanish Music/Fiesta (Shadows)/This Day/Paella/Finders Keepers/My Way/Paella/Fiesta (Shadows)/Run To The Door/Where Did The Summer Go/Into Each Life Some Rain Must Fall
Mono SX 6079 Stereo SCX 6079
December 1966

Cinderella
Welcome To Stoneybroke/Why Wasn't I Born Rich/Peace And Quiet/The Flyder And The Spy (Shadows)/ Poverty/The Hunt/In The Country/Come Sunday/Dare I Love Him Like I Do/If Our Dreams Come True/ Autumn/The King's Place/Peace And Quiet/She Needs Him More Than Me/Hey Doctor Man
Mono SX 6103 Stereo SCX 6103 Jan.1967

Don't Stop Me Now
Shout/One Fine Day/I'll Be Back/Heartbeat/I Saw Her Standing There/Hang On To A Dream/You Gotta Tell Me/Homeward Bound/Good Golly Miss Molly/Don't Make Promises/Move It/Don't/Dizzy Miss Lizzy/Baby It's You/My Babe/Save The Last Dance For Me
Mono SX 6133 Stereo SCX6133 April 1967

Good News
Good News/It Is No Secret/We Shall Be Changed/23rd Psalm/Go Where I Send Thee/What A Friend We Have In Jesus/All Glory Laud And Honour/Just A Closer Walk With Thee/The King Of Love My Shepherd Is/Mary What You Gonna Name That Pretty Little Baby/When I Survey The Wondrous Cross/Take My Hand Precious Lord/Get On Board Little Children/May The Good Lord Bless And Keep You
Mono SX 6167 Stereo SCX 6167 Oct.1967

Cliff In Japan
Shout/I'll Come Running/The Minute You're Gone/On The Beach/Hang On To A Dream/Spanish Harlem/Finders Keepers/Visions/Move It/Living Doll/La La La La La/Twist And ShoutEvergreen Tree/What'd I Say/Dynamite/Medley: Let's Make A Memory, The Young Ones, Lucky Lips, Summer Holiday, We Say Yeah
Mono SX 6244 Stereo SCX 6244 May 1968

Two A Penny
Two A Penny/I'll Love You Forever Today/Questions/Long Is The Night (instrumental)/Lonely Girl/And Me (I'm On The Outside Now)/Daybreak (instrumental)/Twist And Shout/Celeste (instrumental)/Wake Up Wake Up/Cloudy/Red Rubber Ball/Close To Cathy/Rattler
Mono SX 6262 Stereo SCX 6262

Established 1958
Don't Forget To Catch Me/Voyage To The Bottom Of The Bath (Shadows)/Not The Way That It Should Be/Poem/ The Dreams I Dream/The Average Life Of A Daily Man (Shadows)/Somewhere By The Sea/Banana Man (Shadows)/Girl On The Bus/The Magical Mrs Clamps (Shadows)/Ooh La La/Here I Go Again Loving You (Shadows)/What's Behind The Eyes Of Mary/Maggie's Samba (Shadows)
Mono SX 6282 Stereo SCX 6282
September 1968

The Best Of Cliff
The Minute You're Gone/On My Word/The Time In Between/Wind Me Up (Let Me Go)/Blue Turns To Grey/Visions/Time Drags By/In The Country/It's All Over/I'll Come Running/The Day I Met Marie/All My Love/Congatulations/Girl You'll Be A Woman Soon
Mono SX 6343 Stereo SCX 6343 Jun.1969

Sincerely Cliff Richard
In The Past/Always/Will You Love Me Tomorrow/You'll Want Me/I'm Not Getting Married/Time/For Emily Whenever I May Find Her/Baby I Could Be So Good At Loving You/Sam/London's Not Too Far/Take Action/Take Good Care Of Her/When I Find You/Punch And Judy
Mono SX 6357 Stereo SCX 6357 Oct.1969

Cliff Live At The Talk Of The Town
Introduction/Congratulations/Shout/All My Love/Ain't Nothing But A House Party/Something Good/If Ever I Should Leave You/Girl You'll Be A Woman Soon/Hank's Medley/London's Not Too Far/The Dreams That I Dream/The Day I Met Marie/La La La La La/A Taste Of Honey/The Lady Came From Baltimore/When I'm 64/What's More I Don't Need Her /Congratulations/ Visions/Congratulations
Regal SRS 5031 July 1970

About That Man
The Birth Of John The Baptist/Sweet Little Jesus Boy/The Visit Of The Wise Men And The Escape Into Egypt/John The Baptist Points Out Jesus/Jesus Recruits His Helpers And Heals The Sick/Where Is That Man/Jesus Addresses The Crowd On The Hillside/Can It Be True/Jesus Is Betrayed And Arrested/The Trial Of Jesus/His Execution And Death/The First Easter - The Empty Tomb/Reflections
SCX 6408 October 1970

His Land
Ezekiel's Vision/Dry Bones/His Land/Jerusalem Jerusalem/The New 23rd/His Land/Hava Nagila/Over In Bethlehem/Keep Me Where Love Is/He's Everything To Me/Hallelujah Chorus
SCX 6443 November 1970

Tracks And Grooves
Early In The Morning/As I Walk Into The Morning Of Your Life/Love Truth And Emily Stone/My Head Goes Around/Put My Mind At Ease/Abraham, Martin And John/The Girl Can't Help It/Bang Bang (My Baby Shot Me Down)/I'll Make It all Up To You/I'd Just Be Fool Enough/Don't Let Tonight Ever End/What A Silly Thing To Do/Your Heart's Not In Your Love/Don't Ask Me To Be Friends/Are You Only Fooling Me
SCX 6435 November 1970

The Best Of Cliff Volume Two
Goodbye Sam, Hello Samantha/Marianne/Throw Down A Line/Jesus/Sunny Honey Girl/I Ain't Got Time Anymore/Flying Machine/Sing A Song Of Freedom/With The Eyes Of A Child/Good Times (Better Times)/I'll Love You Forever Today/The Joy Of Living/Silvery Rain/Big Ship
SCX 6519 November 1972

Take Me High
It's Only Money/Midnight Blue/Hover/Why/Life/Driving/The Game/Brumburger Duet/Take Me High/The Anti-Brotherhood Of Man/Winning/ Driving /Join The Band/The Word Is Love/Brumburger (Finale)
EMI EMC 3016 December 1973

Help It Along
Day By Day/Celestial Houses/Jesus/Silvery Rain/Jesus Loves You/Fire And Rain/ Yesterday Today Forever/ Mr Businessman/ Help It Along/Amazing Grace/Higher Ground/Sing A Song Of Freedom
EMI EMA 768 June 1974

The 31st Of February Street
31st Of February Street Opening/Give Me Back That Old Familiar Feeling/The Leaving/Travellin' Light/There You Go Again/Nothing To Remind Me/Our Love Could Be So Real/No Matter What/Fireside Song/Going Away/Long Long Time/You Will Never Know/The Singer/31st Of February Street Closing
EMI EMC 3048 November 1974

I'm Nearly Famous
I Can't Ask For Any More Than You/It's No Use Pretending/I'm Nearly Famous/ Lovers/Junior Cowboy/Miss You Nights/I Wish You'd Change Your Mind/Devil Woman/Such Is The Mystery/You've Got To Give Me All Your Lovin'/If You Walked Away/Alright It's Alright
EMI EMC 3122 May 1976

Every Face Tells A Story
My Kinda Life/Must Be Love/When Two World's Drift Apart/You Got Me Wondering/Every Face Tells A Story (It Never Tells A Lie)/Try A Smile/Hey Mr Dream Maker/Give Me Love Your Way/Don't Turn The Light Out/It'll Be Me Babe/Up In The World/Spider Man
EMI EMC 3172 March 1977

40 Golden Greats
Move It/Living Doll/Travellin' Light/Fall In Love With You/Please Don't Tease/Nine Times Out Of Ten/Theme For A Dream/Gee Whiz It's You/When The Girl In Your Arms (Is The Girl In Your Heart)/A Girl Like You/The Young Ones/Do You Wanna Dance/I'm Looking Out The Window/It'll Be Me/ Bachelor Boy/The Next Time/ Summer Holiday/ Lucky Lips/It's All In The Game/Don't Talk To Him/Constantly/ On The Beach/I Could Easily Fall (In Love With You)/The Minute You're Gone/Wind me Up (Let Me Go)/Visions/Blue Turns To Grey/In The Country/The Day I Met Marie/All My Love/Congratulations/ Throw Down A Line/ Goodbye Sam, Hello Samantha/Sing A Song Of Freedom/Power To All Our Friends/ (You Keep Me) Hangin' On/Miss You Nights/Devil Woman/I Can't Ask For Anymore Than You/My Kinda Life
EMI EMTVS 6/TCEMTVS 6/CDEMTV 6
September 1977

Small Corners
Why Should The Devil Have All The Good Music/I Love/Why Me Lord/I've Got News For You/Hey Watcha Say/I Wish We'd All Been Ready/Joseph/Good On The Sally Army/Going Home/Up In Canada/Yes He Lives/ When I Survey The Wondrous Cross
EMI EMC 3219 February 1978

Green Light
Green Light/Under Lock And Key/She's A Gypsy/Count Me Out/Please Remember Me/Never Even Thought/ Free My Soul/Start All Over Again/While She's Young/Can't Take The Hurt Anymore/Ease Along
EMI EMC 3231 September 1978

Thank You Very Much
The Young Ones/Do You Wanna Dance/The Day I Met Marie/Shadoogie (Shadows)/Atlantis (Shadows)/ Nivram (Shadows)/Apache (Shadows)/ Please Don't Tease/Miss You Nights/Move It/Willie And The Hand Jive/All Shook Up/Devil Woman/Why Should The Devil Have All The Good Music/End Of The Show
EMI EMTV 15 February 1979

Rock And Roll Juvenile
Monday Thru Friday/Doin' Fine/Cities May Fall/You Know That I Love You/My Luck Won't Change/Rock And Roll Juvenile/Carrie/Hot Shot/Language Of Love/We Don't Talk Anymore/Sci Fi/Fallin' In Luv
EMI EMC 3307/TCEMC 3307 September 1979

I'm No Hero
Take Another Look/Anything I Can Do/A Little In Love/Here (So Doggone Blue)/Give A Little Bit More/In The Night/I'm No Hero/Dreamin'/A Heart Will Break/Everyman
EMI EMA 796 September 1980

Love Songs
Miss You Nights/Constantly/Up In The World/Carrie/A Voice In The Wilderness/The Twelfth Of Never/ I Could Easily Fall (In Love With You)/The Day I Met Marie/Can't Take The Hurt Anymore/A Little In Love/ The Minute You're Gone/Visions/When Two Worlds Drift Apart/The Next Time/It's All In The Game/ Don't Talk To Him/When The Girl In Your Arms (Is The Girl In Your Heart)/Theme For A Dream/Fall In Love With You/We Don't Talk Anymore
EMTV 27/TCEMTV 27/CDEMTV27 Jul.1981

Wired For Sound
Wired For Sound/Once In A While/Better Than I Know Myself/Oh No Don't Let Go/'Cos I Love That Rock And Roll/Broken Doll/Lost In A Lonely World/Summer Rain/Young Love/Say You Don't Mind/Daddy's Home
EMC 3377/TCEMI 5221 September 1981

Now You See Me Now You Don't
The Only Way Out/First Date/Thief In The Night/Where Do We Go From Here/Son Of Thunder/Little Town/It Has To Be You It Has To Be Me/The Water Is Wide/Now You See Me Now You Don't/Be In My Heart/Discovering
EMC 3415/TCEMC 3415 August 1982

Dressed For The Occasion
Green Light/We Don't Talk Anymore/True Love Ways/Softly As I Leave You/Carrie/Miss You Nights/ Galadriel/Mabe Someday/Thief In The Night/Up In The World/Treasure Of Love/Devil Woman
EMC 3432/TCEMC 3432 May 1983

Silver
Silver's Home Tonight/Hold On/Never Say Die (Give A Little Bit More)/Front Page/Ocean Deep/Locked Inside Your Prison/Please Don't Fall In Love/Baby You're Dynamite/The Golden Days Are Over/Love Stealer
Rock And Roll Silver
Makin' History/Move It/Donna/Teddy Bear/It'll Be Me/ Lucille/Little Bitty Pretty One/There'll Never Be Anyone Else But You/Be Bop A Lula/Tutti Frutti
EMC 1077871 October 1983

(Note: The above two albums were released as a limited edition Box set including a booklet)

The Rock Connection
Heart User/Willie And The Hand Jive/Lovers And Friends/Never Be Anyone Else But You/La Gonave/Over You/Shooting From The Heart/Learning How To Rock And Roll/Lucille/Be Bop A Lula/Donna/Dynamite/She Means Nothing To Me/Makin' History
Clif 2/TCCLIF 2 November 1984

20 Original Greats
On The Beach/Do You Wanna Dance/Lucky Lips/Don't Talk To Him/A Voice In The Wilderness/A Girl Like You/Fall In Love With You/Gee Whiz Its You/Mean Streak/In The Country/Move It/Nine Times Out Of Ten/Dancing Shoes/Theme For A Dream/Willie And The Hand Jive/I'm The Lonely One/When The Girl In Your Arms (Is The Girl In Your Heart)/Time Drags By/I Could Easily Fall/We Say Yeah
EMI CRS1 July 1984

Always Guaranteed
One Night/Once Upon A Time/Some People/Forever/Two Hearts/Under Your Spell/This Time Now/My Pretty One/Remember Me/Always Guaranteed
EMD 1004/TCEMD 1004 September 1987

Always Guaranteed:
The Album Box Set
Limited edition box set featuring the same tracks as the album, includes a large colour poster, calendar, autographed colour prints, four colour postcards plus a 7" single including Another Christmas Day and an engraved message from Cliff.
September 1987

Private Collection
Some People/Wired For Sound/All I Ask Of You/Carrie/Remember Me/True Love Ways/Dreamin'/Green Light/She Means Nothing To Me/Heart User/A Little In Love/Daddy's Home/We Don't Talk Anymore/Never Say Die/The Only Way Out/Suddenly/Slow/ Rivers/Please Don't Fall In Love/Little Town/My Pretty One/ Ocean Deep/She's So Beautiful/Two Hearts/Mistletoe And Wine
CRTV 30/TCCRTV 30/CDCRTV 30
November 1988

(Note: The CD version of Private Collection does not contain the following titles:
Remember Me/Green Light/Heart User/Slow Rivers/Two Hearts)

Stronger
Stronger Than That/Who's In Love/The Best Of Me/Clear Blue Skies/Keep Me Warm/Lean On You/I Just Don't Have The Heart/Joanna/Everybody Knows/Share A Dream/Better Day/Forever You Will Be Mine
EMD 1012/TCEMD 1012/CDEMD 1012
October 1989

From A Distance – The Event
Oh Boy Medley/Zing Went The Strings Of My Heart (Dallas Boys)/Always/When (Kalin Twins)/The Glory Of Love/Hoots Mon (Oh Boy Band)/Don't Look Now (Vernons Girls)/The Girl Can't Help It/Sea Cruise/Oh Boy Medley/From A Distance/Some People/We Don't Talk Anymore/Shake Rattle And Roll/Silhouettes/Move It/ Summer Holiday/The Young Ones/In The Country/ Good Golly Miss Molly/Fighter/Thief In The Night/Share A Dream/All The Time You Need/Saviour's Day
CRTV 31/TCCRTV 31/CDCRTV 31
November 1990

From A Distance - The Event:
The Album Box Set/The Cassette Box Set/The CD Box Set
Limited edition box set featuring the same tracks as the double album, includes 6 exclusive prints, giant poster with lyrics, plus engraved 7" single including acappella version of Miss You Nights
CRTVB 31/TCCRTVB 31/CDCRTVB 31
December 1990

(Note: The CD version of From A Distance – The Event does not contain the following titles:
The Glory Of Love/Hoots Mon/Summer Holiday/In The Country/Good Golly Miss Molly)

Together With Cliff Richard
Have Yourself A Merry Little Christmas/Venite (O Come All Ye Faithful)/We Should Be Together/Mistletoe And Wine/Christmas Never Comes/Christmas Alphabet/Saviour's Day/The Christmas Song (Merry Christmas To You)/Little Town/Scarlet Ribbons/Silent Night/White Christmas/This New Year
EMD 1028/TCEMD 1028/CDEMD 1028
November 1991

My Kinda Life (French Import)
Born To Rock And Roll/Hot Shot/Devil Woman/Remember/Carrie/Lean On You/We Don't Talk Anymore/ Monday Thru Friday/Lucille/You've Got Me Wondering/Never Even Thought/Two Hearts/Language Of Love/
My Kinda Life
EMD 1034/TCEMD 1034/CDEMD 1034
May 1992

Cliff Richard – The Album
Peace In Our Time/Love's Salvation/I Still Believe In You/Love Is The Strongest Emotion/Only Angel/Handle My Heart With Love/Little Mistreater/You Move Heaven/I Need Love/Hold Us Together/Never Let Go/Human Work Of Art/Healing Love/Brother To Brother
CDEMD 1043/TCEMD 1043
April 1993

The Hit List
Move It/Livin' Doll/Travelin' Light/A Voice In The Wilderness/Fall In Love With You/Please Don't Tease/Nine Times Out of Ten/I Love You/Theme For A Dream/Gee Whiz It's You/A Girl Like You/When The Girl In Your Arms Is The Girl In Your Heart/The Young Ones/Do You Wanna Dance/It'll Be Me/The Next Time /Bachelor Boy/Summer Holiday/Lucky Lips/It's All In The Game/Don't Talk To Him/Constantly/ The Minute You're Gone/Wind Me Up (Let Me Go)/Congratulations/Power To All Our Friends/We Don't Talk Anymore/ Carrie/Wired For Sound/Daddy's Home/ Some People/Mistletoe & Wine/The Best Of Me/I Just Don't Have The Heart/ Saviour's Day/Miss You Nights/Green Light
EMI 7243 8 30917 2 0 October 1994

CHART STATISTICS

NOTES
NME: New Musical Express
MM: Melody Maker
RM: Record Mirror
D: Disc
RR: Record Retailer

SINGLES

	NME	MM	RM	D	RR	Weeks on Chart
Move It	2	3	3	2		17
High Class Baby	7	6	5	4		10
Livin' Lovin' Doll	20			17		6
Mean Streak/Never Mind	10/21	7	8	5		9
Living Doll	1	1	1	1		21
Travellin' Light/Dynamite	1/16	1	1	1		17
A Voice In The Wilderness	2	2	2	2		17
Fall In Love With You/Willie And The Hand Jive	2/18	2	2	2	2/18	15
Please Don't Tease	1	1	1	1	1	18
Nine Times Out Of Ten	2	3	2	2	3	12
I Love You/'D' In Love	2/26	1	2	1	1	16
Theme For A Dream	2	3	4	3	3	14
Gee Whiz It's you	6	7	8	7	4	14
A Girl Like You	4	3	3	1	3	14
When The Girl In Your Arms/ Got A Funny Feeling	2/23	2	2	2	3	15
The Young Ones	1	1	1	1	1	21
I'm Looking Out The Window/ Do You Want To Dance	2/10	2		2	2	12
It'll Be Me	2	2		2	2	12
The Next Time/Bachelor Boy	1/3	1		1	1	18
Summer Holiday/Dancing Shoes	1/25	1		1	1	18
Lucky Lips	4	5		3	4	15
It's All In The Game	2	2		2	2	13
Don't Talk To Him	2	2		3	2	14
I'm The Lonely One	10	10		9	8	10
Constantly	5	4		4	4	13
On The Beach	6	7		7	7	13
The Twelfth Of Never	3	9		10	8	11
I Could Easily Fall (In Love With You)	7	7		6	6	11
The Minute You're Gone	1	1		2	1	14
On My Word	15	12		13	12	10
The Time In Between	20	23		25	22	8
Wind Me Up	4	4		4	2	16
Blue Turns To Grey	18	15		16	15	9
Visions	7	7		7	7	12
Time Drags By	9	5		9	10	12
In The Country	8	5		7	6	10
It's All Over	8	5		8	9	10
I'll Come Running	19	22		21	26	8
The Day I Met Marie	11	10		10	10	14
All My Love	8	7		7	6	12
Congratulations	1	2			1	13
I'll Love You Forever Today	22	23			27	6
Marianne	23	20			22	8
Don't Forget To Catch Me	24	21			21	10
Good Times	12	11			12	11
Big Ship	8	8			8	10
Throw Down A Line	7	5			7	9
With The Eyes Of A Child	18	25			20	11
Joy Of Living	24	28			25	8
Goodbye Sam, Hello Samantha	5	3			6	15
Ain't Got Time Anymore	25	28			24	7
Sunny Honey Girl					19	8
Silvery Rain					27	6
Flying Machine					37	7
Sing A Song Of Freedom					13	12
Jesus					35	3
Living In Harmony					10	10
Brand New Song					-	-
Power To All Our Friends					4	12
Help It Along					29	6
Take Me High					27	12
Hangin' On				13	9	
It's Only Me You've Left Behind					-	-
Honky Tonk Angel					-	-
Miss You Nights					15	10
Devil Woman					9	8
I Can't Ask For Anything More Than You					17	8

	RR	Weeks on Chart
Hey Mr Dream Maker	31	5
My Kinda Life	15	8
When Two Worlds Drift Apart	46	3
Yes He Lives	-	-
Please Remember Me	-	-
Can't Take The Hurt Anymore	-	-
Green Light	57	3
We Don't Talk Anymore	1	14
Hot Shot	46	5
Carrie	3	10
Dreaming	8	10
Suddenly	15	7
A Little In Love	15	8
Wired For Sound	4	9
Daddy's Home	2	12
The Only Way Out	10	9
Where Do We Go From Here	60	3
Little Town	11	7
She Means Nothing To Me	9	9
True Love Ways	8	8
Drifting	64	2
Never Say Die	15	7
Please Don't Fall In Love	7	9
Baby You're Dynamite	27	7
Two To The Power	-	-
Shooting From The Heart	51	4
Heart User	46	3
She's So Beautiful	17	9
It's In Every One Of Us	45	7
Living Doll	1	11
Born To Rock 'n' Roll	78	3
All I Ask Of You	3	16
Slow Rivers/	44	8
My Pretty One	6	10
Some People	3	10
Remember Me	35	4
Two Hearts/	34	3
Mistletoe And Wine	1	8
The Best Of Me	2	7
Just Don't Have The Heart	3	8
Lean On Me	17	6
Stronger Than That	14	5
Silhouettes	10	7
From A Distance	11	6
Saviours Day	1	7
More To Life	26	5
We Should Be Together	10	6
This New Year	30	2
I Still Believe In You	6	4
Peace In Our Time	8	

LPs

	RR	Weeks on Chart
Oh Boy!	-	-
Cliff	4	31
Cliff Sings	2	36
Me And My Shadows	2	33
Listen To Cliff	2	28
21 Today	1	16
The Young Ones	1	42
32 Minutes And 17 Seconds With Cliff Richard	3	21
Summer Holiday	1	36
Cliff's Hit Album	2	19
When In Spain	8	10
Wonderful Life	2	23
Aladdin And His Wonderful Lamp	13	5
Cliff Richard	9	5
More Hits By Cliff	20	1
When In Rome	-	-
Love Is Forever	19	1
Kinda Latin	9	12
Finders Keepers	6	18
Cinderella	30	6
Don't Stop Me Now	23	9
Good News	37	1
Cliff In Japan	29	2
Two A Penny	-	-
Established 1958	30	4
Best Of Cliff	5	17
Sincerely Cliff	24	3

	RR	Weeks on Chart
Cliff 'Live At The Talk Of The Town'	-	-
About That Man	-	-
Tracks 'n' Grooves	37	2
His Land	-	-
Best Of Cliff Vol 2	49	2
Take Me High	41	4
Help It Along	-	-
31st Of February Street	-	-
I'm Nearly Famous	5	21
Every Face Tells A Story	8	10
40 Golden Greats	1	19
Small Corners	33	5
Green Light	25	3
Thank You Very Much	5	12
Rock 'N' Roll Juvenile	3	22
I'm No Hero	4	11
Love Songs	1	43
Wired For Sound	4	25
Now You See Me, Now You Don't	4	14
Dressed For The Occasion	7	17
Silver	7	24
The Rock Connection	43	5
Always Guaranteed	5	25
Private Collection 1979 1988	1	22
Stronger	7	
From A Distance The Event	3	
Together With Cliff Richard	10	
My Kinda Life	-	-
Cliff Richard – The Album	1	

EXTENDED PLAY

	RR
Serious Charge	-
Cliff No. 1	-
Cliff No. 2	-
Expresso Bongo	1
Cliff Sings No 1	4
Cliff Sings No 2	3
Cliff Sings No 3	2
Cliff Sings No 4	-
Cliff's Silver Discs	1
Me And My Shadows No 1	5
Me And My Shadows No 2	8
Me And My Shadows No 3	6
Listen To Cliff No 1	17
Dream	3
Listen To Cliff No 2	-
Cliff's Hit Parade	4
Cliff Richard No 1	4
Hits From The Young Ones	11
Cliff Richard No 2	19
Time For Cliff Richard And The Shadows	-
Holiday Carnival	1
Hits From Summer Holiday	4
More Hits From Summer Holiday	-
Cliff's Lucky Lips	17
Love Songs	4
When In France	-
Cliff Sings Don't Talk To Him	15
Cliff's Palladium Successes	-
Wonderful Life	3
A Forever Kind Of Love	-
Wonderful Life No 2	-
Hits From Wonderful Life	-
Why Don't They Understand	-
Cliff Hits From 'Aladdin And His Wonderful Lamp'	20
Look In My Eyes Maria	15
Angel	-
Take Four	4
Wind Me Up	-
Hits From 'When In Rome'	-
Love Is Forever	-
Thunderbirds Are Go	-
La, La, La, La, La	-
Cinderella	-
Carol Singers	-
Congratulations	-

Over the last 35 years various music papers have published charts. This information gives the highest position reached on each of the main charts. During the sixties certain papers (Record Mirror/New Musical Express/Melody Maker/Disc) ceased producing their own charts. The establishment of the BMRB/Gallup chart soon became the industry standard.

PICTURE CREDITS

Malcolm Addey's Private Collection: 21, 25
Sue Andrews: 299 above right, 301 below right, 308 above, 309 above right, 310 above, 311 above, 312 below left, 313 above
BBC Photo Library: 140
David Bryce: 221
Andre Csillag: 228 left
EMI: 18, 34 right, 45, 106, 189, 203, 214, 217, 236, 265, 267, 270. 292
Brian and Tricia Hercoe: 274
Hulton Deutsch Collection: 129
H. Jordan: 256
Vera Knook: 278 bottom left, 279 bottom right, 282
Lella/BBC: 210 top right
London Features International: 8,10, 11, 16, 28, 30, 85, 127, 131, 145, 154, 159, 160, 175, 177, 185, 205, 209, 211, 219, 220, 222, 223 top right and bottom right, 226, 227, 243, 244 bottom right, 247 bottom left, 257, 268
John McGoran: 246, 276
Edward Parker: 286
Photofeatures: 194
PIC Photos: 117, 135 Pictorial Press: 87, 95, 107, 108, 109, 114, 115, 126, 138, 146, 163, 170, 196, 231, 234, 239, 242, 247 top right, 250, 251, 254, 255, 258
Mike Read: 306 above
Relay Photos Ltd/David Wainwright: 304 above right
Retna/Jean Havilland: 298 below right, 305 above right
Rex Features: 9,137, 155, 157, 164, 183, 186, 193, 206 top left, 230 bottom right, 235, 240, 248, 302
David Steen: 96
Surrey Comet: 56
Syndication International: 82, 176, 197, 216, 262 bottom left and top right

With thanks to EMI for a number of other illustrations used in this book.

Every effort has been made to acknowledge correctly and contact the source and/or copyright holder of each illustration, and Hamlyn apologises for any unintentional errors or omissions, which will be corrected in future editions of this book.